Street by Stre

CW00497932

HERTFO**RDSHIRE**

PLUS CHALFONT ST PETER, HARLOW, LUTON, STANSTED AIRPORT, WALTHAM ABBEY

Enlarged Areas Hemel Hempstead, St Albans, Stevenage, Watford

1st edition May 2001

© Automobile Association Developments Limited 2001

Published by AA Publishing (a trading name of Automobile Association Developments Limited, whose registered office is Norfolk House, Priestley Road, Basingstoke, Hampshire, RG24 9NY. Registered number 1878835).

Mapping produced by the Cartographic Department of The Automobile Association.

A CIP Catalogue record for this book is available from the British Library.

Printed in Italy by Printer Trento srl

Ref: MD117

Key to map pages   ii-iii

Key to map symbols   iv-1

Enlarged scale pages   2-13

Street by Street   14-231

Index – towns & villages   232-235

Index – streets   236-283

Index – featured places   283-293

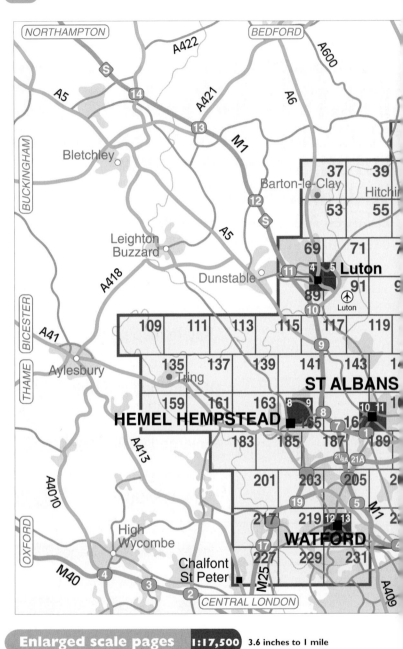

ii

NORTHAMPTON — A422 — BEDFORD

A5 — A421 — A6 — A600

14

M1

13

Bletchley

Barton-le-Clay

BUCKINGHAM

| 37 | 39 |
| 53 | 55 |

Hitchin

12

Leighton Buzzard

A5

S

| 69 | 71 | 7 |

A418

Dunstable

11

4 5 **Luton**

BICESTER

A41

89 91 9

10

Luton ✈

9

| 109 | 111 | 113 | 115 | 117 | 119 |

THAME

Aylesbury

Tring

| 135 | 137 | 139 | 141 | 143 | 1 |

ST ALBANS

| 159 | 161 | 163 | 8 9 | 10 11 | 1 |

HEMEL HEMPSTEAD 165 16 8 7

A413

1

189

| 183 | 185 | 187 | 189 |

21/6A 21A

| 201 | 203 | 205 | 2 |

A4010

19

5

M1

High Wycombe

| 217 | 219 12 13 | 2 |

WATFORD

OXFORD

17

| 227 | 229 | 231 |

M40

Chalfont St Peter

A4

4

3

2

M25

CENTRAL LONDON

A409

Enlarged scale pages   1:17,500   3.6 inches to 1 mile

0 — 1/2 — miles — 1

0 — 1/2 — 1 — kilometres — 1 1/2

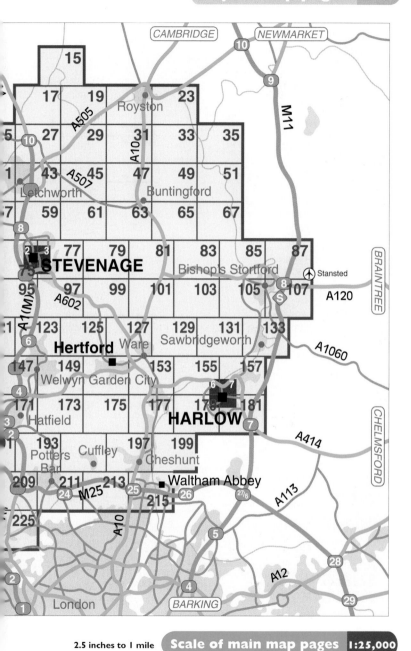

CAMBRIDGE · NEWMARKET · 10 · 9 · M11 · BRAINTREE

15

17 · 19 · Royston · 23

A505 · A10

5 · 10 · 27 · 29 · 31 · 33 · 35

1 · 43 · A507 · 45 · 47 · 49 · 51

Letchworth · Buntingford

7 · 59 · 61 · 63 · 65 · 67

8

2 · 3 · 77 · 79 · 81 · 83 · 85 · 87

STEVENAGE · Bishop's Stortford · Stansted

95 · 97 · 99 · 101 · 103 · 105 · 107 · A120

A11(M) · A602 · 8 · S

1 · 123 · 125 · 127 · 129 · 131 · 133 · A1060

6 · Hertford · Ware · Sawbridgeworth

147 · 149 · 153 · 155 · 157

4 · Welwyn Garden City

171 · 173 · 175 · 177 · 179 · 181

3 · Hatfield · 6 · 7 · HARLOW · 7 · A414

2

11 · 193 · 197 · 199 · CHELMSFORD

Potters Bar · Cuffley · Cheshunt

209 · 211 · 213 · Waltham Abbey

24 · M25 · 25 · 26 · 27/6 · A113

215

225 · A10 · 5

2 · A12 · 28

1 · London · BARKING · 4 · 29

2.5 inches to 1 mile   **Scale of main map pages**   **1:25,000**

| 0 | 1/2 | miles | 1 | 1 1/2 |

| 0 | 1/2 | 1 | kilometres | 1 1/2 | 2 |

iv

Junction 9	Motorway & junction
Services	Motorway service area
	Primary road single/dual carriageway
Services	Primary road service area
	A road single/dual carriageway
	B road single/dual carriageway
	Other road single/dual carriageway
	Restricted road
	Private road
← ←	One way street
	Pedestrian street
----------	Track/ footpath
	Road under construction
}= = ={	Road tunnel
P	Parking

P+☐☐☐	Park & Ride
🚌	Bus/coach station
⇌	Railway & main railway station
■⇌	Railway & minor railway station
⊖	Underground station
⊖	Light railway & station
++++++++	Preserved private railway
LC	Level crossing
●—●—●	Tramway
----------	Ferry route
··············	Airport runway
— · — · — ·	Boundaries- borough/ district
⋎⋎⋎⋎⋎⋎⋎	Mounds
93	Page continuation 1:25,000
7	Page continuation to enlarged scale 1:17,500

	River/canal lake, pier	🚾	Toilet with disabled facilities
	Aqueduct lock, weir	⛽	Petrol station
465 ▲ Winter Hill	Peak (with height in metres)	PH	Public house
	Beach	PO	Post Office
	Coniferous woodland	📖	Public library
	Broadleaved woodland	i	Tourist Information Centre
	Mixed woodland	♜	Castle
	Park		Historic house/ building
	Cemetery	Wakehurst Place NT	National Trust property
	Built-up area	M	Museum/ art gallery
	Featured building	†	Church/chapel
⊓⊔⊓⊔⊓	City wall	⛹	Country park
A&E	Accident & Emergency hospital	🎭	Theatre/ performing arts
🚻	Toilet	🎬	Cinema

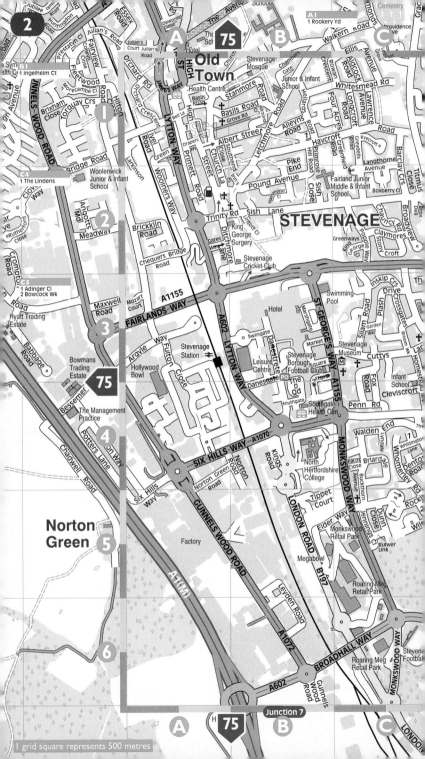

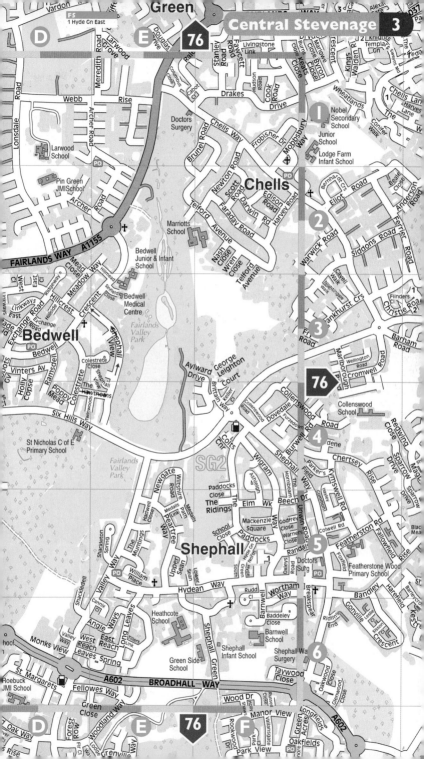

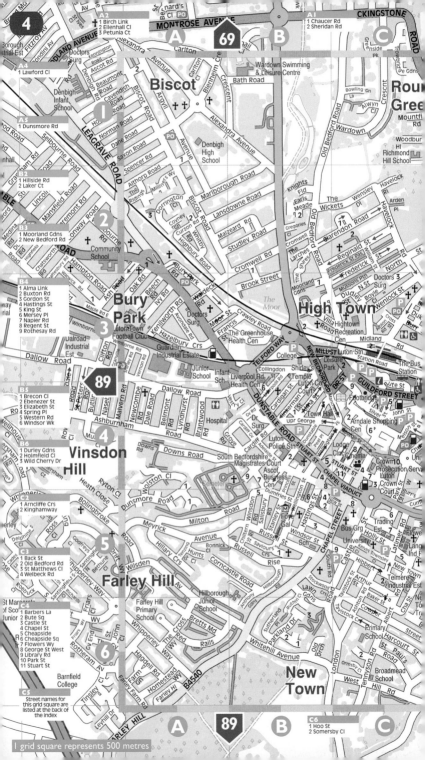

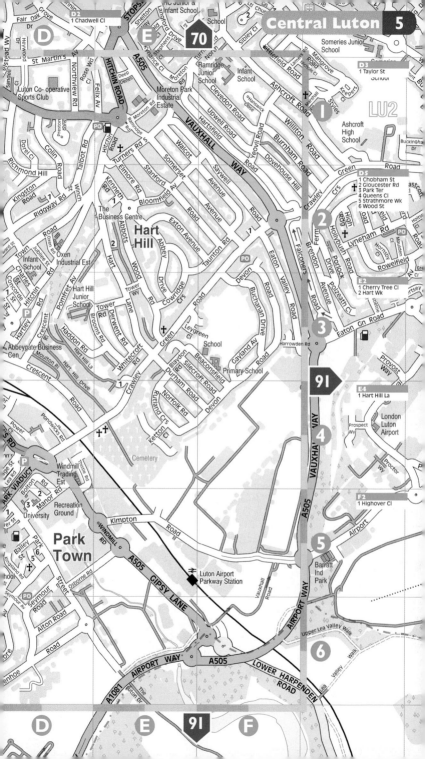

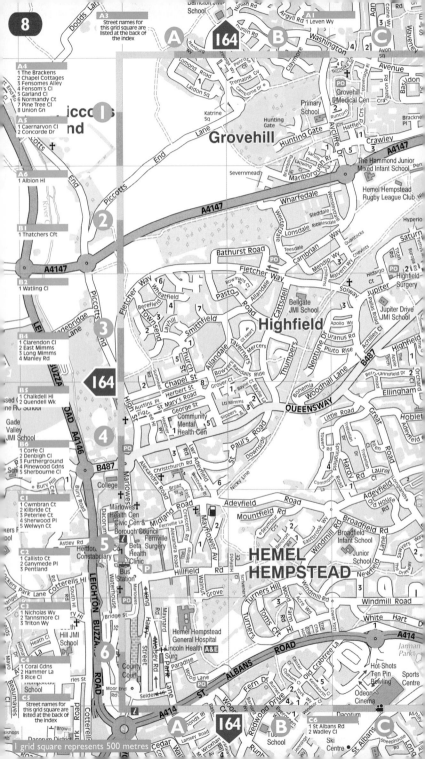

Cupid Green

D3
1 Sainfoin End
2 Winds End Cl

D4
1 Saracens Head
2 Southernwood Cl

Eaton Lodge

D6
1 Grange Cl
2 Haddon Cl
3 Mariner Wy
4 Marston Cl
5 Sandmere Cl

E4
1 Duxons Turn
2 Wellswood Cl

Brickfields Industrial Est

Grovelands Business Cen

E6
1 Tile Kiln Cl

HP2

A M F Bowling

Hobletts Manor Junior School

Stocks Meadow

F3
1 Grovelands

The Coppice

Adeyfield

Adeyfield School

Hemel Hempstead United Football Club

Hotel

F4
1 Hales Park Cl
2 Romany Ct
3 Welkin Gn
4 Wood End Cl

Leverstock Green JMI School

St Margarets Way

Leverstock Green

Leverstock Green Lawn Tennis Club

Woodfield

F5
1 Chartridge Wy
2 Pelham Ct

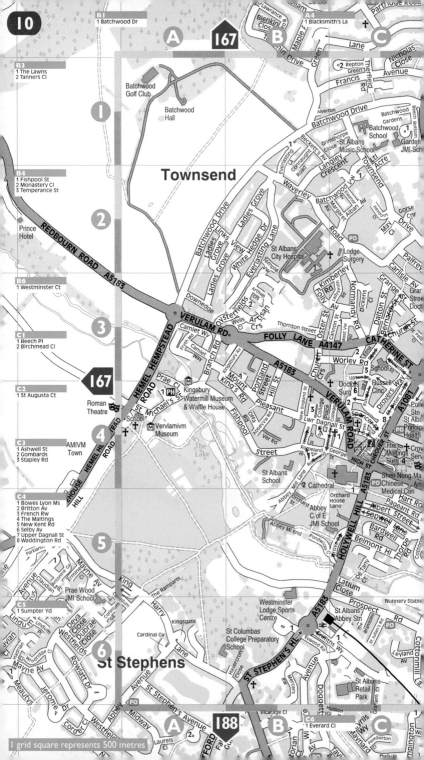

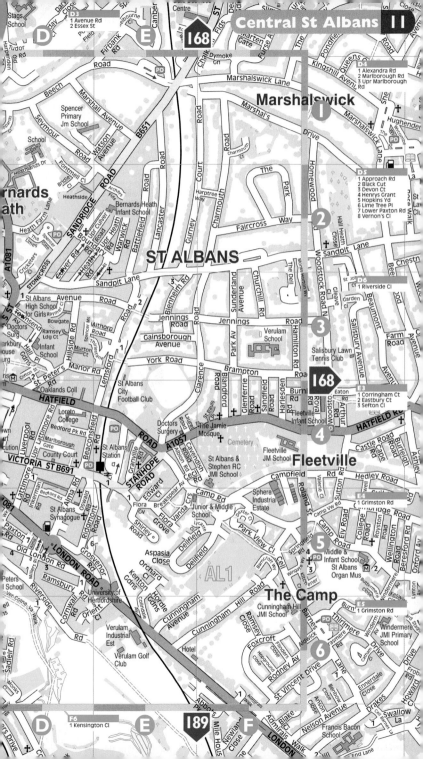

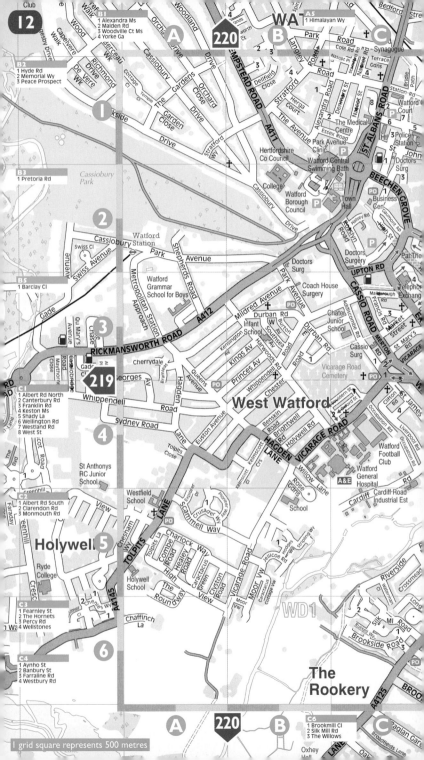

Central Watford 13

F G H J K

1
2
3
4
5
6
7
8

River Cam or Rhee

Flecks Lane

Potton Road

Little Green

North Brook End Road

Great Green

New Road

Cemetery

Fox Hill Road

North Brook End

Guilden Morden

Dublin Pound Road

Guilden Morden School

Worboys Court

Church Street

Church Lane

Thompsons Meadow

Swan Lane

High Street

Silver Street

Morden House

Buxtons Lane

Hay Street

Trap Road

Bogs Gap Lane

Brook End

Hillside Farm

Steeple Morden

Craft Way

Steeple Morden School

Jubilee Way

Coiffee End

Cheyney Close

Cheyney Street

Ashwell Road

Church Street

Highfield Farm

Church Farm Lane

The Green

Litlington Road

Morden Green

Ashwell Road

Westbrooks Close

Bragg Road

Wyndmere Farm

A B C D E

1

2

Edworth

Lower Farm

Manor
Farm

Hinxworth

Arnolds Lane

3

Manor
Farm

Culpe
Street

✝

High Street

Francis
Road

PH

✝

Ashwell

4

A1(M)

New Inn Road

Road

5

A1(M)

Bedfordshire County
Hertfordshire County

Glebe
Farm

Pulter's
Farm

6

Saltmore
Farm

Hinxworth Road

7

Astwick

Astwick Road

✝

8

Taylor's Road

Caldecote

Road

Caldecote Road

A B C D E

Bedfordshire County
Hertfordshire County

1 grid square represents 500 metres

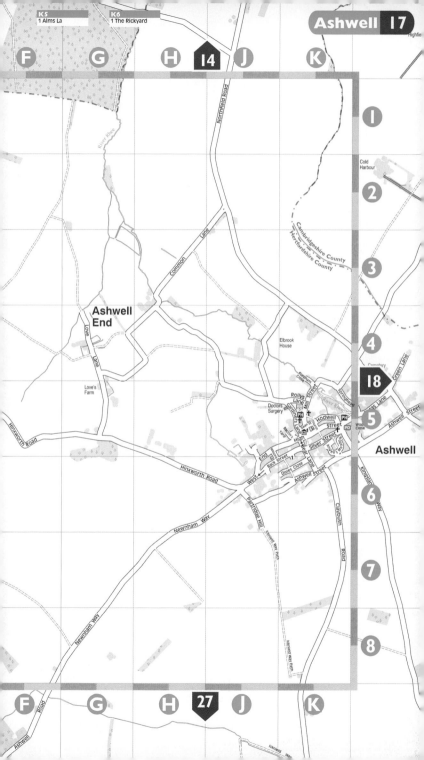

K5
1 Alms La

K6
1 The Rickyard

F G H **14** J K

I

2

3

4

18

5

6

7

8

F G H **27** J K

Cold Harbour

Cambridgeshire County
Hertfordshire County

Elbrook House

Ashwell End

Love Lane

Love's Farm

Hinxworth Road

Common Lane

Northfield Road

Cemetery

Green Lane

Rollys Lane

Doctors Surgery

Hodwell Street

Silver Street

Back Street

High End

Ashwell Street

Oliver Close

Newnham Way

Partridge Hill

Hinxworth Road

Ickleton Way Path

Claybush Road

Kinsey Way

Ashwell Street

Wood Close

Ashwell

Newnham Way

Ashwell Road

Ickleton Way

18

Highfield Farm

A **B** **15** **C** **D** **E**

Ashwell Road

Ashwell Road

Church Farm Lane

The Green

Westbrooks Close

Station Road

1

Wyndmere Farm

2

Cold Harbour

Gat
End

Cambridgeshire County
Hertfordshire Co

3

High Farm

Ickneild Way Path

Station Road

4

Cemetery

17

Green Lane

Rollys Lane

Lucas Lane

Mill Street

Woodforde Close

5

Ashwell Street

Station Road

PH

PO

High

Silver Street

Ashwell

Cambridgeshire County
Hertfordshire County

6

Ashwell Street

Claybush

Kingsland Way

7

Road

Redlands Farm

Station Road

8

Ickneild Way Path

A **B** **28** **C** **D** **E**

The Knoll

Pembroke Farm

1 grid square represents 500 metres

Utlington

Road

Anvil Ave

Coombe C

Coombe C

Roxton Road

F G H J K

Ickneild Way Path

I

Highfield Cottages

2

3

Highfield Farm

Morden Grange Farm

4

20

Morden Grange Plantation

A505

5

BALDOCK ROAD

Kings Ride

Cheyneys Lodge

Chain Walk

Cambridgeshire County

Hertfordshire County

The Thrift

6

Chain Walk

Lower Coombe Farm

7

Chain Walk

A505

A505

Ashwell & Morden Station

8

Coombe Road

Coombe Farm

F **29** G H J K

Chain Walk

Heath Farm

Coombe Road

Royston 21

F2
1 Stephenson Cl

G1
1 Donne Cl
2 Isherwood Cl
3 Keats Cl
4 The Quadrant
5 Willowside Wy

G2
1 Maltings Cl
2 Rose Wk
3 Saddlers Pl

G3
1 Copperfields

H1
1 Rochester Wy

H3
1 George La
2 The Green
3 Jepps La
4 John St

H4
1 Cartwright Rd
2 Hargreaves Rd
3 Nash Rd

J2
1 Poplar Cl

J3
1 Clydesdale Rd
2 Lingfield Rd
3 Martingale Rd
4 Wheatfield Crs
5 Woodlands

K4
1 Foxglove Bank
2 Primrose Vw

K3
1 Goodwood Rd
2 Haydock Rd

K2
1 Hawthorn Cl

K4 (J4)
1 Fordham Rd
2 Furze Gv
3 Kingston V
4 Mallow Wk
5 Whydale Rd

ROYSTON

F8
1 Greenbury Cl

F

G North Hall Farm

H

J

K

New Road

Icknield Way Path

I

Icknield Way Path

2

Icknield Way Path

B1368

BARLEY ROAD

New Buildings Farm

3

4

5

B1368

New Road

6

The Pudgell

ROYSTON RD

B1368

Bakers Lane

CAMBRIDGE ROAD

PICKNAGE ROAD B1039

BARLEY ROAD

Chishill Windmill

Heydon

B1039

7

May Street

Maltings Lane

The Surgery

HIGH STREET

St John

CHISHILL ROAD

B1039

Hertfordshire County

Cambridgeshire County

Barley

Hanger Dr

PO

Barley Vp School

Church End

LONDON ROAD

Churchfield

Church Lane

Shaftenhoe End

8

Smiths End Lane

F

St h's End

G

Bogm

H

33

Sh kenhoe End

Little

J

K

Heydon

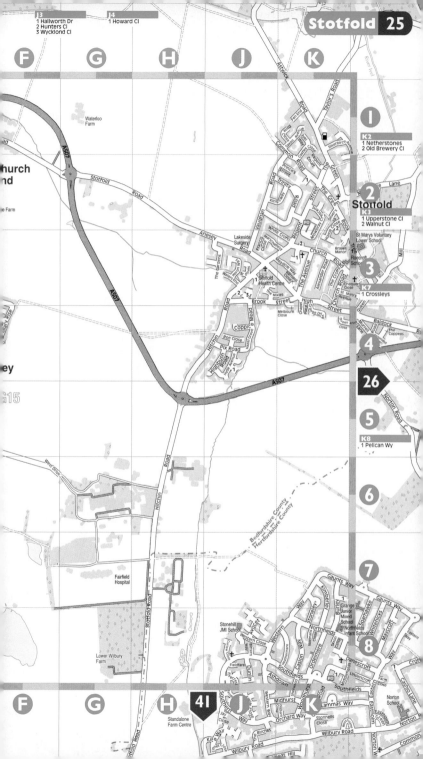

J3
1 Hallworth Dr
2 Hunters Cl
3 Wycklond Cl

J4
1 Howard Cl

F G H J K

I

K2
1 Netherstones
2 Old Brewery Cl

2 Stotfold

K3
1 Upperstone Cl
2 Walnut Cl

St Marys Voluntary
Lower School

3

K7
1 Crossleys

4

26

5

K8
1 Pelican Wy

6

7

8

41

26

A   B   16   C   D   E

E8
1 Aldridge Ct
2 Brewery La
3 Farriers Cl
4 Jackson St
5 Lavender Ct
6 Meeting Ho La

A8
1 Paynes Cl

A3
1 Rook Tree Cl

Taylor's Ro

Caldecote

Caldecote Road

1

Stotfold
Stotfold

River Ivel

Wraxfields

Malthouse Lane

Radwell Grange

2

St Marys Voluntary
Lower School

Cemetery

Roecroft School

3

Church Road

The Avenue

Chequers Close

St Mary's Avenue

High Street

Junction 10

Baldock Road

The Coppens

A507

Newnham Road

4

25

Norton Road

Radwell

Radwell Lane

5

River Ivel

6

Norton Road

Norton

Norton Mill Lane

Norton Bury Lane

Blackhorse Farm

7

Gaunts Way

Kimberley

Grange Junior Mixed School

Northfields Infant School

Whitehinks

Maycroft

8

Danescroft

Croft Lane

Lindencroft

Lammas Way

Southfields

Wilbury Road

Church Lane
St Nicholas
Junior & Infant School

Norton Road

NORTH ROAD

A1(M)

A507

Blackhorse Road

HITCHIN ROAD

A   B   42   C   D   E

1 grid square represents 500 metres

F8
1 Bramley Cl
2 Grosvenor Rd W
3 Icknield Wy East

G8
1 Downlands

F G H 17 J K

The Knoll

I

H8
1 Chauncy Gdns
2 Constantine Pl
3 Eisenberg Cl
4 Maltings Cl
5 Merchants Wk
6 Ringtale Pl
7 Rye Gdns

2

Newnham

SG7

3

Ashwell Road

Hullockpit Hill

4

Bygrave

Manor House

28

Ashwell Road

5

Wedon Way

6

ROYSTON ROAD

A505

7

Ashwell Road

Wallington Rd

8

Half Way Farm

Byroad Road

A505

Marquis Business Centre

ROYSTON ROAD

Wallington Road

Ashville Trading Estate

Rhee Spring

Orwell View

Yeomanry Drive

Saxon Way

Sale Ave

Rivett Close

Jevons Close

Bush Close

Spring Drive

Mercia Road

Hartsfield Junior Middle & Infant School

A507

F G H 43 J K

Baldock

Cll Common

Wallington Road

WHITEHALL ROAD

28

A B 18 C D E

The
Knoll

1

SG7

2

Slip
End

3

Hare Park
Farm

ROYSTON ROAD A505

4

Bygrave Lodge
Farm

27

5

ROYSTON ROAD A505

6

Lodge
Farm

7

Wallington Road

8

Wallingt

A B 44 C D E

Kit's Lane

The Street

Icknield Way Path

1 grid square represents 500 metres

Ashwell Road

Way Path

Cat Ditch

F G H **19** J K

Coombe Farm

I

Chain Walk

Heath Farm

Gatleyway Farm

2

Chain Walk

3

Mount Hill

4

30

Bury Barns

5

Gannock Farm

6

Lodge Farm

7

Partridge Hall Farm

Payne End

Dark La

Sandon

Sandon Infant S

8

Roe Wood

Chain Walk

F G H **45** J K

Rushden

Roe Green

F G H 21 J K

I

2

3

Hatchpen

Hertfordshire Way

The Joint

Reed End

Brickyard La

Jackson's Lane

Crown Lane

Blacksmith's Lane

Willow C

Reed First School

Church Lane

Wisbridge Farm

32

High Street

Reed

Driftway

Dane End

Reed Hall

Grannock Green

4

5

6

7

8

Bull Lane

HILL VIEW

Back Lane

F G H 47 Buckland J K

A10(T)

Hanaper Dr
PH
LONDON ROAD
Barley Vp
School
Church End
Shaftenhoe End
Church End
Churchfield

F
Smith's End Lane
G
H
23
J
K

Smith's
End

Bogmoor Road
Shaftenhoe
End

Road

Little Chishill Road

I

Road

Abbotsbury
House

Li
Chishill
2

3

Cross
Leys

Walk
Wood

4

34

5

Morrice Green
Farm

6

Nuthampstead
Bury

Hertfordshire Way

Bell Farm

Hertfordshire Way

7

Bell Lane
Park Farm Lane

Nuthampstead

Hertfordshire Way

Stocking Lane

8

F
G
H
49
J
K

Scales Park

34

A B C D E

B1039

1

Building
End

2 Little
Chishill

Common Lane

Building
End Road

Building End Road

3

Chrishall
Common

Cross
Leys

Cambridgeshire County

Essex County

4

33

5

River Stort

Park Lane

ice Green
m

6

The Hall

7

Park Lane

Bull Lane

Langl

8

Waterwick Hill

Lower
Green

New Farm

Scales Park

A B 50 C D E

River Stort

Essex County
Hertfordshire County

1 grid square represents 500 metres

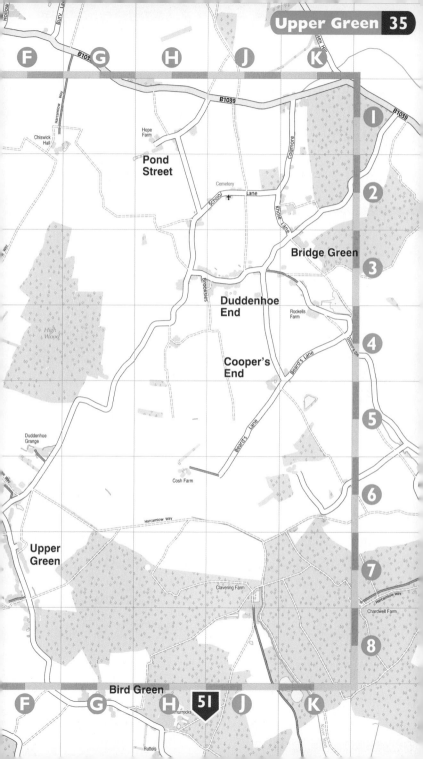

F   G   H   J   K

B103
B1039

I
B1039

2

Chiswick Hall

Hope Farm

Pond Street

Cemetery
School   Lane

Coombre

Knole Lane

3

Bridge Green

Brooksies

Duddenhoe End

Rockells Farm

4

Cooper's End

Beard's Lane

Offers cn

Harcamlow Way

5

6

Duddenhoe Grange

Beards   Lane

Cosh Farm

Upper Green

Harcamlow Way

7

Clavering Farm

Harcamlow Way

Chardwell Farm

8

Bird Green

Thurrocks

51

Ruttels

Knole Stort

Bury Lane

Holloway

Harcamlow Way

sex Hill

F   G   H   J   K

C5
1 Tudor Cl

B7
1 Shortcroft Ct

B6
1 Ravensburgh Cl

A B C D E

Fielden Court

Hillfoot
Farm

Dagmansbury

Barton Road

New Inn
Farm

Fielden
House

Sand Lane

C6
1 Ashby Dr
2 Bradshaws Cl
3 Churchill Rd

C7
1 Old School Gdns

Kitchenend
Farm

Barton Road

D5
1 Lancaster Cl

A6IT

Westhey
Manor

Higham Road

Barton Road

BEDFORD ROAD

York
Close

Faldo
Farm

Barton
Industrial
Estate

Faldo Road

Hanover

Windsor Road

Norman Road

Hastings
Road

Dane
Road

D6
1 Ivel Cl

B655

BEDFORD ROAD

Manor Road

BARTON-LE-CLAY

John Bunyan Trail

Grange Road

Mill Lane

Crays
Close

Arnold
Close

Brook End
Green Farm

Longcroft
Road

Nicholls
Close

Ramsey Manor
Lower School

A6IT

Sharpenhoe Road

Barton Road

Barton Rovers
Football Club

Dunstall Road

Arnold
Middle
School

B655 HEXTON ROAD

LUTON ROAD

Orchard
Close

Washbrook
Close

Church Road

John Bunyan Trail

Cemetery

A B 52 C D E

John Bunyan Trail

Lower

Church View
Hillfoot
Hillside
Brookside

F **G** **H** **J** **K**

John Bunyan
Trail

Church

High Road

Ion Bridge
Farm

I

Little
Ion

**Hanscombe
End**

Hanscombe End Road

2

**Apsle
End**

Apsley End

Manor
Farm

3

**Higham
Gobion**

Apsley Bury
Farm

4

Shillington

38

Hexton
Common

5

Bedfordshire County
Hertfordshire County

Bunyan Trail

6

John Bunyan Trail

Mill Lane

7

Manor
Farm

Bury Farm

Hexton

PH
PO

Hexton
Manor

Pegsdon

Pegsdon Way

BARTON RD B655

Hexton Junior
Middle & Infant
School

HITCHIN R

8

B655

F **G** **H** **53** **J** **K**

Ravensburgh
Castle

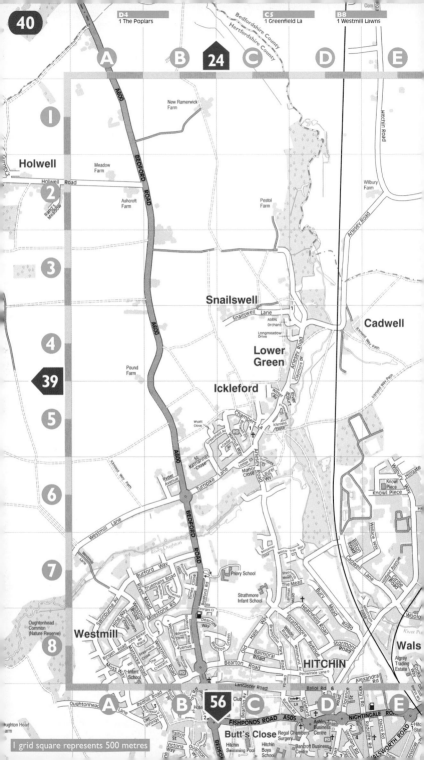

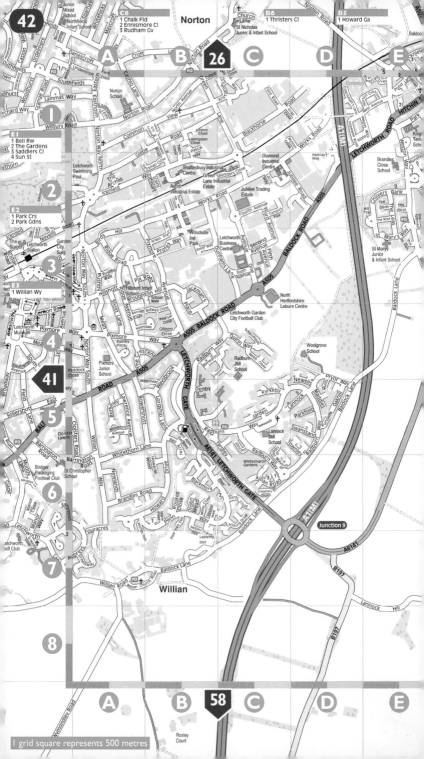

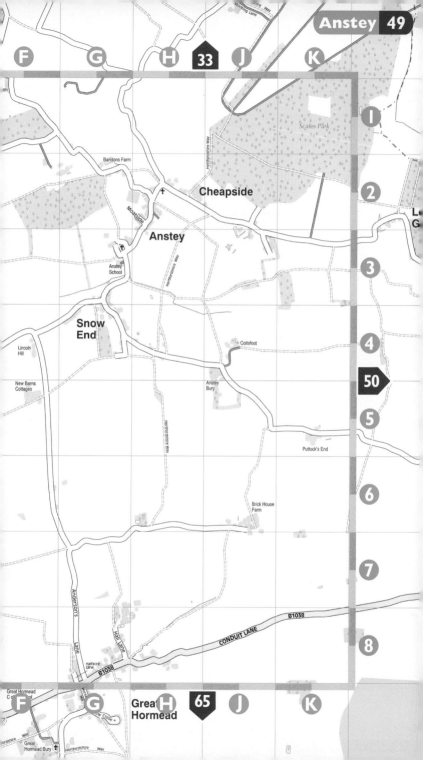

F G H 33 J K

I

2

L
G

3

4

50

5

6

7

8

Scales Park

Bandons Farm

Cheapside

Montside

Anstey

Anstey
School

Snow
End

Lincoln
Hill

New Barns
Cottages

Coltsfoot

Anstey
Bury

Herefordshire Way

Puttock's End

Brick House
Farm

Anderson's
Lane

Hall Lane

Halfacre
Lane

B1038

Conduit Lane

B1038

Great Hormead
C... ...ool

Great Hormead
Bury

Herefordshire Way

F G Great
Hormead H 65 J K

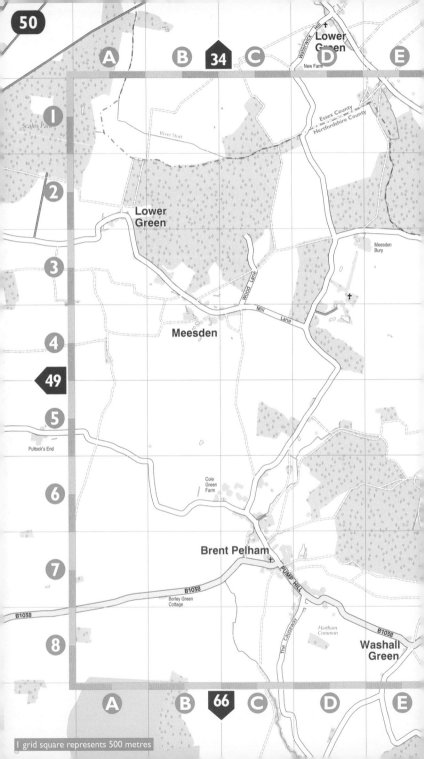

A   B   34   C   D   Lower Green   E

Lower Green
New Farm

1
Scales Park

River Stort

Essex County
Hertfordshire County

2

Lower
Green

Meesden
Bury

3

Wood Lane

Mill Lane

Meesden

4

49

5

Pultock's End

Cole
Green
Farm

6

Brent Pelham

PUMP HILL

7

B1038
Borley Green
Cottage

Hartham
Common

B1038

8

The Causeway

B1038

Washall
Green

A   B   66   C   D   E

1 grid square represents 500 metres

Chardwell Farm

F **G** **H** **35** **J** **K**

Bird Green

Thurrocks

Ruttels

River Stort

I

Valance

2

Clavering Place Farm

Valance Road

Further Ford End

Roast Green

3

4

Clavering

Deer's Green

Ford End

Chamberlaynes Farm

Cock Lane

5

Saville Close

PELHAM Rd

Stortford Road

Clavering Primary School

HI

Starling's Green

Honey Lane

Curles Manor

6

B1038

Parsonage Lane

Essex County Hertfordshire County

7

B1038

Dewes Green

Berden Priory Farm

8

Dewes Green Road

F **G** **H** **67** **J** Green Road **K**

Gull Lane

Vicarage Lane

Church Drive

Street

Berden

Pegsdon Way

HITCHIN ROAD   B655

B655

Icknield Way Path

Old Wellbury

New Wellbury

Bedfordshire County
Hertfordshire County

Icknield Way Path

Wellbury House

Little Offley

Lilley Hoo

Cloudshill

Westend Farm

School Lane

Offley

Lilley Hoo Farm

A505

PO

High St

Luton Road

West Lane

Gn Acres

John Bunyan Rd   East Street

The Bury

Lilleyhoo Lane

Luton Road

Salusbury Lane

Lawns

Cottage Cl

Lilley

Hollough Hill

Luton White Hill

Lilley Wood

West Street

Lilley Bottom

Luton Road

Luton Road

HILL   A505

Dog Kennel Farm

Luton Hill

Westbury Wood

1 grid square represents 500 metres

F G H 39 J K

I

Oughtonhead Lane

HEXTON ROAD B655

Hitchin Road

Oughton Head Farm

Hitc
Cric
Clu

2

Pirton Cross

Manley Way

Foxholes

PIRTON ROAD B

Offley Bottom

Carters Lane

Welbury

Wellbury Lane

3

Offley Cross

4

56

Offley Grange

A505

5

Temple Close

Temple End

6

Great
Offley

7

Harris Lane

Walden

8

Offleyholes Farm

Road

Offley Hoo

West
Wood

F G H 72 J K

56

Westmill

B3
1 Tudor Ct

B1
1 Chestnut Ct
2 Firs Cl
3 Spellbrooke

A1
1 Friday Furlong

Walsw

Wals

40

HIT**D**IN

E

C2
1 West Alley

A B C

FISHPONDS ROAD A505

Lancaster Road

Baliol Rd

Nightingale Road

WALSWORTH ROAD

Butt's Close

C3
1 Wratten Cl

Oughtonhead Lane

Ashley
Business
Centre

Regal Chambers
Surgery

Bancroft Business
Centre

Hitchin
Boys School

Hitchin
Swimming Pool

Health
Centre

Doctors
Surgery

St Andrews Benslow
JMI School

Hitchin Cricket
Club

Lavender
Way

Gaping Lane

Queen Mother
Theatre

Hitchin
Girls School

2

West Hill

D1
1 Bunyan Rd
2 Forge Cl
3 Hazelwood Cl
4 St Anne's Rd
5 St Augustine Cl
6 Water La
7 Whinbush Gv

Gray's Lane

Foxholes

ROAD B655

MOORMEAD HILL

OFFLEY ROAD

UPR TILEHOUSE STREET

Natural Art Gallery
& Science Pictures

Highbury
Infant School

3

D2
1 Harrison Cl
2 Storehouse La

The Ridgeway

Hawthorn

Cranborne Av

Willow Lane

Offley
Cross

PARK WAY

HITCHIN

Cemetery

4

55

Hitchin
Hill

Charlton

STEVENAGE ROAD

LONDON ROAD

Brick Kiln

Gosmore Ley

5

D3
1 St Andrew's Pl

Close

Wellhead

Priory W'y

Temple
End

Maydencroft Lane

Maydencroft
Manor

6

Gosmore

D4
1 St Elmo Ct
2 St John's Rd
3 Traherne Cl

Waterdell

Mill Road

7

Preston Road

D5
1 New England Cl
2 Newlands Cl East
3 Newlands Cl West
4 Ransom Cl

Offleyholes
Farm

8

St Ib

E1
1 Station Ap

Tatmore
Place

E3
Street names for
this grid square are
listed at the back of
the index

A B **73** C D E

E4
1 The Paddock

E5
1 Chestnut Wk
2 Elderberry Dr

I grid square represents 500 metres

F1
1 Arnold Cl
2 Burns Cl
3 Campbell Cl

F2
1 Mermaid Cl
2 Peppercorn Wk
3 Pullman Dr
4 Spurrs Cl
5 Worsdell Wy

F G H 41 J K

Willian Road

CAMBRIDGE ROAD

North Hertfordshire College

Purwell

I

F3
1 Bramfield
2 Hensley Cl

2

G2
1 Holden Cl
2 Nimbus Wy
3 Stirling Cl

3

Great Wymondley

Wymondley Road

Hitchin Road

Graveley Road

Graveley Lane

akfield

Uplands Avenue

4

Kingshott School

58

Ashbrook

5

A602

Ashbrook Lane

Stevenage Road

Little Wymondley

Arch Road

Wymondley Junior & Infant School

Grimsdyke Road

Sicott Road

Priory Lane

Priory View

Elms Close

Bladon Cl

Church Path

6

St Ippollitts School

Cemetery

Bakemore End Road

Wymondley Bury

A602

Country Lane

7

ppollitts

Stevenage Road

Redcoats

Titmore Green

Todd's Green

Stevenage Road

B656

Fishers Green

8

F G H 74 J K shers Green

E8
1 St Albans Link

E7
1 Gloucester Cl

D8
1 Newbury Cl

A   B   **42**   C   D   E

1

Wymondley Road

Roxley Court

Hertfordshire Way

Jack's Hill

2

Killian Road

Hertfordshire Way

B197

3

Road

Graveley Lane

Hertfordshire Way

4

Priory Lane

Mercer Way

57

Church Lane

Turf Lane

Oak Lane

HIGH STREET

Ashwell Close

Ashwell Common

Food Walk

Graveley

Doctors Surgery

Chesfield Park

5

Graveley Junior Mixed School

6

Wymondley Bury

Corton Close

B197

GRAVELEY ROAD

B197

A602

A602 HITCHIN ROAD

Junction 8

7

Champ Lane

Old Charity Lane

A1(M)

Stevenage Road

Todd's Green

Lister Hospital

A&E

NORTH ROAD

Underwood Road

Granby Road

Chorley Gardens

Chancellors Road

Rook's Nest

Corey's Mill Lane

Whitney Drive

Burymead

RECTORY ROAD

The Bury

Cemetery

8

Fishers Green

Chander Road

John Henry Newman RC School

Nicholas Place

Chestnut Walk

Trent Close

Fishers Green

Corton Close

A1(M)

75

MARTINS WAY

A1072

Almonds Hill Junior Mixed School

Weston Road

A   B   **75**   C   D   E

Thomas Alleyne School

Ellis

Providence Grove

Cemetery

F G H **45** J K

I

Cottered

2

Brook End

3

62

4

Cottered Warren

5

6

Gardners End

7

8

Hare Street

B1057

Cromer

B1057

Bury Grange

Ardeley Bury

Ardeley School

The Crescent

PH Ardeley

School Lane

Warren Lane

Blind Lane

Walkern Bury Farm

Bassus Green

St John's Wood

F G H **78** J K

A507

Chain Walk

Spring Lane

Blue Lane

The Cr

Lane

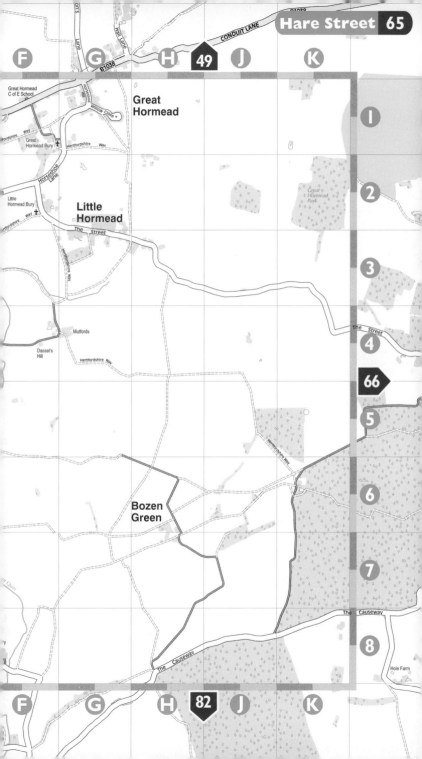

CONDUIT LANE

F **G** **H** 49 **J** **K**

B1038

Hall Lane

Great Hormead
C of E School

Great
Hormead

I

Willow Close

Hertfordshire Way

Great
Hormead Bury

2

Great
Hormead Park

Horseshoe Lane

Little
Hormead Bury

Little
Hormead

3

The Street

Hertfordshire Way

The Street

Hertfordshire Way

Mutfords

4

66

Dassel's
Hill

Hertfordshire Way

5

Hertfordshire Way

6

Bozen
Green

7

The Causeway

Quin

8

Hole Farm

The Causeway

F **G** **H** 82 **J** **K**

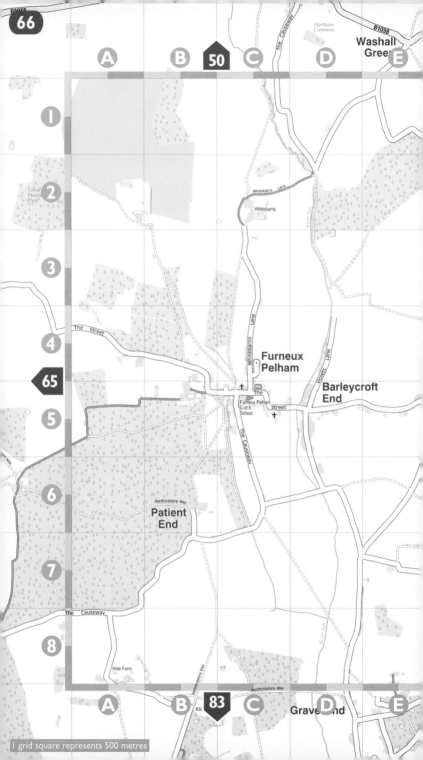

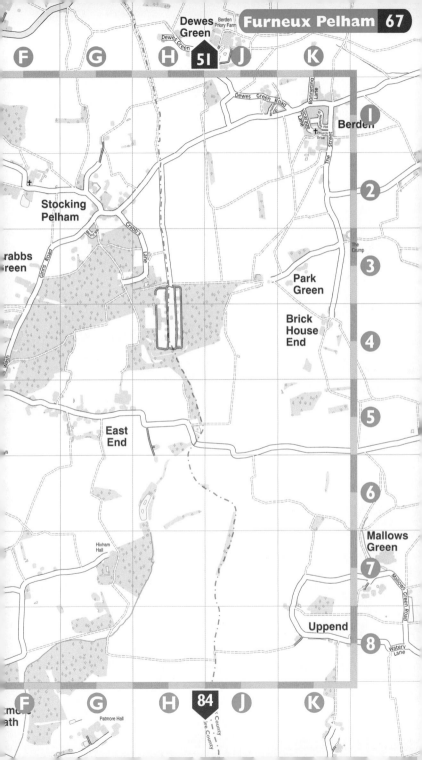

Dewes Green

Berden Priory Farm

Dewes Green Road

Bonnecting Lane

Vicarage Lane

Church Drive

Berden

The Street

Stocking Pelham

Crabb's

Crabb's Lane

Gimms Road

Crabbs Green

The Crump

Park Green

Brick House End

East End

Hixham Hall

Mallows Green

Mallows Green Road

Uppend

Watery Lane

Patmore Hall

County

F **G** **H** 51 **J** **K**

I

2

3

4

5

6

7

8

F **G** **H** 84 **J** **K**

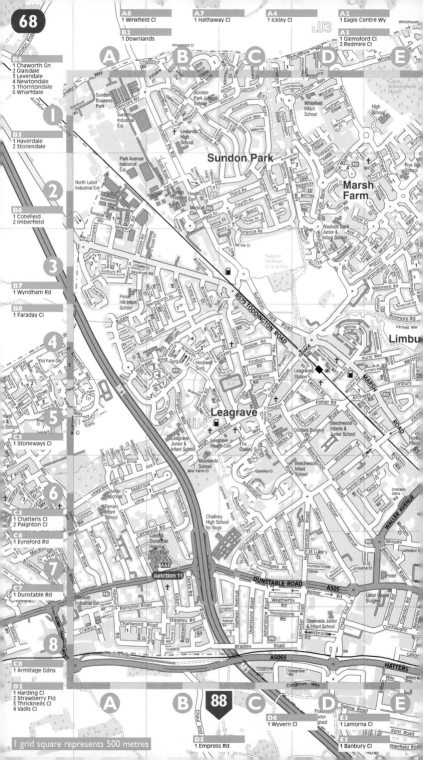

F7
1 Beanley Cl
2 Berrow Cl
3 Branton Cl
4 Manning Pl
5 Renshaw Cl
6 Trescott Cl

F8
1 Ardleigh Gn
2 Baylam Dell
3 Nayland Cl
4 Radstone Pl
5 Tanfield Gn

F G H 54 J K

I

G7
1 Greenriggs
2 Lennox Gn
3 Reedsdale
4 Thaxted Cl

2

G8
1 Whittingham Cl

3

4

72

5

6

7

8

Offley Hoo

Dog Kennel Farm

Westbury Wood

Luton White Hill

Lilley Bottom

Lilley Bottom

Chalk Hill

Offley Chase

Lodge Farm

Mangrove Green

Chalk Hill

Mangrove Rd

Prior

Elmtree Av

ernhoe

Stony Lane

Stony Lane

Bricklin Wood

Tea Green

Tankards Farm

Windmill Road

Windmill Road

The Heath

Darley Road

Heath Road

Wandon End

Darleyhall

Darley Road

St Mary's Cl

Colemans Road

Eaton Gn Rd

F G H 91 J K

Winch Hill Farm

Hertfordshire Co.

Luton

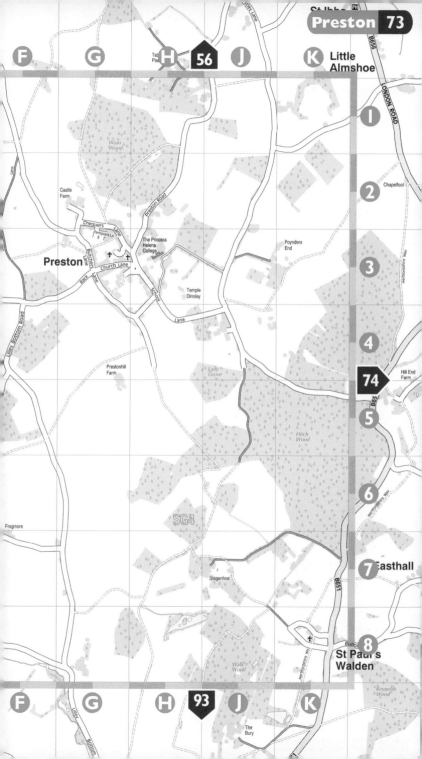

St Ibbs PH

F G H 56 J K Little Almshoe

London Road

B656

1

Chapelfoot 2

Wain Wood

Castle Farm

Chequers
Templars La

Preston Road

The Princess Helena College

Poynders End

3

Back Lane

Butchers Lane

Church Lane

School Lane

Temple Dinsley

Hertfordshire Way

Lilley Bottom Road

Lane

4

Prestonhill Farm

Lady Grove

Hill End Farm

74

B655

5

Hitch Wood

6

Hertfordshire Way

Frogmore

SG4

7 Easthall

Stagenhoe

B651

8

Walk Wood

St Paul's Walden

Butlers

Hertfordshire Way

F G H 93 J K

The Bury

Reynolds Wood

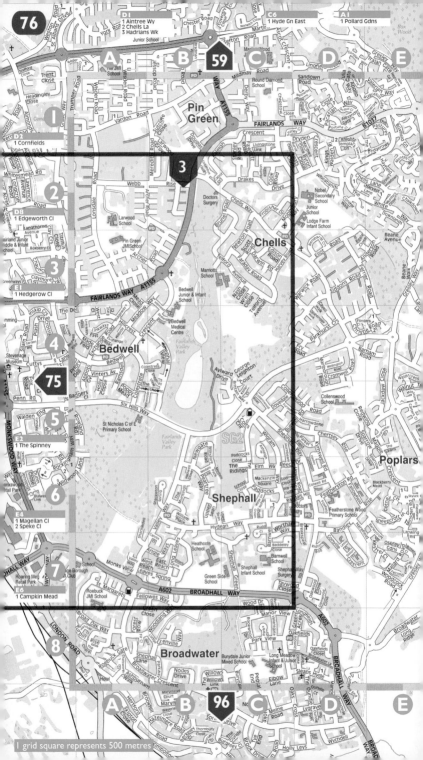

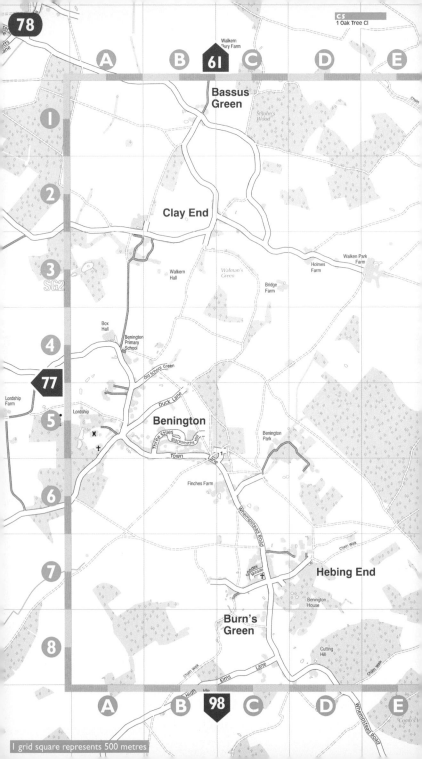

Ⓐ Ⓑ **61** Ⓒ Ⓓ Ⓔ

CS
1 Oak Tree Cl

Walkern
Bury Farm

**Bassus
Green**

St John's
Wood

1

2

Clay End

3

SG2

Walkern
Hall

Walman's
Green

Holmes
Farm

Walken Park
Farm

Bridge
Farm

Box
Hall

Benington
Primary
School

4

77

Old School Green

Lordship
Farm

5

Lordship

Duck Lane

Benington

Benington
Park

Three Stiles

Blacksmiths

Town Lane

6

Finches Farm

Whempstead Road

7

Cooley
Mead

Chain Walk

Hebing End

Benington
House

8

**Burn's
Green**

Chain Walk

Elms Lane

Cutting
Hill

Chain Walk

High

Ⓐ Ⓑ **98** Ⓒ Ⓓ Ⓔ

Whempstead Road

Comb's

I grid square represents 500 metres

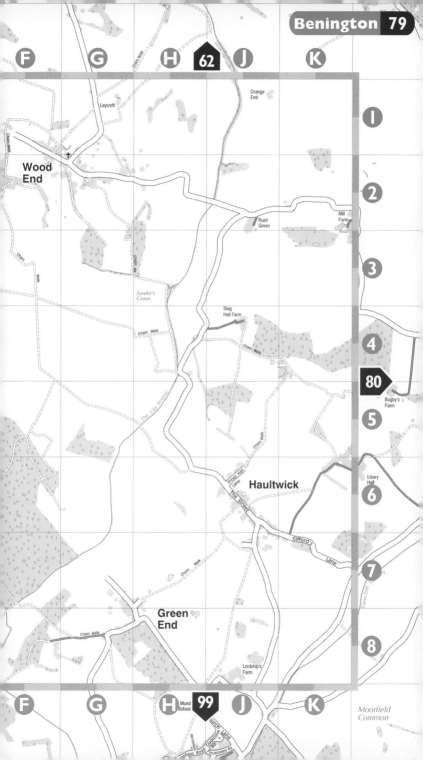

F G H 62 J K

I

2

3

4

80

5

6

7

8

F G H 99 J K

Orange
End

Leycroft

Wood
End

Rush
Green

Mill
Farm

Sander's
Green

Stag
Hall Farm

Chain Walk

Chain Walk

Chain Wa

Chain Walk

Chain Walk

The Old Bourne

Chain Walk

Frogg Hall Lane

Haultwick

The Street

Gifford's
Lane

Libury
Hall

Bugby's
Farm

Dane End

Chain Walk

Green
End

Chain Walk

Lordship's
Farm

Mund
School

Moorfield
Common

A B 63 C D E

Cherry Green

Tillers Farm

Peasefield

Hamels Lane

I

2

Mill Farm

3

Nasty

Nobles Farm

Great Munden

4

79

Bugby's Farm

Mentley Lane

5

6

Libury Hall

Stockalls

Gifford's

7

Lane End Tributary

Brockhold's Farm

8

Levens Green

Old Hall Green

Moor Common

A B 100 C D E

High Trees

Beggarman's Lane

Hill F

J5
1 Mentley La East

J6
1 Roman Wy

64

Quinbury Farm

Coles Park

Knights Hill Farm

I
J7
1 Plashes Cl
2 Sadlier Rd
3 St Mary's Rd

Green End

2
K6
1 Gatesbury Wy
2 Wickham Wy

Hamels Lane

Hamels Lane

Braughing

3
K7
1 Churchfields

Hamels Park

East Herts Golf Club

4

82

Mentley Lane

Mentley Lane West

Gatesbury

5

Mentley Farm

6 SG11

Puckeridge

Park Lane

St Thomas of Canterbury Catholic School

Station Road

Roger De Clare School

Standon Health Centre

7

Town Farm Crescent

Aston Road

Southfields

Aston Road

STANDON HILL   A120   KENT'S LANE   STORTFORD ROAD

Standon

8

Edmunds College

Paper Mill Lane

Hadham Road

F   G   H   101   J   K

82
Hay Street

Quinbury Farm

A3
1 Green Hill Cl

A2
1 The Causeway
2 Northfield
3 Quin Ct
4 Southfield

A **B** **65** **C** useway **D** **E**

I

Gravelly Lane

Cockhan

en End

2

Hull Lane

Malting Lane

PO

Palman Road

Church End

Old Boys School

Green Lane

Friars Road

Harcam

Uplands

Green

Ford Street

Harcamlow Way

Braughing

3

STATION ROAD

4

Braughin Friars

81

5

The Warren

Puckeridge

6

SG11

Harcamlow Way

Pockendon Field

Horse Cross

A120

Roger De Clare School

Standon Health Centre

7

Poor's Land

Broken Green

Southfields

Vicarage

Town Farm Crescent

KENT'S LANE

STORTFORD ROAD

A120

Harcamlow Way

High Street

Standon

8

Standon Friars

Wellpond Green

Paper Mill Lane

Hadham Road

A **B** **102** **C** **D** **E**

Balsams

Bromley

I grid square represents 500 metres

Upper

A B **67** C D E

Patmore
Heath

Patmore Hall

Essex County
Hertfordshire County

Farnham
Green

Harcamlow Way

2

Clapgate

3

The
Common

Mill Lane

Hertfordshire Way

Upwick
Green

4

Upwick Hall

Albury
Lodge

83

Hertfordshire Way

Walnuttree
Green

5

River Ash

6

Tilbury Road

Little
Hadh **7**

Church
End

STORTFORD ROAD

Band End

Hertfordshire Way

Hadham
Park

A120

8

HADHAM ROAD

Green
Street

A B **104** C Cradle D E
End

A120

Millbridge Lane

Hertfordshire Way

F G H J K

I
2
3
4
5
6
7
8

Leigh Drive

STANSTED RD

HENH
HA
Hall Road
Church Lane

Fuller's End

Tye Green Road

Stansted House

M11

B1051

The Arthur Findlay College

Burton Bower

Tye Green

Clayton Hill

Burton End

Belmer Road

Sixth Avenue

Monks Farm

Thirtieth St

Bassingbourn Street

Bury Lodge

Bury Lodge Lane

P

Long Border Road

Threm
BASSINI
ROUND

F G H 107 J K

Round Coppice Road

PRIORY WOOD
ROUNDABOUT

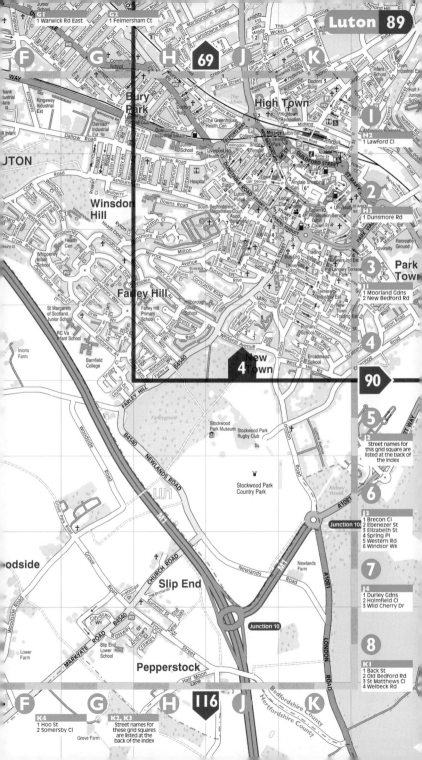

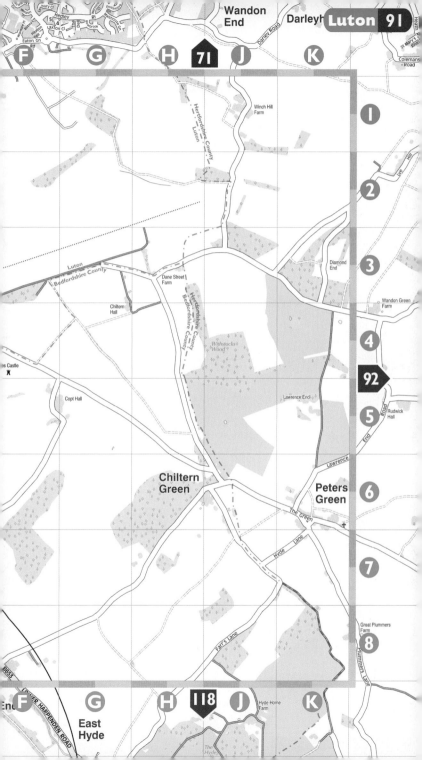

92

A   B   **72**   C   D   E

St Mary's
Colemans
Road

Heath Road

Chapel Road

Orchard

Oxford Rd

Tower Road

Law Hall
Farm

Holroute Lane

**Breachwood
Green**

Bailey's
Farm

Pasture

Grove
Farm

Law Hall Lane

I

Lye Hill

Bendish

2

Long Lane

3

Pond

Whiteway
Bottom

Wandon Green
Farm

Whitewaybottom

Lane

4

91

Lawrence End

End Road

Rudwick
Hall

5

Whitewaybottom

Lawrence

Barleybeans

Lane

6

Peters
Green

The Green

Lane

Luton Road

Claggy Cott

7

Kimpton Road

**Ansells
End**

Claggy

Luton Road

Great Plummers
Farm

8

Plummers Lane

Ramridge
Farm

Sledsbury

Kimpton
Grange

B652

Cooper's
Hill

A   B   **119**   C   D   E

Lane

Tallents
Farm

BOTTOM

1 grid square represents 500 metres

F3
1 Parkins Cl

St Edmunds College

F **G** **H** 81 **J** **K**

Paper Mill Lane

Hadham Road

1

2

3

Latchford
Arches Hall

4

102

5

6

Biggin's Farm

7

8

Rush Green

Dowsett's Farm

Colliers End

Plashes Wood

Plashes Farm

Barwick

Barwick Lane

Gore Lane

Great Barwick Manor

Sutes Woods

Harcamlow Way

River Rib

Harcamlow Way

Harcamlow Way

Sawtrees Wood

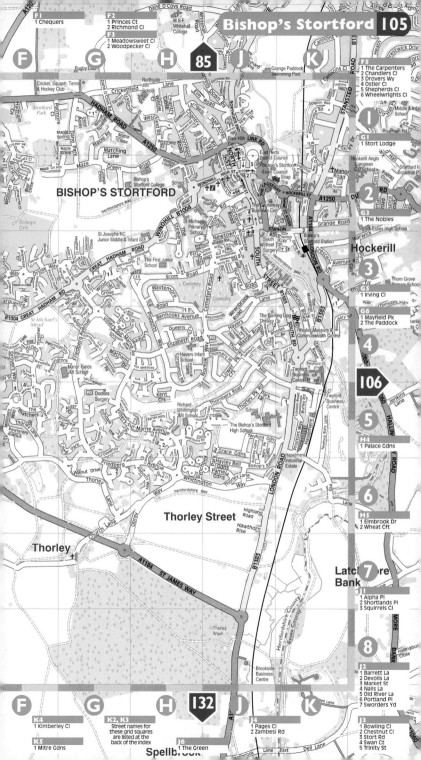

BISHOP'S STORTFORD

Hockerill

Thorley Street

Thorley

Latchmore Bank

Spellbrook

F1
1 Chequers

F2
1 Princes Ct
2 Richmond Cl

F3
1 Meadowsweet Cl
2 Woodpecker Cl

F5
1 The Carpenters
2 Chandlers Cl
3 Drovers Wy
4 Ostler Cl
5 Shepherds Cl
6 Wheelwrights Cl

G1
1 Stort Lodge

G3
1 The Nobles

G5
1 Irving Cl

G6
1 Mayfield Pk
2 The Paddock

H4
1 Palace Gdns

H5
1 Elmbrook Dr
2 Wheat Cft

J1
1 Alpha Pl
2 Shortlands Pl
3 Squirrels Cl

J2
1 Barrett La
2 Devoils La
3 Market St
4 Nails La
5 Old River La
6 Portland Pl
7 Sworders Yd

J3
1 Bowling Cl
2 Chestnut Cl
3 Storrt Rd
4 Swan Ct
5 Trinity St

K4
1 Kimberley Cl

K5
1 Mitre Gdns

K2, K3
Street names for these grid squares are listed at the back of the index

J4
1 Pages Cl
2 Zambesi Rd

J6
1 The Green

85

106

132

P

F G H **87** J K

PRIORY WOOD
ROUNDABOUT

Round Coppice Road

Bury Lodge Lane

Thremhall
Priory Farm

I

CM22

A120 DUNMOW ROAD
Filtch Way

2 20

**Takeley
Street**

iln
en

s Farm

3

Hatfield
Forest

edlar's
reen

Road

Beggar's Hall

The Street

Three Forest Way

Harcamlow Way

Forest Way

4

Hatfield
Forest NT

Three Forests Way

Three Forests Way

Three Forests Way

Harcamlow Way

Three Forests Way

Harcamlow Way

Three Forests Way

5

**Hallingbury
Street**

Forest
Lodge

Collins
Coppice

Little Barrington
Hall Farm

6

Forest Way

Three Forests Way

Lodge
Farm

7

ot
arm

Wall
Wood

The
Woods

8

Three Forests Way

F G H J K

Forest
Hall

Forest
Farm

Mank's
Wood

Three Forests Way

Barrington
Hall

110

C5
1 Greenacres

A7
1 Vicarage Gdns

A2
1 Chaseside Cl
2 Keepers Cl
3 Manor Pound Rd
4 Town Farm

A B C D E

1

D4
1 Newells Hedge

2

D5
1 Cheyne Cl

Cheddington

3

E4
1 Green La
2 Rushendon Furlong

4

109

5

6

Church Farm

Manor Farm

Marsworth

7

Marsworth Church of England Primary School

8

Startop's End

The Street

Station Road

West End Road

Ivinghoe Bridge

Vicarage Farm

Whistle Brook

Little Seabrook

Greatgap

Great Seabrook

Watermill

Ford End Farm

Swing Bridge

Brookmead School

Doctors Surg

Lower School

Church Lane

Station Road

High Street

Club House

Cheddington

Checkers Lane

Pitstone Surgery

Yardley Avenue

Doctors Surgery

Pitstone Green

Old Farm

Morton Close

Marsworth Road

Pitstone

Meadow Lane

Chu End

Grand Union Canal

Church Farm

Grand Union Canal

Manor Road

Church Lane

ICKNIELD WAY

College Lake Wildlife Centre

ICKNIELD

LOWER

UPPER

Folly Farm

Manor House Farm

Startop's End

Nature Reserve
Startops End Reservoir
(Grand Union Canal)

Marsworth Reservoir
(Grand Union Canal)

A B **135** C D E

Bulbourne

Ivinghoe
Aston

F **G** **H** **J** **K**

I

TRING ROAD

2

B489

Coombe
Bottom

Coombe
Hole

Two Ridges Link

Two Ridges Link

● Hill Fort

3

Crabtree
Cottage

Ivinghoe
Golf Club

Town
Farm

B489

Icknield Way

4

112

Ivinghoe

ROAD

B489

Icknield Way

5

6

Hurst Farm

B489

Icknield Way

Clipper
Down

7

Ivinghoe
Common

Ridgeway

Down Farm

Icknield Way

Pitstone Hill

8

Duncombe
Farm

County

Ridgeway

Icknield Way

F **G** **H** **136** **J** **K**

arley
End

Icknield Way

Farm

B4540

F   G   H   J   K

Tree
Cathedral

Icknield

Whipsnade

Whipsnade
Heath

I

Dukes Avenue

**The
Green**

Studham

Buckwood Lane

Lane

Woodcock

Hoe

Oakway

2

Mrs Joans Way

Central

Avenue

Holywell Road

Road

Holywell

Cut Throat

Avenue

**Whipsnade
Park Zoo**

St Peter's Wy

Cut

Valley

Throat

Humphret
Talbot   Avenue

Pitkin Way

Holywell

Rd

Schools

3

Dunstable Road

Icknield Way

Icknield Way

**Whipsnade
Park Golf Club**

Studham

Lane

Studham

Swanells Wy

Manor
Farm

Southern   Wy

II4

4

PO

Ker

Church

Dunstable

Road

5

Valley

Vale
Close

Road

**Studham
VC Lower
School**

Mansgrove
Farm

Common Road

6

Bury
Farm

7

Ravensdell
Wood

Yong
Wood

SOUTH

A4146

Lamsey
Farm

Mileburn
Farm

A4146

Predley Hill

8

HEMEL   HEMPST.

ROAD

Church
Farm

F   G   H   **I38**   J   K

Aley Green

orth

F **G** **H** **88** **J** **K**

H3
1 Old Vicarage Gdn

J4
1 Summer Wk
2 Sursham Ct
3 William St

Tillfield arm

Pipers Lane

Cemetery

Mancroft Road

Lower Farm

Hill Farm

Pipers

Woodside Farm & Wildfowl Park

I

Red Cow Farm

A5(T)

Caddington Common

LUTON ROAD B4540

Caddington Hall

2

Markyate Cell

Cemetery

A5(T)

3

Windmill Road

Markyate Primary School

Cavendish Road

Roman Way

The Railings

Hicks Road

Markyate

Cowper Road

Cowper Court

Hicks Cl

Sherd Court

A5(T)

Long Meadow

4

Green Lane

Rainbow Hall Farm

Parkfield Road

Park Cl

The Coppings

Pickford Road

Chestnut Wood

Cheshunt Cl

London Road

Carter

Dammersden

116

Sebright School

Cheverell's Green

5

A5(T)

oe End

Cheverells

6

Friendless Lane

Cotton Spring Farm

7

Mill Lane

Valleybottom Farm

Valley Lane

Pietley

Mill

8

Hill Farm

F **G** **H** **140** **J** **K**

Wood End Lane

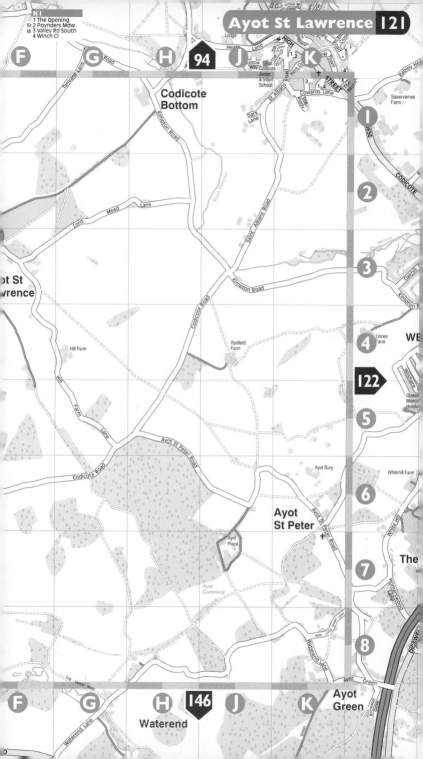

K1
1 The Opening
Ki 2 Poynders Mdw
Mi 3 Valley Rd South
4 Winch Cl

F **G** **H** 94 **J** **K**

Codicote
Bottom

Lodge
Heath

HIGH
Green

Codicote
Junior
& Infant
School

St Albans

Cowards Lane

STREET

I

Sisservernes
Farm

CODICOTE

2

Tanyard Lane

Kimpton Road

Dark
Lane

River Mimram

Saint Albans Road

River Mimram

3

Kimpton Road

ot St
wrence

Lord
Mead
Lane

Codicote Road

Ryefield
Farm

4

Linces
Farm

WE

Hill Farm

Hill
Farm
Lane

122

Queen
Memorial
Hospital

5

Ayot St Peter Road

Codicote Road

Ayot Bury

Whitehill Farm

6

Ayot
St Peter

Ayot St Peter Road

7

The

Ayot
Place

Ayot
Greenway

8

DIGSWE

F **G** **H** 146 **J** **K**

Waterend

Waterend Lane

Ayot Green

Ayot Green

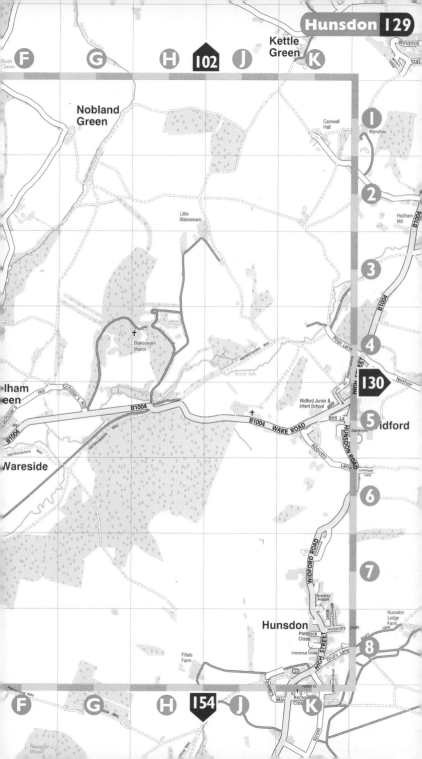

K8
1 Blacksmiths Wy

F   G   H   104   J   K

Hertfordshire Way

Blount's
Farm

Sacombs Ash

Sacombs Ash Lane

Warrens

Allen's
Green

I

Shingle
Hall

2
Trims
Green

3

Tharbies

4

132

Miller's Brook

Hardings

Bearfield Road

Gangies

Gangies Hill

Carters

Hoskins

Crumps

West Road

West Road

5 21

Claylane
Farm

6

Fryars

The Manor of
Groves Golf Club

Jeffs

High Wych

SAWBRIDGEW

7

Bakers
Farm

Mabey's
Walk

Maltings
Lane

Brook Walk

High
Wych

The Thomas Rivers
Medical Centre

Wisem

8

Farnham

Wycherford Drive

Rowney

Blakemo

High Wych Road

F   G   H   156   J   K

Say
Far

Rowney
Farm

Chaseways

Blenheim

Beech

Oak Drive

Wycherford Drive

Hand Lane

Rowney Gardens

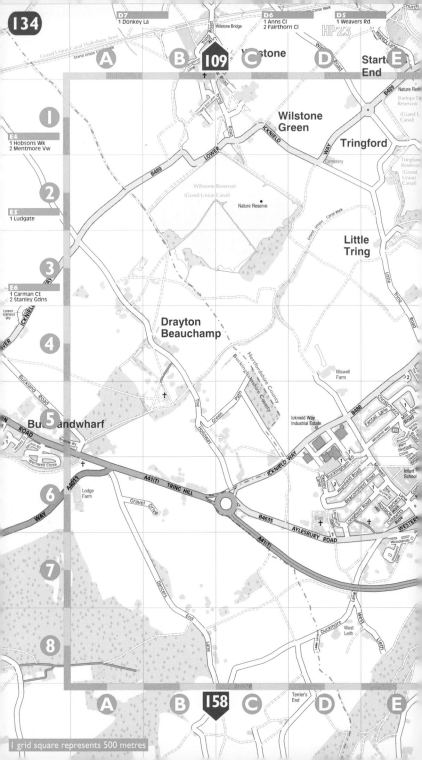

F2
1 Bulbourne Ct

F3
1 Icknield Gn
2 Longbridge Cl

F **G** **H** **110** **J** **K**

I

F4
1 Emma Rothschild Ct
2 Mulberry Cl

2

F5
1 Kingsley Wk
2 Parsonage Cl

3

F6
1 Akeman St
2 Mansard Cl
3 Parsonage Pl
4 Surrey Pl
5 Woods Pl

4

136

5

G3
1 Meadowbrook
2 Pheasant Cl
3 Sutton Cl

6

G5
1 Evans Wy
2 Mill Gdns
3 Mortimer Ri
4 Treehanger Cl

7

G6
1 Dunsley Pl

8

Bulbourne

Tring Wharf

New Mill

Tring & New Mill Pre-school

Grand Union Canal Walk

Manor House Farm

Marsworth Reservoir

Grand Union Canal

Union Canal (Lower Arm)

Tring Ford Road

BULBOURNE ROAD

B488

B488

Parkhill Farm

Marshcroft Lane

Grand Union Canal Walk

Netherby Close

Grove Road Primary School

WINGRAVE ROAD

BROOK STREET

Dundale Infants School

Grove Road

Station Road

Hotel

Football Club

COW LANE

Tring School

Tring Sports Centre

Tring Health Centre

Doctors Surgery

HIGH STREET

B4635

LONDON ROAD

TRING

Tring Town Council

Akeman Business Park

The Arts Educational School

British Museum (Natural History) Zoological Museum

Park Street

Junior School

Friars Walk

Upper Dunsley

A4251

A41(T)

A41(T)

Oddy Hill

Tring Park

The Twist

Ridgeway

Park Farm

Wigginton

Vicarage Road

Hemp Lane

Hill Green Farm

Hastoe

Martin Hill

Fox Road

The Twist

Highfield Road

Ridgeway WW

The Bit

School

Chesham Road

Wigginton Bottom

F **G** **H** **159** **J** **K**

J8
1 Belmers Rd
2 Grimsdyke Rd
3 Pollywick Rd

H5
1 The Beeches
2 Hawkwell Dr

Wick Farm

H4
1 Danvers Cft
2 Hollyfield
3 Sulgrave Crs

Ringshall

F   G   H   **112**   J   K

Church Farm

Deer Leap Swimming Pool

Allerton Drive
Atterton Drive
Ringshall Drive
Castadene Close
PO

I

Church Road

Little Gaddesden JMI School

Little **2** Gaddesden

3

Hudnall Lane

Sallow Copse

Pitstone Common

Bridgewater Monument

B4506

Ashridge Golf Club

Old Park Lodge

Ashridge Park

4

Ashridge Estate (NT)

138

Aldbury Common

5

Woodyard Cotts

Berkhamsted Common

B4506

Coldharbour Farm

6

HP4

7

Northchurch Common

B4506

Hill Farm

Brickkiln Cott

Frithsden Beeches

8

F   G   H   **161**   J   K

Northchurch Farm

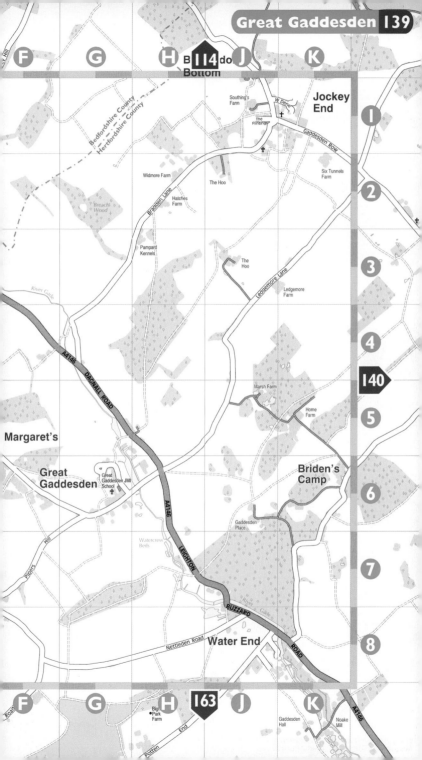

F   G   H   B **114** do   J   K

Bottom

Jockey End

Southing's Farm

W Dere

The Flinting's

Gaddesden Row

1

Bedfordshire County
Hertfordshire County

Widmore Farm

The Hoo

Six Tunnels Farm

2

Braxden Lane

Hatches Farm

Breach Wood

Pampard Kennels

The Hoo

Ledgemore Lane

Ledgemore Farm

3

River Gade

4

140

Marsh Farm

Home Farm

5

Margaret's

A4146 DAGNALL ROAD

Briden's Camp

Great Gaddesden

Great Gaddesden JMI School

6

Watercress Beds

Gaddesden Place

A4146 LEIGHTON

Piner's Hill

7

BUZZARD

River Gade

Nettleden Road

Water End

ROAD

8

F   G   H   **163**   J   K   A4146

Road

Bigg Park Farm

Potten End

Gaddesden Hall

Noake Mill

1 Hadleigh Ct
2 Tiverton Ct

Leasey B

A3
1 Bewdley Cl
2 Camberley Pl
3 Ennis Cl
4 Lilac Wy
5 Newton Cl
6 Ravenscroft
7 Sandhurst Ct

A2
1 Pendennis Ct

A   B   119   C   D   E

Wheathampstead Road

Dornings Close

Harpenden

Long Butlers

Cortwell

Wheathampstead Rd

Green Lane

Down Green Lane

Pipers

The Grove

The Grove JMI School

The Grove Infant School

Aldwick Rd

Alston

Green La

GROVE AV

Pipers Lane

Pipers Av

Sibley Avenue

Paddock Wood

Oakley Road

Broadstone

Cross Farm

Cranstone Dr

Welbeck

Acacia

Ayres End Lane

Cross Lane

Grange Ct Rd

Beech Cl

143

A1081

Ayres End

West End Farm

Ferrers Lane

Bull Lane

Hi

Childwick Bury

Cheapside Farm

Sandridgebury La

Sandridgebury

Sandridge Youth Club & Sports Ce

Reynolds Cres

St Heliers

A   B   168   C   D   E

HARPENDEN

Townsend C of E School

New Greens

ROAD B651

Sandring

1 grid square represents 500 metres

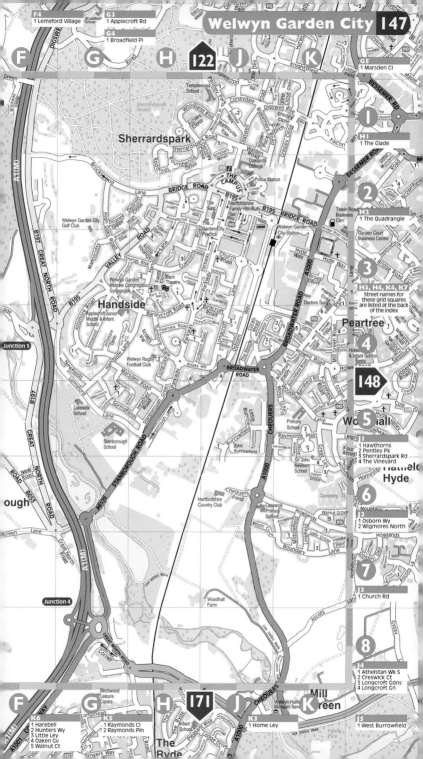

F4
1 Lemsford Village

G3
1 Applecroft Rd

G4
1 Broadfield Pl

G5
1 Marsden Cl

H1
1 The Glade

H2
1 The Quadrangle

H3, H4, K4, K7
Street names for these grid squares are listed at the back of the index

I1
1 Hawthorns
2 Pentley Pk
3 Sherrardspark Rd
4 The Vineyard

I2
1 Osborn Wy
2 Wigmores North

J3
1 Church Rd

I4
1 Athelstan Wk S
2 Creswick Ct
3 Longcroft Gdns
4 Longcroft Gn

K6
1 Harebell
2 Hunters Wy
3 Little Ley
4 Oaken Gv
5 Walnut Ct

K5
1 Raymonds Cl
2 Raymonds Pln

K3
1 Home Ley

J5
1 West Burrowfield

Sherrardspark

Handside

Peartree

Woodhall

Hatfield Hyde

Mill Green

122

148

171

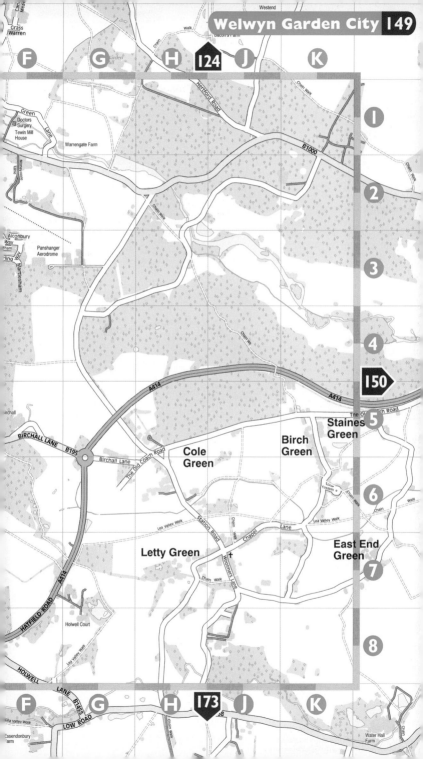

124

150

173

Westend

Dacon's Farm

Hertford Road

B1000

Green
Doctors Surgery
Tewin Mill House

Warrengate Farm

Lane

Chain Walk

Alconbury Way

Panshanger Aerodrome

Chain Walk

Chain Walk

A414

A414

The Old Coach Road

Birch Green

Staines Green

BIRCHALL LANE

B195

Birchall Lane

The Old Coach Road

Cole Green

Ermine Walk

Foxdells

Chain Walk

Lea Valley Walk

Lane

Lea Valley Walk

East End Green

Letty Green

Station Road

Chapel

Chain Walk

Woodmans Lane

Chain Walk

HATFIELD ROAD

A414

Holwell Court

Lea Valley Walk

HOLWELL

LANE B1455

LOW ROAD

Lea Valley Walk

Essendonbury Farm

Water Hall Farm

Chain Walk

F1
1 Cumberland Cl
2 Mansfield Gdns
3 Woodhall Cl

F2
1 Archers Cl
2 Redwoods

F3
Street names for
this grid square are
listed at the back of
the index

F5
1 Glovers Cl
2 Pearsons Cl
3 Waterdale
4 Wilton Wy

F6
1 Mandeville Cl

G1
1 Glebe Cl

G3, J3
Street names for
these grid squares
are listed at the
back of the index

G4
1 Peg's La
2 Queen's Rd

G5
1 The Arbour
2 Morgans Cl

H4
1 Greencoates

K3
1 Foxholes Av
2 Honeysuckle Cl
3 Spinney St

K2
1 King's Rd

J2
1 Meadow Cl

F2
1 Black Smiths Cl

F7
1 Galley Gn

Watersplace Farm

Mardocks Farm

F — VIDBURY HILL
B1004
G
H
128
J
K

Harcamlow Way

Harcamlow Way

I
F8
1 Beyers Prospect
2 Bridle Wy
3 The Coppings

2
G4
1 Meridian Wy

All Nations Christian College
Easneye

Holycross Road

Cappell Lane

3
G5
1 Hillside Crs
2 The Nook

Little Briggens

Newlands

4
Home Farm Industrial Estate

St Johns La
Amwell Lane
St John Baptist School

Lea Valley Walk

B180

154

French's Close
Folly View
Durham Rd
River Meads
St Margarets Station
LC

Chapell Lane
Chambers St
School
Abbotts Wy

Stanstead Abbots

Margarets

Gilpin's Garden
Scott Av
New River

HIGH ST
STATION RD
Millers Lane
Scott Orch

ROYDON

HUNSDON ROAD

5
G7
1 Chelsea Flds

B181
Amwell View School

Lawrence Ave
Rush
Cat's Hill

B181

A414

Hoddesdon Rd

Robin Close
The Granary

Marsh Lane

Netherfield House
Netherfield Lane

6

A414

Ryegate Farm

G8
1 Chittenden Cl
2 Estfeld Cl
3 Parkland Cl
4 Theleway Cl

Saint Margaret's Road
Beechfield
Caxton Rd
Field Rd North
Field Rd
Riverlea

7

Bridle Way
Halley Av
Molesworth
Cranbourne Drive
Dymokes Way
Nursery Road
Wallers Way
Field Rd South

Lea Valley Walk

Cranbourne School
The John Warner School

Rye Meads

H5
1 Lee Cl
2 Woodham Wy

Ditchfield Road
The Drive
Forres Close
Murchison Road

Rye Road

8

River Stort

F — STOCKFORD
G — Rowley Road
H
177
J
K

Ashby Road
Stanstead Hawthorn Road
Lilac Road

J5
1 Abbotts Ri

H6
Rye House Station
Rye House Stadium

1 Kingfisher Cl

River Stort Navigation
Stort Valley Way

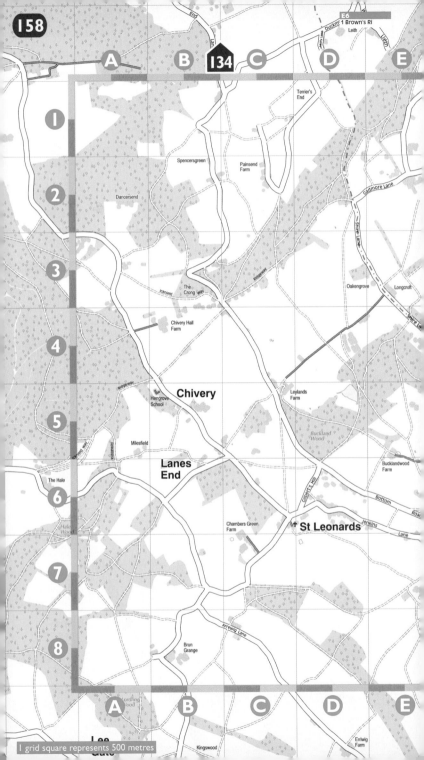

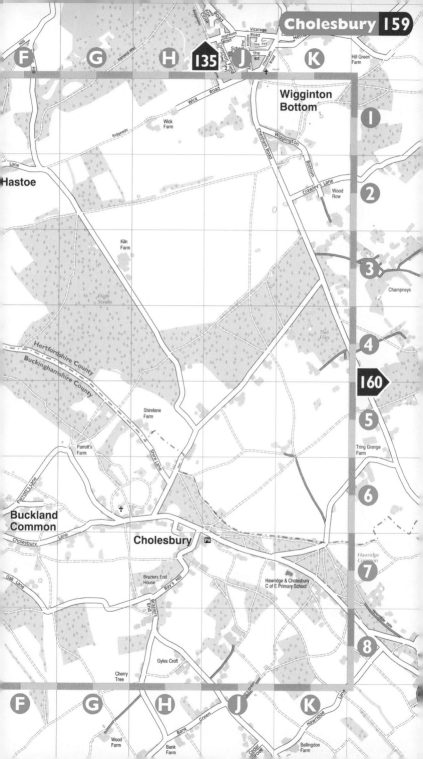

135

F G H **135** J K

I

Wigginton
Bottom

Hill Green
Farm

Hastoe

2

Crawley's Lane

Wood
Row

Wick
Farm

Ridgeway

Wick Road

Cheshm Road

Wigginton Bottom

Lane

Kiln
Farm

3

Champneys

High
Scrubs

The
Flats

4

Hertfordshire County

160

Buckinghamshire County

5

Shire Lane

Shirelane
Farm

Tring Grange
Farm

Parrott's
Farm

6

Parrott's Lane

Buckland
Common

Cholesbury Lane

Cholesbury PH

Hawridge
Common

7

Braziers End
House

Ray's Hill

Hawridge & Cholesbury
C of E Primary School

Oak Lane

Braziers End

Hawridge Vale

8

Gyles Croft

Cherry
Tree

F G H J K

Wood
Farm

Bank
Farm

Bank Green

Cedar Grove

Hawridge Lane

Bellingdon
Farm

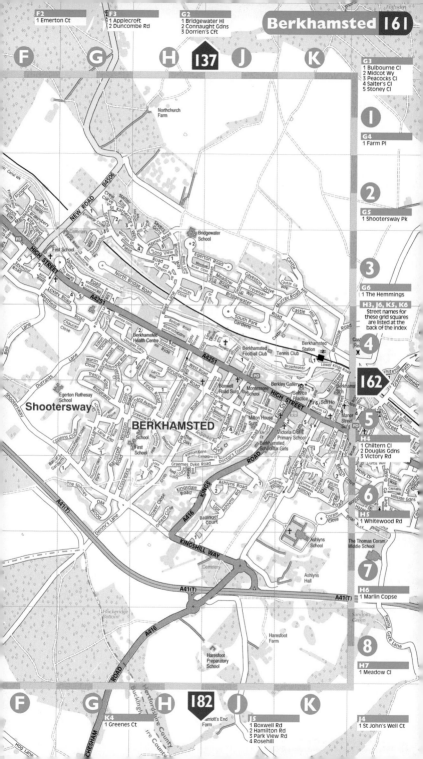

Berkhamsted 161

F2
1 Emerton Ct

F3
1 Applecroft
2 Duncombe Rd

G2
1 Bridgewater Hl
2 Connaught Gdns
3 Dorrien's Cft

G3
1 Bulbourne Cl
2 Midcot Wy
3 Peacocks Cl
4 Salter's Cl
5 Stoney Cl

G4
1 Farm Pl

G5
1 Shootersway Pk

G6
1 The Hemmings

H3, J6, K5, K6
Street names for these grid squares are listed at the back of the index

H4
1 Chiltern Cl
2 Douglas Gdns
3 Victory Rd

H5
1 Whitewood Rd

H6
1 Marlin Copse

H7
1 Meadow Cl

K4
1 Greenes Ct

J5
1 Boxwell Rd
2 Hamilton Rd
3 Park View Rd
4 Rosehill

J4
1 St John's Well Ct

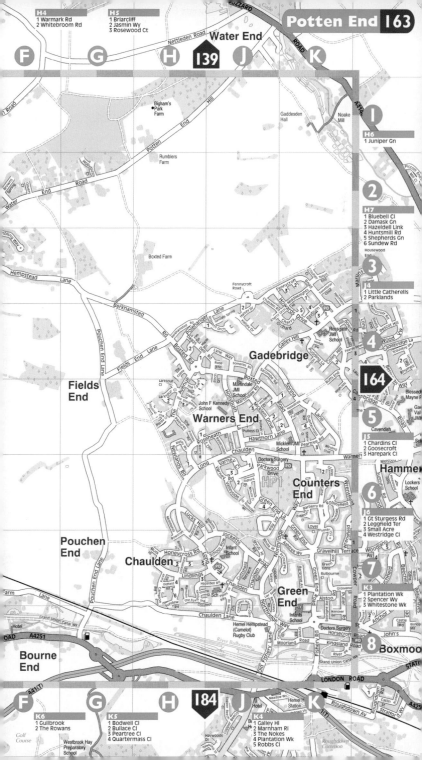

Potten End 163

F   **G**   **H** 139 **J**   **K**

Water End

ROAD

BUZZARD

Nettieden Road

H4
1 Warmark Rd
2 Whitebroom Rd

H5
1 Briarcliff
2 Jasmin Wy
3 Rosewood Ct

Gaddesden Hall

Noake Mill

I

H6
1 Juniper Gn

2

H7
1 Bluebell Cl
2 Damask Gn
3 Hazeldell Link
4 Huntsmill Rd
5 Shepherds Gn
6 Sundew Rd

Housewood End

3

I4
1 Little Catherells
2 Parklands

Bigham's Park Farm

Potten End Hill

Rumbiers Farm

Boxted Farm

Hempstead Lane

Berkhamsted

Pouchen End Lane

Fields End Lane

Boxted Rd

Fennycroft Road

Gadebridge

Rossgate JMI School

Gadebridge La

4

164

Fields End

Warners End

John F Kennedy School

Martindale JMI School

Micklem JMI School

peartree Rd

Hawthorn Lane

Cavendish

5

J5
1 Chardins Cl
2 Goosecroft
3 Harepark Cl

Hamme

Lockers School

6

J6
1 Gt Sturgess Rd
2 Leggfield Ter
3 Small Acre
4 Westridge Cl

Pouchen End

Chaulden

Doctors Surgery

Parkwood Drive

HP1

Counters End

Robbsfield

Gravelhill Terrace

Woodgate Av

7

K3
1 Plantation Wk
2 Spencer Wy
3 Whitestone Wk

Honeycross Rd

Infant School

Lindlings

Chaulden Lane

Chaulden JMI School

Green End

Infants School

Nettleden Way

Doctors Surgery

Horsecroft Road

Kingsland

8

John's

Boxmo

Bourne End

A4251

Grand Union Canal Wk

Hotel

OAD A4251

River Bulbourne

Grand Union Canal Wk

River

LONDON ROAD

F   **G**   **H** 184 **J**   **K**

Hemel H Station

Roughdown Av

A425

K6
1 Gullbrook
2 The Rowans

K5
1 Bodwell Cl
2 Bullace Cl
3 Peartree Cl
4 Quartermass Cl

Westbrook Hay Preparatory School

K4
1 Galley Hl
2 Marnham Ri
3 The Nokes
4 Plantation Wk
5 Robbs Cl

Golf Course

Roughdown Common

B5
1 Bury Gn

B6
1 Combe St

A8
1 Foster Rd
2 Veysey Cl

A6
1 The Farthings
2 Park Hill Rd

A7
1 Linden Gld
2 The Poplars
3 Thistlecroft
4 Woodland Cl
5 Woodland Pl

A4, A5, C5, D1
Street names for
these grid squares
are listed at the back
of the index

B7
1 Vicarage Cl

B8
1 Cotterells
2 Vicarage Cl

C1
1 Tintagel Cl

C2
1 Leven Wy

C4
1 Andrews Cl
2 The Bounce
3 Boxhill
4 Broadcroft
5 Mead Temple
6 Sharpcroft
7 Typleden Cl

C6
1 Caernarvon Cl
2 Concorde Dr

C7
1 Albion Hl

C8
1 Charlesworth Cl
2 Corner Hall
3 Forest Av
4 Ranworth Cl
5 Stuarts Cl
6 Talbot Ct

D2
1 Thatchers Cft

D3
1 Watling Cl

D5
1 Clarendon Cl
2 East Mimms
3 Long Mimms
4 Manley Rd

D7
1 Corfe Cl
2 Denbigh Cl
3 Furtherground
4 Pinewood Gdns
5 Sherbourne Cl

D6, D8, E1, E2
Street names for
these grid squares
are listed at the
back of the index

E3, E5, E7, E8
Street names for
these grid squares
are listed at the
back of the index

E4
1 Nicholas Wy
2 Tannsmore Cl
3 Triton Wy

E6
1 The Queen's Sq
2 Sawyers Wy
3 Sheepcote Rd

A   B   140   C   D   E

163

185

8

Piccotts
End

Grovehill

Highfield

HEMEL
HEMPSTEAD

Hammerfield

Counters
End

Boxmoor

Two
Waters

1 grid square represents 500 metres

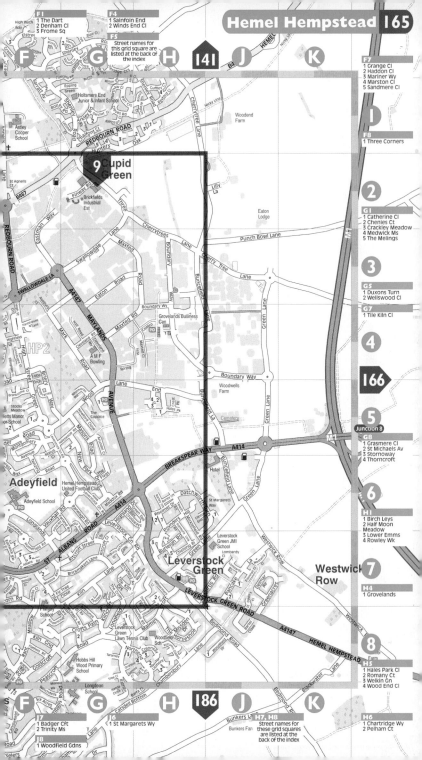

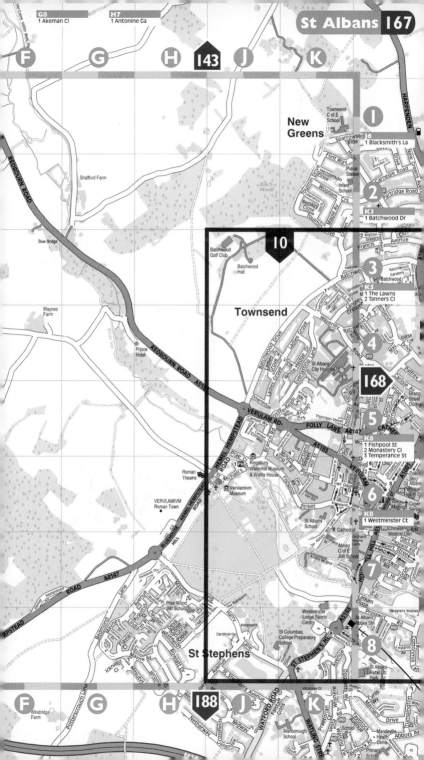

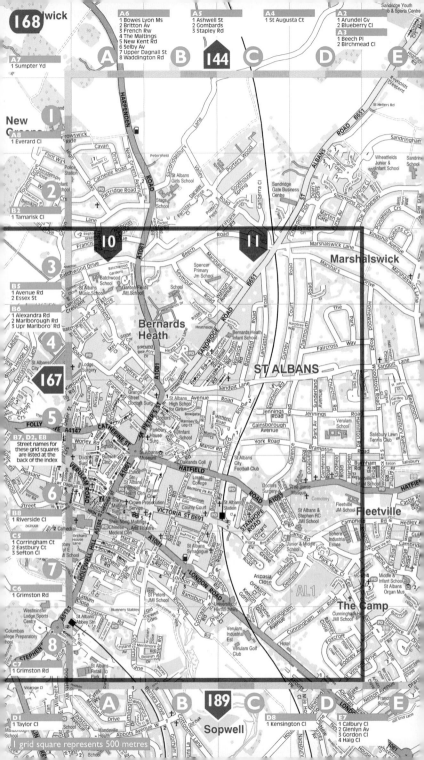

A6
1 Bowes Lyon Ms
2 Britton Av
3 French Rw
4 The Maltings
5 New Kent Rd
6 Selby Av
7 Upper Dagnall St
8 Waddington Rd

A5
1 Ashwell St
2 Gombards
3 Stapley Rd

A4
1 St Augusta Ct

A2
1 Arundel Gv
2 Blueberry Cl

A3
1 Beech Pl
2 Birchmead Cl

A7
1 Sumpter Yd

144

New Greens
A8
1 Everard Cl

Marshalswick

B2
1 Tamarisk Cl

10

11

B5
1 Avenue Rd
2 Essex St

Bernards Heath

B6
1 Alexandra Rd
2 Marlborough Rd
3 Upr Marlboro' Rd

ST ALBANS

167

B7, D2, E8
Street names for
these grid squares
are listed at the
back of the index

B8
1 Riverside Cl

Fleetville

C5
1 Corringham Ct
2 Eastbury Ct
3 Sefton Cl

C6
1 Grimston Rd

The Camp

C7
1 Grimston Rd

D1
1 Taylor Cl

189

Sopwell

D8
1 Kensington Cl

E7
1 Calbury Cl
2 Glenlyn Av
3 Gordon Cl
4 Haig Cl

1 grid square represents 500 metres

F1
1 Aldbury Cl
2 Cotswold Cl
3 Ivinghoe Cl
4 Mendip Cl
5 Pitstone Cl
6 Tilsworth Wk

F2
1 Belgrave Cl
2 Quantock Cl
3 Summersland Rd

I F4
1 Wheatleys

2 F7
1 Edison Cl
2 Greensleeves Cl
3 Grenadier Cl
4 Sturmer Cl

3 F8
1 Ashbourne Ct

5 G2
1 Harley Ct

6 G3
1 Eastfield Ct
2 Hunt Cl
3 Thorpefield Cl
4 Westfield Ct

7 G6
1 Wynches Farm Dr

G8
1 Newfield Wy

G7
1 St Edmunds Wk

Mill Green

The Ryde

Birchwood

Old Hatfield

Oxlease

Roe Green

South Hatfield

Marshmoor

Welham

F2
1 Burfield Cl
2 Lemsford Rd
3 Wellands

F3
1 The Paddock
2 St Peters Cl
3 Town Flds

F4
1 Croft Fld
2 Maryland

F5
1 Maple Cl

F6
1 Mcdonald Ct
2 Rickfield Cl
3 Swallow Gdns

F7
1 Grove Lea
2 Mcdonald Ct
3 Southdown Ct
4 Whitebeams

G1
1 Little Mead

G2
1 Corncroft
2 Strawmead

G3
1 Brain Cl
2 Breaks Rd
3 French Horn La
4 Kennelwood La
5 Wellfield Rd
6 Wheatfield

G4
1 Old Rectory Dr
2 Rectory Gdns

G5
1 Foxglove Cl
2 Lamb Cl
3 Primrose Cl

G6
1 Allen Ct
2 Coney Cl
3 Hamilton Ct
4 Kingsmill Ct

G7, H1
Street names for
these grid squares
are listed at the
back of the index

H3
1 Endymion Ct
2 Endymion Ms

H4
1 St Etheldreda's
Dr

172

172

A B 148 C FORD D ROAD E

Burnside

Welwyn Hatfield
Museum Service

Mill
Green

1

River Lea or Lee

Lea Valley Walk

Home
Park

Lea Valley Walk

The
Vineyard

2

Hillend
Farm

3

West End

4

171

West End Lane

Coombe
Wood

5

Pope's
Farm

Park
Dairy

6

Carnfield
Place

Woodside
Place

Woodside

7

Wildhill

Wildhill Road

8

AL9

Lower
Woodside

Woodhill
House

Woodside

Westfield Lane

Grubbs Lane

A B 193 C D E

A1000 GREAT NORT

1 grid square represents 500 metres

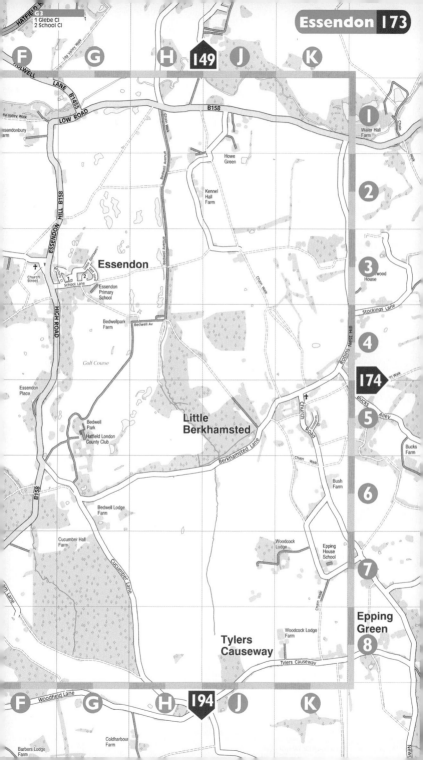

F G H **149** J K

1 Glebe Cl
2 School Cl

HATFIELD L...

HOLWELL
LANE B1455

Hill Valley Walk

LOW ROAD

B158

Hill Valley Walk

Essendonbury
Farm

Water Hall
Farm

Chain Walk

I

ESSENDON HILL B158

Bedwell Avenue

Howe
Green

Kennel
Hall
Farm

2

Church
Street

School Lane

Essendon

1 2

Essendon
Primary
School

Chain Walk

Wood
House

3

Stockings Lane

HIGH ROAD

Bedwellpark
Farm

Bedwell Av

4

Robins Nest Hill

Golf Course

Essendon
Place

**Little
Berkhamstead**

Church
Road

174

In Walk

Bucks Alley

5

Bedwell
Park

Hatfield London
County Club

Berkhamstead Lane

Chain Walk

Bucks
Farm

B158

Bush
Farm

6

Bedwell Lodge
Farm

Woodcock
Lodge

Epping
House
School

7

Cucumber Hall
Farm

Cumber Lane

Cucumber Lane

Chain Walk

**Epping
Green**

8

**Tylers
Causeway**

Woodcock Lodge
Farm

Tylers Causeway

F **Woodfield Lane** G H **194** J K

Barbers Lodge
Farm

Coldharbour
Farm

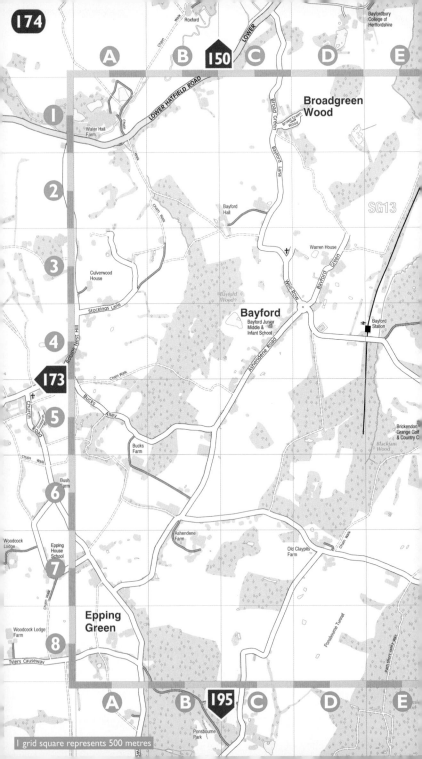

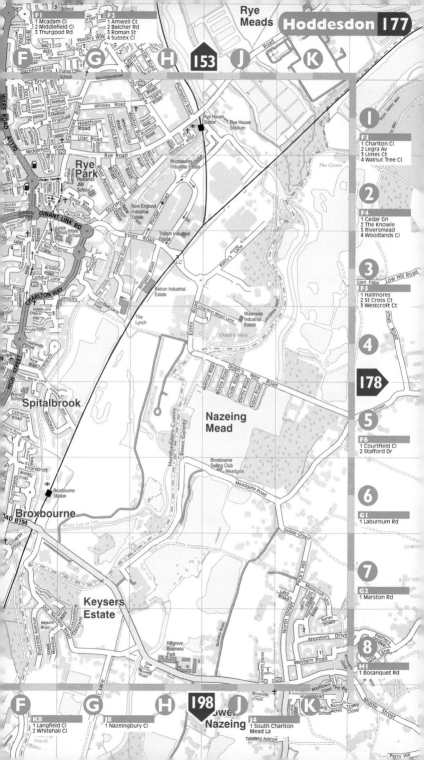

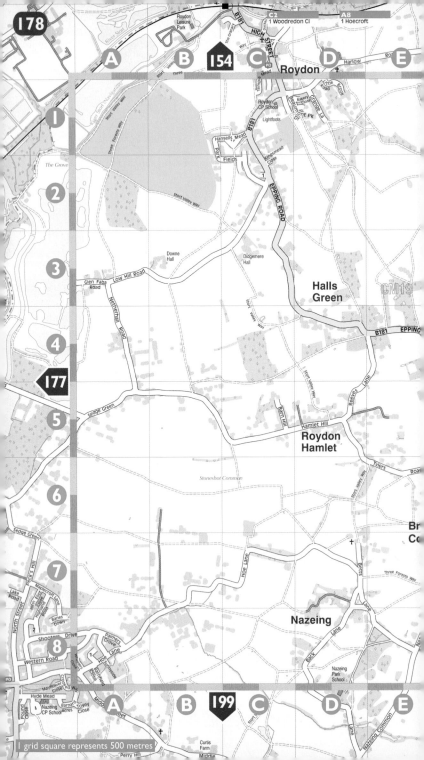

A B C D E

Roydon Leisure Park

River Stort

The Green

HIGH STREET

C2 1 Woodredon Cl

A8 1 Hoecroft

Harlow

Roydon

Stort Lane Three

PO

River Stort Navigation

Stort Valley Way

Three Forests Way

The Grove

Stort Valley Way

B181

Roydon CP School

Lightfoots

Beaumont Ct

Grange La

Bakers Ct

Beaumont Pk

The Maze

The Road

Hansells Mead

Park Fields

Longmead Close

Downe Hall

Diddemere Hall

EPPING ROAD

Halls Green

CM19

Stort Valley Way

B181 EPPING

Glen Faba Road

Low Hill Road

Netherhall Road

Sedge Green

Reeves Lane

Barn Hill

Stort Valley Way

Hamlet Hill

Roydon Hamlet

Tylers Road

Sedge Green

Stoneshot Common

Peck's Hill

North Street

Hoe Lane

Stort Valley Way

Betts Lane

Three Forests Way

Br Co

Nazeing

Lake Road

Manlecroft Lane

Barnet Close

Banes Down

Shooters Drive

Painters Grove

Western Road

Hoe Lane

Back Lane

Nazeing Park School

Maylower Close

Hyde Mead

Nazeing CP School

Barn Acres

Tovey Close

Pound Close

A B C D E

Stort Lane

Nazeing Common

Curtis Farm

Perry Hill

Middle

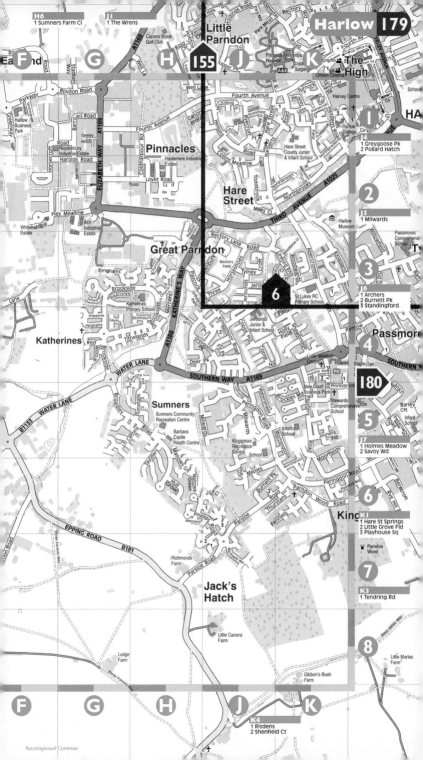

H6
1 Sumners Farm Cl

J1
1 The Wrens

Ea **F** nd

G

H

155

J

K

I

HA

The High

Little Parndon

Canons Brook Golf Club

Princess Alexandra Hospital

A&E

Docs Surgery

Post Office

Odeon Cinema

Co Court

Westgate

Harvey Centre

School

Roydon Road

Parkway

Greenway

Harlow Business Park

Cawley Hatch

Roydonbury Industrial Estate

Harolds Road

Barrows Road

A1169

ELIZABETH WAY

Coldharbour Rd

Fourth Avenue

Pinnacles

Haslemere Industrial Estate

Lovet Road

Well Lane

Fourth Avenue

Canon Brook

Collins Meadow

Road

Hare Street County Junior & Infant School

Harlow College

Velizy Avenue

I4
1 Greygoose Pk
2 Pollard Hatch

Flex Meadow

Ash Industrial Estate

Whitehall Estate

Hare Street

THIRD AVENUE

A1025

Northbrooks

Miles Cl

Harlow Museum

2

J5
1 Milwards

Great Parndon

Rectory Lane

Road

Rectory Field

Tylney

Three

3

I6
1 Archers
2 Burnett Pk
3 Standingford

Bynghams

Brookside

Peacocks

Sylves

Katherines Primary School

Sheppards

Seymours

Heighams

6

St Lukes RC Primary School

Jerounds Junior & Infant School

Penlow

Passmore

Katherines

KATHERINE'S WAY

MERCERS WAY

Titthelands

Red

Brookside

Willow

WATER LANE

Deer Pk

Greygoose

SOUTHERN WAY

A1169

Abercrombie

Ulster Medical Centre

4

180

Stewards Comprehensive School

New Court Business Park

SOUTHERN

Staple Tye

Pinceywood

Barley Cft

Infant School

WATER LANE

B1153

Sycamores

Broadley

Dunstalls

Sumners

Sumners Community Recreation Centre

Barbara Castle Health Centre

Kingsmoor Recreation Centre

Milwards

Paringdon Road

Moorfields

Infant School

Joyners Fld

5

J7
1 Holmes Meadow
2 Savoy Wd

Tanys

Clarkes Road

Mallards Ct

Mallards Green

Hill Grove

Maples

Burnett Pk

Thurstans

Parndon Wood Road

Paringdon Road

Eye Hill

6

K1
1 Hare St Springs
2 Little Grove Fld
3 Playhouse Sq

Phillips Road

Parsloe

Fennells

Parndon Wood

King

Richmonds Farm

EPPING ROAD

B181

Parsloe Road

7

K3
1 Tendring Rd

Little Canons Farm

Jack's Hatch

Lodge Farm

Three Forests Way

Gibbon's Bush Farm

Little Marles Farm

8

F

G

H

J

K

K4
1 Risdens
2 Shenfield Ct

Nazeingwood Common

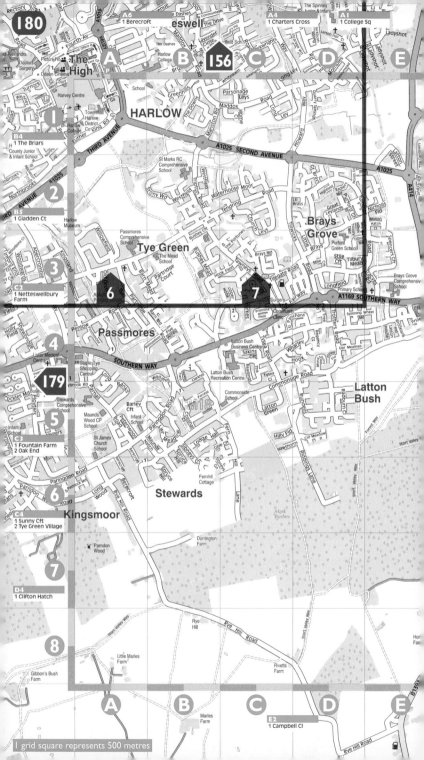

F3
1 Florence Cl
2 Jack Stevens Cl
3 Larkswood

F G H 157 J K

Church Langley

Florence
Nightingale
Health Centre

CM17

Roffey
Hall

I

New Way La

Threshers
Bush

2

Green

Foster
Street

Foster Street

Potter
Street

Harlow
Common

3

Harlow Common

Forest Way

Mill Street

4

Hastingwood Road

Wynter's
Farm

Latton Street

A414

London Road

Park
Av

Stort Valley Way

Harlow
Park

Wynter's
Grange

5

Latton
Park

Hastingwood

Stort Brook

Junction 7

Hastingwood Road

PH

6

Sewel
Hall
Farm

Paris
Hall

Stort Valley Way

Glovers
Farm

Stort Valley Way

M11

A414

7

Rundells

Canes

Canes
Farm

8

Stort

Lane

Little
Weald
Hall

F G H J K

North Weald
Golf Club

Crowsey Brook

Lane

A414

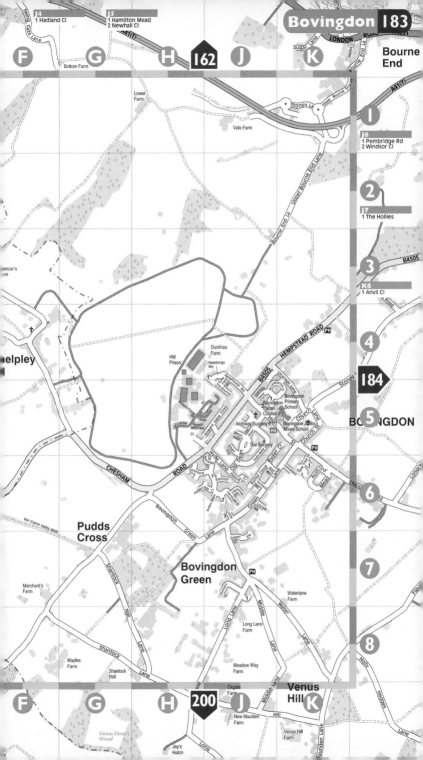

F G H 162 J K

Bourne End

J4
1 Hadland Cl

J5
1 Hamilton Mead
2 Newhall Cl

Bottom Farm

1

Lower Farm

Bourne Gutter

Vale Farm

J6
1 Pembridge Rd
2 Windsor Cl

2

J7
1 The Hollies

3

B4505

K6
1 Anvil Cl

PH

HEMPSTEAD ROAD

4

Spencer's Farm

elpley

HM Prison

Duckhau Farm

Hawkings Wy

184

Bovingdon Primary School

Bovingdon Parish Council

Archway Surgery

Bovingdon Junior Mixed School

BOVINGDON

5

The Surgery

PH

6

CHESHAM ROAD

Bovingdon Green Lane

Pudds Cross

7

Bovingdon Green

PH

Marchant's Farm

Shantock Hall Lane

Waterlane Farm

8

Ver-Colne Valley Walk

Maples Farm

Shantock Hall

Shantock Lane

Long Lane Farm

Middle Lane

Water Lane

Meadow Way Farm

Holly

F G H 200 J K

Venus Hill

Simon Dean's Wood

Jay's Hatch

Long Lane

Oxgate Farm

New Maulden Farm

Hill

Venus Hill Farm

Maunden Lane

Heddes Lane

F1
1 Grindcobbe Cl
2 Tavistock Cl

F2
1 Deacon Cl
2 Martyr Cl

F ● G ● H ● **168** ● J ● K

Sopwell

Verulam Golf Club

River Ver

Abbots Avenue W

Sopwell House Hotel & Country Club

NORTH ORBITAL ROAD A414

Hedges Farm

NAPSBURY LANE
NORTH ORBITAL ROAD A414

North Orbital Trading Est

THE CAMP
Cunningham Hill JMI School

LONDON ROAD A1081

Francis Bacon School

Old Albanians Rugby Football Club

I

F4
1 Magnolia Cl

2

F5
1 The Beeches
2 Sycamore Dr

3

G1
1 Abbots Av
2 Glengall Pl

4

190
LONDON COLNEY

5

G2
1 Cloister Garth
2 Lectern La

6

G6
1 Moorlands

Park Street Station

RADLETT ROAD A5183

PARK STREET

AL2
Park Industrial Estate
Stroud Wood Business Cen

FROGMORE

Frogmore

Radlett Aerodrome

The Drive

Napsbury Hospital

M25

Moor Mill La

Old Ventura Park

Old Parkbury La

7

K1
1 Mountbatten Cl
2 Parkway Ct

8

HARPER LANE

Colney Street

Old Parkbury

F ● G ● H ● **206** ● J ● K

Harperbury Hospital

K2
1 The Poplars

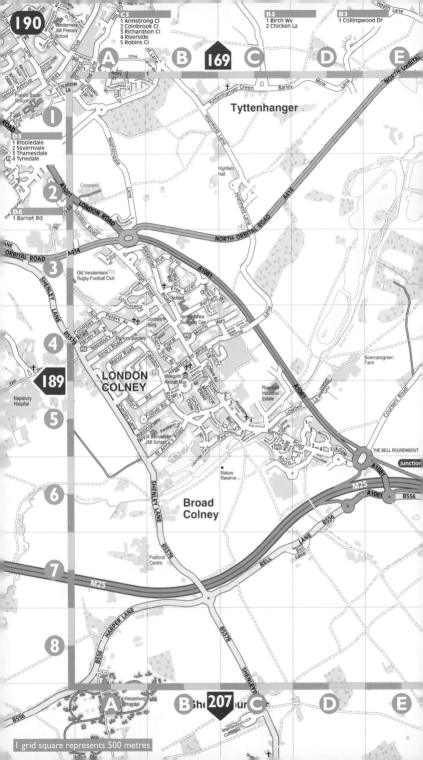

C5
1 Armstrong Cl
2 Coinbrook Cl
3 Richardson Cl
4 Riverside
5 Robins Cl

B5
1 Birch Wy
2 Chicken La

B3
1 Collingwood Dr

A   B   C   D   E

Windermere JMI Primary School

Francis Bacon School

Swallow La

I

D5
1 Ribbledale
2 Severnvale
3 Thamesdale
4 Tynedale

Tyttenhanger

Highfield Hall

Cemetery

2
LONDON ROAD
A1081

D6
1 Barnet Rd

NORTH ORBITAL ROAD
A414

ORBITAL ROAD
A414

3

Old Verulamians Rugby Football Club

Five Acres

Five Acres School

Hertfordshire Business Cen

Doctors' Surg

4

189

Napsbury Hospital

LONDON COLNEY

Doctors Surgery

Mosquito Aircraft Mus

Riverside Industrial Estate

5

Bowmansgreen Farm

THE BELL ROUNDABOUT

Junction

6

River Colne

Broad Colney

Nature Reserve

Barnet

Eskdale

M25
A1081
B556

7

M25

SHENLEY LANE
B5378

Pastoral Centre

BELL LANE
B556

8

HARPER LANE

B556

Harperbury Hospital

A   B   C   **207**   D   E

Shenley

Shenleybury Cottages

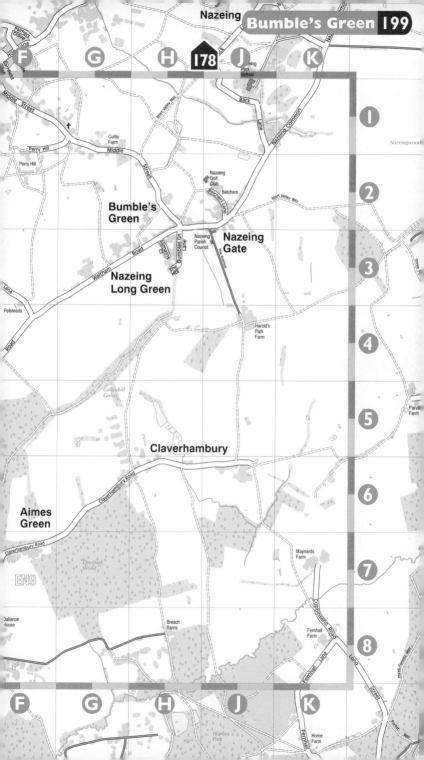

F G H **178** J K

Nazeing wood

I

Nazeing Golf Club Belchers

2

Bumble's Green

Nazeing Gate

3

Nazeing Long Green

4

Harold's Park Farm

Felsteads

Galleyhill Green

5

Parvill Farm

Claverhambury

6

Aimes Green

Deerpark Wood

EN9

7

Maynards Farm

Dallance House

Breach Barns

Fernhall Farm

8

Warlies Park

Home Farm

F G H J K

Middle Street

Perry Hill

Curtis Farm

Middle Street

Perry Hill

Waltham Road

Bumbles Gn Lane

The Hall

Nazeing Parish Council

The Avenue

Claverhambury Road

Claverhambury Road

Copthall Road

Fernhall Lane

Long Street

Nazeing Common

Back Lane

Stort Valley Way

Stort Valley Way

200

ey Hill

A Maples Farm B 183 Shantoc Sha Hall C Long Lane Long Lane Farm D Way E

Venus Hill

Ley Hill Cricket Club
Golf Course

1

Ashridge Farm

Oxgate Farm
Venus
New Mauklton Farm

Long Lane

Middle Lane

Venus Hill

Simon Dean's Wood

Venus Hill Farm

2

Pinner Green

Jay's Hatch

Long Lane

Hogpits Bottom

PH

Ho Bo

Hockley Farm

Flaunden

Sharlowe's Farm

PH

3

Wood

Great White End

Road

Flaunden Hill

Birch Lane

4

Flaunden Bottom

Hollin's Hall

Frith Wood

5

Flaunden Bottom

Martin Top Farm

Baldwin's Wood

6

Chess Valley Walk

The Grove

The Bridge

Close

School

The Grove

Flaunden Bottom

Mill Farm

Chev

7

Latimer House

Latimer

Chess Valley Walk

Chenies Place

Latimer Park Farm

Chess Valley Walk

Latimer Road

Chenies School

8

Chandos Close

Beechwood Avenue

Chess to Hills

South Road

Chenies School

Hol

Boughton Way

Lane

A Chessfield Park B 216 Church Grove C D E

440

andycroft Road

Elizabeth Avenue

Farm Drive

Russell Close

Bedford

Amentia Way

School

Avenue

STATION

Oakington

1 grid square represents 500 metres

202

185

A B C D E

Chipperfield

WD4

A411

1

Chapel Croft

Pale Fm

PO

The School

Hotel

Chipperfield Junior & Infant School

PH

King's Croft C

Havenfield

P

The Common

Rookery Wood

Langley Lodge La

Langley Lodge Farm

Langley Lodge Lane

2

Chipperfield Common

The Common

3

Imeads Fm

Bucks Hill

Callipers Hall

Jeffery's Farm

Berrybushes Wood

Commonwood

PH

Quickmoor Lane

Baytree Farm

Bucks Hill

Mod

4

P

201

Red Lane

5

Sarratt

Ash Lane

Great Westwood

Bottom Lane

Bucks Hill

Newhall Farm

Buck's Hill Bottom

Tom's Hill

6

Alexandra

PO

Sarratt JMI School

The Surgery

Dimmock Lane

Sarratt Road

Cardoon Drive

7

Church Lane

Green E Business Centre

White House

Templepan Lane

Yew Court Farm

Chandlers

M25

Mod

8

Micklefield Green

M25

Chandl Cross

White Shack Lane

Redhall Lane

Roberts

A B C D E

218

Sarratt

Redhall

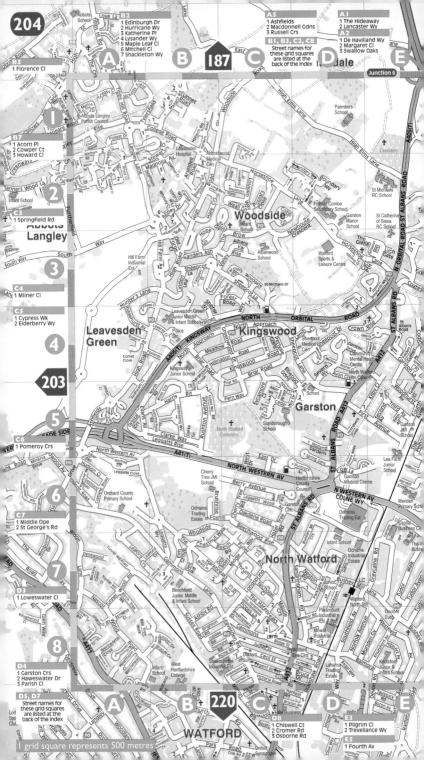

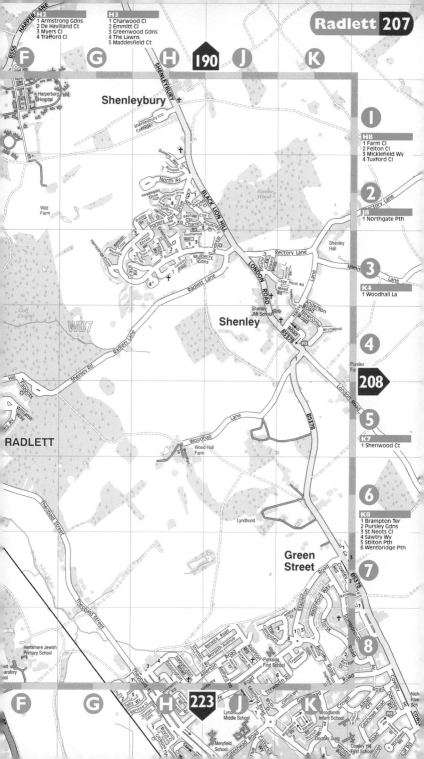

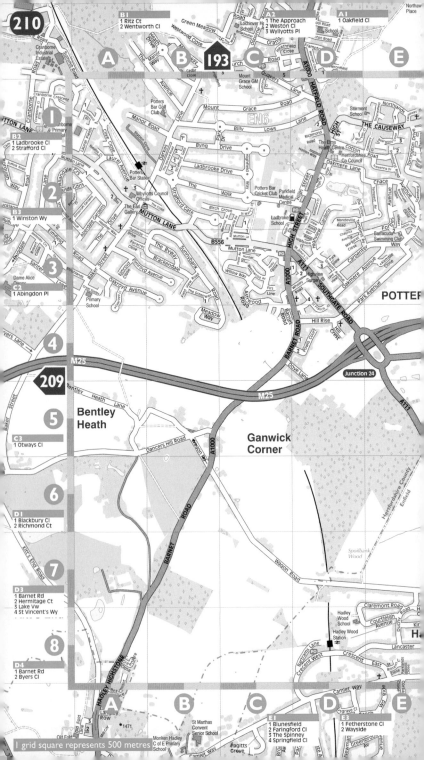

F8
1 Bedale Rd
2 York Ter

G7
1 St John's Ter

196

F G H J K

Infant School
Franklin Avenue
Frank Martin Court
Cromwell Avenue

Laser
Clinic
Road

Woodgreen
Farm

Barrow Lane

Broadfield
Farm

Beverley Gardens

Cemetery
Woodside

Portland Drive
Mews Close
Primrose Farm

Greenwood
Stuart
Way
Hawthorne
Close
Tudor
Crescent

I

G8
1 Violet Av

B
G

Oldpark Ride

Spring
Farm

Theobalds
Manor

Temple
House

LIEUTENANT ELLIS WAY

2

B196

H8
1 Adelaide Cl
2 Henry Cl
3 Portland Dr

3

The
Park

Hertfordshire County
Enfield

Chain Walk

Bullscross

Bulls Cross Ride

K1
1 Warrenfield Cl

Cemetery

4
Junction 25

Sloemans Farm

M25

214

Whitewebbs Lane

Gilmour Close

5

Capel Manor
Primary School

Hillsmoor
Road

Herron Road

Manor Court

Monklands
Junior & Infant
School

Lovell Ev

University
of London

Bull's Cross

6

Bulls
Cross

GREAT CAMBRIDGE ROAD

London Loop

Turkey Street

St Ignatius
College

Dendridge Close

Clay Hill

lay
ill

ill
Loop

Forty Hill

Forty
Hill C of E
School

7

London Loop

Worcesters
Infant &
Primary School

Goat Lane

8

Hoe Lane

Malds Drive

Phipps Hatch Lane

Park Nook
Gardens

Hillside Crescent

Elm
Gardens

Cedar
Park
Road

Woodbine
Grove
Myrtle
Grove

Conway
Gardens

Burnham
Grove

St George's Road

Russell Road

Benton
Drive
Worces
ter Av

Petrich Drive
Tymmswood Close

St Martin's
Drive

Russet
House
School

Brodie Road

Hawthorn Grove

Merton Rd

Lea Rd

Infant
School

Carnonbury
Road
Elmwood
Road

Ridler Road

Willow Road

Melling Drive

Burland
Gardens

Carterhatch
School

F G H J K

Ripley Road

Gordon Hill

Cedar
House

Burlington
Road

Glenville Avenue

Beeling Av

Primrose Av

Myddelton
Avenue

Hadden Road
Manton Cl

Clare House

Gater
Drive

Farr Road

Bell Road

Chase Community
School

Chase Community
House Surgery

Adath Yisroel
Cemetery

Cartbrook
Tene

Baxter
Close

Newland
Close

Monros
Close

Forty

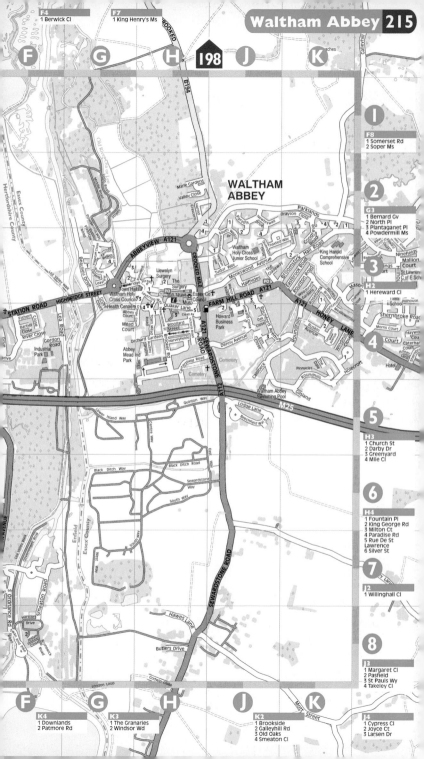

Waltham Abbey 215

WALTHAM ABBEY

F4
1 Berwick Cl

F7
1 King Henry's Ms

F8
1 Somerset Rd
2 Soper Ms

G3
1 Bernard Gv
2 North Pl
3 Plantaganet Pl
4 Powdermill Ms

H2
1 Hereward Cl

H3
1 Church St
2 Darby Dr
3 Greenyard
4 Mile Cl

H4
1 Fountain Pl
2 King George Rd
3 Milton Ct
4 Paradise Rd
5 Rue De St Lawrence
6 Silver St

J2
1 Willinghall Cl

J3
1 Margaret Cl
2 Pasfield
3 St Pauls Wy
4 Takeley Cl

J4
1 Cypress Cl
2 Joyce Ct
3 Larsen Dr

K2
1 Brookside
2 Galleyhill Rd
3 Old Oaks
4 Smeaton Cl

K3
1 The Granaries
2 Windsor Wd

K4
1 Downlands
2 Patmore Rd

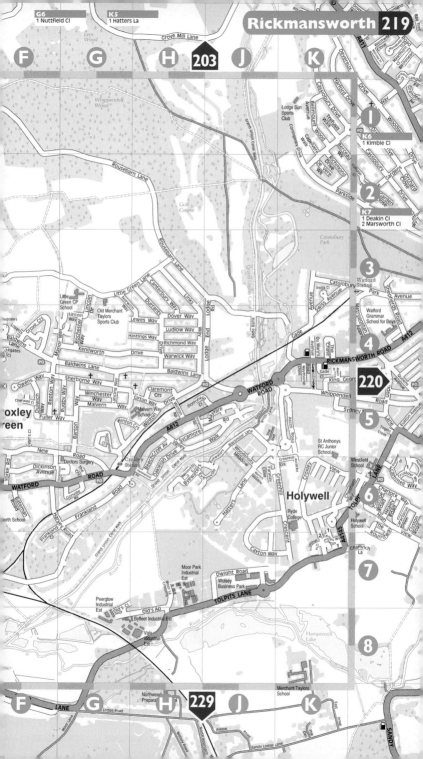

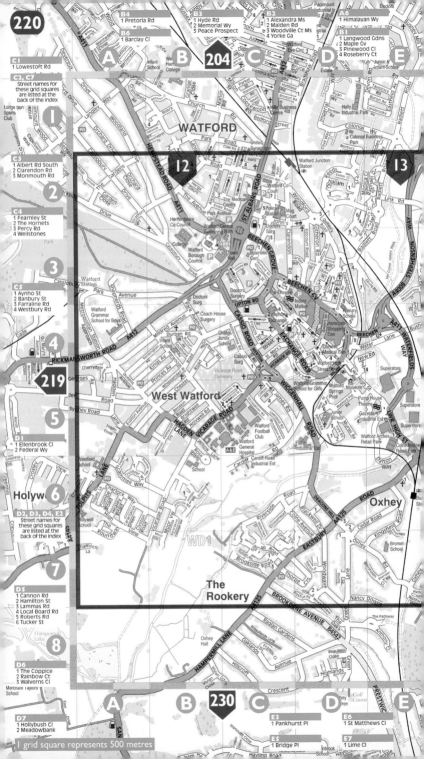

C1
1 Lowestoft Rd

C2, C7
Street names for
these grid squares
are listed at the
back of the index

C3
1 Albert Rd South
2 Clarendon Rd
3 Monmouth Rd

C4
1 Fearnley St
2 The Hornets
3 Percy Rd
4 Wellstones

C5
1 Aynho St
2 Banbury St
3 Farraline Rd
4 Westbury Rd

D1
1 Ellenbrook Cl
2 Federal Wy

D2, D3, D4, E2
Street names for
these grid squares
and squares are
listed at the
back of the index

D5
1 Cannon Rd
2 Hamilton St
3 Lammas Rd
4 Local Board Rd
5 Roberts Rd
6 Tucker St

D6
1 The Coppice
2 Rainbow Ct
3 Walverns Cl

D7
1 Hollybush Cl
2 Meadowbank

B4
1 Pretoria Rd

B6
1 Barclay Cl

A1
1 Hyde Rd
2 Memorial Wy
3 Peace Prospect

B2
1 Alexandra Ms
2 Maiden Rd
3 Woodville Ct Ms
4 Yorke Ga

A6
1 Himalayan Wy

B1
1 Langwood Gdns
2 Maple Gv
3 Pinewood Cl
4 Roseberry Ct

E3
1 Pankhurst Pl

E6
1 St Matthews Cl

E5
1 Bridge Pl

E7
1 Lime Cl

WATFORD

West Watford

Holyw

Oxhey

The Rookery

1 grid square represents 500 metres

Borehamwood 223

BOREHAMWOOD

Elstree

Deacons Hill

Junction 4

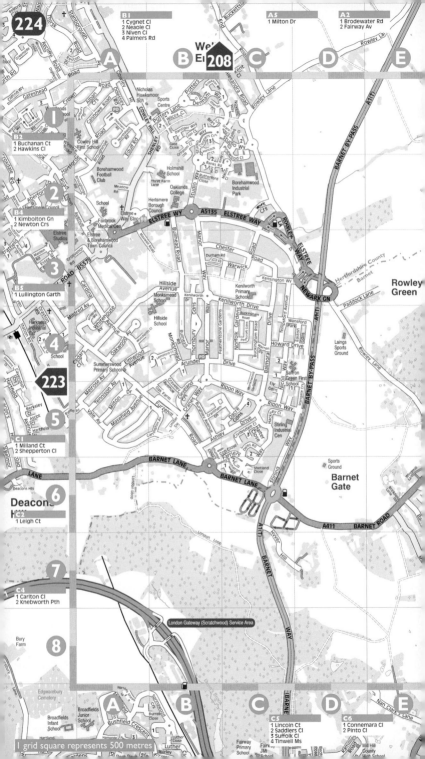

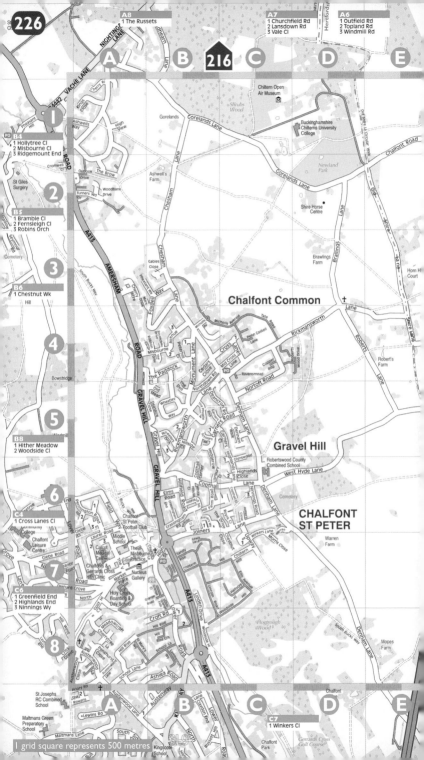

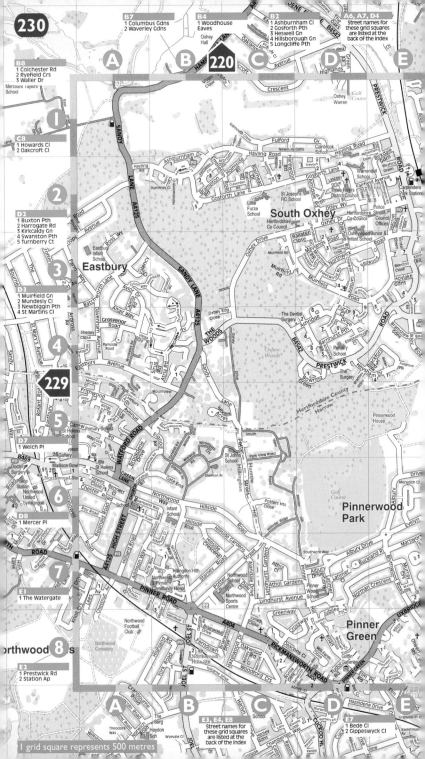

Abbots Langley 203 K2
Adeyfield 9 D5
Aimes Green 199 F6
Albury 83 H3
Albury End 83 G5
Aldbury 136 D3
Aldenham 205 H7
Aley Green 88 D8
Allen's Green 131 H3
Amwell 145 F2
Ansells End 92 C7
Anstey 49 H3
Apsley 185 H2
Apsley End 38 A2
Ardeley 61 J6
Arkley 225 G5
Arlesey 24 E4
Ashley Green 182 B2
Ashwell 18 A5
Ashwell End 17 G4
Aspenden 63 H4
Aston 77 G7
Aston End 77 F4
Astrope 109 F6
Ayot Green 146 E1
Ayot St Lawrence 121 F3
Ayot St Peter 121 K6
Ayres End 144 C4
Babbs Green 128 D5
Bakers End 128 E2
Baldock 43 F1
Ballingdon Bottom 114 C8
Barkway 32 D5
Barley 23 G7
Barleycroft End 66 D5
Barley End 136 D1
Barnet Gate 224 D6
Barton-le-Clay 36 D6
Barwick 101 H5
Bassus Green 78 B1
Batchworth 228 E1
Batchworth Heath 229 F3
Batford 119 G6
Batlers Green 206 C8
Bayford 174 C4
Bedlar's Green 107 F4
Bedmond 186 E5
Bedwell 3 D3
Bell Bar 193 G2
Belsize 201 H2
Bendish 92 D2
Bengeo 150 E1
Benington 78 B5
Bennetts End 185 K1
Bentfield Bury 86 A1
Bentfield Green 86 B1
Bentley Heath 210 A5
Berden 67 K1
Berkhamsted 161 H5
Bernards Heath 10 C2
Birchanger 86 D7
Birch Green 149 K5
Birchwood 171 G2
Bird Green 51 G1
Biscot 4 A1
Bishop's Stortford 105 F2
Blackmore End 119 J3
Blue Hill 98 A4
Borehamwood 223 H3
Botany Bay 212 A6
Botley 182 C8
Bourne End 163 F8
Bovingdon 183 K5
Bovingdon Green 183 H7
Bower Heath 119 F3
Boxmoor 164 A8
Bozen Green 65 G6
Bragbury End 96 E2
Bramfield 124 E5
Braughing 82 A3
Braughing Friars 82 E4
Brays Grove 7 F5
Breachwood Green 92 B1
Brent Pelham 50 B7
Brickendon 175 F5
Bricket Wood 205 F1
Brick House End 67 K4
Briden's Camp 139 K6
Bridge Green 35 K3
Broad Colney 190 B6
Broadgreen Wood 174 D1
Bradley Common 178 E6
Broadoak End 150 C1
Broadwater 76 B8

Broken Green 82 D7
Bromley 102 D1
Brook End 62 A3
Brookmans Park 192 E4
Broxbourne 177 F6
Buckland 47 H1
Buckland Common 159 F6
Bucks Hill 202 B4
Building End 34 C2
Bulbourne 135 G1
Bullen's Green 170 D8
Bulls Cross 213 K6
Bull's Green 123 K2
Bulstrode 184 C6
Bumble's Green 199 G2
Buntingford 63 K2
Burge End 39 F4
Burnham Green 123 J3
Burn's Green 78 C8
Burton End 87 H5
Bury Green 104 B2
Bury Green 214 A1
Bury Park 89 G1
Bushey 221 K7
Bushey Heath 222 B7
Butt's Close 56 C1
Bygrave 27 J4
Caddington 88 E5
Cadwell 40 E4
Caldecote 16 D8
Caldecote Hill 222 C7
Campions 157 J4
The Camp 11 F6
Carpenders Park 231 G1
Chalfont Common 226 C3
Chalfont St Peter 226 D6
Chandler's Cross 218 E1
Chapmore End 126 A4
Charlton 56 B4
Chatter End 84 E2
Chaulden 163 G7
Chaul End 88 C2
Cheapside 49 H2
Cheddington 109 K3
Chells 3 F2
Chenies 201 F8
Cherry Green 63 H8
Cheshunt 197 F8
Cheverell's Green 115 H5
Childwick Bury 143 K8
Childwick Green 143 J7
Chiltern Green 91 H6
Chipperfield 202 A1
Chipping 47 H4
Chipping Barnet 225 K4
Chiswell Green 188 B3
Chivery 158 B5
Cholesbury 159 H7
Chorleywood 217 G4
Chorleywood Bottom ... 217 G6
Chorleywood West 216 D5
Church End 25 F2
Church End 84 A7
Church End 110 E7
Church End 142 B5
Church End 201 J8
Churchgate 197 F7
Churchgate Street 157 J5
Church Langley 181 G1
Clapgate 83 K3
Claverhambury 199 H5
Clay End 78 B2
Clay Hill 213 F7
Clement's End 114 B6
Clothall 43 K5
Clothall Common 43 H1
Cockernhoe 70 E6
Codicote 94 E8
Codicote Bottom 121 H1
Codmore 182 A8
Cokenach 32 E4
Cold Christmas 128 A3
Cold Harbour 118 E4
Cole Green 149 H5
Coleman Green 145 K4
Colliers End 101 F3
Colney Heath 170 B8
Colney Street 189 G8
Commonwood 201 K4
Cooper's End 35 J4
Cooper's Green 170 A1
Cottered 62 A1
Counters End 163 K6
Cow Roast 136 B8

Crabbs Green 67 F3
Cradle End 104 C1
Crews Hill 212 E5
Cromer 61 F4
Cromer-Hyde 146 B4
Croxley Green 219 F5
Cuffley 195 K3
Cumberlow Green 45 G7
Cupid Green 9 E1
Dagnall 112 E3
Damask Green 59 F3
Dancers Hill 209 H5
Dane End 99 J2
Danesbury 122 C3
Darleyhall 71 K8
Dassels 64 D6
Datchworth 97 F2
Datchworth Green 96 D6
Deacons Hill 223 K6
Deer's Green 51 J5
Dewes Green 51 H8
Digswell 123 F6
Digswell Park 122 D2
Digswell Water 123 G2
Drayton Beauchamp 134 B4
Driver's End 95 F7
Duck End 86 D8
Ducks Island 225 J7
Duddenhoe End 35 J1
Dudswell 160 E7
Eastbury 230 A3
East End 67 G5
Eastend 155 F6
East End Green 149 K1
Easthall .... 74 A
East Hyde 118 B3
Eastwick 155 J5
Edworth 16 B3
Ellenbrook .... 170 C
Elstree 223 H6
Enfield Lock .... 214 E
Enfield Wash 214 D6
Epping Green .... 174 A
Essendon .... 173 G
Eyeworth .... 14 A
Farley Hill .... 89 G
Farnham .... 85 F
Farnham Green .... 84 E
Felden .... 184 E
Fields End .... 163 G
Fishers Green .... 74 E
Flamstead .... 116 C
Flamstead End .... 197 F
Flaunden .... 200 D
Fleetville .... 11 F
The Folly .... 119 K
Ford End .... 51 G
Foster Street .... 181 G
Freezy Water .... 214 D
Friar's Wash .... 116 C
Frithsden .... 162 D
Frithsden Gardens .... 138 B
Frogmore .... 189 G
The Frythe .... 122 A
Fuller's End .... 87 H
Furneux Pelham .... 66 C
Further Ford End .... 51 F
Gadebridge .... 163 J
Ganwick Corner .... 210 D
Garston .... 204 D
Gaston Green .... 133 F
Gatley End .... 18 E
Gilston .... 156 A
Gilston Park .... 155 K
Goff's Oak .... 196 A
Goose Green .... 176 C
Gorhambury 166 E6
Gosmore .... 56 C
Graveley .... 58 C
Gravel Hill .... 226 C
Gravesend .... 83 H
Great Amwell .... 152 D
Great Gaddesden .... 139 F
Greatgap .... 110 D
Great Green .... 15 H
Great Hallingbury .... 106 C
Great Hormead .... 65 H
Great Munden .... 80 C
Great Offley .... 55 F
Great Parndon .... 179 F
Great Wymondley .... 57 J
Green End .... 43 J
Green End .... 46 E
Green End .... 79 H

Green End 81 J2
Green End 163 J7
Green Street 84 B8
Green Street 207 K7
The Green 113 H1
Green Tye 103 K8
Grovehill 8 A1
The Grove 203 H7
Gubblecote 109 H7
Guilden Morden 15 F4
Gustard Wood 120 A5
Hadham Cross 103 F7
Hadham Ford 103 J1
Hadley Wood 210 E8
Hailey 152 E7
Haldens 123 G7
Hall Grove 148 C5
Hallingbury Street 107 G5
Halls Green 178 D3
Hall's Green 60 A3
Hammerfield 164 A6
Hammond Street 196 A4
Handside 147 G4
Hanscombe End 37 J1
Harefield 228 B8
Harefield Grove 228 C6
Hare Street 6 A5
Hare Street 61 H3
Hare Street 64 D1
Harlow 6 C4
Harmer Green 123 G4
Harpenden 143 G1
Harpenden Common 143 J2
Hartham 151 G2
Hart Hill 5 E2
Hastingwood 181 J5
Hastoe 159 F2
Hatch End 231 F6
Hatching Green 143 G3
Hatfield 170 E5
Hatfield Garden Village 170 D1
Hatfield Hyde 148 A6
Haultwick 79 J6
Hay Green 30 E3
Hay Street 64 E8
Hazel End 85 K3
Heath End 160 B7
Hebing End 78 D7
Helham Green 129 F5
Hemel Hempstead 8 B5
Heronsgate 217 G7
Hertford 151 H4
Hertford Heath 152 A6
Hertingfordbury 150 D4
Hexton 37 H7
Higham Gobion 37 G3
High Barnet 225 H4
High Cross 100 E7
High Cross 206 A6
Highfield 8 B3
The High 6 B3
High Town 4 B3
High Wych 131 K8
Hill End 228 A5
Hinxworth 16 C3
Hitchin 40 D8
Hitchin Hill 56 C4
Hobbs Cross 157 K8
Hockerill 106 A3
Hoddesdon 176 D4
Hogpits Bottom 200 E2
Holwell 39 K2
Holyfield 198 C6
Holywell 114 A2
Holywell 219 K6
Hoo End 93 H7
Hook's Cross 97 H3
Howe Green 106 D7
How Wood 188 E5
Hudnall 138 B2
Hudnall Corner 138 D2
Hunsdon 129 J8
Hunsdonbury 154 D3
Hunton Bridge 203 G3
Ickleford 40 B5
Ippinghoe 111 F4
Jack's Hatch 179 J7
Jockey End 139 K1
Katherines 179 F4
Kelshall 30 B3
Kettle Green 102 D8
Keysers Estate 177 G7
Kimpton 93 G7
Kings Langley 185 J6
Kingsmoor 179 K6
King's Walden 72 C6
Kingswood 204 C4
Kinsbourne Green 117 H4
Kitt's End 209 K8
Lanes End 158 B6
Langley 34 E7
Langley 74 E8
Langleybury 203 G4
Latchford 102 A4
Latchmore Bank 105 K7
Latimer 200 B7
Latton Bush 180 D5
Leagrave 68 B5
Leasey Bridge 119 H8
Lea Valley 119 H6
Leavesden Green 204 A4
Lemsford 146 E4
Letchmore Heath 222 B1
Letchworth 41 H3
Letty Green 149 H7
Level's Green 85 F4
Levens Green 80 C8
Leverstock Green 9 F6
Ley Green 72 C4
Ley Hill 182 D8
Lilley 53 K7
Limbury 68 E4
Little Almshoe 56 E8
Little Berkamstead 173 H5
Little Chishill 34 A2
Little Gaddesden 138 A2
Little Green 15 H3
Little Hadham 83 K7
Little Hallingbury 133 G1
Little Heath 162 D4
Little Heath 193 H4
Little Hormead 65 G2
Little Offley 54 C3
Little Parndon 6 A3
Little Tring 134 D3
Little Wymondley 57 H5
London Colney 190 A4
Long Marston 109 F6
Loudwater 218 C3
Lower Green 34 D8
Lower Green 40 C4
Lower Green 50 A2
Lower Nazeing 198 D1
Lower Sheering 132 E8
Lower Woodside 172 A8
Lucas End 196 A5
Luffenhall 60 E3
Luton 89 F2
Lye Green 182 B6
Mackerye End 119 G5
Mangrove Green 71 G5
Maple Cross 227 G3
Mardleybury 96 C7
Mark Hall North 7 F1
Mark Hall South 7 F2
Markyate 115 K4
Marshalls Heath 119 J6
Marshalswick 11 F1
Marsh Farm 68 D2
Marshmoor 171 J8
Marsworth 110 A7
Meesden 50 B4
Meriden 205 F6
Merry Hill 221 J8
Micklefield Green 201 K8
Mill End 46 C3
Mill End 217 J8
Mill Green 171 K1
Moneyhill 218 A8
Monken Hadley 225 K2
Moor Green 62 B7
Moor Park 229 H3
Morden Green 15 K8
Mott's Green 133 H3
Mount Pleasant 228 A7
Much Hadham 103 F6
Nash Mills 186 A3
Nast Hyde 170 C5
Nasty 80 C3
Nazeing 178 C8
Nazeing Gate 199 J3
Nazeing Long Green 199 J3
Nazeing Mead 177 J5
Nether Street 130 B4
Netteswell 7 D3
Nettleden 138 E7
Newgate Street 195 G2
New Greens 167 K1
New Ground 136 B7
New Mill 135 G3
New Mill End 117 K1
Newnham 27 F2
Newsells 32 D2
New Town 4 B6
Nobland Green 129 G1
The Node 94 E4
Nomansland 145 F3
Northaw 194 C8
North Brook End 15 K4
Northchurch 160 E3
North Watford 204 C7
Northwood 229 H7
Northwood Hills 229 J8
Norton 26 B8
Norton Green 75 G6
Nup End 95 G5
Nuthampstead 33 H7
Oakfield 57 F3
Oaklands 123 G2
Odsey 18 E8
Old Hall Green 80 E8
Old Harlow 157 F5
Old Hatfield 171 J3
Old Knebworth 95 J3
Old Town 2 A1
Orchard Leigh 182 D5
Otterspool 205 G2
Oxhey 13 E5
Oxlease 171 G5
Painter's Green 96 E7
Panshanger 148 B2
Park Green 67 K3
Park Street 188 E4
Park Town 5 D5
Passmores 180 A4
Patchetts Green 221 K1
Patient End 66 B6
Patmore Heath 84 A1
Peartree 147 K4
Pegsdon 37 J8
Pepperstock 89 H8
Perry Green 130 D1
Peters Green 91 K6
Piccotts End 164 B2
Pimlico 186 E2
Pin Green 76 B1
Pinnacles 179 H1
Pinner Green 230 D8
Pinnerwood Park 230 D6
Pirton 38 E5
Pitstone 110 D6
Pitstone Green 110 E5
Pitstone Hill 111 G8
Pond Street 35 H2
Poplars 76 E6
Porter's End 119 J2
Potten End 162 D3
Potter's Bar 210 E3
Potters Crouch 187 K2
Pottersheath 95 H8
Potter Street 181 G3
Pouchen End 163 G7
Presdales 152 D2
Preston 73 F3
Puckeridge 81 K6
Pudds Cross 183 G6
Purwell 57 H1
Puttenham 108 D7
Rableyheath 95 H7
Radlett 206 B4
Radlett 207 F3
Radwell 26 C5
Redbourn 142 C3
Redbournbury 143 F7
Redhill 45 G3
Reed 31 K5
Reed End 31 G3
Rickmansworth 217 K7
Ridge 208 E4
The Ridgeway 194 D5
Ringshall 112 D8
Roast Green 51 H3
Roe End 115 F5
Roe Green 45 K1
Roe Green 171 F4
Roestock 191 H1
The Rookery 12 B6
Rosedale 196 D6
Round Bush 206 A8
Round Green 4 C1
Rowley Green 224 E3

Roydon 154 C8
Roydon Hamlet 178 D5
Royston 21 F2
Rucklers Lane 185 J4
Rushden 45 G5
Rush Green 74 C5
Rush Green 152 B3
Rusling End 94 C2
The Ryde 171 H1
Rye Meads 153 J8
Rye Park 177 G2
Sacombe 99 H6
Sacombe Green 100 A5
St Albans 11 E2
St Ibbs 56 E8
St Ippollitts 56 E7
St Julians 188 E2
St Leonards 158 D6
St Margarets 153 F5
St Margaret's 139 F5
St Nicholas 59 G7
St Paul's Walden 73 K8
St Stephens 167 H8
Sandon 29 K8
Sandridge 145 F8
Sarratt 201 K5
Sarratt Bottom 201 H6
Sawbridgeworth 131 K7
Shaftenhoe End 33 H1
Shaw Green 45 F4
Shenley 207 J4
Shenleybury 207 G1
Shephall 3 E5
Sherrardspark 147 G1
Shootersway 161 F5
Sleapshyde 170 B7
Slip End 28 D3
Slip End 89 H7
Smallford 170 A5
Smith's End 33 G1
Smug Oak 188 D8
Snailswell 40 B3
Snow End 49 G4
Sopwell 189 G1
South-end 130 D3
Southern Green 45 J5
South Hatfield 171 G7
South Mimms 209 G2
South Oxhey 230 C2
Spellbrook 132 C1
Spitalbrook 177 F5
Staines Green 149 K5
Stanborough 146 E6
Standon 81 K8
Standon Green End 100 D5
Stanstead Abbots 153 K5
Stansted Mountfitchet 86 B2
Stapleford 125 G2
Starling's Green 51 H6
Start Hill 107 F2

Startop's End 109 K8
Steeple Morden 15 H7
Stet 112 A1
Stevenage 2 B2
Stewards 180 B6
Stocking Pelham 67 F2
Stopsley 70 B5
Stotfold 26 A2
Studham 113 K4
Sumners 179 H5
Sundon Park 68 B2
Swanley Bar 193 H6
The Swillett 217 F7
Symonds Green 75 F2
Tea Green 71 J6
Temple Fields 156 D5
Tewin 124 A6
Tewin Wood 123 K4
Therfield 30 D2
Thorley 105 F7
Thorley Houses 104 D4
Thorley Street 105 H6
Threshers Bush 181 K2
The Thrift 19 K6
Throcking 46 C8
Thundridge 127 J2
Tilekiln Green 106 E3
Titmore Green 57 J7
Todd's Green 58 A7
Tolmers 195 G4
Tonwell 126 D2
Totteridge 225 K7
Tower Hill 184 D7
Townsend 10 A2
Trims Green 132 A2
Tring 135 G6
Tringford 134 D1
Tring Wharf 135 G2
Trowley Bottom 141 G1
Turnford 197 H3
Two Waters 185 G1
Tye Green 6 C6
Tye Green 87 K3
Tylers Causeway 173 J8
Tyttenhanger 190 C1
Uppend 67 K8
Upper Dunsley 135 H6
Upper Green 35 F7
Upwick Green 84 B4
Venus Hill 200 E1
Wadesmill 127 H1
Wakeley 62 D7
Walkern 60 D8
Wallington 44 E1
Walsworth 40 E8
Waltham Abbey 215 J2
Waltham Cross 214 B3
Wandon End 71 J2
Ware 127 K7
Wareside 129 F6

Warners End 163 H5
Warren's Green 59 K3
Washall Green 50 D8
Waterdale 187 J8
Water End 139 J8
Water End 192 C4
Waterend 146 C1
Waterford 125 H7
Watford 220 B1
Watford Heath 13 F6
Watton at Stone 97 K5
Welham Green 192 B1
Well End 208 B8
Wellpond Green 82 D8
Welwyn 122 A4
Welwyn Garden City 148 C1
Westbrook Hay 184 A2
West End 172 E4
West Hyde 117 J2
West Hyde 227 H6
Westland Green 103 F1
Westmill 40 A8
Westmill 63 K7
Weston 43 J8
West Watford 12 B4
Westwick Row 165 K7
Wheathampstead 119 K8
Whelpley Hill 183 F4
Whempstead 99 F3
Whippendell Botton 185 G8
Whipsnade 113 J1
Whitehall 46 C5
White Hall 97 J1
Whitwell 93 H3
Widford 130 A5
Wigginton 135 J7
Wigginton Bottom 159 K1
Wildhill 172 D7
Willian 42 B7
Wilstone 109 H8
Wilstone Green 134 C1
Winsdon Hill 89 G2
Woodcock Hill 228 D3
Wood End 79 F2
Woodhall 147 K5
Woodside 89 F7
Woodside 172 B7
Woodside 204 C2
Woodside Green 106 E8
Woollensbrook 152 C8
Woolmer Green 96 C7
Wormley 197 J2
Wormleybury 197 F7
Wormley West End 175 K8
Wright's Green 133 H2
Wyddial 48 A5
Wymondley Bury 57 K6
Youngsbury 127 K4

USING THE STREET INDEX

Street names are listed alphabetically. Each street name is followed by its postal town or area locality, the Postcode District, the page number, and the reference to the square in which the name is found.

Example: **Abbey Rd** *CHES/WCR* EN8.............................. **214** D4 🗓

Some entries are followed by a number in a blue box. This number indicates the location of the street within the referenced grid square. The full street name is listed at the side of the map page.

GENERAL ABBREVIATIONS

ACC	ACCESS	GA	GATE
ALY	ALLEY	GAL	GALLERY
AP	APPROACH	GDN	GARDEN
AR	ARCADE	GDNS	GARDENS
ASS	ASSOCIATION	GLD	GLADE
AV	AVENUE	GLN	GLEN
BCH	BEACH	GN	GREEN
BLDS	BUILDINGS	GND	GROUND
BND	BEND	GRA	GRANGE
BNK	BANK	GRG	GARAGE
BR	BRIDGE	GT	GREAT
BRK	BROOK	GTWY	GATEWAY
BTM	BOTTOM	GV	GROVE
BUS	BUSINESS	HGR	HIGHER
BVD	BOULEVARD	HL	HILL
BY	BYPASS	HLS	HILLS
CATH	CATHEDRAL	HO	HOUSE
CEM	CEMETERY	HOL	HOLLOW
CEN	CENTRE	HOSP	HOSPITAL
CFT	CROFT	HRB	HARBOUR
CH	CHURCH	HTH	HEATH
CHA	CHASE	HTS	HEIGHTS
CHYD	CHURCHYARD	HVN	HAVEN
CIR	CIRCLE	HWY	HIGHWAY
CIRC	CIRCUS	IMP	IMPERIAL
CL	CLOSE	IN	INLET
CLFS	CLIFFS	IND EST	INDUSTRIAL ESTATE
CMP	CAMP	INF	INFIRMARY
CNR	CORNER	INFO	INFORMATION
CO	COUNTY	INT	INTERCHANGE
COLL	COLLEGE	IS	ISLAND
COM	COMMON	JCT	JUNCTION
COMM	COMMISSION	JTY	JETTY
CON	CONVENT	KG	KING
COT	COTTAGE	KNL	KNOLL
COTS	COTTAGES	L	LAKE
CP	CAPE	LA	LANE
CPS	COPSE	LDG	LODGE
CR	CREEK	LGT	LIGHT
CREM	CREMATORIUM	LK	LOCK
CRS	CRESCENT	LKS	LAKES
CSWY	CAUSEWAY	LNDG	LANDING
CT	COURT	LTL	LITTLE
CTRL	CENTRAL	LWR	LOWER
CTS	COURTS	MAG	MAGISTRATE
CTYD	COURTYARD	MAN	MANSIONS
CUTT	CUTTINGS	MD	MEAD
CV	COVE	MDW	MEADOWS
CYN	CANYON	MEM	MEMORIAL
DEPT	DEPARTMENT	MKT	MARKET
DL	DALE	MKTS	MARKETS
DM	DAM	ML	MALL
DR	DRIVE	ML	MILL
DRO	DROVE	MNR	MANOR
DRY	DRIVEWAY	MS	MEWS
DWGS	DWELLINGS	MSN	MISSION
E	EAST	MT	MOUNT
EMB	EMBANKMENT	MTN	MOUNTAIN
EMBY	EMBASSY	MTS	MOUNTAINS
ESP	ESPLANADE	MUS	MUSEUM
EST	ESTATE	MWY	MOTORWAY
EX	EXCHANGE	N	NORTH
EXPY	EXPRESSWAY	NE	NORTH EAST
EXT	EXTENSION	NW	NORTH WEST
F/O	FLYOVER	O/P	OVERPASS
FC	FOOTBALL CLUB	OFF	OFFICE
FK	FORK	ORCH	ORCHARD
FLD	FIELD	OV	OVAL
FLDS	FIELDS	PAL	PALACE
FLS	FALLS	PAS	PASSAGE
FLS	FLATS	PAV	PAVILION
FM	FARM	PDE	PARADE
FT	FORT	PH	PUBLIC HOUSE
FWY	FREEWAY	PK	PARK
FY	FERRY	PKWY	PARKWAY
		PL	PLACE
		PLN	PLAIN
		PLNS	PLAINS
		PLZ	PLAZA
		POL	POLICE STATION
		PR	PRINCE
		PREC	PRECINCT
		PREP	PREPARATORY
		PRIM	PRIMARY
		PROM	PROMENADE
		PRS	PRINCESS
		PRT	PORT
		PT	POINT
		PTH	PATH
		PZ	PIAZZA
		QD	QUADRANT
		QU	QUEEN
		QY	QUAY
		R	RIVER
		RBT	ROUNDABOUT
		RD	ROAD
		RDG	RIDGE
		REP	REPUBLIC
		RES	RESERVOIR
		RFC	RUGBY FOOTBALL CLUB
		RI	RISE
		RP	RAMP
		RW	ROW
		S	SOUTH
		SCH	SCHOOL
		SE	SOUTH EAST
		SER	SERVICE AREA
		SH	SHORE
		SHOP	SHOPPING
		SKWY	SKYWAY
		SMT	SUMMIT
		SOC	SOCIETY
		SP	SPUR
		SPR	SPRING
		SQ	SQUARE
		ST	STREET
		STN	STATION
		STR	STREAM
		STRD	STRAND
		SW	SOUTH WEST
		TDG	TRADING
		TER	TERRACE
		THWY	THROUGHWAY
		TNL	TUNNEL
		TOLL	TOLLWAY
		TPK	TURNPIKE
		TR	TRACK
		TRL	TRAIL
		TWR	TOWER
		U/P	UNDERPASS
		UNI	UNIVERSITY
		UPR	UPPER
		V	VALE
		VA	VALLEY
		VIAD	VIADUCT
		VIL	VILLA
		VIS	VISTA
		VLG	VILLAGE
		VLS	VILLAS
		VW	VIEW
		W	WEST
		WD	WOOD
		WHF	WHARF
		WK	WALK
		WKS	WALKS
		WLS	WELLS
		WY	WAY
		YD	YARD
		YHA	YOUTH HOSTEL

POSTCODE TOWNS AND AREA ABBREVIATIONS

ABLGY	Abbots Langley	BROX	Broxbourne	DUN/HR/TOD	Dunstable/Houghton Regis/Toddington
AMP/FLIT/BLC	Ampthill/Flitwick/Barton-le-Clay	BSF	Bishop's Stortford	DUN/WHIP	Dunstable/Whipsnade
AMS	Amersham	BUNT	Buntingford	EBAR	East Barnet
AMSS	Amersham south	BUSH	Bushey	EDGW	Edgware
ARL/CHE	Arlesey/Church End	CFSP/GDCR	Chalfont St Peter/Gerrards Cross	EN	Enfield
BAR	Barnet	CHES/WCR	Cheshunt/Waltham Cross	ENC/FH	Enfield Chase/Forty Hill
BERK	Berkhamsted	CHESW	Cheshunt west	EPP	Epping
BGSW	Biggleswade	CHING	Chingford	GSTN	Garston
BLDK	Baldock	CSHM	Chesham	GTMIS/PWD	Great Missenden/Prestwood
BORE	Borehamwood	CSTG	Chalfont St Giles	HARP	Harpenden
BRKMPK	Brookmans Park	DEN/HRF	Denham/Harefield	HAT	Hatfield

236

HERT/BAY ....Hertford/Bayford
HERT/WAS ....Hertford/Watton at Stone
HHNE ....Hemel Hempstead northeast
HHS/BOV ....Hemel Hempstead south/Bovingdon
HHW ....Hemel Hempstead west
HLW ....Harlow
HLWE ....Harlow east
HLWS ....Harlow south
HLWW/ROY ....Harlow west/Roydon
HNLW ....Henlow
HOD ....Hoddesdon
HTCH/STOT ....Hitchin/Stotfold
HTCHE/RSTV ....Hitchin east/Rural Stevenage
KGLGY ....Kings Langley
KNEB ....Knebworth
KTN/HRWW/WS ....Kenton/Harrow Weald/Wealdstone
LBUZ ....Leighton Buzzard
LCOL/BKTW ....London Colney/Bricket Wood
LOU ....Loughton
LTN ....Luton
LTNE ....Luton east
LTNN/LIM ....Luton north/Limbury
LTNW/LEA ....Luton west/Leagrave
LWTH ....Letchworth
MHAD ....Much Hadham

MLHL ....Mill Hill
NTHWD ....Northwood
OXHEY ....Oxhey
PEND ....Ponders End
PIN ....Pinner
POTB/CUF ....Potters Bar/Cuffley
RAD ....Radlett
RAYLNE/WEN ....Rural Aylesbury north & east/Wendover
RBSF ....Rural Bishop's Stortford
RKW/CH/CXG ....Rickmansworth/Chorleywood/Croxley Green
ROY ....Royston
RYLN/HDSTN ....Rayners Lane/Headstone
SAFWS ....Saffron Walden south
SBW ....Sawbridgeworth
SDY/GAM/POT ....Sandy/Gamlingay/Potton
STAL ....St Albans
STALE/WH ....St Albans east/Wheathampstead
STALW/RED ....St Albans west/Redbourn
STAN ....Stanmore
STDN ....Standon
STSD ....Stansted
STVG ....Stevenage
STVGE ....Stevenage east
TRDG/WHET ....Totteridge/Whetstone
TRING ....Tring

WAB ....Waltham Abbey
WARE ....Ware
WAT ....Watford
WATN ....Watford north
WATW ....Watford west
WGCE ....Welwyn Garden City east
WGCW ....Welwyn Garden City west

Abb - All

Index - streets

A

Abbey Av STALW/RED AL3 .... 188 C1
Abbey Ct WAB EN9 .... 215 G4
Abbey Dale Cl HLWE CM17 .... 181 F2
Abbey Dr ABGLY WD5 .... 204 B2
　LTNE LU2 .... 5 E2
Abbey Mill End STALW/RED AL3 .... 10 B5
Abbey Mill La STALW/RED AL3 .... 10 B5
Abbey Rd CHES/WCR EN8 .... 214 D4
Abbey Vw RAD WD7 .... 206 C5
Abbeyview WAB EN9 .... 215 G3
Abbey View Rd STALW/RED AL3 .... 10 B4
Abbis Orch HTCH/STOT SG5 .... 40 C1
Abbot John Ms STALE/WH AL4 .... 120 B8
Abbots Av STAL AL1 .... 189 G1
Abbots Av West STAL AL1 .... 189 F1
Abbots Cl KNEB SG3 .... 96 E8
Abbots Gv STVG SG1 .... 3 D4
Abbots Pk STAL AL1 .... 11 E6
Abbots Ri WARE SG12 .... 153 J5
Abbots Rd ABGLY WD5 .... 186 B8
Abbots Vw KGLGY WD4 .... 185 K5
Abbotsweld HLWS CM18 .... 180 A4
Abbots Wood Rd LTNE LU2 .... 5 E2
Abbotts La WARE SG12 .... 129 K5
Abbotts Ri WARE SG12 .... 153 J5
Abbotts Rd LWTH SG6 .... 41 H3
Abbotts Wy BSF CM23 .... 105 H6
　WARE SG12 .... 153 J5
Abdale La BRKMPK AL9 .... 192 C3
Abel Cl HHNE HP2 .... 9 D5
Abercrombie Wy HLWW/ROY CM19 .... 6 B6
Aberdale Gdns POTB/CUF EN6 .... 210 A3
Aberford Rd BORE WD6 .... 223 K2
Abigail Cl LTNN/LIM LU3 .... 69 J6
Abingdon Pl POTB/CUF EN6 .... 210 C2
Abingdon Rd LTNN/LIM LU4 .... 68 B6
Abridge Cl CHES/WCR EN8 .... 214 C5
Abstacle Hl TRING HP23 .... 134 E6
Acacia Cl CHESW EN7 .... 196 C5
Acacia Gv BERK HP4 .... 161 J6
Acacia St HAT AL10 .... 171 F7
Acacia Wk HARP AL5 .... 144 A3
Acers LCOL/BKTW AL2 .... 188 E6
Achilles Cl HHNE HP2 .... 8 C5
Ackroyd Rd ROY SG8 .... 21 J1
Acme Rd WATN WD24 .... 204 B8
Acorn Gld WLYN AL6 .... 123 F5
Acorn La POTB/CUF EN6 .... 195 G2
Acorn Pl WATN WD24 .... 204 B7
Acorn Rd HHS/BOV HP3 .... 9 D6
Acorn St WARE SG12 .... 154 E2
Acremore St STDN SG11 .... 104 A2
Acre Piece HTCHE/RSTV SG4 .... 56 E3
Acre Wy HHNE HP2 .... 8 B6
Acrewood Wy STALE/WH AL4 .... 169 J6
Acton Cl CHES/WCR EN8 .... 214 D1
Acworth Crs LTNW/LEA LU4 .... 68 B4
Adamsfield CHESW EN7 .... 196 D4
Adams House HLW CM20 .... 6 C3
Adams Wy TRING HP23 .... 135 G4
Addington Wy LTNW/LEA LU4 .... 68 C6
Addiscombe Rd WATW WD18 .... 12 C3

Addison Cl NTHWD HA6 .... 230 B7
Addison Wy NTHWD HA6 .... 230 A7
Adelaide Cl EN EN1 .... 213 H8
Adelaide St LTN LU1 .... 4 A4
　STALW/RED AL3 .... 10 C5
Adele Av WLYN AL6 .... 123 F6
Adeyfield Gdns HHNE HP2 .... 8 C4
Adeyfield Rd HHNE HP2 .... 8 C5
Adhara Rd NTHWD HA6 .... 230 A4
Adinger Cl STVG SG1 .... 2 C5
Admirals Cl STALE/WH AL4 .... 191 J1
Admiral St HERT/BAY SG13 .... 151 K3
Admirals Wk HOD EN11 .... 177 F5
　STAL AL1 .... 11 F6
Admiral Wy BERK HP4 .... 161 G3
Adrian Cl DEN/HRF UB9 .... 228 C7
Adrian Rd ABGLY WD5 .... 203 K1
Adstone Rd LTN LU1 .... 88 E6
Ailsworth Rd LTNN/LIM LU3 .... 69 F3
Ainsdale Rd OXHEY WD19 .... 230 D2
Aintree Bd ROY SG8 .... 21 K3
Aintree Wy STVGE SG2 .... 76 D1
Airport Approach Rd LTNE LU2 .... 90 E1
Airport Wy LTN LU1 .... 89 K6
　LTNE LU2 .... 90 D3
Aitken Rd BAR EN5 .... 225 H5
Akeman Cl STALW/RED AL3 .... 167 G8
Akeman St TRING HP23 .... 135 F6
Alamein Cl BROX EN10 .... 176 C6
Alandale Dr LTNN/LIM LU3 .... 69 F6
Alandale St WARE SG12 .... 153 F5
Alban Av STALW/RED AL3 .... 10 C2
Alban Crs BORE WD6 .... 224 A1
Alban Rd LWTH SG6 .... 42 C6
Albans Vw GSTN WD25 .... 204 C3
Albany Cl BUSH WD23 .... 222 A6
Albany Rd PEND EN3 .... 214 C7
Albemarle Av CHES/WCR EN8 .... 197 G6
　POTB/CUF EN6 .... 210 C3
Albert Gdns HLWE CM17 .... 181 G2
Albert Rd ARL/CHE SG15 .... 24 E5
　LTN LU1 .... 4 C6
Albert Rd North WAT WD17 .... 12 C1
Albert Rd South WAT WD17 .... 12 C2
Albert St STAL AL1 .... 11 E6
　STALW/RED AL3 .... 115 J4
　STVG SG1 .... 2 A1
　TRING HP23 .... 135 F6
Albion Hl HHNE HP2 .... 8 A6
Albion Rd LBUZ LU7 .... 110 C4
　LTNE LU2 .... 4 C3
　STAL AL1 .... 11 E4
Albury Cl LTNN/LIM LU3 .... 52 A8
Albury Dr PIN HA5 .... 230 D7
Albury Grove Rd CHES/WCR EN8 .... 197 H8
Albury Ride CHES/WCR EN8 .... 214 C1
Albury Rd STDN SG11 .... 83 K7
Albury Wk CHES/WCR EN8 .... 197 G8
Alconbury BSF CM23 .... 86 A8
　WGCE AL7 .... 149 F3
Aldbury Cl GSTN WD25 .... 204 E6
　STALE/WH AL4 .... 169 F1
Aldbury Gv WGCE AL7 .... 148 C3
Aldbury Rd RKW/CH/CXG WD3 .... 217 J3
Aldcock Rd STVG SG1 .... 75 K1
Aldeburgh Cl STVG SG1 .... 58 A8
Aldenham Av RAD WD7 .... 206 D7

Aldenham Gv RAD WD7 .... 206 E4
Aldenham Rd BUSH WD23 .... 13 F4
　GSTN WD25 .... 222 C2
　OXHEY WD19 .... 13 E5
　RAD WD7 .... 206 D5
Alderbury Rd STSD CM24 .... 86 D1
Alder Cl BLDK SG7 .... 42 E2
　BSF CM23 .... 105 G5
　HOD EN11 .... 177 G1
　LCOL/BKTW AL2 .... 188 D6
Alder Crs LTNN/LIM LU3 .... 69 F6
Alderman Cl BRKMPK AL9 .... 192 C3
Alders End La HARP AL5 .... 118 B7
Alders Wk SBW CM21 .... 132 C7
Alderton Cl LTNE LU2 .... 70 E8
Alderton Dr BERK HP4 .... 137 H1
Alder Wk GSTN WD25 .... 204 C5
Aldock Rd LTNN/LIM LU3 .... 69 G4
Aldous Cl LTNN/LIM LU3 .... 68 D3
Aldridge Av PEND EN3 .... 215 F8
Aldridge Ct BLDK SG7 .... 26 E8
Aldwick STAL AL1 .... 11 F6
Aldwickbury Crs HARP AL5 .... 119 F5
Aldwick Rd HARP AL5 .... 144 B1
Aldwyke Ri WARE SG12 .... 127 G6
Aldykes HAT AL10 .... 170 E4
Alesia Rd LTNN/LIM LU3 .... 68 D3
Alexander Ga STVGE SG2 .... 76 D1
Alexander Rd HERT/WAS SG14 .... 150 D3
　HTCH/STOT SG5 .... 25 K3
　LCOL/BKTW AL2 .... 190 A3
Alexandra Av LTNN/LIM LU3 .... 69 G6
Alexandra Ms WAT WD17 .... 12 B1
Alexandra Rd BORE WD6 .... 208 C8
　HHNE HP2 .... 8 A4
　HTCH/STOT SG5 .... 40 D8
　KGLGY WD4 .... 184 E8
　KGLGY WD4 .... 186 A7
　RKW/CH/CXG WD3 .... 201 K6
　STAL AL1 .... 11 D4
　WAT WD17 .... 12 B1
Alexandra Wy CHES/WCR EN8 .... 214 E4
Aleyn Wy BLDK SG7 .... 27 H8
Alfriston Cl LTNE LU2 .... 70 D6
Alington La LWTH SG6 .... 41 K6
Allandale HHNE HP2 .... 8 A3
　STALW/RED AL3 .... 188 D7
Allandale Crs POTB/CUF EN6 .... 209 K2
Allandale Rd PEND EN3 .... 214 C8
Allard Cl CHESW EN7 .... 196 D5
Allard Crs BUSH WD23 .... 231 K1
Allard Wy BROX EN10 .... 176 D7
Alldicks Rd HHS/BOV HP3 .... 164 E8
Allen Cl RAD WD7 .... 207 H2
　STALE/WH AL4 .... 145 G2
Allen Ct HAT AL10 .... 171 G6
Allendale LTNN/LIM LU3 .... 69 F1
Allerton Cl BORE WD6 .... 207 J8
Allerton Rd BORE WD6 .... 207 H8
Aileyns Rd STVG SG1 .... 2 B5
Allmains Cl WAB EN9 .... 199 J5
All Saints Cl BSF CM23 .... 105 K1
Allsaints Crs GSTN WD25 .... 204 E2
All Saints La RKW/CH/CXG WD3 .... 219 F6
Allum La BORE WD6 .... 223 H4
Allwood Rd CHESW EN7 .... 196 D5

Alma Cut *STAL* AL1 11 D5
Alma Link *LTN* LU1 4 B4
Alma Rd *BERK* HP4 161 F3
STAL AL1 11 D5
Alma St *LTN* LU1 4 B4
Almonds La *STVG* SG1 75 K1
The Almonds *STAL* AL1 189 K2
Almond Wy *BORE* WD6 224 A4
RYLN/HDSTN HA2 231 K8
Almshouse La *EN* EN1 214 A7
Alms La *BLDK* SG7 17 K5
Alnwick Dr *TRING* HP23 108 D2
Alpha Pl *BSF* CM23 105 J1
Alpine Cl *HTCHE/RSTV* SG4 56 E4
Alpine Wy *LTNN/LIM* LU3 68 C1
Alsop Cl *LCOL/BKTW* AL2 190 C6
Alston Rd *BAR* EN5 225 K3
HHW HP1 163 K7
Altair Wy *NTHWD* HA6 230 A4
Altham Gv *HLW* CM20 7 D2
Altham Rd *PIN* HA5 231 F6
Althorp Cl *TRDG/WHET* N20 225 F7
Althorp Rd *LTNN/LIM* LU3 4 A2
STAL AL1 11 D3
Alton Rd *LTN* LU1 5 D6
Altwood *HARP* AL5 119 F8
Alva Wy *OXHEY* WD19 230 E1
Alverton *STALW/RED* AL3 10 B1
Alwin Pl *WATW* WD18 219 K4
Alwyn Cl *BORE* WD6 223 J6
LTNE LU2 4 C1
Alyngton *BERK* HP4 161 F2
Alzey Gdns *HARP* AL5 144 A1
Amberley Cl *HARP* AL5 118 D7
LTNE LU2 70 E5
Amberley Gn *WARE* SG12 127 G5
Ambleside *LTNN/LIM* LU3 68 E4
Ambrose La *HARP* AL5 118 C6
Amenbury La *HARP* AL5 118 C8
Amersham Rd *AMS* HP6 216 A1
CSTG HP8 226 A3
RKW/CH/CXG WD3 216 E1
Amersham Wy *AMS* HP6 216 B1
Amor Wy *LWTH* SG6 42 B3
Amwell Cl *GSTN* WD25 205 F5
Amwell Common *WGCE* AL7 148 C4
Amwell Ct *HOD* EN11 177 F2
WAB EN9 215 K3
Amwell End *WARE* SG12 127 H8
Amwell Hl *WARE* SG12 152 E3
Amwell La *STALE/WH* AL4 144 E2
WARE SG12 153 F3
Amwell St *HOD* EN11 177 F2
Anchor Cl *CHES/WCR* EN8 197 H6
Anchor La *HHW* HP1 164 A7
WARE SG12 127 F3
Anchor Rd *BLDK* SG7 43 F2
Anchor St *BSF* CM23 105 K3
Anderson Cl *DEN/HRF* UB9 227 K7
Anderson Rd *RAD* WD7 207 K3
STVGE SG2 76 D3
Anderson's La *BUNT* SG9 49 G7
Andover Cl *LTNW/LEA* LU4 68 B3
Andrew Cl *RAD* WD7 207 J3
Andrews Cl *HHNE* HP2 8 A3
Andrewsfield *WGCE* AL7 148 D3
Andrew's La *CHESW* EN7 196 C6
Anelle Ri *HHS/BOV* HP3 185 K2
Angell's Meadow *BLDK* SG7 17 K5
Anglefield Rd *BERK* HP4 161 H5
Anglesey Cl *BSF* CM23 105 F2
Anglesey Rd *OXHEY* WD19 230 D4
Angle Ways *STVGE* SG2 3 D6
Anglian Cl *WATN* WD24 13 D1
Angotts Md *STVG* SG1 75 G3
Anmer Gdns *LTNW/LEA* LU4 68 A5
Annables La *HARP* AL5 117 F5
Anns Cl *TRING* HP23 134 D6
Anselm Rd *PIN* HA5 231 G6
Anson Cl *HHW* HP1 183 H5
STAL AL1 168 E8
STALE/WH AL4 145 F8
Anson Wk *NTHWD* HA6 229 H3
Anstee Rd *LTNW/LEA* LU4 68 A3
Anthony Cl *OXHEY* WD19 220 E8
Anthony Gdns *LTN* LU1 4 B6
Anthony Rd *BORE* WD6 223 H2
Anthorne Cl *POTB/CUF* EN6 210 C1
Anthus Ms *NTHWD* HA6 229 J6
Antoneys Cl *PIN* HA5 230 E8
Antonine Ga *STALW/RED* AL3 167 H7
Anvil Cl *HHS/BOV* HP3 183 K6
Aplins Cl *HARP* AL5 118 B7
Apollo Av *NTHWD* HA6 230 B4
Apollo Wy *HHNE* HP2 8 B3
STVG SG1 76 D1
Appleby St *CHESW* EN7 196 C4
Applecroft *BERK* HP4 161 F3
LCOL/BKTW AL2 188 D6
Applecroft Rd *LTNE* LU2 70 D5
WGCW AL8 147 G3
Appleford's Cl *HOD* EN11 176 E1
Apple Glebe *AMP/FLIT/B* MK45 36 C7
The Apple Orch *HHNE* HP2 8 C3
Appleton Av *WARE* SG12 128 E4
Appleton Cl *HLWW/ROY* CM19 6 B5
Appleton Flds *BSF* CM23 105 H5
Appletree Wk *GSTN* WD25 204 C5
Applewood Cl *HARP* AL5 118 A6
Approach Rd *STAL* AL1 11 D5
The Approach *POTB/CUF* EN6 210 A2
Appspond La *LCOL/BKTW* AL2 187 J2
Apsley Cl *BSF* CM23 105 H5
Apsley End Rd *HTCH/STOT* SG5 38 A4
Apton Ct *BSF* CM23 105 J2
Apton Flds *BSF* CM23 105 J3
Apton Rd *BSF* CM23 105 J2
Aquarius Wy *NTHWD* HA6 230 B4
Aragon Cl *ENC/FH* EN2 212 C8
HHNE HP2 165 H1
Aran Cl *HARP* AL5 144 A3
Arbour Cl *LTNN/LIM* LU3 52 A8
The Arbour *HERT/BAY* SG13 151 G5
Arbroath Gn *OXHEY* WD19 230 B2
Archer Cl *KGLGY* WD4 185 K7
Archer Rd *STVG* SG1 3 D1
Archers *BUNT* SG9 63 K1
EPP CM16 179 J6
Archers Cl *HERT/WAS* SG14 151 F2
Archers Flds *STAL* AL1 11 E2
Archers Green La *WLYN* AL6 148 E1
Archers Ride *WGCE* AL7 148 C5
Archers Wy *LWTH* SG6 41 H3
The Arches *LWTH* SG6 42 A2
Archfield *WGCE* AL7 122 E8
Arch Rd *HTCHE/RSTV* SG4 57 H5
Archway Rd *LTNW/LEA* LU4 68 D5
Arden Cl *BUSH* WD23 222 C7
HHS/BOV HP3 183 J6
Arden Gv *HARP* AL5 118 D8
Arden Pl *LTNE* LU2 4 C2
Arden Press Wy *LWTH* SG6 42 B3
Ardens Wy *STALE/WH* AL4 169 G4
Ardleigh Gn *LTNE* LU2 71 F8
Ardross Av *NTHWD* HA6 229 K4
Argent Wy *CHESW* EN7 196 B5
Argyle Rd *BAR* EN5 225 H4
Argyle Wy *STVG* SG1 2 A3
Argyll Av *LTNN/LIM* LU3 4 A1
Argyll Rd *HHNE* HP2 164 D1
Arkley Dr *BAR* EN5 225 F4
Arkley La *BAR* EN5 225 F3
Arkley Rd *HHNE* HP2 165 G1
Arkley Vw *BAR* EN5 225 G4
Arkwrights *HLW* CM20 7 E3
Arlesey New Rd *LWTH* SG6 41 G2
Arlesey Rd *HNLW* SG16 24 B1
HTCH/STOT SG5 25 H3
HTCH/STOT SG5 40 C5
Arlington Crs *CHES/WCR* EN8 214 D4
Armand Cl *WAT* WD17 204 A8
Armitage Cl *RKW/CH/CXG* WD3 218 C4
Armitage Gdns *LTNW/LEA* LU4 68 C8
Armourers Cl *BSF* CM23 104 E5
Armour Ri *HTCHE/RSTV* SG4 41 F7
Armstrong Cl *LCOL/BKTW* AL2 190 C5
Armstrong Gdns *RAD* WD7 207 H2
Arncliffe Crs *LTNE* LU2 4 C2
Arnett Cl *RKW/CH/CXG* WD3 217 K6
Arnett Wy *RKW/CH/CXG* WD3 217 K6
Arnold Av East *PEND* EN3 214 E8
Arnold Cl *AMP/FLIT/B* MK45 36 C7
HTCHE/RSTV SG4 57 F1
LTNE LU2 70 B6
STVG SG1 58 D8
Arnolds La *BLDK* SG7 16 D3
Arran Cl *HHS/BOV* HP3 165 H8
Arretine Cl *STALW/RED* AL3 167 G8
Arrewig La *TRING* HP23 158 B8
Arrow Cl *LTNN/LIM* LU3 68 D3
Arthur Rd *STAL* AL1 168 E6
Arthur St *BUSH* WD23 13 E2
LTN LU1 4 C5
Artisan Crs *STALW/RED* AL3 10 B3
Arundel Cl *CHES/WCR* EN8 197 F6
HHNE HP2 9 E4
STVGE SG2 77 F6
Arundel Dr *BORE* WD6 224 B4
Arundel Gv *STALW/RED* AL3 168 A2
Arundell Rd *ABLGY* WD5 204 B2
Arundel Rd *LTNW/LEA* LU4 69 F7
Ascot Cl *BORE* WD6 223 K5
BSF CM23 106 B1
Ascot Crs *STVG* SG1 59 H8
Ascot Gdns *PEND* EN3 214 B7
Ascot Rd *LTNN/LIM* LU3 69 G7
ROY SG8 21 K3
WATW WD18 219 K5
Ascots La *BRKMPK* AL9 147 K8
Ashanger La *BLDK* SG7 43 K5
Ashborurne Sq *NTHWD* HA6 229 K5
Ashbourne Cl *LWTH* SG6 42 B5
Ashbourne Ct *STALE/WH* AL4 169 F8
Ashbourne Rd *BROX* EN10 176 E7
Ashbrook La *HTCHE/RSTV* SG4 57 G5
Ashburnam Wk *STVGE* SG2 76 A8
Ashburnham Cl *OXHEY* WD19 230 B2
Ashburnham Dr *OXHEY* WD19 230 B2
Ashburnham Rd *LTN* LU1 89 G2
Ashbury Cl *HAT* AL10 170 D4
Ashby Dr *AMP/FLIT/B* MK45 36 C6
Ashby Gdns *STAL* AL1 189 F2
Ashby Ri *BSF* CM23 86 A8
Ashby Rd *BERK* HP4 160 E2
WATN WD24 204 B8
Ash Cl *ABLGY* WD5 203 J2
BRKMPK AL9 193 G3
DEN/HRF UB9 228 C7
GSTN WD25 204 C5
Ashcombe *WGCW* AL8 122 E7
Ash Copse *LCOL/BKTW* AL2 205 G1
Ashcroft *PIN* HA5 231 H5
Ashcroft Cl *HARP* AL5 144 B1
Ashcroft Rd *LTNE* LU2 70 C5
Ashdale *BSF* CM23 105 G5
Ashdale Gdns *LTNN/LIM* LU3 52 A8
Ashdales *STAL* AL1 189 F2
Ashdown *LWTH* SG6 25 J8
Ashdown Crs *CHES/WCR* EN8 197 J6
Ashdown Dr *BORE* WD6 223 J2
Ashdown Rd *BUSH* WD23 13 E2
STVGE SG2 96 C2
Ash Dr *HAT* AL10 171 F7
HTCHE/RSTV SG4 56 E5
Ashendene Rd *CHESW* EN7 195 K3
HERT/BAY SG13 174 C4
Ashfield Av *BUSH* WD23 221 J6
Ashfields *GSTN* WD25 204 A5
Ashfield Wy *LTNN/LIM* LU3 69 F3
Ashford Gn *OXHEY* WD19 230 E4
Ash Gv *DEN/HRF* UB9 228 C7
HHS/BOV HP3 185 K2
STALE/WH AL4 120 A8
Ash Groves *SBW* CM21 132 E7
Ash Hill Cl *BUSH* WD23 221 J8
Ashlea Rd *CFSP/GDCR* SL9 226 B8
Ashleigh *STVGE* SG2 3 F4
Ashley Cl *HHS/BOV* HP3 164 E8
PIN HA5 230 C8
WGCW AL8 147 H1
Ashley Dr *BORE* WD6 224 B5
Ashley Gdns *HARP* AL5 117 K6
Ashley Rd *HERT/WAS* SG14 150 D4
STAL AL1 169 F6
Ashleys *RKW/CH/CXG* WD3 217 J7
Ashlyn Cl *BUSH* WD23 13 F3
Ashlyns Ct *BERK* HP4 161 J6
Ashlyns Rd *BERK* HP4 161 J6
Ash Meadow *MHAD* SG10 103 G7
Ash Ml *ROY* SG8 32 C6
Ashmore Gdns *HHS/BOV* HP3 9 E6
Ash Ride *ENC/FH* EN2 212 D5
Ashridge Cl *HHS/BOV* HP3 183 J6
Ashridge Dr *LCOL/BKTW* AL2 188 A8
OXHEY WD19 230 D4
Ashridge La *CSHM* HP5 200 A1
Ashridge Ri *BERK* HP4 161 G4
Ash Rd *LTNW/LEA* LU4 89 G1
TRING HP23 134 E5
WARE SG12 128 A6
Ashton Rd *LTN* LU1 4 C6
PEND EN3 214 D6
Ashton's La *BLDK* SG7 42 E3
Ash Tree Fld *HLW* CM20 155 H7
Ash Tree Rd *WATN* WD24 204 C6
Ashtree Wy *HHW* HP1 163 K7
Ashurst Cl *NTHWD* HA6 229 K6
Ash V *RKW/CH/CXG* WD3 227 G4
Ashville Wy *BLDK* SG7 27 G8
Ashwell Av *LTNN/LIM* LU3 68 B1
Ashwell Cl *HTCHE/RSTV* SG4 58 B5
Ashwell Common *HTCHE/RSTV* SG4 58 B5
Ashwell Pk *HARP* AL5 119 F8
Ashwell Rd *BLDK* SG7 16 D4
BLDK SG7 27 F1
BLDK SG7 27 H7
ROY SG8 15 G8
Ashwell St *BLDK* SG7 17 K6
STALW/RED AL3 10 C3
Ashwood Rd *POTB/CUF* EN6 210 C3
Ashworth Pl *HLWE* CM17 181 G1
Askew Rd *NTHWD* HA6 229 J1
Aspasia Cl *STAL* AL1 11 E5
Aspen Cl *STVGE* SG2 96 C2
Aspenden Rd *BUNT* SG9 63 J4
Aspen Park Dr *GSTN* WD25 204 C5
The Aspens *BSF* CM23 86 A7
HTCHE/RSTV SG4 56 E3
Aspen Wy *PEND* EN3 214 C5
WGCE AL7 148 D4
Aspfield Rw *HHW* HP1 164 A4
Ass House La *KTN/HRWW/W* HA3 231 J3
Aster Cl *BSF* CM23 105 G3
The Asters *CHESW* EN7 196 B6
Astley Gn *LTNE* LU2 70 E7
Astley Rd *HHW* HP1 164 B6
Aston Cl *BUSH* WD23 221 K6
WATN WD24 13 D1
Aston End Rd *STVGE* SG2 77 F6
Aston La *STVGE* SG2 97 F2
Aston Ri *HTCHE/RSTV* SG4 57 F3
Aston Rd *STDN* SG11 81 J7
Astons Rd *NTHWD* HA6 229 H2
Aston Vw *HHNE* HP2 141 F8
Aston Wy *POTB/CUF* EN6 210 E2

Astrope La TRING HP23 108 E6
Astwick Av HAT AL10 170 E1
Athelstan Rd HHS/BOV HP3 185 J1
Athelstan Wk North WGCE AL7 147 K4
Athelstan Wk South WGCE AL7 147 J4
Athena Pl NTHWD HA6 230 A7
Atherstone Rd LTNW/LEA LU4 68 C8
Atherton End SBW CM21 132 C6
Athlone Cl RAD WD7 206 E6
Athol Cl PIN HA5 230 C7
Athol Gdns PIN HA5 230 C7
Atholl Cl LTNN/LIM LU3 68 C1
Atria Rd NTHWD HA6 230 B4
Attenborough Cl OXHEY WD19 231 F2
Attimore Cl WGCW AL8 147 G4
Attimore Rd WGCW AL8 147 G4
Aubrey Av LCOL/BKTW AL2 190 A4
Aubrey La STALW/RED AL3 141 K7
Aubreys LWTH SG6 41 K7
Aubreys Rd HHW HP1 163 H7
Aubries STVGE SG2 77 J1
Auckland Cl EN EN1 214 A7
Auckland Rd POTB/CUF EN6 209 J2
Audley Cl BORE WD6 223 K3
Audley Ct PIN HA5 230 D8
Audley Gdns WAB EN9 215 H4
Audrey Gdns BSF CM23 105 J6
Audwick Cl CHES/WCR EN8 197 H6
Augustine Rd KTN/HRWW/W HA3 231 J7
Augustus Cl STALW/RED AL3 167 H8
Augustus Ga STVGE SG2 76 D1
Austenwood La CFSP/GDCR SL9 226 A8
Austin Rd LTNN/LIM LU3 69 G5
Austins Md HHS/BOV HP3 183 K6
Austins Pl HHNE HP2 8 A4
Autumn Glades HHS/BOV HP3 165 H8
Autumn Gv WGCE AL7 148 C5
Avalon Cl GSTN WD25 205 F2
Avebury Av LTNE LU2 69 J5
Avenue Ap KGLGY WD4 186 A8
Avenue Ct WLYN AL6 122 E2
Avenue One LWTH SG6 42 C3
Avenue Ri BUSH WD23 221 H5
Avenue Rd BSF CM23 105 K3
HOD EN11 177 J5
STAL AL1 11 D3
Avenue Ter OXHEY WD19 13 F5
The Avenue BAR EN5 225 K3
BUSH WD23 221 G4
HERT/WAS SG14 150 E1
HHW HP1 163 H5
HOD EN11 176 E5
HTCH/STOT SG5 25 K3
HTCHE/RSTV SG4 56 E2
LTNW/LEA LU4 68 C4
NTHWD HA6 229 H5
PIN HA5 231 G5
POTB/CUF EN6 193 F8
RAD WD7 206 D4
STVG SG1 75 H1
WAB EN9 199 J3
WAT WD17 12 B1
WLYN AL6 122 D2
Avia Cl HHS/BOV HP3 185 H2
Avior Dr NTHWD HA6 230 A3
Avocet LWTH SG6 25 J8
Avon Cl GSTN WD25 204 D4
Avondale Rd LTN LU1 4 A3
Avon Sq HHNE HP2 164 E1
Axe Cl LTNN/LIM LU3 68 D3
Aycliffe Dr HHNE HP2 8 B1
Aycliffe Rd BORE WD6 207 K8
Aydon Rd LTNN/LIM LU3 69 G3
Aylands Rd PEND EN3 214 C6
Aylesbury Rd TRING HP23 134 D6
Aylets Fld HLWS CM18 180 B4
Aylotts Cl BUNT SG9 63 H1
Aylsham Rd HOD EN11 177 H1
Aylward Dr STVGE SG2 3 E3
Aynho St WATW WD18 12 C4
Aynsley Gdns HLWE CM17 181 F1
Aynsworth Av BSF CM23 85 K7
Ayot Gn WGCW AL8 121 K8
Ayot Little Green La WLYN AL6 121 K8
Ayot St Peter Rd WLYN AL6 121 H5
Ayr Cl STVGE SG2 76 D1
Ayres End La HARP AL5 144 B3
Aysgarth Cl HARP AL5 143 J1
Aysgarth Rd STALW/RED AL3 142 B3

B

Baas Hl BROX EN10 176 C7
Baas Hill Cl BROX EN10 176 D7
Baas La BROX EN10 176 D7
Babbage Rd STVG SG1 75 G4
Back La BUNT SG9 47 H1
GSTN WD25 222 B1
HTCHE/RSTV SG4 73 G3
RBSF CM22 133 F2
WAB EN9 199 J1
WLYN AL6 124 A7
Back St BLDK SG7 17 J6
LTNE LU2 4 C3
The Back BERK HP4 162 E2
Bacons Dr POTB/CUF EN6 195 G6
Bacon's Yd BLDK SG7 17 K5
Baddeley Cl STVGE SG2 3 F6
Bader Cl STVG SG1 58 E8
WGCE AL7 148 D3
Badger Cl KNEB SG3 96 A3
Badger Cft HHNE HP2 165 J7
Badgers BSF CM23 105 H4
Badgers Cl BORE WD6 223 J2
HERT/BAY SG13 152 A3
STVG SG1 2 C4
Badgers Cft BROX EN10 176 D7
TRDG/WHET N20 225 K7
Badgers Wk RKW/CH/CXG WD3 217 J4
WLYN AL6 123 J4
Badger Wy HAT AL10 171 G6
Badingham Dr HARP AL5 118 A8
Badminton Cl BORE WD6 223 K2
STVGE SG2 96 C2
Badminton Pl BROX EN10 176 D6
Bagwicks Cl LTNN/LIM LU3 68 D2
Bailey St LTN LU1 5 D5
Baines La KNEB SG3 96 D6
Baird Cl BUSH WD23 221 J6
Bairstow Cl BORE WD6 223 H1
Bakers Gv WGCE AL7 148 D2
Bakers La DUN/WHIP LU6 114 C1
ROY SG8 23 F6
WLYN AL6 94 E8
Bakers Rd CHESW EN7 197 F8
Baker St HERT/BAY SG13 151 H3
LTN LU1 4 C5
POTB/CUF EN6 209 K5
Bakery Cl HLWW/ROY CM19 178 D1
Bakewell Cl LTNW/LEA LU4 68 B8
Balcary Gdns BERK HP4 161 F6
Balcombe Cl LTNE LU2 70 D5
Balcon Wy BORE WD6 224 B1
Baldock La LWTH SG6 42 B7
Baldock Rd BUNT SG9 63 F2
HTCH/STOT SG5 26 A4
LWTH SG6 42 B4
ROY SG8 19 K6
Baldock St ROY SG8 21 G3
WARE SG12 127 H7
Baldock Wy BORE WD6 223 J1
Baldwins WGCE AL7 148 C3
Baldwins La RKW/CH/CXG WD3 219 F4
Balfour St HERT/WAS SG14 151 F2
Baliol Rd HTCH/STOT SG5 56 D1
Ballater Cl OXHEY WD19 230 C3
Ballinger Ct BERK HP4 161 H6
Ballslough Hl HTCHE/RSTV SG4 93 G8
Balmoral Cl CHES/WCR EN8 214 C4
LCOL/BKTW AL2 188 E6
STVGE SG2 96 D2
Balmoral Dr BORE WD6 224 C4
Balmoral Rd GSTN WD25 204 B2
HTCH/STOT SG5 40 C8
PEND EN3 214 C6
WATN WD24 204 D8
Balmore Wd LTNN/LIM LU3 52 B8
Balsams Cl HERT/BAY SG13 151 G5
Bampton Rd LTNW/LEA LU4 68 A8
Banbury Cl LTNW/LEA LU4 68 E5
Banbury St WATW WD18 12 C4
Bancroft HTCH/STOT SG5 56 D2
Bancroft Gdns
KTN/HRWW/W HA3 231 K7
Bancroft Rd KTN/HRWW/W HA3 231 K8
LTNN/LIM LU3 69 G5
Bandley Ri STVGE SG2 76 D6
Banes Down WAB EN9 177 K8
Bank Cl LTNW/LEA LU4 68 B5
Bank Ml BERK HP4 162 B5
Bankmill Br BERK HP4 162 C6
Bank Mill La BERK HP4 162 B6
Banks Rd BORE WD6 224 B2
Barbel Cl CHES/WCR EN8 215 F4
Barberry Rd HHW HP1 163 K6
Barbers La LTN LU1 4 C4
Barbers Wk TRING HP23 134 E6
Barclay Cl HERT/BAY SG13 152 A5
WATW WD18 12 B5
Barclay Ct HOD EN11 177 F4
Barclay Crs STVG SG1 2 C1
Barden Cl DEN/HRF UB9 228 B7
Bards Cnr HHW HP1 164 A5
Bardwell Rd STAL AL1 10 C5
Barford Ri LTNE LU2 70 E8
Bargrove Av HHW HP1 163 K7
Barham Av BORE WD6 223 J3
Barham Rd STVGE SG2 76 D4
Barkham Cl LBUZ LU7 109 K2
Barking Cl LTNW/LEA LU4 68 A3
Barkway Hl ROY SG8 32 E3
Barkway Rd ROY SG8 21 J4
Barkway St ROY SG8 21 H4
Barley Cl BUSH WD23 221 J5
Barleycroft BUNT SG9 63 J3
Barley Cft HERT/WAS SG14 125 J6
HERT/WAS SG14 151 G1
HHNE HP2 9 F5
HLWS CM18 180 A5
Barleycroft STVGE SG2 76 E6
WARE SG12 126 D2
Barleycroft Gn WGCW AL8 147 H3
Barleycroft Rd WGCW AL8 147 H4
Barley Hills BSF CM23 105 H5
Barley La LTNW/LEA LU4 68 B4
Barley Mow La STALE/WH AL4 190 C1
Barley Ponds Cl WARE SG12 127 K8
Barley Ponds Rd WARE SG12 127 K8
Barley Ri BLDK SG7 43 H1
Barley Rd ROY SG8 23 G3
Barleyvale LTNN/LIM LU3 69 F1
Barlings Rd HARP AL5 143 J4
Barmor Cl RYLN/HDSTN HA2 231 J8
Barnacres Rd HHS/BOV HP3 185 K2
Barnard Acres WAB EN9 198 E1
Barnard Gn WGCE AL7 148 A4
Barnard Rd LTN LU1 89 F2
SBW CM21 132 C6
Barnard Wy HHS/BOV HP3 8 B6
Barn Cl HHS/BOV HP3 185 K1
RAD WD7 206 D5
WGCW AL8 147 H3
Barncroft STDN SG11 83 K2
Barncroft Rd BERK HP4 161 G6
Barncroft Wy STAL AL1 11 F5
Barndell Cl HTCH/STOT SG5 25 K3
Barndicott WGCE AL7 148 D3
Barnes La KGLGY WD4 185 G6
Barnes Ri KGLGY WD4 185 K5
Barnet By-pass BORE WD6 224 D5
Barnet Gate La BAR EN5 224 E6
Barnet La BORE WD6 223 J6
Barnet Rd EBAR EN4 210 B7
LCOL/BKTW AL2 190 D6
MLHL NW7 224 D6
POTB/CUF EN6 210 D3
POTB/CUF EN6 210 D4
Barnet Way (Barnet By-pass)
MLHL NW7 224 C7
Barnfield HHS/BOV HP3 185 K1
Barnfield Av LTNE LU2 69 J4
Barnfield Cl HOD EN11 177 F1
WAB EN9 178 A8
Barnfield Ct HARP AL5 143 K1
Barnfield Rd HARP AL5 143 K1
STALE/WH AL4 169 F4
WGCE AL7 147 K5
Barn Hl HLWW/ROY CM19 178 C5
Barnhurst Pth OXHEY WD19 230 D4
Barn Lea RKW/CH/CXG WD3 217 K8
Barn Md HLWS CM18 6 C6
Barns Ct EPP CM16 179 J6
Barnsdale Cl BORE WD6 223 J1
Barns Dene HARP AL5 118 A7
Barnside Ct WGCW AL8 147 H3
Barnston Cl LTNE LU2 70 E8
Barnsway KGLGY WD4 185 J6
Barnwell STVGE SG2 3 F6
Baron Ct STVG SG1 58 B8
Barons Rw HARP AL5 144 A2
The Barons BSF CM23 105 G4
Barra Cl HHS/BOV HP3 186 B1
Barrells Down Rd BSF CM23 85 H8
Barrett La BSF CM23 105 J2
Barrington Dr DEN/HRF UB9 227 K6
Barrington Rd LWTH SG6 41 K5
Barrowby Cl LTNE LU2 70 E8
Barrowdene Cl PIN HA5 231 F8
Barrow La CHESW EN7 213 J
Barrow Point Av PIN HA5 231 F8
Barrow Point La PIN HA5 231 F8
Barrows Rd HLWW/ROY CM19 179 G1
Barr Rd POTB/CUF EN6 210 D3
Barry Cl LCOL/BKTW AL2 188 D3
Bartel Cl HHS/BOV HP3 165 J8
Bartholomew Rd BSF CM23 105 J3
Bartletts Md HERT/WAS SG14 126 B8
Barton Cl HARP AL5 118 E6
Barton Rd AMP/FLIT/B MK45 36 A
HTCH/STOT SG5 37 F8
LTNE LU2 69 H2
LTNN/LIM LU3 52 B6
STALE/WH AL4 145 F
The Bartons BORE WD6 223 G6
Barton Wy BORE WD6 223 K2
RKW/CH/CXG WD3 219 G5
Bartrams La EBAR EN4 210 D8
Barwick La STDN SG11 101 H6
Basbow La BSF CM23 105 J
Basildon Cl WATW WD18 219 H6
Basildon Sq HHNE HP2 8 C
Basils Rd STVG SG1 2 A
Basing Rd RKW/CH/CXG WD3 217 J8
Bassett Cl STALW/RED AL3 142 C4
Bassil Rd HHS/BOV HP3 8 A6
Bassingbourne Cl BROX EN10 176 E6
Bassingburn Wk WGCE AL7 148 A4
Batchelors STDN SG11 81 J
Batchwood Dr STALW/RED AL3 10 B1
Batchwood Gdns STALW/RED AL3 10 C
Batchwood Vw STALW/RED AL3 10 B

Batchworth Hill London Rd
RKW/CH/CXG WD3 228 D1
Batchworth La NTHWD HA6 229 H4
Bateman Rd RKW/CH/CXG WD3 219 F6
Batford Cl WGCE AL7 148 C4 2
Batford Rd HARP AL5 119 F6
Bath Rd LTNN/LIM LU3 4 B1
Bathurst Rd HHNE HP2 8 A2
Batterdale BRKMPK AL9 171 H3
Battlefield Rd STAL AL1 11 E2
Battlers Green Dr RAD WD7 206 B7
Battleview STALE/WH AL4 145 H1
The Baulk LBUZ LU7 109 K2
LBUZ LU7 111 F4
LTNE LU2 53 K7
Bawdsey Cl STVG SG1 75 G1
Bay Cl LTNW/LEA LU4 68 A3
Bayford Cl HERT/BAY SG13 151 F5
HHNE HP2 165 H1
Bayford Gn HERT/BAY SG13 174 D3
Bayford La HERT/BAY SG13 174 C1
Bayhurst Dr NTHWD HA6 230 A5
Baylam Dell LTNE LU2 71 F8 2
Baylie Ct HHNE HP2 8 B4
Baylie La HHNE HP2 8 B4
Bay Tree Cl CHESW EN7 196 D5 1
LCOL/BKTW AL2 188 E5
Bay Tree Wk WAT WD17 204 A8
Bayworth LWTH SG6 42 B4
Beacon Cl CFSP/GDCR SL9 226 B6
Beacon Rd BERK HP4 112 B7
WARE SG12 128 A7
Beaconsfield LTNE LU2 5 E3
Beaconsfield Rd HAT AL10 171 H3
PEND EN3 214 C7
STAL AL1 11 D4
TRING HP23 134 D6
Beacon Wy RKW/CH/CXG WD3 218 A7
TRING HP23 135 H4
The Beadles RBSF CM22 133 F1 1
Beagle Cl RAD WD7 206 C7
Beale Cl STVGE SG2 76 D3
Beamish Dr BUSH WD23 221 K8
Beane Av STVGE SG2 76 E3
Beane River Vw HERT/WAS SG14 151 F3
Beane Rd HERT/WAS SG14 98 A5
HERT/WAS SG14 150 E3
The Beaneside HERT/WAS SG14 98 A5 1
Beane Wk STVGE SG2 76 E3
Beanfield Rd SBW CM21 131 J5
Beanley Cl LTNE LU2 71 F7 1
Beard's La SAFWS CB11 35 J5
Bear La BLDK SG7 17 K5
Bearton Av HTCH/STOT SG5 56 C1
Bearton Gn HTCH/STOT SG5 40 B8
Bearton Rd HTCH/STOT SG5 40 C8
Bearwood Cl POTB/CUF EN6 210 E1
Beasant House WATN WD24 13 E1 1
Beatty Rd CHES/WCR EN8 214 E4
Beauchamp Gdns
RKW/CH/CXG WD3 217 K8 2
Beauchamp Pl BORE WD6 208 A7 1
Beaulieu Cl OXHEY WD19 220 D8
Beaulieu Dr WAB EN9 215 G3
Beaumayes Cl HHW HP1 164 A7
Beaumont Av STAL AL1 168 E5
Beaumont Ga RAD WD7 206 D5
Beaumont Hall La STALW/RED AL3 142 C7
Beaumont Park Dr
HLWW/ROY CM19 178 C1
Beaumont Rd BROX EN10 196 D2
LTNN/LIM LU3 69 G7
Beaumont Vw CHESW EN7 196 B4 1
Beazley Cl WARE SG12 127 J7 1
Becket Gdns WLYN AL6 122 C5
Beckets Sq BERK HP4 161 H3 1
Becketts HERT/WAS SG14 150 D4
Beckett's Av STALW/RED AL3 10 B1
Beckfield La BUNT SG9 46 A2
Beckham Cl LTNE LU2 69 J2 1
Becks Cl STALW/RED AL3 115 H4
Bedale Rd ENC/FH EN2 213 F8 1
Bede Cl PIN HA5 230 E7 1
Bedford Cl RKW/CH/CXG WD3 200 E8
Bedford Crs PEND EN3 214 D5
Bedford Park Rd STAL AL1 11 D4
Bedford Rd AMP/FLIT/B MK45 36 C4
HTCH/STOT SG5 40 A2
LWTH SG6 41 H2
NTHWD HA6 229 H3
STAL AL1 11 D5
Bedford St BERK HP4 162 A5
WATN WD24 220 C1
Bedmond La ABLGY WD5 187 G4
STALW/RED AL3 167 G8
Bedmond Rd ABLGY WD5 187 F7
HHS/BOV HP3 165 J8
Bedwell Av BRKMPK AL9 173 H4
HERT/BAY SG13 173 H2
Bedwell Cl WGCE AL7 147 K4
Bedwell Crs STVG SG1 3 D3
Bedwell Ri STVG SG1 2 C3
Beech Av ENC/FH EN2 212 D5
RAD WD7 206 D3
Beech Bottom STALW/RED AL3 10 C1
Beech Cl HARP AL5 143 K4
HAT AL10 171 F5
Beech Ct BERK HP4 162 A4
Beech Crs STALE/WH AL4 145 G2
Beechcroft BERK HP4 161 K6
Beechcroft Av RKW/CH/CXG WD3 219 H6
Beechcroft Rd BUSH WD23 13 F4
Beech Dr BERK HP4 161 K6
BORE WD6 223 J2
SBW CM21 157 F1
STVGE SG2 3 F5
Beechen Gv WAT WD17 12 C2
The Beeches HTCHE/RSTV SG4 56 E3
LCOL/BKTW AL2 189 F5 1
RKW/CH/CXG WD3 217 J5
TRING HP23 135 H5 1
Beech Farm Dr STALE/WH AL4 169 J2
Beechfield HOD EN11 153 F7
KGLGY WD4 185 K8
SBW CM21 132 D7
Beechfield Cl STALW/RED AL3 142 C4 1
Beechfield Rd HHW HP1 164 A7
WARE SG12 127 K7
WGCE AL7 147 K5
Beechfield Wk WAB EN9 215 J5
Beech Gv TRING HP23 135 H5
Beech Hl EBAR EN4 210 E8
LTNE LU2 70 D2
LWTH SG6 41 H2
Beech Hyde La STALE/WH AL4 145 J2
Beeching Cl HARP AL5 118 D5
Beechlands BSF CM23 105 J4
Beech Ms WARE SG12 152 C2
Beechpark Wy WAT WD17 203 K7
Beech Pl STALW/RED AL3 10 C1 1
Beech Rd LTN LU1 4 A3
STALW/RED AL3 11 D1
WATN WD24 204 B7
Beechtree La STALW/RED AL3 166 C8
Beech Wy STALE/WH AL4 119 K3
Beechwood Av POTB/CUF EN6 210 C3
RKW/CH/CXG WD3 216 E4
STAL AL1 168 E4
Beechwood Cl BLDK SG7 43 F4
CHESW EN7 196 C4 1
HERT/BAY SG13 151 J3 1
HTCH/STOT SG5 40 B7
Beechwood Dr TRING HP23 136 E4 1
Beechwood Pk HHS/BOV HP3 184 D2
RKW/CH/CXG WD3 217 J4
Beechwood Ri WATN WD24 204 C6
Beechwood Rd LTNW/LEA LU4 68 D5
Beecroft La STVGE SG2 60 D7
Beehive Cl BORE WD6 223 G6
Beehive Gn WGCE AL7 148 B5
Beehive La WGCE AL7 148 B6 1
Beehive Rd CHESW EN7 195 K6
Beesonend La HARP AL5 143 G6
STALW/RED AL3 142 E7
Beeston Cl OXHEY WD19 230 E3
Beeston Dr CHES/WCR EN8 197 H5
Beethoven Rd BORE WD6 223 F7
Beeton Cl PIN HA5 231 H6 1
Beggarman's La STDN SG11 100 C1
Beggars Bush La WATW WD18 219 J5
Beggars La TRING HP23 136 A5
Belcher Rd HOD EN11 177 F2 2
Belchers La WAB EN9 199 J2
Beldam Av ROY SG8 21 H4
Beldams La BSF CM23 106 A4
Belfairs OXHEY WD19 230 E4
Belford Rd BORE WD6 207 J8
Belfry Av DEN/HRF UB9 227 K7
The Belfry LTNE LU2 69 K3
Belgrave Cl STALE/WH AL4 169 F2 1
Belgrave Rd LTNW/LEA LU4 68 C4
Belham Rd KGLGY WD4 185 K6
Bell Acre LWTH SG6 42 B5
Bell Acre Gdns LWTH SG6 42 B5
Bellamy Cl KNEB SG3 96 A4
WAT WD17 220 B1
Bellamy Rd CHES/WCR EN8 197 J7
Bell Cl ABLGY WD5 187 F5
HTCHE/RSTV SG4 57 F3
KNEB SG3 96 B4
Bellerby Ri LTNW/LEA LU4 68 A3
Belle Vue La BUSH WD23 222 A8
Belle Vue Rd WARE SG12 127 K8 2
Bellfield Gdns HLWE CM17 181 F2
Bell La ABLGY WD5 187 G5
BERK HP4 161 F4
BRKMPK AL9 193 G2
BROX EN10 176 D7
HERT/WAS SG14 151 G3 1
HOD EN11 177 F3
LCOL/BKTW AL2 190 C7
PEND EN3 214 C8
ROY SG8 33 H7
STVG SG1 2 A1
WARE SG12 129 K5
Bell Md SBW CM21 132 C7
Bellmount Wood Av WAT WD17 219 K1
The Bell Rbt LCOL/BKTW AL2 190 E5
Bell Rw BLDK SG7 42 E1 1
Bells Hl BAR EN5 225 J5
BSF CM23 105 H2
Bells Meadow ROY SG8 15 H4
Bell St SBW CM21 132 C7
Bell Vw STALE/WH AL4 169 G6
Belmer Rd STSD CM24 87 J5
Belmers Rd TRING HP23 135 J8 1
Belmont Hl STAL AL1 10 C5
Belmont Rd BUSH WD23 13 F3
HHS/BOV HP3 185 J1
LTN LU1 4 A4
Belmor BORE WD6 223 K5
Belper Rd LTNW/LEA LU4 68 D7
Belsize Cl HHS/BOV HP3 9 D6
STALE/WH AL4 169 F1
Belsize Rd HHS/BOV HP3 9 D6
Belswains La HHS/BOV HP3 185 J2
Beltona Gdns CHES/WCR EN8 197 H5
Belton Rd BERK HP4 161 H4
Belvedere Gdns LCOL/BKTW AL2 188 B5
Belvedere Rd LTNN/LIM LU3 69 G4 1
Bembridge Gdns LTNN/LIM LU3 68 E2
Ben Austins STALW/RED AL3 142 B5
Benbow Cl STAL AL1 168 E8
Benchley Hl HTCHE/RSTV SG4 57 G1
Benchleys Rd HHW HP1 163 J7
Bencroft CHESW EN7 196 E4
Bencroft Rd HHNE HP2 8 B5
Bendish La HTCHE/RSTV SG4 93 G2
Bendysh Rd BUSH WD23 13 F2
Benford Rd HOD EN11 176 E5
Bengeo St HERT/WAS SG14 151 F2
Benhooks Av BSF CM23 105 H4
Benington Cl LTNE LU2 70 A4
Benington Rd STVGE SG2 77 G7
Bennett Cl BRKMPK AL9 148 A7
NTHWD HA6 230 A6
Bennett Ct LWTH SG6 42 A4
Bennetts Cl STALE/WH AL4 191 H1 1
Bennetts End Cl HHS/BOV HP3 164 E8 1
Bennetts End Rd HHS/BOV HP3 8 C6
Benningfield WARE SG12 129 K4
Benningfield Rd WARE SG12 129 K5
Benskin Rd WATW WD18 12 B4
Benskins Cl BSF CM23 67 J1
Benslow La HTCHE/RSTV SG4 56 E2
Benslow Ri HTCHE/RSTV SG4 56 E2
Benson Cl LTNN/LIM LU3 68 E2
Benstede STVGE SG2 96 D1
Bentfield End Cswy STSD CM24 86 C2
Bentfield Gdns STSD CM24 86 C2
Bentfield Rd STSD CM24 86 C2
Bentick Wy HTCHE/RSTV SG4 94 E7
Bentley Cl BSF CM23 105 J4
Bentley Dr HLWE CM17 181 F2
Bentley Heath La BAR EN5 209 K5
Bentley Rd HERT/WAS SG14 150 B2
Benton Rd OXHEY WD19 230 E4
Bentsley Cl STALE/WH AL4 168 E2
Berceau Wk WAT WD17 219 K1
Berecroft HLWS CM18 180 A6 1
Berefield HHNE HP2 8 A3
Beresford Rd LTNW/LEA LU4 69 F8
RKW/CH/CXG WD3 217 J8
STAL AL1 169 F7
Bericot Wy WGCE AL7 148 D3 2
Berkeley LWTH SG6 42 A5
Berkeley Cl ABLGY WD5 204 A2
BORE WD6 223 K5
POTB/CUF EN6 209 K2
STVGE SG2 96 B1
WARE SG12 127 G7
Berkeley Sq HHNE HP2 141 H8
Berkhamsted La HERT/BAY SG13 173 J6
Berkhamsted Rd HHW HP1 163 G4
Berkley Av CHES/WCR EN8 214 C4
Berkley Cl STALE/WH AL4 169 F2
Berks Hl RKW/CH/CXG WD3 217 F5
Bermer Rd WATN WD24 220 D1
Bernard Gv WAB EN9 215 G3 1
Bernard St STALW/RED AL3 10 C3
Berners Dr STAL AL1 189 F1
Berners Wy BROX EN10 197 K1
Bernhardt Crs STVGE SG2 76 D3
The Berries STALE/WH AL4 168 D2 1
Berrow Cl LTNE LU2 71 F7 2
Berry Av WATN WD24 204 C6
Berry Cl RKW/CH/CXG WD3 218 A7
Berryfield LBUZ LU7 109 K2 1
Berry Grove La BUSH WD23 205 F8
Berrygrove La GSTN WD25 221 H1
Berry La RKW/CH/CXG WD3 217 G6
RKW/CH/CXG WD3 218 A8
Berry Leys LTNN/LIM LU3 68 D2
Berrymead HHNE HP2 8 C3
Berry Wy RKW/CH/CXG WD3 218 A7
Berwick Cl CHES/WCR EN8 215 F4 1
STVG SG1 75 F1
Berwick Rd BORE WD6 207 J8
Besford Cl LTNE LU2 70 E7
Bessemer Cl HTCH/STOT SG5 40 C7
Bessemer Dr STVG SG1 75 G5
Bessemer Rd WGCE AL7 148 A1
WGCW AL8 122 E7
Bethune Cl LTN LU1 89 G3
Betjeman Cl CHESW EN7 196 E6 1

Betjeman Wy HHW HP1 ... 164 A4
Betony V ROY SG8 ... 21 J4
Bettespol Mdw STALW/RED AL3 ... 142 B3
Betts La WAB EN9 ... 178 D7
Betty's La TRING HP23 ... 135 F5
Bevan Cl HHS/BOV HP3 ... 164 C8
Bevan House WATN WD24 ... 13 E1 🔟
Beverley Cl ROY SG8 ... 21 F1
Beverley Gdns CHESW EN7 ... 213 J1
 STALE/WH AL4 ... 169 G2
 WGCE AL7 ... 148 D3 🔟
Beverley Rd LTNW/LEA LU4 ... 68 E3
 STVG SG1 ... 59 H7
Beverly Cl BROX EN10 ... 176 D7
Bewdley Cl HARP AL5 ... 144 A3 🔟
Bewley Cl CHES/WCR EN8 ... 214 C1
Bexhill Rd LTNE LU2 ... 70 E7
Beyers Gdns HOD EN11 ... 153 F8
Beyers Prospect HOD EN11 ... 153 F8 🔟
Beyers Ride HOD EN11 ... 153 F8
Bibbs Hall La HTCHE/RSTV SG4 ... 120 C3
Biddenham Turn GSTN WD25 ... 204 D5 🔟
Bideford Gdns LTNN/LIM LU3 ... 69 J3
Bideford Rd PEND EN3 ... 214 E8
Bidwell Cl LWTH SG6 ... 42 B4
Biggin Hl BUNT SG9 ... 48 D2
Biggin La HTCH/STOT SG5 ... 56 C2
Bignells Cnr POTB/CUF EN6 ... 209 G4
Billet La BERK HP4 ... 161 H3
Billy Lows La POTB/CUF EN6 ... 210 C1
Bilton Rd HTCHE/RSTV SG4 ... 68 E8
Bilton Wy LTN LU1 ... 88 E1
 LTN LU1 ... 88 E1
Bingen Rd HTCH/STOT SG5 ... 40 A8
Bingley Rd HOD EN11 ... 177 H3
Binham Cl LTNE LU2 ... 69 J2
Birchall La HERT/WAS SG14 ... 149 F5
Birchalls STSD CM24 ... 86 D1 🔟
Birchanger La BSF CM23 ... 86 C7
Birch Copse LCOL/BKTW AL2 ... 188 A3
Birch Dr HAT AL10 ... 171 F5
 RKW/CH/CXG WD3 ... 227 G4
Birchen Cv LTNE LU2 ... 70 A6
Bircherley Ct HERT/WAS SG14 ... 151 G3 🔟
Bircherley St HERT/WAS SG14 ... 151 G3
The Birches BUSH WD23 ... 221 K5
 HHS/BOV HP3 ... 184 D1
 LWTH SG6 ... 41 J1
 WLYN AL6 ... 121 K1
Birchfield Rd CHES/WCR EN8 ... 197 F7
Birch Gn HHW HP1 ... 163 J5
Birch Gv POTB/CUF EN6 ... 210 B2
 WLYN AL6 ... 122 E1
Birch La HHS/BOV HP3 ... 200 E3
Birch Leys HHNE HP2 ... 165 H1 🔟
Birch Link LTNW/LEA LU4 ... 4 A2 🔟
Birchmead WAT WD17 ... 204 A8
Birchmead Cl STALW/RED AL3 ... 10 C1 🔟
Birch Pk KTN/HRWW/W HA3 ... 231 K6
Birch Rd BERK HP4 ... 160 E2
 KNEB SG3 ... 96 C8
Birch Tree Gv CSHM HP5 ... 182 D8
Birch Tree Wk WAT WD17 ... 204 A7
Birch Wy HARP AL5 ... 143 K1
Birchway HAT AL10 ... 171 F7
Birch Wy LCOL/BKTW AL2 ... 190 B5 🔟
Birchwood BSF CM23 ... 86 C7
 RAD WD7 ... 207 K4
Birchwood Av HAT AL10 ... 171 F2
Birchwood Cl HAT AL10 ... 171 F2
Birchwood Wy LCOL/BKTW AL2 ... 188 D6
Birdcroft Rd WGCW AL8 ... 147 J4
Birdie Wy HERT/BAY SG13 ... 152 A2 🔟
Birds Cl WGCE AL7 ... 148 C5
Birdsfoot La LTNN/LIM LU3 ... 69 G3
Birds Hl LWTH SG6 ... 42 G3
Birkbeck Rd ENC/FH EN2 ... 213 G8
Birkdale Gdns OXHEY WD19 ... 230 E5
Birkett Wy CSTG HP8 ... 216 A3
Birklands La STAL AL1 ... 189 K2
Birling Dr LTNE LU2 ... 70 D4
Birstal Gn OXHEY WD19 ... 230 E3
Birtley Cft LTNE LU2 ... 71 F8
Biscot Rd LTNN/LIM LU3 ... 4 A1
Bishops Av BORE WD6 ... 223 J5
 BSF CM23 ... 105 J4
 NTHWD HA6 ... 229 K3
Bishops Cl BAR EN5 ... 225 J6
 HAT AL10 ... 170 E4
 STALE/WH AL4 ... 168 D2
Bishopscote Rd LTNN/LIM LU3 ... 69 G6
Bishopsfield HLWS CM18 ... 180 A4
Bishops Md HHW HP1 ... 164 A8
Bishops Park Wy BSF CM23 ... 104 E2
Bishops Ri HAT AL10 ... 170 E5
Bishops Rd WLYN AL6 ... 123 K3
Biskra WAT WD17 ... 220 B1
Bisley Cl CHES/WCR EN8 ... 214 C3
Bittern Cl CHESW EN7 ... 195 K3
 STVGE SG2 ... 76 E7
Bittern Wy LWTH SG6 ... 25 J8
The Bit TRING HP23 ... 135 J8
Blackberry Md STVGE SG2 ... 76 E6
Blackbirds La GSTN WD25 ... 205 K4

Black Boy Wd LCOL/BKTW AL2 ... 188 C8
Blackbury Cl POTB/CUF EN6 ... 210 D1 🔟
Blackbushe BSF CM23 ... 86 B8
Blackbush Spring HLW CM20 ... 7 F3
Black Cut STAL AL1 ... 11 D5 🔟
Blackdale CHESW EN7 ... 196 E5
Black Ditch Rd WAB EN9 ... 215 H6
Black Ditch Wy WAB EN9 ... 215 G6
Blacketts Wood Dr
 RKW/CH/CXG WD3 ... 216 E4
Black Fan Rd WGCE AL7 ... 148 A2 🔟
Blackford Rd OXHEY WD19 ... 230 E4
Blackhorse Cl HTCHE/RSTV SG4 ... 56 E4
Blackhorse La HTCHE/RSTV SG4 ... 56 E5
 POTB/CUF EN6 ... 191 H8
 STALW/RED AL3 ... 142 B3
Blackhorse Rd LWTH SG6 ... 42 C1
Blackley Cl WAT WD17 ... 204 A7
Black Lion Ct HLWE CM17 ... 157 F5 🔟
Black Lion Hl RAD WD7 ... 207 H2
Blackmoor La WATW WD18 ... 219 J5
Blackmore Wy STALE/WH AL4 ... 119 K3
Blacksmiths Cl BSF CM23 ... 104 C4
Black Smiths Cl WARE SG12 ... 153 F7 🔟
Blacksmiths Hl STVGE SG2 ... 78 B5
Blacksmith's La ROY SG8 ... 31 H4
 STALW/RED AL3 ... 10 A4 🔟
Blacksmiths Wy SBW CM21 ... 131 K8 🔟
Black Swan La LTNN/LIM LU3 ... 69 F4
Blackthorn Cl GSTN WD25 ... 204 C2
 STALE/WH AL4 ... 169 F3
Blackthorn Dr LTNE LU2 ... 70 D5
Blackthorne Cl HAT AL10 ... 170 E7 🔟
Blackwater La HHS/BOV HP3 ... 186 E1
Blackwell Dr OXHEY WD19 ... 13 D5
Blackwell Rd KGLCY WD4 ... 186 A7
Bladon Cl HTCHE/RSTV SG4 ... 57 K6
Blair Cl BSF CM23 ... 105 F2
 HHNE HP2 ... 141 G8
 STVGE SG2 ... 76 A8
Blairhead Dr OXHEY WD19 ... 230 C2
Blake Cl STAL AL1 ... 189 J1
Blakelands AMP/FLIT/B MK45 ... 36 D7
Blakemere Rd WGCW AL8 ... 147 J1
Blakemore End Rd
 HTCHE/RSTV SG4 ... 57 H6
Blakeney Dr LTNE LU2 ... 69 H2
Blakeney Rd STVG SG1 ... 75 F2
Blakes Wy WLYN AL6 ... 122 C3
Blanche La POTB/CUF EN6 ... 208 E4
Blandford Av LTNE LU2 ... 69 J3
Blandford Rd STAL AL1 ... 11 F3
The Blanes WARE SG12 ... 127 G6 🔟
Blattner Cl BORE WD6 ... 223 H4
Blaydon Rd LTNE LU2 ... 5 E3
Blenheim Cl OXHEY WD19 ... 13 D6
 SBW CM21 ... 156 E1
Blenheim Ct BSF CM23 ... 105 F2
 WGCE AL7 ... 148 A2
Blenheim Crs LTNN/LIM LU3 ... 4 A1
Blenheim Rd BAR EN5 ... 225 J3
 STAL AL1 ... 11 E3
Blenheim Wy HGDN SG3 ... 96 D2
Blenheim Rd GSTN WD25 ... 204 B3
Blenkin Cl STALW/RED AL3 ... 167 K2
Blind La STVGE SG2 ... 61 H4
Blindman's La CHES/WCR EN8 ... 197 H8
Bloomfield Av LTNE LU2 ... 5 E2
Bloomfield Rd CHESW EN7 ... 196 A3 🔟
 HARP AL5 ... 118 B6
Bluebell Cl HERT/BAY SG13 ... 151 K3
 HHW HP1 ... 163 H7 🔟
Bluebell Dr ABLGY WD5 ... 187 F5
 CHESW EN7 ... 196 B6
Bluebells WLYN AL6 ... 122 E2
Bluebell Wood Cl LTN LU1 ... 68 E7
Blueberry Cl STALW/RED AL3 ... 168 A2 🔟
Bluebridge Av BRKMPK AL9 ... 192 E5
Blue Bridge Rd BRKMPK AL9 ... 192 E5
Bluecoats Av HERT/WAS SG14 ... 151 G3 🔟
Bluecoat Yd WARE SG12 ... 127 H8 🔟
Bluehouse Hill
 Hemel Hempstead Rd
 STALW/RED AL3 ... 167 H7
Bluett Rd LCOL/BKTW AL2 ... 190 B5
Blundell Cl STALW/RED AL3 ... 168 A2
Blundell Rd LTNN/LIM LU3 ... 69 F6
Blunesfield POTB/CUF EN6 ... 210 E1 🔟
Blunts La LCOL/BKTW AL2 ... 187 K2
Blyth Cl BORE WD6 ... 223 J1
 STVG SG1 ... 75 F2
Blythe Rd HOD EN11 ... 177 J5
Blythway WGCE AL7 ... 123 F8 🔟
Blythwood Gdns STSD CM24 ... 86 C3
Blythwood Rd PIN HA5 ... 230 E7
Boardman Rd BAR EN5 ... 225 K5
Bockings STVGE SG2 ... 60 E8
Bodmin Rd LTNN/LEA LU4 ... 68 E5
Bodwell Cl HHW HP1 ... 163 K5 🔟
Bogmoor Rd ROY SG8 ... 33 F3
Bognor Gdns OXHEY WD19 ... 230 D4 🔟
Bogs Gap La ROY SG8 ... 15 J6
Bohemia HHNE HP2 ... 8 B4

Boissy Cl STALE/WH AL4 ... 169 H7
Boleyn Cl HHNE HP2 ... 165 H1
Boleyn Ct BROX EN10 ... 176 D7
Boleyn Dr STAL AL1 ... 10 C6
Bolingbroke Rd LTN LU1 ... 89 G3
Bolingbrook STALE/WH AL4 ... 168 D2 🔟
Bolney Gn LTNE LU2 ... 70 E6 🔟
Bolton Rd LTN LU1 ... 5 D5
Boniface Gdns
 KTN/HRWW/W HA3 ... 231 J6
Boniface Wk KTN/HRWW/W HA3 ... 231 J6
Bonks Hl SBW CM21 ... 132 B8
Bonneting La BSF CM23 ... 67 K1
Bonney Gv CHESW EN7 ... 196 E8
Bonnick Cl LTN LU1 ... 4 A5
Booths Cl BRKMPK AL9 ... 192 D2
Bornedene POTB/CUF EN6 ... 209 K1
Borough Wy POTB/CUF EN6 ... 209 K2
Borrell Cl BROX EN10 ... 176 D6
Bosanquet Rd HOD EN11 ... 177 H1 🔟
Bosmore Rd LTNN/LIM LU3 ... 68 E4
Boswell Cl RAD WD7 ... 207 H2
Boswell Dr HTCH/STOT SG5 ... 40 C5
Boswell Gdns STVG SG1 ... 58 D8
Boswick La BERK HP4 ... 160 E1
Botley La CSHM HP5 ... 182 C8
Botley Rd CSHM HP5 ... 182 A8
 HHNE HP2 ... 165 F1
Bottom House La TRING HP23 ... 136 B7
Bottom La KGLGY WD4 ... 202 B5
Bottom Rd TRING HP23 ... 158 E6
The Boulevard WATW WD18 ... 219 J5
 WGCE AL7 ... 148 A1
Boulton Rd STVG SG1 ... 59 J7
The Bounce HHNE HP2 ... 8 A3 🔟
Boundary Dr HERT/WAS SG14 ... 151 C1
Boundary La WGCE AL7 ... 147 K7
Boundary Rd BSF CM23 ... 105 K4
 STAL AL1 ... 11 D2
Boundary Wy GSTN WD25 ... 204 C2
 HHNE HP2 ... 9 F2
Bourne Cl BROX EN10 ... 176 E6
 WARE SG12 ... 127 H7 🔟
Bourne End La HHW HP1 ... 163 F8
Bourne End Rd NTHWD HA6 ... 229 K3
Bournehall Av BUSH WD23 ... 221 H5
Bournehall La BUSH WD23 ... 221 H6
Bournehall Rd BUSH WD23 ... 221 H6
Bourne Honour WARE SG12 ... 126 C2
Bournemouth Rd STVG SG1 ... 75 G1 🔟
Bourne Rd BERK HP4 ... 161 G4
 BUSH WD23 ... 221 H5
The Bourne BSF CM23 ... 106 A1
 HHW HP1 ... 183 J5
 WARE SG12 ... 127 H7
Bouvier Rd PEND EN3 ... 214 B8
Bovingdon Crs GSTN WD25 ... 204 E4
Bovingdon Green La
 HHS/BOV HP3 ... 183 H6
Bow Br STALW/RED AL3 ... 167 F3
Bowbrook V LTNE LU2 ... 71 G8
Bowcock Wk STVG SG1 ... 2 C5 🔟
Bower Heath La HARP AL5 ... 118 E4
Bowershott LWTH SG6 ... 42 A5
Bower's Pde HARP AL5 ... 118 C8
Bowers Wy HARP AL5 ... 118 C7
Bowes Lyon Ms STALW/RED AL3 ... 10 C4 🔟
Bowgate STAL AL1 ... 11 D3
Bowlers Md BUNT SG9 ... 63 H1
Bowles Gn EN EN1 ... 214 A6
Bowling Cl BSF CM23 ... 105 J3 🔟
 HARP AL5 ... 143 J2
Bowling Gn STVG SG1 ... 75 H1 🔟
Bowling Green La BUNT SG9 ... 63 H1
 LTNE LU2 ... 4 C1
Bowling Rd WARE SG12 ... 127 J8
Bowmans Av HTCHE/RSTV SG4 ... 57 F2
Bowmans Cl POTB/CUF EN6 ... 210 E2
 WLYN AL6 ... 122 C2
Bowmans Ct HHNE HP2 ... 8 A3
Bowmans Gn GSTN WD25 ... 205 F6
Bowring Gn OXHEY WD19 ... 230 D4
Bowyers HHNE HP2 ... 8 A3
Bowyer's Cl HTCH/STOT SG5 ... 40 B8
Boxberry Cl STVG SG1 ... 2 C2
Boxfield WGCE AL7 ... 148 C6
Boxfield Gn STVG SG2 ... 76 E7
Boxgrove Cl LTNE LU2 ... 70 D4 🔟
Boxhill HHNE HP2 ... 8 A3 🔟
Box La HHW HP1 ... 184 B3
 HOD EN11 ... 176 D2
Boxted Cl LTNW/LEA LU4 ... 68 B4
Boxted Rd HHW HP1 ... 163 H4
Boxtree La KTN/HRWW/W HA3 ... 231 K7
Boxwell Rd BERK HP4 ... 161 J5 🔟
Boyce Cl BORE WD6 ... 223 H1
Boyd Cl BSF CM23 ... 106 A1
Boyle Cl LTNE LU2 ... 4 C3
Braceby Cl LTNN/LIM LU3 ... 68 E3
Brace Cl CHESW EN7 ... 195 K3
Brache Cl STALW/RED AL3 ... 142 B4
Brackendale POTB/CUF EN6 ... 210 B3
Brackendale Gv HARP AL5 ... 117 K6
 LTNN/LIM LU3 ... 69 F4
Brackendene LCOL/BKTW AL2 ... 188 B8

Bracken Hl BERK HP4 162 B4
Bracken La WLYN AL6 123 F2
The Brackens HHNE HP2 8 A4 1
Bracklesham Gdns LTNE LU2 70 E6
Bracknell Pl HHNE HP2 8 C1
Bradbery RKW/CH/CXG WD3 227 G4
Bradbury Cl BORE WD6 224 A1
Bradden La HHNE HP2 139 H2
Bradford Rd RKW/CH/CXG WD3 217 F7
Bradford St HTCH/STOT SG5 56 B2
Bradgate POTB/CUF EN6 195 F5
Bradgate Cl POTB/CUF EN6 195 F6
Bradgers Hill Rd LTNE LU2 69 K5
Bradley Common BSF CM23 86 B6
Bradley Rd LTNW/LEA LU4 68 C8
PEND EN3 214 D8
Bradleys Cnr HTCHE/RSTV SG4 57 G1
Bradman Wy STVG SG1 59 G8
Bradmore Gn BRKMPK AL9 192 E4
Bradmore La BRKMPK AL9 192 D4
Bradmore Wy BRKMPK AL9 192 E4
Bradshaw Rd WATN WD24 220 D1
Bradshaws HAT AL10 170 E8
Bradshaws Cl AMP/FLIT/B MK45 36 C6 2
Bradway HTCHE/RSTV SG4 93 H3
Braemar Cl KNEB SG3 96 C2
Braeside Cl PIN HA5 231 H6 2
Bragbury Cl STVGE SG2 96 E2
Bragbury La KNEB SG3 96 D5
Bragmans La RKW/CH/CXG WD3 201 G3
The Braid CSHM HP5 182 A8
Brain Cl HAT AL10 171 G3 1
Brakynbery BERK HP4 161 F2
Brallings La CFSP/GDCR SL9 226 D3
Bramble Cl CFSP/GDCR SL9 226 B5 1
GSTN WD25 204 B4
HARP AL5 118 B6 1
LTNW/LEA LU4 68 B5
Bramble Ri HLW CM20 6 B3
Bramble Rd HAT AL10 170 B5
LTNW/LEA LU4 68 B5
The Brambles BSF CM23 105 F3
CHES/WCR EN8 214 C1
ROY SG8 21 J4
STAL AL1 10 C6
STVG SG1 58 D7
WARE SG12 127 G6 3
WLYN AL6 122 E1 1
Brambling Cl BUSH WD23 13 F3 1
Brambling Ri HHNE HP2 8 B2
Bramfield GSTN WD25 205 F4
HTCHE/RSTV SG4 57 F3 1
Bramfield La HERT/WAS SG14 125 G6
Bramfield Pl HHNE HP2 141 F8
Bramfield Rd HERT/WAS SG14 150 B1
KNEB SG3 96 E8
Bramhanger Acre LTNN/LIM LU3 68 C2
Bramingham Rd LTNN/LIM LU3 69 F2
Bramleas WATW WD18 12 A4
Bramley Cl BLDK SG7 27 F8 1
Bramley Ct GSTN WD25 204 C2 1
Bramley Gdns OXHEY WD19 230 D5
Bramley Wy STALE/WH AL4 169 F7
Brampton Cl CHESW EN7 196 E6
HARP AL5 119 F8
Brampton Park Rd HTCH/STOT SG5 40 C8
Brampton Rd OXHEY WD19 230 B2
ROY SG8 21 K3
STAL AL1 11 F3
Brampton Ter BORE WD6 207 K8 1
Bramshaw Gdns OXHEY WD19 230 E4
Bramshott Cl HTCHE/RSTV SG4 56 D5
Branch Cl HAT AL10 171 H2
Branch Rd LCOL/BKTW AL2 189 F5
STALW/RED AL3 10 A3
Brandles Rd LWTH SG6 42 A6
Brandon Cl CHESW EN7 196 C4
Brand St HTCH/STOT SG5 56 C2
Branksome Cl HHNE HP2 9 D4
Branton Cl LTNE LU2 71 F7 3
Brantwood Rd LTN LU1 4 A4
Bray Cl BORE WD6 224 B1
Brayes Mnr HTCH/STOT SG5 25 K3
Brays Md HLWS CM18 7 E6
Brays Rd LTNE LU2 70 C6
Brazier Cl AMP/FLIT/B MK45 36 B6
Braziers End CSHM HP5 159 H7
Braziers Fld HERT/BAY SG13 151 J3 2
Braziers Quay BSF CM23 105 K3
Bread And Cheese La BROX EN10 196 C2
Breadcroft La HARP AL5 118 D7
Breakmead WGCE AL7 148 C5 2
Breakspear STVGE SG2 76 D6
Breakspear Av STAL AL1 11 E5
Breakspear Ct ABLGY WD5 187 F8
Breakspeare Cl WATN WD24 204 C8
Breakspeare Rd ABLGY WD5 203 K1
Breakspear Wy HHNE HP2 9 F5
Breaks Rd HAT AL10 171 G3 2
Brecken Cl STALE/WH AL4 168 D2
Brecon Cl LTN LU1 4 B5 1
Brendon Av LTNE LU2 70 D8
Brett Pl WATN WD24 204 B7
Brett Rd BAR EN5 225 H5
Bretts Md LTN LU1 4 A6
Brewers Cl BSF CM23 105 F4
Brewery La BLDK SG7 26 E8 2
STSD CM24 86 D2
Brewery Rd HOD EN11 177 F3
Brewhouse Hl STALE/WH AL4 145 F1
Brewhouse La HERT/WAS SG14 151 F3 1
Briants Cl PIN HA5 231 F7
Briarcliff HHW HP1 163 H5 1
Briar Cl BERK HP4 162 D2
CHES/WCR EN8 197 G7
LTNE LU2 70 D5
Briardale STVG SG1 2 C4
WARE SG12 127 G6
Briarley Cl BROX EN10 176 E8
Briar Patch La LWTH SG6 41 H6
Briar Rd GSTN WD25 204 B4
STALE/WH AL4 169 F3
Briars Cl HAT AL10 171 F4
Briars La HAT AL10 171 F4
The Briars CHES/WCR EN8 214 D1
HERT/BAY SG13 151 K3
HLWS CM18 180 B4 1
RKW/CH/CXG WD3 201 K6
Briars Wd HAT AL10 171 F4
Briar Wy BERK HP4 161 K6
Briarwood Dr NTHWD HA6 230 B8
Briary La ROY SG8 21 G4
Briary Wood End WLYN AL6 123 F1
Briary Wood La WLYN AL6 123 F1
Brickcroft BROX EN10 197 J4 1
Brickendon La HERT/BAY SG13 151 F6
HERT/BAY SG13 175 G4
Bricket Rd STAL AL1 11 D4
Brickfield HAT AL10 171 F7
Brickfield Av HHS/BOV HP3 9 E6
Brickfield La BAR EN5 224 E6
The Brickfields WARE SG12 127 F7
Brick Kiln Cl BUSH WD23 13 F5 2
Brick Kiln La HTCH/STOT SG5 56 C4
Brickkiln Rd STVG SG1 2 A2
Brick Knoll Pk STALE/WH AL4 169 F7
Brickly Rd LTNW/LEA LU4 68 A4
Brickmakers La HHS/BOV HP3 9 E6
Brickwall Cl WGCW AL8 147 F1
Brickyard La ROY SG8 31 J4
Bride Hall La WLYN AL6 120 E5
Bridewell Cl BUNT SG9 63 J1
Bridge End BUNT SG9 63 J1
Bridgefields WGCE AL7 148 A2 2
Bridgefoot BUNT SG9 63 J2 1
Bridge Foot WARE SG12 127 H8 2
Bridgend Rd EN EN1 214 B5
Bridge Pl WAT WD17 13 E4 1
Bridger Cl GSTN WD25 204 E3
Bridge Rd KGLGY WD4 203 H3
KNEB SG3 96 B7
LWTH SG6 41 K3
STVG SG1 75 G3
WGCE AL7 147 K2
WGCW AL8 147 H2
Bridge Rd East WGCE AL7 147 K2
Bridges Ct HERT/WAS SG14 151 F3 2
Bridge St BERK HP4 162 A5
BSF CM23 105 J2
HHW HP1 164 B7
HTCH/STOT SG5 56 C3
LTN LU1 4 C4
Bridgewater Hl BERK HP4 161 G2 1
Bridgewater Rd BERK HP4 161 J3
Bridgewater Wy BUSH WD23 221 J6
Bridle Cl HOD EN11 153 F7
PEND EN3 214 E7
STALW/RED AL3 11 D2
Bridle La RKW/CH/CXG WD3 218 B3
Bridle Pth WAT WD17 12 C1
Bridle Wy BERK HP4 161 H3
HOD EN11 153 F8 2
WARE SG12 153 F3
Bridle Wy (North) HOD EN11 153 F7
Bridle Wy (South) HOD EN11 153 F8
Bridlington Rd OXHEY WD19 230 E2
Brierley Cl LTNE LU2 70 E7 1
Briery Fld RKW/CH/CXG WD3 217 K3
Briery Wy HHNE HP2 9 D3
Brigadier Hl ENC/FH EN2 213 F8
Brighton Rd WATN WD24 204 B8
Brighton Wy STVG SG1 75 F1
Brightview Cl LCOL/BKTW AL2 188 A7 1
Brightwell Rd WATW WD18 12 B4
Brill Cl LTNE LU2 70 E7
Brimfield Cl LTNE LU2 70 E7 2
Brimstone Wy BERK HP4 161 G3
Brinklow Ct STAL AL1 188 D1 1
Brinley Cl CHES/WCR EN8 214 C1
Brinsmead LCOL/BKTW AL2 189 F5
Briscoe Cl HOD EN11 176 E1
Briscoe Rd HOD EN11 176 E1
Bristol Rd LTNN/LIM LU3 69 F5
Britannia STDN SG11 81 K7
Britannia Av LTNN/LIM LU3 69 G4
Britannia Rd CHES/WCR EN8 214 E4
Brittain Wy STVGE SG2 3 F3
Britten Cl BORE WD6 223 G6
Britton Av STALW/RED AL3 10 C4 2
Brixham Cl STVG SG1 75 G2
Brixton Rd WATN WD24 220 C1
Broad Acre LCOL/BKTW AL2 188 A8
Broad Acres HAT AL10 170 E1
Broadacres LTNE LU2 69 J3 1
Broad Ct WGCE AL7 147 K3
Broadcroft HHNE HP2 8 A3 4
LWTH SG6 41 K7 1
Broadfield BSF CM23 85 J7
HLW CM20 7 D3
Broadfield Cl MHAD SG10 103 G8
Broadfield Pl WGCW AL8 147 G4 1
Broadfield Rd HHNE HP2 8 C5
KNEB SG3 96 C8
Broadfields CHESW EN7 195 K7
HARP AL5 118 B7
PIN HA5 231 J8
RYLN/HDSTN HA2 231 J8
SBW CM21 131 K8
Broadfields La OXHEY WD19 220 C8
Broadfield Wy MHAD SG10 103 G8
Broad Gn HERT/BAY SG13 174 C1
Broad Green Wd HERT/BAY SG13 174 C1
Broadhall Wy STVGE SG2 3 E6
Broadlake Cl LCOL/BKTW AL2 190 B5
Broadleaf Av BSF CM23 105 F5
Broadleaf Gv WLYN AL6 122 B8
Broadley Rd HLWW/ROY CM19 179 G5
Broadmead HTCHE/RSTV SG4 56 E4
Broad Md LTNN/LIM LU3 69 F6
Broadmead Cl PIN HA5 231 F6 1
Broadmeadow Ride
HTCHE/RSTV SG4 56 E5
Broadmeads WARE SG12 127 H8
Broadoak Av PEND EN3 214 C5
Broad Oak Wy STVGE SG2 76 A8
Broadstone Rd HARP AL5 143 K3
Broad St HHNE HP2 8 A5
Broadview STVG SG1 2 C2
The Broad Wk NTHWD HA6 229 H8
Broadwater BERK HP4 161 K4
POTB/CUF EN6 193 H8
Broadwater Av LWTH SG6 41 J4
Broadwater Crs STVGE SG2 76 A8
WGCE AL7 147 J4
Broadwater Dl LWTH SG6 41 J4
Broadwater La STVGE SG2 76 D8
Broadwater Rd WGCE AL7 147 K4
WGCW AL8 147 J4
Broadway LWTH SG6 41 J6
Broadway Av HLWE CM17 156 E5
The Broadway BRKMPK AL9 171 H4
PIN HA5 231 G6
STALE/WH AL4 119 K4
WAT WD17 13 D2 1
Brocket Rd HOD EN11 177 F3
WGCW AL8 146 E5
Brockett Cl WGCW AL8 147 G3
Brocket Vw STALE/WH AL4 145 G1
Brocklesbury Cl WATN WD24 13 D2
Brockles Md HLWW/ROY CM19 179 K5
Brockswood La WGCW AL8 147 G2
Brockwell Shott STVGE SG2 60 D8
Brodewater Rd BORE WD6 224 A2 1
Brodie Rd ENC/FH EN2 213 F8
Bromborough Gn OXHEY WD19 230 D4 2
Bromet Cl WAT WD17 204 A8
Bromleigh Cl CHES/WCR EN8 197 J6 1
Bromley TRING HP23 108 E5
Brompton Cl LTNN/LIM LU3 68 E1
Bronte Crs HHNE HP2 141 G8 1
Brookbridge La KNEB SG3 96 E7
Brookdene Av OXHEY WD19 12 C6
Brookdene Dr NTHWD HA6 230 A6
Brook Dr RAD WD7 206 C3
STVGE SG2 96 C1
Brooke Cl BUSH WD23 221 K7
Brooke End STALW/RED AL3 142 B5
Brooke Gdns BSF CM23 106 B2
Brook End ROY SG8 15 K6
SBW CM21 132 B7
Brooke Rd ROY SG8 21 H1
Brooker Rd WAB EN9 215 H4
Brooke Wy BUSH WD23 221 K7 1
Brook Fld STVGE SG2 77 F7
Brookfield Cl TRING HP23 135 G5
Brookfield Gdns CHES/WCR EN8 197 H5
Brookfield La CHES/WCR EN8 197 F6
STVGE SG2 77 G5
Brookfield La East
CHES/WCR EN8 197 H5
Brookfield La West
CHES/WCR EN8 197 G5
Brookfields SBW CM21 132 B7
Brookhill STVGE SG2 96 A1
Brooklands Cl LTNW/LEA LU4 68 B3
Brooklands Gdns POTB/CUF EN6 209 K2
Brook La BERK HP4 161 J4
SBW CM21 132 B7
Brooklane Fld HLWS CM18 180 E4
Brookmans Av BRKMPK AL9 193 F4
Brookmill Cl OXHEY WD19 12 C6 1
Brook Rd BORE WD6 223 K1
CHES/WCR EN8 214 E4
SBW CM21 132 B8
STSD CM24 86 D3

Brooksfield WGCE AL7 148 C2
Brookside HAT AL10 170 C4
HERT/BAY SG13 151 H4
HLWW/ROY CM19 179 G3
HOD EN11 177 F3
LWTH SG6 41 K4 1
POTB/CUF EN6 209 F2
WAB EN9 215 K2 1
Brookside Cl BAR EN5 225 J6
Brookside Crs POTB/CUF EN6 195 G5
Brookside Gdns EN EN1 214 A7
Brookside Rd OXHEY WD19 12 C6
Brooksies SAFWS CB11 35 H3
Brook St HTCH/STOT SG5 25 J3
LTN LU1 4 B3
TRING HP23 135 G5
Brook Vw HTCHE/RSTV SG4 57 G3
Broom Cl CHESW EN7 196 E5
HAT AL10 170 E7
Broomer Pl CHES/WCR EN8 197 G7
Broomfield HLW CM20 156 E6
LCOL/BKTW AL2 188 E5 1
Broomfield Av BROX EN10 197 J4
Broomfield Cl WLYN AL6 122 C5 1
Broomfield Ri ABLGY WD5 203 J2
Broomfield Rd WLYN AL6 122 C5
Broom Gv KNEB SG3 96 A4
WAT WD17 204 B8
Broom Hl HHW HP1 163 H7
WLYN AL6 123 G1
Broomhills WGCE AL7 148 B2
Broomleys STALE/WH AL4 169 F3
Brooms Cl WGCW AL8 122 D8 1
Brooms Rd LTNE LU2 5 D3
Broomstick Hall Rd WAB EN9 215 K3
Broomstick La CSHM HP5 182 C8
Broom Wk STVG SG1 2 C3
Broughinge Rd BORE WD6 224 A2
Broughton Av LTNN/LIM LU3 69 H4
Broughton Hl LWTH SG6 42 A3
Broughton Wy RKW/CH/CXG WD3 217 K7
Brownfields WGCE AL7 148 A2
Brownfield Wy STALE/WH AL4 119 K3
Browning Dr HTCHE/RSTV SG4 57 F1
Browning Rd ENC/FH EN2 213 G8
HARP AL5 118 E7
Brownlow La LBUZ LU7 109 K2
Brownlow Rd BERK HP4 161 K4
BORE WD6 223 K4 1
Brown's Cl LTNW/LEA LU4 68 C4
Brown's Ri TRING HP23 158 E6 1
Browns Spring BERK HP4 163 F2
The Brow CSTG HP8 226 A2
GSTN WD25 204 C3
Brox Dell STVG SG1 2 C2
Broxley Md LTNW/LEA LU4 68 B4
Bruce Gv WATN WD24 204 C8
Bruce Rd BAR EN5 225 K3 1
Bruce Wy CHES/WCR EN8 214 C3
Brunel Rd STVGE SG2 3 E1
Brunswick Rd WAB EN9 215 F8
Brunswick St LTNE LU2 4 C3
Brushrise WATN WD24 204 B6
Brushwood Dr RKW/CH/CXG WD3 217 F4
Bryan Rd BSF CM23 105 J1
Bryanstone Rd CHES/WCR EN8 214 E4
Bryant Ct HARP AL5 118 C6
Bryce Cl WARE SG12 127 H6
Buchanan Ct BORE WD6 224 B2 1
Buchanan Dr LTNE LU2 5 F3
Buckettsland La BORE WD6 208 C8
Buckingham Dr LTNE LU2 70 D7
Buckingham Rd BORE WD6 224 C4
TRING HP23 134 D6
WATN WD24 204 D7 1
Buckland Ri PIN HA5 230 D7
Buckle Cl LTNN/LIM LU3 68 E2
Bucklersbury HTCH/STOT SG5 56 C3
Bucklers Cl BROX EN10 176 E8
Bucknalls Cl GSTN WD25 205 F2
Bucknalls Dr LCOL/BKTW AL2 205 G1
Bucknalls La GSTN WD25 205 F2
Bucks Aly HERT/BAY SG13 174 A5
Bucks Av OXHEY WD19 13 F6
Bucks Hl KGLGY WD4 202 B3
Buckthorn Av STVG SG1 2 C4
Buckton Rd BORE WD6 207 J8
Buckwood La DUN/WHIP LU6 114 A2
Buckwood Rd DUN/WHIP LU6 114 E3
Buddcroft WGCE AL7 148 C2 1
Bude Crs STVG SG1 75 F3 1
Building End Rd ROY SG8 34 D1
Bulbourne Cl BERK HP4 161 G3 1
HHW HP1 163 K7
Bulbourne Ct TRING HP23 135 F2 1
Bulbourne Rd TRING HP23 135 G2
Bullace Cl HHW HP1 163 K5 2
Bullbeggars La BERK HP4 162 D5
Bullen's Green La STALE/WH AL4 191 J1
Bullfields SBW CM21 132 C5
Bullhead Rd BORE WD6 224 B2
Bull La BUNT SG9 47 G1
BUNT SG9 62 A1
SAFWS CB11 34 D7
STALE/WH AL4 144 D3
Bullock's Hl HTCHE/RSTV SG4 73 K8
Bullock's La HERT/BAY SG13 151 F5
Bull Pln HERT/WAS SG14 151 G3
Bull Rd HARP AL5 143 J1
Bullrush Cl HAT AL10 171 G5
Bull's Cross ENC/FH EN2 213 K6
Bulls Cross Ride CHESW EN7 213 K4
Bullsland Gdns RKW/CH/CXG WD3 216 E6
Bullsland La RKW/CH/CXG WD3 216 E6
Bulls La BRKMPK AL9 192 E2
Bullsmoor Cl CHES/WCR EN8 214 B5 1
Bullsmoor Gdns
CHES/WCR EN8 214 A5 1
Bullsmoor La EN EN1 214 A5
PEND EN3 214 C5
Bullsmoor Ride CHES/WCR EN8 214 B5
Bullsmoor Wy CHES/WCR EN8 214 A5
Bull Stag Gn BRKMPK AL9 171 H2
Bullwell Crs CHES/WCR EN8 197 J7
Bulstrode Cl KGLGY WD4 184 C7
Bulstrode La KGLGY WD4 184 C7
Bulwer Link STVG SG1 2 C5
Bumbles Green La WAB EN9 199 H3
Buncefield La HHNE HP2 9 F2
The Bungalows HARP AL5 118 E6 1
Bunkers La HHS/BOV HP3 186 A3
Bunnsfield WGCE AL7 148 D2
Bunstrux TRING HP23 134 E5
Buntingford Rd STDN SG11 81 J5
Bunyan Cl HTCH/STOT SG5 39 F5
TRING HP23 135 G4
Bunyan Rd HTCH/STOT SG5 56 D1 1
Bunyans Cl LTNN/LIM LU3 69 F4
Burbage Cl CHES/WCR EN8 214 D1
Burchell Ct BUSH WD23 221 K7 2
Burfield Cl HAT AL10 171 F2 1
Burfield Rd RKW/CH/CXG WD3 216 E5
Burford Gdns HOD EN11 177 G2
Burford St HOD EN11 177 F2
Burford Wy HTCH/STOT SG5 40 A7
Burge End La HTCH/STOT SG5 38 E4
Burghley Av BORE WD6 224 B5
BSF CM23 105 F2
Burghley Cl STVGE SG2 96 B1
Burgundy Cft WGCE AL7 148 A5 1
Burhill Gv PIN HA5 231 F8 2
Burleigh Md BRKMPK AL9 171 H2
Burleigh Rd CHES/WCR EN8 214 D2 1
HERT/BAY SG13 151 K2
HHS/BOV HP3 9 F6
STAL AL1 168 E6
Burleigh Wy POTB/CUF EN6 195 G8
Burley LWTH SG6 25 K8
Burley Hl HLWE CM17 181 G2
Burley Rd BSF CM23 105 K5
Burnell Ri LWTH SG6 41 H4
Burnells Wy STSD CM24 86 D2
Burnell Wk LWTH SG6 41 J4
Burnet Cl HHS/BOV HP3 8 B6
Burnett Pk HLWW/ROY CM19 179 J6 2
Burnett Sq HERT/WAS SG14 150 C2
Burnham Cl ENC/FH EN2 213 H8
WLYN AL6 123 J3
Burnham Green Rd WLYN AL6 123 K3
Burnham Rd LTNE LU2 5 F1
STAL AL1 11 F4
Burnley Cl OXHEY WD19 230 D4
Burnsall Pl HARP AL5 143 K3
Burns Cl HTCHE/RSTV SG4 57 F1 2
STVGE SG2 76 C1
Burns Dr HHNE HP2 165 G1
Burnside HERT/WAS SG14 150 D4
HOD EN11 176 E3
SBW CM21 132 B7
STAL AL1 168 E8
Burns Rd ROY SG8 21 G1
Burnt Cl LTNN/LIM LU3 68 E2
Burntfarm Ride CHESW EN7 212 E2
Burntmill Cl HLW CM20 6 B1 1
Burntmill La HLW CM20 6 B1
Burr Cl AMP/FLIT/B MK45 36 C5
LCOL/BKTW AL2 190 C5
Burrowfield WGCE AL7 147 J5
Burrs La ROY SG8 32 C6
Burr's Pl LTN LU1 4 C5
Burr St LTNE LU2 4 C3
Bursland LWTH SG6 41 H3
Burston Dr LCOL/BKTW AL2 188 E6
Burton Av WATW WD18 12 B3
Burton Cl STALE/WH AL4 120 A4
Burton La CHESW EN7 196 C6
Burton's La CSTG HP8 216 B4
RKW/CH/CXG WD3 216 C5
Burwell Rd STVGE SG2 3 F4
Burycroft WGCW AL8 122 E8
Burydale STVGE SG2 76 C8
Burydell La LCOL/BKTW AL2 189 F5
Bury End HTCH/STOT SG5 39 F5
Bury Gn HHW HP1 164 B5 1
STALE/WH AL4 145 F1
Bury Green Rd CHESW EN7 197 F8
Bury Hl HHW HP1 164 B5
Bury Hill Cl HHW HP1 164 B5
Bury Holme BROX EN10 197 K1
Bury La HERT/WAS SG14 124 D5
KNEB SG3 96 E6
LTNN/LIM LU3 52 A4
RKW/CH/CXG WD3 218 C8
WLYN AL6 94 E8
Bury Lodge La RBSF CM22 107 H1
STSD CM24 87 F6
Bury Md ARL/CHE SG15 24 E2
Burymead STVG SG1 58 C8
Bury Mdw RKW/CH/CXG WD3 218 C8
Bury Mead Rd HTCH/STOT SG5 40 D7
Bury Park Rd LTN LU1 4 A2
Bury Ri HHS/BOV HP3 184 B3
Bury Rd HAT AL10 171 H3
HHW HP1 164 B5
HLWE CM17 157 F5
Burywick HARP AL5 143 J4
Bushbarns CHESW EN7 196 E7
Bushby Av BROX EN10 176 E8
Bushel Whf TRING HP23 135 F3
Bushey Cl WGCE AL7 148 C4
Bushey Cft HLWS CM18 7 D6
Bushey Gn WGCE AL7 148 C4
Bushey Grove Rd BUSH WD23 13 E3
Bushey Hall Dr BUSH WD23 13 F3
Bushey Hall Rd BUSH WD23 13 E3
Bushey Ley WGCE AL7 148 C4
Busheymill Br BUSH WD23 205 F8
Bushey Mill Crs WATN WD24 204 D7
Bushey Mill La BUSH WD23 221 G2
WATN WD24 204 D7
Bushfield Rd HHS/BOV HP3 184 A3
Bush Hall La BRKMPK AL9 171 J
Bushmead Rd LTNE LU2 69 K4
Bush Spring BLDK SG7 27 G8
Bushwood Cl BRKMPK AL9 192 B1
Butchers La HTCHE/RSTV SG4 73 G3
Butely Rd LTNW/LEA LU4 68 A4
Bute Sq LTN LU1 4 C4
Bute St LTN LU1 4 C4
Butlers Dr CHING E4 215 H8
Butlin Rd LTN LU1 89 G2
Butterfield Green Rd LTNE LU2 70 B2
Butterfield La STAL AL1 189 G2
Butterfield Rd STALE/WH AL4 145 F2
Butterfly La BORE WD6 222 E3
Buttermere Cl STAL AL1 168 E
Buttersweet Ri SBW CM21 132 C8
Butterwick GSTN WD25 205 F
Butt Field Vw LCOL/BKTW AL2 188 E
Buttlehide RKW/CH/CXG WD3 227 G4
Buttondene Crs BROX EN10 177 G
Butts End HHW HP1 163 K
Buttsmead NTHWD HA6 229 H
The Butts BROX EN10 197 J
Buxton Cl STALE/WH AL4 169 G
Buxton Pth OXHEY WD19 230 D2
Buxton Rd LTN LU1 4 B4
Buxtons La ROY SG8 15 G
Byde St HERT/WAS SG14 151 F
Byers Cl POTB/CUF EN6 210 D4
Byewaters WATW WD18 219 H
The Byeway RKW/CH/CXG WD3 228 D
Byfield WGCW AL8 122 E
Byfield Cl LTNW/LEA LU4 68 A
Bygrave Rd BLDK SG7 27 F
Bylands Cl BSF CM23 105 G
Byng Dr POTB/CUF EN6 210 B
Bynghams HLWW/ROY CM19 179 G
Byng Rd BAR EN5 225 J
Byrd Wk BLDK SG7 43 F
Byron Av BORE WD6 223 K
WATN WD24 220 E
Byron Cl HTCHE/RSTV SG4 57 F
STVGE SG2 76 D
Byron Pl HHNE HP2 141 G
Byron Rd HARP AL5 118 C
LTNW/LEA LU4 68 A
ROY SG8 21 H
Byslips Rd DUN/WHIP LU6 114 B
By the Wd OXHEY WD19 230 E
Byways BERK HP4 162 B
The Byway POTB/CUF EN6 210 E

C

Cabot Cl STVGE SG2 3 E
Caddington Common
STALW/RED AL3 115 J
Cade Cl LWTH SG6 26 C
Cades Cl LTN LU1 89 F
Cades La LTN LU1 89 F
Cadmore La CHES/WCR EN8 197 J
Cadwell La HTCH/STOT SG5 40 D
Caernarvon Cl HHNE HP2 8 A5
STVGE SG2 96 C
Caesars Rd STALE/WH AL4 145 C
Cage Pond Rd RAD WD7 207 K
Caishowe Rd BORE WD6 224 A
Caister Cl HHS/BOV HP3 8 E
STVG SG1 58 A
Calbury Cl STAL AL1 168 E7
Caldbeck WAB EN9 215 J

Caldecot Av CHESW EN7 196 D7 1
Caldecote Gdns BUSH WD23 222 B6
Caldecote La BUSH WD23 222 C7
Caldecote Rd BLDK SG7 16 D8
Caldecot Wy BROX EN10 176 E8 1
Calder Av BRKMPK AL9 193 G4
Caldwell Rd OXHEY WD19 230 E3
Caleb Cl LTNW/LEA LU4 68 E7
Caledon Rd LCOL/BKTW AL2 190 A4
California BLDK SG7 27 F8
California La BUSH WD23 222 A8
Callisto Ct HHNE HP2 8 C2 1
Callowland Pl WATN WD24 204 C8 1
Calnwood Rd LTNW/LEA LU4 68 A7
Calton Av HERT/WAS SG14 150 C2
Calverley Cl BSF CM23 105 H6
Calverton Rd LTNN/LIM LU3 68 E3
Calvert Rd BAR EN5 225 J2
Camberley Pl HARP AL5 144 A3 2
Camborne Dr HHNE HP2 8 B1
Cambrian Wy HHNE HP2 8 B2
Cambridge Cl CHES/WCR EN8 197 G7 1
Cambridge Dr POTB/CUF EN6 209 K1
Cambridge Rd HLW CM20 157 F3
HTCHE/RSTV SG4 41 G8
ROY SG8 23 G6
ROY SG8 32 D4
SBW CM21 132 C4
STAL AL1 168 E7
STDN SG11 81 H7
STSD CM24 86 D1
WATW WD18 13 D3 1
Cambridge St LTN LU1 5 D6
Cambridge Ter BERK HP4 162 A5 1
Cameron Dr CHES/WCR EN8 214 C4
Camfield WGCE AL7 148 A7
Camlet Wy STALW/RED AL3 10 A3
Campania Gv LTNN/LIM LU3 69 F1
Campbell Cl BUNT SG9 63 H2
HLWE CM17 180 E2 1
HTCHE/RSTV SG4 57 F1 3
Campers Av LWTH SG6 41 J4
Campers Rd LWTH SG6 41 H4
Campers Wk LWTH SG6 41 J4
Campfield Rd HERT/WAS SG14 150 E3
STAL AL1 11 F4
Campfield Wy LWTH SG6 41 G4
Campine Cl CHES/WCR EN8 197 H6 1
Campion Cl GSTN WD25 204 B3
Campion Rd HHW HP1 163 H7
Campions Ct BERK HP4 161 H6
The Campions BORE WD6 207 J8
STSD CM24 86 D1 2
Campion Wy ROY SG8 21 J4
Campkin Md STVGE SG2 76 E6 1
Camp Rd STAL AL1 11 E5
Campus Five LWTH SG6 42 C2
The Campus WGCW AL8 147 J2
Camp View Rd STAL AL1 168 E7
Canada La BROX EN10 197 J3
The Canadas BROX EN10 197 J3 1
Canberra Cl STALW/RED AL3 168 C2
Canberra Gdns LTNN/LIM LU3 69 G3
Candlefield Rd HHS/BOV HP3 186 A1
Canes La HLWE CM17 181 H8
Canfield BSF CM23 105 H1
Cangelis Cl HHW HP1 163 K8
Canham Cl HTCHE/RSTV SG4 93 G8
Cannix Cl STVGE SG2 3 E6
Cannon La LTNE LU2 70 C4
Cannon Ms WAB EN9 215 G3
Cannon Rd WATW WD18 13 D4 1
Cannons Cl BSF CM23 85 K8
ROY SG8 15 G4
Cannons Ct STDN SG11 81 J6
Cannons Md STSD CM24 86 C2
Cannons Meadow WLYN AL6 124 A8
Cannons Mill La BSF CM23 85 K7
Cannon St STALW/RED AL3 10 C3
Canons Brook HLWW/ROY CM19 179 H1
Canons Cl RAD WD7 206 E5
Canons Fld STALE/WH AL4 120 B8 2
WLYN AL6 122 E1
Canonsfield Rd WLYN AL6 122 E1
Canons Ga CHES/WCR EN8 197 K4
HLW CM20 155 H7
Canons Rd WARE SG12 127 G7
Canopus Wy NTHWD HA6 230 B3
Canterbury Cl LTNW/LEA LU4 68 E5
NTHWD HA6 230 A5
Canterbury Rd BORE WD6 223 K2
WAT WD17 12 C1 2
Canterbury Wy
RKW/CH/CXG WD3 219 H3
STVG SG1 59 F7
Capella Rd NTHWD HA6 230 A4
Capell Av RKW/CH/CXG WD3 217 F5
Capell Rd RKW/CH/CXG WD3 217 G5
Capell Wy RKW/CH/CXG WD3 217 G5
Capel Rd EN EN1 214 A6
OXHEY WD19 13 E5
Capelvere Wk WAT WD17 219 K1
Cape Rd STAL AL1 168 E6
Caponfield WGCE AL7 148 C5
Cappell La WARE SG12 153 H4
Capron Rd LTNW/LEA LU4 68 D5
Captains Wk BERK HP4 162 A6
Caractacus Cottage Vw
WATW WD18 12 B6
Caractacus Gn WATW WD18 12 A5
Caravan La RKW/CH/CXG WD3 218 D7
Carbone Hl POTB/CUF EN6 195 F4
Carde Cl HERT/WAS SG14 150 C2
Cardiff Cl STVGE SG2 96 C2
Cardiff Gv LTN LU1 4 B4
Cardiff Rd LTN LU1 4 B4
WATW WD18 12 C5
Cardiff Wy ABLGY WD5 204 B2
Cardigan St LTN LU1 4 B4
Cardinal Av BORE WD6 224 A3
Cardinal Cl CHESW EN7 196 D4 1
Cardinal Gv STALW/RED AL3 10 A6
Cardy Rd HHW HP1 164 A7
Carew Rd NTHWD HA6 229 K5
Carew Wy OXHEY WD19 231 G2
Careys Cft BERK HP4 161 G2
Carisbrooke Av WATN WD24 220 E1
Carisbrooke Rd HARP AL5 118 E7
LTNW/LEA LU4 68 D8
Carisbrook Rd LCOL/BKTW AL2 188 D4
Carleton Ri WLYN AL6 122 B3 1
Carleton Rd CHES/WCR EN8 197 H5
Carlisle Av STALW/RED AL3 10 C2
Carlton Cl BORE WD6 224 C4 1
LTNN/LIM LU3 4 A1
Carlton Crs LTNN/LIM LU3 69 H6
Carlton Rd HARP AL5 118 C7
Carman Ct TRING HP23 134 E6 1
Carmelite Rd KTN/HRWW/W HA3 231 K7
Carnaby Rd BROX EN10 176 D6
Carnarvon Rd BAR EN5 225 K3
Carnegie Gdns LTNN/LIM LU3 69 F1
Carnegie Rd STALW/RED AL3 168 A2
Caro La HHS/BOV HP3 165 F8
Carol Cl LTNN/LIM LU3 69 G5
Caroline Pl OXHEY WD19 13 F5 3
Caroon Dr RKW/CH/CXG WD3 202 A6
Carpenders Av OXHEY WD19 231 F2
Carpenders Cl HARP AL5 117 K5 1
Carpenters Rd EN EN1 214 B6
The Carpenters BSF CM23 105 F5 1
Carpenters Wood Dr
RKW/CH/CXG WD3 216 E4
Carpenter Wy POTB/CUF EN6 210 D3
Carrigans BSF CM23 105 H1
Carrington Av BORE WD6 224 A5
Carrington Cl BAR EN5 225 F5
Carrington Pl TRING HP23 135 G4
Carrington Sq
KTN/HRWW/W HA3 231 K6 1
Carsdale Cl LTNN/LIM LU3 69 F3 1
Carteret Rd LTNE LU2 70 D8
Carters Cl ARL/CHE SG15 24 E2
STVGE SG2 76 E5
Cartersfield Rd WAB EN9 215 H4
Carters Lane
(Wibbly Wobbley Lane)
HTCH/STOT SG5 55 J2
Carters Leys BSF CM23 105 G1
Carters Md HLWE CM17 180 E2
Carters Wy ARL/CHE SG15 24 E2
Cart Pth GSTN WD25 204 D3
Cartwright Rd ROY SG8 21 H4 1
STVG SG1 59 J7
Carve Ley WGCE AL7 148 C4
Carvers Cft KNEB SG3 96 C8
Cary Wk RAD WD7 206 E4
Cashio La LWTH SG6 26 A8
Caslon Wy LWTH SG6 25 K8
Cassandra Ga CHES/WCR EN8 197 K5
Cassiobridge Rd WATW WD18 219 K4
Cassiobury Dr WAT WD17 12 B2
Cassiobury Park Av WATW WD18 219 K3
Cassio Rd WATW WD18 12 C3
Castle Cl BUSH WD23 221 J6
HOD EN11 153 H8
Castle Croft Rd LTN LU1 89 F3
Castle Gate Wy BERK HP4 161 K3
Castle Hl BERK HP4 161 K3
Castle Hill Av BERK HP4 161 K4
Castle Hill Cl BERK HP4 161 J4
Castle Md HHW HP1 164 A8
Castle Ri STALE/WH AL4 119 H7
Castle Rd HOD EN11 153 G8
STAL AL1 168 E6
Castles Cl HTCH/STOT SG5 25 K2
Castle St BERK HP4 161 K5
BSF CM23 105 J3
HERT/BAY SG13 151 G4
HERT/WAS SG14 151 F3 3
LTN LU1 4 C4 3
Castle Vw BSF CM23 105 K2
Catesby Gn LTNN/LIM LU3 52 A8
Catham Cl STAL AL1 168 E8
Catherall Rd LTNN/LIM LU3 69 G3
Catherine Cl HHNE HP2 165 G1 1
Catherine Rd PEND EN3 214 D6
Catherine St STALW/RED AL3 10 C3
Catisfield Rd PEND EN3 214 D7
Catkin Cl HHW HP1 164 A5
Catlin St HHS/BOV HP3 185 F1
Catsbrook Rd LTNN/LIM LU3 69 G3
Catsdell Bottom HHS/BOV HP3 186 B1
Catsey La BUSH WD23 221 K7
Catsey Wd BUSH WD23 221 K7
Catterick Wy BORE WD6 223 J1
Cattlegate Rd POTB/CUF EN6 212 A1
Cattlegate Road Crews Hl
ENC/FH EN2 212 C4
Cattley Cl BAR EN5 225 K4
Cattlins Cl CHESW EN7 196 C7
Cattsdell HHNE HP2 8 B3
Causeway Cl POTB/CUF EN6 210 E1
The Causeway BSF CM23 105 J2
BUNT SG9 50 C8
BUNT SG9 63 J1
POTB/CUF EN6 210 D1
ROY SG8 30 D1
SAFWS CB11 34 E6
STDN SG11 65 H8
STDN SG11 82 A2 1
Cautherly La WARE SG12 152 E4
Cavalier Cl LTNN/LIM LU3 69 F3
Cavalier Ct BERK HP4 161 K5 1
Cavan Dr STALW/RED AL3 168 A1
Cavan Rd STALW/RED AL3 142 B3
Cavell Rd CHESW EN7 196 D5
Cavell Wk STVGE SG2 76 D3
Cavendish Crs BORE WD6 223 K4
Cavendish Rd BAR EN5 225 H3
LTNN/LIM LU3 69 G7
STAL AL1 11 E4
STALW/RED AL3 115 H3
STVG SG1 75 F3
Cavendish Wy HAT AL10 170 D4
Cawkell Cl STSD CM24 86 C2
Caxton Hl HERT/BAY SG13 151 J3 3
Caxton Rd HOD EN11 153 G7
Caxton Wy STVG SG1 75 G5
WATW WD18 219 J7
Cecil Cl BSF CM23 106 C2
Cecil Ct BAR EN5 225 J3
HLWS CM18 179 K4
Cecil Crs HAT AL10 171 G2
Cecil Rd CHES/WCR EN8 214 C2
HERT/BAY SG13 151 F6
HOD EN11 177 H1
POTB/CUF EN6 209 G2
STAL AL1 11 E4
Cecil St WATN WD24 204 C8
Cedar Av CHES/WCR EN8 214 C3
HTCH/STOT SG5 40 C5
Cedar Cl HERT/WAS SG14 150 E3 1
POTB/CUF EN6 193 G8
SBW CM21 132 C8
WARE SG12 152 C1
Cedar Ct BSF CM23 85 J8
STALE/WH AL4 169 G6
Cedar Crs ROY SG8 21 F3
Cedar Dr PIN HA5 231 H5
Cedar Gn HOD EN11 177 F4 1
Cedar Lawn Av BAR EN5 225 K5
Cedar Pk BSF CM23 105 G5
Cedar Park Rd ENC/FH EN2 213 F8
Cedar Rd BERK HP4 162 A6
ENC/FH EN2 212 E8
HAT AL10 171 F5
OXHEY WD19 13 D5
Cedars Av RKW/CH/CXG WD3 218 C7
Cedars Cl BORE WD6 223 K4
CFSP/GDCR SL9 226 B4
Cedar Wk HHS/BOV HP3 164 C8
Cedar Wy BERK HP4 162 A6 1
Cedar Wood Dr GSTN WD25 204 C5
Cedarwood Dr STALE/WH AL4 169 G6
Celandine Dr LTNN/LIM LU3 69 F1
Cell Barnes Cl STAL AL1 168 E8 1
Cell Barnes La STAL AL1 11 F5
Cemetery Hl HHW HP1 164 B7
Cemetery Rd BSF CM23 105 J4
Cemmaes Court Rd HHW HP1 164 B5
Cemmaes Meadow HHW HP1 164 B6
Central Av CHES/WCR EN8 214 D3
DUN/WHIP LU6 113 G1
Central Dr STAL AL1 169 F5
WGCE AL7 148 A1
Central Rd HLW CM20 156 D5
Central Wy NTHWD HA6 229 K6 2
Centre Wy WAB EN9 215 H5
Century Rd HOD EN11 177 F2
WARE SG12 127 H7 2
Cervantes Ct NTHWD HA6 230 A6 1
Chace Av POTB/CUF EN6 210 E2
The Chace STVGE SG2 76 A8
Chad La STALW/RED AL3 116 C4
Chadwell WARE SG12 152 B1
Chadwell Av CHES/WCR EN8 197 G6
Chadwell Cl LTNE LU2 5 D2 1
Chadwell Ri WARE SG12 152 B1
Chadwell Rd STVG SG1 75 G5
Chaffinches Gn HHS/BOV HP3 186 A2 1
Chaffinch La WATW WD18 12 A6
Chagney Cl LWTH SG6 41 J3
Chain Wk BLDK SG7 19 F7
BUNT SG9 29 K8

BUNT SG9 .... 45 K3
CHESW EN7 .... 196 A8
ENC/FH EN2 .... 212 D6
HERT/BAY SG13 .... 173 H1
HERT/WAS SG14 .... 98 A2
HERT/WAS SG14 .... 124 C7
HERT/WAS SG14 .... 149 H7
ROY SG8 .... 19 H6
ROY SG8 .... 30 C3
STVGE SG2 .... 78 B8
WARE SG12 .... 99 K8
Chalet Cl BERK HP4 .... 161 G5
Chalfont Av AMS HP6 .... 216 A1
Chalfont Cl HHNE HP2 .... 165 G1
Chalfont La RKW/CH/CXG WD3 .... 216 E5
  RKW/CH/CXG WD3 .... 227 F6
Chalfont Rd CFSP/GDCR SL9 .... 226 E2
Chalfont Wy LTNE LU2 .... 70 D7
Chalgrove WGCE AL7 .... 148 E2
Chalk Dl WGCE AL7 .... 148 C2
Chalkdell Flds STAL AL1 .... 11 F1
Chalkdell Hl HHNE HP2 .... 8 B5
Chalkdown LTNE LU2 .... 69 J2
  STVGE SG2 .... 76 E2
Chalk Fld LWTH SG6 .... 42 C6
Chalk Hl LTNE LU2 .... 71 G5
  OXHEY WD19 .... 13 F5
Chalk Hills BLDK SG7 .... 43 F4
Chalk La CMI7 .... 157 K7
Chalks Av SBW CM21 .... 132 B6
Challinor HLWE CM17 .... 181 H1
Challney Cl LTNW/LEA LU4 .... 68 C7
Chalton Rd LTNW/LEA LU4 .... 68 B4
Chamberlain Cl HLWE CM17 .... 181 F1
Chamberlaines HARP AL5 .... 117 G4
Chambersbury La HHS/BOV HP3 .... 186 A1
Chambers Ga STVG SG1 .... 2 B1
Chambers La HTCH/STOT SG5 .... 40 C5
Chambers' St HERT/WAS SG14 .... 151 F5
Champions Cl BORE WD6 .... 208 A7
Champions Wy HOD EN11 .... 153 F8
Chancellors Rd STVG SG1 .... 58 C8
Chancery Cl STALE/WH AL4 .... 169 G1
Chandler's La RKW/CH/CXG WD3 .... 202 D7
Chandlers Rd STALE/WH AL4 .... 169 F3
Chandlers Wy HERT/WAS SG14 .... 150 D5
Chandos Rd BORE WD6 .... 223 J2
  LTNW/LEA LU4 .... 68 E8
Chantry Cl BSF CM23 .... 105 F5
  ENC/FH EN2 .... 213 F8
  KGLGY WD4 .... 186 A7
Chantry La HAT AL10 .... 170 E5
  HTCHE/RSTV SG4 .... 57 K7
  LCOL/BKTW AL2 .... 190 B4
Chantry Rd BSF CM23 .... 105 H1
  KTN/HRWW/W HA3 .... 231 J7
The Chantry HLW CM20 .... 7 F1
Chaomans LWTH SG6 .... 41 K6
Chapel Cl BERK HP4 .... 138 A3
  GSTN WD25 .... 204 A4
  LTNE LU2 .... 69 H1
  STAL AL1 .... 189 F1
Chapel Cottages HHNE HP2 .... 8 A4
Chapel Cft KGLGY WD4 .... 201 K1
Chapel Crofts BERK HP4 .... 161 F3
Chapel End BUNT SG9 .... 63 J2
  HOD EN11 .... 177 F4
Chapel End La TRING HP23 .... 134 B1
Chapel Flds HLWE CM17 .... 181 F3
Chapelfields WARE SG12 .... 153 J4
Chapel Hl STSD CM24 .... 86 C2
Chapel La HERT/WAS SG14 .... 149 J7
  HLWE CM17 .... 181 F3
  STDN SG11 .... 103 H1
  TRING HP23 .... 109 F5
Chapel Pl HTCH/STOT SG5 .... 25 K4
Chapel Rd HTCHE/RSTV SG4 .... 72 B8
  STALW/RED AL3 .... 116 B7
Chapel Rw DEN/HRF UB9 .... 228 B7
Chapel St BERK HP4 .... 161 K5
  BLDK SG7 .... 16 D3
  HHNE HP2 .... 8 A4
  LTN LU1 .... 4 C4
  TRING HP23 .... 134 E6
Chapel Viad LTN LU1 .... 4 B4
Chapel Wy ABLGY WD5 .... 187 F5
Chapman Rd STVG SG1 .... 58 B8
Chapmans End STDN SG11 .... 81 J6
Chapmans Yd WAT WD17 .... 13 D3
Chappell Ct WARE SG12 .... 126 C2
Chappel Meadow TRING HP23 .... 135 G3
Chard Dr LTNN/LIM LU3 .... 52 B8
Chardins Cl HHW HP1 .... 163 J5
Charles Dr BERK HP4 .... 161 J5
  HHW HP1 .... 164 B7
  LTNE LU2 .... 5 D2
  TRING HP23 .... 135 F6
Charlesworth Cl HHS/BOV HP3 .... 164 C8
Charlock Wy WATW WD18 .... 12 A5
Charlotte Cl STALE/WH AL4 .... 169 H6
Charlton Cl HOD EN11 .... 177 F3
Charlton Mead La HOD EN11 .... 177 H4
Charlton Rd HTCH/STOT SG5 .... 56 B4

Charlton Wy HOD EN11 .... 177 F4
Charlwood Rd LTNW/LEA LU4 .... 68 A8
Charmbury Ri LTNE LU2 .... 70 B5
Charmouth Ct STAL AL1 .... 11 F1
Charmouth Rd STAL AL1 .... 11 F2
Charndon Rd LTNN/LIM LU3 .... 52 B8
Charnwood Rd EN EN1 .... 214 A6
Charters Cross HLWS CM18 .... 180 A1
Chartridge Cl BAR EN5 .... 225 J3
  BUSH WD23 .... 221 K6
Chartridge Wy HHNE HP2 .... 9 F5
Chartwell Cl WAB EN9 .... 215 K3
Chartwell Dr LTNE LU2 .... 69 K6
Chartwell Rd NTHWD HA6 .... 230 A5
Charwood Cl RAD WD7 .... 207 H3
Chasden Rd HHW HP1 .... 163 J3
Chase Cl ARL/CHE SG15 .... 24 E1
Chase Hill Rd ARL/CHE SG15 .... 24 E2
Chaseside Cl LBUZ LU7 .... 110 A2
Chase St LTN LU1 .... 4 C6
The Chase BSF CM23 .... 105 J3
  CHESW EN7 .... 195 K6
  HERT/BAY SG13 .... 151 J4
  HHNE HP2 .... 8 B6
  RAD WD7 .... 206 C5
  WARE SG12 .... 153 F3
  WATW WD18 .... 219 K4
  WLYN AL6 .... 123 F2
Chaseways SBW CM21 .... 156 E1
Chasten Hl LWTH SG6 .... 41 H2
Chatsworth Cl BORE WD6 .... 223 K3
  BSF CM23 .... 105 F2
Chatsworth Ct STVGE SG2 .... 76 A8
Chatsworth Rd LTNW/LEA LU4 .... 69 G8
Chatteris Cl LTNN/LIM LU3 .... 68 C5
Chatterton LWTH SG6 .... 42 B4
Chatton Cl LTNE LU2 .... 71 F7
Chaucer Cl BERK HP4 .... 161 G4
Chaucer Rd LTNN/LIM LU3 .... 4 A1
  ROY SG8 .... 21 G1
Chaucer Wk HHNE HP2 .... 141 G8
Chaucer Wy HOD EN11 .... 153 F7
  HTCHE/RSTV SG4 .... 57 G2
Chaulden House Gdns HHW HP1 .... 163 J8
Chaulden La HHW HP1 .... 163 H8
Chaulden Ter HHW HP1 .... 163 J8
Chaul End La LTNW/LEA LU4 .... 68 D8
Chaul End Rd LTN LU1 .... 68 A8
Chauncy Av POTB/CUF EN6 .... 210 D3
Chauncy Cl WARE SG12 .... 127 G6
Chauncy Gdns BLDK SG7 .... 27 H8
Chauncy Rd STVG SG1 .... 2 C2
Chaworth Gn LTNW/LEA LU4 .... 68 A4
Cheapside LTN LU1 .... 4 C4
Cheapside Sq LTN LU1 .... 4 C4
Chedburgh WGCE AL7 .... 148 E2
Cheddington La TRING HP23 .... 109 G4
Cheddington Rd LBUZ LU7 .... 110 B4
Cheffins Rd HOD EN11 .... 152 E8
Chells La STVGE SG2 .... 76 D1
Chells Wy STVGE SG2 .... 3 F1
Chelmsford Rd HERT/WAS SG14 .... 150 D4
Chelsea Flds HOD EN11 .... 153 G7
Chelsea Gdns HLWE CM17 .... 181 H2
Chelsing Ri HHNE HP2 .... 9 F6
Chelsworth Cl LTNE LU2 .... 70 E8
Chelveston WGCE AL7 .... 148 E2
Chelwood Av HAT AL10 .... 171 F2
Chelwood Cl NTHWD HA6 .... 229 H6
Cheney Rd LTNW/LEA LU4 .... 68 B4
Chenies Av AMS HP6 .... 216 A1
Chenies Ct HHNE HP2 .... 165 G1
Chenies Rd RKW/CH/CXG WD3 .... 217 G6
Chenies Wy WATW WD18 .... 219 K7
Chennells HAT AL10 .... 170 E5
Chennells Cl HTCHE/RSTV SG4 .... 41 F7
The Chennies HARP AL5 .... 143 K2
Chepstow Cl STVG SG1 .... 76 C1
Chequer La STALW/RED AL3 .... 142 B5
Chequers BRKMPK AL9 .... 175 J1
  BSF CM23 .... 105 F1
  WGCE AL7 .... 147 J5
Chequers Bridge Rd STVG SG1 .... 2 A2
Chequers Cl BUNT SG9 .... 63 H1
  HTCH/STOT SG5 .... 25 K3
  LBUZ LU7 .... 110 C5
Chequers Fld WGCE AL7 .... 147 J6
Chequers Hl STALW/RED AL3 .... 116 C3
Chequers La GSTN WD25 .... 187 H8
  HTCHE/RSTV SG4 .... 73 C2
  LBUZ LU7 .... 110 C5
Chequer St LTN LU1 .... 5 D5
  STAL AL1 .... 10 C4
Cheriton Cl STALE/WH AL4 .... 169 C2
Cherry Acre CFSP/GDCR SL9 .... 226 A3
Cherry Cl KNEB SG3 .... 96 A5
Cherry Cft WCCW AL8 .... 122 D7
Cherry Croft Gdns PIN HA5 .... 231 G6
Cherrydale WATW WD18 .... 12 A3
Cherry Dr ROY SG8 .... 21 J2
Cherry Gdns BSF CM23 .... 105 K1
  SBW CM21 .... 132 C5
Cherry Hl LCOL/BKTW AL2 .... 188 C5
  RKW/CH/CXG WD3 .... 218 A3
Cherry Hollow ABLGY WD5 .... 204 A1

Cherry Orch HHW HP1 .... 163 J4
Cherry Ri CSTG HP8 .... 226 A1
Cherry Rd PEND EN3 .... 214 B8
Cherry Tree Av LCOL/BKTW AL2 .... 190 B4
Cherry Tree Cl LTNE LU2 .... 5 E2
Cherry Tree Gn HERT/WAS SG14 .... 150 C1
Cherrytree La CFSP/GDCR SL9 .... 226 A8
Cherry Tree La HHNE HP2 .... 9 F2
Cherrytree La HHNE HP2 .... 165 H1
Cherry Tree La RKW/CH/CXG WD3 .... 217 F8
  STALE/WH AL4 .... 119 J7
Cherry Tree Ri STVGE SG2 .... 60 D8
Cherry Tree Rd HOD EN11 .... 177 F2
  WATN WD24 .... 204 C6
Cherry Wk RKW/CH/CXG WD3 .... 218 B2
Cherry Wy HAT AL10 .... 171 F7
Chertsey Cl LTNE LU2 .... 90 D7
Chertsey Ri STVGE SG2 .... 76 D5
Cherwell Cl RKW/CH/CXG WD3 .... 219 F5
Chesfield Cl BSF CM23 .... 105 J1
Chesford Rd LTNE LU2 .... 70 D5
Chesham La CFSP/GDCR SL9 .... 226 B3
Chesham Rd BERK HP4 .... 161 K6
  CSHM HP5 .... 182 B5
  HHS/BOV HP3 .... 183 G6
  TRING HP23 .... 135 J3
Chesham Wy WATW WD18 .... 219 K6
Cheshunt Wash CHES/WCR EN8 .... 197 J3
Cheslyn Cl LTNE LU2 .... 71 F7
Chess Cl CSHM HP5 .... 200 A6
  RKW/CH/CXG WD3 .... 218 C6
Chessfield Pk AMS HP6 .... 216 B7
Chess Hl RKW/CH/CXG WD3 .... 218 C6
Chess La RKW/CH/CXG WD3 .... 218 C6
Chess Vale Ri RKW/CH/CXG WD3 .... 218 E6
Chess Valley Wk CSHM HP5 .... 200 B3
Chess Wy RKW/CH/CXG WD3 .... 217 K3
Chesswood Wy PIN HA5 .... 230 E8
Chester Av LTNW/LEA LU4 .... 68 C5
Chester Cl LTNW/LEA LU4 .... 68 C5
Chesterfield Rd BAR EN5 .... 225 J2
  PEND EN3 .... 214 D7
Chester Rd BORE WD6 .... 224 B3
  NTHWD HA6 .... 230 A4
  STVG SG1 .... 59 G2
  WATW WD18 .... 12 B4
Chesterton Av HARP AL5 .... 118 E1
Chestnut Av NTHWD HA6 .... 230 A4
  RKW/CH/CXG WD3 .... 217 K2
  WARE SG12 .... 127 G4
Chestnut Cl BERK HP4 .... 112 E4
  BERK HP4 .... 162 E1
  BSF CM23 .... 105 J3
  CFSP/GDCR SL9 .... 226 C2
  WARE SG12 .... 129 K1
Chestnut Ct HTCH/STOT SG5 .... 56 B1
Chestnut Dr BERK HP4 .... 162 A1
  STAL AL1 .... 168 E2
Chestnut La TRDG/WHET N20 .... 225 K2
Chestnut Ri BUSH WD23 .... 221 J2
Chestnut Rd PEND EN3 .... 214 D7
The Chestnuts HERT/BAY SG13 .... 151 G2
  HHS/BOV HP3 .... 184 D1
  WLYN AL6 .... 94 E1
Chestnut Wk CFSP/GDCR SL9 .... 226 B6
  HTCHE/RSTV SG4 .... 56 E5
  STVG SG1 .... 58 D3
  WATN WD24 .... 204 B6
  WLYN AL6 .... 123 F2
Cheverells Cl STALW/RED AL3 .... 115 H1
Cheviot Cl BUSH WD23 .... 221 K5
Cheviot Rd LTNN/LIM LU3 .... 68 C3
Cheviots HAT AL10 .... 171 F2
  HHNE HP2 .... 8 C1
Cheyne Cl LBUZ LU7 .... 110 C3
  WARE SG12 .... 127 H4
Cheyney Cl ROY SG8 .... 15 J3
Cheyneys Wy ROY SG8 .... 15 J3
Chicheley Rd KTN/HRWW/W HA3 .... 231 K3
Chichester Wy GSTN WD25 .... 205 F3
Chicken La LCOL/BKTW AL2 .... 190 B5
Chilcott Rd WATN WD24 .... 203 A4
Chilcourt ROY SG8 .... 21 C
Childs Av DEN/HRF UB9 .... 228 B3
Childwick Ct HHS/BOV HP3 .... 186 B6
Chilham Ct HHS/BOV HP3 .... 8 E
Chiltern Av BUSH WD23 .... 221 K5
Chiltern Cl BERK HP4 .... 161 H4
  BORE WD6 .... 223 J2
  BUSH WD23 .... 221 K5
  CHESW EN7 .... 195 K6
  WARE SG12 .... 127 H4
Chiltern Dr RKW/CH/CXG WD3 .... 217 K2
Chiltern Gdns LTNW/LEA LU4 .... 68 A6
Chiltern Hl CFSP/GDCR SL9 .... 226 A6
Chiltern Park Av BERK HP4 .... 161 H3
Chiltern Ri LTN LU1 .... 4 A6
Chiltern Rd AMP/FLIT/B MK45 .... 36 C2
  BLDK SG7 .... 43 F2
  HTCHE/RSTV SG4 .... 56 E4
  WARE SG12 .... 127 H4
Chilterns HAT AL10 .... 169 F1
  HHNE HP2 .... 8 C1
The Chilterns DUN/WHIP LU6 .... 114 C7
  HTCHE/RSTV SG4 .... 56 E1

Chiltern Vw LWTH SG6 .... 41 H4
Chiltern Wy TRING HP23 .... 135 H4
Chilton Gn WGCE AL7 .... 148 D3
Chilvers Bank BLDK SG7 .... 42 E2
Chilwell Gdns OXHEY WD19 .... 230 D3
Chilworth Rd BROX EN10 .... 176 E8
Chindit Cl BROX EN10 .... 176 C6
Chinnery HI BSF CM23 .... 105 J4
Chipperfield Rd HHS/BOV HP3 .... 183 K6
  HHS/BOV HP3 .... 185 G2
  KGLGY WD4 .... 185 H7
Chipping Cl BAR EN5 .... 225 K3
Chippingfield HLWE CM17 .... 157 F6
Chishill Rd ROY SC8 .... 23 J7
Chiswell Ct WATN WD24 .... 204 D8
Chiswellgreen La LCOL/BKTW AL2 .. 188 A3
Chittenden Cl HOD EN11 .... 153 G8
Chobham St LTN LU1 .... 5 D5
Cholesbury La TRING HP23 .... 159 F7
Church Langley Wy HLWE CM17 ..... 181 F1
Church Leys HLWS CM18 .... 7 E5
Church Md DUN/WHIP LU6 .... 113 K5
  HLWW/ROY CM19 .... 154 C8
Church Pth HTCHE/RSTV SG4 .... 57 K6
Church Pl WLYN AL6 .... 122 C4
Church Rd AMP/FLIT/B MK45 .... 36 C7
  BERK HP4 .... 137 K1
  BERK HP4 .... 137 J4
  DUN/WHIP LU6 .... 113 K5
  HERT/BAY SG13 .... 173 K5
  HERT/WAS SG14 .... 150 E2
  HHS/BOV HP3 .... 9 F6
  HLWE CM17 .... 181 F4
  HTCH/STOT SG5 .... 25 K3
  HTCHE/RSTV SG4 .... 72 B6
  LBUZ LU7 .... 110 E4
  LTN LU1 .... 89 H7
  LTNN/LIM LU3 .... 52 A3
  NTHWD HA6 .... 230 A6
  POTB/CUF EN6 .... 193 H8
  RBSF CM22 .... 106 B7
  RBSF CM22 .... 107 F4
  STALW/RED AL3 .... 116 B7
  STSD CM24 .... 86 C4
  WAT WD17 .... 220 B1
  WGCW AL8 .... 147 J3
Church Rw BROX EN10 .... 176 E6
  TRING HP23 .... 108 E5
Church Wk BUSH WD23 .... 221 H6
  SBW CM21 .... 132 C7
Church Yd TRING HP23 .... 135 F5
Cicero Dr LTNN/LIM LU3 .... 69 F1
Cillocks Cl HOD EN11 .... 177 F2
Claggy Rd HTCHE/RSTV SG4 .... 92 C7
Clapgate Rd BUSH WD23 .... 221 J6
Clare Cl BORE WD6 .... 223 J6
Clare Ct NTHWD HA6 .... 229 H3
Clare Crs BLDK SG7 .... 43 F3
Claremont CHESW EN7 .... 196 D7
  LCOL/BKTW AL2 .... 205 H1
Claremont Crs RKW/CH/CXG WD3 ... 219 H5
Claremont Rd EBAR EN4 .... 210 D8
  LTNW/LEA LU4 .... 69 G8
Clarence Cl BUSH WD23 .... 222 C7
Clarence Rd BERK HP4 .... 161 K5
  HARP AL5 .... 118 C7
  STAL AL1 .... 11 F4
  STSD CM24 .... 86 D2
Clarendon Cl HHNE HP2 .... 8 B4
Clarendon Ms BORE WD6 .... 223 K3
Clarendon Rd BORE WD6 .... 223 K3
  CHES/WCR EN8 .... 197 H7
  HARP AL5 .... 118 D6
  LTNE LU2 .... 4 C2
  WAT WD17 .... 12 C2
Clarion Cl HTCH/STOT SG5 .... 54 E7
Clarke's Rd HAT AL10 .... 171 G2
Clarke's Spring TRING HP23 .... 136 A4
Clarke Wy GSTN WD25 .... 204 C6
Clarkfield RKW/CH/CXG WD3 .... 217 K8
Clarkhill HLWS CM18 .... 180 B5
Clark Rd ROY SG8 .... 21 H2
Clarks Cl WARE SG12 .... 127 H6
Clarks Md BUSH WD23 .... 221 K7
Claudian Pl STALW/RED AL3 .... 167 H7
Claverhambury Rd WAB EN9 .... 199 F7
Claverley Gn LTNE LU2 .... 71 F7
Claverton Cl HHS/BOV HP3 .... 183 J7
Claybury BUSH WD23 .... 221 J7
Claybush Rd BLDK SG7 .... 17 K6
Claycroft WGCE AL7 .... 148 C2
Claydon Cl LTNN/LIM LU3 .... 69 J2
Claydown Wy LTN LU1 .... 89 G8
Claygate Av HARP AL5 .... 118 A7
Clay Hall Rd DUN/WHIP LU6 .... 114 D2
Clay HI ENC/FH EN2 .... 213 F7
Clay La BUSH WD23 .... 222 B7
Claymore HHNE HP2 .... 8 B1
Claymore Dr HTCH/STOT SG5 .... 40 D4
Claymores STVG SG1 .... 2 C2
Claypit HI RBSF CM22 .... 87 K4
Clayponds BSF CM23 .... 105 K2
Cleall Av WAB EN9 .... 215 H4
The Cleave HARP AL5 .... 119 F8
Clement Rd CHES/WCR EN8 .... 197 J5
Clements End Rd DUN/WHIP LU6 .. 114 C7
Clements Rd RKW/CH/CXG WD3 .... 217 G5
Clements St WARE SG12 .... 127 J8
Clevedon Rd LTNE LU2 .... 5 F1
Cleveland Crs BORE WD6 .... 224 B5
Cleveland Rd HHNE HP2 .... 9 E3
  STALW/RED AL3 .... 115 J4
Cleves Rd HHNE HP2 .... 165 G1
Clewiscroft STVG SG1 .... 2 C4
Clifford Crs LTNW/LEA LU4 .... 68 B4
Clifton Cl CHES/WCR EN8 .... 197 J7
Clifton Hatch HLWS CM18 .... 180 D4
Clifton Rd LTN LU1 .... 89 G1
  WATW WD18 .... 12 C4
Clifton St STAL AL1 .... 11 D3
Clifton Wy BORE WD6 .... 223 K1
  WARE SG12 .... 127 H6
The Climb RKW/CH/CXG WD3 .... 218 A6
Clinton Av LTNE LU2 .... 70 A5
Clinton End HHNE HP2 .... 9 F5
Clitheroe Gdns OXHEY WD19 .... 230 E2
Clive Cl POTB/CUF EN6 .... 210 A1
Clive Wy WATN WD24 .... 220 D1
Cloister Garth BERK HP4 .... 161 K5
  STAL AL1 .... 189 C2
Cloister Lawns LWTH SG6 .... 41 K5
Cloisters Rd LTNW/LEA LU4 .... 68 A6
The Cloisters RKW/CH/CXG WD3 ... 218 D7
  WGCW AL8 .... 147 J3
Clonard Wy PIN HA5 .... 231 H5
Closemead Cl NTHWD HA6 .... 229 H5
The Close BLDK SG7 .... 42 E2
  BRKMPK AL9 .... 192 E4
  BUNT SG9 .... 45 F3
  BUSH WD23 .... 221 J6
  HARP AL5 .... 117 K5
  LTNN/LIM LU3 .... 69 F4
  POTB/CUF EN6 .... 210 B2
  RAD WD7 .... 206 C3
  RKW/CH/CXG WD3 .... 218 A8
  ROY SG8 .... 21 K2
  STAL AL1 .... 188 E1
  STALW/RED AL3 .... 115 J4
  WARE SG12 .... 127 J8
  WLYN AL6 .... 94 E8
Clothall Rd BLDK SG7 .... 43 F1
Clovelly Wy STVG SG1 .... 75 F2
Clover Av BSF CM23 .... 104 E3
Clover Fld HLWS CM18 .... 180 D4
Cloverfield WGCE AL7 .... 123 F6
The Clover Fld BUSH WD23 .... 221 G6
Cloverland HAT AL10 .... 170 E7
Clover Wy HHW HP1 .... 164 A5
The Clump RKW/CH/CXG WD3 ...... 217 K5
Clusterbolts HERT/WAS SG14 .... 125 J3
Clutterbucks RKW/CH/CXG WD3 ... 201 K6
Clyde Rd HOD EN11 .... 177 J5
Clydesdale Cl BORE WD6 .... 224 C5
Clydesdale Rd ROY SG8 .... 21 J3
Clyde Sq HHNE HP2 .... 164 E1
Clyde Ter HERT/BAY SG13 .... 151 K3
Clyfton Cl BROX EN10 .... 197 K1
Clyston Rd WATW WD18 .... 12 A5
Coach Dr HTCHE/RSTV SG4 .... 56 D4
The Coach House
  AMP/FLIT/B MK45 .... 36 C6
Coachman's La BLDK SG7 .... 42 D1
Coalport Cl HLWE CM17 .... 181 F2
Coates Dell GSTN WD25 .... 205 F3
Coates Rd BORE WD6 .... 223 G7
Coates Wy GSTN WD25 .... 204 E3
Cobbett Cl PEND EN3 .... 214 B6
Cobbetts Ride TRING HP23 .... 134 E6
Cobb Gn GSTN WD25 .... 204 C2
Cobbinsend Rd WAB EN9 .... 199 K7
The Cobbins WAB EN9 .... 215 K2
Cobbins Wy HLWE CM17 .... 157 H5
Cobb Rd BERK HP4 .... 161 G5
Cob Cl BORE WD6 .... 224 B5
Cobden HI RAD WD7 .... 206 E6
Cobden St LTNE LU2 .... 4 C2
Cobham Rd WARE SG12 .... 127 K7
Cobmead HAT AL10 .... 171 G2
Cockbush Av HERT/BAY SG13 .... 151 K2
Cocker Rd EN EN1 .... 214 A6
Cockfosters Rd EBAR EN4 .... 211 G8
Cock La BROX EN10 .... 176 B5
  SAFWS CB11 .... 51 H6
Cockle Wy RAD WD7 .... 207 H3
Cockrobin La HLW CM20 .... 155 H2
Codicote Dr GSTN WD25 .... 204 E4
Codicote Rd HTCHE/RSTV SG4 .... 93 J3
  STALW/RED AL3 .... 120 D8
  WLYN AL6 .... 120 D7
Codicote Rw HHNE HP2 .... 165 F1
Codmore Crs CSHM HP5 .... 182 A8
Cogmore SAFWS CB11 .... 35 K2
Cohen Cl CHES/WCR EN8 .... 214 D2
Colburn Av PIN HA5 .... 231 F5
Colchester Rd NTHWD HA6 .... 230 B8

Cold Christmas La *WARE* SG12 .... 127 H3
Coldham Gv *PEND* EN3 .... 214 D7 ⬚
Coldharbour La *BUSH* WD23 .... 221 J6
   HARP AL5 .... 118 D5
Coldharbour Rd
   HLWW/ROY CM19 .... 179 K2
Colebrook Av *LTNN/LIM* LU3 ..... 68 B2
Cole Green La *WGCE* AL7 .... 148 A5
Cole Green Wy *HERT/WAS* SG14 ... 150 D5
Coleman Green La *STALE/WH* AL4 .. 145 J4
Coleman's La *WAB* EN9 .... 198 D4
Colemans Rd *HTCHE/RSTV* SG4 ...... 72 A8
Coleridge Cl *CHESW* EN7 .... 196 C5
   HTCHE/RSTV SG4 .... 57 F1
Coleridge La *HHNE* HP2 .... 141 G8
Colesdale *POTB/CUF* EN6 .... 195 G8
Coles Hl *HHW* HP1 .... 163 K4
Colestrete *STVG* SG1 .... 3 D4
Colestrete Cl *STVG* SG1 .... 3 D3
Coleswood Rd *HARP* AL5 .... 143 K2
Colgrove *WGCW* AL8 .... 147 H4
Colindale Av *STAL* AL1 .... 11 E6
Colin Rd *LTNE* LU2 .... 5 D1
College Ct *CHES/WCR* EN8 .... 197 G8 ⬚
College Gn *BSF* CM23 .... 105 G2
   STALW/RED AL3 .... 116 B8
   WARE SG12 .... 152 C1 ⬚
College La *HAT* AL10 .... 170 D5
College Pl *HERT/BAY* AL3 .... 10 B4
College Rd *ABLGY* WD5 .... 204 B1
   CHES/WCR EN8. .... 197 G8
   CHESW EN7 .... 197 F8
   HERT/BAY SG14 .... 152 D7
   HOD EN11 .... 176 E1
   STAL AL1 .... 168 E7
College Sq *HLW* CM20 .... 6 C4 ⬚
College St *STALW/RED* AL3 .... 10 C4
College Wy *NTHWD* HA6 .... 229 J5
   WGCW AL8. .... 147 J2
Collens Rd *HARP* AL5 .... 143 J4
Collenswood Rd *STVGE* SG2 .... 3 F4
Collet Cl *CHES/WCR* EN8. .... 197 H6
Collett Rd *HHW* HP1 .... 164 B6
   WARE SG12 .... 127 H7
Colley Land *RKW/CH/CXG* WD3 ... 217 G4
Collingdon St *LTN* LU1 .... 4 B3
Collingtree *LTNE* LU2 .... 70 C5 ⬚
Collingwood Dr
   LCOL/BKTW AL2 .... 190 B3
Collins Cross *BSF* CM23 .... 86 A8
Collins Meadow *HLWW/ROY* CM19... 6 A4
Collison Cl *HTCHE/RSTV* SG4 .... 41 G7
Collyer Rd *LCOL/BKTW* AL2 ..... 190 B5
Colnbrook Cl *LCOL/BKTW* AL2 ... 190 C5
Colne Av *OXHEY* WD19 .... 12 C5
   RKW/CH/CXG WD3 .... 227 K1
Colne Gdns *LCOL/BKTW* AL2 ..... 190 C5
Colne Md *RKW/CH/CXG* WD3 ..... 227 K1
Colne Valley Trail
   RKW/CH/CXG WD3 .... 228 B1
Colne Wy *HHNE* HP2 .... 164 C1
Colney Heath La *STALE/WH* AL4 .. 169 H7
Colonial Wy *WATN* WD24 .... 220 D1
The Colonnade *CHES/WCR* EN8 .. 197 H6 ⬚
Colonsay *HHS/BOV* HP3 .... 165 H8
Colston Crs *CHESW* EN7 .... 195 K5
Colts Cnr *STVGE* SG2 .... 3 F4
Coltsfield *STSD* CM24 .... 86 D2
Coltsfoot *WGCE* AL7 .... 148 C5
Coltsfoot Dr *ROY* SG8 .... 21 J3
Coltsfoot La *KNEB* SG3 .... 123 K2
Coltsfoot Rd *WARE* SG12 .... 127 J6
The Coltsfoot *HHW* HP1 .... 163 H4
The Colts *BSF* CM23 .... 105 H6
Columbus Cl *STVG* SG1 .... 3 E1
Columbus Gdns *NTHWD* HA6 ..... 230 B7 ⬚
Colvin Gdns *CHES/WCR* EN8 ..... 214 C8
Colwell Ri *LTNE* LU2 .... 71 F7
Colwell Rd *STVGE* SG2 .... 76 D6
Colwyn Cl *STVG* SG1 .... 75 C1
Colyer Cl *WLYN* AL6 .... 123 F6
Combe Rd *WAT* WD18 .... 12 A5
Combe St *HHW* HP1 .... 164 B6 ⬚
Comet Cl *GSTN* WD25 .... 204 A4
Comet Rd *HAT* AL10 .... 170 E4
Comet Wy *HAT* AL10 .... 170 D4
Common Fld *TRING* HP23 .... 135 J8
Commonfields *HLW* CM20 .... 7 D3
Common Gdns *BERK* HP4 .... 162 B3
Common Gate Rd
   RKW/CH/CXG WD3 .... 217 G5
Common La *BLDK* SG7 .... 17 H3
   GSTN WD25 .... 206 B8
   HARP AL5. .... 119 F4
   HTCHE/RSTV SG4 .... 92 E8
   KGLGY WD4 .... 185 K6
   ROY SG8 .... 34 D2
Common Ri *HTCHE/RSTV* SG4 .... 40 E8
Common Rd *DUN/WHIP* LU6 ..... 113 J6
   HTCH/STOT SG5 .... 25 J1
   RKW/CH/CXG WD3 .... 217 G4
   WAB EN9 .... 179 F7
Commonside Rd *HLWS* CM18 ..... 180 C5

Commons La *HHNE* HP2 .... 8 B4
The Commons *WCCE* AL7 .... 148 B6
The Common *BERK* HP4. .... 162 C3
   HARP AL5. .... 117 H5
   HAT AL10 .... 171 F3
   KGLGY WD4 .... 201 K2
Common Vw *LWTH* SG6 .... 42 A1
Common Whf *WARE* SG12 .... 127 J8 ⬚
Compton Av *LTNW/LEA* LU4 .... 68 C5
Compton Gdns *LCOL/BKTW* AL2 .. 188 D4
Compton Pl *OXHEY* WD19 .... 231 F3
Comyne Rd *WATN* WD24 .... 204 A6
The Comyns *BUSH* WD23 .... 221 K8
Concorde Dr *HHNE* HP2 .... 8 A5 ⬚
Concorde St *LTNE* LU2 .... 5 D3
Conduit La *BUNT* SG9 .... 49 J8 ⬚
   HOD EN11 .... 177 F3
Conduit La East *HOD* EN11 ..... 177 G3
Coney Cl *HAT* AL10 .... 171 G6 ⬚
Coneydale *WGCW* AL8 .... 147 J1
Coney Gn *SBW* CM21 .... 132 B6
Congreve Rd *WAB* EN9 .... 215 K3
Conifer Cl *CHESW* EN7 .... 196 D7
The Conifers *GSTN* WD25 .... 204 D5 ⬚
Conifer Wk *STVGE* SG2 .... 76 D2
Coningesby Dr *WAT* WD17 .... 219 K1
Coningsby Bank *STAL* AL1 .... 188 E2
Coningsby Cl *BRKMPK* AL9 ..... 192 D2 ⬚
Coningsby Dr *POTB/CUF* EN6 .... 210 E3
   HHS/BOV HP3 .... 9 F6 ⬚
Coniston Rd *KGLGY* WD4 .... 185 K6
   LTNN/LIM LU3 .... 68 E4
Connaught Cl *HHNE* HP2 .... 9 D3
Connaught Gdns *BERK* HP4 ..... 161 G2 ⬚
Connaught Rd *BAR* EN5 .... 225 J2
   HARP AL5. .... 118 D7 ⬚
   LTNW/LEA LU4 .... 68 E8
   STALW/RED AL3 .... 10 B2
Connemara Cl *BORE* WD6 .... 224 C6 ⬚
Conner's Cl *ROY* SG8 .... 15 C5
Connop Rd *PEND* EN3 .... 214 C8
Conquerors Hl *STALE/WH* AL4 .. 145 H1
Conquest Cl *HTCHE/RSTV* SG4 ... 56 D4
Constantine Cl *STVG* SG1 .... 59 F8 ⬚
Constantine Pl *BLDK* SG7 .... 27 H8 ⬚
Convent Cl *HTCH/STOT* SG5 ..... 56 D1
Conway Gdns *ENC/FH* EN2 ..... 213 H8
Conway Rd *LTNW/LEA* LU4 ..... 69 G8
Conyers *HLW* CM20 .... 6 B2
Cook Rd *STVGE* SG2 .... 5 F1
Cook's Hole Rd *ENC/FH* EN2 .... 212 E8
Cooks Md *BUSH* WD23 .... 221 J6
Cooks Spinney *HLW* CM20 .... 7 F2
Cooks Vennel *HHW* HP1 .... 164 A4 ⬚
Cooks Wy *HAT* AL10 .... 171 G6
   HTCHE/RSTV SG4 .... 40 E8
Coombe Av *BERK* HP4 .... 161 G4
Coombe Hill Rd
   RKW/CH/CXG WD3 .... 217 K2 ⬚
Coombelands Rd *ROY* SG8 .... 21 J1
Coombe Rd *BUSH* WD23 .... 221 K7
   ROY SG8. .... 19 K8
Coombes Rd *LCOL/BKTW* AL2 ... 190 A4
Coopers Cl *BSF* CM23 .... 104 E5
   HTCHE/RSTV SG4 .... 119 K1
   STVGE SG2 .... 76 E1
Coopers Crs *BORE* WD6 .... 224 B1
Coopers Green La *HAT* AL10 ..... 146 B8
   STALE/WH AL4 .... 169 J3
   WGCW AL8. .... 146 E7
Cooper's Hl *HTCHE/RSTV* SG4 ... 92 E8
Coopers La *POTB/CUF* EN6 ..... 194 A7
Coopers Lane Rd *POTB/CUF* EN6 .. 211 H3
Coopers Meadow *STALW/RED* AL3.. 142 B3
Coopers Rd *POTB/CUF* EN6 ..... 193 J8
Cooters End La *HARP* AL5 .... 118 B5
Copenhagen Cl *LTNN/LIM* LU3 ... 68 C1
Copmans Wick *RKW/CH/CXG* WD3.. 217 G5
The Coppens *HOD* EN11 .... 153 F8 ⬚
Coppins Cl *BERK* HP4 .... 161 F5
The Coppins *STALW/RED* AL3 .... 115 H4
Copse Cl *NTHWD* HA6 .... 229 H7
Copse Hl *HLWW/ROY* CM19 ..... 179 J4
   WLYN AL6 .... 123 C1
Copse Hill Cl *HHS/BOV* HP3 ..... 184 B6
The Copse *BSF* CM23 .... 106 B1 ⬚
   HERT/BAY SG13 .... 151 K3
   HHW HP1 .... 163 H4
Copse Wy *LTNN/LIM* LU3 .... 68 C1
Copsewood Rd *WATN* WD24 ..... 220 C1

Copse Wood Wy *NTHWD* HA6 .... 229 H7
Copthall Cl *HLWS* CM18 .... 180 B5
Copthall Dr *CFSP/GDCR* SL9 ..... 226 C6
Copthall Cnr *CFSP/GDCR* SL9. ... 226 B6
Copthall La *CFSP/GDCR* SL9. ... 226 B6
Copthorne *LTNE* LU2............. 70 E6
Copthorne Av *BROX* EN10 .... 176 E2
Copthorne Cl
   RKW/CH/CXG WD3 .... 218 E5 ⬚
Copthorne Rd *RKW/CH/CXG* WD3.. 218 E6
Coral Gdns *HHNE* HP2 .... 8 C4 ⬚
Corals Md *WCCE* AL7 .... 147 J4
Coram Cl *BERK* HP4 .... 161 K6
Corbar Cl *EBAR* EN4 .... 210 E8
Corbridge Dr *LTNE* LU2 .... 71 F7
Corby Cl *LCOL/BKTW* AL2 .... 188 C3
Cordell Cl *CHES/WCR* EN8 .... 197 J6 ⬚
Corder Cl *STALW/RED* AL3 .... 188 C1
Coreys Mill La *STVG* SG1 .... 58 B8
Corfe Cl *HHS/BOV* HP3 .... 8 B6 ⬚
Corinium Gdns *LTNN/LIM* LU3 ... 69 F1 ⬚
Corinium Rd *STALW/RED* AL3 .... 167 H8
Corncastle Rd *LTN* LU1 .... 4 A5
Corncrake Cl *LTNE* LU2 .... 70 D4
Corncroft *HAT* AL10 .... 171 G2 ⬚
Cornel Cl *LTN* LU1 .... 89 F2
Cornerfield *HAT* AL10 .... 171 G1
Corner Hall *HHS/BOV* HP3 .... 164 C8 ⬚
Corner Hall Av *HHS/BOV* HP3 ... 164 C8
Corner Meadow *HLWS* CM18 .... 180 D5
Corners *WCCE* AL7 .... 148 B2 ⬚
Corner Wd *STALW/RED* AL3 ..... 115 H4
Cornfield Crs *BERK* HP4 .... 160 E2
Cornfield Rd *BUSH* WD23 .... 221 J4
Cornfields *HHW* HP1 .... 164 A7
   STVGE SG2 .... 76 D2
Cornhill Dr *PEND* EN3 .... 214 D7 ⬚
Corn Md *WGCW* AL8 .... 122 C6
Cornwall Cl *CHES/WCR* EN8 .... 214 D3
Cornwall Rd *HARP* AL5 .... 118 D2
   PIN HA5 .... 231 G2 ⬚
   STAL AL1 .... 11 D6
Coronation Av *ROY* SG8 .... 21 G4
Coronation Rd *BSF* CM23 .... 105 H4
   WARE SG12 .... 127 H7
Corringham Ct *STAL* AL1 .... 11 E3 ⬚
Corton Cl *STVG* SG1 .... 75 C7
Cory-wright Wy *STALE/WH* AL4 .. 120 C9
Cosgrove Wy *LTN* LU1 .... 88 C5
Cotefield *LTNW/LEA* LU4 .... 68 B6 ⬚
Cotesmore Rd *HHW* HP1 .... 163 H1
Cotlandswick *LCOL/BKTW* AL2 ... 190 A3
Cotney Cft *STVGE* SG2 .... 76 E6
Cotswold Av *BUSH* WD23 .... 221 K6
Cotswold Business Pk *LTN*... LU1..... 88 C
Cotswold Cl *STALE/WH* AL4 ..... 169 F1 ⬚
Cotswold Gdns *LTNN/LIM* LU3... 68 B
Cotswolds *HAT* AL10 .... 171 F
Cottage Cl *RKW/CH/CXG* WD3 ... 218 E
   WAT WD17 .... 12 A
Cottage Gdns *CHES/WCR* EN8. ... 197 G
Cottered Rd *BUNT* SG9 .... 46 D
Cotterells *HHS/BOV* HP3 .... 164 B8 ⬚
   HHW HP1 .... 164 B
Cotterells Hi *HHW* HP1 .... 164 B
Cotton Dr *HERT/BAY* SG13 ..... 152 A2 ⬚
Cotton Fld *HAT* AL10 .... 171 G
Cottonmill Crs *STAL* AL1 .... 10 C
Cottonmill La *STAL* AL1. .... 10 C
Cotton Rd *POTB/CUF* EN6 .... 210 D
Coulser Cl *HHW* HP1 .... 163 K
Coulter Cl *POTB/CUF* EN6 .... 195 F
Council Rd *BSF* CM23 .... 106 A
Counters Cl *HHW* HP1 .... 163 K
Countess Cl *DEN/HRF* UB9 ..... 228 B8
Coursers Rd *STALE/WH* AL4 ..... 190 E
Courtaulds *KGLGY* WD4 .... 185 F
Courtenay Av *KTN/HRWW/W* HA3 .. 231 J
Courtfield Cl *BROX* EN10 .... 177 F6
Courtfields *HARP* AL5 .... 119 F
Courtlands *WATN* WD24 .... 203 K
Courtlands Dr *WAT* WD17 .... 203 K
Courtleigh Av *EBAR* EN4 .... 210 E
The Courtway *OXHEY* WD19 ..... 231 F
The Courtyard *STALE/WH* AL4 ... 169 J
Covent Garden Cl *LTNW/LEA* LU4 .. 68 E
Coventry Cl *STVG* SG1 .... 59 H
Coverdale *LTNW/LEA* LU4 .... 68 A
Covert Cl *BERK* HP4 .... 160 E
Covert Rd *BERK* HP4 .... 160 E
The Covert *NTHWD* HA6 .... 229 H
Cowards La *WLYN* AL6 .... 121 K
Cowbridge *HERT/WAS* SG14 ..... 151 F
Cowdray Cl *LTNE* LU2 .... 70 D6
Cow La *BUSH* WD23 .... 221 H6
   GSTN WD25 .... 204 D
   TRING HP23 .... 135 J
Cowles *CHESW* EN7 .... 196 D
Cowley Hl *BORE* WD6 .... 207 K
Cowlins *HLWE* CM17 .... 157 G5
Cowper Ct *STALW/RED* AL3 ..... 115 H
   WATN WD24 .... 204 B7
Cowper Crs *HERT/WAS* SG14 ..... 125 K
Cowper Ri *STALW/RED* AL3 .... 115 J
Cowper Rd *BERK* HP4 .... 161 G

HARP AL5 118 D8
HHW HP1 164 A7
STALW/RED AL3 115 H4
WGCE AL7 148 A5
Cowper St LTN LU1 4 C6
Cowpers Wy WLYN AL6 123 K4
Cowridge Crs LTNE LU2 5 E3
Cowslip Hl LWTH SG6 41 J2
Cox Cl RAD WD7 207 H2
Cox's Wy ARL/CHE SG15 24 E4
Coyney Gn LTNN/LIM LU3 4 A2
Cozens La East BROX EN10 176 E8
Cozens La West BROX EN10 176 D8
Cozens Rd WARE SG12 127 K7
Crabb's La BUNT SG9 67 G2
Crab La GSTN WD25 205 J4
Crabtree Cl BUSH WD23 221 J5
HHS/BOV HP3 164 C8
Crabtree Dell LWTH SG6 42 C6
Crabtree La HARP AL5 119 F8
HHS/BOV HP3 164 C8
Crab Tree La HTCH/STOT SG5 39 F5
Crab Tree Rd KNEB SG3 96 A6
Crackley Meadow HHNE HP2 165 G1 3
Cradock Rd LTNW/LEA LU4 68 A8
Craft Wy ROY SG8 15 J7
Cragg Av RAD WD7 206 C6
Cragside KNEB SG3 96 D2 1
Craigavon Rd HHNE HP2 8 C1
Craiglands STALE/WH AL4 169 G2
Craig Mt RAD WD7 206 E5
Craigs Wk CHES/WCR EN8 197 H6
Craigweil Av RAD WD7 206 E5
Cranborne Av HTCH/STOT SG5 56 B3
Cranborne Cl HERT/BAY SG13 151 F6
POTB/CUF EN6 209 K1
Cranborne Crs POTB/CUF EN6 209 K1
Cranborne Gdns WGCE AL7 148 A4 1
Cranborne Rd CHES/WCR EN8 214 C2 1
HAT AL10 171 G3
HOD EN11 177 G2
POTB/CUF EN6 192 E8
Cranbourne Dr HARP AL5 143 K3
HOD EN11 153 G7
Cranbrook Cl WARE SG12 127 H6 1
Cranbrook Dr LTNN/LIM LU3 68 C1
STALE/WH AL4 169 H6
Cranefield Dr GSTN WD25 205 F2
Crane Md WARE SG12 152 D1
Cranes Wy BORE WD6 224 B5
Cranfield Crs POTB/CUF EN6 195 G7
Cranleigh Cl CHESW EN7 196 E6
Cranleigh Gdns LTNN/LIM LU3 69 H6
Cranmer Cl POTB/CUF EN6 193 J8
Cranwell Gdns BSF CM23 86 B8
Cravells Rd HARP AL5 143 K3
Crawford Rd HAT AL10 171 F2
Crawley Cl LTN LU1 89 H8
Crawley Dr HHNE HP2 8 C1
Crawley Green Rd LTNE LU2 5 E4
Crawley Rd LTN LU1 4 B3
Crawley's La TRING HP23 159 K2
Creamery Ct LWTH SG6 42 C6
Crecy Gdns STALW/RED AL3 142 B3
Creighton Av STAL AL1 189 F2
Crescent East EBAR EN4 210 D8
Crescent Ri LTNE LU2 5 D3
Crescent Rd BSF CM23 105 K3
HHNE HP2 8 A5
LTNE LU2 5 D3
The Crescent ABLGY WD5 187 F8
BUNT SG9 62 A2
GSTN WD25 205 J8
HLWE CM17 157 F3
HTCH/STOT SG5 40 B8
HTCHE/RSTV SG4 56 E6
LBUZ LU7 110 C5
LCOL/BKTW AL2 188 C8
LTN LU1 88 D5
LWTH SG6 42 A4
RKW/CH/CXG WD3 219 G6
STVGE SG2 61 H6
TRING HP23 110 A8
WAT WD17 13 D3 4
WLYN AL6 122 C5
Crescent West EBAR EN4 210 D8
Cress End RKW/CH/CXG WD3 217 K8
Cresset Cl WARE SG12 153 H6
Cresswick HTCHE/RSTV SG4 93 H2
Crest Dr PEND EN3 214 B8
Crest Pk HHNE HP2 9 F4
The Crest CHESW EN7 195 K5
LTNN/LIM LU3 69 G2 1
SBW CM21 132 B7
WARE SG12 127 H5
WLYN AL6 122 D1
Creswick Ct WGCE AL7 147 J4 2
Crew Curve BERK HP4 161 G2
Crib St WARE SG12 127 H7
Cricketers Cl STAL AL1 11 D3
Cricketer's Rd ARL/CHE SG15 24 E4
Cricketfield La BSF CM23 105 G1
Crispin Fld LBUZ LU7 110 C5
Croasdaile Rd STSD CM24 86 D1
Croasdale Cl STSD CM24 86 D1
Croft Cl KGLGY WD4 184 E8
Croft End Rd KGLGY WD4 184 E8
Crofters SBW CM21 132 C6
Crofters End SBW CM21 132 C5
Crofters Rd NTHWD HA6 229 K3
Croft Fld HAT AL10 171 F4 1
KGLGY WD4 184 E8
Croft La KGLGY WD4 184 E8
LWTH SG6 26 A8
Croft Meadow KGLGY WD4 184 E8
Croft Mdw LBUZ LU7 110 A2
Croft Rd CFSP/GDCR SL9 226 B8
LTNE LU2 70 C6 1
WARE SG12 127 G7
Crofts Pth HHS/BOV HP3 165 G8
The Crofts HHS/BOV HP3 9 E6
HTCH/STOT SG5 25 K3
The Croft BAR EN5 225 K4
BROX EN10 197 J1
LCOL/BKTW AL2 188 C3
LTNN/LIM LU3 68 C1
WARE SG12 128 E5
WGCE AL7 148 A6
Croftwell HARP AL5 144 C1
Cromer Cl BERK HP4 138 B5
Cromer Rd WATN WD24 204 D8 2
Cromer Wy LTNE LU2 69 J2
Crompton Rd STVG SG1 75 F3
Cromwell Av CHESW EN7 197 F8
Cromwell Cl BSF CM23 104 E2
STALE/WH AL4 169 G1
Cromwell Gn LWTH SG6 42 B1
Cromwell Hl LTNE LU2 4 B2
Cromwell Rd AMP/FLIT/B MK45 36 C5
BORE WD6 223 H1
HERT/BAY SG13 151 J2
LTNN/LIM LU3 4 B2
LWTH SG6 42 B1
STVGE SG2 76 D4
WARE SG12 127 K8
Cromwell Wy HTCH/STOT SG5 39 F5
Crooked Mile WAB EN9 198 C8
Crooked Wy WAB EN9 177 K8
Crookhams WGCE AL7 148 B1
Crop Common HAT AL10 171 G2
Crosby Cl LTNW/LEA LU4 69 F7 1
STALE/WH AL4 190 A1
Crossbrook HAT AL10 170 D5
Crossbrook St CHES/WCR EN8 197 H8 1
Crossett Gn HHS/BOV HP3 165 H8 1
Crossfell Rd HHS/BOV HP3 165 G8
Crossfield Cl BERK HP4 161 G5
Crossfield Rd HOD EN11 177 G1
Crossfields STALW/RED AL3 188 D1
Crossgates STVG SG1 2 C3
Crosslands LTN LU1 88 D6
Cross La HARP AL5 143 K4
HERT/WAS SG14 150 E3 2
CFSP/GDCR SL9 226 C4
Cross Lanes Cl CFSP/GDCR SL9 226 C4 1
Crossleys LWTH SG6 25 K7 1
Crossmead OXHEY WD19 12 C5
Cross Oak Rd BERK HP4 161 H6
Crossoaks La BORE WD6 208 C5
POTB/CUF EN6 208 D4
Crosspaths HARP AL5 117 J5
The Crosspath RAD WD7 206 D5
Cross Rd BUSH WD23 13 F5
CHES/WCR EN8 214 D3 1
HERT/WAS SG14 151 F2
Cross St LTNE LU2 4 C3
LWTH SG6 41 K2
STALW/RED AL3 10 C4
WARE SG12 127 J8
WAT WD17 13 D2
Crossway CSHM HP5 182 A8
Cross Wy HARP AL5 118 E6
Crossway PIN HA5 230 C8
WGCW AL8 122 B7
Crossways BERK HP4 161 G6
HHS/BOV HP3 9 E5
The Cross Wy LTN LU1 4 A6
Crouchfield HERT/WAS SG14 126 B8 1
HHW HP1 164 A7
Crouchfield La WARE SG12 126 C5 1
Crouch Hall Gdns STALW/RED AL3 142 B3
Crouch Hall La STALW/RED AL3 142 B3
Crouch La CHESW EN7 196 A5
Crowborough Pth
OXHEY WD19 230 E3 1
Crow Furlong HTCH/STOT SG5 56 B3
Crowland Rd LTNE LU2 70 D4
Crownfield BROX EN10 177 F7
Crown Ga HLW CM20 6 C4
Crown La ROY SG8 31 J4
Crown Ri GSTN WD25 204 D4
Crown Rd BORE WD6 223 K1
Crown St STALW/RED AL3 142 C4
Crown Ter BSF CM23 105 K2
Croxdale Rd BORE WD6 223 J2
Croxley Vw WATW WD18 219 K6
Croxton Cl LTNN/LIM LU3 69 F2 1
Crozier Av BSF CM23 105 F1
Crusader Wy WATW WD18 12 A5
Cubbington Cl LTNN/LIM LU3 69 F2 2
Cubitt Cl HTCHE/RSTV SG4 57 G2
Cubitts Cl WLYN AL6 123 F6
Cublands HERT/BAY SG13 152 A3
Cuckmans Dr LCOL/BKTW AL2 188 C3
Cucumber La BRKMPK AL9 173 G7
Cuffley Av GSTN WD25 204 E4
Cuffley Cl LTNN/LIM LU3 68 E6
Cuffley Ct HHNE HP2 165 H1
Cuffley Hl CHESW EN7 195 J7
Cullera Cl NTHWD HA6 230 A5
Culverden Rd OXHEY WD19 230 C2
Culverhouse Rd LTNN/LIM LU3 69 H5
Culver Rd STAL AL1 11 D3
Culworth Cl LTN LU1 88 D6
Cumberland Cl HERT/WAS SG14 151 F1 1
HHS/BOV HP3 186 E2
Cumberland Dr STALW/RED AL3 142 C4
Cumberland St LTN LU1 4 C5
Cumberlow Pl HHS/BOV HP3 9 F6 3
Cundalls Rd WARE SG12 127 J7
Cunningham Av PEND EN3 214 D6
STAL AL1 11 E6
Cunningham Hill Rd STAL AL1 11 E6
Cunningham Rd CHES/WCR EN8 197 J5
Cupid Green La HHNE HP2 140 D6
Curlew Cl BERK HP4 161 K6
LWTH SG6 25 J8
Curlew Rd LTNE LU2 70 D4
Currie St HERT/BAY SG13 151 H2
Curteys HLWE CM17 157 G4
Curtis Cl RKW/CH/CXG WD3 217 K8
Curtis Rd HHS/BOV HP3 165 J7
Curtis Wy BERK HP4 162 A6
Curzon Rd LTNN/LIM LU3 4 A2
Cussons Cl CHESW EN7 196 E7
Cutenhoe Rd LTN LU1 5 D6
Cutforth Rd SBW CM21 132 C6
Cuthbert Cl CHESW EN7 196 D7 2
Cutlers Gn LTNE LU2 71 G7
Cutmore Dr STALE/WH AL4 170 A8
Cut Throat Av DUN/WHIP LU6 113 G2
Cuttsfield Ter HHW HP1 163 J7
Cutts La HTCHE/RSTV SG4 93 G8
Cuttys La STVG SG1 2 C3
Cwmbran Ct HHNE HP2 8 C1 1
Cygnet Cl BORE WD6 224 B1 1
NTHWD HA6 229 H6
Cygnet Ct BSF CM23 105 J3
Cylers Thicket WLYN AL6 122 C3 1
Cypress Av ENC/FH EN2 212 D5
WGCE AL7 148 D4
Cypress Cl WAB EN9 215 J4 1
Cypress Wk GSTN WD25 204 C5 1
Cyrils Wy STAL AL1 189 F1

D

Dacorum Wy HHW HP1 164 B6
Dacre Crs HTCHE/RSTV SG4 93 F8
Dacre Gdns BORE WD6 224 C5
Dacre Gn ROY SG8 21 K3
Dacre Rd HTCH/STOT SG5 56 E1
Dagger La BORE WD6 222 D6
Daggs Dell Rd HHW HP1 163 H4
Dagnall Rd HHW HP1 139 G4
Dagnalls LWTH SG6 41 K7 2
Dahlia Cl CHESW EN7 196 A3
LTNE LU2 70 C6
Daintrees WARE SG12 130 A5
Dairyglen Av CHES/WCR EN8 214 C1
Dalby Cl LTNW/LEA LU4 68 A5
Dale Av STALE/WH AL4 119 K4
Dale Cl HTCHE/RSTV SG4 56 D5
PIN HA5 230 C7
Dale Ct SBW CM21 132 B8 1
Dale Rd LTN LU1 4 A4
Daleside Dr POTB/CUF EN6 210 A2
Dales Rd BORE WD6 224 C5
The Dale LWTH SG6 41 J3
WAB EN9 215 K4
Dalewood HARP AL5 119 F8 1
WGCE AL7 148 E4
Dalkeith Rd HARP AL5 118 E7
Dallow Rd LTN LU1 88 D1
Dalton Cl LTNN/LIM LU3 52 B8
Dalton Gdns BSF CM23 105 H6
Dalton St STALW/RED AL3 10 C3
Dalton Wy HTCHE/RSTV SG4 93 H3
WAT WD17 13 E5
Daltry Cl STVG SG1 58 C7
Daltry Rd STVG SG1 58 C7
Damask Cl HTCHE/RSTV SG4 59 H1
TRING HP23 135 H5
Damask Gn HHW HP1 163 H7 2
Damask Green Rd
HTCHE/RSTV SG4 59 H1
Dammersey Cl STALW/RED AL3 115 K5
Damson Wy STALE/WH AL4 169 F4
Dancers End La TRING HP23 134 B7
Dancers Hill Rd BAR EN5 209 J6
Dancote KNEB SG3 96 A4
Dane Acres BSF CM23 105 G1

Dane Br MHAD SG10 103 J6
Dane Bridge La MHAD SG10 103 J7
Danebridge Rd MHAD SG10 103 H7
Dane Cl HARP AL5 118 E5
HTCH/STOT SG5 25 K1
Dane End ROY SG8 31 F4
Dane End La HTCHE/RSTV SG4 60 A4
Dane End Rd STDN SG11 100 C5
Danefield Rd HTCH/STOT SG5 38 E5
Danemead HOD EN11 153 F8
Dane O'coys Rd BSF CM23 85 H8
Dane Pk BSF CM23 105 G1
Dane Rd AMP/FLIT/B MK45 36 D6
LTNN/LIM LU3 69 G7
Danesbury La WLYN AL6 122 C1
Danesbury Pk HERT/WAS SG14 151 G2
Danesbury Park Rd WLYN AL6 122 C2
Danescroft LWTH SG6 25 K8
Danesgate STVG SG1 2 B4
The Danes LCOL/BKTW AL2 188 E6 1
Dane St BSF CM23 105 K2
Danestrete STVG SG1 2 B3
Daniells WGCE AL7 148 B2
Danvers Cft TRING HP23 135 H4 1
Danvers Dr LTNN/LIM LU3 52 C8
Danziger Wy BORE WD6 224 B1
Darblay Cl STALE/WH AL4 145 J4
Darby Dr WAB EN9 215 H3 2
WLYN AL6 95 K6
Darcy Cl CHES/WCR EN8 214 D1
Darkes La POTB/CUF EN6 210 B2
Dark La BUNT SG9 29 K8
CHESW EN7 196 E8
HARP AL5 144 A2
WLYN AL6 121 J1
Darley Rd LTNE LU2 71 J8
Darnicle Hl CHESW EN7 195 J3
Darrington Rd BORE WD6 223 H1
Darr's La BERK HP4 160 E4
The Dart HHNE HP2 165 F1 1
Darwin Cl HHNE HP2 141 G8
STALW/RED AL3 168 B2
Darwin Gdns OXHEY WD19 230 D4 3
Darwin Rd STVGE SG2 3 F2
The Dashes HLW CM20 7 D3
Datchet Cl HHNE HP2 165 G1
Datchworth Turn HHNE HP2 9 F5
Davenham Av NTHWD HA6 230 A3
Davenport HLWE CM17 181 H2
Davies St HERT/BAY SG13 151 H3
Davis Crs HTCH/STOT SG5 39 F4
Davison Cl CHES/WCR EN8 197 H6
Davison Dr CHES/WCR EN8 197 H6
Davis' Rw ARL/CHE SG15 24 E5
Davys Cl STALE/WH AL4 145 H2
Dawes La RKW/CH/CXG WD3 201 J6
Dawley WGCE AL7 123 F8
Dawley Ct HHNE HP2 8 C1
Dawlish Cl STVGE SG2 96 D2
Dawlish Rd LTNW/LEA LU4 68 E6
Dawson Cl HNLW SG16 24 A4
Dayemead WGCE AL7 148 C6 1
Days Cl HAT AL10 170 E4
ROY SG8 21 G4
Days Md HAT AL10 170 E4
Deacon Cl STAL AL1 189 F2 1
Deacons Cl BORE WD6 223 K4
PIN HA5 230 C8
Deaconsfield Rd HHS/BOV HP3 185 H1
Deacons Hts BORE WD6 223 K6
Deacons Hl OXHEY WD19 13 D5
Deacon's Hill Rd BORE WD6 223 J5
Deacons Wy HTCH/STOT SG5 40 B8
Deadhearn La CSTG HP8 216 B8
Deadman's Ash La
RKW/CH/CXG WD3 202 A6
Dead Woman's La
HTCHE/RSTV SG4 73 F3
Deakin Cl WATW WD18 219 K7 1
Deanacre Cl CFSP/GDCR SL9 226 B5
Deancroft Rd CFSP/GDCR SL9 226 B5
Dean Fld HHS/BOV HP3 183 J5
Deans Cl ABLGY WD5 203 J2
TRING HP23 135 F5
Deanscroft KNEB SG3 96 A4
Deans Furlong TRING HP23 135 F5
Dean's Gdns STALE/WH AL4 168 D2
Deans Meadow BERK HP4 112 E4
Deansway HHS/BOV HP3 185 K1
Deard's End La KNEB SG3 96 A3
Deards Wd KNEB SG3 96 A4
Debenham Rd CHESW EN7 197 F5
Deepdene POTB/CUF EN6 209 J1
Deep Denes LTNE LU2 5 E1
Deeping Cl KNEB SG3 96 A5 1
Deer Cl HERT/BAY SG13 151 J3
Deerfield Cl WARE SG12 127 H7
The Deerings HARP AL5 143 H5
Deer Pk HLWW/ROY CM19 179 H4
Deer Park Wk CSHM HP5 182 A6
Deerswood Av HAT AL10 171 G6
The Dee HHNE HP2 164 E1
Deeves Hall La POTB/CUF EN6 208 D3
De Havilland Cl HAT AL10 170 E3
De Havilland Ct RAD WD7 207 H2 2
De Havilland Wy ABLGY WD5 204 A2 1
Deimos Dr HHNE HP2 9 D2
Delahay Ri BERK HP4 161 J3
Delamare Rd CHES/WCR EN8 197 K7
Delamere Rd BORE WD6 224 A1
Delfcroft WARE SG12 127 G6
Delfield Gdns LTN LU1 88 D5
Delius Cl BORE WD6 223 F6
Dell Cl HARP AL5 118 D6
Dellcot Cl LTNE LU2 70 C4
Dellcott Cl WGCW AL8 147 G2
Dellcroft Wy HARP AL5 143 H3
Dellcut Rd HHNE HP2 9 D3
Dellfield BERK HP4 161 H3 2
STAL AL1 11 E5
WARE SG12 127 H1
Dellfield Av BERK HP4 161 J3
Dellfield Cl RAD WD7 206 B5
WAT WD17 12 B1
Dellfield Rd HAT AL10 171 F4
Dell La BSF CM23 105 K2
RBSF CM22 132 E1
Dellmeadow ABLGY WD5 186 E8
Dell Meadow HHS/BOV HP3 185 J2 1
Dellors Cl BAR EN5 225 J5
Dell Ri LCOL/BKTW AL2 188 D4
Dell Rd BERK HP4 160 E2 1
PEND EN3 214 B8
WATN WD24 204 B7
Dell Side WATN WD24 204 B7
Dellsome La BRKMPK AL9 191 K1
STALE/WH AL4 191 J1 1
Dell Springs BUNT SG9 63 J1 1
The Dells HHS/BOV HP3 9 E6
Dellswood Cl HERT/BAY SG13 151 H4
Dells Wood Cl HOD EN11 152 E8
The Dell BLDK SG7 42 E3
CFSP/GDCR SL9 226 B5
HERT/BAY SG13 151 F6
LTN LU1 88 D6
LTNE LU2 71 G8
NTHWD HA6 229 K1
PIN HA5 230 E8
RAD WD7 206 D6
ROY SG8 21 G4
STAL AL1 11 F2
STVG SG1 2 C3
Dellwood Cl RKW/CH/CXG WD3 218 A8
Delmar Av HHNE HP2 165 J7
Delmerend La STALW/RED AL3 116 C8
Delphine Cl LTN LU1 89 F3
Delta Gain OXHEY WD19 230 E1
Demontfort Ri WARE SG12 127 G6
Denbigh Cl HHS/BOV HP3 8 B6 2
Denbigh Rd LTNN/LIM LU3 69 G7
Denby LWTH SG6 42 B5
Denby Gra HLWE CM17 181 H1
Dencora Wy LTNN/LIM LU3 68 A1
Dendridge Cl EN EN1 214 A7
Dene La STVGE SG2 77 F7
Dene Rd NTHWD HA6 229 H5
Denewood Cl WAT WD17 204 A7
Denham Cl HHNE HP2 165 F1 2
LTNN/LIM LU3 68 D1
Denham La CFSP/GDCR SL9 226 C5
Denham Wk CFSP/GDCR SL9 226 C5
Denham Wy BORE WD6 224 B1
Denham Wy
(North Orbital Road)
RKW/CH/CXG WD3 217 H8
Denmark St WAT WD17 12 C1
Denny Av WAB EN9 215 J4
Denny Ct BSF CM23 86 A7
Denny Ga CHES/WCR EN8 197 K5
Denny's La BERK HP4 161 G7
Densley Cl WGCW AL8 147 H1
Denton Cl BAR EN5 225 H5
LTNW/LEA LU4 68 A5
Denton Rd STVG SG1 2 C4
Dents Cl LWTH SG6 42 C6
Derby Rd HOD EN11 177 J5
LTNW/LEA LU4 68 B7
WAT WD17 13 D3 5
Derby Wy STVG SG1 76 C1
Derwent Av LTNN/LIM LU3 69 G2
PIN HA5 231 F5
Derwent Rd HARP AL5 117 J5
HHS/BOV HP3 9 F6
LTNE LU2 5 E3
Desborough Cl HERT/WAS SG14 126 A8
Desborough Dr WLYN AL6 123 J4
Desborough Rd HTCHE/RSTV SG4 57 G1
Desmond Rd WATN WD24 204 A6
De Tany Ct STAL AL1 10 C5
Deva Cl STALW/RED AL3 167 H8
Devereux Dr WAT WD17 203 K8
De Vere Wk WAT WD17 219 K2
Devoils La BSF CM23 105 J2 2
Devon Ct STAL AL1 11 D5 3
Devon Rd LTNE LU2 5 F4
WATN WD24 220 E1
Devonshire Cl STVGE SG2 96 B1
Devonshire Rd HARP AL5 118 D7 2
PIN HA5 231 G7
Dewars Cl WLYN AL6 122 C3
Dewes Green Rd BSF CM23 51 H8
Dewgrass Gv CHES/WCR EN8 214 C5 2
Dewhurst Rd CHES/WCR EN8 197 G7
Dewpond Cl STVG SG1 75 H1
Dewsbury Rd LTNN/LIM LU3 69 G3
Dexter Cl LTNN/LIM LU3 52 B8
STAL AL1 11 F5
Dexter Rd BAR EN5 225 J6
DEN/HRF UB9 228 B8
Diamond Rd WATN WD24 204 B8
Dickens Cl STALW/RED AL3 10 C3
Dickens Ct HHNE HP2 141 G8
Dicket Md WLYN AL6 122 C4
Dickins Cl CHESW EN7 196 E5
Dickinson Av RKW/CH/CXG WD3 219 F6
Dickinson Sq RKW/CH/CXG WD3 219 G6
Dickson CHESW EN7 196 D5
Dig Dag Hl CHESW EN7 196 D5
Digswell Cl BORE WD6 207 K8
Digswell Hl WLYN AL6 122 A8
Digswell La WGCE AL7 123 F7
Digswell Park Rd WGCW AL8 122 D6
Digswell Ri WGCW AL8 147 J1
Digswell Rd WGCW AL8 122 E8
Dimmocks La RKW/CH/CXG WD3 201 K6
Dimsdale Crs BSF CM23 106 A4
Dimsdale St HERT/WAS SG14 151 F3
Dinant Link Rd HOD EN11 177 F2
Dingle Cl BAR EN5 224 E6
Dinmore HHS/BOV HP3 183 H6
Ditchfield Rd HOD EN11 153 F8
Ditchling Cl LTNE LU2 70 D6
Ditchmore La STVG SG1 2 A2
Ditton Gn LTNE LU2 70 E7
Divot Pl HERT/BAY SG13 152 A2 3
Dixies Cl BLDK SG7 17 K6
Dixon Pl BUNT SG9 63 J2
Dixons Hill Cl BRKMPK AL9 192 B3
Dixons Hill Rd BRKMPK AL9 192 B3
Dobb's Weir Rd HOD EN11 177 J4
Docklands HTCH/STOT SG5 39 F5 1
Doctor's Commons Rd BERK HP4 161 J6
Dodds La HHNE HP2 140 D8
Dodwood WGCE AL7 148 C4
Doggetts Wy STAL AL1 10 B6
Dog Kennel La HAT AL10 171 F3
RKW/CH/CXG WD3 217 J5
ROY SG8 21 H3
Dognell Gn WGCW AL8 147 G2
Dolesbury Dr WLYN AL6 95 K8
Dolphin Wy BSF CM23 105 K1
Doncaster Cl STVG SG1 76 D1
Doncaster Gn OXHEY WD19 230 D4
Donkey La TRING HP23 134 D7
Donne Cl ROY SG8 21 G1
Dorchester Av HOD EN11 177 F1
Dordans Rd LTNW/LEA LU4 68 D5
Dorel Cl LTNE LU2 5 D1
Dormans Cl NTHWD HA6 229 J6
Dormer Cl BAR EN5 225 J5
Dorrien's Cft BERK HP4 161 G2
Dorrington Cl LTNN/LIM LU3 4 A2
Dorrofield Cl RKW/CH/CXG WD3 219 H5
Dorset Cl BERK HP4 161 G4
Douglas Av WATN WD24 204 E7
Douglas Dr STVG SG1 76 B1
Douglas Gdns BERK HP4 161 H4
Douglas Rd HARP AL5 118 B7
LTNW/LEA LU4 69 F7
Douglas Wy WGCE AL7 148 D3
Doulton Cl HLWE CM17 181 H2
Dove Cl BSF CM23 105 H6
STSD CM24 86 D2
Dove Ct HAT AL10 171 F6
Dovedale LTNE LU2 69 K3
STVGE SG2 3 F4
WARE SG12 127 G5
Dovedale Cl DEN/HRF UB9 228 B8
Dovehouse Cft HLW CM20 7 F2
Dovehouse Hl LTNE LU2 5 F1
Dove House La DUN/WHIP LU6 114 A2
Dove La POTB/CUF EN6 210 C4
Dove Pk PIN HA5 231 G6
RKW/CH/CXG WD3 216 E5
Dover Cl LTNN/LIM LU3 69 F6
Doverfield CHESW EN7 196 A
Dover Wy RKW/CH/CXG WD3 219 H4
Dowling Ct HHS/BOV HP3 185 H1
Downalong BUSH WD23 222 A8
Downedge STALW/RED AL3 10 A3
Down Edge STALW/RED AL3 142 A4
Downer Dr RKW/CH/CXG WD3 201 J
Downes Rd STALE/WH AL4 168 E
Downfield Cl HERT/BAY SG13 152 B
Downfield Rd CHES/WCR EN8 214 D
HERT/BAY SG13 152 B5
Downfields WGCW AL8 147 G
Down Green La STALE/WH AL4 144 E
Downhall Ley BUNT SG9 63 J
Downings Wd RKW/CH/CXG WD3 227 G4
Downlands BLDK SG7 27 G8
LTNN/LIM LU3 68 B2
ROY SG8 21 G
STVGE SG2 76 E
WAB EN9 215 K4

Downsfield HAT AL10 .... 171 G7 🔲
Downside HHNE HP2 .... 8 B4
Downs La HAT AL10 .... 171 F6
Downs Rd LTN LU1 .... 4 A4
The Downs HAT AL10 .... 171 F6
   HLW CM20 .... 7 D4
Dowry Wk WAT WD17 .... 204 A8
Drakes Cl CHES/WCR EN8 .... 197 H6 🔲
Drakes Dr NTHWD HA6 .... 229 C2
   STAL AL1 .... 189 K1
   STVGE SG2 .... 3 F1
Drakes Wy HAT AL10 .... 171 C6
Drapers Wy STVG SG1 .... 2 A1
Drayman's Cl BSF CM23 .... 104 E4
Drayson Cl WAB EN9 .... 215 G2
Drayton Av POTB/CUF EN6 .... 209 K2
Drayton Rd BORE WD6 .... 223 K4
The Drey CFSP/GDCR SL9 .... 226 B4
Driftway ROY SG8 .... 31 J5
The Driftway HHNE HP2 .... 8 C5
Driftwood Av LCOL/BKTW AL2 .... 188 C4
Driver's End La HTCHE/RSTV SG4 .... 94 E5
The Drive BAR EN5 .... 225 J3
   BRKMPK AL9 .... 193 G3
   CFSP/GDCR SL9 .... 226 B6
   CHESW EN7 .... 195 K6
   CHESW EN7 .... 197 F6
   HARP AL5 .... 118 C8
   HERT/WAS SG14 .... 151 F1
   HLW CM20 .... 7 D3
   HOD EN11 .... 177 F1
   LCOL/BKTW AL2 .... 189 J3
   NTHWD HA6 .... 229 K7
   POTB/CUF EN6 .... 210 A3
   RAD WD7 .... 206 D4
   RKW/CH/CXG WD3 .... 218 A5
   SBW CM21 .... 132 C7
   STALE/WH AL4 .... 119 K2
   WAT WD17 .... 203 J7
   WLYN AL6 .... 96 B8
The Driveway POTB/CUF EN6 .... 195 G6
Drop La LCOL/BKTW AL2 .... 205 J1
Drovers Ride BSF CM23 .... 105 F5 🔲
   HAT AL10 .... 171 G5
   STALW/RED AL3 .... 10 C4
Drummond Ride TRING HP23 .... 135 H5
Drury La WARE SG12 .... 127 K7
Drycroft WCCE AL7 .... 147 K7 🔲
Dryden Crs STVGE SG2 .... 76 D1
Drysdale Cl NTHWD HA6 .... 229 K6 🔲
Dubbs Knoll Rd ROY SG8 .... 15 G4
Dubrae Cl STALW/RED AL3 .... 167 H8
Duchess Cl BSF CM23 .... 104 E2 🔲
Duchy Rd EBAR EN4 .... 210 E8
Ducketts La MHAD SG10 .... 104 A8
Ducketts Md HLWW/ROY CM19 .... 154 C8
Ducketts Wd WARE SG12 .... 127 H2
Duck La STVGE SG2 .... 78 B5
Duckling La SBW CM21 .... 132 C7 🔲
Duckmore La TRING HP23 .... 134 D8
Ducks Hill Rd NTHWD HA6 .... 229 F8
   NTHWD HA6 .... 229 C6
   NTHWD HA6 .... 229 G6
Dudley Av CHES/WCR EN8 .... 214 C2
Dudley Hill Cl WLYN AL6 .... 122 E1 🔲
Dudley St LTNE LU2 .... 4 C3
Dudswell La BERK HP4 .... 160 E1
Dugdale Hill La POTB/CUF EN6 .... 209 K3
Dugdales RKW/CH/CXG WD3 .... 219 K3
Dukes Av DUN/WHIP LU6 .... 113 G1
   LTNN/LIM LU3 .... 69 K3
Duke's La HTCH/STOT SG5 .... 56 C1
Dukes Ride BSF CM23 .... 105 F2
Duke St HOD EN11 .... 177 F2
   LTNE LU2 .... 4 C3
   WAT WD17 .... 13 D2
Dukes Wy BERK HP4 .... 161 H5 🔲
Dulwich Wy RKW/CH/CXG WD3 .... 219 F5
Dumbarton Av CHES/WCR EN8 .... 214 C4 🔲
Dumfries Cl OXHEY WD19 .... 230 B2
Dumfries St LTN LU1 .... 4 B5
Duncan Cl ABLGY WD5 .... 147 K4
Duncan Wy BUSH WD23 .... 221 G2
Duncombe Cl HERT/WAS SG14 .... 151 F1
   LTNN/LIM LU3 .... 69 K3
Duncombe Rd BERK HP4 .... 161 F3 🔲
   HERT/WAS SG14 .... 151 F2
Duncots Cl HTCH/STOT SG5 .... 40 C5
Dundale Rd TRING HP23 .... 135 F5
Dunhams La LWTH SG6 .... 42 B3
Dunlin LWTH SG6 .... 25 J8
Dunlin Rd HHNE HP2 .... 164 D1
Dunmow Rd BSF CM23 .... 106 A2
   RBSF CM22 .... 107 F2
Dunn Cl STVG SG1 .... 2 C5
Dunnock Cl BORE WD6 .... 223 K4 🔲
Dunny La KGLCY WD4 .... 201 J2
   RKW/CH/CXG WD3 .... 201 J3 🔲
Dunsby Rd LTNN/LIM LU3 .... 69 F3
Dunsley Pl TRING HP23 .... 135 G6 🔲
Dunsmore Cl BUSH WD23 .... 222 A6 🔲
Dunsmore Rd LTN LU1 .... 4 A6 🔲
Dunsmore Wy BUSH WD23 .... 221 K6
Dunstable Cl LTNW/LEA LU4 .... 69 F8
Dunstable Pl LTN LU1 .... 4 B4
Dunstable Rd DUN/WHIP LU6 .... 112 E3

LTN LU1 .... 4 B4
LTNW/LEA LU4 .... 68 C7 🔲
STALW/RED AL3 .... 117 F8
Dunstall Rd AMP/FLIT/B MK45 .... 36 C7 🔲
   DEN/HRF UB9 .... 228 A7
Dunstalls RKW/CH/CXG CM19 .... 179 H5
Dunster Cl BAR EN5 .... 225 C7 🔲
   DEN/HRF UB9 .... 228 A7
Dunster HHNE HP2 .... 141 C8 🔲
Dunsters Md WGCE AL7 .... 148 B5
Dunston HI TRING HP23 .... 135 F5
Durban Rd East WATW WD18 .... 12 B3
Durban Rd West WATW WD18... .... 12 B3
Durbar Rd LTNW/LEA LU4 .... 68 A3
Durham Cl SBW CM21 .... 132 A8 🔲
   WARE SG12 .... 153 C4
Durham Rd LTNE LU2 .... 5 E3
   STVG SG1 .... 59 G8
Durley Cdns LTN LU1 .... 4 B6 🔲
Durrants Cl RKW/CH/CXG WD3 .... 219 H3
Durrants Hill Rd HHS/BOV HP3 .... 185 H1
Durrants La BERK HP4 .... 161 F5
Durrants Rd BERK HP4 .... 161 G4
Duxford Cl LTNN/LIM LU3 .... 69 G2
Duxons Turn HHNE HP2 .... 9 E4 🔲
Dwight Rd WATW WD18 .... 219 J3
Dyes La HTCHE/RSTV SG4 .... 74 E6
Dyke La STALE/WH AL4 .... 145 H2
Dylan Cl BORE WD6 .... 223 C7 🔲
Dymoke Gn STALE/WH AL4 .... 11 F1
Dymokes Wy HOD EN11 .... 153 F8
Dyrham La BAR EN5 .... 209 F6
Dysons Cl CHES/WCR EN8 .... 214 C3

E

Eagle Centre Wy LTNW/LEA LU4 .... 68 A2 🔲
Eagle Ct HERT/BAY SG13 .... 152 A2 🔲
Eagle Wy HAT AL10 .... 171 F6
Ealing Cl BORE WD6 .... 224 C1
Earls Cl BSF CM23 .... 105 G3
Earls Hill Gdns ROY SG8 .... 21 G3
Earls La POTB/CUF EN6 .... 208 C2
Earlsmead LWTH SG6 .... 41 K6
Earls Meade LTNE LU2 .... 4 B2
Earl St WAT WD17 .... 13 D2 🔲
Easington Rd WARE SG12 .... 99 H2
Easingwold Gdns LTN LU1 .... 88 E1
Eastbourne Av STVG SG1 .... 75 F3
Eastbrook Rd WAB EN9 .... 215 K3
Eastbrook Wy HHNE HP2 .... 8 B5
East BurrowFields WCCE AL7 .... 147 J5
Eastbury Av NTHWD HA6 .... 229 K4
Eastbury Ct STAL AL1 .... 11 E3 🔲
Eastbury Rd NTHWD HA6 .... 229 K5
   OXHEY WD19 .... 13 D6
Eastcheap LWTH SG6 .... 41 K4
East Cl HTCHE/RSTV SG4... .... 94 E5
   LCOL/BKTW AL2 .... 188 D3 🔲
   STVG SG1 .... 3 D3
Eastcote Dr HARP AL5 .... 144 A3
Eastcott Cl LTNE LU2 .... 70 D8
East Dr GSTN WD25 .... 204 C6
   NTHWD HA6 .... 229 K1
   SBW CM21 .... 132 C8
Eastern Av CHES/WCR EN8 .... 214 E3
   HNLW SG16 .... 24 A6
Eastern Wy LTNE LU2 .... 26 A8
Eastfield Av WATN WD24 .... 220 E1 🔲
Eastfield Cl STALE/WH AL4 .... 169 G3 🔲
Eastfield Rd CHES/WCR EN8 .... 214 C2
   PEND EN3 .... 214 C8
   ROY SG8 .... 21 J2
East Flint HHW HP1 .... 163 H5
East Ga HLW CM20 .... 6 C3
Eastgate STVG SG1 .... 2 B4
Eastglade NTHWD HA6 .... 229 K4
East HI LTNN/LIM LU3 .... 69 G3
Eastholm LWTH SG6 .... 42 A1
Eastholm Gn LWTH SG6 .... 42 A1
East La ABLGY WD5 .... 187 G6
   GSTN WD25 .... 187 H8
   STALE/WH AL4 .... 120 B8
Eastlea Av GSTN WD25 .... 205 F7
East Lodge La ENC/FH EN2 .... 212 A6
Eastman Wy HHNE HP2 .... 9 D2
East Md WCCE AL7 .... 148 C6
East Mimms HHNE HP2 .... 8 B4 🔲
Eastmoor Pk HARP AL5 .... 143 K3
East Mt STALE/WH AL4 .... 120 B8 🔲
Eastnor HHS/BOV HP3 .... 183 J6
Easton Gdns BORE WD6 .... 224 D4
Eastor WCCE AL7 .... 123 G8
East Pk HLWE CM17 .... 157 C6
   SBW CM21 .... 132 C8
East Reach STVGE SG2 .... 3 E6
East Ridgeway POTB/CUF EN6... .... 195 F6
East Riding WLYN AL6 .... 123 K4
East Rd BSF CM23 .... 106 A2
   HLW CM20 .... 156 E5
   PEND EN3 .... 214 B8
East St HHNE HP2 .... 8 A5

LTNE LU2 .... 53 K7
WARE SG12 .... 127 H8
East Vw BRKMPK AL9 .... 173 G5
   HTCHE/RSTV SG4 .... 57 D7
East Wy WAB EN9 .... 215 J5
Eastwick Crs RKW/CH/CXG WD3... .... 227 J1
Eastwick Hall La HLW CM20 .... 155 H3
Eastwick Rd HLW CM20 .... 155 J5
Eastwick Rw HHNE HP2 .... 9 D6
Eaton Ga NTHWD HA6 .... 229 H5
Eaton Green Rd LTNE LU2 .... 90 D1
Eaton Pl LTNE LU2 .... 70 E8
Eaton Rd HHNE HP2 .... 9 E2
   STAL AL1 .... 168 E6
Eaton Valley Rd LTNE LU2 .... 5 F2
Ebberns Rd HHS/BOV HP3 .... 185 J1
Ebenezer St LTN LU1 .... 4 B5 🔲
Ebury Ap RKW/CH/CXG WD3 .... 218 C8
Ebury Cl NTHWD HA6 .... 229 H4
Ebury Rd RKW/CH/CXG WD3 .... 218 C8
   WAT WD17 .... 13 E2
Echo HI ROY SG8 .... 21 G4
Eddy St BERK HP4 .... 161 H4
Edenhall Cl HHNE HP2 .... 165 J7
Edens Cl BSF CM23 .... 106 A2
Edgars Ct WGCE AL7 .... 147 K4 🔲
Edgbaston Dr RAD WD7 .... 207 H2
Edgcott Cl LTNN/LIM LU3 .... 52 B8
Edgecote Cl LTN LU1 .... 88 D6
Edgehill Gdns LTNN/LIM LU3 .... 68 B1
Edgewood Dr LTNE LU2 .... 70 D3
Edgeworth Cl STVGE SG2 .... 76 D8 🔲
Edgwarebury La BORE WD6 .... 223 J7
   EDGE HA8 .... 223 J8
Edinburgh Av RKW/CH/CXG WD3 .... 217 K6
Edinburgh Crs CHES/WCR EN8 .... 214 D3
Edinburgh Dr GSTN WD25 .... 204 B2 🔲
Edinburgh Pl HLW CM20 .... 156 D5
Edinburgh Wy HLW CM20 .... 156 E5
   HLWE CM17 .... 157 F4 🔲
Edison Cl STALE/WH AL4 .... 169 F7 🔲
Edison Rd STVGE SG2 .... 3 F2
Edkins Cl LTNE LU2 .... 69 K4 🔲
Edlyn Cl BERK HP4 .... 161 G4
Edmonds Dr STVGE SG2 .... 76 E5
Edmund Beaufort Dr
   STALW/RED AL3 .... 10 C2
Edmunds Rd HERT/WAS SG14 .... 150 C2
Edridge Cl BUSH WD23 .... 221 K5
Edulf Rd BORE WD6 .... 224 A2
Edward Amey Cl GSTN WD25 .... 204 D6
Edward Cl ABLGY WD5 .... 204 A2
   STAL AL1 .... 11 E5
Edward Ct HHS/BOV HP3 .... 185 H2 🔲
Edward St LTNE LU2 .... 5 D2
Edwin Cl BAR EN5 .... 225 H5
Egdon Dr LTNE LU2 .... 69 J3
Egerton Rd BERK HP4 .... 161 H3
Eight Acres TRING HP23 .... 135 F5
Eighth Av LTNN/LIM LU3 .... 68 C2
Eisenberg Cl BLDK SG7 .... 27 H8 🔲
Elaine Gdns LTN LU1 .... 89 F8
Elbow La HERT/BAY SG13 .... 152 A8 🔲
   STVGE SG2 .... 76 C8
Eldefield LWTH SG6 .... 41 H2
Elderbeck Cl CHESW EN7 .... 196 E6
Elderberry Cl LTNE LU2 .... 70 C5 🔲
Elderberry Dr HTCHE/RSTV SG4 .... 56 E5 🔲
Elderberry Wy GSTN WD25 .... 204 C5 🔲
Elderfield HLWE CM17 .... 157 G5
Elder Rd WARE SG12 .... 127 K6
Elder Wy STVG SG1 .... 2 B5
Eldon Av BORE WD6 .... 223 K2
Eldon Rd HOD EN11 .... 177 J5
   LTNW/LEA LU4 .... 68 B7
Eleanor Av STALW/RED AL3 .... 10 C2
Eleanor Cross Rd CHES/WCR EN8 .... 214 D4
Eleanor Gdns BAR EN5 .... 225 J5 🔲
Eleanor Rd CHES/WCR EN8 .... 214 D3
   HERT/WAS SG14 .... 151 F2
Eleanor Wy CHES/WCR EN8 .... 214 E4
Elfrida Rd WATW WD18 .... 13 D4
Elgar Cl BORE WD6 .... 223 F7
Elgin Dr NTHWD HA6 .... 229 K6
Elgin Rd BROX EN10 .... 197 G8
   CHES/WCR EN8... .... 197 G8
Elgood Av NTHWD HA6 .... 230 B5
Eliot Rd ROY SG8 .... 21 H1
   STVGE SG2 .... 76 D3
Elizabeth Cl BAR EN5 .... 225 J3
   WAB EN9 .... 177 J8
   WGCE AL7 .... 148 D3 🔲
Elizabeth Ct STALE/WH AL4 .... 169 G3
Elizabeth Dr TRING HP23 .... 135 G3
Elizabeth Rd BSF CM23 .... 105 H4
Elizabeth St LTN LU1 .... 4 B5 🔲
Elizabeth Wy HLW CM20 .... 155 H7
   HLWW/ROY CM19... .... 179 G2
Ellenborough Cl BSF CM23 .... 105 G4
Ellenbrook Cl WATN WD24 .... 220 D1 🔲
Ellenbrook Crs HAT AL10 .... 170 C4 🔲
Ellenbrook La HAT AL10 .... 170 C4
Ellen Cl HHNE HP2 .... 8 C4
Ellenhall Cl LTNN/LIM LU3 .... 4 A2 🔲
Ellerdine Rd LTNN/LIM LU3 .... 69 G5 🔲

Ellesborough Cl OXHEY WD19 230 D4
Ellesfield WLYN AL6 122 B4
Ellesmere Rd BERK HP4 162 A5
Ellingham Cl HHNE HP2 9 D3
Ellingham Rd HHNE HP2 8 C4
Elliott Cl WGCE AL7 147 J6
Ellis Av CFSP/GDCR SL9 226 C7
STVG SG1 75 K1
Elliswick Rd HARP AL5 118 D7
Ellwood Gdns GSTN WD25 204 C4
Elm Av LTN LU1 88 D6
OXHEY WD19 13 F6
Elmbank Av BAR EN5 225 H4
Elmbridge HLWE CM17 157 J6
Elmbrook Dr BSF CM23 105 H5 1
Elm Cl WAB EN9 215 J4
Elmcote Wy RKW/CH/CXG WD3 218 E6
Elm Dr CHES/WCR EN8 197 J6
HAT AL10 171 F5
STALE/WH AL4 169 F6
Elmfield Cl POTB/CUF EN6 209 K3 1
Elmfield Rd POTB/CUF EN6 209 K3
Elm Gdns ENC/FH EN2 213 G8
WGCW AL8 147 G3
Elm Gn HHW HP1 163 H4
Elm Gv BERK HP4 161 K5
BSF CM23 106 A2
WATN WD24 204 B7
Elm Hatch PIN HA5 231 G6
Elmhurst Cl BSF CM23 105 H2
Elmhurst Rd PEND EN3 214 B7
Elmoor Av WLYN AL6 122 B4
Elmoor Cl WLYN AL6 122 B5
Elmore Rd LTNE LU2 5 E2
Elm Pk BLDK SG7 43 F1 1
Elm Park Rd PIN HA5 230 D8
Elm Rd BSF CM23 105 H1
Elmroyd Av POTB/CUF EN6 210 A3
Elmroyd Cl POTB/CUF EN6 210 A3
Elms Cl HTCHE/RSTV SG4 57 J6
Elmscroft Gdns POTB/CUF EN6 210 A2
Elmside DUN/WHIP LU6 114 B1
Elmside Wk HTCH/STOT SG5 56 C2
Elms Rd CFSP/GDCR SL9 226 B6
WARE SG12 128 A7
The Elms HERT/BAY SG13 151 K3
WLYN AL6 94 E7
Elmtree Av LTNE LU2 71 F6
Elm Tree Wk RKW/CH/CXG WD3 217 J4 1
TRING HP23 135 F4
Elm Wk RAD WD7 206 C6
ROY SG8 21 K2
STVGE SG2 3 F5
Elm Wy RKW/CH/CXG WD3 218 A8
Elmwood SBW CM21 132 D8
WGCW AL8 147 G4
Elmwood Av BLDK SG7 43 F2 1
BORE WD6 224 A4
Elmwood Crs LTNE LU2 69 K6
Elsinge Rd EN EN1 214 A6
Elstree Hl North BORE WD6 223 G5
Elstree Hl South BORE WD6 223 F7
Elstree Rd BORE WD6 222 D6
BUSH WD23 222 A8
HHNE HP2 141 F8
STAN HA7 222 C7
Elstree Wy BORE WD6 224 B2
Elton Rd HERT/WAS SG14 151 F2
Elveden Cl LTNE LU2 69 K3
Elvington Gdns LTNN/LIM LU3 52 B8
Elwood HLWE CM17 181 H2
Ely Cl HAT AL10 170 E3
STVG SG1 59 H7
Ely Gdns BORE WD6 224 C5
Ely Rd STAL AL1 168 E7
Ely Wy LTNW/LEA LU4 68 C5
Embleton Rd OXHEY WD19 230 B2
Emerton Ct BERK HP4 161 F2 1
Emerton Garth BERK HP4 161 F2
Emmanuel Rd NTHWD HA6 230 A6
Emma Rothschild Ct
TRING HP23 135 F4 1
Emma's Crs WARE SG12 153 G5
Emmer Gn LTNE LU2 71 G7
Emmitt Cl RAD WD7 207 H3 2
Emperor Cl BERK HP4 161 G2
Emperors Ga STVGE SG2 76 D1
Empress Rd LTNN/LIM LU3 68 D5 1
Endeavour Rd CHES/WCR EN8 197 H5
Enderby Rd LTNN/LIM LU3 69 H2
Endersby Rd BAR EN5 225 H5
Endymion Ct HAT AL10 171 H3 1
Endymion Ms HAT AL10 171 H3 2
Endymion Rd HAT AL10 171 H3
Englehurst HARP AL5 119 F8 2
Enid Cl LCOL/BKTW AL2 205 G1
Ennerdale Cl STAL AL1 168 E8
Ennis Cl HARP AL5 144 A3 3
Ennismore Cl LWTH SG6 42 C6 2
Ennismore Gn LTNE LU2 71 G8
Enslow Cl LTN LU1 88 D6
Enterprise Wy LTNN/LIM LU3 69 G1
Epping Gn HHNE HP2 165 G1
Epping Rd WAB EN9 179 G6
Ereswell Rd LTNN/LIM LU3 69 F2
Erin Cl LTNW/LEA LU4 69 F7
Ermine Cl CHESW EN7 214 A1 1
ROY SG8 21 H1
STALW/RED AL3 167 H7
Ermine Ct BUNT SG9 63 J1 2
Ermine St BUNT SG9 47 H6
WARE SG12 127 H2
Escarpment Av DUN/WHIP LU6 113 F1
Escot Wy BAR EN5 225 H5
Esdaile La HOD EN11 177 F4
Eskdale LCOL/BKTW AL2 190 D5
LTNW/LEA LU4 68 B4
Essendon Gdns WGCE AL7 148 A3
Essendon Hl BRKMPK AL9 173 F3
Essex Cl LTN LU1 4 C5 1
Essex La ABLGY WD5 203 J3
Essex Md HHNE HP2 140 E8
Essex Rd BORE WD6 223 K3
HOD EN11 177 G2
STVG SG1 75 G1
WAT WD17 12 B1
Essex St STAL AL1 11 D3 2
Estcourt Rd WAT WD17 13 D2
Estfeld Cl HOD EN11 153 G8 2
Ethelred Cl WGCE AL7 148 A4
Etna Rd STALW/RED AL3 10 C3
Europa Rd HHNE HP2 8 C2
Euston Av WATW WD18 12 A4
Evans Av GSTN WD25 204 A5
Evan's Cl RKW/CH/CXG WD3 219 F5
Evans Gv STALE/WH AL4 169 F2
Evans Wy TRING HP23 135 G5 1
Evedon Cl LTNN/LIM LU3 68 E3
Evelyn Dr PIN HA5 230 E6
Evensyde WATW WD18 219 H6
Everard Cl STAL AL1 10 C6 1
Everest Cl ARL/CHE SG15 25 F4
Everest Wy HHNE HP2 9 D5
Everett Cl BUSH WD23 222 B8
CHESW EN7 196 A3 2
Evergreen Cl KNEB SG3 96 B7
Evergreen Rd WARE SG12 127 K6
Evergreen Wk HHS/BOV HP3 164 D8
Evergreen Wy LTNN/LIM LU3 69 F1
Everlasting La STALW/RED AL3 10 B2
Exchange Rd STVG SG1 3 D3
WATW WD18 12 C3
Exeter Cl STVG SG1 59 H7
WATN WD24 13 D1
Explorer Dr WATW WD18 12 A5
Extension Rd HERT/BAY SG13 151 J3 5
Exton Av LTNE LU2 5 E2
Eynsford Ct HTCHE/RSTV SG4 56 D3
Eynsford Rd LTNW/LEA LU4 68 C6 1
Eywood Rd STAL AL1 10 B6

F

Faggots Cl RAD WD7 207 F5
Faints Cl CHESW EN7 196 C7
Fairacre HHS/BOV HP3 185 K2
Fairacres Cl POTB/CUF EN6 210 A3
Fairburn Cl BORE WD6 223 K1 1
Fair Cl BUSH WD23 221 J7
Faircross Wy STAL AL1 11 F2
Fairfax Av LTNN/LIM LU3 68 C2
Fairfax Rd HERT/BAY SG13 151 J2
Fairfield BUNT SG9 63 J3
Fairfield Av OXHEY WD19 230 D2
Fairfield Cl HARP AL5 119 F8 3
RAD WD7 206 B7 1
Fairfield Dr BROX EN10 197 K2
Fairfield Rd HOD EN11 177 F1
Fairfield Wy HTCHE/RSTV SG4 57 G1
Fairfolds GSTN WD25 205 F5
Fairford Av LTNE LU2 69 K4
Fairgreen Rd LTN LU1 88 E6
Fairhaven Crs OXHEY WD19 230 B2
Fairhill HHS/BOV HP3 185 K2 2
Fairlands Wy STVG SG1 2 A3
STVGE SG2 76 C1
Fairlawns WAT WD17 220 A1
Fairley Wy CHESW EN7 197 F6
Fairmead Av HARP AL5 143 K1
Fair Oak Dr LTNE LU2 70 A6
Fairoaks Gv PEND EN3 214 C7
Fairthorn Cl TRING HP23 134 D6 2
Fair Vw POTB/CUF EN6 193 H8
Fairview Dr WAT WD17 203 K6
Fairview Rd STVG SG1 75 G1
Fairway BSF CM23 106 B3
HHS/BOV HP3 185 K2
SBW CM21 132 D7
WARE SG12 152 B1
Fairway Av BORE WD6 224 A2 2
Fairway Cl HARP AL5 143 H4
LCOL/BKTW AL2 188 E5
Fairways CHES/WCR EN8 197 H4
The Fairway ABLGY WD5 203 J2
HLWS CM18 180 C4
NTHWD HA6 229 K3
Falcon Cl HAT AL10 171 F6
NTHWD HA6 229 K6
SBW CM21 132 A8
STVGE SG2 76 E7
Falconer Rd BUSH WD23 221 H6
Falconers Fld HARP AL5 117 K6
Falconers Pk SBW CM21 132 B8
Falconers Rd LTNE LU2 5 F2
Falconer St BSF CM23 105 F4
Falcon Rdg BERK HP4 161 K6
Falcon Wy GSTN WD25 205 F4
WGCE AL7 147 K1
Faldo Rd AMP/FLIT/B MK45 36 A5
Falkirk Gdns OXHEY WD19 230 E4 2
Falkland Rd BAR EN5 225 K2
Fallowfield LTNN/LIM LU3 69 G5
STVGE SG2 76 D6
WGCE AL7 123 F8
Fallowfield Cl DEN/HRF UB9 228 B7
Fallow Ri HERT/BAY SG13 151 H3
Fallows Gn HARP AL5 118 D6
Falstaff Gdns STAL AL1 188 D1
Falstone Gn LTNE LU2 71 F7
Fanhams Hall Rd WARE SG12 127 J6
Fanhams Rd WARE SG12 127 J7
Fanshaw Ct HERT/WAS SG14 150 E2
Fanshawe Crs WARE SG12 127 F7
Fanshawe St HERT/WAS SG14 150 E2
Fanshaws La HERT/BAY SG13 175 F4
Fantail La TRING HP23 134 E5
Faraday Cl LTNW/LEA LU4 68 B8 1
WATW WD18 219 J6
Faraday Rd STVGE SG2 3 F2
Far End HAT AL10 171 G7
Faringdon Rd LTNW/LEA LU4 68 B6
Faringford Cl POTB/CUF EN6 210 E1 2
Farland Rd HHNE HP2 9 D5
Farley Farm Rd LTN LU1 89 G4
Farley Hl LTN LU1 4 A6
Farm Av HARP AL5 117 K5
Farmbrook LTNE LU2 69 J2
Farm Cl AMS HP6 216 A
BAR EN5 225 G5
BORE WD6 207 H8
CHES/WCR EN8 197 G8
HERT/WAS SG14 150 D3
LWTH SG6 26 A8
POTB/CUF EN6 195 G5
STVG SG1 2 C4
WGCW AL8 147 H3
Farmers Cl GSTN WD25 204 C3
Farm Gn LTN LU1 4 A6
Farm Hill Rd WAB EN9 215 J4
Farmhouse Cl BROX EN10 197 K3
Farmhouse La HHNE HP2 9 D3
Farm La RKW/CH/CXG WD3 218 A3
STDN SG11 101 F
Farm Pl BERK HP4 161 G4
Farm Rd LTN LU1 117 H2
NTHWD HA6 229 H4
RKW/CH/CXG WD3 216 D4
STAL AL1 168 E5
Farm Wy BUSH WD23 221 J4
NTHWD HA6 229 K3
Farnham Cl HHS/BOV HP3 183 J6
SBW CM21 132 A8
Farquhar St HERT/WAS SG14 151 F
Farraline Rd WATW WD18 12 C4
Farrant Wy BORE WD6 223 H1
Farrer Top STALW/RED AL3 115 J
Farriday Cl STALW/RED AL3 168 B2
Farriers WARE SG12 153 F
Farriers Cl BLDK SG7 26 E8
WLYN AL6 94 E8
Farriers End BROX EN10 197 K4
Farriers Wy BORE WD6 224 C
Farringford Cl LCOL/BKTW AL2 188 C4
Farrow Cl LTNN/LIM LU3 52 B
Farr's La LTNE LU2 91 J
Farthing Dr LWTH SG6 42 C
The Farthings HHW HP1 164 A6
Faverolle Gn CHES/WCR EN8 197 H6
Faversham Cl TRING HP23 135 F
Fawcett Rd STVGE SG2 76 C
Fawn Ct BRKMPK AL9 171 H
Fay Gn ABLGY WD5 203 J
Feacey Down HHW HP1 163 K
Fearney Md RKW/CH/CXG WD3 217 K
Fearnley Rd WGCW AL8 147 H
Fearnley St WATW WD18 12 C3
WATW WD18 12 C3
Featherbed La HHS/BOV HP3 185 G
Feather Dell HAT AL10 170 E
Featherstone Gdns BORE WD6 224 C
Featherston Rd STVGE SG2 76 D
Federal Wy WATN WD24 220 D1
Felbrigg Cl LTNE LU2 71 C
Felden Cl GSTN WD25 204 E
Felden Dr HHS/BOV HP3 184 E
Felden La HHS/BOV HP3 184 E
Feldon Cl PIN HA5 231 F
Felix Av LTNE LU2 5 E
Fellowes La STALE/WH AL4 191 H
Fellowes Wy STVGE SG2 3 D
Fells Cl HTCH/STOT SG5 56 D
Felmersham Ct LTN LU1 89 G2

Felmersham Rd *LTN* LU1 .... 89 F2
Felmongers *HLW* CM20 .... 156 E7
Felstead Cl *LTNE* LU2 .... 70 A6 🔢
Felstead Rd *CHES/WCR* EN8 .... 214 D2
Felstead Wy *LTNE* LU2 .... 5 D1
Felton Cl *BORE* WD6 .... 207 H8 🔢
  BROX EN10 .... 197 K5 🔢
  LTNE LU2 .... 70 E8
Fen End *HTCH/STOT* SG5 .... 25 K1
Fennells *HLWW/ROY* CM19 .... 179 J6
Fennycroft Rd *HHW* HP1 .... 163 J3
Fensomes Aly *HHNE* HP2 .... 8 A4 🔢
Fensom's Cl *HHNE* HP2 .... 8 A4 🔢
Fenton Gra *HLWE* CM17 .... 181 F2
Fenwick Cl *LTNN/LIM* LU3 .... 69 G4 🔢
Fermor Crs *LTNE* LU2 .... 70 D8
Fern Cl *BROX* EN10 .... 197 K1 🔢
Ferndale *MHAD* SG10 .... 103 C3
Ferndale Rd *LTN* LU1 .... 89 G2
  PEND EN3 .... 214 D7
Fern Dells *HAT* AL10 .... 170 E5
Ferndene *LCOL/BKTW* AL2 .... 205 G1
Ferndown *NTHWD* HA6 .... 230 B8
Ferndown Cl *PIN* HA5 .... 231 F6
Ferndown Rd *OXHEY* WD19 .... 230 D2
Fern Dr *HHS/BOV* HP3 .... 8 B6
Fernecroft *STAL* AL1 .... 188 E1
Fern Gv *WGCW* AL8 .... 122 D7
Fernheath *LTNN/LIM* LU3 .... 52 A8
Fernhill *HLWS* CM18 .... 180 B5
Fern Hill La *HLWS* CM18 .... 180 C5
Fernhills *ABLGY* WD5 .... 203 J4
Fernleigh Ct *RYLN/HDSTN* HA2 .... 231 J8
Fernleys *STALE/WH* AL4 .... 169 F3
Ferns *PEND* EN3 .... 214 D6 🔢
Fernsleigh Cl *CFSP/GDCR* SL9 .... 226 B5 🔢
Fernville La *HHNE* HP2 .... 8 A5
Fern Wy *STVG* WD25 .... 204 C5
Ferny HI *EBAR* EN4 .... 211 G8
Ferrars Cl *STALE/WH* AL4 .... 68 A8
Ferrers La *STALE/WH* AL4 .... 144 A4
Ferrier Rd *STVGE* SG2 .... 76 D3
Ferryhills Cl *OXHEY* WD19 .... 230 D2
Fesants Cft *HLW* CM20 .... 156 E6
Fetherstone Cl *POTB/CUF* EN6 .... 210 E3 🔢
Fiddle Bridge La *HAT* AL10 .... 170 E3
Fidler Pl *BUSH* WD23 .... 221 J6 🔢
Field Cl *CSHM* HP5 .... 182 A6
  HARP AL5 .... 144 A2
  STALE/WH AL4 .... 168 D2
Field Crs *ROY* SG8 .... 21 K2
Field End *LTNE* LU2 .... 70 D5 🔢
  OXHEY WD19 .... 13 F6 🔢
Fielders Wy *RAD* WD7 .... 207 H3
Fieldfare *LWTH* SG6 .... 25 J8
  STVGE SG2 .... 76 E6
Fieldfares *LCOL/BKTW* AL2 .... 190 B5
Fieldgate Rd *LTNW/LEA* LU4 .... 68 C6
Fieldings Rd *CHES/WCR* EN8 .... 197 K7
Field La *LWTH* SG6 .... 41 K5
Field Wy *HHNE* HP2 .... 9 D6
  OXHEY WD19 .... 13 F5
Fields End *TRING* HP23 .... 135 F3
Fields End La *HHW* HP1 .... 163 G4
Field Vw *BAR* EN5 .... 225 G4
Field View Ri *LCOL/BKTW* AL2 .... 188 A7
Field View Rd *POTB/CUF* EN6 .... 210 B3
Fieldway *BERK* HP4 .... 162 B7
Field Wy *CFSP/GDCR* SL9 .... 226 A6 🔢
  HHW HP1 .... 183 J5
  HOD EN11 .... 153 G7
  RKW/CH/CXG WD3 .... 218 A3
Fieldway *TRING* HP23 .... 135 J8
  WARE SG12 .... 153 C5
Fifth Av *GSTN* WD25 .... 204 E5
  LWTH SG6 .... 42 C2
Fifth Avenue Allende Av *HLW* CM20 .... 6 C3
Figtree HI *HHNE* HP2 .... 8 A4
Filey Cl *STVG* SG1 .... 75 F2
Filmer Rd *LTNW/LEA* LU4 .... 68 C5
Finch Cl *HAT* AL10 .... 171 F4
Finchdale *HHW* HP1 .... 163 K6
Finches End *STVGE* SG2 .... 77 J1
The Finches *HERT/BAY* SG13 .... 152 A3 🔢
  HTCHE/RSTV SG4 .... 56 E2
Finch Gn *RKW/CH/CXG* WD3 .... 217 J4
Finch La *BUSH* WD23 .... 221 H4
Finchmoor *HLWS* CM18 .... 180 A4
Finch Rd *BERK* HP4 .... 161 H5
Finley Rd *HARP* AL5 .... 119 F6
Finsbury Rd *LTNW/LEA* LU4 .... 68 C5
Finucane Ri *BUSH* WD23 .... 231 K1
Finway *LTN* LU1 .... 89 F1
Finway Rd *HHNE* HP2 .... 9 E1
Firbank Cl *LTNN/LIM* LU3 .... 68 B1
Firbank Dr *OXHEY* WD19 .... 13 F6
Firbank Rd *STALE/WH* AL4 .... 168 C2
Fir Cl *STVGE* SG2 .... 76 A8
Firecrest *LWTH* SG6 .... 25 J8
Firlands *BSF* CM23 .... 105 H3
Fir Pk *HLWW/ROY* CM19 .... 179 J4
Firs Cl *HAT* AL10 .... 171 C5
  HTCH/STOT SG5 .... 56 B1 🔢
Firs Dr *STALE/WH* AL4 .... 120 A4
Firs La *POTB/CUF* EN6 .... 210 C3

First Av *GSTN* WD25 .... 204 D5
First Avenue Mandela Av *HLW* CM20... 6 C3
  HLWE CM17 .... 156 E6
The Firs *CHESW* EN7 .... 196 C4
  STAL AL1 .... 189 K2
  TRING HP23 .... 135 J8
  WGCW AL8 .... 122 C7
Firs Wk *NTHWD* HA6 .... 230 A6
  WLYN AL6 .... 123 K4
Fir Tree Cl *HHS/BOV* HP3 .... 9 D6
Fir Tree Ct *BORE* WD6 .... 223 J4
Fir Tree HI *RKW/CH/CXG* WD3 .... 203 F7
Firway *WLYN* AL6 .... 123 F2
Firway Cl *WLYN* AL6 .... 123 F2
Firwood Av *STALE/WH* AL4 .... 169 H6
Fisher Cl *KGLGY* WD4 .... 186 A7
Fishers Cl *CHES/WCR* EN8 .... 215 F4
  STDN SG11 .... 81 J6
Fishers Gn *STVG* SG1 .... 58 A8
Fisher's Green Rd *STVG* SG1 .... 75 G3
Fishers Md *STDN* SG11 .... 81 J6
Fishery Rd *HHW* HP1 .... 163 K8
Fish Farm St *STALW/RED* AL3 .... 142 C4 🔢
Fish HI *ROY* SG8 .... 21 H3
Fishponds Rd *HTCH/STOT* SG5 .... 56 C1
Fishpool St *STALW/RED* AL3 .... 10 B4 🔢
Fish St *STALW/RED* AL3 .... 142 C4
Fitzjohn Av *BAR* EN5 .... 225 K5
Fitzroy Av *LTNN/LIM* LU3 .... 69 G6
Fitzwarin Cl *LTNN/LIM* LU3 .... 68 D2
Fitzwilliams Ct *HLWE* CM17 .... 157 H5 🔢
Five Acres *HLWS* CM18 .... 180 B4
  KGLGY WD4 .... 185 K7
  LCOL/BKTW AL2 .... 190 B3
  STSD CM24 .... 86 D1
Five Acres Av *LCOL/BKTW* AL2 .... 188 B7
Five Fields Cl *OXHEY* WD19 .... 231 G1
Five Oaks *LTN* LU1 .... 88 C5
Five Springs *LTNN/LIM* LU3 .... 68 D3
Flagstaff Cl *WAB* EN9 .... 215 G3
Flagstaff Rd *WAB* EN9 .... 215 G2
The Flags *HHNE* HP2 .... 9 E5
Flamsteadbury La
  STALW/RED AL3 .... 142 B5
Flamstead End Rd
  CHESW EN8 .... 197 F6
Flash La *ENC/FH* EN2 .... 213 F7
Flatfield Rd *HHS/BOV* HP3 .... 165 F8
Flaunden Bottom *CSHM* HP5 .... 200 B7
Flaunden HI *HHS/BOV* HP3 .... 200 C3
Flaunden La *HHS/BOV* HP3 .... 200 C3
  RKW/CH/CXG WD3 .... 201 H3
Flavian Cl *STALW/RED* AL3 .... 167 G8
Flecks La *STDN* SG11 .... 81 K5
The Fleet *ROY* SG8 .... 21 G3
Fleetwood Crs *STVG* SG1 .... 75 G2
Fleetwood Wy *OXHEY* WD19 .... 230 D3
Fleming Cl *CHESW* EN7 .... 196 E4
Fleming Crs *HERT/WAS* SG14 .... 150 D3 🔢
Fletcher Wy *HHNE* HP2 .... 164 B4
Flexley Wd *WGCE* AL7 .... 123 F8
Flex Meadow *HLWW/ROY* CM19 .... 179 F2
Flinders Cl *STAL* AL1 .... 11 F6
  STVGE SG2 .... 76 D4
Flint Cl *LTNN/LIM* LU3 .... 68 D2
Flint Copse *STALW/RED* AL3 .... 142 D3
The Flintings *HHNE* HP2 .... 139 J1
Flint Rd *LWTH* SG6 .... 42 C1
Flint Wy *STALW/RED* AL3 .... 167 K2
Flitch Wy *RBSF* CM22 .... 107 J2
Flora Gv *STAL* AL1 .... 11 E5
Floral Dr *LCOL/BKTW* AL2 .... 190 B4
Florence Av *LTNN/LIM* LU3 .... 68 C3
Florence Cl *GSTN* WD25 .... 204 B5 🔢
  HLWE CM17 .... 181 F3 🔢
Florence St *HTCH/STOT* SG5 .... 56 D1
Flowers Wy *LTN* LU1 .... 4 C4 🔢
Flowton Gv *HARP* AL5 .... 143 H2
Fold Cft *HLW* CM20 .... 155 H8
Foldingshott *KNEB* SG3 .... 96 E6
Follett Dr *ABLGY* WD5 .... 204 A1
Folly Av *STALW/RED* AL3 .... 10 B3
  RAD WD7 .... 206 C6
Folly Flds *STALE/WH* AL4 .... 119 K7
Folly La *LTN* LU1 .... 88 C5
  STALW/RED AL3 .... 10 B3
Folly Pathway *RAD* WD7 .... 206 C5
The Folly *BUNT* SG9 .... 63 H2
  HERT/WAS SG14 .... 151 G3
Folly Vw *WARE* SG12 .... 153 C4
Fontmell Cl *STALW/RED* AL3 .... 11 D1
Football Cl *BLDK* SG7 .... 26 E8
Forbes Av *POTB/CUF* EN6 .... 210 E3
Ford Cl *BUSH* WD23 .... 221 K4 🔢
Ford Fld *STDN* SG11 .... 103 H1
Fordham Cl *BLDK* SG7 .... 17 K4
Fordham Rd *ROY* SG8 .... 21 J4 🔢
Ford HI *STDN* SG11 .... 103 J1
Ford St *STDN* SG11 .... 81 K3
Fordwich Cl *HERT/WAS* SG14 .... 150 D3 🔢
Fordwich HI *HERT/WAS* SG14 .... 150 D3
Fordwich Ri *HERT/WAS* SG14 .... 150 D3
Fordwich Rd *WGCW* AL8 .... 147 H4 🔢
Forebury Av *SBW* CM21 .... 132 D7

The Forebury *SBW* CM21 .... 132 D7
Forefield *LCOL/BKTW* AL2 .... 188 C5
Forest Av *HHS/BOV* HP3 .... 164 C8 🔢
Foresters Cl *CHESW* EN7 .... 196 C5
Foresthall Rd *STSD* CM24 .... 86 C5
Fore St *BRKMPK* AL9 .... 171 H3
  HERT/WAS SG14 .... 151 C3
  LTN LU1 .... 157 F5
  HTCHE/RSTV SG4 .... 43 H8
Forest Rd *CHES/WCR* EN8 .... 197 H2
  GSTN WD25 .... 204 C3
  PEND EN3 .... 214 D6
Forest Rw *STVG* SG2 .... 76 A8
Forest Wy *HLWE* CM17 .... 180 E5
  RBSF CM22 .... 107 H3
Forge Cl *HTCH/STOT* SG5 .... 56 D1 🔢
  KGLGY WD4 .... 201 K1
Forge End *LCOL/BKTW* AL2 .... 188 C5
Forge La *NTHWD* HA6 .... 229 K6
  WLYN AL6 .... 122 B4
Forres Cl *HOD* EN11 .... 177 F1
Forrest Crs *LTNE* LU2 .... 70 B1
Foresters Dr *WGCE* AL7 .... 148 D4 🔢
Fortuna Cl *STVGE* SG2 .... 76 D1
Fortune La *BORE* WD6 .... 223 G6
The Fortunes *HLWS* CM18 .... 7 E6
Forty HI *EN* EN1 .... 213 J7
Foster Cl *CHES/WCR* EN8 .... 197 J8 🔢
  STVG SG1 .... 58 C8
Foster Dr *HTCHE/RSTV* SG4 .... 56 E4
Foster Rd *HHW* HP1 .... 164 A8 🔢
Foster St *HLWE* CM17 .... 181 J3
Foston Cl *LTNN/LIM* LU3 .... 68 E4
Fotherley Rd *RKW/CH/CXG* WD3 .... 227 J1
Founceley Av *WARE* SG12 .... 99 J1
Founders Rd *HOD* EN11 .... 153 G8
Fountain Farm *HLWS* CM18 .... 7 E6 🔢
Fountain Pl *WAB* EN9 .... 215 H4 🔢
Fountains Dr *HHS/BOV* HP3 .... 164 C8
Fouracres *LWTH* SG6 .... 42 A7
Four Acres *STVG* SG1 .... 2 B1
  WGCE AL7 .... 147 K5
Fouracres Dr *HHS/BOV* HP3 .... 164 C8 🔢
The Four Acres *SBW* CM21 .... 132 E7
Fouracres Wk *HHS/BOV* HP3 .... 164 C8
Four Limes *STALE/WH* AL4 .... 145 C1
Fourth Av *GSTN* WD25 .... 204 E5 🔢
  HLW CM20 .... 6 B3
  HLWW/ROY CM19 .... 179 H1
  LTNN/LIM LU3 .... 68 C2
  LWTH SG6 .... 42 C2
The Four Tubs *BUSH* WD23 .... 222 A7 🔢
  BUSH WD23 .... 222 A7 🔢
Fovant Cl *HARP* AL5 .... 143 K3
Fowley Cl *CHES/WCR* EN8 .... 214 E4
Foxbury Cl *LTNE* LU2 .... 69 J3
Fox Cl *BORE* WD6 .... 223 G6 🔢
  BUSH WD23 .... 221 J5
  TRING HP23 .... 135 H8
Fox Cnr *ROY* SG8 .... 15 G4
Foxcroft *STAL* AL1 .... 11 F6
Foxdell *NTHWD* HA6 .... 229 J5
Foxdells *HERT/WAS* SG14 .... 149 K6
Foxdells La *BSF* CM23 .... 85 J7
Foxdell Wy *CFSP/GDCR* SL9 .... 226 B4
Foxes Cl *HERT/BAY* SG13 .... 152 A3
Foxes Dr *CHESW* EN7 .... 196 D7
Foxes La *POTB/CUF* EN6 .... 195 G6
Foxfield *STVGE* SG2 .... 76 D6
Foxfield Cl *NTHWD* HA6 .... 230 A5
Foxglove Bank *ROY* SG8 .... 21 K4 🔢
Foxglove Cl *BSF* CM23 .... 105 F3
  HAT AL10 .... 171 G3 🔢
The Foxgloves *HHW* HP1 .... 163 H7
Foxglove Wy *WLYN* AL6 .... 122 E1 🔢
Foxgrove Pth *OXHEY* WD19 .... 230 E4
Foxhill *LTNE* LU2 .... 69 K4
Fox HI *ROY* SG8 .... 15 G4
Foxhill *WATN* WD24 .... 204 B6
Fox Hill Rd *ROY* SG8 .... 15 G4
Foxholes Av *HERT/BAY* SG13 .... 151 K3 🔢
Foxhollows *HAT* AL10 .... 171 G2
Foxlands Cl *GSTN* WD25 .... 204 A4
Foxley Dr *BSF* CM23 .... 105 K1
Foxley Gv *WLYN* AL6 .... 122 E5
Foxleys *OXHEY* WD19 .... 231 F2
Fox Rd *STVG* SG2 .... 2 C3
  TRING HP23 .... 135 H7
Fox's La *BRKMPK* AL9 .... 192 E2
Foxton Rd *HOD* EN11 .... 176 E6
Frampton Rd *POTB/CUF* EN6 .... 193 J8
Frampton St *HERT/WAS* SG14 .... 151 G3
Francis Av *STALW/RED* AL3 .... 10 C1
Francis Cl *HTCH/STOT* SG5 .... 25 J1
  HTCHE/RSTV SG4 .... 56 E4
Francis Rd *BLDK* SG7 .... 16 C3
  WARE SG12 .... 127 H7
  WATW WD18 .... 12 C3
Francis St *LTN* LU1 .... 4 A3
Frankland Cl *RKW/CH/CXG* WD3 .... 219 F7
Frankland Rd *RKW/CH/CXG* WD3 .... 219 G6
Franklin Av *AMP/FLIT/B* MK45 .... 36 B6
  CHESW EN7 .... 196 E8
Franklin Cl *HTCH/STOT* SG5 .... 39 F5
  STALE/WH AL4 .... 170 D8

Franklin Gdns *HTCHE/RSTV* SG4 .... 41 F8
Franklin Rd *WAT* WD17 .... 12 C1 🔲
Franklin's Rd *STVG* SG2 .... 75 H1
Frank Martin Ct *CHESW* EN7 .... 196 E8
Fraser Rd *CHES/WCR* EN8 .... 197 J6 🔲
Frederick St *LTNE* LU2 .... 4 C3
Frederick Street Pas *LTNE* LU2 .... 4 B3
Freeman Av *LTNN/LIM* LU3 .... 69 G1
Freemans Cl *HTCH/STOT* SG5 .... 40 A8
Freewaters Cl *HTCH/STOT* SG5 .... 40 C5
Freman Dr *BUNT* SG9 .... 63 H1 🔲
French Horn La *HAT* AL10 .... 171 G3 🔲
French Rw *STAL* AL1 .... 10 C4 🔲
French's Cl *WARE* SG12 .... 153 F4
Frensham *CHESW* EN7 .... 196 D5
Frensham Dr *HTCHE/RSTV* SG4 .... 41 G7
Freshwater Cl *LTNN/LIM* LU3 .... 68 E2
Freshwaters *HLW* CM20 .... 7 D3 🔲
Fretherne Rd *WGCW* AL8 .... 147 J3
Friars Cl *LTN* LU1 .... 89 G4
Friarscroft *BROX* EN10 .... 177 F6
Friars Fld *BERK* HP4 .... 161 F2
Friars Rd *HTCHE/RSTV* SG4 .... 43 H8
    STDN SG11 .... 82 B2
Friars Wk *TRING* HP23 .... 135 F5
Friars Wy *BUSH* WD23 .... 221 G1
    KGLGY WD4 .... 186 A8
    LTN LU1 .... 89 G4
Friars Wd *BSF* CM23 .... 105 K2 🔲
Friday Furlong *HTCH/STOT* SG5 .... 56 A1 🔲
Friedberg Av *BSF* CM23 .... 105 G4
Friendless La *HTCHE/RSTV* AL3 .... 115 J6
Friends Av *CHES/WCR* EN8 .... 214 C2
Frimley Rd *HHW* HP1 .... 163 H5
Fringewood Cl *NTHWD* HA6 .... 229 G7
Frinton Cl *OXHEY* WD19 .... 230 C1
Friston Gn *LTNE* LU2 .... 70 E8 🔲
Frithsden Copse *BERK* HP4 .... 162 C1
Frithwood Av *NTHWD* HA6 .... 230 A5
Frobisher Cl *BUSH* WD23 .... 221 H6
Frobisher Dr *STVGE* SG2 .... 3 F1
Frobisher Rd *STAL* AL1 .... 169 F8
Frobisher Wy *STVGE* SG2 .... 3 F1
Froghall La *STDN* SG11 .... 60 D8
Frogmoor La *RKW/CH/CXG* WD3 .... 228 C3
Frogmore *LCOL/BKTW* AL2 .... 189 G5
Frogmore Hl *HERT/WAS* SG14 .... 97 J3 🔲
Frogmore Rd *HHS/BOV* HP3 .... 185 H2 🔲
Frogmore St *TRING* HP23 .... 135 F5
Frogs Hall La *STDN* SG11 .... 79 J6
Frome Cl *LTNW/LEA* LU4 .... 68 C5
Frome Sq *HHNE* HP2 .... 165 F1 🔲
Front St *LTN* LU1 .... 89 H8
The Front *BERK* HP4 .... 162 E2
Frowick Cl *BRKMPK* AL9 .... 192 B1
Frowyke Crs *POTB/CUF* EN6 .... 209 F2
Fry Rd *STVGE* SG2 .... 76 D4
Fryth Md *STALW/RED* AL3 .... 10 A3
Fulbeck Wy *RYLN/HDSTN* HA2 .... 231 K8
Fulbourne Cl *LTNW/LEA* LU4 .... 68 D7
Fulford Gv *OXHEY* WD19 .... 230 C1
Fuller Ct *BSF* CM23 .... 105 K2 🔲
Fuller Gdns *WATN* SG24 .... 204 C7
Fuller Rd *WATN* SG24 .... 204 C7
Fullers Cl *LWTH* SG6 .... 41 J2
Fullers Md *HLWE* CM17 .... 181 F2
Fuller Wy *RKW/CH/CXG* WD3 .... 219 F5
Fulling Mill La *WLYN* AL6 .... 122 B3
Fulmar Crs *HHW* HP1 .... 163 K7
Fulmore Cl *HARP* AL5 .... 119 F5
Fulton Cl *STVG* SG1 .... 2 A3
Fulton Crs *BSF* CM23 .... 86 B8
Furham Fld *PIN* HA5 .... 231 H6
Furlay Cl *LWTH* SG6 .... 41 H2
Furlongs *HHW* HP1 .... 163 K5
Furlong Wy *WARE* SG12 .... 152 E2
Furriers *BSF* CM23 .... 105 F4
The Furrows *LTNN/LIM* LU3 .... 69 G2
Furse Av *STALE/WH* AL4 .... 11 F1
Furtherfield *ABLGY* WD5 .... 203 K2 🔲
Furtherground *HHNE* HP2 .... 8 B6 🔲
Furzebushes La *LCOL/BKTW* AL2 .... 188 A3
Furze Cl *LTNE* LU2 .... 69 J2
    OXHEY WD19 .... 230 D4
Furzedown *STVGE* SG2 .... 3 F4
Furzedown Ct *HARP* AL5 .... 143 J1
Furzefield *WGCE* AL7 .... 147 K4
Furze Gv *ROY* SG8 .... 21 J4 🔲
Furzehill Rd *BORE* WD6 .... 224 B5
Furzen Crs *HAT* AL10 .... 170 E7
Furze Rd *HHW* HP1 .... 163 H7
Furze Vw *RKW/CH/CXG* WD3 .... 217 F6

G

Gable Cl *ABLGY* WD5 .... 203 K2
    PIN HA5 .... 231 H6
Gables Av *BORE* WD6 .... 223 J3
Gables Cl *CFSP/GDCR* SL9 .... 226 B3
Gaddesden Crs *WATN* SG24 .... 204 E4
Gaddesden Gv *WGCE* AL7 .... 148 C3 🔲
Gaddesden La *STALW/RED* AL3 .... 141 F5
Gaddesden Rw *HHNE* HP2 .... 139 K1
Gade Av *WATW* WD18 .... 219 K4
Gade Bank *RKW/CH/CXG* WD3 .... 219 J4
Gadebridge La *HHW* HP1 .... 164 A4
Gadebridge Rd *HHW* HP1 .... 164 A5
Gade Cl *HHW* HP1 .... 164 A3
    WATW WD18 .... 219 K4
Gade Valley Cl *KGLGY* WD4 .... 186 A6
Gade View Rd *HHS/BOV* HP3 .... 185 G2
Gadmore La *TRING* HP23 .... 158 D2
Gadswell Cl *GSTN* WD25 .... 205 F6
Gage Cl *ROY* SG8 .... 21 H1
Gainsborough Av *STAL* AL1 .... 11 E3
Gainsford Crs *HTCHE/RSTV* SG4 .... 41 C7
Gainswood *WGCE* AL7 .... 147 K4
Gall End La *STSD* CM24 .... 86 C2
Galley Gn *HERT/BAY* SG13 .... 153 F7 🔲
Galley Hl *HHW* HP1 .... 163 K4 🔲
Galleyhill Rd *WAB* EN9 .... 215 K2 🔲
Galley La *BAR* EN5 .... 209 F8
Galliard Cl *LTNN/LIM* LU3 .... 69 G5
Galloway Cl *BROX* EN10 .... 197 K4
    BSF CM23 .... 105 J1
Galloway Rd *BSF* CM23 .... 105 J1
Gallows Hl *KGLGY* WD4 .... 203 H1
Gallows Hill La *ABLGY* WD5 .... 203 H2
Galston Rd *LTNN/LIM* LU3 .... 68 C1
Gammon Cl *HHS/BOV* HP3 .... 9 D6
Gammons La *WATN* SG24 .... 204 B7
Gandhi Ct *WATN* SG24 .... 131 E1 🔲
Gangies Hl *SBW* CM21 .... 131 J6
Ganton Vw *OXHEY* WD19 .... 231 F3 🔲
Ganymede Pl *HHNE* HP2 .... 8 C2 🔲
Gaping La *HTCH/STOT* SG5 .... 56 B2
Garden Av *HAT* AL10 .... 171 F7
Garden Cl *BAR* EN5 .... 225 H4
    HARP AL5 .... 143 H4
    ROY SG8 .... 21 J2
    STAL AL1 .... 168 C5
    WAT WD17 .... 12 A1
Garden Ct *STALE/WH* AL4 .... 120 B8
Garden Field La *BERK* HP4 .... 162 C7
Gardenia Av *LTNN/LIM* LU3 .... 69 F5
Garden La *ROY* SG8 .... 21 H4
Garden Reach *CSTG* HP8 .... 216 A3
Garden Rd *ABLGY* WD5 .... 203 K1 🔲
    BUNT SG9 .... 63 J1
    KNEB SG3 .... 96 C7
Garden Rw *HTCH/STOT* SG5 .... 56 B1
The Gardens *BLDK* SG7 .... 42 E1 🔲
    BRKMPK AL9 .... 192 E5
    HTCH/STOT SG5 .... 25 J3
    WAT WD17 .... 12 A1
Garden Terrace Rd *HLWE* CM17 .... 157 F5
Garden Wk *ROY* SG8 .... 21 J2
Gardiners La *BLDK* SG7 .... 17 K5
The Gardiners *HLWE* CM17 .... 180 E2
Garfield St *WATN* SG24 .... 204 C8
Garland Rd *WARE* SG12 .... 127 J8
    HHNE HP2 .... 8 A4 🔲
Garnault Rd *EN* EN1 .... 213 J8
Garner Dr *BROX* EN10 .... 197 J4
Garners Cl *CFSP/GDCR* SL9 .... 226 B5
Garners End *CFSP/GDCR* SL9 .... 226 B5
Garners Rd *CFSP/GDCR* SL9 .... 226 B5
Garnett Cl *WATN* SG24 .... 204 E6
Garnett Rd *DEN/HRF* UB9 .... 228 C8
Garrard Wy *STALE/WH* AL4 .... 145 G1
Garratts Rd *BUSH* WD23 .... 221 K7
Garretts Md *LTNE* LU2 .... 70 C2
Garrisan Wy *GSTN* WD25 .... 204 E6
Garston Crs *GSTN* WD25 .... 204 D4
Garston Dr *GSTN* WD25 .... 204 D4
Garston La *GSTN* WD25 .... 204 E4
Garthland Dr *BAR* EN5 .... 225 G5
Garth Rd *LWTH* SG6 .... 41 J6
The Garth *ABLGY* WD5 .... 203 J3
Gartlet Rd *WAT* WD17 .... 12 C2
Gascoyne Wy *HERT/BAY* SG13 .... 151 G4
Gas La *ROY* SG8 .... 32 C5
Gate Cl *BORE* WD6 .... 224 B1
Gatecroft *HHS/BOV* HP3 .... 164 B8
Gate End *NTHWD* HA6 .... 230 B6
Gatehill Gdns *LTNN/LIM* LU3 .... 52 B8 🔲
Gatehill Rd *NTHWD* HA6 .... 230 A6
Gatesbury Wy *STDN* SG11 .... 81 K6 🔲
Gatesdene Cl *BERK* HP4 .... 137 K1
Gateshead Rd *BORE* WD6 .... 223 J2
Gates Wy *STVG* SG1 .... 2 A2
Gateway Cl *NTHWD* HA6 .... 229 H5
The Gateways *CHESW* EN7 .... 196 B6
Gatwick Cl *BSF* CM23 .... 86 A8 🔲
Gauldie Wy *STDN* SG11 .... 81 J7
Gaumont Ap *WATW* WD18 .... 12 C2
Gaunts Wy *LWTH* SG6 .... 25 K7
Gaveston Dr *BERK* HP4 .... 161 J3
Gayland Av *LTNE* LU2 .... 5 F3
Gayton Cl *LTNN/LIM* LU3 .... 69 F5
Gaywood Av *CHES/WCR* EN8 .... 197 H8
Geddes Rd *BUSH* WD23 .... 221 K4 🔲
Geddings Rd *HOD* EN11 .... 177 G3
The Generals Wk *PEND* EN3 .... 214 D7 🔲

Gentlemens Fld *WARE* SG12 .... 127 F6
George La *ROY* SG8 .... 21 H3 🔲
George Leighton Ct *STVGE* SG2 .... 3 F3
Georges Md *BORE* WD6 .... 223 G6 🔲
George St *BERK* HP4 .... 162 A5
    HERT/WAS SG14 .... 151 F3
    HHNE HP2 .... 8 C4
    LTN LU1 .... 4 C4
    STALW/RED AL3 .... 10 C4
    STALW/RED AL3 .... 115 J4
    WATW WD18 .... 13 D3
George St West *LTN* LU1 .... 4 C4 🔲
George's Wood Rd *BRKMPK* AL9 .... 193 G4
George V Av *PIN* HA5 .... 231 G8
George V Wy *RKW/CH/CXG* WD3 .... 201 K6
George Wk *WARE* SG12 .... 127 H8 🔲
Georgewood Rd *HHS/BOV* HP3 .... 185 K3
Gerard Av *BSF* CM23 .... 105 H5
Gernon Rd *LWTH* SG6 .... 41 K4
Gernon Wk *LWTH* SG6 .... 41 K4
Gew's Cnr *CHES/WCR* EN8 .... 197 H7
Ghibert Wy *BERK* HP4 .... 161 H5
Gibb Cft *HLWS* CM18 .... 180 B5
Gibbons Wy *KNEB* SG3 .... 96 A5
Gibbs Cl *CHES/WCR* EN8 .... 197 H7
Gibbs Couch *OXHEY* WD19 .... 230 E2
Gibbs Fld *BSF* CM23 .... 105 G4
Gibson Cl *HTCHE/RSTV* SG4 .... 57 F2
Gifford's La *STDN* SG11 .... 79 K7
Gilbert Rd *DEN/HRF* UB9 .... 228 C8
Gilbert's Hl *TRING* HP23 .... 158 D6
Gilbert St *PEND* EN3 .... 214 B7
Gilbey Av *BSF* CM23 .... 106 A3
Gilbey Crs *STSD* CM24 .... 86 D1
Gildea Cl *PIN* HA5 .... 231 H6
Gilden Cl *HLWE* CM17 .... 157 H5 🔲
Gilden Wy *HLWE* CM17 .... 157 G6
Gilder Cl *LTNN/LIM* LU3 .... 69 F1
Gilderdale *LTNW/LEA* LU4 .... 68 A3
Gilders *SBW* CM21 .... 132 B7
Giles Cl *STALE/WH* AL4 .... 145 F8
Gillam St *LTNE* LU2 .... 4 C3
Gillan Gn *BUSH* WD23 .... 231 K1 🔲
Gillian Av *STAL* AL1 .... 188 E2
Gilliat's Gn *RKW/CH/CXG* WD3 .... 217 G4
Gillison Cl *LWTH* SG6 .... 42 B4
Gills Hl *RAD* WD7 .... 206 C5
Gills Hill La *RAD* WD7 .... 206 C5
Gills Hollow *RAD* WD7 .... 206 C6
Gilmour Ct *ENC/FH* EN2 .... 213 K5
Gilpin Gn *HARP* AL5 .... 118 E8
Gilpin Rd *WARE* SG12 .... 152 D1
Gilpin's Gallop *WARE* SG12 .... 153 C5
Gilpin's Ride *BERK* HP4 .... 162 B4
Gilsland *WAB* EN9 .... 215 K5
Ginns Rd *BUNT* SG9 .... 67 F3
Gippeswyck Cl *PIN* HA5 .... 230 E7 🔲
Gipsy La *BSF* CM23 .... 86 B5
    KNEB SG3 .... 95 K4
    LTN LU1 .... 5 E5
Girdle Rd *HTCHE/RSTV* SG4 .... 40 E7
Girons Rd *HTCHE/RSTV* SG4 .... 57 F2
Girtin Rd *BUSH* WD23 .... 221 J5
Girton Ct *CHES/WCR* EN8 .... 197 J8
Girton Wy *RKW/CH/CXG* WD3 .... 219 H5
Gisburne Wy *WATN* SG24 .... 204 B7
Gladden Ct *HLWS* CM18 .... 180 B5 🔲
Gladding Rd *CHESW* EN7 .... 195 K3
Gladeside *STALE/WH* AL4 .... 169 G3
The Glades *HHW* HP1 .... 163 H5
The Glade *BLDK* SG7 .... 42 E2
    LWTH SG6 .... 41 K6
    WGCW AL8 .... 147 H1 🔲
The Gladeway *WAB* EN9 .... 215 J3
Gladsmuir Rd *BAR* EN5 .... 225 K2
Gladstone Rd *HOD* EN11 .... 177 G2
    WARE SG12 .... 99 J1
    WARE SG12 .... 127 G7
    WAT WD17 .... 13 D2
Glaisdale *LTNW/LEA* LU4 .... 68 B4 🔲
Glamis Cl *CHESW* EN7 .... 196 E7
    HHNE HP2 .... 141 G8
Gleave Av *ARL/CHE* SG15 .... 24 E2
Glebe Av *BRKMPK* AL9 .... 173 G3 🔲
    CFSP/GDCR SL9 .... 226 A3
    HERT/WAS SG14 .... 98 A6
    HERT/WAS SG14 .... 151 G1 🔲
    HHS/BOV HP3 .... 185 J1
    LBUZ LU7 .... 110 D4
Glebe Cottages *BRKMPK* AL9 .... 173 G3
Glebe Ct *BSF* CM23 .... 106 A1
Glebelands *HLW* CM20 .... 7 E1
Glebe La *BAR* EN5 .... 225 F5
Glebe Rd *HERT/WAS* SG14 .... 151 G1
    LWTH SG6 .... 42 A2
    WLYN AL6 .... 122 B4
The Glebe *GSTN* WD25 .... 204 D3
    KGLGY WD4 .... 186 A7 🔲
Glemsford Cl *LTNW/LEA* LU4 .... 68 A3 🔲
Glemsford Dr *HARP* AL5 .... 119 F7
Glencoe Rd *BUSH* WD23 .... 221 H6
Glencorse Gn *OXHEY* WD19 .... 230 E3 🔲

Glendale HHW HP1 164 A6
Gleneagles Cl OXHEY WD19 230 E4 3
Gleneagles Dr LTNE LU2 69 K3
Glenester Cl HOD EN11 153 F8
Glen Faba Rd HLWW/ROY CM19 178 A3
Glenferrie Rd STAL AL1 11 F4
Glenfield Ct HERT/WAS SG14 150 C2 1
Glenfield Rd LTNN/LIM LU3 69 H3
Glengall Pl STAL AL1 189 G1 2
Glenhaven Av BORE WD6 223 K3
Glenlyn Av STAL AL1 168 E7 2
The Glen HHNE HP2 165 F1
LTN LU1 88 D6
NTHWD HA6 229 J6
Glenview Rd HHW HP1 164 A6
Glenville Av ENC/FH EN2 213 F8
Glen Wy WAT WD17 203 K8
Glenwood BROX EN10 176 E5
WGCE AL7 148 D4 5
Glenwood Cl STVGE SG2 76 D7
Glevum Cl STALW/RED AL3 167 G8
Globe Cl HARP AL5 118 E8
Globe Crs BSF CM23 85 G3
Gloucester Av CHES/WCR EN8 214 D3
Gloucester Cl STVG SG1 58 E7 1
Gloucester Rd ENC/FH EN2 213 F8
LTN LU1 5 D5 2
Glover Cl CHESW EN7 196 D5 2
Glovers Cl HERT/BAY SG13 151 F5 1
Glovers La HLWE CM17 181 H6
The Glynde STVGE SG2 96 C1
Glynswood CFSP/GDCR SL9 226 C6
Goat La EN EN1 213 J8
Goblins Gn WGCE AL7 147 J4
Goddard End STVGE SG2 76 D8
Goddards Cl HERT/BAY SG13 173 K5
Godfrey Cl STVGE SG2 3 F5
Godfreys Cl LTN LU1 89 G3
Godfries Cl WLYN AL6 124 A6
Godwin Cl CHING E4 215 H8
Goffs Crs CHESW EN7 196 A7
Goff's La CHESW EN7 196 A7
Goff's Oak Av CHESW EN7 195 K6
Golda Cl BAR EN5 225 J6
Gold Cl BROX EN10 176 D6
Goldcrest Wy BUSH WD23 221 K8
Goldcroft HHS/BOV HP3 165 F8
Golden Dell WGCE AL7 148 A7
Goldfield Rd TRING HP23 134 E6
Goldfinch Wy BORE WD6 223 K4 5
Gold Hl East CFSP/GDCR SL9 226 A8
Goldings BSF CM23 106 A1
Goldings Crs HAT AL10 171 G3
Goldings La HERT/WAS SG14 125 J8
Goldington Cl HOD EN11 152 E8 1
Goldon LWTH SG6 42 B5
Goldstone Cl WARE SG12 127 H7 3
Golf Cl BUSH WD23 13 E2
Golf Club Rd BRKMPK AL9 193 G4
Golf Ride ENC/FH EN2 212 D5
Gombards STALW/RED AL3 10 C3 2
Gomer Cl HTCHE/RSTV SG4 94 D8
Gonville Av RKW/CH/CXG WD3 219 G6
Gonville Crs STVGE SG2 76 D7
Goodey Meade STVGE SG2 78 C7
Goodliffe Pk BSF CM23 86 A7
Goodrich Cl GSTN WD25 204 B5
Goodwin Ct CHES/WCR EN8 197 J6 4
Goodwins Md LBUZ LU7 110 A2
Goodwin Stile BSF CM23 105 G4
Goodwood Av PEND EN3 214 B7
WATN WD24 203 K5
Goodwood Cl HOD EN11 176 E2
Goodwood Rd ROY SG8 21 K3 1
Goodyers Av RAD WD7 206 C3
Goose Acre CSHM HP5 182 C8
LBUZ LU7 110 A2
Gooseacre WGCE AL7 148 A5
Gooseberry Hl LTNN/LIM LU3 69 G2
Goosecroft HHW HP1 163 J5 2
Goosefields RKW/CH/CXG WD3 218 B6
Goose La RBSF CM22 133 H2
Goral Md RKW/CH/CXG WD3 218 C8
Gordian Wy STVG SG1 59 J8
Gordon Cl STAL AL1 168 E7 3
Gordon Rd CHES/WCR EN8 215 F4
Gordon St LTN LU1 4 B4 3
Gordons Wk HARP AL5 143 K1 2
Gorelands La CSTG HP8 226 B1
Gore La STDN SG11 101 H6
Gorham Dr STAL AL1 189 G1
Gorle Cl GSTN WD25 204 B4
Gorleston Cl STVG SG1 58 A8
Gorse Cl HAT AL10 170 E7
Gorse Cnr STALW/RED AL3 10 C2
Gorselands HARP AL5 143 K2 2
Gorst Cl LWTH SG6 41 J4
Gosforth La OXHEY WD19 230 B2
Gosforth Pth OXHEY WD19 230 B2 2
Gosling Av HTCH/STOT SG5 54 E7
Gosmore Ley Cl HTCHE/RSTV SG4 56 D6
Gosmore Rd HTCHE/RSTV SG4 56 D4
The Gossamers GSTN WD25 205 F5
Gosselin Rd HERT/WAS SG14 151 F1
Gossoms Ryde BERK HP4 161 H4
Gothic Wy ARL/CHE SG15 24 E4
Gould Cl BRKMPK AL9 192 B2
Government Rw PEND EN3 215 F7
Gowar Fld POTB/CUF EN6 209 F1
Gower Rd ROY SG8 21 G2
The Gowers HLW CM20 7 F2
Grace Av RAD WD7 207 G3
Grace Cl BORE WD6 224 C1
Grace Gdns BSF CM23 105 J5
Grace Wy STVG SG1 75 K1
Graemes Dyke Rd BERK HP4 161 H6
Grafton Cl STALE/WH AL4 169 G7
Graham Av BROX EN10 176 D6
Graham Cl STAL AL1 189 F1
Graham Gdns LTNN/LIM LU3 69 H5
Grailands BSF CM23 105 G1
Grammar School Wk
HTCH/STOT SG5 56 C2
Grampian Wy LTNN/LIM LU3 68 B1
The Granaries WAB EN9 215 K3 1
Granary Cl STALE/WH AL4 145 G1 1
Granary La HARP AL5 118 D8
The Granary HLWW/ROY CM19 154 C8
WARE SG12 153 H6
Granby Av HARP AL5 118 E7
Granby Park Rd CHESW EN7 196 D6
Granby Rd LTNW/LEA LU4 68 C6
STVG SG1 58 C7
Grandfield Av WAT WD17 220 A1
Grand Union Canal Wk BERK HP4 161 F2
HHW HP1 163 F8
LBUZ LU7 110 C3
RKW/CH/CXG WD3 227 K3
TRING HP23 110 A7
Grange Av LTNN/LIM LU3 68 D4
LTNW/LEA LU4 68 C5
TRDG/WHET N20 225 K7
Grange Bottom ROY SG8 21 J4
Grange Cl CFSP/GDCR SL9 226 B7
HERT/WAS SG14 150 E3 3
HHNE HP2 9 D6 1
HTCHE/RSTV SG4 56 E5
STALW/RED AL3 115 H3
WAT WD17 220 B1
Grange Ct WAB EN9 215 H4
Grange Court Rd HARP AL5 143 K3
Grangedale Cl NTHWD HA6 229 K7 1
Grange Dr HTCH/STOT SG5 25 K3
Grange Flds CFSP/GDCR SL9 226 B7
Grange Gdns WARE SG12 152 D1
Grange Hl WLYN AL6 122 C3
Grange La GSTN WD25 222 A1
HLWW/ROY CM19 178 D1
Grange Pk BSF CM23 85 J8
Grange Ri WLYN AL6 94 E8
Grange Rd AMP/FLIT/B MK45 36 B6
BORE WD6 223 J5
BSF CM23 105 K2
BUSH WD23 13 F4
CFSP/GDCR SL9 226 A7
LBUZ LU7 110 D5
LWTH SG6 41 K1
TRING HP23 109 G8
Grangeside BSF CM23 85 J7
Grange St STALW/RED AL3 10 C3
Grange Wk BSF CM23 105 K2
Grangewood POTB/CUF EN6 193 H8
Gransden Cl LTNN/LIM LU3 69 F2
Grant Gdns HARP AL5 118 D7
Grantham Cl ROY SG8 21 F1
Grantham Gdns WARE SG12 127 J7
Grantham Gn BORE WD6 224 B5
Grantham Rd LTNW/LEA LU4 69 F8
Granville Dene HHS/BOV HP3 183 J5
Granville Gdns HOD EN11 153 F7
Granville Rd BAR EN5 225 H4
HTCHE/RSTV SG4 41 G8
LTN LU1 89 G1
STAL AL1 11 E4
WATW WD18 13 D3 6
Grasmere Av HARP AL5 118 E7
LTNN/LIM LU3 69 G2
Grasmere Cl GSTN WD25 204 C2
HHS/BOV HP3 165 G8 1
Grasmere Rd LTNN/LIM LU3 69 G2
STAL AL1 168 E8
WARE SG12 127 J6 1
Grassingham End CFSP/GDCR SL9 226 B6
Grassingham Rd CFSP/GDCR SL9 226 B6
Grassington Cl LCOL/BKTW AL2 188 C8 1
Grass Mdw STVGE SG2 76 E2
Grass Warren WLYN AL6 124 A8
Grassy Cl HHW HP1 163 K5
Gravel Dr TRING HP23 134 B6
Graveley Av BORE WD6 224 B4
Graveley Dell WGCE AL7 148 C4 5
Graveley La HTCHE/RSTV SG4 57 K4
Graveley Rd HTCHE/RSTV SG4 57 J3
STVG SG1 58 B6
Gravel Hl CFSP/GDCR SL9 226 A5
Gravelhill Ter HHW HP1 163 K7
Gravel La HHW HP1 163 K6
Gravelly La STDN SG11 81 K2
Gravel Pth BERK HP4 162 A5
Gravely Ct HHS/BOV HP3 9 F6 4
The Graylings ABLGY WD5 203 K3
Grays Cl AMP/FLIT/B MK45 36 C6
ROY SG8 21 G1
Grays Ct BSF CM23 105 H1
Graysfield WGCE AL7 148 B6
Gray's La HTCH/STOT SG5 56 B2
The Grazings HHNE HP2 8 C3
Greasy Cl ABLGY WD5 204 A1
Great Ashby Wy STVG SG1 59 G6
Great Braitch La HAT AL10 146 D7
Great Brays HLWS CM18 7 F5
Great Break WGCE AL7 148 C4
Great Cambridge Rd BROX EN10 197 J4
CHES/WCR EN8 214 B1
Great Conduit WGCE AL7 148 D2
Great Dell WGCW AL8 147 J1
Great Eastern Cl BSF CM23 105 K3 1
Great Elms Rd HHS/BOV HP3 185 K2
Greatfield Cl HARP AL5 117 J5
Great Ganett WGCE AL7 148 C5
Great Gn HTCH/STOT SG5 39 F5
Great Gv BUSH WD23 221 J4
Great Groves CHESW EN7 196 C6
Great Hadham Rd BSF CM23 104 C4
Greatham Rd BUSH WD23 13 E2
Great Heart HHNE HP2 8 B3
Great Heath HAT AL10 171 G1
Great Innings North
HERT/WAS SG14 98 A6
Great Innings South
HERT/WAS SG14 98 A6 1
Great Lawne KNEB SG3 96 E7
Great Ley WGCE AL7 147 K5
Great Leylands HLWS CM18 7 F5
Great Meadow BROX EN10 177 F8
Great Molewood HERT/WAS SG14 125 K8
Great North Rd BRKMPK AL9 147 G8
HAT AL10 171 H1
WGCW AL8 147 F3
WLYN AL6 122 D3
Great Palmers HHNE HP2 164 E1 2
Great Pk KGLGY WD4 186 A8
Great Plumtree HLW CM20 7 E2
Great Rd HHNE HP2 8 C4
Great Slades POTB/CUF EN6 210 A3
Great Sturgess Rd HHW HP1 163 J6 1
Great Whites Rd HHS/BOV HP3 164 E8
Greenacre Cl BAR EN5 210 A8
Greenacres HHS/BOV HP3 165 J8
LBUZ LU7 110 C5 1
Green Acres LTNE LU2 53 K7
STVGE SG2 76 D8
WGCE AL7 148 A6 1
Greenall Cl CHES/WCR EN8 197 J8
Greenbank CHESW EN7 197 F6
Greenbank Rd WAT WD17 203 J6
Greenbury Cl RKW/CH/CXG WD3 217 F3
ROY SG8 23 F8 1
Green Cl BRKMPK AL9 192 E4
CHES/WCR EN8 214 D2
LTNW/LEA LU4 68 A4
STVGE SG2 76 A8
Greencoates HERT/BAY SG13 151 H4 1
Green Cft HAT AL10 171 F1
Green Dell Wy HHS/BOV HP3 9 E5
Green Drift ROY SG8 21 F3
Greene Field Rd BERK HP4 161 K5 3
Green End WLYN AL6 122 B5 1
Green End Gdns HHW HP1 163 K7
Green End La HHW HP1 163 J6
Green End Rd HHW HP1 163 K6
Greenes Ct BERK HP4 161 K4 1
Greene Wk BERK HP4 162 A6
Greenfield BRKMPK AL9 171 J1
ROY SG8 21 F2
WGCW AL8 122 D8 2
Greenfield Av HTCH/STOT SG5 40 B5
OXHEY WD19 231 F1
Greenfield End CFSP/GDCR SL9 226 C6 1
Greenfield La HTCH/STOT SG5 40 C5 1
Greenfield Rd STVG SG1 2 C1
Greenfields STSD CM24 86 D2
Greenfield St WAB EN9 215 H4
Greengate LTNN/LIM LU3 68 B1
Greenheys Cl NTHWD HA6 229 K7
Greenhill Av LTNE LU2 69 J6
Green Hill Cl STDN SG11 82 A3 1
Greenhill Crs WATW WD18 219 K6
Greenhill Pk BSF CM23 105 G4
Greenhills HLW CM20 7 D4
WARE SG12 127 G6
Greenhills Cl RKW/CH/CXG WD3 218 A5
Greenland Rd BAR EN5 225 H6
Green La BLDK SG7 18 A4
BROX EN10 198 B1
DUN/WHIP LU6 114 C1
HHNE HP2 9 F6
HHS/BOV HP3 183 J6
HTCHE/RSTV SG4 41 F8
LBUZ LU7 110 E4 1
LCOL/BKTW AL2 189 J2
LTNE LU2 70 C5
LWTH SG6 26 B8
NTHWD HA6 229 J6
OXHEY WD19 220 D8

RKW/CH/CXG WD3 .... 218 E5
STALW/RED AL3 .... 10 B1
STALW/RED AL3 .... 115 K5
STDN SG11 .... 82 A2
WGCE AL7 .... 148 D5
Green Lane CI HARP AL5 .... 144 B1
Green La HAT AL10 .... 170 E1
WGCW AL8 .... 146 E5
Green Meadow POTB/CUF EN6 .... 193 C8
Green Milverton LTNN/LIM LU3 .... 69 F2
Green Oaks LTNE LU2 .... 70 A6
Green Pth TRING HP23 .... 134 B5
Greenriggs LTNE LU2 .... 71 G7
Greenside BORE WD6 .... 207 K8
Greenside Dr HTCH/STOT SG5 .... 56 B1
Greenside Pk LTNE LU2 .... 69 K6
Greensleeves CI STALE/WH AL4 .... 169 F7
Greenstead SBW CM21 .... 132 C8
Green St RAD WD7 .... 207 K5
RKW/CH/CXG WD3 .... 217 F2
ROY SG8 .... 21 H1
STVG SG1 .... 2 A1
Greensward BUSH WD23 .... 221 J6
The Green BSF CM23 .... 105 J6
CHES/WCR EN8 .... 197 G6
HTCH/STOT SG5 .... 25 K2
KNEB SG3 .... 95 G4
LTNE LU2 .... 91 K6
LTNW/LEA LU4 .... 68 D4
RKW/CH/CXG WD3 .... 218 E4
ROY SG8 .... 15 K8
ROY SG8 .... 21 H3
WARE SG12 .... 127 H6
WLYN AL6 .... 94 D8
WLYN AL6 .... 122 B4
Green V WGCE AL7 .... 148 B4
Green View CI HHS/BOV HP3 .... 183 J7
Greenway BERK HP4 .... 161 H5
BSF CM23 .... 106 D3
HARP AL5 .... 144 A1
HLWW/ROY CM19 .... 179 F1
LWTH SG6 .... 42 A7
PIN HA5 .... 230 C8
STVGE SG2 .... 77 J1
Greenways ABLGY WD5 .... 203 J1
BUNT SG9 .... 63 H1
CHESW EN7 .... 195 K7
HERT/WAS SG14 .... 150 E3
LTNE LU2 .... 70 C4
STVG SG1 .... 2 C2
The Greenway PEND EN3 .... 214 C5
POTB/CUF EN6 .... 210 B2
RKW/CH/CXG WD3 .... 217 K7
TRING HP23 .... 134 B4
Greenwood Av CHESW EN7 .... 214 A1
Greenwood CI CHESW EN7 .... 214 A1
RAD WD7 .... 207 H2
Greenwood Dr GSTN WD25 .... 204 C4
Greenwood Gdns RAD WD7 .... 207 H3
Greenyard WAB EN9 .... 215 H3
Greer Rd KTN/HRWW/W HA3 .... 231 K7
Gregories CI LTNE LU2 .... 4 B2
Gregory Av POTB/CUF EN6 .... 210 D3
Gregson CI BORE WD6 .... 224 D3
Grenadier CI STALE/WH AL4 .... 169 F7
Grenadine CI CHESW EN7 .... 196 D5
Grenadine Wy TRING HP23 .... 135 F4
Grenfell CI BORE WD6 .... 224 B1
Grenville Av BROX EN10 .... 176 E7
Grenville CI CHES/WCR EN8 .... 214 C2
Grenville Wy STVGE SG2 .... 76 B8
Gresford CI STALE/WH AL4 .... 169 G6
Gresham CI LTNE LU2 .... 70 E8
Gresham Ct BERK HP4 .... 161 J6
Gresley CI WGCW AL8 .... 147 K2
Gresley Wy STVGE SG2 .... 59 K8
Greville CI BRKMPK AL9 .... 192 B4
Greycaine Rd WATN WD24 .... 204 E7
Greydells Rd STVG SG1 .... 2 C1
Greyfriars WARE SG12 .... 127 F6
Greyfriars La HARP AL5 .... 143 H2
Greygoose Pk HLWW/ROY CM19 .... 179 J4
Greyhound La POTB/CUF EN6 .... 209 F3
Greystoke CI BERK HP4 .... 161 H6
Griffiths Wy STAL AL1 .... 10 B6
Grimaldi Av LTNN/LIM LU3 .... 69 F6
Grimsdyke Crs BAR EN5 .... 225 H3
Grimsdyke Rd PIN HA5 .... 231 F6
TRING HP23 .... 135 J8
Grimstone Rd HTCHE/RSTV SG4 .... 57 J5
Grimston Rd STAL AL1 .... 11 E4
STAL AL1 .... 11 E5
Grinthorpe CI STALW/RED AL3 .... 10 B1
Grindcobbe CI STAL AL1 .... 189 F1
Grinstead La HARP AL5 .... 143 G3
Groom Rd BROX EN10 .... 197 K4
Groomsby Dr LBUZ LU7 .... 110 E4
Grooms Cottages CSHM HP5 .... 182 D8
Grosvenor CI BSF CM23 .... 105 G6
Grosvenor Rd BLDK SG7 .... 27 F8
BORE WD6 .... 223 K3
BROX EN10 .... 176 E5
LTNN/LIM LU3 .... 69 G4
NTHWD HA6 .... 230 A4
STAL AL1 .... 11 D5

WAT WD17 .... 13 D3
Grosvenor Rd West BLDK SG7 .... 27 F8
Grosvenor Ter HHW HP1 .... 163 K7
The Grotto WARE SG12 .... 152 C1
Ground La HAT AL10 .... 171 G2
Grove Av HARP AL5 .... 144 A2
Groveberry Gdns
LCOL/BKTW AL2 .... 188 E5
Grove Ct WAB EN9 .... 215 G3
Grove Crs RKW/CH/CXG WD3 .... 219 F4
Grovedale CI CHESW EN7 .... 196 D5
Grove End LTNE LU1 .... 89 C4
Grove Farm Pk NTHWD HA6 .... 229 J4
Grove Gdns TRING HP23 .... 135 G4
Grove Hall Rd BUSH WD23 .... 13 F3
Grove HI STSD SM24 .... 86 D2
Grovelands HHNE HP2 .... 9 F3
LCOL/BKTW AL2 .... 188 D5
Grovelands Av HTCHE/RSTV SG4 .... 41 G7
Groveland Wy HTCH/STOT SG5 .... 26 A4
Grove La CSHM HP5 .... 181 F7
Grove Lea HAT AL10 .... 171 F7
Grove Md HAT AL10 .... 170 E4
Grove Meadow WGCE AL7 .... 148 D5
Grove Mill La RKW/CH/CXG WD3 .... 203 H8
Grove Pk TRING HP23 .... 135 H4
Grove Park Rd LTN LU1 .... 89 F6
Grove PI BRKMPK AL9 .... 192 C2
Grove Rd BORE WD6 .... 223 K1
HARP AL5 .... 144 A2
HHW HP1 .... 163 K8
HTCH/STOT SG5 .... 56 D1
LTN LU1 .... 4 B4
NTHWD HA6 .... 229 J4
RKW/CH/CXG WD3 .... 227 K1
STAL AL1 .... 10 C5
STVG SG1 .... 2 A1
TRING HP23 .... 135 G4
WARE SG12 .... 127 K2
Grove Rd West PEND EN3 .... 214 B7
Grover Rd OXHEY WD19 .... 13 E5
The Grove BRKMPK AL9 .... 193 C5
CSHM HP5 .... 200 A6
LTN LU1 .... 89 C4
POTB/CUF EN6 .... 210 D2
RAD WD7 .... 206 D4
RBSF CM22 .... 106 E5
STDN SG11 .... 104 B2
Grove Wk HERT/WAS SG14 .... 151 F1
Grove Wy RKW/CH/CXG WD3 .... 216 E4
Grovewood CI RKW/CH/CXG WD3 .... 216 E5
Grubbs La BRKMPK AL9 .... 172 C8
Guessens Gv WGCW AL8 .... 147 K5
Guessens Rd WGCW AL8 .... 147 H5
Guessens Wk WGCW AL8 .... 147 H5
Guildford CI STVG SG1 .... 58 E7
Guildford Rd STAL AL1 .... 168 E7
Guildford St LTN LU1 .... 4 C3
The Guilfords HLWE CM17 .... 157 K5
Guinery Gv HHS/BOV HP3 .... 185 K2
Guinevere Gdns CHES/WCR EN8 .... 197 J8
Gulland CI BUSH WD23 .... 221 K5
Gullbrook HHW HP1 .... 163 K6
Gullet Wood Rd GSTN WD25 .... 204 B5
The Gulphs HERT/BAY SG13 .... 151 G3
Gun La KNEB SG3 .... 96 A4
Gun Meadow Av KNEB SG3 .... 96 B5
Gunnels Wood Rd STVG SG1 .... 2 A5
Gun Rd KNEB SG3 .... 96 B5
Gun Road Gdns KNEB SG3 .... 96 A5
Gurney Court Rd STAL AL1 .... 11 E2
Gurney's La HTCH/STOT SG5 .... 39 K2
Gwent CI GSTN WD25 .... 204 E4
Gwynfa CI WLYN AL6 .... 122 D2
Gwynne CI TRING HP23 .... 135 F4
Gwynns Wk HERT/BAY SG13 .... 151 H3
Gypsy CI WARE SG12 .... 152 E5
Gypsy La BRKMPK AL9 .... 148 A8
GSTN WD25 .... 203 J5
WARE SG12 .... 152 E5

H

Hackforth CI BAR EN5 .... 225 G5
Hackney St BORE WD6 .... 224 C5
Haddestoke Ga BROX EN10 .... 197 K4
Haddon CI BORE WD6 .... 223 K2
HHS/BOV HP3 .... 9 D6
STVGE SG2 .... 96 D2
Haddon Rd LTNE LU2 .... 5 D3
RKW/CH/CXG WD3 .... 217 F5
Hadham CI BSF CM23 .... 105 J2
Hadham Gv BSF CM23 .... 105 F1
Hadham Rd BSF CM23 .... 84 D3
STDN SG11 .... 82 A8
Hadland CI HHW HP1 .... 183 J4
Hadleigh Rd BROX EN10 .... 176 E8
HARP AL5 .... 144 B3
Hadley CI BORE WD6 .... 223 J5
Hadley Gra HLWE CM17 .... 181 F1
Hadley Gn West BAR EN5 .... 225 K2

Hadley Gv BAR EN5 .... 225 K2
Hadley Rd EBAR EN4 .... 211 H8
ENC/FH EN2 .... 212 B8
Hadlow Down CI LTNN/LIM LU3 .... 69 F4
Hadrian CI STALW/RED AL3 .... 167 G8
Hadrians Wk STVGE SG2 .... 76 D1
Hadrian Wy LWTH SG6 .... 42 D2
Hadwell CI STVGE SG2 .... 3 E5
Hagdell Rd LTN LU1 .... 4 A6
Hagden La WATW WD18 .... 12 A3
Haggerston Rd BORE WD6 .... 207 H8
Hagsdell Rd HERT/BAY SG13 .... 151 G4
Haig CI STAL AL1 .... 168 E7
Hailey Av HOD EN11 .... 153 F7
Hailey La HOD EN11 .... 152 C8
Haines Wy GSTN WD25 .... 204 B4
Haldens WGCE AL7 .... 123 F6
Hale Rd HERT/BAY SG13 .... 151 G4
Hales Meadow HARP AL5 .... 118 C7
Hales Pk HHNE HP2 .... 9 F4
Hales Park CI HHNE HP2 .... 9 F4
Haleswood Rd HHNE HP2 .... 9 D4
Half Acre HTCH/STOT SG5 .... 56 B5
Halfacre HI CFSP/GDCR SL9 .... 226 C5
Halfacre La BUNT SG9 .... 49 G8
Half Acres BSF CM23 .... 105 J2
Halfhide La CHES/WCR EN8 .... 197 H4
Halfhides WAB EN9 .... 215 J2
Half Moon La LTN LU1 .... 116 C5
Half Moon Meadow HHNE HP2 .... 165 H1
Halfway Av LTNW/LEA LU4 .... 68 C5
Halifax Rd RKW/CH/CXG WD3 .... 217 F7
Halifax Wy WGCE AL7 .... 149 F5
Hallam CI WATN WD24 .... 13 D3
Hallam Gdns PIN HA5 .... 231 F5
Halland Wy NTHWD HA6 .... 229 J3
Hall CI RKW/CH/CXG WD3 .... 217 K6
Hall Dr DEN/HRF UB9 .... 228 B3
Halleys Rdg HERT/WAS SG14 .... 150 D3
Hall Gdns STALE/WH AL4 .... 191 H6
Hall Gv WGCE AL7 .... 148 C5
Hall Heath CI STAL AL1 .... 168 E2
Halliday CI RAD WD7 .... 207 H4
Halliday CI BAR EN5 .... 225 K7
Hallingbury CI RBSF CM22 .... 106 A2
Hallingbury Rd BSF CM23 .... 106 A4
SBW CM21 .... 132 E2
Halling HI HLWE CM20 .... 7 E
Hall La BUNT SG9 .... 49 G2
HTCHE/RSTV SG4 .... 120 A2
KNEB SG3 .... 96 B5
Hall Md LWTH SG6 .... 41 G5
Hallmores BROX EN10 .... 177 H5
Hallowell Rd NTHWD HA6 .... 229 K7
Hallowes Crs OXHEY WD19 .... 230 B5
Hall Pk BERK HP4 .... 162 E6
Hall Park Ga BERK HP4 .... 162 E6
Hall Park HI BERK HP4 .... 162 E6
Hall Place Gdns STAL AL1 .... 11 E3
Halls CI WLYN AL6 .... 122 C5
Hallside Rd EN EN1 .... 213 K7
Hallwicks Rd LTNE LU2 .... 70 D6
Hallworth Dr HTCH/STOT SG5 .... 25 J3
Halsey Dr HHW HP1 .... 163 J2
HTCHE/RSTV SG4 .... 57 C8
Halsey Pk LCOL/BKTW AL2 .... 190 C5
Halsey PI WATN WD24 .... 204 C8
Halsey Rd WATW WD18 .... 12 C4
Halstead HI CHES/WCR EN7 .... 196 B8
Halter CI BORE WD6 .... 224 D2
Haltside HAT AL10 .... 170 C4
Halwick CI HHW HP1 .... 164 D6
Halyard CI LTNN/LIM LU3 .... 69 C3
Hamberlins La BERK HP4 .... 160 D5
Hamblings CI RAD WD7 .... 207 G3
Hambridge Wy HTCH/STOT SG5 .... 39 J8
Hambro CI STAL AL1 .... 118 E2
Hamburgh Ct CHES/WCR EN8 .... 197 H6
Hamels Dr HERT/BAY SG13 .... 152 A8
Hamels La BUNT SG9 .... 80 E6
Hamer CI HHS/BOV HP3 .... 183 K6
Hamilton Av HOD EN11 .... 177 F1
Hamilton CI LCOL/BKTW AL2 .... 188 D7
POTB/CUF EN6 .... 209 F2
Hamilton Ct HAT AL10 .... 171 G6
Hamilton Md HHS/BOV HP3 .... 185 J3
Hamilton Rd BERK HP4 .... 161 J5
KGLGY WD4 .... 203 F7
OXHEY WD19 .... 230 C2
STAL AL1 .... 11 E4
Hamilton St WATW WD18 .... 13 D4
Hamlet HI HLWW/ROY CM19 .... 178 D5
The Hamlet BERK HP4 .... 162 E4
Hammarskjold Rd HLW CM20 .... 6 B4
Hammer La HHNE HP2 .... 8 C4
Hammers Ga LCOL/BKTW AL2 .... 188 E3
Hammond CI CHESW EN7 .... 196 B5
STVG SG1 .... 2 D3
Hammonds HI HARP AL5 .... 143 G5
Hammonds La HAT AL10 .... 146 A7
STALE/WH AL4 .... 145 K8
Hammondstreet Rd CHESW EN7 .... 195 K3
Hammondswick HARP AL5 .... 143 G5
Hampden HTCHE/RSTV SG4 .... 93 G1
Hampden CI LWTH SG6 .... 42 C5
Hampden Crs CHESW EN7 .... 214 A4

Hampden Hl WARE SG12 127 K8
Hampden Hill Cl WARE SG12 127 K7 1
Hampden Pl LCOL/BKTW AL2 189 G7
Hampden Rd HTCHE/RSTV SG4 41 G8
KTN/HRWW/W HA3 231 K7
Hampden Wy WAT WD17 203 K6
Hampermill La OXHEY WD19 220 B8
Hampton Cl STVGE SG2 96 D2
Hampton Gdns SBW CM21 156 E2
Hampton Rd LTNW/LEA LU4 69 G8
Hamstel Rd HLW CM20 6 A2
Hanaper Dr ROY SG8 23 F8
Hanbury Cl CHES/WCR EN8 197 H8
WARE SG12 127 H7
Hanbury Dr WARE SG12 127 G3
Hancock Ct BORE WD6 224 B1
Hancock Dr LTNE LU2 69 K3
Hancroft Rd HHS/BOV HP3 164 E8
Handa Cl HHS/BOV HP3 186 B1
Handcross Rd LTNE LU2 70 E6
Hand La SBW CM21 132 A8
Handside Cl WGCW AL8 147 H3 2
Handside Gn WGCW AL8 147 H2
Handside La WGCW AL8 147 G4
Handsworth Cl OXHEY WD19 230 B2
Hangar Ruding OXHEY WD19 231 G2
Hanger Cl HHW HP1 164 A7
Hangmans La WLYN AL6 123 F1
Hanover Cl STVGE SG2 76 A8
Hanover Gn HHW HP1 163 K8
Hanover Pl AMP/FLIT/B MK45 36 C5
Hanover Wk HAT AL10 170 E7 2
Hanscombe End Rd
HTCH/STOT SG5 37 K1
Hansells Md HLWW/ROY CM19 178 B1
Hanswick Cl LTNE LU2 5 F1
Hanworth Cl LTNE LU2 69 J2 2
Hanyards La POTB/CUF EN6 195 F6
Harbert Gdns LCOL/BKTW AL2 188 D7
Harberts Rd HLWW/ROY CM19 6 A5
Harborne Cl OXHEY WD19 230 D4 5
Harbury Dell LTNN/LIM LU3 69 G2
Harcamlow Wy RBSF CM22 107 G5
STDN SG11 82 A8
WARE SG12 154 B1
Harcourt Rd BUSH WD23 221 K5
TRING HP23 135 H5
Harcourt St LTN LU1 4 C6
Harding Cl GSTN WD25 204 D3
LTNN/LIM LU3 68 D2 1
STALW/RED AL3 142 C4 3
Hardings WGCE AL7 148 D2
Hardwick Cl STVGE SG2 96 D2
Hardwicke Pl LCOL/BKTW AL2 190 B5
Hardwick Gn LTNN/LIM LU3 69 F2
Hardy Cl BAR EN5 225 K5
HTCHE/RSTV SG4 57 G2
Hardy Dr ROY SG8 21 H1
Hardy Rd HHNE HP2 8 C4
Harebell WGCE AL7 147 K6 1
Harebell Cl HERT/BAY SG13 152 A3
The Harebreaks WATN WD24 204 B7
Hare Crs GSTN WD25 204 B2
Harefield HLW CM20 7 F3
STVGE SG2 76 D6
Harefield Pl STALE/WH AL4 169 G3
Harefield Rd LTN LU1 88 E1
RKW/CH/CXG WD3 228 C1
Hare La HAT AL10 171 G6
Harepark Cl HHW HP1 163 J5 3
Hare St HLWW/ROY CM19 6 A4
Hare Street Rd BUNT SG9 63 K2
Hare Street Springs
HLWW/ROY CM19 6 B4 1
Harewood RKW/CH/CXG WD3 218 B5
Harewood Rd OXHEY WD19 230 C1
Harford Dr WAT WD17 203 K8
Hargrave Cl STSD CM24 86 D1
Hargreaves Av CHESW EN7 214 A1
Hargreaves Cl CHESW EN7 214 A1 3
Hargreaves Rd ROY SG8 21 H4 2
Harkness Wy HTCHE/RSTV SG4 41 G7
Harlech Rd ABLGY WD5 204 B1
Harlesden Rd STAL AL1 11 F4
Harlestone Cl LTNN/LIM LU3 52 A8
Harley Ct STALE/WH AL4 169 G2 1
The Harlings HERT/BAY SG13 152 B7
Harlow Common HLWE CM17 181 G4
Harlow Ct HHNE HP2 8 C1
Harlow Rd HLWW/ROY CM19 154 D8
SBW CM21 157 F1
Harmer Dell WLYN AL6 123 G5
Harmer Green La WLYN AL6 123 F5
Harmony Cl HAT AL10 171 F2
Harness Wy STALE/WH AL4 169 G3
Harold Crs WAB EN9 215 H2
Harold Rd AMP/FLIT/B MK45 36 C6
Harolds Rd HLWW/ROY CM19 179 G2
Harpenden La STALW/RED AL3 142 C3
Harpenden Ri HARP AL5 118 A6
Harpenden Rd HARP AL5 143 J2
STALE/WH AL4 144 E1
STALW/RED AL3 143 K5
Harper La RAD WD7 206 D1
Harpsfield Broadway HAT AL10 170 E3
Harptree Wy STAL AL1 11 E2
Harriet Walker Wy
RKW/CH/CXG WD3 217 J7 1
Harriet Wy BUSH WD23 222 A7
Harris Ct AMP/FLIT/B MK45 36 B5
Harris La HTCH/STOT SG5 55 F7
RAD WD7 207 K4
Harrison Cl HTCHE/RSTV SG4 56 D2 1
NTHWD HA6 229 H5
Harrisons BSF CM23 86 C7
Harrison Wk CHES/WCR EN8 197 H8
Harris Rd GSTN WD25 204 B5
Harris's La WARE SG12 127 G8
Harrogate Rd OXHEY WD19 230 D2 2
Harrowdene STVGE SG2 76 D5
Harrowden Rd LTNE LU2 5 F3
Harrow Wy OXHEY WD19 231 F2
Harrow Yd TRING HP23 135 F6
Harry Scott Ct LTNW/LEA LU4 68 B3
Harston Dr PEND EN3 215 F8
Hartfield Av BORE WD6 223 K4
Hartfield Cl BORE WD6 223 K5
Hartforde Rd BORE WD6 223 K2
Harthall La KGLGY WD4 186 B6
Hartham La HERT/WAS SG14 151 F3
Hart Hill Dr LTNE LU2 5 D3
Hart Hill La LTNE LU2 5 E4 1
Hartland Rd CHES/WCR EN8 197 H8
Hart La LTNE LU2 5 E2
Hartley Rd LTNE LU2 5 D3
Hartmoor Ms PEND EN3 214 C7 1
Hart Rd HLWE CM17 157 F4
STAL AL1 10 C5
Hartsbourne Av BUSH WD23 231 K1
Hartsbourne Wy HHNE HP2 9 F6 5
Harts Cl BUSH WD23 221 H2 1
Hartsfield Rd LTNE LU2 5 E1
Hartspring La GSTN WD25 221 H2
Hart Wk LTNE LU2 5 E2 2
Hartwell Gdns HARP AL5 118 A8
Harvest Ct STALE/WH AL4 169 F2
WLYN AL6 122 E2
Harvest End GSTN WD25 204 E6
Harvest La STVGE SG2 76 D2
Harvest Md HAT AL10 171 G3
Harvest Rd BUSH WD23 221 J4
Harveyfields WAB EN9 215 H4
Harvey Rd LCOL/BKTW AL2 190 A4
RKW/CH/CXG WD3 219 F6
STVGE SG2 3 F2
Harvey's Hl LTNE LU2 70 A4
Harwood Cl WGCW AL8 122 E7 2
WLYN AL6 124 A7
Harwood Hl WGCW AL8 122 E8
Harwoods Rd WATW WD18 12 B3
Hasedines Rd HHW HP1 163 K5
Haseldine Mdw HAT AL10 170 E5
Haseldine Rd LCOL/BKTW AL2 190 B4
Haselfoot LWTH SG6 41 J3
Hasketon Dr LTNW/LEA LU4 68 A3
Haslemere BSF CM23 105 K5
Haslewood Av HOD EN11 177 F2
Haslingden Cl HARP AL5 117 K6
Hastings Cl STVG SG1 75 F1
Hastings Rd AMP/FLIT/B MK45 36 C6
Hastings St LTN LU1 4 B4 4
Hastings Wy BUSH WD23 13 F3 2
RKW/CH/CXG WD3 219 G4
Hastingwood Rd HLWE CM17 181 H6
Hastoe Hl TRING HP23 135 F8
Hastoe La TRING HP23 135 F7
Hatch Gn RBSF CM22 133 F1
Hatching Green Cl HARP AL5 143 H3
Hatch La BLDK SG7 43 F4
Hatfield Av HAT AL10 170 E1
Hatfield Crs HHNE HP2 8 C1
Hatfield Rd BRKMPK AL9 148 B8
POTB/CUF EN6 210 D1
STAL AL1 168 E6
STALE/WH AL4 169 F6
WATN WD24 220 C1
Hathaway Cl LTNW/LEA LU4 68 A7 1
Hathaway Ct STALE/WH AL4 169 H6
Hatherleigh Gdns POTB/CUF EN6 210 E2
Hatters La WATW WD18 219 K5 1
Hatters Wy LTN LU1 68 E8
Hatton Rd CHES/WCR EN8 197 H7
Havelock Ri LTNE LU2 4 C2
Havelock Rd KGLGY WD4 185 K6
LTNE LU2 4 C2
Haven Cl HAT AL10 170 E3
Havenfield KGLGY WD4 202 A1
Havercroft Cl STAL AL1 10 B6
Haverdale LTNW/LEA LU4 68 B5 1
Havers La BSF CM23 105 J4
Haward Rd HOD EN11 177 H1
Hawbush Cl WLYN AL6 122 B5 2
Hawbush Ri WLYN AL6 122 B4
Hawes Cl NTHWD HA6 230 A6
Hawes La WAB EN9 215 H8
Haweswater Dr GSTN WD25 204 D4 2
Hawfield Gdns LCOL/BKTW AL2 189 F4
Hawkenbury HLWW/ROY CM19 179 H3
Hawkesworth Cl NTHWD HA6 229 K6 4
Hawkfields LTNE LU2 69 K3
Hawkings Wy HHW HP1 183 J4
Hawkins Cl BORE WD6 224 B2 2
Hawkins Hall La KNEB SG3 97 F7
Hawkshead La BRKMPK AL9 192 E6
Hawkshill Dr HHW HP1 184 C1
Hawksmead Cl PEND EN3 214 C5 4
Hawksmoor RAD WD7 207 K3
Hawkwell Dr TRING HP23 135 H5 2
Hawridge V CSHM HP5 160 A8
Hawsley Rd HARP AL5 143 H5
Hawthorn Av LTNE LU2 70 C5
Hawthorn Cl ABLGY WD5 204 A2
HARP AL5 144 A2
HERT/WAS SG14 150 D2 1
HTCH/STOT SG5 56 B3
ROY SG8 21 K2 1
WAT WD17 204 A8
Hawthorn Crs LTN LU1 88 D6
Hawthorne Av CHESW EN7 197 F8
Hawthorne Cl CHESW EN7 214 A1
Hawthorne Rd RAD WD7 206 D4 1
Hawthornes HAT AL10 170 E6 1
Hawthorn Gv ENC/FH EN2 213 G8
Hawthorn Hl LWTH SG6 41 J2
Hawthorn La HHW HP1 163 J5
Hawthorn Ri BSF CM23 105 J6
Hawthorn Rd HOD EN11 177 G1
Hawthorns HLWS CM18 180 C5
WGCW AL8 147 J1 1
The Hawthorns BERK HP4 161 H4
HHS/BOV HP3 184 D2
RKW/CH/CXG WD3 227 G4
STVG SG1 3 D4
WARE SG12 127 F6
Hawthorn Wy LCOL/BKTW AL2 188 C2
ROY SG8 21 K2
Hawtrees RAD WD7 206 C5
Haybourn Md HHW HP1 164 A7
Hay Cl BORE WD6 224 B2
Haycroft BSF CM23 106 B3
LTNE LU2 69 K3 1
Haycroft Rd STVG SG1 2 B1
Haydens Rd HLWW/ROY CM19 6 B4
Haydock Rd ROY SG8 21 K3 2
Haydon Rd OXHEY WD19 13 F5
Hayes Cl LTNE LU2 70 C4
Hayfield STVGE SG2 76 E2
Hayfield Cl BUSH WD23 221 J4
Haygarth KNEB SG3 96 B5
Hayhurst Rd LTNW/LEA LU4 68 A7
Hay La HARP AL5 118 C8
Hayley Bell Gdns BSF CM23 105 J6
Hayley Common STVGE SG2 76 D5
Hayling Dr LTNE LU2 70 D6
Hayling Rd OXHEY WD19 230 A2
Haymeads WGCW AL8 122 E8
Haymeads La BSF CM23 106 B3
Haymoor LWTH SG6 41 J2
Haynes Cl WGCE AL7 148 B4
Haynes Md BERK HP4 161 H3
Haysman Cl LWTH SG6 42 A2
Hay St ROY SG8 15 J7
Hayton Cl LTNN/LIM LU3 52 B7
Haywood Cl PIN HA5 230 E8
Haywood La ROY SG8 30 E3
Haywood Pk RKW/CH/CXG WD3 217 J5
Haywoods Dr HHW HP1 184 D1
Haywoods La ROY SG8 21 J2
Hazelbury Av ABLGY WD5 203 H2
Hazelbury Crs LTN LU1 4 A3
Hazel Cl CHESW EN7 196 C4 2
WLYN AL6 122 E6
Hazelcroft PIN HA5 231 H5
Hazeldell HERT/WAS SG14 98 A6
Hazeldell Link HHW HP1 163 H7 3
Hazeldell Rd HHW HP1 163 H7
Hazeldene CHES/WCR EN8 214 D2
Hazelend Rd BSF CM23 86 A6
Hazel Gv GSTN WD25 204 C5
HAT AL10 170 E7
HTCH/STOT SG5 25 J4
WGCE AL7 148 C2
Hazel Md BAR EN5 225 G5
Hazelmere Rd STALE/WH AL4 169 F3
STVGE SG2 96 B1
Hazel Rd BERK HP4 162 A6
LCOL/BKTW AL2 188 D6
The Hazels WLYN AL6 124 A7 1
Hazel Tree Rd WATN WD24 204 C7
Hazelwood Cl HTCH/STOT SG5 56 D1 3
LTNE LU2 70 C5
Hazelwood Dr PIN HA5 230 C8
STALE/WH AL4 169 F4
Hazelwood La ABLGY WD5 203 J2
Hazelwood Rd RKW/CH/CXG WD3 219 H6
Hazely TRING HP23 135 H5
Heacham Cl LTNW/LEA LU4 68 A5
Headingley Cl CHESW EN7 196 D4 2
RAD WD7 207 H2
STVG SG1 75 K1
Headstone La KTN/HRWW/W HA3 231 J7
RYLN/HDSTN HA2 231 J8
Healey Rd WATW WD18 12 A5
Heath Av ROY SG8 21 G3
STALW/RED AL3 10 C2

Heathbourne Rd BUSH WD23 ...... 222 C8
Heath Brow HHW HP1 ...... 164 B8
Heathcroft Rd WLYN AL6 ...... 122 C1
Heath Cl HARP AL5 ...... 143 J2
  HHW HP1 ...... 164 B7
  LTN LU1 ...... 89 C2
  POTB/CUF EN6 ...... 193 H8
Heathcote Av HAT AL10 ...... 171 F2
Heathcote Gdns HLWE CM17 ...... 181 H1
Heath Dr POTB/CUF EN6 ...... 193 G8
  WARE SG12 ...... 127 H6
Heather Cl ABLGY WD5 ...... 204 B2
  BSF CM23 ...... 86 A8
Heathermere LWTH SG6 ...... 25 K8
Heather Ri BUSH WD23 ...... 221 G2
Heather Rd WGCW AL8 ...... 147 H5
Heather Wy HHNE HP2 ...... 8 A4
  POTB/CUF EN6 ...... 210 A2
Heath Farm La STALW/RED AL3 ...... 11 D2
Heathfield ROY SG8 ...... 21 F3
Heathfield Cl LTN LU1 ...... 88 E5
  POTB/CUF EN6 ...... 193 H8
Heathfield Rd BUSH WD23 ...... 13 F3
  HTCHE/RSTV SG4 ...... 40 D7
  LTNN/LIM LU3 ...... 69 H5
Heathgate HERT/BAY SG13 ...... 152 A6
Heathlands WLYN AL6 ...... 96 A8
Heathlands Dr STALW/RED AL3 ...... 11 D2
Heath La HERT/BAY SG13 ...... 152 B7
  HHW HP1 ...... 164 B8
  HTCHE/RSTV SG4 ...... 94 D8
  WLYN AL6 ...... 94 E8
Heath Rd HTCHE/RSTV SG4 ...... 72 A8
  OXHEY WD19 ...... 13 E6
  POTB/CUF EN6 ...... 193 H8
  STAL AL1 ...... 11 D3
  WLYN AL6 ...... 96 A8
Heath Rw BSF CM23 ...... 86 A8
Heathside STALE/WH AL4 ...... 191 F1
  STALW/RED AL3 ...... 11 D2
Heathside Rd NTHWD HA6 ...... 229 J3
The Heath HTCHE/RSTV SG4 ...... 72 A7
  RAD WD7 ...... 206 D5
Heaton Dell LTN LU2 ...... 71 F8
Heay Flds WCCE AL7 ...... 148 D2
Hebden Cl LTNW/LEA LU4 ...... 68 A5
Hedgebrooms WGCE AL7 ...... 148 D2
Hedgerow CFSP/GDCR SL9 ...... 226 B5
Hedge Rw HHW HP1 ...... 163 K6
Hedgerow Cl STVGE SG2 ...... 76 E1
Hedgerows SBW CM21 ...... 132 D7
The Hedgerows STVGE SG2 ...... 76 E1
The Hedgerow LTNW/LEA LU4 ...... 68 B4
Hedges Cl HAT AL10 ...... 171 G3
Hedgeside BERK HP4 ...... 162 D2
Hedley Ri LTNE LU2 ...... 71 F7
Hedley Rd STAL AL1 ...... 168 E6
Hedworth Av CHES/WCR EN8 ...... 214 C3
Heighams HLWW/ROY CM19 ...... 179 G4
The Heights WAB EN9 ...... 199 H3
Helena Cl EBAR EN4 ...... 213 E8
Helens Ga CHES/WCR EN8 ...... 197 K4
Helions Rd HLWW/ROY CM19 ...... 6 A4
Hellards Rd STVG SG1 ...... 2 B1
Helmsley Cl LTNW/LEA LU4 ...... 68 A5
Helston Cl PIN HA5 ...... 231 G6
Helston Gv HHNE HP2 ...... 164 D1
Helston Pl ABLGY WD5 ...... 204 A2
Hemel Hempstead Rd BERK HP4 ...... 113 H8
  HHS/BOV HP3 ...... 165 K8
  STALW/RED AL3 ...... 141 J8
Hemingford Dr LTNE LU2 ...... 69 J4
Hemingford Rd WAT WD17 ...... 203 K6
The Hemmings BERK HP4 ...... 161 G6
Hemming Wy GSTN WD25 ...... 204 B5
Hemp La TRING HP23 ...... 135 K8
Hempstall WCCE AL7 ...... 148 C5
Hempstead La BERK HP4 ...... 163 F3
Hempstead Rd HHS/BOV HP3 ...... 183 K4
  KGLGY WD4 ...... 185 K5
  WAT WD17 ...... 12 B1
Henbury Wy OXHEY WD19 ...... 230 E2
Henderson Cl STALW/RED AL3 ...... 167 K2
Henderson Pl ABLGY WD5 ...... 187 F5
Hendon Wood La MLHL NW7 ...... 225 F7
Henge Wy LTNN/LIM LU3 ...... 68 C2
Henry Cl ENC/FH EN2 ...... 213 H8
Henrys Grant STAL AL1 ...... 11 D5
Henry St HHS/BOV HP3 ...... 185 H2
  TRING HP23 ...... 135 F6
Hensley Cl HTCHE/RSTV SG4 ...... 57 F3
  WLYN AL6 ...... 122 C3
Henstead Pl LTNE LU2 ...... 70 E8
Herald Cl BSF CM23 ...... 105 G3
Herbert St HHNE HP2 ...... 8 A4
Hereward Cl WAB EN9 ...... 215 H2
Herga Ct WAT WD17 ...... 12 B1
Herkomer Cl BUSH WD23 ...... 221 J6
Herkomer Rd BUSH WD23 ...... 221 H5
Hermitage Ct POTB/CUF EN6 ...... 210 D3
Hermitage Rd HTCH/STOT SG5 ...... 56 D2
Herne Rd BUSH WD23 ...... 221 J6
  STVG SG1 ...... 3 G8
Herneshaw HAT AL10 ...... 170 E6
Herns La WGCE AL7 ...... 148 C3

Herns Wy WGCE AL7 ...... 148 B1
Heron Cl HHS/BOV HP3 ...... 185 K3
  RKW/CH/CXG WD3 ...... 228 C3
  SBW CM23 ...... 132 B8
Heron Ct BSF CM23 ...... 105 K2
Heron Dr LTNE LU2 ...... 69 K3
  WARE SG12 ...... 153 H6
Heronfield POTB/CUF EN6 ...... 193 J8
Herongate Rd CHES/WCR EN8 ...... 197 H5
Herons Elm BERK HP4 ...... 161 F2
Heronsgate Rd RKW/CH/CXG WD3 ...... 216 E6
Heronslea GSTN WD25 ...... 204 D6
Herons Wd HLW CM20 ...... 6 A2
Heronswood Pl WGCE AL7 ...... 148 B4
Heronswood Rd WGCE AL7 ...... 148 A3
Heron Wk NTHWD HA6 ...... 229 K3
Heron Wy HAT AL10 ...... 171 F6
  HTCH/STOT SG5 ...... 25 J3
Hertford Rd BRKMPK AL9 ...... 148 C8
  HOD EN11 ...... 176 D1
  PEND EN3 ...... 214 B8
  STVGE SG2 ...... 96 A1
  WARE SG12 ...... 152 C1
  WGCW AL8 ...... 122 D5
  WLYN AL6 ...... 122 C5
Hertfordshire Wy BLDK SG7 ...... 44 B5
  BUNT SG9 ...... 64 E2
  BUNT SG9 ...... 65 G1
  BUNT SG9 ...... 65 G3
  HERT/WAS SG14 ...... 125 J7
  HERT/WAS SG14 ...... 58 B2
  HTCHE/RSTV SG4 ...... 93 H3
  MHAD SG10 ...... 130 B3
  ROY SG8 ...... 21 K8
  ROY SG8 ...... 33 G7
  STDN SG11 ...... 84 B5
  WARE SG12 ...... 128 D2
Hertingfordbury Rd
  HERT/WAS SG14 ...... 150 B3
  HERT/WAS SG14 ...... 151 F3
Heswell Gn OXHEY WD19 ...... 230 B2
Hetchleys HHW HP1 ...... 163 K3
Hewitt Cl STALE/WH AL4 ...... 145 G4
Hewlett Cl LTNW/LEA LU4 ...... 68 D5
Hexton Rd AMP/FLIT/B MK45 ...... 36 C7
  HTCH/STOT SG5 ...... 55 G1
  LTNE LU2 ...... 53 H5
Heybridge Ct HERT/WAS SG14 ...... 150 C2
Heydons Cl STALW/RED AL3 ...... 10 C2
Heyford Rd RAD WD7 ...... 206 C7
Heyford St HAT AL10 ...... 171 H2
Heysham Dr OXHEY WD19 ...... 230 D4
Heywood Dr LTNE LU2 ...... 70 A6
Hibbert Av WATN WD24 ...... 204 E8
Hibbert St LTN LU1 ...... 4 C5
Hickling Cl LTNE LU2 ...... 70 E8
Hickling Wy HARP AL5 ...... 118 E6
Hickman Cl BROX EN10 ...... 176 D6
Hicks Rd STALW/RED AL3 ...... 115 J4
Hidalgo Ct HHNE HP2 ...... 8 C3
The Hideaway ABLGY WD5 ...... 204 A1
The Hides HLW CM20 ...... 6 C3
High Acres ABLGY WD5 ...... 203 J2
High Dr LTNE LU2 ...... 70 E8
Higham Rd AMP/FLIT/B MK45 ...... 36 C5
High Ash Rd STALE/WH AL4 ...... 145 F2
High Av LWTH SG6 ...... 41 H4
Highbanks Rd PIN HA5 ...... 231 J5
Highbarns HHS/BOV HP3 ...... 186 A3
High Beech Rd LTNN/LIM LU3 ...... 68 C2
Highbridge St WAB EN9 ...... 215 F4
Highbury Av HOD EN11 ...... 177 F1
Highbury Rd HTCHE/RSTV SG4 ...... 56 E7
  LTN LU1 ...... 4 A2
Highbush Rd HTCH/STOT SG5 ...... 25 J4
High Canons BORE WD6 ...... 208 B7
Highclere Dr HHS/BOV HP3 ...... 186 B2
High Cl RKW/CH/CXG WD3 ...... 218 B5
Highcroft Rd HHS/BOV HP3 ...... 184 E3
High Cross GSTN WD25 ...... 206 A7
High Dane HTCHE/RSTV SG4 ...... 40 E7
High Dells HAT AL10 ...... 170 E5
High Elms HARP AL5 ...... 143 H3
High Elms Cl NTHWD HA6 ...... 229 H5
High Elms La GSTN WD25 ...... 204 C1
  STVGE SG2 ...... 98 B1
Highfield HLWS CM18 ...... 7 F5
  KGLGY WD4 ...... 185 J6
  LWTH SG6 ...... 41 H5
  OXHEY WD19 ...... 231 G2
Highfield Av BSF CM23 ...... 106 B3
  HARP AL5 ...... 143 K1
Highfield Cl NTHWD HA6 ...... 229 K7
Highfield Crs NTHWD HA6 ...... 229 K7
Highfield Dr BROX EN10 ...... 176 D7
Highfield La HHNE HP2 ...... 8 C3
  STALE/WH AL4 ...... 169 F8
Highfield Ov HARP AL5 ...... 118 C5
Highfield Rd BERK HP4 ...... 162 A6
  BUSH WD23 ...... 13 F4
  CHESW EN7 ...... 196 C4
  HERT/BAY SG13 ...... 151 G5
  LTNW/LEA LU4 ...... 69 G8
  NTHWD HA6 ...... 229 K7
  STALE/WH AL4 ...... 144 E8

TRING HP23 ...... 134 D6
Highfields POTB/CUF EN6 ...... 195 G6
  RAD WD7 ...... 206 C5
Highfield Wy POTB/CUF EN6 ...... 210 C1
  RKW/CH/CXG WD3 ...... 217 K6
High Firs RAD WD7 ...... 206 C5
High Firs Crs HARP AL5 ...... 144 A1
Highgate Ov SBW CM21 ...... 132 B7
High Gv WGCW AL8 ...... 147 G2
Highland Dr BUSH WD23 ...... 221 J7
  HHS/BOV HP3 ...... 9 E5
Highland Rd BSF CM23 ...... 105 J6
  NTHWD HA6 ...... 230 B8
  WAB EN9 ...... 177 K8
Highlands BRKMPK AL9 ...... 171 H1
  OXHEY WD19 ...... 220 D8
  ROY SG8 ...... 21 J3
Highlands Cl CFSP/GDCR SL9 ...... 226 C6
Highlands End CFSP/GDCR SL9 ...... 226 C6
Highlands La CFSP/GDCR SL9 ...... 226 C5
The Highlands POTB/CUF EN6 ...... 193 J8
  RKW/CH/CXG WD3 ...... 218 A7
High La STSD SM24 ...... 86 D1
High Md LTNN/LIM LU3 ...... 69 F6
Highmead STSD CM24 ...... 86 D1
High Meads STALE/WH AL4 ...... 145 F1
Highmoor HARP AL5 ...... 118 C5
High Oak Rd WARE SG12 ...... 127 H7
High Oaks ENC/FH EN2 ...... 212 C8
  STALW/RED AL3 ...... 167 K1
High Oaks Rd WGCW AL8 ...... 147 G2
Highover Cl LTNE LU2 ...... 5 F2
Highover Rd LWTH SG6 ...... 41 H4
Highover Wy HTCHE/RSTV SG4 ...... 41 F8
  LTNE LU2 ...... 70 D8
  POTB/CUF EN6 ...... 195 G5
High Rdg HARP AL5 ...... 118 A6
High Ridge Cl HHS/BOV HP3 ...... 185 H3
High Ridge Rd HHS/BOV HP3 ...... 185 H3
High Rd BRKMPK AL9 ...... 173 F4
  BROX EN10 ...... 176 E6
  BUSH WD23 ...... 222 A8
  GSTN WD25 ...... 204 A4
  HERT/WAS SG14 ...... 125 H3
  HTCH/STOT SG5 ...... 38 A2
High Road Broxbourne
  BROX EN10 ...... 176 E7
High Road Turnford BROX EN10 ...... 197 H6
High Road Wormley BROX EN10 ...... 197 K2
High St ABLGY WD5 ...... 187 F5
  ARL/CHE SG15 ...... 24 E3
  BERK HP4 ...... 161 F2
  BLDK SG7 ...... 16 C3
  BLDK SG7 ...... 43 H1
  BORE WD6 ...... 223 G6
  BROX EN10 ...... 197 J3
  BSF CM23 ...... 105 J2
  BUNT SG9 ...... 63 J1
  BUSH WD23 ...... 221 H6
  CFSP/GDCR SL9 ...... 226 B7
  CHES/WCR EN8 ...... 197 H6
  CHES/WCR EN8 ...... 214 C2
  DEN/HRF UB9 ...... 228 B8
  HARP AL5 ...... 118 C7
  HERT/WAS SG14 ...... 98 A5
  HHNE HP2 ...... 164 B8
  HHS/BOV HP3 ...... 183 J5
  HLWE CM17 ...... 157 F7
  HLWW/ROY CM19 ...... 178 A4
  HOD EN11 ...... 177 F3
  HTCH/STOT SG5 ...... 25 K3
  HTCH/STOT SG5 ...... 39 F5
  HTCH/STOT SG5 ...... 54 E8
  HTCHE/RSTV SG4 ...... 56 D6
  HTCHE/RSTV SG4 ...... 58 C5
  HTCHE/RSTV SG4 ...... 93 F8
  HTCHE/RSTV SG4 ...... 93 J3
  KGLGY WD4 ...... 186 A3
  LBUZ LU7 ...... 110 A2
  LCOL/BKTW AL2 ...... 190 A3
  LTNW/LEA LU4 ...... 68 B5
  MHAD SG10 ...... 103 G6
  NTHWD HA6 ...... 230 A2
  POTB/CUF EN6 ...... 210 C3
  RKW/CH/CXG WD3 ...... 218 C6
  ROY SG8 ...... 15 G5
  ROY SG8 ...... 21 H3
  ROY SG8 ...... 23 F7
  ROY SG8 ...... 31 J4
  ROY SG8 ...... 32 C4
  SDY/GAM/PO SG19 ...... 14 C1
  STAL AL1 ...... 10 C4
  STALE/WH AL4 ...... 120 B8
  STALE/WH AL4 ...... 144 E4
  STALE/WH AL4 ...... 170 A4
  STALW/RED AL3 ...... 115 J3
  STALW/RED AL3 ...... 116 B2
  STALW/RED AL3 ...... 142 C3
  STDN SG11 ...... 81 J4
  STVG SG1 ...... 2 A5
  STVGE SG1 ...... 60 D8
  TRING HP23 ...... 135 F6
  WARE SG12 ...... 127 H4
  WARE SG12 ...... 129 K3
  WARE SG12 ...... 153 H4

WAT WD17 ...... 12 C2
WATW WD18 ...... 12 C2
WLYN AL6 ...... 94 E8
WLYN AL6 ...... 122 C4
High Street Gn HHNE HP2 ...... 9 D2
High Town Rd LTNE LU2 ...... 5 D3
High Vw BSF CM23 ...... 86 B6
  CSTG HP8 ...... 226 A1
  HAT AL10 ...... 170 E6
  HTCH/STOT SG5 ...... 56 B3
  RKW/CH/CXG WD3 ...... 217 K4
  STALW/RED AL3 ...... 115 J5
  WATW WD18 ...... 12 A5
Highview Cl POTB/CUF EN6 ...... 210 D3
Highview Gdns POTB/CUF EN6 ...... 210 D3
  STALE/WH AL4 ...... 169 F1
High Wickfield WCCE AL7 ...... 148 D4
Highwood Av BUSH WD23 ...... 221 G1
High Wood Cl LTN LU1 ...... 88 E2
Highwoodhall La HHS/BOV HP3 ...... 186 A3
High Wood Rd HOD EN11 ...... 152 E8
High Wych La SBW CM21 ...... 131 J7
  SBW CM21 ...... 132 B8
High Wych Wy HHNE HP2 ...... 141 F8
Hilbury HAT AL10 ...... 170 E5
Hilfield La GSTN WD25 ...... 221 J1
Hiljon Crs CFSP/GDCR SL9 ...... 226 B7
Hillary Cl LTN LU1 ...... 68 C2
Hillary Crs LTN LU1 ...... 4 A5
Hillary Ri ARL/CHE SG15 ...... 25 F4
Hillary Rd HHNE HP2 ...... 9 D4
Hillborough Rd LTN LU1 ...... 4 B5
Hillbrow LWTH SG6 ...... 41 H4
Hill Cl BAR EN5 ...... 225 H5
  HARP AL5 ...... 118 C5
  LTNN/LIM LU3 ...... 69 H2
Hill Common HHS/BOV HP3 ...... 186 A1
Hill Ct BERK HP4 ...... 162 A4
Hill Crest HTCHE/RSTV SG4 ...... 93 H3
  POTB/CUF EN6 ...... 210 D3
Hillcrest BLDK SG7 ...... 43 F2
  HAT AL10 ...... 171 F5
  STVG SG1 ...... 3 D3
Hillcrest Av LTNE LU2 ...... 69 H1
Hillcrest Rd WD7 ...... 207 K3
Hill Croft Cl LTNN/LEA LU4 ...... 68 C3
Hillcroft Crs OXHEY WD19 ...... 220 C8
Hilldown Rd HHW HP1 ...... 163 K4
Hill Dyke Rd STALE/WH AL4 ...... 145 C2
Hill End La STAL AL1 ...... 189 K1
  STALE/WH AL4 ...... 190 A1
Hill End Rd DEN/HRF UB9 ...... 228 A5
Hill Farm Av CSTN WD25 ...... 204 B3
Hill Farm La STALW/RED AL3 ...... 142 C8
  WLYN AL6 ...... 121 C4
Hill Farm Rd CFSP/GDCR SL9 ...... 226 B6
Hillfield HAT AL10 ...... 171 G1
Hillfield La HTCHE/RSTV SG4 ...... 40 E7
Hillfield Ct HHNE HP2 ...... 8 B5
Hillfield La South BUSH WD23 ...... 222 B6
Hillfield Rd CFSP/GDCR SL9 ...... 226 B6
  HHNE HP2 ...... 8 A5
Hillfield Sq CFSP/GDCR SL9 ...... 226 B6
Hillgate HTCHE/RSTV SG4 ...... 40 E6
Hilliard Rd NTHWD HA6 ...... 230 A7
Hillingdon Rd GSTN WD25 ...... 204 B4
Hillingdon Trail DEN/HRF UB9 ...... 227 K6
Hill Ley HAT AL10 ...... 170 E4
Hill Leys POTB/CUF EN6 ...... 195 G6
Hill Md BERK HP4 ...... 161 H6
Hillmead STVG SG1 ...... 3 E2
Hill Milford HARP AL5 ...... 119 F6
Hill Pickford HARP AL5 ...... 119 F5
Hill Ri CFSP/GDCR SL9 ...... 226 A8
  LTNN/LIM LU3 ...... 68 B2
  POTB/CUF EN6 ...... 195 F5
  POTB/CUF EN6 ...... 210 A7
  RKW/CH/CXG WD3 ...... 218 A7
Hillrise Av WATN WD24 ...... 204 E8
Hill Rise Crs CFSP/GDCR SL9 ...... 226 B8
Hill Rd HTCHE/RSTV SG4 ...... 94 D8
  NTHWD HA6 ...... 229 H3
Hillsborough Gn OXHEY WD19 ...... 230 B2
Hillshott LWTH SG6 ...... 42 A5
Hill Side LBUZ LU7 ...... 109 K3
Hillside HAT AL10 ...... 171 F4
  HLWE CM17 ...... 181 F3
  HOD EN11 ...... 176 E2
  ROY SG8 ...... 21 H4
  STVG SG1 ...... 3 D3
  WARE SG12 ...... 152 C1
  WCCE AL7 ...... 148 C6
  WLYN AL6 ...... 94 E8
Hillside Av BORE WD6 ...... 224 B3
  BSF CM23 ...... 105 K2
  CHES/WCR EN8 ...... 214 C1
Hillside Cl ABLGY WD5 ...... 203 K2
  CFSP/GDCR SL9 ...... 226 B5
Hillside Crs CHES/WCR EN8 ...... 214 C1
  ENC/FH EN2 ...... 213 G8
  NTHWD HA6 ...... 230 B7
  OXHEY WD19 ...... 13 F5
  WARE SG12 ...... 153 G5
Hillside Gdns BAR EN5 ...... 225 K4

BERK HP4 ...... 162 A6
  NTHWD HA6 ...... 230 B6
Hillside La WARE SG12 ...... 153 F4
Hillside Ri NTHWD HA6 ...... 230 B6
Hillside Rd BUSH WD23 ...... 13 F4
  HARP AL5 ...... 118 B6
  LTNN/LIM LU3 ...... 4 B2
  NTHWD HA6 ...... 230 B6
  PIN HA5 ...... 230 C6
  RAD WD7 ...... 206 E5
  RKW/CH/CXG WD3 ...... 217 F5
  STAL AL1 ...... 11 D3
Hillside Ter HERT/BAY SG13 ...... 151 F5
Hillside Wy WLYN AL6 ...... 123 G1
Hills La NTHWD HA6 ...... 229 K7
Hill St STALW/RED AL3 ...... 10 C1
The Hill HLWE CM17 ...... 157 F5
  STALE/WH AL4 ...... 145 C4
Hill Top BLDK SG7 ...... 42 E2
Hilltop STALW/RED AL3 ...... 142 A3
Hilltop Cl CHESW EN7 ...... 196 D4
Hilltop Rd BERK HP4 ...... 161 K6
  KGLGV WD4 ...... 186 D5
Hill Tree Cl SBW CM21 ...... 132 B5
Hill Vw BERK HP4 ...... 161 H3
  BUNT SG9 ...... 47 H1
  HTCHE/RSTV SG4 ...... 93 H3
Hillview Cl PIN HA5 ...... 231 C5
Hillview Crs LTNE LU2 ...... 69 H2
Hillview Gdns CHES/WCR EN8 ...... 197 J5
Hillview Rd PIN HA5 ...... 231 C6
Hilly Flds HLWS CM18 ...... 180 C2
Hilly Flds WCCE AL7 ...... 148 D2
Hilmay Dr HHW HP1 ...... 164 A7
Hilton Cl STVG SG1 ...... 75 G2
Himalayan Wy WATW WD18 ...... 12 A5
Hindhead Gn OXHEY WD19 ...... 230 D4
Hine Wy HTCH/STOT SG5 ...... 40 A8
Hinxworth Rd BLDK SG7 ...... 16 B7
Hipkins BSF CM23 ...... 105 H5
Hitchens Cl HHW HP1 ...... 163 J5
Hitchin Hl HTCHE/RSTV SG4 ...... 56 C3
Hitchin Rd ARL/CHE SG15 ...... 24 E6
  HTCH/STOT SG5 ...... 25 H6
  HTCH/STOT SG5 ...... 37 K8
  HTCHE/RSTV SG4 ...... 43 H8
  HTCHE/RSTV SG4 ...... 56 D5
  HTCHE/RSTV SG4 ...... 93 C7
  LTNE LU2 ...... 5 D3
  LWTH SG6 ...... 41 J6
  STVG SG1 ...... 58 B7
Hitchin St BLDK SG7 ...... 42 E1
Hitherbank WCCE AL7 ...... 147 J5
Hither Fld WARE SG12 ...... 127 J6
Hitherfield La HARP AL5 ...... 118 C7
Hither Meadow CFSP/GDCR SL9 ...... 226 B8
Hitherway WGCW AL8 ...... 122 D7
Hobbs Cl CHES/WCR EN8 ...... 197 H7
  STALE/WH AL4 ...... 169 H7
Hobbs Cross Rd HLWE CM17 ...... 157 J6
Hobbs Hill Rd HHS/BOV HP3 ...... 185 J2
Hobbs Wy WGCW AL8 ...... 147 H4
Hobletts Rd HHNE HP2 ...... 8 E3
Hobsons Cl HOD EN11 ...... 152 E8
Hobsons Wk HP23 ...... 134 E4
Hobtoe Rd HLW CM20 ...... 155 H8
Hockerill HERT/WAS SG14 ...... 98 B6
Hockerill St BSF CM23 ...... 105 K2
Hocklands WGCE AL7 ...... 148 D2
Hockwell Ring LTNN/LEA LU4 ...... 68 A4
Hoddesdon Rd WARE SG12 ...... 153 H6
Hodges Wy WATW WD18 ...... 12 B5
Hodings Rd HLW CM20 ...... 6 A3
Hodwell BLDK SG7 ...... 17 K5
Hoecroft WAB EN9 ...... 178 A8
Hoe La EN EN1 ...... 214 A8
  PEND EN3 ...... 214 B8
  WAB EN9 ...... 178 A8
  WARE SG12 ...... 152 C3
Hoestock Rd SBW CM21 ...... 132 B7
The Hoe OXHEY WD19 ...... 230 B3
Hogg End La STALW/RED AL3 ...... 166 B4
Hogg Rd BORE WD6 ...... 222 D4
Hog Hall La BERK HP4 ...... 112 C4
Hog La CSHM HP5 ...... 160 C8
Hogpits Bottom HHS/BOV HP3 ...... 200 D2
Hogsdell La HERT/BAY SG13 ...... 152 A5
Holbeck La CHESW EN7 ...... 196 D4
Holborn Cl STALE/WH AL4 ...... 169 G1
Holcroft Rd HARP AL5 ...... 119 F4
Holdbrook HTCHE/RSTV SG4 ...... 57 F2
Holden Cl HERT/BAY SG13 ...... 151 H2
  HTCHE/RSTV SG4 ...... 57 G2
Holders La STVGE SG2 ...... 77 F4
The Holdings BRKMPK AL9 ...... 171 J2
Holecroft WAB EN9 ...... 215 K4
Holford Wy LTNN/LIM LU3 ...... 52 B8
Holgate Dr LTNN/LEA LU4 ...... 68 A6
Holland Gdns GSTN WD25 ...... 204 D5
Holland La LTNN/LIM LU3 ...... 69 G7
Holland's Cft WARE SG12 ...... 129 K8
Holliday St BERK HP4 ...... 162 A5
Holliers Wy HAT AL10 ...... 171 F4
Hollies Cl ROY SG8 ...... 21 J3

The Hollies HHS/BOV HP3 ...... 183 J7
  RKW/CH/CXG WD3 ...... 217 F7
  TRING HP23 ...... 135 J8
Hollies Wy POTB/CUF EN6 ...... 210 D1
Holloway La RKW/CH/CXG WD3 ...... 200 E8
Holloways La BRKMPK AL9 ...... 192 D1
The Holloway RAYLNE/WEN HP2 ...... 134 B5
Hollow La HTCHE/RSTV SG4 ...... 56 D2
Hollybush Av LCOL/BKTW AL2 ...... 188 C2
Hollybush Cl BERK HP4 ...... 163 G2
  OXHEY WD19 ...... 13 D6
  WLYN AL6 ...... 122 E1
Hollybush Hl LTNE LU2 ...... 54 B8
Hollybush La BRKMPK AL9 ...... 148 A7
  HARP AL5 ...... 118 B6
  HHW HP1 ...... 163 J5
  HTCHE/RSTV SG4 ...... 92 E1
  KNEB SG3 ...... 96 D6
  STALW/RED AL3 ...... 116 A6
  WGCE AL7 ...... 147 K6
Hollybush Rd LTNE LU2 ...... 70 D8
Hollybush Wy CHESW EN7 ...... 196 E6
Holly Cl HAT AL10 ...... 170 E5
Holly Copse STVG SG1 ...... 3 D4
Holly Cft HERT/WAS SG14 ...... 150 C2
Hollycross Rd WARE SG12 ...... 152 E1
Holly Dell HERT/BAY SG13 ...... 151 F5
Holly Dr BERK HP4 ...... 162 A6
  POTB/CUF EN6 ...... 210 C3
Holly Farm Cl LTN LU1 ...... 88 D5
Hollyfield HAT AL10 ...... 171 F7
Holly Fld HLWW/ROY CM19 ...... 179 K4
Hollyfield TRING HP23 ...... 135 H4
Hollyfield Cl TRING HP23 ...... 135 H4
Hollyfields BROX EN10 ...... 197 J4
Hollygrove BUSH WD23 ...... 222 A7
Holly Gv PIN HA5 ...... 231 F7
Holly Grove Rd HERT/WAS SG14 ...... 124 E6
Holly Hall Ct WLYN AL6 ...... 122 C4
Holly Hedges La HHS/BOV HP3 ...... 184 A8
Holly La HARP AL5 ...... 119 G2
Holly Leys STVGE SG2 ...... 96 C1
Holly Rd KNEB SG3 ...... 96 B8
  PEND EN3 ...... 214 C6
Holly Shaws STVGE SG2 ...... 3 F6
Holly St LTN LU1 ...... 4 C5
Hollytree Cl CFSP/GDCR SL9 ...... 226 B4
Holly Tree Ct HHNE HP2 ...... 9 E5
Holly Wk HARP AL5 ...... 119 F8
  WGCW AL8 ...... 122 C7
Holmbrook Av LTNN/LIM LU3 ...... 69 H4
Holmdale LWTH SG6 ...... 42 A4
Holmdale Cl BORE WD6 ...... 223 J2
Holme Cl CHES/WCR EN8 ...... 214 D1
  HAT AL10 ...... 170 E1
Holme Lea GSTN WD25 ...... 204 D4
Holme Pk BORE WD6 ...... 223 J2
Holme Rd HAT AL10 ...... 170 E1
Holmesdale CHES/WCR EN8 ...... 214 B5
Holmes Meadow EPP CM16 ...... 179 J7
Holmfield Cl LTN LU1 ...... 4 B6
Holmscroft Rd LTNN/LIM LU3 ...... 68 E3
Holmshill La BORE WD6 ...... 208 E7
Holmside Ri OXHEY WD19 ...... 230 C2
Holmwood Rd PEND EN3 ...... 214 C6
Holroyd Crs BLDK SG7 ...... 42 E2
Holt Cl BORE WD6 ...... 223 J4
Holts Meadow STALW/RED AL3 ...... 142 C3
Holtsmere Cl GSTN WD25 ...... 204 D5
  LTNE LU2 ...... 70 C2
Holtsmere End La HHNE HP2 ...... 141 G7
The Holt HHNE HP2 ...... 8 B6
  WGCE AL7 ...... 148 E4
Holwell Hyde WGCE AL7 ...... 148 D4
Holwell Hyde La BRKMPK AL9 ...... 148 D7
Holwell La BRKMPK AL9 ...... 148 F8
Holwell Rd HTCH/STOT SG5 ...... 39 H5
  WGCE AL7 ...... 147 K4
Holy Cross Hl BROX EN10 ...... 196 E1
Holyfield Rd WAB EN9 ...... 198 C7
Holyrood Crs STAL AL1 ...... 189 F2
Holywell Cl DUN/WHIP LU6 ...... 113 K3
  STAL AL1 ...... 10 B6
Holywell Hl STAL AL1 ...... 10 B6
Holywell Rd DUN/WHIP LU6 ...... 113 K2
  WATW WD18 ...... 12 B4
Home Cl BROX EN10 ...... 197 K2
  HLW CM20 ...... 7 E4
  HTCH/STOT SG5 ...... 25 K3
  LTNN/LEA LU4 ...... 68 B5
Homedale Dr LTNN/LEA LU4 ...... 68 C7
Home Farm Rd BERK HP4 ...... 160 E2
  RKW/CH/CXG WD3 ...... 229 F3
Homefield BERK HP4 ...... 162 E2
  BLDK SG7 ...... 16 D3
  HHS/BOV HP3 ...... 183 K6
Homefield La HTCHE/RSTV SG4 ...... 74 E7
Homefield Rd BUSH WD23 ...... 221 H5
  HHNE HP2 ...... 9 D5
  RAD WD7 ...... 206 C7
  RKW/CH/CXG WD3 ...... 217 G4
  WARE SG12 ...... 127 J7
Homeleigh Ct CHES/WCR EN8 ...... 197 F8
Home Ley WCCE AL7 ...... 147 K3
Home Meadow WGCE AL7 ...... 148 A3

Home Park Mill Link Rd
KGLGY WD4 203 G1
Home Pastures RBSF CM22 133 K6
Homerfield WGCW AL8 147 H3
Homerswood La WLYN AL6 122 A7
Homerton Rd LTNN/LIM LU3 69 F3
Homestead Cl LCOL/BKTW AL2 188 E5
Homestead La WGCE AL7 148 A6
Homestead Moat STVG SG1 2 C3
Homestead Rd HAT AL10 171 F1
RKW/CH/CXG WD3 218 C7
Homestead Wy LTN LU1 4 A6
Home Wy RKW/CH/CXG WD3 217 J8
Homewood Av POTB/CUF EN6 195 G5
Homewood La POTB/CUF EN6 194 E5
Homewood Rd STAL AL1 168 E3
Honeybourne BSF CM23 105 H5
Honey Brook WAB EN9 215 K3
Honeycroft WGCW AL8 147 H4 3
Honeycroft Dr STALE/WH AL4 190 A1
Honeycross Rd HHW HP1 163 H7
Honeygate LTNE LU2 69 K5
Honey La BUNT SG9 63 J1
CHES/WCR EN8 214 E4
SAFWS CB11 51 H6
WAB EN9 215 K4
Honeymeade HLW CM20 157 F2
Honeysuckle Cl BSF CM23 105 F3
HERT/BAY SG13 151 K3 2
Honeysuckle Gdns HAT AL10 171 G5
Honeyway ROY SG8 21 J2
Honeywood Cl POTB/CUF EN6 210 E3
Hook Fld HLWS CM18 7 D6
Hook Ga EN EN1 214 A7
Hook La POTB/CUF EN6 211 G2
Hoops La ROY SG8 30 D3
Hoo St LTN LU1 4 C6 1
The Hoo HLWE CM17 157 F4
Hope Gn GSTN WD25 204 B3
Hopewell Rd BLDK SG7 42 D1
Hopground Cl STAL AL1 11 F6
Hopkins Crs STALE/WH AL4 144 E8
Hopkins Yd STAL AL1 11 D5 5
Hopton Rd STVG SG1 75 F2
Horace Gay Gdns LWTH SG6 41 J4 1
Horbeam Cl BORE WD6 223 K1 3
Hordle Gdns STAL AL1 11 E5
Hornbeam La BRKMPK AL9 173 F7
Hornbeams LCOL/BKTW AL2 188 B8
Hornbeams Av EN EN1 214 B5
Hornbeam Spring KNEB SG3 96 A5
The Hornbeams HLW CM20 6 B2
STVGE SG2 3 F4
Hornbeam Wy CHESW EN7 196 D7
The Hornets WATW WD18 12 C3 2
Horn Hl HTCHE/RSTV SG4 93 H3
Hornhill Rd RKW/CH/CXG WD3 227 F4
Hornsby Cl LTNE LU2 70 D8
Horns Cl HERT/BAY SG13 151 F5
Hornsfield WGCE AL7 148 D2
Horns Mill Rd HERT/BAY SG13 150 E6
Horns Rd HERT/BAY SG13 151 F4
Horrocks Cl WARE SG12 127 H6
Horsecroft Rd HHW HP1 163 K8
HLWW/ROY CM19 179 F2
Horse Hl CSHM HP5 200 A2
Horselers HHS/BOV HP3 186 A1
Horsemans Dr LCOL/BKTW AL2 188 C4
Horseshoe Hl BUNT SG9 65 G1
Horseshoe La BUNT SG9 65 F2
GSTN WD25 204 C2
TRDG/WHET N20 225 J8
Horseshoes Cl LBUZ LU7 109 K2 2
The Horseshoe HHS/BOV HP3 165 H8
Horsham Cl LTNE LU2 70 E6
Horsler Cl AMP/FLIT/B MK45 36 C7
Horsleys RKW/CH/CXG WD3 227 G4
Horton Gdns HHNE HP2 141 F8 1
Hospital Rd ARL/CHE SG15 24 D6
Housden Cl STALE/WH AL4 145 H2 1
Housefield Wy STALE/WH AL4 190 A1
House La ARL/CHE SG15 24 E2
STALE/WH AL4 145 F8
Housewood End HHW HP1 164 A3
Howard Agne Cl HHW HP1 183 J5
Howard Cl BUSH WD23 222 B7
HTCH/STOT SG5 25 J4 1
LTNN/LIM LU3 69 F5 1
STALE/WH AL4 190 A1
WAB EN9 215 J4
WATN WD24 204 B7 3
Howard Dr BORE WD6 224 C4
LWTH SG6 42 B6
Howard Ga LWTH SG6 42 B5 1
Howards Cl PIN HA5 230 C8 1
Howards Dr HHW HP1 163 J3
Howardsgate WGCW AL8 147 J3
Howards Wd LWTH SG6 42 B6
Howard Wy BAR EN5 225 J5
HLW CM20 7 E1
Howe Cl RAD WD7 207 H2
Howe Dell HAT AL10 171 G4
Howe Rd HHS/BOV HP3 165 F8
How Fld HARP AL5 118 A6
Howfield Gn HOD EN11 152 E8
Howicks Gn WGCE AL7 148 B6
Howland Garth STAL AL1 188 E2
Howlands WGCE AL7 148 B6 2
Howton Pl BUSH WD23 222 A8
How Wd LCOL/BKTW AL2 188 D6
Hoylake Gdns OXHEY WD19 230 E3
Hubbards Rd RKW/CH/CXG WD3 217 G5
Huckleberry Cl LTNN/LIM LU3 69 F1 3
Hudnall La BERK HP4 138 A3
Hudson Cl STAL AL1 188 E1
WATN WD24 204 A6
Hudson Rd STVGE SG2 3 F1
Huggins La BRKMPK AL9 192 B1
Hughenden Rd STALE/WH AL4 168 E3
Hull Gv HLWW/ROY CM19 179 H6
Hull La STDN SG11 81 K2
Humberstone Cl LTNW/LEA LU4 68 D7
Humberstone Rd LTNW/LEA LU4 68 D7
Humphrey Talbot Av
DUN/WHIP LU6 113 H2
Hunsdon WGCE AL7 148 E3 1
Hunsdon Rd WARE SG12 129 K5
Hunston Cl LTNW/LEA LU4 68 A4
Hunt Cl STALE/WH AL4 169 G3 2
Hunter Cl BORE WD6 224 B5
POTB/CUF EN6 210 C3
Huntercrombe Gdns
OXHEY WD19 230 D4 6
Hunters Cl HHS/BOV HP3 183 J7
HTCH/STOT SG5 25 J3 2
STVGE SG2 76 E2
TRING HP23 135 G4
Hunter's La GSTN WD25 204 A4
Hunters Oak HHNE HP2 165 G1
Hunters Pk BERK HP4 162 B4
Hunters Reach CHESW EN7 196 D7
Hunters Ride LCOL/BKTW AL2 205 H1
Hunters Wy ROY SG8 21 J3
WGCE AL7 147 K6 2
Huntingdon Cl BROX EN10 197 J2
Huntingdon Rd STVG SG1 75 G1
Hunting Ga HHNE HP2 8 B1
HTCHE/RSTV SG4 40 E6
Hunton Bridge Hl KGLGY WD4 203 H3
Hunts Cl LTN LU1 4 A5
Huntsman Cl STDN SG11 81 J6
Huntsmans Cl BERK HP4 112 E4 2
Huntsmill Rd HHW HP1 163 H7 4
Hurlock Wy LTNW/LEA LU4 68 B4
Hurricane Wy GSTN WD25 204 B2 2
Hurst Cl BLDK SG7 27 G8
WGCE AL7 148 D4
Hurst Dr CHES/WCR EN8 214 C4
Hurstlings WGCE AL7 148 C5
Hurst Pl NTHWD HA6 229 G7
Hurst Wy LTNN/LIM LU3 68 D4
Hutton Cl HERT/WAS SG14 150 D3
Hutton La KTN/HRWW/W HA3 231 K6
Hutton Wk KTN/HRWW/W HA3 231 K6
Hyburn Cl HHS/BOV HP3 9 E6
LCOL/BKTW AL2 188 B8
Hydean Wy STVGE SG2 3 E5
Hyde Av HTCH/STOT SG5 25 J4
POTB/CUF EN6 210 C3
Hyde Cl HARP AL5 118 D5
Hyde Gn East STVGE SG2 3 F5 1
Hyde Gn North STVGE SG2 3 F5
Hyde Gn South STVGE SG2 3 F5
Hyde La HHS/BOV HP3 183 J5
KGLGY WD4 186 B5
LCOL/BKTW AL2 188 E6
LTNE LU2 91 J7
Hyde Md WAB EN9 198 E1
Hyde Mdw HHS/BOV HP3 183 J6
Hyde Rd LTN LU1 88 E5
WAT WD17 12 B2 1
The Hyde WARE SG12 127 F7
Hyde Va WGCE AL7 148 A5
Hyde View Rd HARP AL5 118 D5
Hyde Wy WGCE AL7 147 K3
Hyperion Ct HHNE HP2 8 C2
Hyver Hl MLHL NW7 224 C6

I

Ibberson Wy HTCHE/RSTV SG4 56 E2
Iceni Ct LWTH SG6 42 B2
Ickleford Rd HTCH/STOT SG5 56 D1
Ickley Cl LTNW/LEA LU4 68 A4 1
Icknield Cl HTCH/STOT SG5 40 C5
STALW/RED AL3 167 G8
Icknield Gn LWTH SG6 41 J3
TRING HP23 135 F3 1
Icknield Rd LTNN/LIM LU3 68 E5
Icknield Wk ROY SG8 21 J2
Icknield Wy BERK HP4 113 G4
BLDK SG7 26 E8
BUNT SG9 30 A7
LTNN/LIM LU3 69 G1
LWTH SG6 41 G3
ROY SG8 30 D2
TRING HP23 134 C6
TRING HP23 158 B3
Icknield Wy East BLDK SG7 27 F8 3
Icknield Way Pth
AMP/FLIT/B MK45 52 A1
BLDK SG7 26 E6
HTCH/STOT SG5 38 E6
HTCH/STOT SG5 40 D4
HTCH/STOT SG5 53 K3
LTNN/LIM LU3 69 F3
LTNW/LEA LU4 68 B6
ROY SG8 18 D3
ROY SG8 23 F2
Ilford Cl LTNE LU2 70 D6
Ilkley Rd OXHEY WD19 230 E4
Imberfield LTNW/LEA LU4 68 B6 2
Imperial Wy WATN WD24 220 D1
Indells HAT AL10 170 E5
Ingelheim Ct STVG SG1 2 B1 1
Ingersoll Rd PEND EN3 214 B8
Inglefield POTB/CUF EN6 193 G8
Ingles WGCW AL8 122 E8
Ingleside Dr STVG SG1 58 B8
Ingram Gdns LTNE LU2 69 J3
Inkerman Rd STAL AL1 11 D5
Inkerman St LTN LU1 4 B4
Innes Ct HHS/BOV HP3 164 C8
Inn's Cl STVG SG1 2 B2
Inskip Crs STVG SG1 2 C3
Iona Cl STVG SG1 59 F7
Iredale Vw BLDK SG7 27 G8
Iron Dr HERT/BAY SG13 152 A2
Irving Cl BSF CM23 105 G5 1
Irving Crs LBUZ LU7 110 A1
Isabel Ga CHES/WCR EN8 197 K4
Isabelle Cl CHESW EN7 196 A7
Isenburg Wy HHNE HP2 164 C1
Isherwood Cl ROY SG8 21 G1 2
Islington Wy STVG SG1 59 F7
Iveagh Cl NTHWD HA6 229 G7
Ivel Cl AMP/FLIT/B MK45 36 D6 1
Ivel Rd STVG SG1 2 A1
Ivel Wy BLDK SG7 43 G3
HTCH/STOT SG5 25 K1
Ives Rd HERT/WAS SG14 150 E2
Ivinghoe Br LBUZ LU7 110 C1
Ivinghoe Cl GSTN WD25 204 E5
STALE/WH AL4 169 F1 3
Ivinghoe Rd BUSH WD23 222 A6
RKW/CH/CXG WD3 217 J7
Ivory Cl STALE/WH AL4 169 F8
Ivory Ct HHS/BOV HP3 185 J1
Ivybridge BROX EN10 177 F5
Ivy House La BERK HP4 162 A5 2
Ivy Lea RKW/CH/CXG WD3 217 K8 3
Ivy Rd LTN LU1 4 A3
Ivy Ter HOD EN11 177 H1

J

Jackdaw Cl STVGE SG2 76 E5
Jackdaws WGCE AL7 148 D3
Jackets La DEN/HRF UB9 229 F6
Jacketts Fld ABLGY WD5 187 F8
Jackman's Pl LWTH SG6 42 B3
Jacks La DEN/HRF UB9 227 K7
Jacksons Dr CHESW EN7 196 E6
Jackson's La ROY SG8 31 J4
Jackson St BLDK SG7 26 E8
Jack Stevens Cl HLWE CM17 181 F3
James Cl BUSH WD23 13 F4
James Ct LTN LU1 4 C5
Jameson Rd HARP AL5 118 D6
James Wy STVG SG1 2 A
Jane Cl HHNE HP2 165 G
Jarden LWTH SG6 42 C5
Jarman Cl HHS/BOV HP3 164 D8
Jarman Wy ROY SG8 21 F
Jarvis Cleys CHESW EN7 196 D4
Jarvis Cl BAR EN5 225 J5
Jasmin Cl BSF CM23 105 F
NTHWD HA6 230 A
Jasmine Dr HERT/BAY SG13 151 K
Jasmine Gdns HAT AL10 170 E
Jasmin Wy HHW HP1 163 H5
Jasons Hl CSHM HP5 182 D
Jasper Cl PEND EN3 214 B
Jay Cl LWTH SG6 41 J
Jaywood LTNE LU2 70 D
Jeans La BSF CM23 105 H
Jeffrey Cl ROY SG8 21 G
Jellicoe Rd WATW WD18 12 B
Jenkins Av LCOL/BKTW AL2 188 A
Jenkins La BSF CM23 106 A
TRING HP23 158 D
Jennings Cl STVG SG1 2 C
Jennings Rd STAL AL1 11 E
Jennings Wy BAR EN5 225 H
HHS/BOV HP3 164 D
Jenning Wd WLYN AL6 123 F
Jepps La ROY SG8 21 H3
Jerome Dr STALW/RED AL3 167 H
Jerounds HLWW/ROY CM19 6 A

Jersey Cl *HOD* EN11 177 F2
Jersey La *STAL* AL1 168 E4
STALE/WH AL4 145 F8
Jervis Av *PEND* EN3 214 D5
Jervis Rd *BSF* CM23 105 J3
Jessop Rd *STVG* SG1 59 G8
Jeve Cl *BLDK* SG7 27 G8
Jill Grey Pl *HTCH/STOT* SG5 56 D3
The Jinnings *WGCE* AL7 148 C6
Jocelyns *HLWE* CM17 157 F5
Jocketts Hl *HHW* HP1 163 J6
Jocketts Rd *HHW* HP1 163 J7
Joel St *NTHWD* HA6 230 B8
John Barker Pl *HTCH/STOT* SG5 40 A8
John Bunyan Trail *HTCH/STOT* SG5 37 G6
LTNE LU2 53 J7
LTNN/LIM LU3 52 B7
Johnby Cl *PEND* EN3 214 D7 4
John Eliot Cl *WAB* EN9 177 K8
John Howland Cl *HNLW* SG16 24 B1
Johns La *CSHM* HP5 160 E8
Johnson Ct *HHS/BOV* HP3 164 D8
Johns Rd *BSF* CM23 85 K8
John St *LTN* LU1 4 C4
ROY SG8 21 H3 4
John Tate Rd *HERT/BAY* SG13 151 J4
Joiner's Cl *CFSP/GDCR* SL9 226 C6
Joiners La *CFSP/GDCR* SL9 226 B7
Joiners Wy *CFSP/GDCR* SL9 226 B6
The Joint *ROY* SG8 32 A3
Jones Rd *CHESW* EN7 195 K8
Jonquil Cl *WGCE* AL7 148 C5
Jordan Cl *GSTN* WD25 204 A5
Jordans Rd *RKW/CH/CXG* WD3 217 K7
Jordan's Wy *LCOL/BKTW* AL2 188 A8
Joslyn Cl *PEND* EN3 215 F8
Joyce Ct *WAB* EN9 215 J4 2
Joyners Fld *HLWS* CM18 179 K5
Jubilee Av *LCOL/BKTW* AL2 190 B4
WARE SG12 127 K7 2
Jubilee Cl *PIN* HA5 230 D8
Jubilee Crs *ARL/CHE* SG15 24 D7
Jubilee End *ROY* SG8 15 J7
Jubilee Rd *LWTH* SG6 42 C2
STVG SG1 75 G1
WATN WD24 204 B8
Jubilee St *LTNE* LU2 5 D2
Jubilee Wy *ROY* SG8 15 J7
Judge's Hl *POTB/CUF* EN6 194 B7
Judge St *WATN* WD24 204 C8
Julia Ga *STVG* SG1 76 D1
Julian's Ct *STVG* SG1 75 H1
Julian's Rd *STVG* SG1 75 G1
Julius Gdns *LTNN/LIM* LU3 68 E2
Juniper Av *LCOL/BKTW* AL2 205 H1 1
Juniper Cl *BAR* EN5 225 J5
BROX EN10 197 K3 3
LTNW/LEA LU4 68 D7
Juniper Gdns *RAD* WD7 207 H3
Juniper Ga *RKW/CH/CXG* WD3 228 C1
Juniper Gn *HHW* HP1 163 H6 1
Juniper Gv *WAT* WD17 204 B8
Jupiter Dr *HHNE* HP2 8 C3
Juxon Cl *RYLN/HDSTN* HA2 231 J7

K

Kardwell Cl *HTCHE/RSTV* SG4 56 E3 1
Katescroft *WGCE* AL7 147 K7 2
Katherine Pl *ABLGY* WD5 204 B2 3
Katherine's Wy *HLWW/ROY* CM19 179 H4
Katrine Sq *HHNE* HP2 8 A1
Keats Cl *HHNE* HP2 141 G8
ROY SG8 21 G1 3
STVGE SG2 76 C1
Keats Wy *HTCHE/RSTV* SG4 57 G2
Keble Ter *ABLGY* WD5 204 A2
Kecksy's *SBW* CM21 132 D5
Keeble Cl *LTNE* LU2 71 F8
Keele Cl *WATN* WD24 13 D1 3
Keepers Cl *LBUZ* LU7 110 A2 2
LTNE LU2 70 D7
Keiths Rd *HHS/BOV* HP3 9 D6
Keiths Wd *KNEB* SG3 96 A4
Kelbys *WGCE* AL7 148 D2
Keller Cl *STVGE* SG2 3 F4
Kelling Cl *LTNE* LU2 69 H1
Kelly Cl *BORE* WD6 224 C2
Kelman Cl *CHES/WCR* EN8 214 C1 1
Kelmscott Cl *WATW* WD18 12 B5
Kelmscott Crs *WATW* WD18 12 B4
Kelshall *GSTN* WD25 205 F6
Kelshall St *ROY* SG8 30 C4
Kelvin Cl *LTN* LU1 4 C5
Kemble Cl *POTB/CUF* EN6 210 E3
Kempe Cl *STAL* AL1 188 E2
Kempe Rd *EN* EN1 214 A6
Kemp Pl *BUSH* WD23 221 H6
Kemprow *GSTN* WD25 206 A5
Kemps Dr *NTHWD* HA6 230 A6 3
Kempsey Cl *LTNE* LU2 70 E7
Kendal Cl *LTNN/LIM* LU3 68 C2
Kendale *HHS/BOV* HP3 9 E6
Kendale Rd *HTCHE/RSTV* SG4 56 D3
LTNW/LEA LU4 68 A7
Kendall Cl *WGCE* AL7 148 A7
Kendals Cl *RAD* WD7 206 B6
Kenerne Dr *BAR* EN5 225 K5
Kenford Cl *GSTN* WD25 204 C2
Kenilworth Cl *HHS/BOV* HP3 8 B6
STVGE SG2 96 D2
Kenilworth Ct *WAT* WD17 220 B1
Kenilworth Dr *BORE* WD6 224 B3
RKW/CH/CXG WD3 219 G4
Kenilworth Gdns *OXHEY* WD19 230 D4 7
Kenilworth Rd *LTN* LU1 4 A3
Kennedy Av *HOD* EN11 176 E3
Kennedy Cl *CHES/WCR* EN8 197 J6
PIN HA5 231 G5
Kennedy Rd *WARE* SG12 99 H2
Kennel La *HARP* AL5 117 G4
Kennelwood La *HAT* AL10 171 G3 4
Kenneth Rd *LTNE* LU2 5 E2
Kenning Rd *HOD* EN11 177 F1
Kennington Rd *LTNN/LIM* LU3 69 G7
Kensington Av *WATW* WD18 12 A3
Kensington Cl *STAL* AL1 11 F6 1
Kensington Wy *BORE* WD6 224 C3
Kensworth Rd *DUN/WHIP* LU6 114 A5
Kent Cl *BORE* WD6 208 C8
Kent Crs *BSF* CM23 105 H5
Kentish La *BRKMPK* AL9 193 J2
Kenton Gdns *STAL* AL1 11 E5
Kent Rd *LTN* LU1 88 E1
Kents Av *HHS/BOV* HP3 185 H2 4
Kent's La *STDN* SG11 81 K7
Kenwood Dr *RKW/CH/CXG* WD3 227 J1
Kenworth Cl *CHES/WCR* EN8 214 C3
Kerdistone Cl *POTB/CUF* EN6 193 H8
Kerr Cl *KNEB* SG3 96 A4
Kerri Cl *BAR* EN5 225 H4
Kerril Cft *HLW* CM20 155 H8
Kershaw Cl *LTNN/LIM* LU3 69 F1
Kershaw's Hl *HTCHE/RSTV* SG4 56 D3
Kessingland Av *STVG* SG1 58 A8
Keston Ms *WAT* WD17 12 C1 4
Kestrel Cl *BERK* HP4 161 K6
GSTN WD25 205 F4
STVGE SG2 76 E7
Kestrel Gdns *BSF* CM23 105 F3
Kestrel Gn *HAT* AL10 171 F5
The Kestrels *LCOL/BKTW* AL2 205 F1
Kestrel Wk *LWTH* SG6 42 B6
Kestrel Wy *WGCE* AL7 148 A1
Keswick Cl *STAL* AL1 168 E7
Keswick Dr *PEND* EN3 214 B6
Kettering Rd *PEND* EN3 214 C7
Kettle Green Rd *MHAD* SG10 103 F7
Ketton Cl *LTNE* LU2 5 E4
Kewferry Dr *NTHWD* HA6 229 G4
Kewferry Rd *NTHWD* HA6 229 H5
Keyfield Ter *STAL* AL1 10 C5
Keymer Cl *LTNE* LU2 70 D6 2
Keynton Cl *HERT/WAS* SG14 150 C2
Keysers Rd *BROX* EN10 177 F8
Kibes La *WARE* SG12 127 H8
Kidner Cl *LTNE* LU2 69 K4
Kilbride Ct *HHNE* HP2 8 C1 2
Kilby Cl *GSTN* WD25 204 E5
Kilfillan Gdns *BERK* HP4 161 H6
Kilmarnock Dr *LTNE* LU2 69 K4
Kilmarnock Rd *OXHEY* WD19 230 E3
Kilncroft *HHS/BOV* HP3 165 G8
Kilnfield *WGCE* AL7 123 F8
Kiln Gnd *HHS/BOV* HP3 165 F8
Kiln House Cl *WARE* SG12 127 J7
Kiln La *HLWE* CM17 181 F2
Kiln Wy *NTHWD* HA6 229 K5
Kilsmore La *CHES/WCR* EN8 197 H6
Kilvinton Dr *ENC/FH* EN2 213 G8
Kilworth Cl *WGCE* AL7 148 C5
Kimberley *LWTH* SG6 25 K7
Kimberley Cl *BSF* CM23 105 K4 1
Kimberley Rd *STALW/RED* AL3 10 B3
Kimble Cl *WATW* WD18 219 K6 1
Kimble Crs *BUSH* WD23 221 K7
Kimbolton Crs *KNEB* SG3 96 B1
Kimbolton Gn *BORE* WD6 224 B4 1
Kimps Wy *HHS/BOV* HP3 186 A1
Kimpton Bottom *HARP* AL5 119 G2
Kimpton Cl *HHNE* HP2 165 G1
Kimpton Pl *GSTN* WD25 204 E4
Kimpton Rd *HTCHE/RSTV* SG4 94 B8
LTN LU1 5 E5
LTNE LU2 92 B7
STALE/WH AL4 120 A3
WLYN AL6 121 J3
Kimptons Cl *POTB/CUF* EN6 209 J3
Kimptons Md *POTB/CUF* EN6 209 J3
Kinderscout *HHS/BOV* HP3 165 F8
Kindersley Cl *WLYN* AL6 122 C3 3
Kindersley Wy *ABLGY* WD5 203 H1
King Arthur Ct *CHES/WCR* EN8 214 D1
King Charles Rd *RAD* WD7 207 H2
King Croft Rd *HARP* AL5 144 A2
King Edward Rd *CHES/WCR* EN8 214 D3
OXHEY WD19 13 F5
RAD WD7 207 J3
King Edward's Rd *WARE* SG12 127 J7
King Edward St *HHS/BOV* HP3 185 H2
Kingfisher Cl *NTHWD* HA6 229 G7
STALE/WH AL4 120 B8
WARE SG12 153 H6 1
Kingfisher Ct *HTCHE/RSTV* SG4 56 E3 2
Kingfisher Dr *HHS/BOV* HP3 185 K3
Kingfisher Lure
RKW/CH/CXG WD3 218 A4
Kingfisher Ri *STVGE* SG2 76 E7
Kingfisher Wy *BSF* CM23 105 K2
King George Av *BUSH* WD23 221 J6
King George Cl *STVG* SG1 2 C2
King George Rd *WAB* EN9 215 H4 2
WARE SG12 127 J7
King Georges Av *WATW* WD18 219 K5
King Georges Cl *HTCH/STOT* SG5 40 B7
King George's Wy *HTCHE/RSTV* SG4 93 H3
Kingham Rd *WARE* SG12 128 E4
Kinghamway *LTNE* LU2 4 C2 2
King Harry La *STALW/RED* AL3 167 H7
King Harry St *HHNE* HP2 8 A5
King Henry's Ms *PEND* EN3 215 F7 1
King James Av *POTB/CUF* EN6 195 G7
King James Wy *ROY* SG8 21 H3
Kings Av *HHS/BOV* HP3 185 K2
WATW WD18 12 B3
Kingsbridge Rd *BSF* CM23 105 K1
Kingsbury Av *STALW/RED* AL3 10 A3
Kings Cl *CSTG* HP8 226 A1
KGLGY WD4 202 A1
NTHWD HA6 230 A5
WATW WD18 13 D3 7
Kings Ct *BSF* CM23 105 K1
Kingscroft *WGCE* AL7 148 C2 3
Kingsdale Rd *BERK* HP4 161 H6
Kingsdon La *HLWE* CM17 181 F2
Kingsdown *HTCHE/RSTV* SG4 57 F2
Kingsdown Av *LTNE* LU2 69 J5
Kings Farm Rd *RKW/CH/CXG* WD3 217 G6
Kingsfield *HOD* EN11 177 F1
Kingsfield Ct *OXHEY* WD19 13 E5
Kingsfield Dr *PEND* EN3 214 C5
Kingsfield Rd *OXHEY* WD19 13 E6
WARE SG12 99 H2
Kingsfield Wy *PEND* EN3 214 C5 5
Kingsgate *STALW/RED* AL3 10 A6
Kingshill Av *STALE/WH* AL4 168 E3
Kingshill Wy *BERK* HP4 161 H7
Kingsland *HLWS* CM18 6 B6
Kingsland Rd *HHW* HP1 163 K8
LTN LU1 5 D5
Kingsland Wy *BLDK* SG7 18 A6
King's La *KGLGY* WD4 201 K1
Kingsley Av *BORE* WD6 223 J2
CHES/WCR EN8 197 F7
Kingsley Ct *BRKMPK* AL9 148 A7
Kingsley Rd *LTNN/LIM* LU3 69 F4
Kingsley Wk *TRING* HP23 135 F5 1
Kingsmead *CHES/WCR* EN8 197 H6
POTB/CUF EN6 195 G6
SBW CM21 132 C8
STALE/WH AL4 169 G3
Kingsmead Cl *HLWW/ROY* CM19 178 C2
Kings Meadow *KGLGY* WD4 186 A6
Kingsmill Ct *HAT* AL10 171 G6 4
Kingsmoor Rd *HLWW/ROY* CM19 179 J4
Kings Rd *BAR* EN5 225 H3
BERK HP4 161 J6
CHES/WCR EN8 214 D4
HERT/BAY SG13 151 K2 1
HTCH/STOT SG5 56 D1
LCOL/BKTW AL2 190 A4
STALW/RED AL3 10 A3
STVG SG1 2 B4
Kingston Rd *LTNE* LU2 5 D2
Kingston V *ROY* SG8 21 J4 3
King St *BSF* CM23 105 J2
LTN LU1 4 B4 5
STALW/RED AL3 115 J4
TRING HP23 135 F6
WATW WD18 13 D3
Kings Walden Ri *STVGE* SG2 76 D2
King's Walden Rd *HTCH/STOT* SG5 54 E7
Kingsway *HTCH/STOT* SG5 25 J2
LTN LU1 89 F1
LTNW/LEA LU4 69 F8
POTB/CUF EN6 195 G8
ROY SG8 21 G1
WARE SG12 127 H6
Kingsway North Orbital Rd
GSTN WD25 204 B4
Kingswell Ride *POTB/CUF* EN6 195 G8
Kingswood Av *HTCHE/RSTV* SG4 57 H1
Kingswood Rd *GSTN* WD25 204 C4
Kingwell Rd *EBAR* EN4 210 E8
King William Cl *AMP/FLIT/B* MK45 36 D5
Kinmoor Cl *LTNN/LIM* LU3 68 C1
Kinross Crs *LTNN/LIM* LU3 68 C1
Kinsbourne Cl *HARP* AL5 117 J5
Kinsbourne Crs *HARP* AL5 117 K5 2
Kinsbourne Green La *HARP* AL5 117 H6
Kipling Cl *HTCHE/RSTV* SG4 57 G2
Kipling Gv *HHNE* HP2 141 G8

The Kipling *LTNN/LIM* LU3 ..... **69** G3 1
Kipling Wy *HARP* AL5 ..... **118** D8
Kirby Cl *NTHWD* HA6 ..... **230** A5
Kirkcaldy Gn *OXHEY* WD19 ..... **230** D2 3
Kirkdale Rd *HARP* AL5 ..... **118** C7
Kirklands *WGCW* AL8 ..... **122** E7
Kirkwick Av *HARP* AL5 ..... **118** B8
Kitchener Cl *STAL* AL1 ..... **11** F5
Kitcheners La *STVGE* SG2 ..... **60** D8
Kitching La *STVG* SG1 ..... **74** E4
Kite Fld *BERK* HP4 ..... **161** F2
Kite Wy *LWTH* SG6 ..... **41** J1
Kitsbury Rd *BERK* HP4 ..... **161** J5
Kitsbury Ter *BERK* HP4 ..... **161** J5
Kit's La *BLDK* SG7 ..... **44** E1
Kitson Wy *HLW* CM20 ..... **6** B3 1
Kitswell Wy *RAD* WD7 ..... **206** C3
Kitt's End Rd *BAR* EN5 ..... **209** K7
Knap Cl *LWTH* SG6 ..... **42** C1
Knebworth Pth *BORE* WD6 ..... **224** C4 2
Kneesworth St *ROY* SG8 ..... **21** G2
Knella Gn *WGCE* AL7 ..... **148** B3
Knella Rd *WGCE* AL7 ..... **148** A4
Knights Cl *BSF* CM23 ..... **104** E1
BUNT SG9 ..... **63** J3
Knights Fld *LTNE* LU2 ..... **4** B2
Knightsfield *WGCW* AL8 ..... **122** D7
Knights Orch *HHW* HP1 ..... **163** J4
Knights Templars Gn *STVGE* SG2 ..... **76** D1
Knight St *SBW* CM21 ..... **132** C7
Knole La *SAFWS* CB11 ..... **35** J2
Knoll Crs *NTHWD* HA6 ..... **229** K8
Knolles Crs *BRKMPK* AL9 ..... **192** B2
Knoll Ri *LTNE* LU2 ..... **69** K5
The Knoll *HERT/BAY* SG13 ..... **152** A2
Knowle Dr *HARP* AL5 ..... **144** A2
The Knowle *HOD* EN11 ..... **177** F4 2
Knowl Piece *HTCHE/RSTV* SG4 ..... **40** E6
Knowl Wy *BORE* WD6 ..... **223** H5
Knutsford Av *WATN* WD24 ..... **204** E8
Koh-i-noor Av *BUSH* WD23 ..... **221** H6
Kristiansand Wy *LWTH* SG6 ..... **42** C1
Kymswell Rd *STVGE* SG2 ..... **76** D5
Kynance Cl *LTNE* LU2 ..... **70** B6
Kyrkeby *LWTH* SG6 ..... **42** C5
Kytes Dr *GSTN* WD25 ..... **204** E3

L

Laburnum Cl *CHES/WCR* EN8 ..... **214** C1
LTNN/LIM LU3 ..... **69** H2
Laburnum Gv *LCOL/BKTW* AL2 ..... **188** C3
LTNN/LIM LU3 ..... **69** G2
Laburnum Rd *HOD* EN11 ..... **177** G1 1
Lachbury Cl *LTN* LU1 ..... **89** F3
Lackmore Rd *EN* EN1 ..... **214** B5 2
Lacre Wy *LWTH* SG6 ..... **42** C2
Ladbrooke Cl *POTB/CUF* EN6 ..... **210** B2 1
Ladbrooke Dr *POTB/CUF* EN6 ..... **210** B2
Ladies Gv *STALW/RED* AL3 ..... **10** A2
Lady Gv *WGCE* AL7 ..... **147** K7
Ladyhill *LTNW/LEA* LU4 ..... **68** A3
Ladymeadow *HHS/BOV* HP3 ..... **185** H5
Lady's Cl *WATW* WD18 ..... **13** D3
Ladyshot *HLW* CM20 ..... **7** F3
Ladysmith Rd *LBUZ* LU7 ..... **110** E4
STALW/RED AL3 ..... **10** C3
Ladywalk *RKW/CH/CXG* WD3 ..... **227** H4
Ladywell Prospect *SBW* CM21 ..... **132** D8
Ladywood Cl *RKW/CH/CXG* WD3 ..... **218** A3
Ladywood Rd *HERT/WAS* SG14 ..... **150** C3
Laidon Sq *HHNE* HP2 ..... **8** A1
Lake Dr *BUSH* WD23 ..... **231** K1
Laker Ct *LTNE* LU2 ..... **4** B2 2
Lake Rd *WAB* EN9 ..... **177** K7
Lakeside *TRING* HP23 ..... **135** F4
Lakeside Pl *LCOL/BKTW* AL2 ..... **190** B6
Lakeside Rd *CHES/WCR* EN8 ..... **197** G6
The Lake *BUSH* WD23 ..... **222** A8
Lake Vw *POTB/CUF* EN6 ..... **210** D3 3
Lalleford Rd *LTNE* LU2 ..... **70** D8
Lamb Cl *GSTN* WD25 ..... **204** D4
HAT AL10 ..... **171** G5 2
Lambert Ct *BUSH* WD23 ..... **13** E3
Lamb La *STALW/RED* AL3 ..... **142** C4
Lamb Meadow *ARL/CHE* SG15 ..... **24** D6
Lambourn Cha *RAD* WD7 ..... **206** C6 1
Lambourn Dr *LTNE* LU2 ..... **69** K3
Lambourn Gdns *HARP* AL5 ..... **118** B6 2
Lambs Cl *POTB/CUF* EN6 ..... **195** H7
Lambscroft Wy *CFSP/GDCR* SL9 ..... **226** B8
Lambton Av *CHES/WCR* EN8 ..... **214** C3 1
Lamer La *STALE/WH* AL4 ..... **120** B5
Lamers Rd *LTNE* LU2 ..... **5** F1
Lammasmead *BROX* EN10 ..... **197** K1
Lammas Md *HTCH/STOT* SG5 ..... **40** C7
Lammas Rd *HERT/WAS* SG14 ..... **98** A5
LBUZ LU7 ..... **110** A2
WATW WD18 ..... **13** D4 3
Lammas Wy *LWTH* SG6 ..... **41** K1
Lamorna Cl *LTNN/LIM* LU3 ..... **68** E3 1
RAD WD7 ..... **206** E4
Lampits *HOD* EN11 ..... **177** G3
Lampitts Cross *LTNN/LIM* LU3 ..... **69** F4 1
Lamsey Rd *HHS/BOV* HP3 ..... **164** C8
Lancaster Av *EBAR* EN4 ..... **210** E8
LTNE LU2 ..... **69** H1 1
Lancaster Cl *AMP/FLIT/B* MK45 ..... **36** D5 1
STVG SG1 ..... **58** E7
Lancaster Dr *HHW* HP1 ..... **183** H5
Lancaster Rd *HTCH/STOT* SG5 ..... **56** C1
STAL AL1 ..... **11** E2
Lancaster Wy *ABLGY* WD5 ..... **204** A1 2
BSF CM23 ..... **104** E1
Lancing Rd *LTNE* LU2 ..... **70** E6
Lancing Wy *RKW/CH/CXG* WD3 ..... **219** G5
Landau Wy *BROX* EN10 ..... **197** K4
Landford Cl *RKW/CH/CXG* WD3 ..... **228** D1
Landmead Rd *CHES/WCR* EN8 ..... **197** J7
Lands' End *BORE* WD6 ..... **223** G6
Lane End *BERK* HP4 ..... **161** G5
HAT AL10 ..... **170** E7
HLWE CM17 ..... **181** H2
Lanefield Wk *WGCW* AL8 ..... **147** H3 3
Lane Gdns *BUSH* WD23 ..... **222** B8
Lanercost Cl *WLYN* AL6 ..... **123** F2
Langbridge Cl *HTCHE/RSTV* SG4 ..... **56** E4
Langdale Av *HARP* AL5 ..... **119** F7
Langdale Gdns *PEND* EN3 ..... **214** C5
Langdon St *TRING* HP23 ..... **135** F6
Langfield Cl *WAB* EN9 ..... **177** K8 1
Langford Dr *LTNE* LU2 ..... **70** B6
Langham Cl *LTNE* LU2 ..... **69** J2
STALE/WH AL4 ..... **169** F1
Langholme *BUSH* WD23 ..... **221** K8 1
Langland Ct *NTHWD* HA6 ..... **229** H6
Langland Dr *PIN* HA5 ..... **231** F6
Langley Av *HHS/BOV* HP3 ..... **185** J1
Langleybury La *KGLGY* WD4 ..... **203** G4
WAT WD17 ..... **203** G7
Langley Crs *KGLGY* WD4 ..... **186** A8
STALW/RED AL3 ..... **10** B2
Langley Gv *STALE/WH* AL4 ..... **145** F7
Langley Hl *KGLGY* WD4 ..... **185** K7
Langley Hill Cl *KGLGY* WD4 ..... **186** A7 3
Langley La *ABLGY* WD5 ..... **204** A1
HTCHE/RSTV SG4 ..... **74** C7
Langley Lodge La *KGLGY* WD4 ..... **202** D1
Langley Rd *ABLGY* WD5 ..... **203** K1
KGLGY WD4 ..... **185** F8
WAT WD17 ..... **220** A1
Langley St *LTN* LU1 ..... **4** C5 3
Langley Wy *WAT* WD17 ..... **220** A1
Langmead Dr *BUSH* WD23 ..... **222** A8
Langthorne Av *STVG* SG1 ..... **2** C1
Langton Gv *NTHWD* HA6 ..... **229** H4
Langton Rd *HOD* EN11 ..... **176** E3
KTN/HRWW/W HA3 ..... **231** K6
Langwood Gdns *WAT* WD17 ..... **220** B1 1
Lankester Rd *ROY* SG8 ..... **21** G4
Lannock *LWTH* SG6 ..... **42** C5
Lannock Hl *HTCHE/RSTV* SG4 ..... **42** D7
Lanrick Copse *BERK* HP4 ..... **162** B4
Lansdowne Rd *LTNN/LIM* LU3 ..... **4** A2
Lansdown Rd *CFSP/GDCR* SL9 ..... **226** A7 2
Lanterns La *STVGE* SG2 ..... **76** E3
Laporte Wy *LTNW/LEA* LU4 ..... **68** E8
Lapwing Cl *HHNE* HP2 ..... **8** B1
Lapwing Dell *LWTH* SG6 ..... **42** B7
Lapwing Ri *STVGE* SG2 ..... **76** E7
Lapwing Wy *ABLGY* WD5 ..... **204** B1 1
Larch Av *HTCHE/RSTV* SG4 ..... **56** E5
LCOL/BKTW AL2 ..... **188** A8
Larch Cl *CHESW* EN7 ..... **196** C5 1
Larches Av *EN* EN1 ..... **214** B5
The Larches *BERK* HP4 ..... **160** E4
BUSH WD23 ..... **13** F4
LTNE LU2 ..... **4** B2
STALE/WH AL4 ..... **169** G2
WARE SG12 ..... **127** G5
Larch Ri *BERK* HP4 ..... **161** H4
Larchwood *BSF* CM23 ..... **105** G4
Larchwood Rd *HHNE* HP2 ..... **8** C3
Larken Cl *BUSH* WD23 ..... **221** K8
Larken Dr *BUSH* WD23 ..... **221** K8
Larkens Cl *STDN* SG11 ..... **81** J6
Larkins Cl *BLDK* SG7 ..... **27** F8
Larkinson *STVG* SG1 ..... **2** A1
Lark Ri *HAT* AL10 ..... **171** F6
Larksfield *WARE* SG12 ..... **127** J6
Larkspur Cl *BSF* CM23 ..... **105** G3
HHW HP1 ..... **163** H5
Larkspur Gdns *LTNW/LEA* LU4 ..... **68** E7
Larks Rdg *LCOL/BKTW* AL2 ..... **188** C4
Larksway *BSF* CM23 ..... **105** F3
Larkswood *HLWE* CM17 ..... **181** F3 3
Larkswood Ri *STALE/WH* AL4 ..... **169** F1
Larmans Rd *PEND* EN3 ..... **214** B6 1
Larsen Dr *WAB* EN9 ..... **215** J4 3
Larwood Gv *STVG* SG1 ..... **76** B1
Latchmore Bank *RBSF* CM22 ..... **106** A7
Latchmore Cl *HTCHE/RSTV* SG4 ..... **56** D4
Latimer Cl *HHNE* HP2 ..... **165** G1
PIN HA5 ..... **230** D7
WATW WD18 ..... **219** K7
Latimer Gdns *PIN* HA5 ..... **230** D7
WGCE AL7 ..... **148** C3
Latimer Rd *AMS* HP6 ..... **200** C8
LTN LU1 ..... **4** C5
Latium Cl *STAL* AL1 ..... **10** C5
Lattimore Rd *STAL* AL1 ..... **11** D5
STALE/WH AL4 ..... **145** F1
Latton Gn *HLWS* CM18 ..... **180** C5
Latton Hall Cl *HLW* CM20 ..... **7** F3
Latton House *HLWS* CM18 ..... **180** E4
Latton St *HLW* CM20 ..... **180** E1
HLWE CM17 ..... **180** E2
Lauderdale Rd *ABLGY* WD5 ..... **203** H3
Laundry La *WAB* EN9 ..... **199** F3
Launton Cl *LTNN/LIM* LU3 ..... **52** B8
Laureate Wy *HHW* HP1 ..... **164** A4
Laurel Av *POTB/CUF* EN6 ..... **210** A2
Laurel Bank *HHS/BOV* HP3 ..... **184** D1
Laurel Cl *HHNE* HP2 ..... **8** C4
Laureldene *MHAD* SG10 ..... **103** G8 1
Laurel Flds *POTB/CUF* EN6 ..... **210** A1
Laurel Rd *CFSP/GDCR* SL9 ..... **226** A7
STAL AL1 ..... **11** E4
Laurels Cl *STALW/RED* AL3 ..... **188** D1
The Laurels *BERK* HP4 ..... **162** E3
CHESW EN7 ..... **196** C5
Laurel Wy *HTCH/STOT* SG5 ..... **40** C6
Lauries Cl *HHW* HP1 ..... **162** E8
Laurino Pl *BUSH* WD23 ..... **231** K1
Lavender Cl *BSF* CM23 ..... **105** G3
CHESW EN7 ..... **196** D5 4
HLW CM20 ..... **7** D3
LTNE LU2 ..... **69** K2
Lavender Ct *BLDK* SG7 ..... **26** E8 3
Lavender Gdns *ENC/FH* EN2 ..... **212** E8
Lavender Wy *HTCH/STOT* SG5 ..... **56** B2
Lavinia Av *GSTN* WD25 ..... **204** D4
Lavrock La *RKW/CH/CXG* WD3 ..... **218** E7
Lawford Av *RKW/CH/CXG* WD3 ..... **217** F6
Lawford Cl *LTN* LU1 ..... **4** A4 1
RKW/CH/CXG WD3 ..... **217** F6
Law Hall La *HTCHE/RSTV* SG4 ..... **92** D1
Lawn Av *HTCHE/RSTV* SG4 ..... **93** F8
Lawn Gdns *LTN* LU1 ..... **4** B5
Lawn La *HHS/BOV* HP3 ..... **164** C8
Lawns Cl *HTCH/STOT* SG5 ..... **54** E7
The Lawns Dr *BROX* EN10 ..... **176** E8
The Lawns *HHW* HP1 ..... **163** H5
PIN HA5 ..... **231** J6
RAD WD7 ..... **207** H3 4
STALW/RED AL3 ..... **10** B3 1
STVGE SG2 ..... **76** E5
WGCW AL8 ..... **122** D8
Lawn V *PIN* HA5 ..... **230** E8
Lawrance Gdns *CHES/WCR* EN8 ..... **197** H6
Lawrance Rd *STALW/RED* AL3 ..... **167** K2
Lawrence Av *LWTH* SG6 ..... **42** A5
SBW CM21 ..... **132** C5
STVG SG1 ..... **2** C1
WARE SG12 ..... **153** H5
Lawrence Cl *HERT/WAS* SG14 ..... **150** B2
Lawrence End Rd *LTNE* LU2 ..... **91** K6
Lawrence Moorings *SBW* CM21 ..... **132** D8
Laxton Cl *LTNE* LU2 ..... **71** F8
Laxton Gdns *BLDK* SG7 ..... **43** G2
Lay Brook *STALE/WH* AL4 ..... **168** D2 3
Layham Dr *LTNE* LU2 ..... **70** E8
Layhill *HHNE* HP2 ..... **8** A3
Layston Meadow *BUNT* SG9 ..... **63** K3
Layston Pk *ROY* SG8 ..... **21** H4
Lea Bushes *GSTN* WD25 ..... **205** F5
Lea Cl *BSF* CM23 ..... **86** A8
BUSH WD23 ..... **221** J5 1
Leaf Cl *NTHWD* HA6 ..... **229** J6
Leafield *LTNN/LIM* LU3 ..... **68** E5
Leaford Crs *WATN* WD24 ..... **204** A7
Leaforis Rd *CHESW* EN7 ..... **196** E6
Leafy La *TRING* HP23 ..... **134** D8
Leagrave Rd *LTNN/LIM* LU3 ..... **69** F6
Lea Gv *BSF* CM23 ..... **86** A8
Leamington Rd *LTNN/LIM* LU3 ..... **69** F2
Lea Mt *CHESW* EN7 ..... **196** C6
Leander Gdns *GSTN* WD25 ..... **205** F7 1
Lea Rd *HARP* AL5 ..... **118** D6
HOD EN11 ..... **177** H1
LTN LU1 ..... **5** D4
WAB EN9 ..... **215** F4
WATN WD24 ..... **204** C8 3
Leasey Bridge La *STALE/WH* AL4 ..... **119** H8
Leasey Dell Dr *STALE/WH* AL4 ..... **119** J7
Leaside *HHNE* HP2 ..... **9** F6
The Leas *BLDK* SG7 ..... **42** E2
BUSH WD23 ..... **221** G2
HHS/BOV HP3 ..... **186** A2
Leat Cl *SBW* CM21 ..... **132** D6
Leathwaite Cl *LTNN/LIM* LU3 ..... **68** E4
Lea Valley Wk *BRKMPK* AL9 ..... **147** H7
BRKMPK AL9 ..... **149** G8
BRKMPK AL9 ..... **171** K1
HERT/BAY SG13 ..... **151** H2
HERT/WAS SG14 ..... **149** K6
LTNE LU2 ..... **90** D4
WAB EN9 ..... **198** A4
WAB EN9 ..... **215** F3
WARE SG12 ..... **153** F3
WGCW AL8 ..... **146** E3
Leavesden Rd *WATN* WD24 ..... **204** C8

Leaves Spring *STVGE* SG2 3 D6
Leaview *WAB* EN9 215 G3
Lea Wk *HARP* AL5 118 E5
Lebanon Cl *WAT* WD17 203 J6
Le Corte Cl *KGLGY* WD4 185 K7
Lectern La *STAL* AL1 189 G2 2
Ledgemore La *HHNE* HP2 139 J3
Ledwell Rd *LTN* LU1 88 E6
Leeches Wy *LBUZ* LU7 110 A2
Lee Cl *HERT/BAY* SG13 151 F5
WARE SG12 153 H5 1
Leecroft Rd *BAR* EN5 225 K4
Lee Farm Cl *CSHM* HP5 182 B8
Leefe Wy *POTB/CUF* EN6 195 F6
Leeming Rd *BORE* WD6 223 J1
Lees Av *NTHWD* HA6 230 A7
Leeside *BAR* EN5 225 K5
POTB/CUF EN6 210 E2
Leete Pl *ROY* SG8 21 G2
Leggatts Cl *WATN* WD24 204 A6
Leggatts Ri *GSTN* WD25 204 B5
Leggatts Wy *WATN* WD24 204 B6
Leggatts Wood Av *WATN* WD24 204 C6
Leggett Gv *STVG* SG1 75 K1
Leggfield Ter *HHW* HP1 163 J6 2
Legions Wy *BSF* CM23 105 K1
Legra Av *HOD* EN11 177 F3 2
Leicester Rd *LTNW/LEA* LU4 68 D8
Leigh Common *WGCE* AL7 147 K5
Leigh Ct *BORE* WD6 224 C2 1
Leigh Rodd *OXHEY* WD19 231 F2
Leighton Buzzard Rd *HHW* HP1 139 H7
Lemon Field Dr *GSTN* WD25 205 F3 2
Lemsford Ct *BORE* WD6 224 B4
Lemsford La *WGCW* AL8 147 G4
Lemsford Rd *HAT* AL10 171 F2 2
STAL AL1 11 E4
Lemsford Village *WGCW* AL8 147 F4 1
Lennox Gn *LTNE* LU2 71 G7 2
Lensbury Cl *CHES/WCR* EN8 197 J6 5
Leonard's Cl *WLYN* AL6 122 E1
Lesbury Cl *LTNE* LU2 71 F8
Leslie Cl *STVGE* SG2 76 D7
Letchmore Rd *RAD* WD7 206 D6
STVG SG1 2 B1
Letchworth Cl *OXHEY* WD19 230 E4 4
Letchworth Ga *LWTH* SG6 42 B4
Letchworth La *LWTH* SG6 41 K6
Letchworth Rd *BLDK* SG7 42 D2
LTNN/LIM LU3 68 E5
LWTH SG6 42 D2
Levenage La *WARE* SG12 130 A6
Leven Cl *CHES/WCR* EN8 214 C3 2
OXHEY WD19 230 E4 5
Levendale *LTNW/LEA* LU4 68 B4 3
Leven Dr *CHES/WCR* EN8 214 C3
Leven Wy *HHNE* HP2 8 A1 1
Leveret Cl *GSTN* WD25 204 B4
Leverstock Green Rd *HHNE* HP2 9 D4
HHS/BOV HP3 9 F6
Leverton Wy *WAB* EN9 215 H3
Lewes Wy *RKW/CH/CXG* WD3 219 G4
Lewis Cl *DEN/HRF* UB9 228 B8
Lewis La *ARL/CHE* SG15 24 E3
CFSP/GDCR SL9 226 B7
Lewsey Rd *LTNW/LEA* LU4 68 A6
Lexington Cl *BORE* WD6 223 K3 3
Lexington Wy *BAR* EN5 225 J4
Leyburne Rd *LTNN/LIM* LU3 69 G3
Leycroft Wy *HARP* AL5 144 B2
Leyden Rd *STVG* SG1 2 B5
Leygreen Cl *LTNE* LU2 5 E3
Leyhill Dr *LTN* LU1 89 G5
Leyland Av *STAL* AL1 10 C6
Leyland Cl *CHES/WCR* EN8 197 G6 1
Leys Av *LWTH* SG6 41 K3
Leys Cl *DEN/HRF* UB9 228 C7
Leysdown *WGCE* AL7 148 E3
Leys Rd *HHS/BOV* HP3 164 E8
The Leys *STALE/WH* AL4 169 G3
TRING HP23 135 H5
Leyton Gn *HARP* AL5 118 C8
Leyton Rd *HARP* AL5 118 C8
Ley Wk *WGCE* AL7 148 D3
Liberty Cl *HERT/BAY* SG13 151 F5
Library Rd *LTN* LU1 4 C4 9
Lichfield Wy *BROX* EN10 176 E8 2
Liddel Cl *LTNN/LIM* LU3 69 F6
Lidgate Cl *LTNW/LEA* LU4 68 A3
Lieutenant Ellis Wy *CHESW* EN7 213 J1
Lighthorne Ri *LTNN/LIM* LU3 69 F2
Lilac Av *EN* EN1 214 B6
Lilac Cl *CHESW* EN7 214 A1 4
Lilac Rd *HOD* EN11 177 G1
Lilac Wy *HARP* AL5 144 A3 4
Lilley Bottom *LTNE* LU2 54 A8
Lilley Bottom Rd *HTCHE/RSTV* SG4 72 B7
Lilleyhoo La *LTNE* LU2 54 B7
Lilliard Cl *HOD* EN11 153 G7
Lilly La *HHNE* HP2 165 J2
The Limberlost *WLYN* AL6 122 B2
Limbrick Rd *HARP* AL5 143 J3
Limbury Rd *LTNN/LIM* LU3 68 E5
Lime Av *LTNW/LEA* LU4 68 A6
STALE/WH AL4 119 K3
Lime Cl *AMP/FLIT/B* MK45 36 C6
OXHEY WD19 13 E6 1
STVGE SG2 76 E5
WARE SG12 127 J7
Limedene Cl *PIN* HA5 230 E7
Lime Gv *ROY* SG8 21 J1
TRDG/WHET N20 225 K8
Limekiln La *BLDK* SG7 43 F2
STSD CM24 86 B3
Limes Ct *HOD* EN11 177 F3 3
Limes Crs *BSF* CM23 105 K2
Limes Rd *CHES/WCR* EN8 214 C2
The Limes *ARL/CHE* SG15 24 E1
HTCH/STOT SG5 56 B3
STALW/RED AL3 11 D2
WGCE AL7 148 B5
Limetree Av *LTN* LU1 117 G2
Lime Tree Pl *STAL* AL1 11 D5 6
Lime Tree Wk *BUSH* WD23 222 B8
ENC/FH EN2 213 F8
RKW/CH/CXG WD3 218 A5
Lime Wk *HHS/BOV* HP3 164 E8
Linacres *LTNW/LEA* LU4 68 C5
Linbridge Wy *LTNE* LU2 71 F7
Linces Wy *WGCE* AL7 148 C5
Lincoln Cl *BSF* CM23 105 G4
WGCE AL7 148 D2
Lincoln Ct *BERK* HP4 161 J5
BORE WD6 224 C5 1
Lincoln Dr *OXHEY* WD19 230 D2
RKW/CH/CXG WD3 219 G4
Lincoln Rd *CFSP/GDCR* SL9 226 B7
LTNW/LEA LU4 69 G8
STVG SG1 59 H7
Lincoln's Cl *STALE/WH* AL4 169 F1
Lincoln Wy *RKW/CH/CXG* WD3 219 G4
Lincot La *HTCHE/RSTV* SG4 94 B2
Lindbergh *WGCE* AL7 148 D3 7
Linden Cl *CHESW* EN7 197 F8 2
Linden Ct *HARP* AL5 143 J1
Linden Crs *STAL* AL1 169 F6
Lindencroft *LWTH* SG6 26 A8
Linden Dr *CFSP/GDCR* SL9 226 B7
Linden Gld *HHW* HP1 164 A7 1
Linden Lea *GSTN* WD25 204 B3
Linden Rd *LTNW/LEA* LU4 68 D5
STALW/RED AL3 142 B3
The Lindens *BSF* CM23 105 J3
HHS/BOV HP3 184 D1
STVG SG1 2 C4 1
Lindley Cl *HARP* AL5 118 C5
Lindlings *HHW* HP1 163 H7
Lindsay Av *HTCHE/RSTV* SG4 57 F4
Lindsay Pl *CHESW* EN7 197 F8 3
Lindsey Cl *BSF* CM23 85 J8
Lindsey Rd *BSF* CM23 85 J8
LTNE LU2 70 E8
Lindum Pl *STALW/RED* AL3 167 G8
Linford Cl *HLWW/ROY* CM19 6 B6
Linford End *HLWW/ROY* CM19 6 B6
Lingfield Cl *NTHWD* HA6 229 K6
Lingfield Rd *ROY* SG8 21 J3 2
STVG SG1 59 J8
Lingfield Wy *WAT* WD17 204 A8
Lingholm Wy *BAR* EN5 225 J5
Lingmoor Dr *GSTN* WD25 204 D4
Linington Av *CSHM* HP5 182 C8
Link Cl *HAT* AL10 171 G4
Link Dr *HAT* AL10 171 G4
Linkfield *WGCE* AL7 147 K7
Link Rd *BSF* CM23 105 J1
WATN WD24 13 E1
WLYN AL6 123 F2 1
Links Av *HERT/BAY* SG13 152 A2
Links Dr *BORE* WD6 223 J4 1
RAD WD7 206 C3
The Links *CHES/WCR* EN8 197 H4 1
Links Vw *STALW/RED* AL3 10 A2
Links Wy *RKW/CH/CXG* WD3 219 H3
LTNE LU2 69 J1
NTHWD HA6 229 H7
Linksway *NTHWD* HA6 229 J7
Link Wy *BSF* CM23 105 H3
Linkway *PIN* HA5 230 E7
Linkways East *STVG* SG1 3 D3
Linkways West *STVG* SG1 3 D3
Linnet Cl *BUSH* WD23 221 K8
LWTH SG6 41 J1
Linnet Rd *ABLGY* WD5 204 B1
Linsey Cl *HHS/BOV* HP3 186 A2
Linster Gv *BORE* WD6 224 B5
Linten Cl *HTCHE/RSTV* SG4 57 G3
Linton Av *BORE* WD6 223 J2
Lintott Cl *STVG* SG1 2 B2
Linwood *SBW* CM21 132 C7 3
Linwood Rd *HARP* AL5 143 K2 3
WARE SG12 127 K6
Lion Ct *BORE* WD6 224 B1
Liphook Rd *OXHEY* WD19 230 E3
Lippitts Hl *LTNE* LU2 69 K4
Lismore *HHS/BOV* HP3 165 H8
STVGE SG2 76 D8
Lister Av *HTCHE/RSTV* SG4 56 D4
Liston Cl *LTNW/LEA* LU4 68 A4
Litlington Rd *ROY* SG8 15 K8
Little Acre *STALW/RED* AL3 10 C1
Little Acres *WARE* SG12 152 C1
Little Berries *LTNN/LIM* LU3 68 D2
Little Brays *HLWS* CM18 7 F5
Little Bridge Rd *BERK* HP4 162 A5 3
Littlebrook Gdns *CHES/WCR* EN8 197 H8
Little Brook Rd *HLWW/ROY* CM19 178 D1
Little Burrow *WGCE* AL7 147 J5
Little Bushey La *BUSH* WD23 221 H3
Little Catherells *HHW* HP1 163 J4 1
Little Cattins *HLWW/ROY* CM19 179 G5
Little Chishill Rd *ROY* SG8 33 J1
Little Church Rd *LTNE* LU2 70 C6
Littlecote Pl *PIN* HA5 231 G7 1
Little Dell *WGCW* AL8 147 J1
Littlefield Rd *LTNE* LU2 70 C6
Little Ganett *WGCE* AL7 148 C5
Little Graylings *ABLGY* WD5 203 K3
Littlegreen La *LTN* LU1 88 D7
Little Green La *RKW/CH/CXG* WD3 218 E3
Little Gv *BUSH* WD23 221 J4
Little Grove Fld *HLWW/ROY* CM19 6 B4 2
Little Hardings *WGCE* AL7 148 D2
Little Hayes *KGLGY* WD4 186 A7 4
Little Heath *RBSF* CM22 133 K6
Little Heath La *BERK* HP4 162 E7
Little Hl *RKW/CH/CXG* WD3 217 F6
Little Hoo *TRING* HP23 134 E5
Little How Cft *ABLGY* WD5 203 H1
Little Lake *WGCE* AL7 148 C6
Little La *HARP* AL5 143 K3
HTCH/STOT SG5 39 F4
Little Ley *WGCE* AL7 147 K6 3
Little Martins *BUSH* WD23 221 J5
Little Md *HAT* AL10 171 G1 1
Little Mimms *HHNE* HP2 8 A4
Little Moss La *PIN* HA5 231 F8
Little Mundells *WGCE* AL7 148 A2
Little Orchard Cl *ABLGY* WD5 203 J1
PIN HA5 231 F8 3
Little Oxhey La *OXHEY* WD19 231 F4
Little Pk *HHS/BOV* HP3 183 J6
Little Piper's Cl *CHESW* EN7 195 K7
Little Potters *BUSH* WD23 222 A7
Little Pynchons *HLWS* CM18 180 C4
Little Rdg *WGCE* AL7 148 B3
Little Rivers *WGCE* AL7 148 B2
Little Rd *HHNE* HP2 8 B4
Little Stream Cl *NTHWD* HA6 229 K4
Little Thistle *WGCE* AL7 148 D5
Little Tring Rd *TRING* HP23 134 E3
Little Twye Rd *TRING* HP23 158 E5
Little Wade *WGCE* AL7 148 A6
Little Widbury *WARE* SG12 127 K8
Little Widbury La *WARE* SG12 127 K8
Little Windmill Hl *KGLGY* WD4 201 H2
Little Wood Cft *LTNN/LIM* LU3 68 D2
Little Youngs *WGCW* AL8 147 H3
Liverpool Rd *LTN* LU1 4 B4
STAL AL1 11 D4
WATW WD18 12 C4
Livingstone Link *STVGE* SG2 76 C1
Llanbury Cl *CFSP/GDCR* SL9 226 B6
Lloyd-taylor Cl *STDN* SG11 83 J7
Lloyd Wy *HTCHE/RSTV* SG4 93 F8
Loates La *WAT* WD17 13 D2
Local Board Rd *WAT* WD17 13 D4 4
Locarno Av *LTNW/LEA* LU4 68 B3
Lochnell Rd *BERK* HP4 161 G3
Lockers Park La *HHW* HP1 164 A5 2
Lockley Crs *HAT* AL10 171 G2
Lockleys Dr *WLYN* AL6 122 C4
Lodge Av *BORE* WD6 223 J5
Lodge Cl *HERT/WAS* SG14 151 F1
Lodge Ct *HTCH/STOT* SG5 40 C6
Lodge Crs *CHES/WCR* EN8 214 D4 2
Lodge Dr *BRKMPK* AL9 171 J1
RKW/CH/CXG WD3 218 B4
Lodge End *RAD* WD7 206 E4
RKW/CH/CXG WD3 219 J4
Lodge Fld *WGCE* AL7 122 E8
Lodge Gdns *HARP* AL5 118 C7
Lodge Hall *HLWS* CM18 180 B5
Lodge La *CSTG* HP8 216 C2
WAB EN9 215 J5
Lodge Rd *RKW/CH/CXG* WD3 219 J4
Lodge Wy *STVGE* SG2 76 B8
Loftus Cl *LTNW/LEA* LU4 68 A5
Lombardy Cl *HHNE* HP2 165 J7
Lombardy Dr *BERK* HP4 162 A6
Lombardy Wy *BORE* WD6 223 H1
Lomond Rd *HHNE* HP2 8 A1
Lomond Wy *STVG* SG1 59 J6
London Loop *BORE* WD6 224 A6
ENC/FH EN2 212 B7
MLHL NW7 224 B7
London Rd *BERK* HP4 162 A5
BLDK SG7 43 F3
BSF CM23 105 J6
BUNT SG9 63 K3
BUSH WD23 13 F5
EPP CM16 180 E8
HARP AL5 117 G3
HERT/BAY SG13 151 H3
HHS/BOV HP3 185 F1

HHW HP1 162 E8
HLWE CM17 157 F6
HTCHE/RSTV SG4 56 D4
HTCHE/RSTV SG4 74 A1
KNEB SG3 96 B4
LTN LU1 4 C6
RAD WD7 207 J3
RKW/CH/CXG WD3 218 D8
ROY SG8 21 H4
SBW CM21 132 C7
STAL AL1 11 D5
STALW/RED AL3 115 J4
STVG SG1 2 B5
TRING HP23 135 G6
WARE SG12 152 C1
WLYN AL6 122 C5
London Rw ARL/CHE SG15 24 E6
Long Acre HLWE CM17 156 E5
Longacres STALE/WH AL4 169 G6
Long Arrotts HHW HP1 164 A4
Long Banks HLWS CM18 180 A4
Long Barn Cl GSTN WD25 204 B2
Long Border Rd RBSF CM22 87 K8
Longbridge Cl TRING HP23 135 F3 2
Long Buftlers HARP AL5 144 C1
Long Chaulden HHW HP1 163 H7
Longcliffe Pth OXHEY WD19 230 B2 5
Long Cl LTNE LU2 70 D6
Long Cft OXHEY WD19 12 C6
STSD CM24 86 C1
Longcroft Av HARP AL5 118 B8
Long Croft Dr CHES/WCR EN8 214 E4
Longcroft Gdns WGCW AL8 147 J4 3
Longcroft Gn WGCW AL8 147 J4 4
Longcroft La HHS/BOV HP3 184 A6
WGCW AL8 147 J4
Longcroft Rd AMP/FLIT/B MK45 36 B7
Long Croft Rd LTN LU1 89 F2
RKW/CH/CXG WD3 227 G4
Longcroft Rd STVG SG1 2 C1
Long Cutt STALW/RED AL3 142 B3
Longdean Pk HHS/BOV HP3 186 A2
Long Elmes KTN/HRWW/W HA3 231 J7
Long Elms ABLGY WD5 203 J3
Long Elms Cl ABLGY WD5 203 J3 1
Long Fallow LCOL/BKTW AL2 188 C5
Longfield HHS/BOV HP3 165 G8
HLWS CM18 7 F6
Longfield Av PEND EN3 214 B7
Longfield Dr LTNW/LEA LU4 68 C8
Longfield Gdns TRING HP23 134 D6
Longfield La CHESW EN7 196 D5
Longfield Rd HARP AL5 143 K2
TRING HP23 134 D6
Longfields STVGE SG2 76 D8
Long John HHS/BOV HP3 164 E8
Longlands HHNE HP2 8 C4
Longlands Cl CHES/WCR EN8 214 C2 2
Longlands Rd WGCE AL7 148 A5
Long La HHS/BOV HP3 200 C1
HTCHE/RSTV SG4 92 D2
RKW/CH/CXG WD3 217 J8
RKW/CH/CXG WD3 217 F6
STVGE SG2 77 F4
Long Leaves STVGE SG2 3 E6
Long Ley HLW CM20 7 E4
LBUZ LU7 110 A2
WGCE AL7 148 D3
Long Marston La LBUZ LU7 109 J3
Long Marston Rd TRING HP23 109 J7
Longmead BUNT SG9 63 H2
HAT AL10 171 G1
KNEB SG3 96 B7 1
LWTH SG6 41 J2
Long Meadow BSF CM23 105 G3
STALW/RED AL3 115 J4
Longmeadow Dr HTCH/STOT SG5 40 C4
Long Mimms HHNE HP2 8 B4 3
Long Moor CHES/WCR EN8 197 J7
Longmore Cl RKW/CH/CXG WD3 227 J3
Longmore Gdns WGCE AL7 148 A3
Long Rdg STVGE SG2 76 E8
Long Spring STALW/RED AL3 168 C2
Longspring WATN WD24 204 C7
Long Vw BERK HP4 161 H3
Long Wk CSTG HP8 216 B3
Long Wd HLWS CM18 180 A6
Longwood Rd HERT/WAS SG14 150 C2
The Loning PEND EN3 214 B8
Lonsdale HHNE HP2 8 B2
Lonsdale Cl LTNN/LIM LU3 69 F4
Lonsdale Rd STVG SG1 3 D1
Loom La RAD WD7 206 C7
Loom Pl RAD WD7 206 D6
Loop Rd WAB EN9 215 G2
Lord Mead La WLYN AL6 121 G2
Lords Av BSF CM23 104 E2
Lords Cl RAD WD7 207 H2
Lordship La LWTH SG6 42 B5
Lordship Rd CHESW EN7 197 F8
Lords Meadow STALW/RED AL3 142 B4
Lord St HOD EN11 176 D3
WAT WD17 13 D2 3
Lords Wd WGCE AL7 148 D3
Loring Rd BERK HP4 161 K6
Lorrimer Cl LTNE LU2 69 K3
Lothair Rd LTNE LU2 70 B5
Loudhams Wood La CSTG HP8 216 A2
Loudwater Dr RKW/CH/CXG WD3 218 B4
Loudwater Hts RKW/CH/CXG WD3 218 A3
Loudwater La RKW/CH/CXG WD3 218 B5
Loudwater Rdg
RKW/CH/CXG WD3 218 B4 1
Louise Wk HHS/BOV HP3 183 J6
Louvain Wy GSTN WD25 204 C2
Lovatts RKW/CH/CXG WD3 219 F4
Love La ABLGY WD5 187 F8
BLDK SG7 17 G4
KGLGY WD4 185 J7
Lovel Cl HHW HP1 163 K6
Lovell Cl HTCHE/RSTV SG4 56 E3 3
Lovell Rd EN EN1 214 A5
Lovering Rd CHESW EN7 196 A3
Lovet Rd HLWW/ROY CM19 179 H2
Lowbell La LCOL/BKTW AL2 190 C5
Lower Adeyfield Rd HHNE HP2 8 A4
Lower Barn HHS/BOV HP3 185 K1
Lower Bourne Gdns WARE SG12 127 G6
Lower Clabdens WARE SG12 127 K8
Lower Dagnall St STALW/RED AL3 10 B4
Lower Derby Rd WAT WD17 13 D3 8
Lower Emms HHNE HP2 165 H1 3
Lowerfield WGCE AL7 148 B4
Lower Gower Rd ROY SG8 21 H1
Lower Harpenden Rd LTN LU1 5 F6
Lower Hatfield Rd
HERT/BAY SG13 150 C8
Lower High St WAT WD17 13 D3
Lower Icknield Wy TRING HP23 109 K8
Lower Innings HTCH/STOT SG5 56 A1
Lower Island Wy WAB EN9 215 G5
Lower Kings Rd BERK HP4 161 K4
Lower King St ROY SG8 21 H3
Lower Luton Rd HARP AL5 118 E6 2
HARP AL5 119 F6 1
LTNE LU2 118 D3
STALE/WH AL4 119 H7
Lower Mardley Hl WLYN AL6 123 F1
Lower Meadow CHES/WCR EN8 197 H5
HLWS CM18 180 B5
Lower Paddock Rd OXHEY WD19 13 F5
Lower Park Crs BSF CM23 105 J4
Lower Paxton Rd STAL AL1 11 D5 7
Lower Plantation
RKW/CH/CXG WD3 218 B3
Lower Rd CFSP/GDCR SL9 226 B7
HHS/BOV HP3 186 A4
HTCHE/RSTV SG4 72 C8
RBSF CM22 133 G2
RKW/CH/CXG WD3 217 G4
WARE SG12 152 E3
Lower Sales HHW HP1 163 J7
Lower Sean STVGE SG2 3 E5
Lower St STSD CM24 86 E2 1
Lower Tail OXHEY WD19 231 F2
Lower Tub BUSH WD23 222 A7 2
Lower Yott HHNE HP2 8 B6
Lowestoft Rd WATN WD24 220 C1 1
Loweswater Cl GSTN WD25 204 D3 1
Lowfield SBW CM21 132 C8
Lowfield La HOD EN11 177 F3
Lowgate La WARE SG12 99 K5
Low Hill Rd HLWW/ROY CM19 178 A3
Lowlands BRKMPK AL9 171 H1 2
Low Rd BRKMPK AL9 173 G1
Lowson Gv OXHEY WD19 13 F6
Lowswood Cl NTHWD HA6 229 H7
Lowther Cl BORE WD6 223 J5 1
Loxley Rd BERK HP4 161 F3
Lucan Rd BAR EN5 225 K3
Lucas Gdns LTNN/LIM LU3 69 G1
Lucas La BLDK SG7 18 A5
HTCH/STOT SG5 56 B2
Lucerne Wy LTNN/LIM LU3 69 H5
Lucks Hl HHW HP1 163 H6
Ludgate TRING HP23 134 E5 1
Ludlow Av LTN LU1 89 K5
Ludlow Md OXHEY WD19 230 C2
Ludlow Wy RKW/CH/CXG WD3 219 H4
Ludwick Wy WGCE AL7 148 A3
Lukes La TRING HP23 109 H6
Lukes Lea TRING HP23 110 A8
Lullington Cl LTNE LU2 70 D6
Lullington Garth BORE WD6 224 A6 1
Lulworth Av CHESW EN7 195 K7
Lumbards WGCE AL7 123 G8
Lumen Rd ROY SG8 21 H2
Lunardi Ct STDN SG11 81 H6
Lundin Wk OXHEY WD19 230 E3 3
Luther King Rd HLW CM20 6 B4
The Luton Dr LTN LU1 5 E6
Luton La STALW/RED AL3 142 B1
Luton Rd AMP/FLIT/B MK45 36 B8
HARP AL5 118 A5
HTCHE/RSTV SG4 92 D7
LTN LU1 88 E5
LTNE LU2 54 C7
LTNN/LIM LU3 52 B4
STALW/RED AL3 115 J2
Luton White Hl LTNE LU2 71 H1
Luxembourg Cl LTNN/LIM LU3 68 C1
Luxford Pl SBW CM21 132 D8
Luynes Ri BUNT SG9 63 J3
Lybury La STALW/RED AL3 141 K2
Lycaste Cl STAL AL1 11 E5
Lych Ga GSTN WD25 204 E3
Lycrome Rd CSHM HP5 182 A6
Lydia Ms BRKMPK AL9 192 C2
Lye Green Rd CSHM HP5 182 A8
Lye Hl HTCHE/RSTV SG4 92 A2
Lye La LCOL/BKTW AL2 188 C6
The Lye BERK HP4 138 A3
Lygean Av WARE SG12 127 J8
Lygetun Dr LTNN/LIM LU3 68 E2
Lygrave STVGE SG2 96 D1
Lyles La WGCW AL8 147 K1
Lyle's Rw HTCHE/RSTV SG4 56 D3
Lymans Rd ARL/CHE SG15 24 E3
Lyme Av BERK HP4 160 E2
Lymington Rd STVG SG1 75 G1
Lynch Hl DUN/WHIP LU6 114 E1
The Lynch HOD EN11 177 G3
Lyndale STVG SG1 2 C4
Lyndhurst Av PIN HA5 230 C7
Lyndhurst Cl HARP AL5 118 E7 1
Lyndhurst Dr HARP AL5 118 E7
Lyndhurst Gdns PIN HA5 230 C7
Lyndhurst Rd LTN LU1 4 A4
Lyndon Av PIN HA5 231 F5
Lyndon Md STALE/WH AL4 145 F7
Lyneham Rd LTNE LU2 70 D8
Lyne Wy HHW HP1 163 J4
Lynmouth Rd WGCE AL7 148 A3
Lynsey Cl STALW/RED AL3 142 B2
Lynton Av ARL/CHE SG15 24 E4
STAL AL1 169 F8
Lynwood Av LTNE LU2 70 B6
Lynwood Dr NTHWD HA6 229 K7
Lynwood Hts RKW/CH/CXG WD3 218 A5
Lyon Wy STALE/WH AL4 169 K6
Lyrical Wy HHW HP1 164 A4
Lysander Cl HHW HP1 183 H5
Lysander Wy ABLGY WD5 204 B2 4
WGCE AL7 148 E2 2
Lys Hill Gdns HERT/WAS SG14 150 E1
Lytham Av OXHEY WD19 230 E4
Lytton Av LWTH SG6 41 K4
PEND EN3 214 D8
Lytton Flds KNEB SG3 96 A5 2
Lytton Gdns WGCW AL8 147 J3
Lytton Rd PIN HA5 231 F6
Lyttons Wy HOD EN11 153 F8
Lytton Wy STVG SG1 2 A3

M

Mabbutt Cl LCOL/BKTW AL2 188 A8
Mabey's Wk SBW CM21 131 K8
Macdonnell Gdns GSTN WD25 204 A5 2
Macer's La BROX EN10 197 K2
Macintosh Cl CHESW EN7 196 B4 2
Mackenzie Sq STVGE SG2 3 F5
Mackerel Hall ROY SG8 21 F3
Maddesfield Ct RAD WD7 207 H3 5
Maddles LWTH SG6 42 D5
Maddox Rd HHNE HP2 9 E5
HLW CM20 7 D3
Made Feld STVG SG1 3 D3
Madgeways Cl WARE SG12 152 E4 1
Madgeways La WARE SG12 152 E4
Magellan Cl STVGE SG2 76 E4 1
Magna Cl HARP AL5 144 A3
Magnaville Rd BSF CM23 105 H5
BUSH WD23 222 B7
Magnolia Av ABLGY WD5 204 A2
Magnolia Cl HERT/BAY SG13 151 K3
LCOL/BKTW AL2 189 F4 1
Magpie Crs STVGE SG2 76 E5
The Magpies LTNE LU2 69 J3
Maidenhall Rd LTNW/LEA LU4 69 F7
Maidenhead St HERT/WAS SG14 151 G3 6
Maidenhead Yd
HERT/WAS SG14 151 G3 7
Maiden St HTCHE/RSTV SG4 43 J8
Main Av NTHWD HA6 229 H2
Main Rd HERT/WAS SG14 124 E6
Main Rd North BERK HP4 112 C2
Main Rd South BERK HP4 112 E4
Maitland Rd STSD CM24 86 D3
Malborough Rd WATW WD18 12 C3
Malden Flds BUSH WD23 13 E4
Malden Rd BORE WD6 223 K3
WAT WD17 12 B1 2
Maldon Ct HARP AL5 118 D7 3
Malham Cl LTNW/LEA LU4 68 E6
Malins Cl BAR EN5 225 H5 1
Mallard Gdns LTNN/LIM LU3 69 F4
Mallard Rd ABLGY WD5 204 B1
ROY SG8 21 G3
STVGE SG2 76 E7
Mallards Ri HLWE CM17 181 F1
The Mallards HHS/BOV HP3 185 K3

Mallard Wy GSTN WD25 205 F6 1
NTHWD HA6 229 H6
Mallows Gn HLWW/ROY CM19 179 H5
Mallow Wk ROY SG8 21 J4 4
The Mall LCOL/BKTW AL2 188 E5
Malm Cl RKW/CH/CXG WD3 228 C1
Malmes Cft HHS/BOV HP3 165 H8
Malmsdale WGCW AL8 122 D7
Maltby Dr EN EN1 214 A8
Malthouse Gn LTNE LU2 71 G8
Malthouse La HTCH/STOT SG5 26 A2
Malting La MHAD SG10 103 G7
STDN SG11 81 K2
TRING HP23 136 E4
Maltings Cl BLDK SG7 27 H8 4
ROY SG8 21 G2 1
Maltings Dr STALE/WH AL4 145 F2
Maltings Orch HTCH/STOT SG5 39 F6
The Maltings KGLGY WD4 203 H3
STAL AL1 10 C4 4
STVGE SG2 77 J1
Malus Cl HHNE HP2 9 D5
Malvern Cl STALE/WH AL4 168 E2
Malvern Rd LTN LU1 89 G2
PEND EN3 214 D7
Malvern Wy HHNE HP2 8 B3
RKW/CH/CXG WD3 219 G5
Malzeard Rd LTNN/LIM LU3 4 A2
Manan Cl HHS/BOV HP3 165 H8 2
Manchester Cl STVG SG1 59 F6
Manchester St LTN LU1 4 B4
Mancroft Rd LTN LU1 88 C6
Mandela Pl WATN WD24 13 E1 4
Mandelyns BERK HP4 161 F2
Mandeville STVGE SG2 76 D8
Mandeville Cl BROX EN10 176 E6
HERT/BAY SG13 151 F6 1
WAT WD17 204 A8
Mandeville Dr STAL AL1 189 F1
Mandeville Ri WGCW AL8 147 J1
Mandeville Rd HERT/BAY SG13 151 F6
PEND EN3 214 D7
POTB/CUF EN6 210 D2
Mangrove Dr HERT/BAY SG13 151 H5
Mangrove La HERT/BAY SG13 151 H6
Mangrove Rd HERT/BAY SG13 151 H4
LTNE LU2 70 D6
Manland Av HARP AL5 118 E7
Manland Wy HARP AL5 118 E7
Manley Hwy HTCH/STOT SG5 55 K2
Manley Rd HHNE HP2 8 B4 4
Manly Dixon Dr PEND EN3 214 D7
Mannicotts WGCW AL8 147 G3
Manning Pl LTNE LU2 71 F7 4
Manor Av HHS/BOV HP3 185 H1 1
Manor Cl BAR EN5 225 K4
BERK HP4 161 K5 4
HAT AL10 170 E1
HERT/WAS SG14 151 G1
HTCH/STOT SG5 40 C6
LWTH SG6 41 K6
Manor Cottages NTHWD HA6 230 A7 1
Manor Ct DEN/HRF UB9 228 B8
EN EN1 214 A6
RAD WD7 206 C7
Manor Crs HTCHE/RSTV SG4 57 F3
Manor Dr LCOL/BKTW AL2 188 C5
Manor Farm Cl LTNW/LEA LU4 68 B6
Manor Farm Rd EN EN1 214 A5
Manor Hatch HLWS CM18 7 F5
Manor Hatch Cl HLWS CM18 180 E2
Manor House Dr NTHWD HA6 229 G6
Manor House Gdns ABLGY WD5 203 J1
Manor Links BSF CM23 106 B2
Manor Pde HAT AL10 170 E1 1
Manor Pound Rd LBUZ LU7 110 A2 3
Manor Rd AMP/FLIT/B MK45 36 D7
BAR EN5 225 K4
BSF CM23 105 K2
HAT AL10 170 E1
HLWE CM17 157 F4
HOD EN11 177 F1
LBUZ LU7 109 K2
LCOL/BKTW AL2 190 A4
LTN LU1 5 D5
POTB/CUF EN6 210 A1
STAL AL1 11 D3
STALE/WH AL4 119 H7
STSD CM24 86 D4
TRING HP23 135 F4
WAB EN9 215 J3
WAT WD17 220 C1
Manorside BAR EN5 225 K4
Manor St BERK HP4 162 A5 4
Manor Vw STVGE SG2 76 C8
Manorville Rd HHS/BOV HP3 185 G2
Manor Wy BORE WD6 224 B3
KNEB SG3 95 H3
LWTH SG6 41 K6
POTB/CUF EN6 193 G8
RKW/CH/CXG WD3 219 F4
Mansard Cl TRING HP23 135 F6 2
Manscroft Rd HHW HP1 164 A4
Mansdale Rd STALW/RED AL3 142 A5
Mansfield SBW CM21 131 J8
Mansfield Gdns
HERT/WAS SG14 151 F1 2
Mansfield Rd BLDK SG7 42 E2
LTNW/LEA LU4 69 G8
Mansion Dr TRING HP23 135 G6
Manston Cl CHES/WCR EN8 197 G8 2
Manston Dr BSF CM23 86 A8
Manston Rd HLW CM20 7 D4
Manton Dr LTNE LU2 69 J5
Manton Rd HTCHE/RSTV SG4 57 G3
Manx Cl LTNW/LEA LU4 69 F7
Maple Av BSF CM23 105 G1
STALW/RED AL3 167 K2
Maple Cl BSF CM23 105 G1
BUSH WD23 13 F1
HAT AL10 171 F5 1
Maplecroft La WAB EN9 177 K7
Maplefield LCOL/BKTW AL2 188 D7
Maple Gn HHW HP1 163 H4
Maple Gv BSF CM23 105 G1
WAT WD17 220 B1 2
WGCE AL7 123 F8
Maple Leaf Cl ABLGY WD5 204 B2 5
Maple Lodge Cl
RKW/CH/CXG WD3 227 H3
Maple Rd HARP AL5 118 B8
Maple Rd East LTN LU1 89 G1
Maple Rd West LTNW/LEA LU4 89 G1
Maple Spring BSF CM23 105 F1
The Maples CHESW EN7 196 C6
HLWW/ROY CM19 179 J6
HTCHE/RSTV SG4 56 D4
Mapleton Crs PEND EN3 214 B8
Maple Wy DUN/WHIP LU6 114 C1
ROY SG8 21 J1
Maplewood WARE SG12 127 G6 4
Maran Av WLYN AL6 122 C5 3
Marconi Wy STALE/WH AL4 169 G6
Mardlebury Rd KNEB SG3 96 B8
Mardley Av WLYN AL6 123 F1
Mardleybury KNEB SG3 96 B7 2
Mardley Dell WLYN AL6 96 A8
Mardley Hts WLYN AL6 123 G1
Mardley Hl WLYN AL6 123 F1
Mardley Wd WLYN AL6 123 F1 1
Mardyke Rd HLW CM20 7 F2
Marford Rd STALE/WH AL4 145 J1
WGCW AL8 146 C2
Margaret Av STALW/RED AL3 10 C2
Margaret Cl ABLGY WD5 204 A2 2
POTB/CUF EN6 210 D3
WAB EN9 215 J3 1
Margeholes OXHEY WD19 231 F1
Margery Wd WGCE AL7 123 G7
Marguerite Wy BSF CM23 105 F3
Marian Gdns GSTN WD25 204 C3
Marigold Pl HLWE CM17 156 E5 1
Marina Gdns CHES/WCR EN8 197 G8
Mariner Wy HHNE HP2 9 D6 3
Marion Cl BUSH WD23 221 G1
Mark Dr CFSP/GDCR SL9 226 A3
Markeston Gn OXHEY WD19 230 E3 4
Market Hl BUNT SG9 63 J2 2
ROY SG8 21 H3
Market Oak La HHS/BOV HP3 186 A2
Market Pl CFSP/GDCR SL9 226 A7
HERT/WAS SG14 151 G3 8
STAL AL1 10 C4
WATW WD18 13 D3 9
Market Sq BSF CM23 105 J2
STVG SG1 2 B3
Market St BSF CM23 105 J2 3
HERT/WAS SG14 151 G3 9
HLWE CM17 157 F5
WATW WD18 12 C3
Markfield Cl LTNN/LIM LU3 69 H3 2
Mark Hall Moors HLW CM20 156 E6
Markham Rd CHESW EN7 196 A4
LTNN/LIM LU3 69 H1
Mark Rd HHNE HP2 9 D3
Markwell Wd EPP CM16 179 J7
Markyate Rd LTN LU1 89 G8
Marlborough Cl BSF CM23 105 J4
HTCHE/RSTV SG4 59 H1
WLYN AL6 123 F1 2
Marlborough Ga STAL AL1 11 D4
Marlborough Ri HHNE HP2 8 B2
Marlborough Rd LTNN/LIM LU3 4 A2
STAL AL1 11 D4 2
STVGE SG2 76 D4
Marle Gdns WAB EN9 215 H2
Marley Rd WGCE AL7 148 B5
Marlin Cl BERK HP4 161 G4
Marlin Copse BERK HP4 161 H6 1
Marlin Hl TRING HP23 135 F8
Marlins Cl RKW/CH/CXG WD3 217 H2
Marlins Meadow WATW WD18 219 J6
Marlin Sq ABLGY WD5 204 A1
The Marlins NTHWD HA6 230 A5
Marlins Turn HHW HP1 164 A3
Marlowe Cl STVGE SG2 76 D1
Marlowes HHNE HP2 8 A5
Marnham Ri HHW HP1 163 K4 2
Marquis Cl BSF CM23 104 E2
HARP AL5 119 F7
Marquis La HARP AL5 119 F7
Marrilyne Av PEND EN3 214 E8
Marriott Rd BAR EN5 225 J3
LTNN/LIM LU3 69 G3
Marriotts Wy HHS/BOV HP3 164 C8
Marriott Ter RKW/CH/CXG WD3 217 J4
Marryat Rd EN EN1 214 A5
Marschefield HTCH/STOT SG5 25 J3
Marsden Cl WGCW AL8 147 G5 1
Marsden Gn WGCW AL8 147 G4
Marsden Rd WGCW AL8 147 G4
Marshall Av STALW/RED AL3 11 D1
Marshall Rd LTNE LU2 70 D7
Marshalls Heath La HARP AL5 119 J4
Marshall's La WARE SG12 99 K5
Marshalls Wy STALE/WH AL4 119 H7
Marshal's Dr STAL AL1 11 F1
Marshalswick La STAL AL1 11 F1
Marshbarns BSF CM23 105 F1
Marsh Cl CHES/WCR EN8 214 E3
Marshcroft Dr CHES/WCR EN8 197 J8
Marshcroft La TRING HP23 135 J3
Marshe Cl POTB/CUF EN6 210 E2
Marshgate STVG SG1 2 B3
Marshgate Dr HERT/BAY SG13 151 H2
Marsh Hl WAB EN9 198 E5
Marsh La HLWE CM17 157 H4
WARE SG12 152 D1
WARE SG12 153 J6
Marshmoor Crs BRKMPK AL9 171 J8
Marshmoor La BRKMPK AL9 171 H8
Marsh Rd LTNN/LIM LU3 68 D4
Marsom Gv LTNN/LIM LU3 69 G1
Marston Cl HHS/BOV HP3 9 D6 4
Marston Gdns LTNE LU2 69 J5
Marston Rd HOD EN11 177 G2 1
Marsworth Av PIN HA5 230 E7
Marsworth Cl WATW WD18 219 K7 2
Marsworth Rd LBUZ LU7 110 D5
Marten Ga STALE/WH AL4 168 D2
Martian Av HHNE HP2 8 C2
Martin Cl HAT AL10 171 F6
Martindale Rd HHW HP1 163 J5
Martinfield WGCE AL7 148 A2 3
Martingale Rd ROY SG8 21 J3 3
Martins Cl RAD WD7 206 B6 1
Martins Dr CHES/WCR EN8 197 J6
HERT/BAY SG13 152 A3
Martins Wy STVG SG1 59 H8
Martin Wy LWTH SG6 41 H4
Martlesham WGCE AL7 149 F3
Martyr Cl STAL AL1 189 F2 2
Marwood Cl KGLGY WD4 185 K7 1
Maryland HAT AL10 171 F4 2
Mary Mcarthur Pl STSD CM24 86 D1 4
Marymead Ct STVGE SG2 96 B1
Marymead Dr STVGE SG2 96 B1
Mary Park Gdns BSF CM23 105 J5
Maryport Rd LTNW/LEA LU4 69 F7
Mary Proud Ct WLYN AL6 122 E2 2
Masefield HTCHE/RSTV SG4 57 G2
Masefield Av BORE WD6 224 A5
Masefield Ct HARP AL5 118 D5 1
Masefield Rd HARP AL5 118 D6
Mason Cl BORE WD6 224 C2
Masons Ct BSF CM23 105 H2
Masons Rd EN EN1 214 A6
HHNE HP2 9 E4
Mason Wy WAB EN9 215 K3
Masters Cl LTN LU1 89 G4
Matching La BSF CM23 105 G1
Mathams Dr BSF CM23 105 G4
Mathews Cl STVG SG1 58 D8
Matlock Cl BAR EN5 225 J5
Matlock Crs LTNW/LEA LU4 68 B8
OXHEY WD19 230 D2
Matthew Ga HTCHE/RSTV SG4 56 E4
Mattocke Rd HTCH/STOT SG5 40 A8
Maude Crs WATN WD24 204 C7
Maud Jane's Cl LBUZ LU7 110 E4
Maulden Cl LTNE LU2 70 D8
Maunds Hatch HLWS CM18 180 A5
Maxted Rd HHNE HP2 9 E3
Maxwell Cl RKW/CH/CXG WD3 227 K1
Maxwell Ri OXHEY WD19 13 F6 2
Maxwell Rd BORE WD6 224 A3
NTHWD HA6 229 J6
STAL AL1 168 E7
STVG SG1 75 G4
Maybury Av CHES/WCR EN8 197 F6
CHESW EN7 197 F6 1
May Cl STALW/RED AL3 10 C2
Maycock Gv NTHWD HA6 230 A5
Maycroft LWTH SG6 26 A8
PIN HA5 230 C8
Maycroft Rd CHESW EN7 196 C4
Maydencroft La HTCH/STOT SG5 56 B5
Maydwell Ldg BORE WD6 223 J2
Mayes Cl BSF CM23 106 C1
Mayfair Cl STALE/WH AL4 169 F1
Mayfare RKW/CH/CXG WD3 219 J5
Mayfield WGCW AL8 122 C7
Mayfield Cl HARP AL5 118 A6
HLWE CM17 157 J5
Mayfield Pk BSF CM23 105 G6 1

Mayfield Rd *LTNE* LU2 ... 70 C5
Mayflower Av *HHNE* HP2 ... 8 A5
Mayflower Cl *HERT/WAS* SG14 ... 150 D5
  WAB EN9 ... 198 E1
  WLYN AL6 ... 94 E8
Mayflower Gdns *BSF* CM23 ... 104 E3
Mayflower Rd *LCOL/BKTW* AL2 ... 188 D5
May Gdns *BORE* WD6 ... 223 G6
Mayhill Rd *BAR* EN5 ... 225 K6
Maylands Av *HHNE* HP2 ... 9 E3
Maylands Rd *OXHEY* WD19 ... 230 D3
Maylin Cl *HTCHE/RSTV* SG4 ... 57 G1
Maylins Dr *SBW* CM21 ... 132 B7
Maynard Dr *STAL* AL1 ... 189 F1
Maynard Pl *POTB/CUF* EN6 ... 195 G7
Maynard Rd *HHNE* HP2 ... 8 A6
Mayne Av *LTNW/LEA* LU4 ... 68 B5
  STALW/RED AL3 ... 167 G8
Mayo Cl *CHES/WCR* EN8 ... 197 G6
Mayo Gdns *HHW* HP1 ... 164 A7
Mayshades Cl *KNEB* SG3 ... 96 B7
Mays La *BAR* EN5 ... 225 G7
May St *LTN* LU1 ... 4 C5
Maythorne Cl *WATW* WD18 ... 219 K4
Maytree Crs *WATN* WD24 ... 204 A6
Maytrees *HTCHE/RSTV* SG4 ... 56 E3
  RAD WD7 ... 206 D7
Maze Green Hts *BSF* CM23 ... 105 F2
Maze Green Rd *BSF* CM23 ... 105 G2
Mazoe Cl *BSF* CM23 ... 105 J4
Mazoe Rd *BSF* CM23 ... 105 J4
Mcadam Cl *HOD* EN11 ... 177 F1
Mcdonald Ct *HAT* AL10 ... 171 F6
  HAT AL10 ... 171 F7
Mc Kellar Cl *BUSH* WD23 ... 231 K1
Mc Kenzie Rd *BROX* EN10 ... 177 F6
Mead Cl *STVG* SG2 ... 3 D2
Mead Ct *WAB* EN9 ... 215 G4
Meadgate Rd *HOD* EN11 ... 177 J6
Mead La *HERT/BAY* SG13 ... 151 H2
Meadowbank *HTCHE/RSTV* SG4 ... 41 F8
  KGLGY WD4 ... 186 A8
  OXHEY WD19 ... 13 D6
Meadowbanks *BAR* EN5 ... 225 F5
Meadowbrook *TRING* HP23 ... 135 G3
Meadow Cl *BERK* HP4 ... 161 H7
  BRKMPK AL9 ... 192 D2
  HERT/BAY SG13 ... 151 J2
  KNEB SG3 ... 96 E7
  LCOL/BKTW AL2 ... 188 C8
  LCOL/BKTW AL2 ... 190 B5
  STALE/WH AL4 ... 169 F3
  TRING HP23 ... 135 F5
Meadowcroft *BERK* HP4 ... 160 E2
  BUSH WD23 ... 221 J6
  CFSP/GDCR SL9 ... 226 A8
Meadow Cft *HAT* AL10 ... 170 E4
Meadowcroft *STAL* AL1 ... 189 J2
  STSD CM24 ... 86 D2
Meadowcross *WAB* EN9 ... 215 K4
Meadow Dell *HAT* AL10 ... 170 E4
Meadow Gn *WGCW* AL8 ... 147 H3
Meadowlands *BAR* EN5 ... 224 E5
  BSF CM23 ... 85 K8
Meadow La *LBUZ* LU7 ... 110 E6
Meadow Rd *BERK* HP4 ... 161 J3
  BORE WD6 ... 224 A2
  BUSH WD23 ... 221 J5
  GSTN WD25 ... 204 B4
  HHS/BOV HP3 ... 186 A3
  LTNN/LIM LU3 ... 69 G5
Meadow Road Cl *BERK* HP4 ... 161 J3
The Meadows *BSF* CM23 ... 105 H4
  HTCHE/RSTV SG4 ... 72 B8
  SBW CM21 ... 132 E7
Meadowsweet Cl *BSF* CM23 ... 105 F3
The Meadow *HERT/BAY* SG13 ... 152 D7
  WGCE AL7 ... 148 D3
Meadow Vw *BUNT* SG9 ... 63 H5
Meadow Wk *HARP* AL5 ... 143 K1
  STDN SG11 ... 81 K7
Meadow Wy *ABLGY* WD5 ... 187 G5
  HHS/BOV HP3 ... 184 D1
  HTCH/STOT SG5 ... 25 J3
  HTCH/STOT SG5 ... 54 E6
  HTCH/STOT SG5 ... 56 B3
  HTCHE/RSTV SG4 ... 94 D8
  KGLGY WD4 ... 186 A8
  LTN LU1 ... 88 D5
  LWTH SG6 ... 41 K4
  POTB/CUF EN6 ... 210 B4
  RKW/CH/CXG WD3 ... 218 B7
  ROY SG8 ... 30 E3
  SBW CM21 ... 132 E8
  STVG SG1 ... 3 D3
Mead Pl *RKW/CH/CXG* WD3 ... 218 A8
Mead Rd *RAD* WD7 ... 207 K3
Meads La *STALE/WH* AL4 ... 120 B8
The Meads *BERK* HP4 ... 161 G3
  LCOL/BKTW AL2 ... 188 B7
  LTNN/LIM LU3 ... 69 F6
  LWTH SG6 ... 41 J3
Mead Temple *HHNE* HP2 ... 8 A3
The Mead *CHES/WCR* EN8 ... 197 C8
  HTCH/STOT SG5 ... 40 C7

OXHEY WD19 ... 231 F2
Mead Vw *BUNT* SG9 ... 67 C3
Meadview Rd *WARE* SG12 ... 152 B1
Meadway *BERK* HP4 ... 162 B4
Mead Wy *BUSH* WD23 ... 13 F1
Meadway *HARP* AL5 ... 144 B2
  HOD EN11 ... 177 F5
  KNEB SG3 ... 96 A5
  PEND EN3 ... 214 C6
  STALE/WH AL4 ... 191 H1
  STVG SG1 ... 75 F3
  WGCE AL7 ... 148 A5
Meadway Cl *PIN* HA5 ... 231 J5
The Meadway *POTB/CUF* EN6 ... 195 H6
Meautys *STALW/RED* AL3 ... 167 G8
Medalls Link *STVGE* SG2 ... 3 E5
Medalls Pth *STVGE* SG2 ... 3 E5
Medcalf Rd *PEND* EN3 ... 214 E7
Medina Rd *LTNW/LEA* LU4 ... 69 F8
Medlows *HARP* AL5 ... 118 A7
Medow Md *RAD* WD7 ... 206 C5
Medway Cl *GSTN* WD25 ... 204 D4
Medway Rd *HHNE* HP2 ... 164 E1
Medwick Ms *HHNE* HP2 ... 165 G1
Meeting House La *BLDK* SG7 ... 26 E8
Megg La *KGLGY* WD4 ... 185 F7
Melbourn Cl *HTCH/STOT* SG5 ... 25 K4
Melbourne Cl *STALW/RED* AL3 ... 168 C2
Melbourne Ct *WGCW* AL8 ... 147 G4
Melbourne Rd *BUSH* WD23 ... 221 J5
Melbourn Rd *ROY* SG8 ... 21 J2
Melbourn St *ROY* SG8 ... 21 H3
Melford Cl *LTNE* LU2 ... 70 E8
The Melings *HHNE* HP2 ... 165 G1
Melne Rd *STVGE* SG2 ... 96 C1
Melrose Av *BORE* WD6 ... 224 A5
  POTB/CUF EN6 ... 210 C3
Melrose Pl *WAT* WD17 ... 204 A8
Melson St *LTN* LU1 ... 4 C4
Melsted Rd *HHW* HP1 ... 164 A6
Melvern Cl *STVGE* SG2 ... 96 C2
Melvyn Cl *CHESW* EN7 ... 195 K6
Memorial Rd *LTNW/LIM* LU3 ... 68 E5
Memorial Wy *WAT* WD17 ... 12 B2
Mendip Cl *STALE/WH* AL4 ... 169 F1
Mendip Rd *BUSH* WD23 ... 221 K6
Mendip Wy *HHNE* HP2 ... 8 B2
  LTNN/LIM LU3 ... 68 B1
Mendlesham *WGCE* AL7 ... 149 F3
Mentley La *STDN* SG11 ... 80 D5
Mentley La East *STDN* SG11 ... 81 G5
Mentley La West *STDN* SG11 ... 81 G5
Mentmore Rd *LBUZ* LU7 ... 109 K1
  STAL AL1 ... 10 C6
Mentmore Rd *TRING* HP23 ... 134 E4
Mepham Crs *KTN/HRWW/W* HA3 ... 231 K6
Mepham Gdns *KTN/HRWW/W* HA3 ... 231 K6
Mercer Pl *PIN* HA5 ... 230 D8
Mercers *HHNE* HP2 ... 8 B3
  HLWW/ROY CM19 ... 179 H4
Mercers Av *BSF* CM23 ... 104 E5
Mercers Rw *STAL* AL1 ... 10 B6
Merchant Dr *HERT/BAY* SG13 ... 151 J2
Merchants Wk *BLDK* SG7 ... 27 H8
Mercia Rd *BLDK* SG7 ... 43 G1
Meredith Cl *PIN* HA5 ... 230 E6
Meredith Rd *STVG* SG1 ... 3 E1
Merefield *SBW* CM21 ... 132 C8
Meriden Wy *GSTN* WD25 ... 205 F7
Meridian Wy *WARE* SG12 ... 153 G4
Merle Av *DEN/HRF* UB9 ... 228 B8
Merling Cft *BERK* HP4 ... 161 F3
Mermaid Cl *HTCHE/RSTV* SG4 ... 57 F2
Merritt Wk *BRKMPK* AL9 ... 192 B2
Merrow Dr *HHW* HP1 ... 163 H5
Merryfield Cl *BORE* WD6 ... 223 J2
Merryfields *STALE/WH* AL4 ... 169 H6
Merry Hill Mt *BUSH* WD23 ... 221 J8
Merry Hill Rd *BUSH* WD23 ... 221 H7
Mersey Pl *HHNE* HP2 ... 164 E1
Merton Rd *ENC/FH* EN2 ... 213 H6
Metropolitan Station Ap *WATW* WD18 ... 12 A2
Meux Cl *CHESW* EN7 ... 213 K1
The Mews *SBW* CM21 ... 132 C6
Meyer Gn *EN* EN1 ... 213 K8
Meyrick Av *LTN* LU1 ... 4 A5
Mezen Cl *NTHWD* HA6 ... 229 J4
Michaels Rd *BSF* CM23 ... 85 K7
Micholls Av *CFSP/GDCR* SL9 ... 226 B4
Micklefield Cl *HHNE* HP2 ... 9 F5
Micklefield Wy *BORE* WD6 ... 207 H8
Micklem Dr *HHW* HP1 ... 163 J5
Midcot Wy *BERK* HP4 ... 161 G3
Mid Cross La *CFSP/GDCR* SL9 ... 226 C4
Middle Drift *ROY* SG8 ... 21 G3
Middlefield *HAT* AL10 ... 171 F3
  WGCE AL7 ... 148 C3
Middlefield Av *HOD* EN11 ... 177 F1
Middlefield Cl *HOD* EN11 ... 177 F1
  STALE/WH AL4 ... 169 F1
Middlefield Rd *HOD* EN11 ... 177 F1

Middlefields *LWTH* SG6 ... 41 K1
Middle Furlong *BUSH* WD23 ... 221 J4
Middlehill *HHW* HP1 ... 163 H6
Middleknights Hl *HHW* HP1 ... 163 K4
Middle La *HHS/BOV* HP3 ... 183 J7
  WAB EN9 ... 215 G2
Middle Rw *BSF* CM23 ... 105 J3
Middlesborough Cl *STVG* SG1 ... 59 F7
Middle St *WAB* EN9 ... 199 F1
Middleton Rd *LTNE* LU2 ... 70 E5
  RKW/CH/CXG WD3 ... 217 K8
Middle Wy *WATN* WD24 ... 204 C7
Midhurst *LWTH* SG6 ... 41 J1
Midhurst Gdns *LTNN/LIM* LU3 ... 69 H4
Midland Rd *HHNE* HP2 ... 8 A5
  LTN LU1 ... 4 C3
Midway *STALW/RED* AL3 ... 188 D1
Milburn Cl *LTNN/LIM* LU3 ... 52 E8
Midmay Rd *STVG* SG1 ... 76 C1
Mildred Av *BORE* WD6 ... 223 K4
  WATW WD18 ... 12 B3
Mile Cl *WAB* EN9 ... 215 H3
Mile House Cl *STAL* AL1 ... 189 H1
Mile House La *STAL* AL1 ... 189 H2
Miles Cl *HLWW/ROY* CM19 ... 6 A5
Milestone Cl *STVGE* SG2 ... 76 E5
Milestone Rd *HTCH/STOT* SG5 ... 40 B8
  KNEB SG3 ... 96 B4
Milford Cl *STALE/WH* AL4 ... 169 G2
Milford Hl *HARP* AL5 ... 119 F5
Milksey La *HTCHE/RSTV* SG4 ... 58 B4
Milland Ct *BORE* WD6 ... 224 C1
Millard Wy *HTCHE/RSTV* SG4 ... 41 G7
Millbank *HHS/BOV* HP3 ... 185 H2
Mill Br *HERT/WAS* SG14 ... 151 F3
Millbrook Rd *BUSH* WD23 ... 221 C1
Mill Cl *BUNT* SG9 ... 63 J2
  HHS/BOV HP3 ... 186 A3
  HHW HP1 ... 164 A2
  HTCH/STOT SG5 ... 26 A3
  WARE SG12 ... 127 H8
  WGCW AL8 ... 147 F4
Millcrest Rd *CHESW* EN7 ... 195 K6
Millcroft *BSF* CM23 ... 85 K8
Mill End *STDN* SG11 ... 82 A7
Millers Cl *BSF* CM23 ... 105 F4
Millersdale *HLWW/ROY* CM19 ... 179 J5
Millers La *WARE* SG12 ... 153 H5
Millers Ri *STAL* AL1 ... 11 C5
Millers Vw *MHAD* SG10 ... 103 F8
Millers Yd *HERT/WAS* SG14 ... 151 C3
Mill Farm Cl *PIN* HA5 ... 230 D8
Mill Fld *HLWE* CM17 ... 157 F5
Millfield *BERK* HP4 ... 162 A4
  WARE SG12 ... 127 J1
  WGCE AL7 ... 148 D2
Millfield La *HTCHE/RSTV* SG4 ... 56 D5
  LTN LU1 ... 88 B6
  STDN SG11 ... 104 A1
Millfield Rd *LTNN/LIM* LU3 ... 69 G6
Millfields *SBW* CM21 ... 132 D6
  STSD CM24 ... 86 D3
Millfield Wk *HHS/BOV* HP3 ... 186 A1
Millfield Wy *LTN* LU1 ... 88 C6
Mill Gdns *TRING* HP23 ... 135 G3
Mill Green La *BRKMPK* AL9 ... 147 K8
Mill Green Rd *WGCE* AL7 ... 147 K4
Mill Hl *BSF* CM23 ... 85 H4
  ROY SG8 ... 21 J5
  STSD CM24 ... 86 C3
Millhouse La *ABLGY* WD5 ... 187 G5
Millhurst Ms *HLWE* CM17 ... 157 H5
Milliners Wy *BSF* CM23 ... 105 F5
  LTNN/LIM LU3 ... 4 A2
Mill La *AMP/FLIT/B* MK45 ... 36 B6
  ARL/CHE SG15 ... 24 D5
  BROX EN10 ... 176 E7
  BUNT SG9 ... 50 C4
  CHES/WCR EN8 ... 19 C6
  HERT/WAS SG14 ... 98 C4
  HLWE CM17 ... 157 H5
  HTCH/STOT SG5 ... 26 A3
  HTCH/STOT SG5 ... 37 H6
  HTCHE/RSTV SG4 ... 43 J8
  HTCHE/RSTV SG4 ... 56 D6
  KGLGY WD4 ... 186 A7
  RBSF CM22 ... 133 K5
  ROY SG8 ... 30 D1
  SBW CM21 ... 132 D6
  STALW/RED AL3 ... 116 A8
  STDN SG11 ... 84 A3
  WLYN AL6 ... 122 C4
Mill Lane Cl *BROX* EN10 ... 176 E7
Mill Race *WARE* SG12 ... 153 J5
Mill Rd *HERT/BAY* SG13 ... 151 G2
  HERT/WAS SG14 ... 151 G2
  HTCHE/RSTV SG4 ... 56 D6
  ROY SG8 ... 21 H2
Mill Side *STSD* CM24 ... 86 C3
Millstream Cl *HERT/WAS* SG14 ... 150 E5
  HTCHE/RSTV SG4 ... 40 E7
Mill St *BERK* HP4 ... 161 K5
  BLDK SG7 ... 17 K5

BSF CM23 .... 105 K4
HHS/BOV HP3 .... 185 H2
HLWE CM17 .... 181 H4
LTN LU1 .... 4 B3
Millthorne CI *RKW/CH/CXG* WD3 ... 218 E5
Mill View Rd *TRING* HP23 .... 134 E5
Millwards *HAT* AL10 .... 171 C7
Mill Wy *BUSH* WD23 .... 13 F1
Millway *HHW/RSTV* SG4 .... 72 A7
Mill Wy *RKW/CH/CXG* WD3 .... 217 J8
Milne CI *LWTH* SG6 .... 42 B6
Milne Fld *PIN* HA5 .... 231 H6
Milner CI *GSTN* WD25 .... 204 C4 🔲
Milner Ct *BUSH* WD23 .... 221 J6
Milneway *DEN/HRF* UB9 .... 228 A7
Milton Rd *HARP* AL5 .... 118 D8
   LTN LU1 .... 4 A5
   WARE SG12 .... 127 H7
Milton St *WATN* WD24 .... 220 C1
Milton Vw *HTCHE/RSTV* SG4 .... 57 C7
Milverton Gn *LTNN/LIM* LU3 .... 69 F2
Milwards *HLWW/ROY* CM19 .... 179 J5 🔲
Mimms Hall Rd *POTB/CUF* EN6 .... 209 J1
Mimms La *BORE* WD6 .... 208 C3
   RAD WD7 .... 207 K3
Mimram CI *HTCHE/RSTV* SG4 .... 93 H2
Mimram Rd *HERT/WAS* SG14 .... 150 C4 🔲
   WLYN AL6 .... 122 C4 🔲
Minchen Rd *HLW* CM20 .... 7 F3
Minehead Wy *STVG* SG1 .... 75 F2
Minerva CI *STVG* SG1 .... 59 J8
Minerva Dr *WAT* WD17 .... 203 K6
The Minims *HAT* AL10 .... 171 F3
Minsden Rd *STVGE* SG2 .... 76 E6
Minster CI *HAT* AL10 .... 171 F6
Minster Rd *ROY* SG8 .... 21 C1
Minstrel CI *HHW* HP1 .... 164 A5 🔲
Minton La *HLWE* CM17 .... 181 F1
Misbourne Av *CFSP/GDCR* SL9 ... 226 B4
Misbourne CI *CFSP/GDCR* SL9 ... 226 B4 🔲
Missden Dr *HARP* AL5 .... 118 B6
Miss Joans Ride *DUN/WHIP* LU6 ... 113 C3
Mistletoe HI *LTNE* LU2 .... 90 D1
Mistley Rd *HLW* CM20 .... 7 F2
Miswell La *TRING* HP23 .... 134 E6
Mitchell CI *ABLGY* WD5 .... 204 B2 🔲
   HHW HP1 .... 183 H5
   STAL AL1 .... 189 F2
   WGCE AL7 .... 148 D3 🔲
Mitre Gdns *BSF* CM23 .... 105 K5 🔲
Mixes Hill Rd *LTNE* LU2 .... 70 A6
The Mixies *HTCH/STOT* SG5 .... 25 J3
The Moakes *LTNN/LIM* LU3 .... 68 D2
Moat CI *BUSH* WD23 .... 221 J5 🔲
Moat La *LTNN/LIM* LU3 .... 69 C5
Moatside *BUNT* SG9 .... 48 A5
The Moat *STDN* SG11 .... 81 J6
Moatwood Gn *WGCE* AL7 .... 147 K4 🔲
Mobbsbury Wy *STVGE* SG2 .... 3 F1
Mobley Gn *LTNE* LU2 .... 70 C6
Moffats CI *BRKMPK* AL9 .... 193 C4
Moffats La *BRKMPK* AL9 .... 192 E5
Moira CI *LTNN/LIM* LU3 .... 68 B3
Molescroft *HARP* AL5 .... 117 K5
Moles La *BUNT* SG9 .... 48 A6
Molesworth *HOD* EN11 .... 153 F7
Molewood Rd *HERT/WAS* SG14 ... 150 C2 🔲
Mollison Av *PEND* EN3 .... 214 D5
Molteno Rd *WAT* WD17 .... 220 B1
Momples Rd *HLW* CM20 .... 7 F3
Monarch's Wy *CHES/WCR* EN8 ... 214 C3 🔲
Monastery CI *STALW/RED* AL3 ... 10 B4 🔲
Money Hill Rd *RKW/CH/CXG* WD3 ... 218 B8
Money Hole La *WLYN* AL6 .... 149 F2
Monica CI *WATN* WD24 .... 13 E1
Monklands *LWTH* SG6 .... 41 H5
Monksbury *HLWS* CM18 .... 180 D4
Monks CI *BROX* EN10 .... 177 F6
   LWTH SG6 .... 41 G3
   STAL AL1 .... 11 D6
   STALW/RED AL3 .... 142 C4
Monks Horton Wy *STAL* AL1 .... 11 F2
Monksmead *BORE* WD6 .... 224 B4
Monks Ri *WGCW* AL8 .... 122 C1
Monks Vw *STVGE* SG2 .... 3 D6
Monks Wk *BUNT* SG9 .... 63 J2
Monkswick Rd *HLW* CM20 .... 7 E2
Monkswood *WGCW* AL8 .... 122 C1
Monkswood Av *WARE* SG12 .... 215 J3
Monkswood Dr *BSF* CM23 .... 105 C3
Monkswood Gdns *BORE* WD6 ... 224 C5
Monkswood Wy *STVG* SG1 .... 2 C6
   STVGE SG2 .... 2 C6
Monmouth Rd *WAT* WD17 .... 12 C2 🔲
Mons Av *BLDK* SG7 .... 43 F3
Mons CI *HARP* AL5 .... 144 A3
Monson Rd *BROX* EN10 .... 176 E6 🔲
Montacute Rd *BUSH* WD23 .... 222 B7
Montague Av *LTNW/LEA* LU4 ... 68 B3
Montague Hall PI *BUSH* WD23 ... 221 H6 🔲
Montague Rd *BERK* HP4 .... 161 J5

Montayne Rd *CHES/WCR* EN8 ...... 214 C2
Montfitchet Wk *STVGE* SG2 .... 76 E2
Montgomerie CI *BERK* HP4 .... 161 H3 🔲
Montgomery Av *HHNE* HP2 .... 9 D4
Montgomery Dr *CHES/WCR* EN8 ... 197 J6
Monton CI *LTNN/LIM* LU3 .... 68 E3
Montrose Av *LTNN/LIM* LU3 .... 69 H6
Monument La *CFSP/GDCR* SL9 ... 226 B5
Moorend *WGCE* AL7 .... 148 B6
Moor End Rd *HHW* HP1 .... 164 B7
Moore Rd *BERK* HP4 .... 161 C3
Moorfields *HLWS* CM18 .... 179 K6
Moor Hall Rd *HLWE* CM17 .... 157 J5
Moorhead CI *HTCH/STOT* SG5 ... 56 B3
Moorhurst Av *CHESW* EN7 .... 195 K7
The Moorings *BSF* CM23 .... 105 K3
Moorland Gdns *LTNE* LU2 .... 4 B3 🔲
Moorland Rd *HARP* AL5 .... 118 D5
   HHW HP1 .... 163 J8
Moorlands *LCOL/BKTW* AL2 ...... 189 C6 🔲
   WGCE AL7 .... 148 B6
Moor La *RKW/CH/CXG* WD3 ...... 201 H6
   RKW/CH/CXG WD3 .... 228 D1
Moor Lane Crossing *WATW* WD18 ... 219 H7
Moor Mill La *LCOL/BKTW* AL2 ... 189 C7
Moor Park Rd *NTHWD* HA6 ...... 229 J5
Moorside *WGCE* AL7 .... 148 B6
Moors Ley *STVGE* SG2 .... 60 C8
The Moors *WGCE* AL7 .... 148 B2
Moor St *LTN* LU1 .... 4 A3
Moors Wk *WGCE* AL7 .... 148 C2
Moortown Rd *OXHEY* WD19 ...... 230 D3
Moor Vw *WATW* WD18 .... 12 B6
Moorymead CI *HERT/WAS* SG14 ... 98 A6
Morecambe CI *STVG* SG1 .... 75 C2
Morefields *TRING* HP23 .... 135 F3
Moremead *WAB* EN9 .... 215 J3
Moreton Av *HARP* AL5 .... 118 B7
Moreton CI *CHESW* EN7 .... 197 F5
Moreton End CI *HARP* AL5 .... 118 B7 🔲
Moreton End La *HARP* AL5 .... 118 B7
Moreton PI *HARP* AL5 .... 118 B6 🔲
Morgan CI *LTNE* LU2 .... 5 E1
   STVG SG1 .... 58 D8
Morgan Gdns *WD25* .... 205 J8 🔲
Morgans Rd *HERT/BAY* SG13 ... 151 C5 🔲
Morgan's Rd *HERT/BAY* SG13 ... 151 G5 🔲
Morgan's Wk *HERT/BAY* SG13 ... 151 G6
Morice Rd *HOD* EN11 .... 176 E1
Morland Av *CHES/WCR* EN8 ...... 197 J4
Morley Gv *HLW* CM20 .... 6 B3
Morley HI *ENC/FH* EN2 .... 213 C6
Mornington *WLYN* AL6 .... 123 C5
Mornington Rd *RAD* WD7 .... 206 D4
Morningtons *HLWW/ROY* CM19 ... 179 J5
Morpeth Av *BORE* WD6 .... 207 J8
Morrell CI *LTNN/LIM* LU3 .... 69 F2
Morris CI *CFSP/GDCR* SL9 ...... 226 C7
   HNLW SG16 .... 24 A4
   LTNN/LIM LU3 .... 68 D1
Morriston CI *OXHEY* WD19 ...... 230 D4 🔲
Morris Wy *LCOL/BKTW* AL2 ...... 190 B4
Morse CI *DEN/HRF* UB9 .... 228 B4
Mortain Dr *BERK* HP4 .... 161 G3
Mortimer Ga *CHES/WCR* EN8 ... 197 K5 🔲
Mortimer HI *TRING* HP23 .... 135 C5
Mortimer Ri *TRING* HP23 .... 135 C5 🔲
Mortimer Rd *ROY* SG8 .... 21 J3
Morton CI *LBUZ* LU7 .... 110 C5
Morton St *ROY* SG8 .... 21 H1
Morven CI *POTB/CUF* EN6 ...... 210 D1
Mossbank Av *LTNE* LU2 .... 90 D1
Mossendew CI *DEN/HRF* UB9 ... 228 C5
Moss Gn *WGCE* AL7 .... 147 K5
Moss La *PIN* HA5 .... 231 F8
Mossman Dr *LTN* LU1 .... 88 D5
Moss Rd *GSTN* WD25 .... 204 C4
Moss Side *HTCH/STOT* SG5 ...... 40 A8
Moss Wy *HTCH/STOT* SG5 ...... 40 A8
Mostyn Rd *BUSH* WD23 .... 221 K5
   LTNW/LEA LU4 .... 68 D5
Motts CI *HERT/WAS* SG14 .... 97 K5
Moulton Ri *LTNE* LU2 .... 5 D3
Mountbatten CI *STAL* AL1 ...... 189 K1 🔲
Mount CI *HHW* HP1 .... 163 J4
Mount Dr *LCOL/BKTW* AL2 ...... 189 F3
   STSD CM24 .... 86 D4
Mounteagle *ROY* SG8 .... 21 H4
Mountfield Rd *HHNE* HP2 .... 8 B5
   LTNE LU2 .... 4 C1
Mountfitchet Rd *STSD* CM24 ...... 86 D4
Mount Garrison *HTCHE/RSTV* SG4 ... 56 D2
Mount Grace Rd *LTNE* LU2 ...... 70 D3
   POTB/CUF EN6 .... 210 B1
Mountjoy *HTCHE/RSTV* SG4 ...... 41 C8
Mount Pleasant *DEN/HRF* UB9 ... 227 C7
   HTCH/STOT SG5 .... 56 B3
   STALW/RED AL3 .... 10 B3
Mount Pleasant CI *BRKMPK* AL9 ... 171 H1

Mount Pleasant La *BRKMPK* AL9 ... 171 H1
   LCOL/BKTW AL2 .... 187 K8 🔲
Mount Pleasant Rd *LTNN/LIM* LU3 ... 68 D4
Mount Rd *HERT/WAS* SG14 ...... 150 D4
   STALE/WH AL4 .... 120 B8
Mountsorrel *HERT/BAY* SG13 ... 151 J3 🔲
The Mount *CHESW* EN7 .... 196 B4 🔲
   POTB/CUF EN6 .... 193 H8
   RKW/CH/CXG WD3 .... 218 B6
   ROY SG8 .... 22 E8
Mount Vw *ENC/FH* EN2 .... 212 C8
   LCOL/BKTW AL2 .... 190 C5
Mountview *NTHWD* HA6 .... 230 B5
Mount Vw *RKW/CH/CXG* WD3 ... 218 A8
Mountview Rd *CHESW* EN7 ...... 196 C4
Mountway *POTB/CUF* EN6 ...... 193 G8
Mount Wy *WGCE* AL7 .... 148 A6
Mountway CI *WGCE* AL7 .... 148 A6
Mowbray Crs *HTCH/STOT* SG5 ... 25 K3
Mowbray Gdns *HTCHE/RSTV* SG4 ... 56 E4
Mowbray Rd *HLW* CM20 .... 7 E2
Moxes Wd *LTNN/LIM* LU3 .... 68 D2
Moxom Av *CHES/WCR* EN8 ...... 197 J8
Mozart Ct *STVG* SG1 .... 2 A3
Muddy La *LWTH* SG6 .... 41 K6
Muirfield *LTNE* LU2 .... 69 K3
Muirfield CI *OXHEY* WD19 ...... 230 D4
   OXHEY WD19 .... 230 D4 🔲
Muirfield Gn *OXHEY* WD19 ...... 230 D3 🔲
Muirfield Rd *OXHEY* WD19 ...... 230 C3
Muirhead Wy *KNEB* SG3 .... 96 A4 🔲
Mulberry CI *BROX* EN10 .... 197 F2
   LCOL/BKTW AL2 .... 188 D6 🔲
   LTN LU1 .... 89 G2
   TRING HP23 .... 135 F4 🔲
Mulberry Ct *BSF* CM23 .... 105 K4
Mulberry Gdns *RAD* WD7 ...... 207 H3
Mulberry Gn *HLWE* CM17 ...... 157 G5
Mulberry Wy *HTCH/STOT* SG5 ... 40 B7
Mullion CI *KTN/HRWW/W* HA3... 231 J7
   LTNE LU2 .... 70 C5
Mullion Wk *OXHEY* WD19 ...... 230 E3 🔲
Mullway *LWTH* SG6 .... 41 G3
Mundells *CHESW* EN7 .... 196 E5
   WGCE AL7 .... 148 A2
Munden Gv *WATN* WD24 .... 204 D8
Munden Rd *WARE* SG12 .... 99 H2
Mundesley CI *STVGE* SG2 .... 58 B8
Mundesly CI *OXHEY* WD19 ...... 230 D3 🔲
Mungo-park CI *BUSH* WD23 ...... 231 K1 🔲
Munro Rd *BUSH* WD23 .... 221 J5
The Muntings *STVGE* SG2 .... 3 E5
Munts Meadow *HTCHE/RSTV* SG4 ... 43 J8
Murchison Rd *HOD* EN11 ...... 177 G1
Muriel Av *WATW* WD18 .... 13 D4
Murray Crs *PIN* HA5 .... 230 E7
Murray Rd *BERK* HP4 .... 161 K4
   NTHWD HA6 .... 229 K7
Murrell La *HTCH/STOT* SG5 ...... 26 A4
Murton Ct *STAL* AL1 .... 11 D3
Musgrave CI *CHESW* EN7 ...... 196 D5 🔲
Muskalls CI *CHESW* EN7 ...... 196 E5 🔲
Muskham Rd *HLW* CM20 .... 7 F1
Musk HI *HHW* HP1 .... 163 H7
Musleigh Mnr *WARE* SG12 ...... 127 K8 🔲
Musley HI *WARE* SG12 .... 127 J7
Musley La *WARE* SG12 .... 127 J7
Mussons Pth *LTNE* LU2 .... 4 C3
Muswell CI *LTNN/LIM* LU3 ...... 69 G3
Mutchetts CI *GSTN* WD25 ...... 205 F8
Mutford Cft *LTNE* LU2 .... 70 E8 🔲
Mutton La *POTB/CUF* EN6 ...... 209 J1
Myddelton Av *EN* EN1 .... 213 H8
Myddelton Rd *WARE* SG12 ...... 152 C1
Myers CI *RAD* WD7 .... 207 H2 🔲
Myles Ct *CHESW* EN7 .... 196 A7
Mylne CI *CHES/WCR* EN8 ...... 197 G5
Mymms Dr *BRKMPK* AL9 ...... 193 G5
Myrtle Gv *ENC/FH* EN2 .... 213 G8
Myrtleside CI *NTHWD* HA6 ...... 229 J5

N

Nails La *BSF* CM23 .... 105 J2 🔲
Nairn CI *HARP* AL5 .... 144 A3
Nairn Gn *OXHEY* WD19 .... 230 B2
Nancy Downs *OXHEY* WD19 ...... 13 D6
Napier CI *LCOL/BKTW* AL2 ...... 190 B3
Napier Dr *BUSH* WD23 .... 13 F3
Napier Rd *LTN* LU1 .... 4 B4 🔲
Nappsbury Rd *LTNW/LEA* LU4 ... 68 C4
Napsbury Av *LCOL/BKTW* AL2 ... 190 A4
Napsbury La *LCOL/BKTW* AL2 ... 189 J5
   STAL AL1 .... 189 J1
The Nap *KGLGY* WD4 .... 186 A7
Nascot CI *HARP* AL5 .... 144 A3
Nascot Rd *WAT* WD17 .... 12 C1
Nascot St *WAT* WD17 .... 12 C1
Nascot Wood Rd *WAT* WD17 ... 204 A7
Naseby Rd *LTN* LU1 .... 89 G2
Nash CI *BORE* WD6 .... 223 J4
   BRKMPK AL9 .... 192 D1

STVGE SG2 3 F2
Nash Mills La HHS/BOV HP3 185 K4
Nash Rd ROY SG8 21 H4 3
Nathaniel Wk TRING HP23 135 F4
Nathans Cl WLYN AL6 122 C2
Nayland Cl LTNE LU2 71 F8 3
Nazeingbury Cl WAB EN9 177 J8 1
Nazeing Common WAB EN9 199 J1
Neal Cl NTHWD HA6 230 B7
Neal Ct HERT/WAS SG14 151 F3
Neal St WATW WD18 13 D4
Neaole Cl BORE WD6 224 B1 2
Necton Rd STALE/WH AL4 145 H1
Needham Rd LTNW/LEA LU4 68 A3
Neild Wy RKW/CH/CXG WD3 217 J7
Nell Gwynn Cl RAD WD7 207 H2
Nelson Av STAL AL1 189 K1
Nelson Rd BERK HP4 112 E4
BSF CM23 105 K4
Nelson St HERT/WAS SG14 150 E2 1
Neptune Dr HHNE HP2 8 B3
Neptune Ga STVGE SG2 59 K8
Neston Rd WATN WD24 204 D7
Netherby Cl TRING HP23 135 G3
Nethercott Cl LTNE LU2 70 D8 1
Netherfield La WARE SG12 153 J6
Netherfield Rd HARP AL5 143 J5
Netherhall Rd HLWW/ROY CM19 178 A3
Netherstones HTCH/STOT SG5 25 K2 1
Nether St WARE SG12 130 A4
Netherway STALW/RED AL3 188 C1
Netley Dell LWTH SG6 42 B6
Netteswellbury Farm HLWS CM18 7 E5 1
Netteswell Orch HLW CM20 6 C3
Netteswell Rd HLW CM20 7 D2
Nettlecroft HHW HP1 164 A7
WGCE AL7 148 C2 4
Nettleden Rd BERK HP4 137 K2
Nevell's Gn LWTH SG6 41 K2
Nevells Rd LWTH SG6 41 K3
Nevil Cl NTHWD HA6 229 J4
Neville Cl POTB/CUF EN6 210 A1
Neville Rd LTNN/LIM LU3 69 F4
Nevill Gv WATN WD24 220 C1
Newark Cl ROY SG8 21 G1
Newark Gn BORE WD6 224 D3
Newark Rd LTNW/LEA LU4 69 F7
New Barnes Av STAL AL1 189 J1
New Barn La RBSF CM22 106 B8
New Barns La MHAD SG10 103 F5
New Bedford Rd LTN LU1 4 B3 2
Newberries Av RAD WD7 206 E5
Newbiggin Pth OXHEY WD19 230 D3 3
Newbold Rd LTNN/LIM LU3 69 G2
Newbury Av PEND EN3 214 E7
Newbury Cl BSF CM23 105 H1
LTNW/LEA LU4 68 D7
STVG SG1 58 D8 1
Newcastle Cl STVG SG1 59 F7 2
New Cl KNEB SG3 96 A3
Newcombe Rd LTN LU1 4 A4
Newcome Rd RAD WD7 207 K4
New Cottages BRKMPK AL9 192 D6
New Ct KNEB SG3 96 B7 3
Newdigate Gn DEN/HRF UB9 228 C7
Newdigate Rd DEN/HRF UB9 228 B7
Newdigate Rd East DEN/HRF UB9 228 C7
Newell La STVGE SG2 60 E2
Newell Ri HHS/BOV HP3 185 J1
Newell Rd HHS/BOV HP3 185 J1
Newells LWTH SG6 42 D5
Newells Hedge LBUZ LU7 110 D4 1
New England Cl
HTCHE/RSTV SG4 56 D5 1
New England St STALW/RED AL3 10 B4
New Farm La NTHWD HA6 229 K7
Newfield La HHNE HP2 8 C5
Newfields WGCW AL8 147 G4
Newfield Wy STALE/WH AL4 169 G8 1
Newford Cl HHNE HP2 9 E4
New Ford Rd CHES/WCR EN8 214 E4
Newgate STVGE SG2 3 E5
Newgate Cl STALE/WH AL4 169 G3
Newgate St HERT/BAY SG13 195 F1
Newgatestreet Rd CHESW EN7 195 K4
Newgate Street Village
HERT/BAY SG13 195 G3
New Greens Av STALW/RED AL3 168 A1
Newground Rd TRING HP23 136 C6
Newhall Cl HHS/BOV HP3 183 J5 2
Newhouse Crs GSTN WD25 204 C3
New House Pk STAL AL1 189 J1
Newhouse Rd HHW HP1 183 J4
New Inn Rd BLDK SG7 16 D5
New Kent Rd STAL AL1 10 C4 5
Newland Cl PIN HA5 231 F5
STAL AL1 189 J1
Newlands LWTH SG6 42 A6
Newlands Av RAD WD7 206 C4
Newlands Cl East
HTCHE/RSTV SG4 56 D5 2
Newlands Cl West
HTCHE/RSTV SG4 56 D5 3
Newlands La HTCHE/RSTV SG4 56 D5
Newlands Pl BAR EN5 225 J5
Newlands Rd HHW HP1 163 H5
LTN LU1 89 H6
Newlands Wk GSTN WD25 204 E3
Newlands Wy POTB/CUF EN6 193 H8 1
Newlyn Cl LCOL/BKTW AL2 188 A8
STVG SG1 75 F3
Newman Av ROY SG8 21 K3
Newmans Dr HARP AL5 118 B7
Newmarket Rd ROY SG8 21 J3
Newnham Cl LTNE LU2 70 E8
Newnham Rd BLDK SG7 26 D4
Newnham Wy BLDK SG7 17 G8
New Park Dr HHNE HP2 9 E4
New Park La STVGE SG2 77 F7
New Park Rd DEN/HRF UB9 228 B7
HERT/BAY SG13 194 E2
New Pl WLYN AL6 122 B5 3
Newport Cl PEND EN3 214 D7 5
Newport Md OXHEY WD19 230 E3 6
Newports SBW CM21 132 A8
Newquay Gdns OXHEY WD19 230 C1
New River Av WARE SG12 153 G5
New River Cl HOD EN11 177 G2
New Rd BERK HP4 161 G2
BERK HP4 162 A4
BROX EN10 176 E5
CSTG HP8 216 B3
GSTN WD25 222 B1
HERT/WAS SG14 151 G1
HLWE CM17 157 G5
KGLGY WD4 184 D8
KNEB SG3 96 C6
POTB/CUF EN6 209 F3
RAD WD7 206 B6
RAD WD7 207 K4
RKW/CH/CXG WD3 217 J1
RKW/CH/CXG WD3 219 F5
ROY SG8 15 H4
STDN SG11 103 H2
TRING HP23 109 G8
TRING HP23 135 G3
WARE SG12 127 J8
WAT WD17 13 D3
WGCW AL8 147 F6
WLYN AL6 123 F6
Newstead HAT AL10 170 E7
New St BERK HP4 162 A5
LBUZ LU7 109 K2
LTN LU1 4 B5
SBW CM21 132 C6
WATW WD18 13 D3 10
Newteswell Dr WAB EN9 215 J2
Newton Cl HARP AL5 144 A3 5
HOD EN11 153 G7
Newton Crs BORE WD6 224 B4 2
Newtondale LTNW/LEA LU4 68 B4 4
Newton Dr SBW CM21 132 B8
Newton Rd STVGE SG2 3 F2
Newtons Wy HTCHE/RSTV SG4 56 D3
New Town WLYN AL6 94 E8
Newtown Rd BSF CM23 105 J3
New Town Rd LTN LU1 4 C5 5
New Town St LTN LU1 4 C5
New Wd WGCE AL7 148 D2
Niagara Cl CHES/WCR EN8 197 H7 1
Nicholas Cl STALW/RED AL3 10 C1
WATN WD24 204 C7
Nicholas La HERT/WAS SG14 151 G3 11
Nicholas Pl STVG SG1 58 D8
Nicholas Rd BORE WD6 223 J6
Nicholas Wy HHNE HP2 8 C3 1
NTHWD HA6 229 H7
Nicholls Cl AMP/FLIT/B MK45 36 B6
STALW/RED AL3 142 A4
Nicholls Fld HLWS CM18 180 E2
Nichols Cl LTNE LU2 5 F1
Nicholson Dr BUSH WD23 221 K8
Nicky Line HHNE HP2 8 B5
STALW/RED AL3 141 K8
Nicoll Wy BORE WD6 224 C5
Nightingale Cl ABLGY WD5 204 B1 2
LTNE LU2 70 D3
RAD WD7 206 C6
Nightingale La STAL AL1 190 A2
STALE/WH AL4 190 A1
Nightingale Pl
RKW/CH/CXG WD3 218 C7 2
Nightingale Rd BUSH WD23 221 H5
CHESW EN7 196 A3
HTCH/STOT SG5 56 D1
RKW/CH/CXG WD3 218 B7
Nightingales La CSTG HP8 216 A5
Nightingale Wk STVGE SG2 76 D4
Nightingale Wy BLDK SG7 42 E3
Nimbus Wy HTCHE/RSTV SG4 57 G2 2
Nimrod Cl STALE/WH AL4 169 F4
Ninesprings Wy HTCHE/RSTV SG4 57 G3
Ninian Rd HHNE HP2 164 D1
Ninning's La WLYN AL6 95 J7
Ninnings Rd CFSP/GDCR SL9 226 C6
Ninnings Wy CFSP/GDCR SL9 226 C6 3
Ninth Av LTNN/LIM LU3 68 C2
Niton Cl BAR EN5 225 J6
Niven Cl BORE WD6 224 B1 3
The Nobles BSF CM23 105 G3 1
Nodes Dr STVGE SG2 76 B8
Noke La LCOL/BKTW AL2 188 A4
Noke Shot HARP AL5 118 E5
Noke Side LCOL/BKTW AL2 188 C5
Nokeside STVGE SG2 96 C
The Nokes HHW HP1 163 K4
The Noke STVGE SG2 96 C
The Nook WARE SG12 153 G5
Norbury Av WATN WD24 220 D
Norfolk Av WATN WD24 204 D
Norfolk Gdns BORE WD6 224 C
Norfolk Rd BUNT SG9 63 H
LTNE LU2 5 E
RKW/CH/CXG WD3 218 D
Norfolk Wy BSF CM23 105 J
Norman Av BSF CM23 105 G
Norman Cl WAB EN9 215 J
Norman Ct POTB/CUF EN6 193 J
Norman Crs PIN HA5 230 D
Normandy Ct HHNE HP2 8 A4
Normandy Dr BERK HP4 161 H
Normandy Rd STALW/RED AL3 10 C
Norman Rd AMP/FLIT/B MK45 36 C
LTNN/LIM LU3 69 G
WLYN AL6 122 B6
Normans Cl LWTH SG6 25 K
Normansfield Cl BUSH WD23 221 J7
Normans La WLYN AL6 95 K
Norman's Wy STSD CM24 86 D
Norris Cl BSF CM23 106 B
Norris Gv BROX EN10 176 D
Norris La HOD EN11 177 F
Norris Ri HOD EN11 176 E
Norris Rd HOD EN11 177 F
North Ap GSTN WD25 204 B
RKW/CH/CXG WD3 229 H
North Av LWTH SG6 42 B
RAD WD7 207 H
Northaw Cl HHNE HP2 165 G
Northaw Rd West POTB/CUF EN6 194 C
North Barn BROX EN10 177 G
North Bridge Rd BERK HP4 161 G
Northbrook Dr NTHWD HA6 229 K
North Brook End ROY SG8 15 J
Northbrook Rd BAR EN5 225 K
Northbrooks HLWW/ROY CM19 6 A
Northchurch La CSHM HP5 160 D
North Cl BAR EN5 225 H
LCOL/BKTW AL2 188 D
ROY SG8 21 G
North Common Rd
STALW/RED AL3 142 E
Northcourt RKW/CH/CXG WD3 217 K8
Northdown Rd CFSP/GDCR SL9 226 B
HAT AL10 171 F
North Drift Wy LTN LU1 89 C
North Dr STDN SG11 100 E
Northend HHS/BOV HP3 165 C
Northfield STDN SG11 82 A2
Northfield Gdns WATN WD24 204 D
Northfield Rd BLDK SG7 17
BORE WD6 224 A
CHES/WCR EN8 214 D
HARP AL5 118 E
SBW CM21 132 C
TRING HP23 135 K
Northfields LWTH SG6 25 K
North Ga HLW CM20 6 B3
Northgate NTHWD HA6 229 H
Northgate End BSF CM23 105
Northgate Pth BORE WD6 207 J8
North Gv HLWS CM18 7 F
North Hl RKW/CH/CXG WD3 217 H
Northlands POTB/CUF EN6 210 E
Northolt Av BSF CM23 86 A
North Orbital Rd LCOL/BKTW AL2 188 A
STALE/WH AL4 170 E
North Orbital Road St Albans Rd
GSTN WD25 204 E
North Pl HLW CM20 156 D
WAB EN9 215 G3
North Ride WLYN AL6 122 C
Northridge Wy HHW HP1 163
North Riding LCOL/BKTW AL2 188
North Rd BERK HP4 161
BLDK SG7 26
CHES/WCR EN8 214
HERT/WAS SG14 150
HOD EN11 177
RKW/CH/CXG WD3 217
STVG SG1 58
North Road Av HERT/WAS SG14 150
North Road Gdns HERT/WAS SG14 150
North St BSF CM23 105
LTNE LU2 4
WAB EN9 177
North Ter BSF CM23 105
Northumberland Av EN EN1 214
Northview Rd LTNE LU2 5
Northway RKW/CH/CXG WD3 218
WGCE AL7 123 F8
Northwell Dr LTNN/LIM LU3 68
North Western Av GSTN WD25 204
WATN WD24 204

North Western Avenue Colne Wy
WATN WD24 204 D6
North Western Avenue Elton Wy
GSTN WD25 221 J2
North Western Avenue Gade Side
KGLGY WD4 203 H5
WAT WD17 203 J5
North Western Avenue
Otterspool Wy GSTN WD25 205 G8
North Western Avenue
(Tylers Way) BUSH WD23 221 K4
North Western Avenue
(Watford By-pass) STAN HA7 222 D6
Northwick Rd OXHEY WD19 230 D3
Northwood WGCE AL7 148 E3 2
Northwood Cl CHESW EN7 196 D5 6
Northwood Rd DEN/HRF UB9 228 D7
Northwood Wy DEN/HRF UB9 228 C7
NTHWD HA6 230 B6
Nortoft Rd CFSP/GDCR SL9 226 C5
Norton Bury La LWTH SG6 26 C7
Norton Cl BORE WD6 223 K1
Norton Crs BLDK SG7 42 E1
Norton Green Rd STVG SG1 2 A5
Norton Mill La LWTH SG6 26 D6
Norton Rd HTCH/STOT SG5 26 A4
LTNN/LIM LU3 68 E5
LWTH SG6 42 A1
STVG SG1 2 B4
Nortonstreet La HTCHE/RSTV SG4 94 B2
Norton Wy North LWTH SG6 42 A1
Norton Wy South LWTH SG6 42 A3
Norvic Rd TRING HP23 110 A8
Norwich Cl STVG SG1 59 H8
Norwich Wy RKW/CH/CXG WD3 219 G3
Norwood Cl HERT/WAS SG14 150 C2
Norwood Rd CHES/WCR EN8 197 J8
Nottingham Cl GSTN WD25 204 B3 2
Nottingham Rd
RKW/CH/CXG WD3 217 F8
Novello Wy BORE WD6 224 C1
Nugent's Pk PIN HA5 231 F7
Nunnery Cl STAL AL1 11 D6
Nunnery La LTNN/LIM LU3 69 G4
Nunnery Stables STAL AL1 10 C6
Nunsbury Dr BROX EN10 197 J3 2
Nun's Cl HTCH/STOT SG5 56 C2
Nuns La STAL AL1 189 G2
Nupton Dr BAR EN5 225 H6
Nurseries Rd STALE/WH AL4 145 H2
Nursery Cl STVGE SG2 96 B1
Nursery Flds SBW CM21 132 B7
Nursery Gdns TRING HP23 135 G5
WGCE AL7 122 E8 2
Nursery Hl WGCE AL7 123 F8 3
Nursery Rd BROX EN10 197 J3 3
BSF CM23 105 J3
HOD EN11 153 G8
LTNN/LIM LU3 68 E4
WAB EN9 177 J8
Nutcroft KNEB SG3 96 E7
Nutfield WGCE AL7 123 G8
Nut Gv WGCW AL8 122 D8
Nuthampstead Rd ROY SG8 32 D7
Nutleigh Gv HTCH/STOT SG5 40 B8
Nut Slip BUNT SG9 63 J3 2
Nuttfield Cl RKW/CH/CXG WD3 219 G6 1
Nye Wy HHS/BOV HP3 183 J6
Nymans Cl LTNE LU2 70 E6

O

Oak Av LCOL/BKTW AL2 188 C8
Oak Cl HHS/BOV HP3 185 K2
WAB EN9 215 J4
Oakcroft Cl PIN HA5 230 C8 2
Oakdale WGCW AL8 122 D8
Oakdale Av NTHWD HA6 230 B8
Oakdale Cl OXHEY WD19 230 D3
Oakdale Rd OXHEY WD19 230 D2
Oakdene CHES/WCR EN8 197 J8
Oakdene Cl PIN HA5 231 G6
Oakdene Rd HHS/BOV HP3 185 K2
WATN WD24 204 C6
Oakdene Wy STAL AL1 169 F6
Oak Dr BERK HP4 162 A6
SBW CM21 157 F1
Oak End BUNT SG9 63 H3
HLWS CM18 7 E6 2
Oaken Gv WGCE AL7 147 K6 4
Oak Farm BORE WD6 224 B5
Oakfield RKW/CH/CXG WD3 217 K7
Oakfield Av HTCHE/RSTV SG4 57 F4
Oakfield Cl POTB/CUF EN6 210 A1 1
Oakfield Rd HARP AL5 143 G4
Oakfields STVGE SG2 76 C8
Oakfields Av KNEB SG3 96 B3
Oakfields Cl STVGE SG2 76 D8
Oakfields Rd KNEB SG3 96 B3
Oak Gld NTHWD HA6 229 G7
Oak Gn ABLGY WD5 203 K2
Oak Gv HAT AL10 170 E4
HERT/BAY SG13 151 H5
Oakhill LWTH SG6 42 D5
Oakhill Av PIN HA5 231 F8
Oakhill Cl RKW/CH/CXG WD3 227 H3
Oakhill Dr WLYN AL6 122 A3
Oakhill Rd RKW/CH/CXG WD3 227 G3
Oakhurst Av HARP AL5 143 G3
Oakhurst Rd PEND EN3 214 C6
Oakington WGCE AL7 148 E3 3
Oakington Av AMS HP6 216 B1
Oaklands BERK HP4 161 H5
Oaklands Av BRKMPK AL9 192 E5
OXHEY WD19 220 C8
Oaklands Cl BSF CM23 86 A7
Oaklands Ct WAT WD17 220 B1
Oaklands Dr BSF CM23 86 A8
HLWE CM17 181 F2
Oaklands Ga NTHWD HA6 229 K5 2
Oaklands Gv BROX EN10 197 J2
Oaklands La BAR EN5 225 G4
STALE/WH AL4 169 J4
Oaklands Pk BSF CM23 86 A7
Oaklands Ri WLYN AL6 123 F1
Oaklands Rd CHESW EN7 196 C4
Oak La HTCHE/RSTV SG4 58 B5
POTB/CUF EN6 195 H6
TRING HP23 159 F7
Oaklea WLYN AL6 122 E2
Oaklea Cl WLYN AL6 122 E1
Oaklea Wd WLYN AL6 122 E2
Oakleigh Dr RKW/CH/CXG WD3 219 H6
Oakleigh Rd PIN HA5 231 G5
Oakley Cl LTNW/LEA LU4 68 C5
Oakley Rd HARP AL5 144 A2
LTNW/LEA LU4 68 C5
Oakmeade PIN HA5 231 H5
Oakmere Av POTB/CUF EN6 210 D3
Oakmere Cl POTB/CUF EN6 210 E1
Oakmere La POTB/CUF EN6 210 D2
Oak Piece WLYN AL6 122 D2
Oakridge LCOL/BKTW AL2 188 B7
Oakridge Av RAD WD7 206 C3
Oakridge La GSTN WD25 206 B4
Oak Rd KNEB SG3 96 C8
LTN LU1 4 A3
Oakroyd Av POTB/CUF EN6 210 A3
Oakroyd Cl POTB/CUF EN6 210 A4
Oaks Cl HTCHE/RSTV SG4 56 D4
RAD WD7 206 C5
Oaks Cross STVGE SG2 96 C1
The Oaks BERK HP4 161 H5
LTN LU1 89 H8
OXHEY WD19 220 D8
Oak St BSF CM23 105 J3
HHS/BOV HP3 185 K2
Oak Tree Cl ABLGY WD5 203 J2
Oaktree Cl BSF CM23 105 J2
Oak Tree Cl HAT AL10 171 F3
HERT/BAY SG13 152 B6
STVGE SG2 78 C5 1
Oak Tree Ct BORE WD6 223 G6 4
Oaktree Garth WGCE AL7 147 K4 4
Oakview Cl CHESW EN7 197 F6
Oakway DUN/WHIP LU6 113 K2
Oak Wy HARP AL5 143 H4
Oakwell Cl STVGE SG2 96 E2
Oakwell Dr POTB/CUF EN6 211 J3
Oak Wd BERK HP4 161 G6
Oakwood Av BORE WD6 224 A4
Oakwood Cl STVGE SG2 76 D7
Oakwood Dr LTNN/LIM LU3 68 B1
STALE/WH AL4 169 F5
Oakwood Rd LCOL/BKTW AL2 188 B7
PIN HA5 230 C8
Oberon Cl BORE WD6 224 B1
Obrey Wy BSF CM23 105 H6
Occupation Rd WATW WD18 12 C4
Octavia Ct WATN WD24 13 D1 4
Oddy Hl TRING HP23 135 H6
Odessey Rd BORE WD6 224 A1
Offa Rd STALW/RED AL3 10 B4
Offas Wy STALE/WH AL4 145 G1
Offley Hl HTCH/STOT SG5 54 E6
Offley Rd HTCH/STOT SG5 56 B3
Ogard Rd HOD EN11 177 H1
Okeford Cl TRING HP23 134 E5
Okeford Dr TRING HP23 134 E6
Okeley La TRING HP23 134 D6
Old Barn La RKW/CH/CXG WD3 218 E5
Old Bedford Rd LTN LU1 4 C3 2
Old Bell Cl STSD CM24 86 C3
Old Bourne Wy STVG SG1 59 G6
Old Brewery Cl HTCH/STOT SG5 25 K2 2
Old Burylodge La STSD CM24 87 F5
Old Chantry La STVG SG1 58 A7
Old Charlton Rd HTCH/STOT SG5 56 C3
Old Church La WARE SG12 127 J2
The Old Coach Rd
HERT/WAS SG14 149 G6
Old Crabtree La HHS/BOV HP3 8 B6
Old Cross HERT/WAS SG14 151 F3 6
Old Cross B158 HERT/WAS SG14 151 F3 7
Old Dean HHS/BOV HP3 183 J5
The Old Dr WGCW AL8 147 G4
Olden Md LWTH SG6 42 B6
Old Farm LBUZ LU7 110 D5
Old Field Cl AMS HP6 216 B1
Oldfield Ri HTCHE/RSTV SG4 93 H2
Oldfield Rd HHW HP1 163 H7
LCOL/BKTW AL2 190 B3
Old Fishery La HHW HP1 163 J8
Old Fold Vw BAR EN5 225 H3
Old Forge Cl GSTN WD25 204 B3
WGCE AL7 123 F7
Old Forge Rd EN EN1 213 J8
Old French Horn La HAT AL10 171 G3
Old Gannon Cl NTHWD HA6 229 H3
Old Hale Wy HTCH/STOT SG5 40 C8
Old Hall Cl PIN HA5 231 F7
Old Hall Dr PIN HA5 231 F7
Old Hall Ri HLWE CM17 181 H1
Oldhall St HERT/WAS SG14 151 G3 12
Old Harpenden Rd
STALW/RED AL3 168 B2
Old Herns La WGCE AL7 148 D1
Old Hertford Rd BRKMPK AL9 171 H2
Old Hwy HOD EN11 177 G1
Oldhouse Cft HLW CM20 7 D2
Old House La HLWW/ROY CM19 178 E4
KGLGY WD4 203 F5
Old House Rd HHNE HP2 8 C5
Oldings Cnr HAT AL10 147 G8
Old Knebworth La KNEB SG3 95 H3
Old La KNEB SG3 96 C4
Old Leys HAT AL10 171 F8
Old London Rd HERT/BAY SG13 151 H3
STAL AL1 11 D5
The Old Maltings BSF CM23 105 K2 2
Old Maple HHNE HP2 140 E8
Old Md CFSP/GDCR SL9 226 B5
Old Mill Gdns BERK HP4 162 A5
Old Mill La RBSF CM22 133 F3
Old Mill Rd KGLGY WD4 203 H4
Old Nazeing Rd BROX EN10 177 F7
WAB EN9 177 H8
Old North Rd ROY SG8 21 G1
Old Oak STAL AL1 189 G1
Old Oak Cl ARL/CHE SG15 24 E1
Old Oaks WAB EN9 215 K2 3
Old Orch HLWS CM18 6 C6
LCOL/BKTW AL2 189 F4
LTN LU1 4 B6
Old Orchard Ms BERK HP4 161 K6 1
Old Parkbury La LCOL/BKTW AL2 189 H7
Oldpark Ride CHESW EN7 213 G2
Old Park Rd HTCH/STOT SG5 56 C2
Old Rectory Cl HARP AL5 118 C7 2
Old Rectory Dr HAT AL10 171 G4 1
Old Rectory Gdns STALE/WH AL4 120 B8
Old Redding KTN/HRWW/W HA3 231 J4
Old River La BSF CM23 105 J2 5
Old Rd AMP/FLIT/B MK45 36 C8
HLWE CM17 157 F3
Old's Ap WATW WD18 219 H8
Old School Cl HTCHE/RSTV SG4 94 E8
Old School Gdns
AMP/FLIT/B MK45 36 C7 1
Old School Gn STVGE SG2 78 B4
Old School Wk ARL/CHE SG15 24 E5
Old's Cl WATW WD18 219 G8
Old Shire La CFSP/GDCR SL9 226 E2
RKW/CH/CXG WD3 216 D6
Old Shire Lane Circular Wk
RKW/CH/CXG WD3 217 F7
Old Sopwell Gdns STAL AL1 11 D6
Old South Cl PIN HA5 230 E7
Old Uxbridge Rd
RKW/CH/CXG WD3 227 H6
Old Vicarage Gdns
STALW/RED AL3 115 H3 1
The Old Walled Gdn STVG SG1 58 C8
Old Watford Rd LCOL/BKTW AL2 188 A8
Old Watling St STALW/RED AL3 116 B5
Oldwood WLYN AL6 122 E2
Oliver Cl HHS/BOV HP3 185 J2
LCOL/BKTW AL2 189 F5
Oliver Ri HHS/BOV HP3 185 J2
Oliver Rd HHS/BOV HP3 185 K2
Olivers Cl BERK HP4 163 F2
Oliver's La HTCH/STOT SG5 25 K2
Olivia Gdns DEN/HRF UB9 228 B7
Olleberrie La RKW/CH/CXG WD3 201 H2
Olwen Ms PIN HA5 230 E8
Onslow Cl HAT AL10 171 G4
Onslow Rd LTNW/LEA LU4 68 C4
On the Hl OXHEY WD19 231 F1
The Opening WLYN AL6 121 K1 1
Openshaw Wy LWTH SG6 42 A3
Oram Pl HHS/BOV HP3 185 H1
Orbital Crs GSTN WD25 204 A5
Orchard BUSH WD23 222 A8
Orchard Av BERK HP4 161 H5
GSTN WD25 204 C1
HARP AL5 118 B8
Orchard Cl AMP/FLIT/B MK45 36 C8
BORE WD6 223 J3 1
HHNE HP2 8 C3
HTCHE/RSTV SG4 56 D6
LWTH SG6 41 K1
POTB/CUF EN6 195 G6

RAD WD7 .... 206 B7
RKW/CH/CXG WD3 .... 217 G3
STAL AL1 .... 11 E5
WARE SG12 .... 127 H7 4
WARE SG12 .... 153 H5
WAT WD17 .... 12 A1
Orchard Crs *STVG* SG1 .... 2 A1
Orchard Cft *HLW* CM20 .... 7 F2
Orchard Dr *LCOL/BKTW* AL2 .... 188 D4
RKW/CH/CXG WD3 .... 217 F3
WAT WD17 .... 220 A1
Orchard Gdns *WAB* EN9 .... 215 G4
Orchard House La *STAL* AL1 .... 10 C5
Orchard Md *HAT* AL10 .... 170 E4
The Orchard on the Gn
RKW/CH/CXG WD3 .... 218 E5
Orchard Rd *BAR* EN5 .... 225 K4
BLDK SG7 .... 42 E1
BSF CM23 .... 86 A8
HTCHE/RSTV SG4 .... 41 F8
ROY SG8 .... 21 F2
STVG SG1 .... 75 G1
WLYN AL6 .... 122 C4 4
Orchard Sq *BROX* EN10 .... 197 K2 1
The Orchards *LTN* LU1 .... 89 H7
SBW CM21 .... 132 C7 4
TRING HP23 .... 134 E6
Orchard St *HHS/BOV* HP3 .... 185 H1 2
STALW/RED AL3 .... 10 B5
The Orchard *BLDK* SG7 .... 43 F1
HERT/WAS SG14 .... 125 K8
KGLGY WD4 .... 186 A7
WARE SG12 .... 126 C2
WGCW AL8 .... 147 J1
WLYN AL6 .... 94 D8
Orchard Wy *CHESW* EN7 .... 195 K5
HHS/BOV HP3 .... 183 J6
HTCHE/RSTV SG4 .... 72 B8
KNEB SG3 .... 95 K4
LBUZ LU7 .... 110 E4
LTNW/LEA LU4 .... 68 B5
LWTH SG6 .... 41 K1
POTB/CUF EN6 .... 193 H6
RKW/CH/CXG WD3 .... 217 K7
ROY SG8 .... 21 G1
Ordelmere *LWTH* SG6 .... 25 K8
Ordnance Rd *PEND* EN3 .... 214 C7
Oregon Wy *LTNN/LIM* LU3 .... 69 F1
Organ Hall Rd *BORE* WD6 .... 223 H1
Orient Cl *STAL* AL1 .... 11 D6
Oriole Cl *ABLGY* WD5 .... 204 B1 3
Oriole Wy *BSF* CM23 .... 105 F3
Orion Wy *NTHWD* HA6 .... 230 A3
Orlando Cl *HTCHE/RSTV* SG4 .... 56 E3 4
Ormesby Dr *POTB/CUF* EN6 .... 209 J2
Ormonde Rd *NTHWD* HA6 .... 229 J3
Ormsby Cl *LTN* LU1 .... 4 C6
Ormskirk Rd *OXHEY* WD19 .... 230 E3
Oronsay *HHS/BOV* HP3 .... 165 G8
Orphanage Rd *WAT* WD17 .... 13 D1 5
Orton Cl *STALE/WH* AL4 .... 168 D2
Orwell Ct *WATN* WD24 .... 13 E1 5
Orwell Vw *BLDK* SG7 .... 27 H8
Osborne Gdns *POTB/CUF* EN6 .... 193 H8 2
Osborne Rd *BROX* EN10 .... 177 F5
CHES/WCR EN8 .... 197 J5 2
LTN LU1 .... 5 D5
POTB/CUF EN6 .... 193 H8
WATN WD24 .... 204 D8 3
Osborne Wy *TRING* HP23 .... 135 J8
Osborn Rd *AMP/FLIT/B* MK45 .... 36 D6
Osborn Wy *WGCW* AL8 .... 147 J2 1
Osbourne Av *KGLGY* WD4 .... 185 K6
Osmington Pl *TRING* HP23 .... 134 E5
Osprey Gdns *STVGE* SG2 .... 76 E7
Osterley Cl *STVGE* SG2 .... 96 D2
Oster St *STALW/RED* AL3 .... 10 B3
Ostler Cl *BSF* CM23 .... 105 F5 4
Ostler's Gn *SAFWS* CB11 .... 35 K4
Oswald Rd *STAL* AL1 .... 11 D5
Otley Wy *OXHEY* WD19 .... 230 D2
Otter Gdns *HAT* AL10 .... 171 G5
Otterspool La *GSTN* WD25 .... 205 F8
Otterspool Wy *GSTN* WD25 .... 221 G1
Otterton Cl *HARP* AL5 .... 118 B6 4
Ottoman Ter *WAT* WD17 .... 13 D2 4
Ottway Wk *WLYN* AL6 .... 122 B5
Otway Gdns *BUSH* WD23 .... 222 B7
Otways Cl *POTB/CUF* EN6 .... 210 C3 1
Oudle La *MHAD* SG10 .... 103 G6
Oughtonhead La *HTCH/STOT* SG5 .... 55 K1
Oughton Head Wy *HTCH/STOT* SG5 .... 56 B1
Oulton Crs *POTB/CUF* EN6 .... 209 J2
Oulton Ri *HARP* AL5 .... 118 E6
Oulton Wy *OXHEY* WD19 .... 231 G3
Oundle Av *BUSH* WD23 .... 221 K6
Oundle Ct *STVGE* SG2 .... 96 D1
Oundle Pth *STVGE* SG2 .... 96 D1
The Oundle *STVGE* SG2 .... 76 D8
Ousden Cl *CHES/WCR* EN8 .... 197 J8
Ousden Dr *CHES/WCR* EN8 .... 197 J8
Ouseley Cl *LTNW/LEA* LU4 .... 68 C6
Outfield Rd *CFSP/GDCR* SL9 .... 226 A6 1
Outlook Dr *CSTG* HP8 .... 226 A2
The Oval *BROX* EN10 .... 197 J3
HNLW SG16 .... 24 A6
Overfield Rd *LTNE* LU2 .... 70 D8
Overlord Cl *BROX* EN10 .... 176 D6 2
Overstone Rd *HARP* AL5 .... 118 E8 1
LTNW/LEA LU4 .... 68 C8
Overstream *RKW/CH/CXG* WD3 .... 218 A4
Oving Cl *LTNE* LU2 .... 70 E7
Owen Jones Cl *HNLW* SG16 .... 24 A4
Owens Wy *RKW/CH/CXG* WD3 .... 219 F5
Owles La *BUNT* SG9 .... 63 K3
Oxcroft *BSF* CM23 .... 105 J6
Oxendon Dr *HOD* EN11 .... 177 F4
Oxen Rd *LTNE* LU2 .... 5 D2
Oxfield Cl *BERK* HP4 .... 161 H6
Oxford Av *STAL* AL1 .... 169 F7
Oxford Cl *CHES/WCR* EN8 .... 197 G7
NTHWD HA6 .... 229 H3
Oxford Rd *HTCHE/RSTV* SG4 .... 72 B8
LTN LU1 .... 4 C5 6
Oxford St *WATW* WD18 .... 12 C4
Oxhey Av *OXHEY* WD19 .... 13 E6
Oxhey Dr *OXHEY* WD19 .... 230 C3
Oxhey La *OXHEY* WD19 .... 13 E6
PIN HA5 .... 231 H4
Oxhey Ridge Cl *OXHEY* WD19 .... 230 B4
Oxhey Rd *OXHEY* WD19 .... 13 D6
Ox La *HARP* AL5 .... 118 D6
Oxlease Dr *HAT* AL10 .... 171 G5
Oxleys Rd *STVGE* SG2 .... 3 F5
The Oxleys *HLWE* CM17 .... 157 G5
Oysterfields *STALW/RED* AL3 .... 10 A3

P

Pacatian Wy *STVGE* SG2 .... 76 D1
Packhorse Cl *STALE/WH* AL4 .... 169 F3
Packhorse La *RAD* WD7 .... 208 C1
Paddick Cl *HOD* EN11 .... 176 E2
Paddock Cl *LWTH* SG6 .... 41 K4
OXHEY WD19 .... 13 F5
WARE SG12 .... 129 K8
Paddock La *BAR* EN5 .... 224 D4
Paddock Md *HLWS* CM18 .... 179 K6
Paddock Rd *BUNT* SG9 .... 63 J1
Paddocks Cl *STVGE* SG2 .... 3 F5
The Paddocks *HERT/BAY* SG13 .... 152 A6 1
RKW/CH/CXG WD3 .... 217 J4
STALE/WH AL4 .... 119 K3
STVGE SG2 .... 3 F5
WGCE AL7 .... 148 C3 2
WLYN AL6 .... 94 E8 5
The Paddock *BROX* EN10 .... 177 F6
BSF CM23 .... 105 G6 2
CFSP/GDCR SL9 .... 226 B4
HAT AL10 .... 171 F3 1
HTCHE/RSTV SG4 .... 56 E4 1
Paddock Wd *HARP* AL5 .... 144 B2
Pageant Rd *STAL* AL1 .... 10 C5
Page Cl *BLDK* SG7 .... 43 F3
Page Hl *WARE* SG12 .... 127 F7
Page Rd *HERT/BAY* SG13 .... 151 K3
Pages Cl *BSF* CM23 .... 105 J4 1
Pages Cft *BERK* HP4 .... 161 H3 5
Paignton Cl *LTNW/LEA* LU4 .... 68 C5 2
Paine's La *PIN* HA5 .... 231 F8
Paines Orch *LBUZ* LU7 .... 110 A1
Painters La *PEND* EN3 .... 214 D5
Palace Cl *KGLGY* WD4 .... 185 K8
Palace Gdns *BSF* CM23 .... 105 H4 1
ROY SG8 .... 21 G3
Palfrey Cl *STALW/RED* AL3 .... 10 C2
Pallas Rd *HHNE* HP2 .... 8 C3
Palmer Av *BUSH* WD23 .... 221 J6
Palmer Cl *HERT/WAS* SG14 .... 151 F1
Palmer Gdns *BAR* EN5 .... 225 J5 2
Palmer Rd *HERT/WAS* SG14 .... 151 G1
Palmers Gv *WAB* EN9 .... 178 A8
Palmers Rd *BORE* WD6 .... 224 B1 4
Palmerston Cl *WGCW* AL8 .... 147 H3 4
Palmers Wy *CHES/WCR* EN8 .... 197 J7
Pamela Av *HHS/BOV* HP3 .... 185 K1
Pamela Gdns *BSF* CM23 .... 105 J6
Pams La *HTCHE/RSTV* SG4 .... 93 G8
Pancake La *HHS/BOV* HP3 .... 165 J7
Pankhurst Crs *STVGE* SG2 .... 76 D4
Pankhurst Pl *WATN* WD24 .... 13 E2 1
Panshanger Dr *WGCE* AL7 .... 148 C3
The Pantiles *BUSH* WD23 .... 222 A7
Panxworth Rd *HHS/BOV* HP3 .... 164 C8
Paper Mill La *STDN* SG11 .... 81 K8
Paradise *HHNE* HP2 .... 8 A6
Paradise Cl *CHESW* EN7 .... 197 F6
Paradise Rd *WAB* EN9 .... 215 H4 4
Paringdon Rd *HLWW/ROY* CM19 .... 179 J5
Parish Cl *GSTN* WD25 .... 204 D4 3
Parishes Md *STVGE* SG2 .... 76 E5
Park Av *BSF* CM23 .... 105 J6
BUSH WD23 .... 13 E1
HLWE CM17 .... 181 F4
LTNN/LIM LU3 .... 68 B2
POTB/CUF EN6 .... 210 D3
RAD WD7 .... 206 E3
RKW/CH/CXG WD3 .... 217 K5
STAL AL1 .... 11 F3
WATW WD18 .... 12 B2
Park Av North *HARP* AL5 .... 118 B8
Park Av South *HARP* AL5 .... 118 A8
Park Cl *BLDK* SG7 .... 42 E2
BRKMPK AL9 .... 171 H3
BRKMPK AL9 .... 193 F4
BUSH WD23 .... 13 E2
RKW/CH/CXG WD3 .... 229 G3
STALW/RED AL3 .... 115 H4
STVGE SG2 .... 76 C8
Park Ct *HLW* CM20 .... 6 C2
Park Crs *BLDK* SG7 .... 42 E2
BORE WD6 .... 223 J3
Park Dr *BLDK* SG7 .... 42 E2
POTB/CUF EN6 .... 210 C1
STDN SG11 .... 81 J6
Parker Av *HERT/WAS* SG14 .... 151 G
Parker Cl *LWTH* SG6 .... 41 J5
Parker's Fld *STVGE* SG2 .... 76 D5
Parker St *WATN* WD24 .... 220 C
Park Farm Cl *HNLW* SG16 .... 24 B
Park Farm La *ROY* SG8 .... 33 J7
Parkfield *LWTH* SG6 .... 42 D5
RKW/CH/CXG WD3 .... 217 J4
Parkfield Av *RYLN/HDSTN* HA2 .... 231 K8
Parkfield Crs *HTCHE/RSTV* SG4 .... 93 G8
RYLN/HDSTN HA2 .... 231 K8
Parkfield Rd *STALW/RED* AL3 .... 115 H4
Park Flds *HLWW/ROY* CM19 .... 178 B
Parkfields *WGCW* AL8 .... 147 J3
Park Gdns *BLDK* SG7 .... 42 E2
Park Ga *HTCHE/RSTV* SG4 .... 56 D3
Parkgate Rd *WATN* WD24 .... 204 D
Park Gv *CSTG* HP8 .... 216 A
Park Hl *HARP* AL5 .... 118 B
HLWE CM17 .... 156 E
Park Hill Rd *HHW* HP1 .... 164 A6
Parkhurst Rd *HERT/WAS* SG14 .... 150 E
Parkins Cl *STDN* SG11 .... 101 F3
Parkinson Cl *STALE/WH* AL4 .... 145 G
Parkland Cl *HOD* EN11 .... 153 G8
Parkland Dr *LTN* LU1 .... 4 B
Parklands *HHW* HP1 .... 163 J4
ROY SG8 .... 21 J
WAB EN9 .... 215 K
Parklands Cl *EBAR* EN4 .... 210 E
Parklands Dr *STALW/RED* AL3 .... 167 H
Park La *BROX* EN10 .... 176 D
BSF CM23 .... 105 J
CHES/WCR EN8 .... 214 C
CHESW EN7 .... 196 E
DEN/HRF UB9 .... 227 K
HHNE HP2 .... 8 A
HLW CM20 .... 6 C
HTCHE/RSTV SG4 .... 93 F
KNEB SG3 .... 95 G
SAFWS CB11 .... 34 C
STALE/WH AL4 .... 191 G
STDN SG11 .... 81 J
Park Lane Paradise *BROX* EN10 .... 196 E
Park Md *HLW* CM20 .... 6 A
Park Meadow *BRKMPK* AL9 .... 171 H
Park Mt *HARP* AL5 .... 118 A
Park Nook Gdns *ENC/FH* EN2 .... 213 C
Park Pl *LCOL/BKTW* AL2 .... 189 F
Park Ri *BERK* HP4 .... 161 F
HARP AL5 .... 118 A
Park Rise Cl *HARP* AL5 .... 118 A
Park Rd *BUSH* WD23 .... 221 H
CHES/WCR EN8 .... 214 C3
HERT/BAY SG13 .... 151 H
HHW HP1 .... 164 E
HOD EN11 .... 177 F
PEND EN3 .... 214 D
POTB/CUF EN6 .... 194 C
RAD WD7 .... 206 D
RKW/CH/CXG WD3 .... 218 D
STSD CM24 .... 86 D
TRING HP23 .... 134 E
WARE SG12 .... 127 F
WAT WD17 .... 220 E
Parkside *BUNT* SG9 .... 47 C
CHES/WCR EN8 .... 214 D
Parkside Dr *WAT* WD17 .... 219 K
Parkside Rd *NTHWD* HA6 .... 230 A
Park St *BERK* HP4 .... 161 J
BLDK SG7 .... 42 E
BRKMPK AL9 .... 171 H
HTCHE/RSTV SG4 .... 56 C
LCOL/BKTW AL2 .... 189 F
LTN LU1 .... 4 C4
TRING HP23 .... 135 F
Park Street La *LCOL/BKTW* AL2 .... 188 D
Park St West *LTN* LU1 .... 4 C
Park Ter *LTN* LU1 .... 5 D5
The Park *STAL* AL1 11
STALW/RED AL3 .... 142 C
Park Viad *LTN* LU1 .... 5 D
Park Vw *BRKMPK* AL9 .... 171 K
HOD EN11 177
PIN HA5 .... 231 C
POTB/CUF EN6 210
STVGE SG2 .... 76 C

Park View Cl *LTNN/LIM* LU3 **68** C3
STAL AL1 **11** F5
Park View Dr *STALW/RED* AL3 **115** H3
Park View Rd *BERK* HP4 **161** J5 3
PIN HA5 **230** C5
Park Wy *HTCH/STOT* SG5 **56** C3
RKW/CH/CXG WD3 **218** B8
Parkway *HLWW/ROY* CM19 **179** F1
SBW CM21 **132** C8
STVGE SG2 **76** B8
WGCW AL8 **147** H4
Parkway Cl *WGCW* AL8 **147** H3
Parkway Ct *STAL* AL1 **189** K1 2
Parkway Gdns *WGCW* AL8 **147** H4
Parkwood Cl *HOD* EN11 **176** D5
Parkwood Dr *HHW* HP1 **163** J6
Parliament Sq
HERT/WAS SG14 **151** G3 13
Parnall Rd *HLWS* CM18 **180** A5
Parndon Mill La *HLW* CM20 **6** A1
Parndon Wood Rd
HLWW/ROY CM19 **179** K6
Parnell Cl *ABLGY* WD5 **187** F8
Parnel Rd *WARE* SG12 **127** K7
Parr Crs *HHNE* HP2 **165** G1
Parrotts Cl *RKW/CH/CXG* WD3 **219** F4
Parrotts Fld *HOD* EN11 **177** G2
Parrott's La *TRING* HP23 **159** F6
Parsloe Rd *EPP* CM16 **179** H7
Parsonage Cl *ABLGY* WD5 **186** E8
TRING HP23 **135** F5 2
Parsonage La *BRKMPK* AL9 **192** B1
BSF CM23 **106** A1
SAFWS CB11 **51** K6
STDN SG11 **83** G3
STSD CM24 **86** E5
Parsonage Leys *HLW* CM20 **7** E4
Parsonage Pl *TRING* HP23 **135** F6 3
Parsonage Rd *BRKMPK* AL9 **192** B1
RKW/CH/CXG WD3 **218** C7
Parson's Cl *STALW/RED* AL3 **116** B8
Parthia Cl *ROY* SG8 **21** J3
Partridge Cl *BAR* EN5 **225** H6
BUSH WD23 **221** K8 2
CSHM HP5 **182** A6
Partridge Ct *HLWS* CM18 **7** D6
Partridge Hl *BLDK* SG7 **17** J6
Partridge Rd *HLWS* CM18 **6** C6
STALW/RED AL3 **168** A2
Parva Cl *HARP* AL5 **144** A3
Parvills *WAB* EN9 **215** J2
Parys Rd *LTNN/LIM* LU3 **69** G3
Pascal Wy *LWTH* SG6 **42** B2
Pasfield *WAB* EN9 **215** J3 2
Passingham Av *HTCHE/RSTV* SG4 **56** E3
Paston Rd *HHNE* HP2 **8** A3
Pasture Cl *BUSH* WD23 **221** K7
Pasture La *HTCHE/RSTV* SG4 **92** B1
Pasture Loates *STSD* CM24 **86** C1
Pasture Rd *LWTH* SG6 **41** J6
The Pastures *HAT* AL10 **171** G5
HHW HP1 **163** H5
LCOL/BKTW AL2 **188** C2 1
OXHEY WD19 **13** D6
STVGE SG2 **76** E1
WARE SG12 **127** G6
WGCE AL7 **148** B5
Path Stort Valley Wy
HERT/BAY SG13 **174** E8
The Pathway *OXHEY* WD19 **220** E8
RAD WD7 **206** C6
Patmore Cl *BSF* CM23 **105** F1
Patmore Link Rd *HHNE* HP2 **9** F5
Patmore Rd *WAB* EN9 **215** K4 2
Patricia Gdns *BSF* CM23 **105** H4
Pauls La *HOD* EN11 **177** F3
Paxton Rd *BERK* HP4 **162** B5 1
STAL AL1 **11** D5
Paycock Rd *HLWW/ROY* CM19 **179** H3
Payne End *BUNT* SG9 **29** K8
Paynes Cl *LWTH* SG6 **26** A8 1
Paynesfield Rd *BUSH* WD23 **222** C7
Paynes La *WAB* EN9 **198** C2
Payne's Pk *HTCH/STOT* SG5 **56** C2
Peace Gv *WLYN* AL6 **123** G2
Peace Prospect *WAT* WD17 **12** B2 3
Peacocks *HLWW/ROY* CM19 **179** G3
Peacocks Cl *BERK* HP4 **161** G3 3
Peakes La *CHESW* EN7 **196** D5
Peakes Wy *CHESW* EN7 **196** D5
Pea La *BERK* HP4 **160** E3
Pearman Dr *WARE* SG12 **99** H2
Pearsall Cl *LWTH* SG6 **42** B4
Pearson Av *HERT/BAY* SG13 **151** F5
Pearsons Cl *HERT/BAY* SG13 **151** F5 2
Peartree Cl *HHW* HP1 **163** K5 3
WGCE AL7 **147** K3
Peartree Ct *WGCE* AL7 **147** K4 3
Pear Tree Dell *LWTH* SG6 **42** B7
Peartree La *WGCE* AL7 **147** K4
Pear Tree Md *HLWS* CM18 **7** F6
Peartree Rd *HHW* HP1 **163** K5
LTNE LU2 **70** D5
Pear Tree Wk *CHESW* EN7 **196** B4
Peartree Wy *STVGE* SG2 **3** E5
Peascroft Rd *HHS/BOV* HP3 **186** A1
Peasmead *BUNT* SG9 **63** J3 3
Peck Ct *AMP/FLIT/B* MK45 **36** B5
Peck's Hl *WAB* EN9 **177** K7
Pedlars La *ROY* SG8 **30** C2
Pedley Hl *DUN/WHIP* LU6 **114** A8
Peel Crs *HERT/WAS* SG14 **125** K8
Peel Pl *LTN* LU1 **4** B4
Pegmire La *GSTN* WD25 **221** K1
Pegrams Rd *HLWS* CM18 **179** K4
Pegsdon Cl *LTNN/LIM* LU3 **69** G2
Pegsdon Wy *HTCH/STOT* SG5 **37** K8
Peg's La *HERT/BAY* SG13 **151** G4 1
WARE SG12 **129** K4
Peldon Rd *HLWW/ROY* CM19 **179** H3
Pelham Ct *HHNE* HP2 **9** F5 2
WGCE AL7 **148** D4 8
Pelham Rd *SAFWS* CB11 **51** K5
STDN SG11 **82** A2
The Pelhams *GSTN* WD25 **204** E5
Pelican Wy *LWTH* SG6 **25** K8 1
Pemberton Cl *STAL* AL1 **189** F1
Pembridge Cl *HHS/BOV* HP3 **183** H6
Pembridge La *BROX* EN10 **175** J7
Pembridge Rd *HHS/BOV* HP3 **183** J6 1
Pembroke Av *LTNW/LEA* LU4 **68** D6
Pembroke Cl *BROX* EN10 **197** J2
Pembroke Dr *CHESW* EN7 **195** K7
Pembroke Rd *BLDK* SG7 **43** F1
NTHWD HA6 **229** H2
Pemsel Ct *HHS/BOV* HP3 **164** D8
Penda Cl *LTNN/LIM* LU3 **68** E3
Pendennis Ct *HARP* AL5 **144** A2 1
Penfold Cl *BLDK* SG7 **43** G2
Pengelly Cl *CHESW* EN7 **197** F8 4
Penhill *LTNN/LIM* LU3 **68** D2
Penlow Rd *HLWS* CM18 **179** K4
Penman Cl *LCOL/BKTW* AL2 **188** C5
Penn Cl *RKW/CH/CXG* WD3 **217** G6
Penne Cl *RAD* WD7 **206** D4
Penn Gaskell La *CFSP/GDCR* SL9 **226** C4
Pennine Av *LTNN/LIM* LU3 **68** B1
Pennine Wy *HHNE* HP2 **8** C2
Pennington La *STSD* CM24 **86** C1
Pennington Rd *CFSP/GDCR* SL9 **226** A6
Penningtons *BSF* CM23 **105** F4
Penn Rd *LCOL/BKTW* AL2 **188** E5
RKW/CH/CXG WD3 **217** J8
STVG SG1 **2** C4
Penn Wy *LWTH* SG6 **42** B6
RKW/CH/CXG WD3 **217** G6
Penny Cft *HARP* AL5 **143** H5
Pennyfather Cl *KNEB* SG3 **97** F7 1
Pennyfathers La *WLYN* AL6 **123** G5
Pennymead *HLW* CM20 **7** F4
Penrose Av *OXHEY* WD19 **231** F1
Penrose Ct *HHNE* HP2 **8** B1
Penscroft Gdns *BORE* WD6 **224** C4
Penshurst *HLWE* CM17 **156** E6
Penshurst Cl *CFSP/GDCR* SL9 **226** A8
HARP AL5 **117** K5 3
Penshurst Rd *POTB/CUF* EN6 **210** E1
Pentland *HHNE* HP2 **8** C2 3
Pentland Rd *BUSH* WD23 **221** K6
Pentley Pk *WGCW* AL8 **147** J1 2
Penton Dr *CHES/WCR* EN8 **197** H7
Pentrich Av *EN* EN1 **213** K8
Penzance Cl *DEN/HRF* UB9 **228** C8 1
Peplins Cl *BRKMPK* AL9 **192** E4
Peplins Wy *BRKMPK* AL9 **192** E3
Peppercorn Wk
HTCHE/RSTV SG4 **57** F2 2
Pepper Hl *WARE* SG12 **152** E4
Pepsal End *STVGE* SG2 **76** C8
Pepsal End Rd *LTN* LU1 **116** C3
Pepys Crs *BAR* EN5 **225** H5
Pepys Wy *BLDK* SG7 **42** D1
Percheron Rd *BORE* WD6 **224** C6
Percival Wy *LTNE* LU2 **90** D2
Percy Rd *WATW* WD18 **12** C3 3
Peregrine Cl *BSF* CM23 **105** G3
GSTN WD25 **205** F4
Perham Wy *LCOL/BKTW* AL2 **190** B4
Perimeter Rd *HAT* AL10 **170** D1
Perivale Gdns *GSTN* WD25 **204** C4
Periwinkle Cl *ROY* SG8 **32** C4
Periwinkle La *HTCH/STOT* SG5 **40** D8
Permain Cl *RAD* WD7 **207** H3
Perowne Wy *STDN* SG11 **81** K6
Perram Cl *BROX* EN10 **197** J4 2
Perriors Cl *CHESW* EN7 **196** E5
Perry Dr *ROY* SG8 **21** J2
Perry Gn *HHNE* HP2 **141** F8
Perry Hl *WAB* EN9 **199** F1
Perry Md *BUSH* WD23 **221** K6
Perrymead *LTNE* LU2 **71** G7
Perry Rd *HLWS* CM18 **179** K4
Perrysfield Rd *CHES/WCR* EN8 **197** J5
Perry Spring *HLWE* CM17 **181** F3
Perrywood La *HERT/WAS* SG14 **124** C3
Pescot Hl *HHW* HP1 **164** A4
Peterhill Cl *CFSP/GDCR* SL9 **226** B4
Peterlee Ct *HHNE* HP2 **8** C1 3
Peters Av *LCOL/BKTW* AL2 **190** A4
Petersfield *STALW/RED* AL3 **168** B2
Peter's Pl *BERK* HP4 **161** F3
Peters Wy *KNEB* SG3 **96** A3
Peterswood *HLWS* CM18 **180** A5
Peters Wood Hl *WARE* SG12 **152** C2
Pettys Cl *CHES/WCR* EN8 **197** H7
Petunia Ct *LTNW/LEA* LU4 **4** A2 3
Petworth Cl *STVGE* SG2 **96** D2
Pevensey Cl *LTNE* LU2 **70** E5 3
Pewterers Av *BSF* CM23 **105** F5
Pheasant Cl *BERK* HP4 **161** K6 2
TRING HP23 **135** G3 2
Pheasant Wk *CFSP/GDCR* SL9 **226** A3
Phelips Rd *EPP* CM16 **179** H6
Phillimore Pl *RAD* WD7 **206** B6
Phillipers *GSTN* WD25 **205** F5 1
Phillips Av *ROY* SG8 **21** G1
Phipps Hatch La *ENC/FH* EN2 **213** F8
Phoenix Cl *NTHWD* HA6 **230** A3
The Phygtle *CFSP/GDCR* SL9 **226** B5
Piccotts End *HHW* HP1 **164** B2
Piccotts End La *HHNE* HP2 **164** B3
Piccotts End Rd *HHW* HP1 **164** A2
Pickets Cl *BUSH* WD23 **222** A8
Picketts *WGCW* AL8 **122** D8
Pickford Hl *HARP* AL5 **118** E6
Pickford Rd *STALW/RED* AL3 **115** G7
Picknage Rd *ROY* SG8 **23** G7
Pie Cnr *STALW/RED* AL3 **116** B8
Pie Gdn *STALW/RED* AL3 **116** C8
Pierian Spring *HHW* HP1 **164** A4 2
Pietley Hl *STALW/RED* AL3 **116** A8
Pigeonwick *HARP* AL5 **118** C6
Piggottshill La *HARP* AL5 **143** K2
Piggotts La *LTNW/LEA* LU4 **68** C5
Piggotts Wy *BSF* CM23 **105** H4
Pightle Cl *ROY* SG8 **21** G2
Pig La *BSF* CM23 **105** K6
Pike End *STVG* SG1 **2** B2
Pilgrim Cl *GSTN* WD25 **204** E3 1
LCOL/BKTW AL2 **188** E5
Pilgrims Wy *STVG* SG1 **59** H7
Pilkingtons *HLWE* CM17 **181** G1
Piltdown Rd *OXHEY* WD19 **230** E3 7
OXHEY WD19 **230** E3 7
Pinceybrook Rd *HLWS* CM18 **179** K5
Pinchfield *RKW/CH/CXG* WD3 **227** G4
Pindar Rd *HOD* EN11 **177** H2
Pine Cl *BERK* HP4 **161** J5
CHES/WCR EN8 **197** G6
NTHWD HA6 **229** K5
Pine Crest *WLYN* AL6 **122** E1
Pinecroft *HHS/BOV* HP3 **185** K2
Pinecroft Crs *BAR* EN5 **225** K4
Pine Gv *BRKMPK* AL9 **193** H3
BSF CM23 **106** A3
BUSH WD23 **13** F1
LCOL/BKTW AL2 **188** B8
Pinehurst Cl *ABLGY* WD5 **203** K2
Pinelands *BSF* CM23 **85** J8
Pine Rd *DUN/WHIP* LU6 **112** B1
Pines Av *EN* EN1 **214** B6
Pines Hl *STSD* CM24 **86** C4
The Pines *BORE* WD6 **223** J2 5
HHW HP1 **184** D2
Pine Tree Cl *HHNE* HP2 **8** A4 7
Pine Wk *BERK* HP4 **160** E2
Pinewood *WGCE* AL7 **147** K5
Pinewood Av *PIN* HA5 **231** J5
Pinewood Cl *BORE* WD6 **224** C1
HLWE CM17 **181** F3
PIN HA5 **231** J5
STAL AL1 **169** F6
WAT WD17 **220** B1 3
Pinewood Dr *POTB/CUF* EN6 **210** A1
Pinewood Gdns *HHS/BOV* HP3 **8** B6 4
HHW HP1 **164** A6
Pinfold Rd *BUSH* WD23 **221** G2
Pinford Dell *LTNE* LU2 **70** E8 8
Pinnacles *WAB* EN9 **215** K4
Pinnate Pl *WGCE* AL7 **147** K7
Pinner Gn *PIN* HA5 **230** D8
Pinner Hl *PIN* HA5 **230** C6
Pinner Hill Rd *PIN* HA5 **230** D7
Pinner Park Av *RYLN/HDSTN* HA2 **231** K8
Pinner Park Gdns
RYLN/HDSTN HA2 **231** K8
Pinner Rd *NTHWD* HA6 **230** A7
OXHEY WD19 **13** E5
PIN HA5 **230** B8
Pinnocks La *BLDK* SG7 **43** F2
Pinto Cl *BORE* WD6 **224** C6 2
Pioneer Wy *WATW* WD18 **12** A5
Pipers Av *HARP* AL5 **144** A2
Pipers Cl *STALW/RED* AL3 **142** B3
Pipers Hl *HHW* HP1 **139** F7
Pipers La *HARP* AL5 **144** B2
STALW/RED AL3 **115** J1
Pippens *WGCW* AL8 **122** E8
Pippin Cl *RAD* WD7 **207** H3
Pirton Cl *HTCH/STOT* SG5 **56** B2
STALE/WH AL4 **169** F1
Pirton Rd *HTCH/STOT* SG5 **39** J3
HTCH/STOT SG5 **55** K2
LTNW/LEA LU4 **68** B4
Pishiobury Dr *SBW* CM21 **157** G1

Pitsfield WGCW AL8 122 D8
Pitstone Cl STALE/WH AL4 169 F1 5
Pitt Dr STALE/WH AL4 190 A1
Pittman's Fld HLW CM20 7 E3
Pix Ct ARL/CHE SG15 24 E1
Pix Farm La HHW HP1 162 E7
Pixies Hill Crs HHW HP1 163 J8
Pixies Hill Rd HHW HP1 163 J7
Pixmore Av LWTH SG6 42 B3
Pixmore Wy LWTH SG6 41 K4
Pix Rd HTCH/STOT SG5 25 J4
LWTH SG6 42 A3
Plaiters Cl TRING HP23 135 F5
Plaitford Cl RKW/CH/CXG WD3 228 D1
Plantaganet Pl WAB EN9 215 G3 3
Plantation Rd LTNN/LIM LU3 68 C2
Plantation Wk HHW HP1 163 K3 1
HHW HP1 163 K4 4
Plash Dr STVG SG1 2 C3
Plashes Cl STDN SG11 81 J7 1
Plashets RBSF CM22 133 G8
Platt Cl LTNW/LEA LU4 68 C5
Plaw Hatch Cl BSF CM23 106 A1
Playhouse Sq HLW CM20 6 B4 3
The Pleasance HARP AL5 117 K5
Pleasant Mt HERT/BAY SG13 152 B5
Pleasant Ri BRKMPK AL9 171 H1
Pleasant Rd BSF CM23 105 H1
Plewes Cl DUN/WHIP LU6 114 C1
Plough Hl POTB/CUF EN6 195 G7
Plough La BERK HP4 162 E2
DEN/HRF UB9 228 B5
HTCHE/RSTV SG4 72 D4
RKW/CH/CXG WD3 201 J3
Ploughmans Cl BSF CM23 105 F4
Ploughmans End WGCE AL7 148 D4 9
Plover Cl BERK HP4 161 K6 3
Ployters Rd HLWW/ROY CM19 179 K5
Plummers La LTNE LU2 92 A8
Plumpton Cl LTNE LU2 70 E6 2
Plumpton Rd HOD EN11 177 H1
Pluto Ri HHNE HP2 8 B3
Poets Cha HHW HP1 164 A4
Poets Cl HHW HP1 164 A5
Poets Ct HARP AL5 118 D8 1
Poets Ga CHESW EN7 196 B6
Polayn Garth WGCW AL8 147 H2
Polegate LTNE LU2 70 E7
Polehanger La HHW HP1 163 H4
Poles Hl RKW/CH/CXG WD3 201 H3
Poles La WARE SG12 127 G3
Police Rw ROY SG8 30 D2
Pollard Gdns STVG SG1 76 A1 1
Pollard Hatch HLWW/ROY CM19 179 J4 2
Pollards RKW/CH/CXG WD3 227 G4
Pollards Cl CHESW EN7 196 A7
Pollards Wy HTCH/STOT SG5 38 E5
Pollywick Rd TRING HP23 135 J8 3
Polzeath Cl LTNE LU2 90 D1
Pomeroy Crs WATN WD24 204 C6 1
Pomeroy Gv LTNE LU2 69 K4
Pomfret Av LTNE LU2 5 D3
Pond Cl DEN/HRF UB9 228 B8
LTNW/LEA LU4 68 A4
Pond Cft HAT AL10 170 E3
WGCE AL7 147 K4
Pondcroft Rd KNEB SG3 96 B4
Pondfield Crs STALE/WH AL4 168 E3
Pond La BLDK SG7 42 E1
Pond Rd HHS/BOV HP3 186 A3
Pondside HTCHE/RSTV SG4 58 C5
Pondsmeade STALW/RED AL3 142 C4 4
Pondwick Rd HARP AL5 118 A7
Pondwicks Cl STALW/RED AL3 10 B5
Pondwicks Rd LTN LU1 5 D4
Pooleys La BRKMPK AL9 192 B1
Popes La WATN WD24 204 C7
Pope's Rd ABLGY WD5 203 K1
Popes Rw WARE SG12 127 H6
Popis Gdns WARE SG12 127 J7
Poplar Av HAT AL10 170 C4
LTNN/LIM LU3 69 H1
Poplar Cl HTCHE/RSTV SG4 56 E4
PIN HA5 230 E7
ROY SG8 21 J2 1
STDN SG11 100 E8
Poplar Dr ROY SG8 21 J2
Poplar Rd DUN/WHIP LU6 114 C1
Poplars WGCE AL7 148 C2
Poplars Cl GSTN WD25 204 C2
HAT AL10 170 C4
LTNE LU2 70 C6
The Poplars ARL/CHE SG15 24 E1
CHESW EN7 196 C4
HHW HP1 164 A7 2
HTCH/STOT SG5 40 D4 1
STAL AL1 189 K2 1
Popple Wy STVG SG1 2 C2
Poppy Cl HHW HP1 163 H5
Poppyfields WGCE AL7 148 D4 10
Poppy Md STVG SG1 3 D4
Poppy Wk CHESW EN7 196 B6
Porlock Dr LTNE LU2 70 D8
Porters Cl BUNT SG9 63 J1
Porters Hl HARP AL5 118 E5
Porters Park Dr RAD WD7 207 H2
Porters Wd STALW/RED AL3 168 C2
Port Hl HERT/WAS SG14 151 F3 8
Portland Dr CHESW EN7 213 K1
ENC/FH EN2 213 H8 3
Portland Pl BSF CM23 105 J2 6
HERT/BAY SG13 152 B5
Portland Rd BSF CM23 105 J2
LTNW/LEA LU4 69 F8
Portland St STALW/RED AL3 10 B4
Port La RBSF CM22 106 A7
Portman Cl HTCH/STOT SG5 40 B7
STALE/WH AL4 169 F1
Portmill La HTCH/STOT SG5 56 D2
Port V HERT/WAS SG14 150 E2
Postfield WGCE AL7 123 G8
Post Office Rd HLW CM20 6 B3
Post Office Rw HTCHE/RSTV SG4 43 H8 1
Postwood Gn HERT/BAY SG13 152 B6
Post Wood Rd WARE SG12 152 D2
Potash La TRING HP23 108 D5
Potten End Hl HHW HP1 163 H1
Potterscrouch La LCOL/BKTW AL2 187 K2
Potters Fld HLWE CM17 181 G3
STALW/RED AL3 168 B2
Pottersheath Rd WLYN AL6 95 J8
Potters Heights Cl PIN HA5 230 C6
Potters La BORE WD6 224 B1
STVG SG1 75 G5
Potter St BSF CM23 105 J2
HLWE CM17 181 F2
NTHWD HA6 230 B7
Potter Street Hl NTHWD HA6 230 C5
Pottery Cl LTNN/LIM LU3 68 E2
Potton Rd ROY SG8 15 F3
Pouchen End La HHW HP1 163 G7
Poulteney Rd STSD CM24 86 D1 5
Poultney Cl RAD WD7 207 H2
Pound Av STVG SG1 2 B2
Pound Cl WAB EN9 198 E1
Pound Fld GSTN WD25 204 A5
Pound Gn ROY SG8 15 G4
Pound La RAD WD7 207 J3
Poundwell WGCE AL7 148 B4 2
Powdermill La WAB EN9 215 G3
Powdermill Ms WAB EN9 215 G3 4
Powdermill Wy WAB EN9 215 G2
Power Ct LTN LU1 5 D4
Powis Ct POTB/CUF EN6 210 D4
Poynders Hl HHNE HP2 9 F6
Poynders Meadow WLYN AL6 121 K1 2
Poynings Cl HARP AL5 144 C1
Prae Cl STALW/RED AL3 10 A3
Praetorian Ct STAL AL1 188 E1
Prebendal Dr LTN LU1 89 G7
Prentice Wy LTNE LU2 90 E2
Prescott Rd CHES/WCR EN8 197 J5
Presdales Dr WARE SG12 152 C1
President Wy LTNE LU2 90 E1
Prestatyn Cl STVG SG1 75 G2
Preston Gdns LTNE LU2 5 D1
PEND EN3 214 D7
Preston Rd HTCHE/RSTV SG4 73 H2
Prestwick Cl LTNE LU2 69 K4
Prestwick Dr BSF CM23 86 A8
Prestwick Rd OXHEY WD19 230 E2 1
Pretoria Rd WATW WD18 12 B3 1
Priestleys LTN LU1 89 F2
Primary Wy ARL/CHE SG15 24 E5
Primett Rd STVG SG1 2 A1
Primley La RBSF CM22 133 G8
Primrose Cl ARL/CHE SG15 24 E5
BSF CM23 105 F3
HAT AL10 171 G5 3
Primrose Dr HERT/BAY SG13 152 A3
Primrose Fld HLWS CM18 180 C4
Primrose Gdns BUSH WD23 221 J7
Primrose Hl KGLGY WD4 186 B6
Primrose Hill Rd STVG SG1 2 B1
Primrose La ARL/CHE SG15 24 E5
Primrose Pth CHESW EN7 213 K1
Primrose Vw ROY SG8 21 K4 2
Prince Andrew's Cl ROY SG8 21 H4
Prince Edward St BERK HP4 161 K5 5
Prince Pk HHW HP1 163 K7
Princes Av PEND EN3 214 D6
WATW WD18 12 B4
Princes Cl BERK HP4 161 H3
Princes Ct BSF CM23 105 F2 1
Princes Ga BSF CM23 105 F2
Princes Ms ROY SG8 21 G4
Princess Diana Dr STALE/WH AL4 169 F7
Princess St LTN LU1 4 B5
Prince's St HTCH/STOT SG5 25 K2
WARE SG12 127 H7
Prince St WAT WD17 13 D2
Prince Wy LTNE LU2 90 E1
Printers Wy HLW CM20 156 D4
Priors Cl HERT/BAY SG13 152 A6
Priors Hl HTCH/STOT SG5 38 E5
Priors Wood Rd HERT/BAY SG13 152 B6
Priory Av HLWE CM17 157 F4
Priory Cl BROX EN10 197 J2 1
HOD EN11 177 F4
ROY SG8 21 J3
Priory Ct BSF CM23 105 H
HLWS CM18 180 E
Priory Dell STVG SG1 2 C
Priory Dr STSD CM24 86 D
Priory End HTCHE/RSTV SG4 56 D
Priory Gdns BERK HP4 161 K
LTNE LU2 69 J
Priory Ga CHES/WCR EN8 197 K5
Priory La HTCHE/RSTV SG4 57 K
ROY SG8 21 H
Priory Orch STALW/RED AL3 116 B
Priory St HERT/WAS SG14 151 G
WARE SG12 127 G
Priory Vw BUSH WD23 222 B
HTCHE/RSTV SG4 57 J
Priory Wk STAL AL1 189 G
Priory Wy HTCHE/RSTV SG4 56 C
Priory Wood Rbt RBSF CM22 107 F
Proctors Wy BSF CM23 105 K
Proctor Wy LTNE LU2 90 D
Progress Wy LTNW/LEA LU4 68 A
Prospect La HARP AL5 143 G
Prospect Pl WLYN AL6 122 C4
Prospect Rd CHES/WCR EN8 197 G
STAL AL1 10 C
Prospect Wy LTNE LU2 90 D
Protea Wy LWTH SG6 42 B
Providence Gv STVG SG1 75 K
Providence Wy BLDK SG7 43 F2
Provost Wy LTNE LU2 90 D
Prowse Av BUSH WD23 231 K
Pryor Cl ABLGY WD5 204 A
Pryor Rd BLDK SG7 43 F
Pryors Cl BSF CM23 105 K
Pryor Wy LWTH SG6 42 D
Puddephat's La STALW/RED AL3 140 C
Pudding La HHW HP1 163 K
ROY SG8 23 C
Pulham Av BROX EN10 176 D
Puller Rd BAR EN5 225 J
HHW HP1 163 K
Pulleys Cl HHW HP1 163 J
Pulleys La HHW HP1 163 J
Pullman Dr HTCHE/RSTV SG4 57 F2
Pulter's Wy HTCHE/RSTV SG4 56 E
Pump Hl BUNT SG9 50 C
Punch Bowl La HHNE HP2 165 J
STALW/RED AL3 166 B
Purbrock Av GSTN WD25 204 D
Purcell Cl BORE WD6 223 G1
WLYN AL6 123 K
Purford Gn HLWS CM18 7 F
Purkiss Rd HERT/BAY SG13 151 F
Purlings Rd BUSH WD23 221
Pursley Gdns BORE WD6 207 K8
Purway Cl LTNN/LIM LU3 68 D
Purwell La HTCHE/RSTV SG4 57 C
Putney Rd PEND EN3 214 C
Puttenham Cl OXHEY WD19 230 D
Putteridge Rd LTNE LU2 70 E
Putters Cft HHNE HP2 164 E
Puttocks Cl BRKMPK AL9 192 C1
Puttocks Dr BRKMPK AL9 192 C
Pyenest Rd HLWW/ROY CM19 179 J
The Pyghtle BUNT SG9 63 H
LTN LU1 89 F
Pyms Cl LWTH SG6 42 E
Pynchbek BSF CM23 105 H
Pynchon Paddocks RBSF CM22 133 H
Pytchley Cl LTNE LU2 69 K4
Pytt Fld HLWE CM17 180 E

Q

The Quadrangle WGCW AL8 147 H2
The Quadrant LWTH SG6 41
ROY SG8 21 G1
STALE/WH AL4 168
STVG SG1 2
Quaker La WAB EN9 215
Quaker Rd WARE SG12 127
Quakers La POTB/CUF EN6 193
Quantock Cl LTNN/LIM LU3 69
STALE/WH AL4 169 F2
Quantock Ri LTNN/LIM LU3 69
Quantocks HHNE HP2 8
Quarry Springs HLW CM20 7
Quartermass Cl HHW HP1 163 K5
Quartermass Rd HHW HP1 163
Queen Anne's Cl HTCH/STOT SG5 25
Queen Hoo La WLYN AL6 124
Queen Mary's Av WATW WD18 219
Queens Av WATW WD18 12
Queens Cl LTN LU1 5 D5
SBW CM21 132
STSD CM24 86
Queens Crs BSF CM23 105
STALE/WH AL4 168
Queens Dr ABLGY WD5 204
CHES/WCR EN8 215
The Queen's Dr
RKW/CH/CXG WD3 217

Queen's Pl WAT WD17 .... 13 D2 ⊡
Queens Rd BAR EN5 .... 225 ⊡
   BERK HP4 .... 161 H4
   CHES/WCR EN8 .... 214 D4
   HARP AL5 .... 143 J2
   HERT/BAY SG13 .... 151 G4 ⊡
   ROY SG8 .... 21 H2
   WARE SG12 .... 127 K7
   WAT WD17 .... 13 D2 ⊡
The Queen's Sq HHNE HP2 .... 8 C5 ⊡
Queen St HTCH/STOT SG5 .... 26 A4
   HTCHE/RSTV SG4 .... 56 D3
   KGLGY WD4 .... 201 K1
   LBUZ LU7 .... 110 D5
   STALW/RED AL3 .... 10 B4
   TRING HP23 .... 135 F6
Queens Wy RAD WD7 .... 207 H1
   CHES/WCR EN8 .... 214 E4 ⊡
Queensway HAT AL10 .... 171 F4
   HHW HP1 .... 164 B5
   ROY SG8 .... 21 H2
Queenswood Crs GSTN WD25 .... 204 B3
Queenswood Dr HTCHE/RSTV SG4 ... 41 G8
Quendell Wk HHNE HP2 .... 8 B5 ⊡
Quendon Dr WAB EN9 .... 215 J3
Quickbeams WGCE AL7 .... 123 G8 ⊡
Quickley La RKW/CH/CXG WD3 ...... 217 F6
Quickley Ri RKW/CH/CXG WD3 ...... 216 E6
Quickly Brow RKW/CH/CXG WD3 .... 216 E6
Quickmoor La KGLGY WD4 .... 202 A3
Quickswood LTNN/LIM LU3 .... 69 F2 ⊡
Quickwood Cl RKW/CH/CXG WD3 .. 217 J6
Quills LWTH SG6 .... 42 D5
Quilter Cl LTNN/LIM LU3 .... 68 C5
Quinces Cft HHW HP1 .... 163 K4
Quincey Rd WARE SG12 .... 127 C6
Quin Ct STDN SG11 .... 82 A2 ⊡
Quinn Wy LWTH SG6 .... 42 C4
Quinta Dr BAR EN5 .... 225 C5
Quinton Wy WAB EN9 .... 215 H5

R

Raban Cl STVGE SG2 .... 76 D3
Rabley Heath Rd WLYN AL6 .... 95 F8
Rackman Dr LTNN/LIM LU3 .... 69 H4
Radburn Cl HLWS CM18 .... 180 D5
Radburn Wy LWTH SG6 .... 42 B5
Radcliffe Rd HTCH/STOT SC5 .... 56 E1
Radlett La RAD WD7 .... 207 G4
Radlett Park Rd RAD WD7 .... 206 D4
Radlett Rd GSTN WD25 .... 205 K8
   LCOL/BKTW AL2 .... 189 G7
   WATN WD24 .... 13 D2
Radstone Pl LTNE LU2 .... 71 F8 ⊡
Radwell La BLDK SG7 .... 26 C5
Raeburn Gdns BAR EN5 .... 225 J3
Raffin Cl KNEB SG3 .... 96 E5
Raffin Green La HERT/WAS SG14 .. 97 G4
   KNEB SG3 .... 96 E5
Raffin Pk KNEB SG3 .... 97 F6
Ragged Hall La LCOL/BKTW AL2 .... 187 F5
Raglan Cl CHES/WCR EN8 .... 214 C4
Raglan Gdns OXHEY WD19 .... 220 C8
Rags La CHESW EN7 .... 196 C5
Railway Pl HERT/BAY SG13 .... 151 H3
Railway Rd CHES/WCR EN8 .... 214 E3
Railway St HERT/WAS SG14 .... 151 G3
Railway Ter KGLGY WD4 .... 186 A5
Rainbow Cl STALW/RED AL3 .... 142 A4
Rainbow Ct OXHEY WD19 .... 13 D5 ⊡
Rainer Cl CHES/WCR EN8 .... 197 H7
Rainsford Rd STSD CM24 .... 86 C1
Raleigh Crs STVGE SG2 .... 3 E1
Raleigh Gv LTNW/LEA LU4 .... 68 C3
Ralston Wy OXHEY WD19 .... 230 E1
Ramblers Wy WGCE AL7 .... 148 C4
Rambling Wy BERK HP4 .... 162 E5
Ramerick Gdns ARL/CHE SG15 ...... 24 D7
Ram Gorse HLW CM20 .... 6 A2
Ramney Dr PEND EN3 .... 214 D6
The Ramparts STALW/RED AL3 ...... 10 A6
Ramridge Rd LTNE LU2 .... 5 E1
Ramsay Cl BROX EN10 .... 176 D7 ⊡
Ramsbury Rd STAL AL1 .... 11 D5
Ramsdell STVG SG1 .... 3 D4
Ramsey Cl BRKMPK AL9 .... 193 K5
   STAL AL1 .... 11 F6
Ramsey Lodge Ct STAL AL1 .... 11 D3
Ramsey Rd AMP/FLIT/B MK45 ...... 36 C6
Ramson Ri HHW HP1 .... 163 H7
Randalls Ride HHNE HP2 .... 8 B3
Randals Hl STVGE SG2 .... 3 E1
Randon Cl PIN HA5 .... 231 J8
Rand's Meadow HTCH/STOT SG5 .. 39 K2
Ranelagh Rd HHNE HP2 .... 9 E5
Ranleigh Wk HARP AL5 .... 144 A3
Ranock Cl LTNN/LIM LU3 .... 68 C1
Ranskill Rd BORE WD6 .... 223 K1
Ransom Cl HTCHE/RSTV SC4 ...... 56 D5 ⊡
   OXHEY WD19 .... 13 D6

Rant Meadow HHS/BOV HP3 .... 9 D6
Ranulf Cl HLWE CM17 .... 157 F3
Ranworth Av HOD EN11 .... 153 C2
   STVGE SG2 .... 96 D2
Ranworth Cl HHS/BOV HP3 .... 164 C8 ⊡
Raphael Cl RAD WD7 .... 207 H2
Raphael Dr WATN WD24 .... 13 E1
Rasehill Cl RKW/CH/CXG WD3 ...... 218 B5
Rathlin HHS/BOV HP3 .... 165 G8
Ratty's La HOD EN11 .... 177 J3
Ravenbank Rd LTNE LU2 .... 70 D4
Raven Cl RKW/CH/CXG WD3 ...... 218 B7
Raven Ct HAT AL10 .... 171 F6
Ravensburgh Cl
   AMP/FLIT/B MK45 .... 36 B6 ⊡
Ravenscroft GSTN WD25 .... 205 F5 ⊡
   HARP AL5 .... 144 A3 ⊡
Ravenscroft Pk BAR EN5 .... 225 J3
Ravensdell HHW HP1 .... 163 J5
Ravens La BERK HP4 .... 162 A5
Ravensmead CFSP/GDCR SL9 ...... 226 C4
Ravensthorpe LTNE LU2 .... 70 C5
Ravenswood Pk NTHWD HA6 ...... 230 B5
Rawdon Dr HOD EN11 .... 177 F4
Rayburn Rd HHW HP1 .... 163 K8
Rayfield WGCW AL8 .... 122 D8 ⊡
Raymer Cl STAL AL1 .... 11 D3
Raymond Cl ABLGY WD5 .... 203 J2 ⊡
Raymonds Cl WGCE AL7 .... 147 K5 ⊡
Raymonds Pln WGCE AL7 .... 147 K5 ⊡
Raynham Cl BSF CM23 .... 106 B2
Raynham Rd BSF CM23 .... 106 A1
Raynham St HERT/BAY SG13 ...... 151 H2
Raynham Wy LTNE LU2 .... 70 E8
Raynsford Rd WARE SG12 .... 127 J8
Raynton Rd PEND EN3 .... 214 C7
Ray's Hl CSHM HP5 .... 159 H7
The Readings HLWS CM18 .... 180 C4
   RKW/CH/CXG WD3 .... 217 H5
Recreation Gnd STSD CM24 .... 86 C3
Rectory Cl BRKMPK AL9 .... 173 F5
   WARE SG12 .... 154 E1
Rectory Fld HLWW/ROY CM19 ...... 6 A6
Rectory Gdns HAT AL10 .... 171 C4 ⊡
   HLWW/ROY CM19 .... 6 A6
   KGLGY WD4 .... 186 A6
Rectory La BERK HP4 .... 161 K5
   BSF CM23 .... 85 F3
   HERT/WAS SG14 .... 98 A6
   HLWW/ROY CM19 .... 6 A6
   KGLGY WD4 .... 186 A6
   KNEB SG3 .... 96 D7
   LTNE LU2 .... 53 K7
   RAD WD7 .... 207 J5
   RAD WD7 .... 208 B1
   RKW/CH/CXG WD3 .... 218 C8
   STVG SG1 .... 58 C8
Rectory Rd RKW/CH/CXG WD3 ...... 218 C7
   WGCW AL8 .... 122 B8
Rectory Wd HLW CM20 .... 6 B3
Redan Rd WARE SG12 .... 127 J6
Redbournbury La STALW/RED AL3.. 142 E7
Redbourn La HARP AL5 .... 143 F3
Redbourn Rd HHNE HP2 .... 9 D1
   STALW/RED AL3 .... 167 F2
Redcar Dr STVG SG1 .... 75 F3
Redding La STALW/RED AL3 ...... 116 E8
Reddings HHS/BOV HP3 .... 164 E8
   WGCW AL8 .... 147 H2
Reddings Av BUSH WD23 .... 221 J5
The Reddings WD6 .... 223 J8 ⊡
Redfern Cl LTN LU1 .... 89 F3
Redgrave Gdns LTNN/LIM LU3 .... 68 E1
Redhall Cl HAT AL10 .... 170 E7
Redhall Dr HAT AL10 .... 170 E7
Redhall La RKW/CH/CXG WD3 .... 218 D1
Redheath Cl GSTN WD25 .... 204 A5
Redhill Rd HTCH/STOT SG5 ...... 56 A1
Redhoods Wy East LWTH SG6 ...... 41 J3
Redhoods Wy West LWTH SG6 .... 41 J3
Red House Cl WARE SG12 .... 152 D2
Red Lion Cl GSTN WD25 .... 205 J7
Red Lion Crs HLWE CM17 .... 181 F5
Red Lion La HHS/BOV HP3 .... 185 K4
   HLWE CM17 .... 181 F5
Red Lodge Gdns BERK HP4 .... 161 H6
Redmire Cl LTNW/LEA LU4 .... 68 A3 ⊡
Red Rails LTN LU1 .... 4 A1
Redricks La HLW CM20 .... 156 C3
Red Rd BORE WD6 .... 223 J3
Redvers Cl BSF CM23 .... 85 K7
Red White And Blue Rd BSF CM23.. 86 A7
Red Willow HLWW/ROY CM19 .... 179 G4
Redwing Cl STVGE SG2 .... 76 D5
Redwing Gv ABLGY WD5 .... 204 B1 ⊡
Redwood Cl OXHEY WD19 .... 230 D3
Redwood Dr HHS/BOV HP3 .... 164 D8
   LTNN/LIM LU3 .... 68 B1
Redwood Ri BORE WD6 .... 207 K7
Redwoods HERT/WAS SG14 ...... 151 F2 ⊡
   WGCW AL8 .... 122 D6 ⊡
Redwood Wy BAR EN5 .... 225 J5
Reed Cl LCOL/BKTW AL2 .... 190 B5
Reedham Cl LCOL/BKTW AL2 ...... 188 C7
Reedings Wy SBW CM21 .... 132 D5
Reeds Crs WATN WD24 .... 13 D1

Reedsdale LTNE LU2 .... 71 G7 ⊡
The Reeds WGCE AL7 .... 147 J4
Reeves Av LTNN/LIM LU3 .... 69 G5
Reeves La HLWW/ROY CM19 ...... 178 D5
Regal Cl STDN SG11 .... 81 K7
Regal Wy WATN WD24 .... 204 D8
Regency Cl BSF CM23 .... 105 F2
Regency Ct HLWS CM18 .... 180 C4
Regent Cl KGLGY WD4 .... 186 A7
   STALE/WH AL4 .... 169 F2
   WGCE AL7 .... 147 K4 ⊡
Regent Ct HTCH/STOT SG5 .... 25 K2
Regents Cl RAD WD7 .... 206 D4
Regent St HTCH/STOT SG5 .... 25 K3
   LTN LU1 .... 4 B4 ⊡
   WATN WD24 .... 204 C8
Reginald Rd NTHWD HA6 .... 230 A7
Reginald St LTNE LU2 .... 4 C2
Rendlesham Av WARE SG12 ...... 206 C7
Rendlesham Cl WARE SG12 ...... 127 C7
Rendlesham Wy
   RKW/CH/CXG WD3 .... 217 F6
Rennison Cl CHESW EN7 .... 196 D5 ⊡
Renshaw Cl LTNN/LIM LU3 .... 71 F7 ⊡
Repton Cl LTNN/LIM LU3 .... 68 E3
Repton Gn STALW/RED AL3 ...... 10 C1
Repton Wy RKW/CH/CXG WD3 .... 219 F5
Reson Wy HHW HP1 .... 164 A7
Reston Cl BORE WD6 .... 207 K8
Retford St HERT/WAS SG14 ...... 151 G1
The Retreat AMS HP6 .... 216 B1
Revels Cl HERT/WAS SC14 ...... 151 G1
Revels Rd HERT/WAS SG14 ...... 151 G1
Reynard Copse BSF CM23 ...... 85 J8
Reynards Rd WLYN AL6 .... 122 B2
Reynard's Wy LCOL/BKTW AL2 .... 188 B7
Reynard Wy HERT/BAY SG13 ...... 151 K3
Reynolds Cl HHW HP1 .... 163 K5
Reynolds Crs STALE/WH AL4 ...... 168 C1
Rhee Spring BLDK SG7 .... 27 H8
Rhodes Av BSF CM23 .... 105 J4
Rhodes Wy WATN WD24 .... 13 E1
Rhymes HHW HP1 .... 164 A4
Ribbledale LCOL/BKTW AL2 ...... 190 D5 ⊡
Ribblesdale HHNE HP2 .... 8 B2
Rib Cl STDN SG11 .... 81 K7
Ribocon Wy LTNW/LEA LU4 ...... 68 A3
Ribston Cl RAD WD7 .... 207 G3
Rib V HERT/WAS SG14 .... 126 B8
Rice Cl HHNE HP2 .... 8 C4 ⊡
Richards Cl BUSH WD23 .... 222 A7
   LTN LU1 .... 89 G3
Richardson Cl LCOL/BKTW AL2 .. 190 C5 ⊡
Richardson Crs CHESW EN7 ...... 195 K4
Richardson Pl STALE/WH AL4 ...... 170 A8
Richard Stagg Cl STAL AL1 ...... 168 E8
Richfield Rd BUSH WD23 .... 222 A8 ⊡
Richmond Cl BSF CM23 .... 105 F2 ⊡
   WARE SG12 .... 127 F6
Richmond Cl BROX EN10 .... 176 E6 ⊡
   HAT AL10 .... 171 G7 ⊡
   POTB/CUF EN6 .... 210 D1 ⊡
Richmond Dr WAT WD17 .... 219 K2
Richmond Hl LTNE LU2 .... 5 D1
Richmond Rd POTB/CUF EN6 ...... 210 D1
   RKW/CH/CXG WD3 .. 219 H4
Richmond Cl HAT AL10 .... 171 F6 ⊡
Rickard Cl LTNE LU2 .... 70 C6 ⊡
Rickyard Meadow
   STALW/RED AL3 .... 142 B4
The Rickyard BLDK SG7 .... 17 K6 ⊡
Riddell Gdns BLDK SG7 .... 43 F1 ⊡
Riddings La HLWS CM18 .... 180 D5
Riddy Hill Cl HTCHE/RSTV SG4 .... 56 E3 ⊡
Riddy La LTNN/LIM LU3 .... 69 G4
The Riddy WLYN AL6 .... 121 K1
Ridge Av HARP AL5 .... 118 A5
   LWTH SG6 .... 42 A3
Ridgedown STALW/RED AL3 ...... 142 B4 ⊡
Ridgefield WAT WD17 .... 203 K7
Ridgehurst Av GSTN WD25 ...... 204 A3
Ridge La WAT WD17 .... 203 K6
Ridge Lea HHW HP1 .... 163 J7
Ridgemount End
   CFSP/GDCR SL9 .... 226 B3 ⊡
Ridge Rd LWTH SG6 .... 42 A3
Ridge St WATN WD24 .... 204 C8
Ridgeview LCOL/BKTW AL2 ...... 190 D6
Ridge Vw TRING HP23 .... 135 H4
Ridgeview Cl BAR EN5 .... 225 J6
Ridge Wy RKW/CH/CXG WD3 .. 218 A7
Ridgeway BERK HP4 .... 161 G5
   DUN/WHIP LU6 .... 114 C1
   HARP AL5 .... 118 A5 ⊡
   LBUZ LU7 .... 111 J3
   STDN SG11 .... 83 J8
   STVG SG1 .... 3 D3
   TRING HP23 .... 111 G7

WGCE AL7	148 C4	
Ridgeway Cl HHS/BOV HP3	185 K3	
Ridgeways HLWE CM17	181 H1	
The Ridgeway ENC/FH EN2	211 K6	
HERT/WAS SG14	150 C2	
HTCH/STOT SG5	56 B3	
POTB/CUF EN6	194 C5	
POTB/CUF EN6	211 G5	
RAD WD7	206 C7	
STALE/WH AL4	168 D2	
WARE SG12	127 G6	
WAT WD17	203 K7	
WLYN AL6	94 E8	
Ridgewood Dr HARP AL5	118 A6	
Ridgewood Gdns HARP AL5	118 A5	
Ridgmont Rd STAL AL1	11 D5	
The Ridings BSF CM23	105 G5	
CSHM HP5	200 A6	
HERT/WAS SG14	150 D4	
LTNN/LIM LU3	4 A2	
STALW/RED AL3	115 J3	
STVGE SG2	3 F5	
Ridler Rd EN EN1	213 H8	
Ridlins End STVGE SG2	76 D7	
Rigery La STDN SG11	100 E3	
Riley Rd PEND EN3	214 B8	
Ringshall Dr BERK HP4	137 J1	
Ringshall Rd BERK HP4	112 D6	
Ringtale Pl BLDK SG7	27 H8	
Ringway Rd LCOL/BKTW AL2	188 D5	
Ringwood Rd LTNE LU2	69 J3	
Ripley Rd LTNW/LEA LU4	68 B8	
Ripley Wy CHESW EN7	197 F8	
HHW HP1	163 H5	
Ripon Rd STVG SG1	59 F7	
Ripon Wy BORE WD6	224 B5	
STALE/WH AL4	169 G8	
Risdens HLWS CM18	179 K4	
Risedale Cl HHS/BOV HP3	185 J1	
Risedale Hl HHS/BOV HP3	185 J1	
Risedale Rd HHS/BOV HP3	185 J1	
The Rise BLDK SG7	42 E2	
BORE WD6	223 J5	
LCOL/BKTW AL2	189 F3	
Rising Hill Cl NTHWD HA6	229 H5	
Risingholme Cl BUSH WD23	221 J7	
Ritcroft Cl HHS/BOV HP3	9 E6	
Ritcroft Dr HHS/BOV HP3	9 E6	
Ritcroft St HHS/BOV HP3	9 E6	
Ritz Ct POTB/CUF EN6	210 B1	
Rivenhall End WGCE AL7	148 D3	
River Av HOD EN11	177 G2	
River Cl CHES/WCR EN8	215 F4	
River Ct HTCH/STOT SG5	40 C5	
Riverfield La SBW CM21	132 C6	
Riverford Cl HARP AL5	118 D5	
River Hl HTCH/STOT SG5	116 B7	
River Md HTCH/STOT SG5	40 C5	
River Meads WARE SG12	153 H4	
Rivermill HLW CM20	6 B2	
River Pk HHW HP1	163 K6	
Riversend Rd HHS/BOV HP3	185 G1	
Rivershill HERT/WAS SG14	98 B6	
Riverside BSF CM23	105 J2	
BUNT SG9	63 J2	
LCOL/BKTW AL2	190 C5	
WLYN AL6	122 B4	
Riverside Av BROX EN10	177 F8	
Riverside Cl KGLGY WD4	186 B7	
STAL AL1	11 D6	
Riverside Ct HLW CM20	157 F3	
Riverside Dr RKW/CH/CXG WD3	218 C3	
Riverside Gdns BERK HP4	161 H4	
Riverside Rd LTNN/LIM LU3	69 F4	
OXHEY WD19	12 C5	
STAL AL1	11 D5	
Riversmead HOD EN11	177 F4	
Riversmeet HERT/WAS SG14	150 E4	
River St WARE SG12	127 J8	
River Vw WGCE AL7	122 E7	
River Wy HLW CM20	156 D4	
LTNN/LIM LU3	68 D4	
Rivett Cl BLDK SG7	27 G8	
Robbery Bottom La WLYN AL6	123 F1	
Robbs Cl HHW HP1	163 K4	
Robe End HHW HP1	163 J4	
Robert Av LCOL/BKTW AL2	188 C2	
Robert Cl POTB/CUF EN6	209 K3	
Roberts Cl CHES/WCR EN8	197 J8	
Roberts La CFSP/GDCR SL9	226 D4	
Robertson Cl BROX EN10	197 J4	
Roberts Rd WATW WD18	13 D4	
Roberts Wy HAT AL10	170 D6	
Robert Wallace Cl BSF CM23	85 J8	
Robeson Wy BORE WD6	224 B1	
Robina Cl NTHWD HA6	230 A8	
Robin Cl WARE SG12	153 H6	
Robin Hl BERK HP4	161 K6	
Robin Hood Dr BUSH WD23	221 J5	
Robin Hood La HAT AL10	171 F3	
Robin Hood Meadow		
HHNE HP2	164 E1	
Robin Md WGCE AL7	123 G8	
Robins Cl LCOL/BKTW AL2	190 C5	
Robinsfield HHW HP1	163 K6	
Robins Nest Hl HERT/BAY SG13	173 K4	
Robinson Av CHESW EN7	195 K6	
Robinson Cl BSF CM23	105 J4	
Robinson Crs BUSH WD23	221 K8	
Robins Orch CFSP/GDCR SL9	226 B5	
Robins Rd HHS/BOV HP3	165 F3	
Robins Wy HAT AL10	170 E7	
Robinswood LTNE LU2	69 K4	
Robin Wy POTB/CUF EN6	195 G6	
Robson Cl CFSP/GDCR SL9	226 B4	
Robsons Cl CHES/WCR EN8	197 G7	
Rochester Av LTNE LU2	70 D5	
Rochester Dr CSTN WD25	204 D5	
Rochester Wy RKW/CH/CXG WD3	219 G4	
ROY SG8	21 H1	
Rochford Av WAB EN9	215 J4	
Rochford Cl BROX EN10	197 J4	
Rochford Dr LTNE LU2	71 F7	
Rochford Rd BSF CM23	86 A8	
Rockcliffe Av KGLGY WD4	186 B8	
Rockfield Av WARE SG12	127 H6	
Rockingham Wy STVG SG1	2 C5	
Rockleigh HERT/WAS SG14	150 E3	
Rockley Rd LTN LU1	89 F3	
Rock Rd ROY SG8	21 G1	
Rockways BAR EN5	224 E6	
Rodeheath LTNW/LEA LU4	68 C6	
Roden Cl HAT AL10	157 J5	
Rodgers Cl BORE WD6	223 G6	
Rodney Av STAL AL1	11 F6	
Rodney Crs HOD EN11	177 F1	
Roebuck Cl HERT/BAY SG13	151 K3	
LTN LU1	89 F3	
Roebuck Ga STVGE SG2	76 A8	
Roe Cl HTCH/STOT SG5	25 J4	
Roedean Cl LTNE LU2	70 E6	
Roe End La STALW/RED AL3	114 E5	
Roefields Cl HHS/BOV HP3	184 E2	
Roe Green Cl HAT AL10	170 D5	
Roe Green La HAT AL10	170 E4	
Roe Hill Cl HAT AL10	170 E5	
Roehyde Wy HAT AL10	170 D8	
Roestock Gdns STALE/WH AL4	170 D8	
Roestock La STALE/WH AL4	191 H1	
Rofant Rd NTHWD HA6	229 K5	
Rogate Rd LTNE LU2	70 D1	
Rogers Ruff NTHWD HA6	229 H7	
Roland St STAL AL1	11 F4	
Rolleston St WGCE SG12	127 G6	
Rollswood WGCE AL7	147 K6	
Rollswood Rd WLYN AL6	122 A2	
Rollys La BLDK SG7	17 K5	
Roman Gdns KGLGY WD4	186 B8	
LWTH SG6	41 J5	
Roman La BLDK SG7	43 F1	
Roman Ri SBW CM21	132 B7	
Roman Rd AMP/FLIT/B MK45	36 D6	
LTNW/LEA LU4	68 D2	
RAD WD7	206 D5	
Roman St HOD EN11	177 F2	
Roman V HLWE CM17	157 F4	
Roman Wy STALW/RED AL3	115 J3	
STDN SG11	81 J6	
WLYN AL6	122 C4	
Romany Cl LWTH SG6	41 G3	
Romany Ct HHNE HP2	9 F4	
Romeland BORE WD6	223 G6	
STALW/RED AL3	10 B4	
WAB EN9	215 H3	
Romeland Hl STALW/RED AL3	10 B4	
Romilly Dr OXHEY WD19	231 F3	
Rondini Av LTNN/LIM LU3	69 G7	
Ronsons Wy STALW/RED AL3	168 C2	
Rookery Cl LTNE LU2	69 K3	
The Rookery STSD CM24	86 D1	
Rookery La STVG SG1	2 A1	
Rookes Cl LWTH SG6	42 B6	
Rooks Hl RKW/CH/CXG WD3	218 D5	
WGCW AL8	147 H4	
Rooks Nest La ROY SG8	30 D2	
Rook Tree Cl HTCH/STOT SG5	26 A3	
Rook Tree La HTCH/STOT SG5	25 K2	
Rookwood Dr STVGE SG2	76 D8	
Rosary Ct POTB/CUF EN6	193 H8	
Rosary Gdns BUSH WD23	222 B7	
Roseacre Gdns WGCE AL7	148 E3	
Roseacres SBW CM21	132 B6	
Rosebank WAB EN9	215 K4	
Rosebarn La TRING HP23	109 H8	
Roseberry Ct WAT WD17	220 B1	
Rosebery Rd BSF CM23	106 B3	
Rosebery Av HARP AL5	118 B7	
Rosebery Rd BUSH WD23	221 J3	
Rosebery Wy TRING HP23	135 C4	
Rosebriar Wk WATN WD24	204 A6	
Rose Ct CHESW EN7	196 E5	
Rosecroft Dr WAT WD17	203 K7	
Rosecroft La WLYN AL6	123 G1	
Rosedale WGCE AL7	147 J7	
Rosedale Av CHESW EN7	196 D7	
Rosedale Cl LCOL/BKTW AL2	188 A8	
LTNW/LEA LU4	68 D2	
Rosedale Wy CHESW EN7	196 E5	
Rose Gdns WATW WD18	12 B4	
Roseheath HHW HP1	163 H5	
Rosehill BERK HP4	161 J5	
Rosehill Gdns ABLGY WD5	203 H2	
Roselands Av HOD EN11	176 E1	
Rose La STALE/WH AL4	120 A7	
Rose Md POTB/CUF EN6	193 J8	
Rose Meadow STDN SG11	64 E5	
Rosemont Cl LWTH SG6	41 J3	
Rosemount HLWW/ROY CM19	179 J4	
Rose V HOD EN11	177 F3	
Rose Wk ROY SG8	21 G2	
STALE/WH AL4	168 E4	
The Rose Wk RAD WD7	206 E6	
Rosewood Ct HHW HP1	163 H5	
Rosewood Dr ENC/FH EN2	212 D5	
Roslyn Cl BROX EN10	176 D7	
Ross Cl KTN/HRWW/W HA3	231 K8	
LTN LU1	89 G3	
Ross Crs GSTN WD25	204 B5	
Rossfold Rd LTNN/LIM LU3	68 C1	
Rossington Av BORE WD6	207 H8	
Rossiter Flds BAR EN5	225 K6	
Rosslyn Crs LTNN/LIM LU3	69 H4	
Rosslyn Rd WATW WD18	12 C2	
Rossway LTN LU1	89 G5	
Ross Wy NTHWD HA6	230 A3	
Rossway Dr BUSH WD23	221 K5	
Rossway La TRING HP23	160 B7	
Roswell Cl CHES/WCR EN8	197 J8	
Rothamsted Av HARP AL5	118 B8	
Rotheram Av LTN LU1	89 G4	
Rother Cl GSTN WD25	204 D2	
Rother Fld LTNE LU2	70 E6	
Rotherfield Rd PEND EN3	214 C2	
Rothesay Rd LTN LU1	4 B4	
Roughdown Av HHS/BOV HP3	184 E2	
Roughdown Rd HHS/BOV HP3	185 F1	
Roughdown Villas Rd		
HHS/BOV HP3	184 E1	
The Roughs NTHWD HA6	229 K2	
Roughwood Cl WAT WD17	203 K6	
Roughwood La CSTG HP8	216 B6	
Roundabout La WLYN AL6	123 F7	
Round Coppice Rd RBSF CM22	107 F5	
Roundcroft CHESW EN7	196 D6	
Roundfield Av HARP AL5	119 J6	
Roundhaye STDN SG11	81 J7	
Roundhedge Wy ENC/FH EN2	212 C8	
Roundhills WAB EN9	215 K4	
The Roundings HERT/BAY SG13	152 A6	
Roundmoor Dr CHES/WCR EN8	197 J3	
The Roundway WATW WD18	12 A4	
Roundwood HHS/BOV HP3	185 J1	
Roundwood Cl HTCHE/RSTV SG4	41 G2	
WLYN AL6	122 D7	
Roundwood Dr WGCW AL8	147 H4	
Roundwood Gdns HARP AL5	118 A7	
Roundwood La HARP AL5	117 H7	
Roundwood Pk HARP AL5	118 A7	
Rounton Rd WAB EN9	215 K2	
Rousebarn La RKW/CH/CXG WD3	202 E4	
Rowan Cl HTCHE/RSTV SG4	59 H4	
LCOL/BKTW AL2	205 H1	
LTN LU1	89 G2	
STALE/WH AL4	169 G4	
Rowan Crs LWTH SG6	41 J3	
STVG SG1	2 B1	
Rowan Dr BROX EN10	197 K2	
Rowan Gv HTCHE/RSTV SG4	56 E2	
Rowans WGCE AL7	123 F7	
The Rowans BLDK SG7	42 E3	
BROX EN10	176 D3	
HHW HP1	163 K6	
Rowan Wk SBW CM21	132 C3	
Rowan Wy HARP AL5	143 K5	
Rowcroft HHW HP1	163 H4	
Rowelfield LTNE LU2	70 D3	
Rowington Cl LTNE LU2	71 F7	
Rowland Rd STVG SG1	2 C6	
Rowlands Av PIN HA5	231 H1	
Rowlands Cl CHES/WCR EN8	197 H4	
Rowland Wy LWTH SG6	41 K3	
Rowlatt Dr STALW/RED AL3	167 H5	
Rowley Cl OXHEY WD19	13 F5	
Rowley Green Rd BAR EN5	225 F2	
Rowley La BAR EN5	224 D3	
BORE WD6	224 C2	
Rowley's Rd HERT/BAY SG13	151 J3	
Rowley Wk HHNE HP2	9 F1	
Rowney Gdns SBW CM21	157 H1	
Rowney La WARE SG12	100 A3	
Rowney Wd SBW CM21	132 A4	
Royal Av CHES/WCR EN8	214 C1	
Royal Ct HHS/BOV HP3	185 G4	
Royal Oak Cl BUNT SG9	47 F8	
Royal Oak Gdns BSF CM23	105 H4	
Royal Oak La HTCH/STOT SG5	39 F6	
Royal Rd STAL AL1	168 E1	
Royce Cl BROX EN10	176 E7	
Roydon Ct HHNE HP2	141 F7	
Roydon Rd HLWW/ROY CM19	155 J3	
WARE SG12	153	

Royle CI CFSP/GDCR SL9...... 226 C6
Roy Rd NTHWD HA6...... 230 A6
Royse Gv ROY SG8...... 21 H5
Royston CI HERT/WAS SG14...... 150 E3
Royston Gv PIN HA5...... 231 G5
Royston Park Rd PIN HA5...... 231 G5
Royston CI BLDK SG7...... 27 G8
  ROY SG8...... 32 C4
  STAL AL1...... 168 E7
Rucklers La KGLGY WD4...... 184 E6
Ruckles CI STVG SG1...... 2 C3
Rudd CI STVGE SG2...... 3 F5
Rudham Gv LWTH SG6...... 42 C6
Rudolph Rd BUSH WD23...... 221 H6
Rudyard CI LTNW/LEA LU4...... 68 C3
Rue De St Lawrence WAB EN9 ...... 215 H4
Rueley Dell Rd LTNE LU2...... 53 K7
Rugby Wy RKW/CH/CXG WD3...... 219 G5
The Ruins STALW/RED AL3...... 142 C4
Rumballs Rd HHS/BOV HP3...... 186 A1
Rumbold Rd HOD EN11...... 177 H1
Rumsley CHESW EN7...... 196 E5
Runcie CI STALE/WH AL4...... 168 C3
Runcorn Crs HHNE HP2...... 8 C1
Rundells HLWS CM18...... 180 D5
  HLWS CM18...... 42 D5
Runfold Av LTNN/LIM LU3...... 69 F4
Runham CI LTNW/LEA LU4...... 68 A5
Runham Rd HHS/BOV HP3...... 164 D8
Runley Rd LTN LU1...... 88 E2
Runnalow LWTH SG6...... 41 H2
Runsley WGCE AL7...... 123 G8
Ruscombe Dr LCOL/BKTW AL2 ...... 188 E4
Rushall Gn LTNE LU2...... 70 E7
Rushby Md LWTH SG6...... 42 A3
Rushby Pl LWTH SG6...... 42 A3
Rushby Wk LWTH SG6...... 42 A3
Rush CI WARE SG12...... 153 H5
Rushden Rd BUNT SG9...... 45 K1
Rushenden Furlong LBUZ LU7 ...... 110 E4
Rushen Dr HERT/BAY SG13...... 152 B6
Rushes Md HLWS CM18...... 7 D6
Rushfield POTB/CUF EN6...... 209 J3
  SBW CM21...... 132 C7
Rushfield Rd WARE SG12...... 127 K6
Rush La RBSF CM22...... 87 H1
Rushleigh Av CHESW EN7...... 197 H8
Rushleigh Gn BSF CM23...... 105 G6
Rushmere La CSHM HP5...... 182 C6
Rushmoor CI
  RKW/CH/CXG WD3...... 228 C1
Rushton Av WATN WD25...... 204 B5
Rushton Gv HLWE CM17...... 181 G1
Ruskin Av WAB EN9...... 215 K4
Ruskin CI CHESW EN7...... 196 E6
Ruskin La HTCHE/RSTV SG4...... 57 G2
Rusper Gn LTNE LU2...... 70 E6
Russell Av STALE/WH AL4...... 10 C4
Russell CI AMS HP6...... 216 A1
  DUN/WHIP LU6...... 114 C1
  NTHWD HA6...... 229 H4
  ROY SG8...... 15 J7
  STVGE SG2...... 3 F6
Russell Ct LCOL/BKTW AL2...... 188 C8
Russell Crs GSTN WD25...... 204 A5
Russellcroft Rd WGCW AL8...... 147 H2
Russell La WAT WD17...... 203 J6
Russell PI HHS/BOV HP3...... 185 F1
Russell Ri LTN LU1...... 4 C4
Russell Rd EN EN1...... 213 J8
  NTHWD HA6...... 229 H2
Russell's Dr CHES/WCR EN8...... 214 D1
Russell's Ride CHES/WCR EN8...... 214 C1
Russell St HERT/WAS SG14...... 151 F3
  LTN LU1...... 4 B5
Russell Wy OXHEY WD19...... 12 C5
Russet CI CHESW EN7...... 196 C4
Russet Dr RAD WD7...... 207 H2
  STALE/WH AL4...... 169 F7
The Russets CFSP/GDCR SL9...... 226 A8
Russett Wd WGCE AL7...... 148 E4
Rutherford CI BORE WD6...... 224 B2
  STVG SG1...... 75 F3
Rutherford Wy BUSH WD23...... 222 A8
Ruthin CI LTN LU1...... 4 B6
Ruthven Av CHES/WCR EN8...... 214 C3
Rutland Crs LTNE LU2...... 5 E4
The Rutts BUSH WD23...... 222 A8
Ryall CI LCOL/BKTW AL2...... 188 A7
Ryan Wy WATN WD24...... 220 D1
Rydal Wy LTNN/LIM LU3...... 68 E4
Ryder CI BUSH WD23...... 221 J6
  HERT/BAY SG13...... 152 A2
  HHS/BOV HP3...... 183 J6
Ryders Av STALE/WH AL4...... 170 D6
The Ryde BRKMPK AL9...... 171 H1
Rye CI HARP AL5...... 118 D5
Ryecroft CI HHNE HP2...... 9 F6
Ryecroft Crs BAR EN5...... 225 G5
Ryecroft Wy LTNE LU2...... 70 B6

Ryefeld CI HOD EN11...... 153 G7
Ryefield LTNN/LIM LU3...... 52 A8
Ryefield Crs NTHWD HA6...... 230 B8
Rye Gdns BLDK SG7...... 27 H8
Rye HI HARP AL5...... 118 D5
Rye Hill Rd HLWS CM18...... 180 A6
Rylands WGCE AL7...... 148 A6
Rye Rd HOD EN11...... 153 J8
Rye St BSF CM23...... 85 J8
Rylands Heath LTNE LU2...... 71 G7
Rymill CI HHS/BOV HP3...... 183 J6
Ryton CI LTN LU1...... 89 G2

S

Saberton CI STALW/RED AL3...... 142 A5
Sacombe Gn LTNN/LIM LU3...... 52 B8
Sacombe Green Rd WARE SG12...... 99 H5
Sacombe Pound WARE SG12...... 99 G7
Sacombe Rd HERT/WAS SG14...... 125 K5
  HHW HP1...... 163 J4
Sacombs Ash La SBW CM21...... 131 G2
Saddlers CI BLDK SG7...... 42 E1
  BORE WD6...... 224 C5
  PIN HA5...... 231 H4
Saddlers PI ROY SG8...... 21 G2
Sadleir Rd STAL AL1...... 11 D6
Sadlers Md HLWS CM18...... 7 F5
Sadlers Wy HERT/WAS SG14...... 150 D3
Sadlier Rd STDN SG11...... 81 J7
Saffron HI LWTH SG6...... 41 J3
Saffron La HHW HP1...... 164 A5
Saffron Mdw STDN SG11...... 81 K7
Saffron St ROY SG8...... 21 K4
Sainfoin End HHNE HP2...... 9 D3
St Agnells Ct HHNE HP2...... 9 D1
St Agnells La HHNE HP2...... 164 E1
St Albans Dr STVG SG1...... 58 E8
St Albans HI HHS/BOV HP3...... 185 J1
St Albans La ABLGY WD5...... 187 F4
St Albans Link STVG SG1...... 58 E8
St Albans Rd BAR EN5...... 225 K1
  GSTN WD25...... 204 D6
  HARP AL5...... 143 J3
  HHNE HP2...... 8 C6
  HHS/BOV HP3...... 8 A6
  POTB/CUF EN6...... 208 D1
  STALE/WH AL4...... 168 D2
  STALW/RED AL3...... 142 D5
  WAT WD17...... 12 C1
  WATN WD24...... 204 C8
  WLYN AL6...... 121 J3
St Albans Rd East HAT AL10...... 171 G5
St Albans Rd West HAT AL10...... 170 B4
St Andrew's Av HARP AL5...... 118 B8
St Andrew's CI LTN LU1...... 89 H8
St Andrews Dr KNEB SG3...... 59 F6
St Andrew's PI HTCHE/RSTV SG4...... 56 D3
St Andrew's Rd HHS/BOV HP3...... 185 H2
St Andrew St HERT/WAS SG14...... 151 F3
St Anna Rd BAR EN5...... 225 J5
St Anne's CI CHESW EN7...... 196 E6
  OXHEY WD19...... 230 D3
St Anne's Pk BROX EN10...... 177 H6
St Anne's Rd HTCHE/RSTV SG5...... 56 D1
  LCOL/BKTW AL2...... 190 B5
St Ann's Rd LTN LU1...... 5 D4
St Anthonys Av HHS/BOV HP3...... 165 G8
St Audreys CI HAT AL10...... 171 G7
St Audreys Gn WGCE AL7...... 148 A4
St Augusta Ct STALW/RED AL3...... 10 C2
St Augustine Av LTNN/LIM LU3...... 69 G6
St Augustine CI HTCHE/RSTV SG5...... 56 D1
St Augustines CI BROX EN10...... 176 E6
St Augustines Dr BROX EN10...... 176 E6
St Bernard's CI LTN LU3...... 69 H6
St Bernard's Rd STALW/RED AL3...... 10 C1
St Catharine's Rd BROX EN10...... 177 F5
St Catharines Av LTNN/LIM LU3...... 69 G5
St Cross St HOD EN11...... 177 F5
St Cuthberts Gdns PIN HA5...... 231 G6
St Cuthberts Rd HOD EN11...... 153 H8
St David's CI HHS/BOV HP3...... 165 J8
  STVG SG1...... 59 F6
St David's Dr BROX EN10...... 176 E5
St Dunstan's Rd WARE SG12...... 154 E1
St Edmunds BERK HP4...... 161 K6
St Edmunds Wk STALE/WH AL4...... 169 G7
St Edmund's Wy HLWE CM17...... 157 G5
St Elmo Ct HTCHE/RSTV SG4...... 56 D4
St Ethelbert Av LTNN/LIM LU3...... 69 G5
St Etheldreda's Dr HAT AL10...... 171 H4
St Faiths CI HTCHE/RSTV SG4...... 41 F8
St Francis CI BUNT SG9...... 63 K3
  OXHEY WD19...... 12 B8
  POTB/CUF EN6...... 210 D3
St George's Dr OXHEY WD19...... 231 F2
St George's Rd EN EN1...... 213 J8

  HHS/BOV HP3...... 185 G2
  WATN WD24...... 204 C7
  WATN WD24...... 204 C8
St George's Wy STVG SG1...... 2 B3
St Giles' Av POTB/CUF EN6...... 209 F3
St Giles Rd HTCHE/RSTV SG4...... 94 E7
St Helen's CI STALE/WH AL4...... 145 G1
St Heliers Rd STALE/WH AL4...... 168 E1
St Ives CI LTNN/LIM LU3...... 69 G6
  WLYN AL6...... 123 F6
St James Rd HARP AL5...... 118 D6
  LTNN/LIM LU3...... 69 G6
  WATW WD18...... 12 C4
St James's Rd CHESW EN7...... 196 A6
St James Wy BSF CM23...... 104 E4
St John CI LTN LU1...... 89 G4
St Johns STDN SG11...... 81 K6
St John's Av HLWE CM17...... 157 F5
St John's CI POTB/CUF EN6...... 210 D3
  WLYN AL6...... 122 C3
St John's Ct HARP AL5...... 143 K2
  STAL AL1...... 168 E5
St John's Crs STSD CM24...... 86 D2
St John's La STSD CM24...... 86 D2
  WARE SG12...... 153 F3
St John's Rd ARL/CHE SG15...... 24 E5
  HARP AL5...... 143 K2
  HHW HP1...... 164 A8
  HTCHE/RSTV SG4...... 56 D4
  STSD CM24...... 86 D2
  WAT WD17...... 12 C1
St John's St HERT/WAS SG14...... 151 G3
St John's Ter ENC/FH EN2...... 213 G7
St Johns Wk HLWE CM17...... 157 F5
St John's Well CI BERK HP4...... 161 J4
St John's Well La BERK HP4...... 161 J4
St Joseph's CI LTNN/LIM LU3...... 69 F5
St Julian's Rd STAL AL1...... 10 C6
St Katharines CI HTCH/STOT SG5...... 40 B6
St Katherine's Wy BERK HP4...... 161 G2
St Laurence Av BROX EN10...... 197 J1
St Lawrence CI ABLGY WD5...... 186 E8
  HHS/BOV HP3...... 183 J5
St Lawrences Av LTNN/LIM LU3...... 69 H5
St Lawrence Wy LCOL/BKTW AL2...... 188 B8
St Leonards CI BUSH WD23...... 13 F3
  HERT/WAS SG14...... 151 H1
St Leonard's Ct STALE/WH AL4...... 145 F8
St Leonards Crs STALE/WH AL4...... 145 F8
St Leonard's Rd HERT/WAS SG14...... 151 G1
  WAB EN9...... 198 D2
St Luke's Av ENC/FH EN2...... 213 G8
St Luke's CI LTNW/LEA LU4...... 68 D7
St Margarets STVGE SG2...... 3 D6
St Margarets Av LTNN/LIM LU3...... 69 G5
St Margaret's CI BERK HP4...... 162 A6
St Margaret's Rd WARE SG12...... 153 F7
St Margarets Wy HHNE HP2...... 165 J6
St Marks CI STALE/WH AL4...... 170 A8
St Martin's Av LTNE LU2...... 5 D1
St Martins CI HARP AL5...... 118 E5
  OXHEY WD19...... 230 D3
St Martin's Rd KNEB SG3...... 96 B4
St Mary's Av BERK HP4...... 160 E3
  HTCH/STOT SG5...... 25 K3
  NTHWD HA6...... 229 K4
St Mary's CI HTCH/STOT SG5...... 39 F5
  LWTH SG6...... 41 K2
  STALW/RED AL3...... 142 B4
  STVGE SG2...... 77 F7
  WLYN AL6...... 122 C4
St Mary's Ct POTB/CUF EN6...... 210 C2
St Mary's Dr STSD CM24...... 86 E5
St Mary's La HERT/WAS SG14...... 150 C5
St Mary's Ri HTCHE/RSTV SG4...... 72 A8
St Mary's Rd CHES/WCR EN8...... 197 G7
  HHNE HP2...... 8 A4
  LTN LU1...... 4 C4
  STDN SG11...... 81 J7
  WATW WD18...... 12 C3
St Marys Wk STALE/WH AL4...... 168 E2
St Mary's Wy BLDK SG7...... 42 E3
  CFSP/GDCR SL9...... 226 A8
St Matthews CI LTNE LU2...... 4 C3
  OXHEY WD19...... 13 E5
St Michael's Av HHS/BOV HP3...... 9 E6
  HHS/BOV HP3...... 165 G8
St Michael's CI HLW CM20...... 7 D3
St Michael's Crs LTNN/LIM LU3...... 69 G5
St Michaels Dr GSTN WD25...... 204 C3
St Michael's Mt HTCHE/RSTV SG4...... 56 E1
St Michael's Rd BROX EN10...... 176 E6
  HTCHE/RSTV SG4...... 57 F1
St Michael's St STALW/RED AL3...... 10 B4
St Michaels Wy POTB/CUF EN6...... 193 H8
St Mildreds Av LTNN/LIM LU3...... 69 G5
St Monicas Av LTNN/LIM LU3...... 69 G5
St Neots CI BORE WD6...... 207 K8
St Nicholas Av HARP AL5...... 118 C8
St Nicholas CI BORE WD6...... 223 C6
St Nicholas Fld BSF CM23...... 67 K1
St Nicholas Mt HHW HP1...... 163 J6
St Olam's CI LTNN/LIM LU3...... 69 G3
St Olives HTCH/STOT SG5...... 25 J3
St Pauls PI STAL AL1...... 11 F4

St Paul's Rd *HHNE* HP2 8 B4
LTN LU1 4 C6
St Pauls Wy *WAB* EN9 215 J3 3
WATN WD24 13 D1 6
St Peter's Av *ARL/CHE* SG15 24 E2
St Peter's Cl *BAR* EN5 225 G5
BUSH WD23 222 A8
HAT AL10 171 F3 2
RKW/CH/CXG WD3 228 A1
STALW/RED AL3 10 C3
St Peters Hl *TRING* HP23 135 F5
St Peters Rd *LTN* LU1 89 G2
STAL AL1 11 D4
St Peter's St *STAL* AL1 10 C3
St Peters Wy *RKW/CH/CXG* WD3 216 E4
St Ronans Cl *EBAR* EN4 210 E8
St Saviours's Crs *LTN* LU1 4 B5
St Stephen's Av *STALW/RED* AL3 10 A6
St Stephen's Cl *STALW/RED* AL3 188 D1 2
St Stephen's Hl *STAL* AL1 10 B6
St Stephens Rd *BAR* EN5 225 J5
PEND EN3 214 C7
St Thomas' Dr *PIN* HA5 231 F7
St Thomas Pl *STALE/WH* AL4 145 G1
St Vincent Dr *STAL* AL1 11 F6
St Vincent's Wy *POTB/CUF* EN6 210 D3 4
St Winifreds Av *LTNN/LIM* LU3 69 H5
St Yon Ct *STALE/WH* AL4 169 G6
Sakins Cft *HLWS* CM18 180 C4
Sale Dr *BLDK* SG7 27 F8
Salisbury Av *HARP* AL5 118 B7
STAL AL1 168 E5
Salisbury Cl *BSF* CM23 105 J4
POTB/CUF EN6 210 D2
Salisbury Crs *CHES/WCR* EN8 214 C2
Salisbury Gdns *WGCE* AL7 148 A4
Salisbury Rd *BAR* EN5 225 K3
BLDK SG7 26 E8
HARP AL5 119 F6
HOD EN11 177 H2
LTN LU1 4 B5
PEND EN3 214 E7
STVG SG1 59 G7
WATN WD24 204 C8
WGCE AL7 148 A4
Salisbury Sq *HERT/WAS* SG14 151 G3 15
Sally Deards La *WLYN* AL6 95 G5
Salmon Cl *WGCE* AL7 123 G8
Salmons Cl *WARE* SG12 127 H6
Saltdean Cl *LTNE* LU2 70 E5
Salters *BSF* CM23 105 F5
Salter's Cl *BERK* HP4 161 G3 4
RKW/CH/CXG WD3 218 D8
Saltfield Cresent *LTNW/LEA* LU4 68 B5
Salusbury La *HTCH/STOT* SG5 54 E7
Salwey Crs *BROX* EN10 176 E6
Samian Ga *STALW/RED* AL3 167 G8
Sampson Av *BAR* EN5 225 J5
Sanctuary Cl *DEN/HRF* UB9 228 B6
Sandalls Spring *HHW* HP1 163 J4
Sandalwood Cl *LTNN/LIM* LU3 69 G2 2
Sanday Cl *HHS/BOV* HP3 165 G8
Sandbrook La *TRING* HP23 109 G8
Sandell Cl *LTNE* LU2 5 D1
Sanderling Cl *LWTH* SG6 41 J1
Sanders Cl *LCOL/BKTW* AL2 190 B5
Sanders Rd *HHS/BOV* HP3 185 K1
Sandfield Rd *STAL* AL1 11 F4
Sandgate Rd *LTNW/LEA* LU4 68 C7
Sandhurst Ct *HARP* AL5 144 A3 7
Sandifield *HAT* AL10 171 G7
Sand La *AMP/FLIT/B* MK45 36 B2
Sandle Rd *BSF* CM23 105 K2
Sandmere Cl *HHNE* HP2 9 D6 5
Sandon Cl *TRING* HP23 134 E5
Sandon Rd *CHES/WCR* EN8 197 G8
Sandover Cl *HTCHE/RSTV* SG4 57 F3
Sandown Rd *STVG* SG1 59 J8
WATN WD24 204 D8
Sandpit La *STAL* AL1 11 E3
Sandpit Rd *WGCE* AL7 147 K5
Sandridgebury La
STALW/RED AL3 144 E7
Sandridge Cl *HHNE* HP2 141 F8
Sandridge Rd *STAL* AL1 11 D2
Sandringham Av
HLWW/ROY CM19 179 F1
Sandringham Crs *STALE/WH* AL4 168 D2
Sandringham Rd
POTB/CUF EN6 193 H8 5
WATN WD24 204 C7
Sandringham Wy *CHES/WCR* EN8 214 B4
Sandy Cl *HERT/WAS* SG14 150 E3
Sandy Gv *HTCHE/RSTV* SG4 56 D3
Sandy La *BUSH* WD23 221 K3
NTHWD HA6 230 A1
Sandy Lodge La *NTHWD* HA6 229 J1
Sandy Lodge Rd
RKW/CH/CXG WD3 229 G1
Sandy Lodge Wy *NTHWD* HA6 229 K4
Sandy Ri *CFSP/GDCR* SL9 226 B7
Sanfoine Cl *HTCHE/RSTV* SG4 57 G1
Santers La *POTB/CUF* EN6 209 K3
Santingfield North *LTN* LU1 89 G3
Santingfield South *LTN* LU1 89 G4
Sappers Cl *SBW* CM21 132 D7
Saracens Head *HHNE* HP2 9 D4 1
Sarratt Av *HHNE* HP2 165 F1
Sarratt La *RKW/CH/CXG* WD3 218 A2
Sarratt Rd *RKW/CH/CXG* WD3 202 A7
Sarum Pl *HHNE* HP2 8 B1
Sarum Rd *LTNN/LIM* LU3 68 D5
Satinwood Ct *HHS/BOV* HP3 164 D8 1
Saturn Wy *HHNE* HP2 8 C2
Sauncey Av *HARP* AL5 118 D6
Sauncey Wd *HARP* AL5 119 F5
Sauncey Wood La *HARP* AL5 119 G4
Saunders Cl *CHES/WCR* EN8 197 G6
LWTH SG6 42 B2
Savill Cl *CHESW* EN7 196 A3 3
Saville Cl *SAFWS* CB11 51 K5
Savoy Cl *DEN/HRF* UB9 228 C8
Savoy Wd *EPP* CM16 179 J7 2
Sawbridgeworth Rd *RBSF* CM22 133 F4
SBW CM21 133 G6
Sawells *BROX* EN10 176 E7
Sawtry Cl *LTNN/LIM* LU3 69 F3
Sawtry Wy *BORE* WD6 207 K8 4
Sawyers La *POTB/CUF* EN6 209 J4
Sawyers Wy *HHNE* HP2 8 C5 2
Saxon Av *HTCH/STOT* SG5 25 K1
Saxon Cl *HARP* AL5 118 E5
LWTH SG6 25 K8
Saxon Ct *BORE* WD6 223 H1 2
Saxon Crs *AMP/FLIT/B* MK45 36 C5
Saxon Rd *LTNN/LIM* LU3 69 G7
STALE/WH AL4 145 G2
WLYN AL6 122 B6
Saxon Wy *BLDK* SG7 27 H8
Saxtead Cl *LTNE* LU2 70 E8
Sayers Gdns *BERK* HP4 161 H2
Sayer Wy *KNEB* SG3 96 A5
Sayesbury Av *SBW* CM21 132 B6
Sayesbury Rd *SBW* CM21 132 C7
Sayes Gdns *SBW* CM21 132 D7
Saywell Rd *LTNE* LU2 5 F2
Scammell Wy *WATW* WD18 12 A5
Scarborough Av *STVG* SG1 75 F2
Scatterdells La *KGLGY* WD4 184 D8
Scholar's Hl *WARE* SG12 129 F5
Scholars Ms *WGCW* AL8 147 J2
Scholars Wk *CFSP/GDCR* SL9 226 B5
School Cl *BRKMPK* AL9 173 G3 2
STVGE SG2 3 F5
Schoolfields *LWTH* SG6 42 C4
School La *BRKMPK* AL9 173 G3
BUSH WD23 221 J7
CFSP/GDCR SL9 226 A8
HAT AL10 171 C3
HERT/WAS SG14 98 B6
HLW CM20 7 D1
HTCH/STOT SG5 54 E6
HTCHE/RSTV SG4 43 J8
HTCHE/RSTV SG4 73 H3
LCOL/BKTW AL2 205 G4
LTNW/LEA LU4 68 C5
ROY SG8 23 G8
SAFWS CB11 35 J2
STVGE SG2 61 H6
STVGE SG2 77 F7
WLYN AL6 122 B5
WLYN AL6 124 A8
School Md *ABLGY* WD5 203 J2
School Rd *POTB/CUF* EN6 193 J8
School Rw *HHW* HP1 163 J7
School Wk *LWTH* SG6 42 B3
Schubert Rd *BORE* WD6 223 G6
Scot Gv *PIN* HA5 230 E6
Scotscraig *RAD* WD7 206 C5
Scots Hl *RKW/CH/CXG* WD3 218 E6
Scots Hill Cl *RKW/CH/CXG* WD3 218 E6
Scots Mill La *RKW/CH/CXG* WD3 218 E6
Scott Av *WARE* SG12 153 G5
Scott Rd *BSF* CM23 105 H3
LTNN/LIM LU3 68 B2
STVGE SG2 3 F2
Scotts Cl *WARE* SG12 152 C1
Scott's Rd *WARE* SG12 152 C1
Scotts Vw *WGCW* AL8 147 H4
Scottswood Cl *BUSH* WD23 13 F1 1
Scottswood Rd *BUSH* WD23 13 F1
Scriveners Cl *HHNE* HP2 8 B5
Scrubbits Sq *RAD* WD7 206 D5 1
Scrubbitts Park Rd *RAD* WD7 206 D5
Seabrook *LTNW/LEA* LU4 68 A6
Seabrook Rd *KGLGY* WD4 186 D6
Seacroft Gdns *OXHEY* WD19 230 E2
Seaford Cl *LTNE* LU2 70 D6
Seaforth Dr *CHES/WCR* EN8 214 C4
Seal Cl *LTNW/LEA* LU4 68 C6
Seaman Cl *LCOL/BKTW* AL2 189 F3
Searches La *ABLGY* WD5 187 H5
HHS/BOV HP3 187 J5
Seaton Rd *HHS/BOV* HP3 185 H1
LCOL/BKTW AL2 190 B5
LTNW/LEA LU4 68 E6
Sebright Rd *BAR* EN5 225 J2
HHW HP1 163 K8
STALW/RED AL3 115 J4
Secker Crs *KTN/HRWW/W* HA3 231 K7
Second Av *GSTN* WD25 204 E5
HLWE CM17 180 E2
HLWS CM18 7 E4
LWTH SG6 42 C3
Sedbury Cl *LTNN/LIM* LU3 69 F3
Sedge Gn *HLWW/ROY* CM19 178 A5
WAB EN9 177 K6
Sedgwick Rd *LTNW/LEA* LU4 68 A2
Seebohm Cl *HTCH/STOT* SG5 40 A8
Seeleys *HLWE* CM17 157 F5
Sefton Cl *STAL* AL1 11 E3
Sefton Rd *STVG* SG1 59 H8
Selbourne Rd *LTNW/LEA* LU4 68 E6
Selby Av *STALW/RED* AL3 10 C4
Selden Hl *HHNE* HP2 8 A6
Sele Ml *HERT/WAS* SG14 150 E3
Sele Rd *HERT/WAS* SG14 150 E3
Selina Cl *LTNN/LIM* LU3 68 B2
Sells Rd *WARE* SG12 127 K7
Sellwood Dr *BAR* EN5 225 J5
Selsey Dr *LTNE* LU2 70 E4
Selwyn Av *HAT* AL10 170 C5
Selwyn Crs *HAT* AL10 170 D4
Selwyn Dr *HAT* AL10 170 D4
Semphill Rd *HHS/BOV* HP3 185 J1
Senate Pl *STVG* SG1 59 H7
Sequoia Cl *BUSH* WD23 222 A8
Sequoia Pk *PIN* HA5 231 J5
Serby Av *ROY* SG8 21 G
Sergehill La *ABLGY* WD5 187 G4
Serpentine Cl *STVG* SG1 59 J7
The Service Rd *POTB/CUF* EN6 210 B2
Seven Acres *NTHWD* HA6 230 B5
The Severalls *LTNE* LU2 70 C6
Severn Dr *EN* EN1 213 K8
Severnmead *HHNE* HP2 8 B2
Severnvale *LCOL/BKTW* AL2 190 D5
Severn Wy *GSTN* WD25 204 D4
Sewardstone Rd *WAB* EN9 215 H4
Sewardstone St *WAB* EN9 215 H4
Sewardstone Wy *WAB* EN9 215 H6
Sewell Cl *STALE/WH* AL4 169 H6
Sewell Harris Cl *HLW* CM20 7 E3
Sewells *WGCW* AL8 122 E8
Sexton Cl *CHESW* EN7 195 K3
Seymour Av *LTN* LU1 5 D5
Seymour Cl *PIN* HA5 231 G
Seymour Crs *HHNE* HP2 8 B
Seymour Rd *BERK* HP4 161 F
LTN LU1 5 D
STALW/RED AL3 11 D
Seymours *HLWW/ROY* CM19 179 G
Shackledell *STVGE* SG2 3 D
Shacklegate La *HTCHE/RSTV* SG4 93 J
Shackleton Spring *STVGE* SG2 3 E
Shackleton Wy *ABLGY* WD5 204 B2
WGCE AL7 148 E
Shady Bush Cl *BUSH* WD23 221 K7
Shady La *WAT* WD17 12 C1
Shaftenhoe End Rd *ROY* SG8 23 G
Shaftesbury Rd *LTNW/LEA* LU4 89 G
WAT WD17 13 D2
Shaftesbury Wy *ROY* SG8 21 J
Shakespeare *ROY* SG8 21 H
Shakespeare Rd *HARP* AL5 118 D
LTNW/LEA LU4 68 A
Shakespeare St *WATN* WD24 204 C
Shalcross Dr *CHES/WCR* EN8 197 K
Shallcross Crs *HAT* AL10 170 E
Shambrook Rd *CHESW* EN7 195 K
Shangani Rd *BSF* CM23 105 J
Shanklin Cl *CHESW* EN7 196 D7
LTNN/LIM LU3 69 F
Shanklin Gdns *OXHEY* WD19 230 D
Shantock Hall La *HHS/BOV* HP3 183 G
Shantock La *HHS/BOV* HP3 183 G
Sharmans Cl *WLYN* AL6 123 F
Sharose Ct *STALW/RED* AL3 115 J
Sharpcroft *HHNE* HP2 8 A3
Sharpecroft *HLWW/ROY* CM19 6 B
Sharpenhoe Rd *AMP/FLIT/B* MK45 36 A
LTNN/LIM LU3 52 B
Sharpes La *HHW* HP1 162 E
Sharples Gn *LTNN/LIM* LU3 69 G
Sharps Wy *HTCHE/RSTV* SG4 56 E
Shawbridge *HLWW/ROY* CM19 179 K
Shaw Cl *CHES/WCR* EN8 197 G
The Shaws *WGCE* AL7 148 D
The Shearers *BSF* CM23 104 E
Sheares Hoppit *WARE* SG12 129 K
Shearwater Cl *STVGE* SG2 76 E
Sheepcot Dr *GSTN* WD25 204 C
Sheepcote *WGCE* AL7 148 E
Sheepcote La *STALE/WH* AL4 120 C
Sheepcote Rd *HHNE* HP2 8 C5
Sheepcot La *GSTN* WD25 204 B
Sheepcroft Hl *STVGE* SG2 76 E
Sheephouse Rd *HHS/BOV* HP3 164 E
Sheering Dr *HLWE* CM17 157 H
Sheering Lower Rd *SBW* CM21 157
Sheering Mill La *SBW* CM21 132 D
Sheering Rd *HLWE* CM17 157 H
Sheethanger La *HHS/BOV* HP3 184 E
Shefton Ri *NTHWD* HA6 230 B
Sheldon Cl *CHESW* EN7 196 E

HLWE CM17 181 H1
Shelford Rd *BAR* EN5 225 H6
Shelley Cl *HTCHE/RSTV* SG4 57 G2
NTHWD HA6 230 A4
Shelley La *DEN/HRF* UB9 227 K6
Shelton Wy *LTNE* LU2 70 B6
Shenfield Ct *HLWS* CM18 179 K4 2
Shenleybury *RAD* WD7 190 C8
Shenleybury Cottages *RAD* WD7 207 H1
Shenley Hl *RAD* WD7 206 E4
Shenley La *LCOL/BKTW* AL2 189 K3
Shenley Rd *BORE* WD6 223 K3
HHNE HP2 141 G8
RAD WD7 207 G5
Shenstone Hl *BERK* HP4 162 B4
Shenwood Ct *BORE* WD6 207 K7 1
BORE WD6 208 A7 3
Shephall Gn *STVGE* SG2 3 F6
Shephall La *STVGE* SG2 76 A8
Shephall Vw *STVG* SG1 3 E3
Shephall Wy *STVGE* SG2 3 F4
Shepherd Cl *ROY* SG8 21 J4
Shepherds Cl *BSF* CM23 105 F5 5
Shepherds Ct *HERT/WAS* SG14 126 A8 1
Shepherds Gn *HHW* HP1 163 H7 5
HHW HP1 163 H7 5
Shepherd's La *RKW/CH/CXG* WD3 217 G6
STVG SG1 74 E3
Shepherds Md *HTCH/STOT* SG5 40 C7
Shepherds Rd *WATW* WD18 12 A2
Shepherds Wy *BRKMPK* AL9 193 J5
HARP AL5 117 K5 4
RKW/CH/CXG WD3 218 A7
Shepley Ms *PEND* EN3 215 F8
Sheppard Cl *EN* EN1 214 A8
Sheppards *HLWW/ROY* CM19 179 G4
Sheppards Cl *STALW/RED* AL3 11 D1
Shepperton Cl *BORE* WD6 224 C1 2
Sheppey's La *KGLGY* WD4 186 E6
Sheraton Cl *BORE* WD6 223 J5
Sherborne Av *LTNE* LU2 69 J3
Sherborne Pl *NTHWD* HA6 229 J5
Sherborne Wy *RKW/CH/CXG* WD3 219 G4
Sherbourne Cl *HHS/BOV* HP3 8 B6 5
Sherd Cl *LTNN/LIM* LU3 68 E2
Sheredes Dr *HOD* EN11 176 E4 1
Sherfield Av *RKW/CH/CXG* WD3 228 C2
Sheridan Cl *HHW* HP1 164 A7
Sheridan Rd *LTNN/LIM* LU3 4 A1 2
OXHEY WD19 13 E6
Sheriden Wk *BROX* EN10 176 D6
Sheriff Wy *GSTN* WD25 204 B3
Sheringham Av *STVG* SG1 58 B8
Sheringham Cl *LTNE* LU2 69 H2 1
Sherington Av *PIN* HA5 231 H6
Sherrardspark Rd *WGCW* AL8 147 J1 3
Sherwood *LWTH* SG6 41 K1
Sherwood Av *POTB/CUF* EN6 209 K2
STALE/WH AL4 168 E3
Sherwood Pl *HHNE* HP2 8 C1 4
Sherwood Rd *LTNW/LEA* LU4 69 F7
Sherwoods Ri *HARP* AL5 144 A1
Sherwoods Rd *OXHEY* WD19 13 F6
Shetland Cl *BORE* WD6 224 C6
Shillington Rd *HTCH/STOT* SG5 38 A3
Shillitoe Av *POTB/CUF* EN6 209 J2
Shingle Cl *LTNN/LIM* LU3 69 F1
Shire Cl *BROX* EN10 197 K4 3
Shire La *CFSP/GDCR* SL9 226 E4
RKW/CH/CXG WD3 216 E5
TRING HP23 158 D2
Shiremeade *BORE* WD6 223 J5
The Shires *LTNE* LU2 4 B3
ROY SG8 21 J3
Shirley Cl *BROX* EN10 197 K2 2
CHES/WCR EN8 197 G7
STVGE SG2 76 C1
Shirley Rd *ABLGY* WD5 204 A2
LTN LU1 4 A3
STAL AL1 11 E5
Shooters Dr *WAB* EN9 177 K8
Shooters Rd *ENC/FH* EN2 212 D8
Shootersway *BERK* HP4 160 C3
Shootersway La *BERK* HP4 161 G6
Shootersway Pk *BERK* HP4 161 G5 1
Shoplands *WGCW* AL8 122 D8
Shoreham Cl *STVG* SG1 75 F1
Shortcroft *BSF* CM23 106 C1
Shortcroft Ct *AMP/FLIT/B* MK45 36 B7 1
Shortlands Gn *WGCE* AL7 148 A4 2
Shortlands Pl *BSF* CM23 105 J1 2
Short La *LCOL/BKTW* AL2 188 A7
STVGE SG2 77 F5
Shortmead Dr *CHES/WCR* EN8 214 D1
Shothanger Wy *HHS/BOV* HP3 184 B3
Shottfield Cl *STALE/WH* AL4 145 F7
Shott La *LWTH* SG6 42 A3
Shott Lower *CHESW* EN7 196 D4
Shrubbery Gv *ROY* SG8 21 H5
The Shrubbery *HHW* HP1 163 H5
Shrub Hill Rd *HHW* HP1 163 J7
Shrublands *BRKMPK* AL9 193 H4
Shrublands Av *BERK* HP4 161 H5
Shrublands Rd *BERK* HP4 161 H4
The Shrublands *POTB/CUF* EN6 209 K3
Shugars Gn *TRING* HP23 135 G4
Sibley Av *HARP* AL5 144 A2
Sibley Cl *LTNE* LU2 70 C6
Sibneys Gn *HLWS* CM18 180 B5
Sibthorpe Rd *BRKMPK* AL9 192 D2 2
Siccut Rd *HTCHE/RSTV* SG4 57 J5
Sicklefield Cl *CHESW* EN7 196 D4 4
Siddons Rd *STVGE* SG2 76 D3
Sidford Cl *HHW* HP1 163 J6
The Sidings *BROX* EN10 176 E8 3
HAT AL10 170 D5 1
HHNE HP2 8 A5
Sidmouth Cl *OXHEY* WD19 230 C1
Sidney Ter *BSF* CM23 105 J3
Silam Rd *STVG* SG1 2 C3
Silecroft Rd *LTNE* LU2 5 E3
Silk Mill Rd *OXHEY* WD19 12 C6 2
STALW/RED AL3 142 C5
Silk Mill Wy *TRING* HP23 135 F4
Silverbirch Av *HTCH/STOT* SG5 25 K1
Silverdale Rd *BUSH* WD23 13 F4
Silver Dell *WATN* WD24 204 A5
Silverfield *BROX* EN10 176 E8
Silver Hl *BORE* WD6 208 B6
Silver St *BLDK* SG7 17 K5
CHESW EN7 196 B8
LTN LU1 4 C4
ROY SG8 15 G6
STSD CM24 86 C3
WAB EN9 215 H4 6
Silverthorn Dr *HHS/BOV* HP3 186 B2
Silver Trees *LCOL/BKTW* AL2 188 B8
Silverwood Cl *NTHWD* HA6 229 H7
Simmonds Ri *HHS/BOV* HP3 164 C8
Simon Dean *HHS/BOV* HP3 183 J5
Simpkins Dr *AMP/FLIT/B* MK45 36 C5
Simpson Cl *LTNW/LEA* LU4 68 C7
Simpson Dr *BLDK* SG7 43 F1
Sinderby Cl *BORE* WD6 223 H1
Sinfield Cl *STVG* SG1 3 E3
Singlets La *STALW/RED* AL3 116 C7
Sir Joseph's Wk *HARP* AL5 143 H1
Sir Peter's Wy *DUN/WHIP* LU6 113 G3
Sirus Rd *NTHWD* HA6 230 B4
Sish Cl *STVG* SG1 2 B2
Sish La *STVG* SG1 2 B2
Siskin Cl *BORE* WD6 223 K4
BUSH WD23 13 F3 3
Sisson Cl *STVGE* SG2 76 D7
Six Acres *HHS/BOV* HP3 186 A1
Six Hills Wy *STVG* SG1 2 A4
Sixth Av *GSTN* WD25 204 E5
LWTH SG6 42 C3
STSD CM24 87 H6
Skegness Rd *STVG* SG1 75 F1
Skegsbury La *HTCHE/RSTV* SG4 92 C8
Skelton Cl *LTNN/LIM* LU3 52 B8
Skidmore Wy *RKW/CH/CXG* WD3 218 D8
Skimpans Cl *BRKMPK* AL9 192 D2
Skinners St *BSF* CM23 105 F5
Skipton Cl *STVGE* SG2 96 A1
Skylark Cnr *STVGE* SG2 76 E6
Skys Wood Rd *STALE/WH* AL4 168 E2
Slade Ct *RAD* WD7 206 E6
Sleaford Gn *OXHEY* WD19 230 E2
Sleapcross Gdns *STALE/WH* AL4 170 B7
Sleaps Hyde *STVGE* SG2 76 D8
Sleapshyde La *STALE/WH* AL4 170 B7
Sleddale *HHNE* HP2 8 B2
Sleets End *HHW* HP1 164 A4
Slimmons Dr *STALE/WH* AL4 168 D2
Slipe La *BROX* EN10 197 K2
The Slipe *LBUZ* LU7 110 A2
Slip La *KNEB* SG3 95 G4
Slippers Hl *HHNE* HP2 8 A4
Sloansway *WGCE* AL7 123 F8
The Slype *STALE/WH* AL4 119 J4
Small Acre *HHW* HP1 163 J6 3
Smallcroft *WGCE* AL7 148 C2 5
Smallford La *STALE/WH* AL4 170 A7
Smallwood Cl *STALE/WH* AL4 145 H2 2
Smarts Gn *CHESW* EN7 196 D4
Smeaton Cl *WAB* EN9 215 K2 4
Smeaton Rd *WAB* EN9 215 F8
Smithfield *HHNE* HP2 8 A3
Smith's End La *ROY* SG8 23 F8
Smiths La *CHESW* EN7 196 B4
Smith St *WATW* WD18 13 D3 11
The Smithy *STDN* SG11 83 J7
Smug Oak La *LCOL/BKTW* AL2 188 D8
Snailswell La *HTCH/STOT* SG5 40 C4
Snatchup *STALW/RED* AL3 142 B4
Snells Md *BUNT* SG9 63 J2
The Snipe *HTCHE/RSTV* SG4 43 G8
Snowdrop Cl *BSF* CM23 105 F3
Snowford Cl *LTNN/LIM* LU3 69 F2
Snowhill Cottages *CSHM* HP5 182 B2
Soham Rd *PEND* EN3 214 E7
Solesbridge Cl *RKW/CH/CXG* WD3 217 J3
Solesbridge La *RKW/CH/CXG* WD3 217 J3
Sollershott East *LWTH* SG6 41 K5
Sollershott West *LWTH* SG6 41 J5
Solomon's Hl
RKW/CH/CXG WD3 218 C7 3
Solway *HHNE* HP2 8 C3
Solway Rd North *LTNN/LIM* LU3 69 F5
Solway Rd South *LTNN/LIM* LU3 69 F6
Somerby Cl *BROX* EN10 177 F7
Someries Rd *HARP* AL5 118 E5 2
HHW HP1 163 J4
Somersby Cl *LTN* LU1 4 C6 2
Somerset Av *LTNE* LU2 5 E1
Somerset Rd *PEND* EN3 215 F8 1
Somersham *WGCE* AL7 148 E3 5
Somers Rd *BRKMPK* AL9 192 C2
Somers Sq *BRKMPK* AL9 192 C1 2
Somers Wy *BUSH* WD23 221 K7
Sonia Cl *OXHEY* WD19 13 D6
Soothouse Spring
STALW/RED AL3 168 C2
Soper Ms *PEND* EN3 215 F8 2
Sopers Rd *POTB/CUF* EN6 195 H7
Sopwell La *STAL* AL1 10 C5
Sorrel Cl *LTNN/LIM* LU3 69 F1
ROY SG8 21 K4
Sorrel Garth *HTCHE/RSTV* SG4 56 E3
Sotheron Rd *WAT* WD17 13 D1
Souberie Av *LWTH* SG6 41 K4
Souldern St *WATW* WD18 12 C4
Southacre Wy *PIN* HA5 230 D7
Southall Cl *WARE* SG12 127 H7
South Ap *NTHWD* HA6 229 J2
South Bank Rd *BERK* HP4 161 G3
Southbrook *SBW* CM21 132 C8
Southbrook Dr *CHES/WCR* EN8 197 H6 6
South Bucks Wy *CFSP/GDCR* SL9 226 D8
South Charlton Mead La
HOD EN11 177 J4 1
Southcliffe Dr *CFSP/GDCR* SL9 226 B4
South Cl *BLDK* SG7 43 F2 3
LCOL/BKTW AL2 188 D3
ROY SG8 21 F2
South Cottage Dr
RKW/CH/CXG WD3 217 J5
South Cottage Gdns
RKW/CH/CXG WD3 217 J5
Southdown Ct *HAT* AL10 171 F7 3
Southdown Rd *HARP* AL5 118 D8
HAT AL10 171 F7
South Drift Wy *LTN* LU1 89 G3
South Dr *POTB/CUF* EN6 195 G8
STALE/WH AL4 169 H5
Southend Cl *STVG* SG1 2 A1
Southern Ri *LTNE* LU2 118 B2
Southern Wy *DUN/WHIP* LU6 114 A5
HLWE CM17 181 F3
HLWS CM18 7 F6
HLWW/ROY CM19 179 H4
LWTH SG6 41 J1
Southernwood Cl *HHNE* HP2 9 D4 2
Southerton Wy *RAD* WD7 207 H3
Southfield *BAR* EN5 225 J6 1
STDN SG11 82 A2 4
WGCE AL7 147 J5
Southfield Av *WATN* WD24 204 D8
Southfield Rd *CHES/WCR* EN8 214 D2
HOD EN11 177 F1
Southfields *LWTH* SG6 25 K8
STDN SG11 81 K7
Southfield Wy *STALE/WH* AL4 169 G3
South Ga *HLW* CM20 6 C4
Southgate *STVG* SG1 2 B4
Southgate Rd *POTB/CUF* EN6 210 D3
South Hill Cl *HTCHE/RSTV* SG4 56 E3 6
South Hill Rd *HHW* HP1 164 B6
South Ley *WGCE* AL7 147 K6
Southmead Crs *CHES/WCR* EN8 197 J8
Southmill Rd *BSF* CM23 105 K3
South Ordnance Rd *PEND* EN3 215 F7
South Park Av *RKW/CH/CXG* WD3 217 J5
South Park Gdns *BERK* HP4 161 J4
South Pl *HLW* CM20 7 F1
HTCH/STOT SG5 56 B1
South Riding *LCOL/BKTW* AL2 188 C8
South Rd *BLDK* SG7 43 F2
BSF CM23 105 K4
HLW CM20 7 F1
LTN LU1 4 B5
RKW/CH/CXG WD3 217 F5
STDN SG11 81 J7
Southsea Av *WATW* WD18 12 B3
Southsea Rd *STVG* SG1 75 G1
South St *BSF* CM23 105 J3
HERT/WAS SG14 151 G3
WARE SG12 153 H5
South Vw *LWTH* SG6 41 K4
Southview Cl *CHESW* EN7 196 C4 4
Southview Rd *HARP* AL5 118 E6
South View Rd *PIN* HA5 230 C5
Southwark Cl *STVG* SG1 59 H8
South Wy *ABLGY* WD5 203 J3
GSTN WD25 203 K3
HAT AL10 171 F8
WAB EN9 215 G7
South Weald Dr *WAB* EN9 215 J3
Southwold Rd *WATN* WD24 204 D7 2
Sowerby Av *LTNE* LU2 70 D6
Sparhawke *LWTH* SG6 26 A8
Sparrow Dr *STVGE* SG2 76 D5
Sparrows Herne *BUSH* WD23 221 J7

Sparrows Wy *BUSH* WD23 **221** K7 4
Sparrowswick Ride
STALW/RED AL3 **167** K1
Spayne Cl *LTNN/LIM* LU3 **69** G1
Spear Cl *LTNN/LIM* LU3 **68** D3
Speedwell Cl *LTNN/LIM* LU3 **69** F1
Speke Cl *STVGE* SG2 **76** E4 2
Spellbrooke *HTCH/STOT* SG5 **56** B1 3
Spellbrook La East *BSF* CM23 **132** D1
Spellbrook La West *SBW* CM21 **132** B2
Spencer Av *CHESW* EN7 **196** C4
Spencer Cl *STSD* CM24 **86** D3 2
Spencer Ga *STAL* AL1 **11** D2
Spencer Ms *STAL* AL1 **11** D3
Spencer Pl *STALE/WH* AL4 **145** F7 1
Spencer Rd *LTNN/LIM* LU3 **4** A2
Spencers Cft *HLWS* CM18 **7** F6
Spencer St *HERT/BAY* SG13 **151** H2
STALW/RED AL3 **10** C4
Spencer Wk *RKW/CH/CXG* WD3 **218** B5
Spencer Wy *HHW* HP1 **163** K3 2
Spenser Rd *HARP* AL5 **118** E8
Sperberry Hl *HTCHE/RSTV* SG4 **57** F7
Spicersfield *CHESW* EN7 **196** E5
Spicer St *STALW/RED* AL3 **10** B4
Spindle Berry Cl *WLYN* AL6 **123** G2 1
Spinney La *WLYN* AL6 **95** J7
Spinney Rd *LTNN/LIM* LU3 **68** C2
Spinney St *HERT/BAY* SG13 **151** K3 3
The Spinney *BERK* HP4 **161** G6
BLDK SG7 **42** E2
BROX EN10 **176** E5 1
HARP AL5 **118** A6 1
HERT/BAY SG13 **151** J3
POTB/CUF EN6 **210** E1 3
STSD CM24 **86** D4
STVGE SG2 **76** E2 1
WAT WD17 **220** B1
WGCE AL7 **147** K4
Spinning Wheel Md *HLWS* CM18 **180** D4
Spooners Dr *LCOL/BKTW* AL2 **188** E5
Spring Cl *BAR* EN5 **225** J5
BORE WD6 **223** K1 4
CSHM HP5 **200** A6
DEN/HRF UB9 **228** C7
Spring Court Rd *ENC/FH* EN2 **212** D8
Spring Crofts *BUSH* WD23 **221** H5
Spring Dr *STVGE* SG2 **96** B1
Springfield *BUSH* WD23 **222** A8
Springfield Cl *POTB/CUF* EN6 **210** E1 4
RKW/CH/CXG WD3 **219** G5
Springfield Crs *HARP* AL5 **118** C5
Spring Field Rd *BERK* HP4 **161** G2
Springfield Rd *CHES/WCR* EN8 **214** D2
GSTN WD25 **204** C3 1
HHNE HP2 **8** C4
LTNN/LIM LU3 **69** H3
STAL AL1 **11** F5
STALE/WH AL4 **170** A6
Springfields *BROX* EN10 **176** E5
WGCW AL8 **147** G5
Spring Gdns *GSTN* WD25 **204** D5
Spring Gln *HAT* AL10 **170** E5
Springhall La *SBW* CM21 **132** C8
Springhall Rd *SBW* CM21 **132** C7
Springhead *BLDK* SG7 **17** K5
Spring Hills *HLW* CM20 **155** H7
Spring La *BUNT* SG9 **62** A4
HHW HP1 **163** K5
Springle La *HERT/BAY* SG13 **152** E6
Spring Pl *LTN* LU1 **4** B5 4
Spring Rd *HARP* AL5 **117** G5
LWTH SG6 **41** J4
Springshott *LWTH* SG6 **41** J4
The Springs *BROX* EN10 **197** J3
Spring View Rd *WARE* SG12 **152** B1
Spring Wk *BROX* EN10 **176** B7
Springwell Av *RKW/CH/CXG* WD3 **227** K1
Springwell La *RKW/CH/CXG* WD3 **227** K2
Springwood *CHESW* EN7 **196** D4
Springwood Cl *DEN/HRF* UB9 **228** C7 1
Springwood Wk *STALE/WH* AL4 **169** F3
Spruce Hl *HLWS* CM18 **180** B5
Spruce Wy *LCOL/BKTW* AL2 **188** D5
Spur Cl *ABLGY* WD5 **203** J3 2
Spurcroft *LTNN/LIM* LU3 **52** C8 1
Spurrs Cl *HTCHE/RSTV* SG4 **57** F2 4
The Spur *CHES/WCR* EN8 **197** H6 7
STVG SG1 **2** C4
The Square *BROX* EN10 **197** K1 2
BUNT SG9 **47** G4
SBW CM21 **132** C7 6
STALW/RED AL3 **142** A3
WATN WD24 **204** C7
Squires Cl *BSF* CM23 **105** F1
Squires Ride *HHNE* HP2 **140** E8
Squirrel Cha *HHW* HP1 **163** H5
Squirrels Cl *BSF* CM23 **105** J1 3
The Squirrels *BUSH* WD23 **222** A6
HERT/BAY SG13 **152** A3 2
Stackfield *HLW* CM20 **156** E6
Stacklands *WGCW* AL8 **147** G5
Staddles *RBSF* CM22 **106** A8
Stadium Wy *HLWW/ROY* CM19 **155** G8
Stafford Cl *CHES/WCR* EN8 **197** F7
Stafford Dr *BROX* EN10 **177** F6 2
Stafford Rd *KTN/HRWW/W* HA3 **231** K6
Staffords *HLWE* CM17 **157** H5
Stagg Hl *POTB/CUF* EN6 **210** E5
Stag Green Av *BRKMPK* AL9 **171** H2
Stag La *BERK* HP4 **161** H4
RKW/CH/CXG WD3 **217** F6
Stainer Rd *BORE* WD6 **223** G1 2
Stainers *BSF* CM23 **105** F4
Stains Cl *CHES/WCR* EN8 **197** J6
Stake Piece Rd *ROY* SG8 **21** G4
Stakers Ct *HARP* AL5 **118** D8
Stamford Av *ROY* SG8 **21** H2
Stamford Cl *POTB/CUF* EN6 **210** E2
Stamford Rd *WAT* WD17 **12** C1
Stanborough Av *BORE* WD6 **207** K8
Stanborough Cl *WGCW* AL8 **147** H4 4
Stanborough Gn *WGCW* AL8 **147** H5
Stanborough La *WGCW* AL8 **147** H5
Stanborough Rd *WGCW* AL8 **147** G6
Stanbury Av *WAT* WD17 **203** K7
Standard Rd *PEND* EN3 **214** D8
Standfield *ABLGY* WD5 **203** K1
Standhill Cl *HTCHE/RSTV* SG4 **56** D3
Standhill Rd *HTCHE/RSTV* SG4 **56** D3
Standingford *EPP* CM16 **179** J6 3
Standon Hl *STDN* SG11 **81** H7
Standon Rd *STDN* SG11 **83** F6
Standring Ri *HHS/BOV* HP3 **185** F1 1
Stane Cl *BSF* CM23 **105** J1
Stane Fld *LWTH* SG6 **42** B6
Stanelow Crs *STDN* SG11 **81** J7
Stane St *BLDK* SG7 **27** G8
Stanford Rd *LTNE* LU2 **5** E2
Stangate Crs *BORE* WD6 **224** D5
Stanhope Rd *BAR* EN5 **225** J6
CHES/WCR EN8 **214** D3
STAL AL1 **11** E5
Stanier Ri *BERK* HP4 **161** G2
Stanley Av *LCOL/BKTW* AL2 **188** C3
Stanley Dr *HAT* AL10 **171** G6
Stanley Gdns *BORE* WD6 **223** H1
TRING HP23 **134** E6 2
Stanley Rd *HERT/BAY* SG13 **151** H4
LTNN/LIM LU3 **52** A4
NTHWD HA6 **230** B7
STVGE SG2 **3** F1
WAT WD17 **13** D2 8
Stanley St *LTN* LU1 **4** B5
Stanmore Crs *LTNN/LIM* LU3 **68** E5
Stanmore Rd *STVG* SG1 **2** A1
WATN WD24 **220** C1
Stanmount Rd *LCOL/BKTW* AL2 **188** C3 1
Stanstead Dr *HOD* EN11 **177** G1
Stanstead Rd *HERT/BAY* SG13 **151** K2
HOD EN11 **153** G8
WARE SG12 **152** C4
Stansted Hl *MHAD* SG10 **103** H8
Stansted Rd *BSF* CM23 **86** B6
RBSF CM22 **87** G1
Stanton Cl *STALE/WH* AL4 **169** G2
Stanton Rd *LTNW/LEA* LU4 **68** B7
Staplefield Cl *PIN* HA5 **231** F6
Stapleford *WGCE* AL7 **148** E3 6
Stapleford Rd *LTNE* LU2 **70** C5
Stapleton Cl *POTB/CUF* EN6 **210** E1
Stapleton Rd *BORE* WD6 **207** K8
Stapley Rd *STALW/RED* AL3 **10** C3 3
Staplyton Rd *BAR* EN5 **225** K3
Star Holme Ct *WARE* SG12 **127** J8
Starkey Cl *CHESW* EN7 **196** A3 4
Starling La *POTB/CUF* EN6 **195** H6
Star St *WARE* SG12 **127** J8
Statham Cl *LTNN/LIM* LU3 **52** B8
Station Ap *CHES/WCR* EN8 **214** D4 3
HARP AL5 **118** D8
HTCHE/RSTV SG4 **56** E1 1
KNEB SG3 **96** A4
NTHWD HA6 **229** K6 5
OXHEY WD19 **230** E2 2
RAD WD7 **206** D5
RKW/CH/CXG WD3 **217** F4
Station Cl *BRKMPK* AL9 **192** E4 1
POTB/CUF EN6 **210** A1
Station Footpath *KGLGY* WD4 **186** B8
Station Pl *LWTH* SG6 **41** K3 2
Station Rd *ARL/CHE* SG15 **24** E5
BERK HP4 **162** A4
BLDK SG7 **18** B5
BLDK SG7 **19** F7
BLDK SG7 **27** F8
BORE WD6 **223** K4
BRKMPK AL9 **192** D3
BROX EN10 **176** E6
BSF CM23 **105** K3 2
BUNT SG9 **63** J2
CHES/WCR EN8 **215** F4
HARP AL5 **118** D8
HERT/WAS SG14 **98** A6
HERT/WAS SG14 **149** H6
HHS/BOV HP3 **164** A8
HLWE CM17 **157** F5
KGLGY WD4 **186** B7
KNEB SG3 **96** A4
LBUZ LU7 **110** E4
LCOL/BKTW AL2 **205** H1
LTN LU1 **4** C3
LTNW/LEA LU4 **68** D4
LWTH SG6 **41** K3
MHAD SG10 **103** F8
POTB/CUF EN6 **195** H7
RAD WD7 **206** D5
RKW/CH/CXG WD3 **218** C7 4
ROY SG8 **18** D1
SBW CM21 **132** D6
STALE/WH AL4 **120** B8
STALE/WH AL4 **170** A5
STDN SG11 **81** J6
STSD CM24 **86** D3 5
TRING HP23 **108** E5
TRING HP23 **135** G5
WAB EN9 **198** E5
WARE SG12 **127** H8
WARE SG12 **153** H5
WAT WD17 **12** C1
WGCW AL8 **122** E6
Station Wy *LWTH* SG6 **41** J3
Staveley Rd *LTNW/LEA* LU4 **68** B8
Steeplands *BUSH* WD23 **221** J7
Steeple Vw *BSF* CM23 **105** J1
Stephens Cl *LTNE* LU2 **70** B6
Stephenson Cl *ROY* SG8 **21** F2
Stephenson Wy *BUSH* WD23 **220** E1
Stephens Wy *STALW/RED* AL3 **142** A4
Stepnells *TRING* HP23 **110** A8
Sterling Av *CHES/WCR* EN8 **214** C4
Stevenage Crs *BORE* WD6 **223** H1
Stevenage Ri *HHNE* HP2 **8** C1
Stevenage Rd *HTCHE/RSTV* SG4 **56** D4
KNEB SG3 **96** A2
STVGE SG2 **77** G1
Stevens Gn *BUSH* WD23 **221** K8
Steward Cl *CHES/WCR* EN8 **197** J8
Stewart Cl *ABLGY* WD5 **204** B2
Stewart Rd *HARP* AL5 **118** D7
The Stewarts *BSF* CM23 **105** H2
Stile Cft *HLWS* CM18 **7** F6
Stilton Pth *BORE* WD6 **207** K8
Stirling Cl *HTCHE/RSTV* SG4 **57** G2
STVGE SG2 **96** D2
Stirling Wy *ABLGY* WD5 **204** B2
BORE WD6 **224** C6
WGCE AL7 **149** F3
Stoat Cl *HERT/BAY* SG13 **151** K3
Stobarts Cl *KNEB* SG3 **96** A3
Stockbreach Cl *HAT* AL10 **171** F3
Stockbreach Rd *HAT* AL10 **171** F3
Stockens Dell *KNEB* SG3 **96** A5
Stockens Gn *KNEB* SG3 **96** A5
Stockers Farm Rd
RKW/CH/CXG WD3 **228** B2
Stockfield Av *HOD* EN11 **177** F
Stockholm Wy *LTNN/LIM* LU3 **68** D
Stocking La *ROY* SG8 **33** J8
Stockings La *HERT/BAY* SG13 **174** A4
Stockingstone Rd *LTNE* LU2 **69** K6
Stockmen Fld *BSF* CM23 **105** F4
Stockport Rd *RKW/CH/CXG* WD3 **217** F7
Stocks Meadow *HHNE* HP2 **9** D4
Stocks Rd *TRING* HP23 **136** E3
Stockwell Cl *CHESW* EN7 **196** E6
Stockwood Crs *LTN* LU1 **4** B5
Stonecroft *KNEB* SG3 **96** A4
Stonecroft Cl *BAR* EN5 **225** G4
Stonecross *STAL* AL1 **11** D3
STALW/RED AL3 **11** D2
Stonecross Rd *HAT* AL10 **171** G
Stonehills *WGCW* AL8 **147** J3
Stonelea Rd *HHS/BOV* HP3 **185** K
Stoneleigh *SBW* CM21 **132** B6
Stoneleigh Av *EN* EN1 **214** A8
Stoneleigh Cl *CHES/WCR* EN8 **214** C3
LTNN/LIM LU3 **69** G2
Stoneleigh Dr *HOD* EN11 **153** G8
Stoneley *LWTH* SG6 **25** K
Stonemason Cl *HARP* AL5 **118** C6
Stonemead *WGCW* AL8 **122** D
Stonesdale *LTNW/LEA* LU4 **68** B5
Stoneways Cl *LTNW/LEA* LU4 **68** C3
Stoney Cl *BERK* HP4 **161** G3
Stoney Common *STSD* CM24 **86** D4
Stoney Common Rd *STSD* CM24 **86** C4
Stoney Cft *TRING* HP23 **136** D4
Stoneycroft *WGCE* AL7 **148** B2
Stoneyfield Dr *STSD* CM24 **86** D4
Stoneygate Rd *LTNW/LEA* LU4 **68** C
Stoney La *HHS/BOV* HP3 **183** K5
HHW HP1 **183** K
KGLGY WD4 **184** C
Stonnells Cl *LWTH* SG6 **41** K
Stony Cft *STVG* SG1 **2** C
Stony Hills *WARE* SG12 **126** A
Stony La *CSHM* HP5 **200** B
LTNE LU2 **71** J
Stonyshotts *WAB* EN9 **215** K
Stony Wd *HLWS* CM18 **6** C
Stopsley Wy *LTNE* LU2 **70** B
Storehouse La *HTCHE/RSTV* SG4 **56** D2
Storey St *HHS/BOV* HP3 **185** H
Stormont Rd *HTCH/STOT* SG5 **40** D

Stornoway HHS/BOV HP3 .... 165 G8
Stortford Hall Pk BSF CM23 ... 106 A1
Stortford Hall Rd BSF CM23 ... 106 A1
Stortford Rd EN11 ... 177 G2
  RBSF CM22 ... 133 J5
  STDN SG11 ... 82 A8
  STDN SG11 ... 83 K7
Stort Ldg BSF CM23 ... 105 G3
Stort Ml HLW CM20 ... 156 E3
Stort Rd BSF CM23 ... 105 J3
Stort Valley Wy HLW CM20 ... 157 G2
  HLWW/ROY CM19 ... 154 B8
  SBW CM21 ... 133 G7
Stotfold Rd ARL/CHE SG15 ... 24 E1
  BLDK SG7 ... 26 C1
  HTCHE/RSTV SG4 ... 41 G5
  LWTH SG6 ... 41 G2
The Stow HLW CM20 ... 7 E2
Strafford Cl BORE EN6 ... 210 B2
Strafford Ct KNEB SG3 ... 96 B4
Strafford Ga POTB/CUF EN6 ... 210 B2
Strafford Rd BAR EN5 ... 225 K3
The Straits WAB EN9 ... 215 G2
Strangers Wy LTNW/LEA LU4 ... 68 B5
Strangeways WAT WD17 ... 203 K6
Stratfield Dr BROX EN10 ... 176 D5
Stratfield Rd BORE WD6 ... 223 J3
Stratford Rd LTNW/LEA LU4 ... 69 G8
  WAT WD17 ... 12 B1
Stratford Wy HHS/BOV HP3 ... 185 F1
  LCOL/BKTW AL2 ... 188 B7
  WAT WD17 ... 12 A1
Strathmore Av HTCH/STOT SG5 ... 40 C8
  LTN LU1 ... 4 C6
Strathmore Rd HTCHE/RSTV SG4 ... 93 H3
Strathmore Wk WATN LU1 ... 5 D5
Stratton Av ENC/FH EN2 ... 213 G2
Stratton Gdns LTNE LU2 ... 69 J5
Strawberry Fieds WARE SG12 ... 127 F7
Strawberry Fld LTNW/LEA LU3 ... 68 D2
Strawfields WCGE AL7 ... 148 D5
Strawmead HAT AL10 ... 171 G2
Straw Plait ARL/CHE SG15 ... 24 D5
Strayfield Rd ENC/FH EN2 ... 212 D6
The Street BLDK SG7 ... 17 K5
  BSF CM23 ... 67 K2
  BUNT SG9 ... 65 G3
  BUNT SG9 ... 66 C5
  KGLGY WD4 ... 201 K1
  RBSF CM23 ... 107 F5
  STDN SG11 ... 79 J6
  STDN SG11 ... 82 A2
Stretton Wy BORE WD6 ... 207 H8
Stringers La STVGE SG2 ... 77 F8
Stripling Wy WATW WD18 ... 12 B5
Stroma Cl HHS/BOV HP3 ... 165 H8
Stronnell Cl LTNE LU2 ... 70 B6
Stronsay HHS/BOV HP3 ... 165 H8
Stuart Cl BORE WD6 ... 223 G6
Stuart Dr HTCHE/RSTV SG4 ... 57 F2
  ROY SG8 ... 21 H1
Stuart Rd AMP/FLIT/B MK45 ... 36 C2
  WLYN AL6 ... 122 B5
Stuarts Cl HHS/BOV HP3 ... 164 C8
Stuart St LTN LU1 ... 4 C4
Stuart Wy CHESW EN7 ... 214 A1
Stud Gn GSTN WD25 ... 204 B2
Studham La BERK HP4 ... 113 G5
The Studios BUSH WD23 ... 221 H6
Studio Wy BORE WD6 ... 224 B1
Studlands Ri ROY SG8 ... 21 J3
Studley Rd LTNN/LIM LU3 ... 4 B2
Sturgeon's Rd HTCHE/RSTV SG4 ... 41 F7
Sturlas Wy CHES/WCR EN8 ... 214 E3
Sturmer Cl STALE/WH AL4 ... 169 F7
Sturrock Wy HTCHE/RSTV SG4 ... 57 G3
Styles Cl LTNE LU2 ... 70 C7
Such Cl LWTH SG6 ... 42 B2
Sudbury Rd LTNW/LEA LU4 ... 68 A3
Suffolk Cl BORE WD6 ... 224 C5
  LCOL/BKTW AL2 ... 190 A3
Suffolk Rd POTB/CUF EN6 ... 209 K2
  ROY SG8 ... 21 J3
Sugar La HHW HP1 ... 162 E8
Sulgrave Crs DEN/HRF UB9 ... 228 C8
Sullivan Wy BORE WD6 ... 223 F6
Summer Dl WCGC AL8 ... 122 D7
Summerfield HAT AL10 ... 171 F7
Summerfield Cl LCOL/BKTW AL2 ... 190 A4
Summerfield Rd GSTN WD25 ... 204 B5
  LTN LU1 ... 88 E1
Summer Gv BORE WD6 ... 223 G6
Summer Hl BORE WD6 ... 223 K5
Summerhouse La DEN/HRF UB9 ... 227 K6
  GSTN WD25 ... 221 K1
Summersland Rd STALE/WH AL4 ... 169 F2
Summers Rd LTNE LU2 ... 70 D8
Summer St LTN LU1 ... 89 H7
Summerswood La BORE WD6 ... 208 D5
Summer Wk STALE/WH AL3 ... 115 J4
Summit Rd POTB/CUF EN6 ... 192 E8
Sumners Farm Cl EPP CM16 ... 179 H6

Sumpter Yd STAL AL1 ... 10 C5
Sunderland Av STAL AL1 ... 11 F3
Sundew Rd HHW HP1 ... 163 H7
Sundon Park Rd LTNN/LIM LU3 ... 68 B1
Sun Hi ROY SG8 ... 21 G4
Sun La HARP AL5 ... 118 C7
Sunmead Rd HHNE HP2 ... 8 A3
Sunningdale BSF CM23 ... 105 H5
  LTNE LU2 ... 70 C7
Sunningdale Ms WCGE AL7 ... 123 F7
Sunny Bank LBUZ LU7 ... 109 K2
Sunnybank Rd POTB/CUF EN6 ... 210 B3
Sunny Cft HLWS CM18 ... 180 C4
Sunnydell LCOL/BKTW AL2 ... 188 D4
Sunnyfield BRKMPK AL9 ... 171 J1
Sunny Hl BUNT SG9 ... 63 J2
Sunnyhill Rd HHW HP1 ... 164 A6
  RKW/CH/CXG WD3 ... 227 G5
Sunnymede Av CSHM HP5 ... 182 A6
Sunnyside STSD CM24 ... 86 D3
  WAB EN9 ... 178 A8
Sunnyside Rd HTCHE/RSTV SG4 ... 56 E3
Sunridge Av LTNE LU2 ... 70 A6
Sunrise Crs HHS/BOV HP3 ... 185 K1
Sunset Dr LTNE LU2 ... 70 A6
Sunset Vw BAR EN5 ... 225 K2
Sun St BLDK SG7 ... 42 E1
  HTCH/STOT SG5 ... 56 C3
  SBW CM21 ... 132 D8
  WAB EN9 ... 215 H3
Surrey Pl TRING HP23 ... 135 F6
Surrey St LTN LU1 ... 4 C4
Sursham Ct STALW/RED AL3 ... 115 J4
Sussex Cl HOD EN11 ... 177 F2
Sussex Pl LTNE LU2 ... 70 E7
Sussex Rd WATN WD24 ... 204 B8
Sutcliffe Cl BUSH WD23 ... 221 K4
  STVG SG1 ... 76 B1
Sutherland Av POTB/CUF EN6 ... 195 F6
Sutherland Cl BAR EN5 ... 225 K4
Sutherland Ct WCGE AL7 ... 148 A2
Sutherland Pl LTN LU1 ... 4 B6
Sutherland Wy POTB/CUF EN6 ... 195 F6
Sutton Acres RBSF CM22 ... 133 H2
Sutton Cl BROX EN10 ... 176 D5
Sutton Crs BAR EN5 ... 225 J5
Sutton Gdns LTNN/LIM LU3 ... 68 C5
Sutton Rd SDY/GAM/PO SG19 ... 14 A1
  STAL AL1 ... 168 E7
  WAT WD17 ... 13 D2
Swallow Cl BUSH WD23 ... 221 J8
  RKW/CH/CXG WD3 ... 218 B7
Swallowdale La HHNE HP2 ... 9 D2
Swallow End WCGE AL7 ... 148 A3
Swallowfields WCGE AL7 ... 148 A3
Swallow Gdns HAT AL10 ... 171 F6
Swallow La STAL AL1 ... 189 K1
Swallow Oaks ABLGY WD5 ... 204 A2
Swallows HLWE CM17 ... 157 F5
The Swallows WCGE AL7 ... 123 F7
Swan and Pike Rd PEND EN3 ... 215 F8
Swan Cl RKW/CH/CXG WD3 ... 218 C7
Swan Ct BSF CM23 ... 105 J3
Swanells Wd DUN/WHIP LU6 ... 113 K5
Swanfield Rd CHES/WCR EN8 ... 214 D3
Swangley's La KNEB SG3 ... 96 B4
Swanhill WCGE AL7 ... 123 G6
Swanland Rd BRKMPK AL9 ... 192 B5
  POTB/CUF EN6 ... 209 G3
Swan La ROY SG8 ... 15 C5
Swanley Bar La POTB/CUF EN6 ... 193 H6
Swanley Crs POTB/CUF EN6 ... 193 H7
Swan Md HHS/BOV HP3 ... 185 K3
Swans Cl STALE/WH AL4 ... 169 H7
Swans Rd CHES/WCR EN8 ... 214 C4
Swanstand LWTH SG6 ... 42 D5
Swanston Pth OXHEY WD19 ... 230 D2
Swan St BLDK SG7 ... 17 K5
Swasedale Rd LTNN/LIM LU3 ... 68 E3
Sweet Briar BSF CM23 ... 104 E3
  WCGE AL7 ... 148 B5
Sweetbriar Cl HHW HP1 ... 163 K3
Sweyne HLWE CM17 ... 181 F4
Sweyns Md STVGE SG2 ... 76 D1
Swift Cl LWTH SG6 ... 41 J1
  WARE SG12 ... 153 H6
Swiftfields WCGE AL7 ... 148 A2
Swifts Green Cl LTNE LU2 ... 70 C4
Swifts Green Rd LTNE LU2 ... 70 C4
Swinburne Av HTCH/STOT SG5 ... 40 A8
Swingate STVG SG1 ... 2 B3
Swing Br LBUZ LU7 ... 110 B4
Swing Gate La BERK HP4 ... 162 A6
Swiss Av WATW WD18 ... 219 K4
Swiss Cl WATW WD18 ... 219 K3
Sworders Yd BSF CM23 ... 105 J2
Sycamore Ap RKW/CH/CXG WD3 ... 219 H5
Sycamore Av HAT AL10 ... 171 F5
Sycamore Cl BUSH WD23 ... 13 F1
  CHESW EN7 ... 196 D5
  GSTN WD25 ... 204 C5
  HTCHE/RSTV SG4 ... 56 E6
Sycamore Dr LCOL/BKTW AL2 ... 189 F5
  TRING HP23 ... 135 G5

Sycamore Fld HLWW/ROY CM19 ... 179 H5
Sycamore Ri BERK HP4 ... 162 A6
Sycamore Rd RKW/CH/CXG WD3 ... 219 H5
The Sycamores BLDK SG7 ... 26 E8
  BSF CM23 ... 106 A3
  HHS/BOV HP3 ... 184 D1
  RAD WD7 ... 206 E4
Sydney Rd WATW WD18 ... 219 K5
Sylam Cl LTNN/LIM LU3 ... 68 D2
Sylvan Cl HHS/BOV HP3 ... 9 D6
Sylvandale WCGE AL7 ... 148 D4
Sylvan Wy WCGE AL7 ... 148 E3
Sylvesters HLWW/ROY CM19 ... 179 G3
Sylvia Av PIN HA5 ... 231 G5
Symonds Ct CHES/WCR EN8 ... 197 H6
Symonds Green STVG SG1 ... 75 F2
Symonds Green Rd STVG SG1 ... 75 F2
Symonds Rd HTCH/STOT SG5 ... 56 B1

Tabbs Cl LWTH SG6 ... 42 B1
Tacitus Cl STVGE SG2 ... 76 D1
Tailors BSF CM23 ... 104 E4
Takeley Cl WAB EN9 ... 215 J3
Talbot Ct HHS/BOV HP3 ... 164 C8
Talbot Rd HAT AL10 ... 171 F1
  LTNE LU2 ... 5 D2
  RKW/CH/CXG WD3 ... 218 D8
Talbot St HERT/BAY SG13 ... 151 H3
  HTCH/STOT SG5 ... 56 B1
Talbot Wy LWTH SG6 ... 42 B1
Talisman St HTCHE/RSTV SG4 ... 57 G2
Tallents Crs HARP AL5 ... 119 F6
Tallis Wy BORE WD6 ... 223 G1
Talls Hill HTCHE/RSTV SG4 ... 56 E5
  ROY SG8 ... 21 J3
Tamar Cl STVG SG1 ... 59 G6
Tamar Gn HHNE HP2 ... 164 E1
Tamarisk Cl STALW/RED AL3 ... 168 B2
Tameton Cl LTNE LU2 ... 71 F7
Tamworth Rd HERT/BAY SG13 ... 151 J2
Tancred Rd LTNE LU2 ... 70 B5
Tanfield Cl CHESW EN7 ... 196 C5
Tanfield Gn LTNE LU2 ... 71 F8
Tanglewood WLYN AL6 ... 123 G2
Tanners Cl STALW/RED AL3 ... 10 B3
Tanners Ct HERT/BAY SG13 ... 151 F5
Tanners Hl ABLGY WD5 ... 204 A1
Tanners Wy WARE SG12 ... 129 J8
Tanners Wood La ABLGY WD5 ... 203 K2
Tannery Cl STVG SG1 ... 21 G3
Tannery Drift ROY SG8 ... 21 G2
The Tannery BUNT SG9 ... 63 J2
Tannsfield Dr HHNE HP2 ... 8 C3
Tansmore Cl HHNE HP2 ... 8 C3
Tansycroft WCGE AL7 ... 148 C2
Tanworth Cl NTHWD HA6 ... 229 H5
Tanworth Gdns PIN HA5 ... 230 C8
Tanyard La HTCHE/RSTV SG4 ... 121 C1
Tany's Dell HLW CM20 ... 7 F1
Taransey HHS/BOV HP3 ... 165 G8
Tarpan Wy BROX EN10 ... 197 K4
Tarrant Dr HARP AL5 ... 143 K2
Tassell Hall STALW/RED AL3 ... 142 A3
Tate Gdns BUSH WD23 ... 222 B7
Tate Rd CFSP/GDCR SL9 ... 226 C4
Tatlers La STVGE SG2 ... 76 E4
Tatsfield La WAB EN9 ... 198 D1
Tattershall Dr HHNE HP2 ... 141 F8
Tattle Hl HERT/WAS SG14 ... 125 C7
Tauber Cl BORE WD6 ... 223 J4
Taunton Rd LTNE LU2 ... 5 F2
Taverners HHNE HP2 ... 8 B3
Taverners Wy HOD EN11 ... 177 F3
Tavistock Av STAL AL1 ... 188 E1
Tavistock Cl POTB/CUF EN6 ... 210 E1
  STAL AL1 ... 189 F1
Tavistock Crs LTN LU1 ... 4 C6
Tavistock Rd WATN WD24 ... 220 E1
Tawneys Rd HLWS CM18 ... 7 E6
Taylifers HLWW/ROY CM19 ... 179 H6
Taylor Cl STALE/WH AL4 ... 168 D1
Taylors Cl HOD EN11 ... 177 F4
Taylors End Rd STSD CM24 ... 87 K8
Taylor's Rd HTCH/STOT SG5 ... 25 K1
Taylor St LTNE LU2 ... 5 D3
Taywood Dr STVGE SG2 ... 3 F6
Teal Dr NTHWD HA6 ... 229 H6
Teasel Cl ROY SG8 ... 21 J4
Tedder Rd HHNE HP2 ... 9 D4
Teesdale HHNE HP2 ... 8 B2
  LTNW/LEA LU4 ... 68 B4
Tee Side HERT/BAY SG13 ... 152 A2
Telford Av STVGE SG2 ... 3 E2
Telford Cl GSTN WD25 ... 204 E5
Telford Ct LCOL/BKTW AL2 ... 190 A5
Telford Wy LTN LU1 ... 4 B3
Telscombe Wy LTNE LU2 ... 70 D6
Temperance St STALW/RED AL3 ... 10 B4
Tempest Av POTB/CUF EN6 ... 210 D2

Templar Av BLDK SG7 43 F3 2
Templars La HTCHE/RSTV SG4 73 G3
Temple Bank HLW CM20 156 E4
Temple Cl CHESW EN7 213 K1
HTCHE/RSTV SG4 55 K5
LTNE LU2 69 K4 3
WAT WD17 12 A1
Temple Flds HERT/WAS SG14 126 A8
Temple Gdns RKW/CH/CXG WD3 229 G2
Temple La WARE SG12 126 C2
Temple Md HLWW/ROY CM19 178 C1
Templepan La RKW/CH/CXG WD3 202 D7
Temple Vw STALW/RED AL3 10 B2
Templewood WGCW AL8 122 D8
Tempsford WGCE AL7 148 E3 3
Tempsford Av BORE WD6 224 C4
Temsford Cl RYLN/HDSTN HA2 231 K8 2
Tenby Dr LTNW/LEA LU4 68 E6
Tenby Ms LTNW/LEA LU4 68 D6
Tendring Rd HLWS CM18 6 B6 1
The Tene BLDK SG7 43 F1
Tennand Cl CHESW EN7 196 D4
Tennison Av BORE WD6 224 A5
Tennyson Av HTCHE/RSTV SG4 57 G2
WAB EN9 215 K4
Tennyson Rd HARP AL5 118 C6
LCOL/BKTW AL2 188 C4
LTN LU1 4 C6
Tenth Av LTNN/LIM LU3 68 B2
Tenzing Gv LTN LU1 4 A5
Tenzing Rd HHNE HP2 9 D5
Teresa Gdns CHES/WCR EN8 214 B4
Terminus St HLW CM20 6 C3
Terrace Gdns WAT WD17 12 C1
Tethys Rd HHNE HP2 8 C2
Tewin Cl STALE/WH AL4 169 F2
WLYN AL6 123 J4
Tewin Ct WGCE AL7 148 A2 5
Tewin Hl WLYN AL6 124 A6
Tewin Rd HHNE HP2 9 F5
WGCE AL7 148 A2
Thames Av HHNE HP2 164 E1
Thamesdale LCOL/BKTW AL2 190 D5 3
Thatchers Cft HHNE HP2 8 B1 1
Thatchers End HTCHE/RSTV SG4 57 H1
The Thatchers BSF CM23 105 F4
Thaxted Cl LTNE LU2 71 G7 4
Thaxted Wy WAB EN9 215 J3
Thaynesfield POTB/CUF EN6 210 E1
Thelby Cl LTNN/LIM LU3 68 E3
Thele Av WARE SG12 153 J5
Theleway Cl HOD EN11 153 G8 4
Thellusson Wy
RKW/CH/CXG WD3 217 K7 1
Thelusson Ct RAD WD7 206 D5 2
Theobald Crs KTN/HRWW/W HA3 231 J7
Theobald's Cl POTB/CUF EN6 195 H8
Theobald's Gv CHES/WCR EN8 214 C2 3
Theobald's La CHES/WCR EN8 214 A2
Theobalds Park Rd ENC/FH EN2 212 E5
Theobald's Rd POTB/CUF EN6 195 G8
Theobald St RAD WD7 206 E6
Therfield Rd STALW/RED AL3 10 C1
Thetford Gdns LTNE LU2 69 J3 3
Thieves La HERT/WAS SG14 150 C3
HERT/WAS SG14 150 C2
Third Av GSTN WD25 204 E5
HLWS CM18 6 C4
HLWW/ROY CM19 6 A5
LTNN/LIM LU3 68 C2
LWTH SG6 42 C2
Thirlestane STAL AL1 11 D3
Thirlestone Rd LTNW/LEA LU4 68 C8
Thirlmere STVG SG1 59 J7
Thirlmere Dr STAL AL1 168 E8
Thirlmere Gdns NTHWD HA6 229 G4
Thirsk Rd BORE WD6 207 K8
Thistle Cl HHW HP1 163 H7
Thistlecroft HHW HP1 164 A7 3
Thistle Gv WGCE AL7 148 D6
Thistle Rd LTN LU1 5 D4
The Thistles HHW HP1 164 A5
Thistley La HTCHE/RSTV SG4 56 D7
Thomas Rochford Wy
CHES/WCR EN8 197 K5
Thompsons Cl CHESW EN7 196 C7
HARP AL5 118 C8 1
Thompsons Meadow ROY SG8 15 H5
Thompson Wy RKW/CH/CXG WD3 217 K7
Thorley Hl BSF CM23 105 J4
Thorley La BSF CM23 104 E4
Thorley Park Rd BSF CM23 105 J5
Thornage Cl LTNE LU2 69 J2
Thorn Av BUSH WD23 221 K8
Thornbera Cl BSF CM23 105 J5
Thornbera Gdns BSF CM23 105 H5
Thornbera Rd BSF CM23 105 J5
Thornbury HARP AL5 119 F8
Thornbury Cl HOD EN11 153 G7
STVGE SG2 96 B1
Thornbury Gdns BORE WD6 224 B4
Thorncroft HHS/BOV HP3 165 G8 4
Thorndyke Ct PIN HA5 231 G6 4
Thorne Cl HHW HP1 164 A8
Thornfield Rd BSF CM23 105 H1
Thorn Gv BSF CM23 106 A3
Thornhill Rd LTNW/LEA LU4 68 E8
NTHWD HA6 229 H3
Thorntondale LTNW/LEA LU4 68 B4 5
Thornton Gv PIN HA5 231 H5
Thornton Rd BAR EN5 225 K3
POTB/CUF EN6 193 J8
Thornton St HERT/WAS SG14 151 G3
STALW/RED AL3 10 B3
Thorn Tree Dr TRING HP23 134 E5
Thorpe Crs OXHEY WD19 12 C6
Thorpefield Cl STALE/WH AL4 169 G3 3
Thorpe Rd STAL AL1 10 C5
Thrales Cl LTNN/LIM LU3 68 D2
Three Cherrytrees La HHNE HP2 9 E1
Three Close La BERK HP4 161 K6
Three Closes HTCH/STOT SG5 38 E5
Three Corners HHS/BOV HP3 165 F8 1
Three Forests Wy
HLWW/ROY CM19 178 A1
RBSF CM22 107 F8
SBW CM21 132 C8
WAB EN9 178 E7
Three Forest Wy RBSF CM22 107 G4
Three Horseshoes Rd
HLWW/ROY CM19 6 A6
Three Houses La HTCHE/RSTV SG4 94 B6
Three Stiles STVGE SG2 78 B5
Three Valleys Wy BUSH WD23 13 E4
Thresher Cl BSF CM23 105 F4
Thricknells Cl LTNN/LIM LU3 68 D2 3
Thrift Farm La BORE WD6 224 A2
Thristers Cl LWTH SG6 42 B6 1
Throcking La BUNT SG9 47 G8
Throcking Rd BUNT SG9 62 B1
Thrums WATN WD24 204 C7
Thrush Av HAT AL10 171 F6
Thrush Gn RKW/CH/CXG WD3 218 B7
Thrush La POTB/CUF EN6 195 G6
Thumbswood WGCE AL7 148 B6
Thumpers HHNE HP2 8 B3
Thundercourt WARE SG12 127 H7
Thundridge Cl WGCE AL7 148 C4 6
Thurgood Rd HOD EN11 177 F1 3
Thurlow Cl STVG SG1 58 D8
Thurnall Av ROY SG8 21 H4
Thurnall Cl BLDK SG7 43 F1
Thurstans HLWW/ROY CM19 179 J6
Tibbles Cl GSTN WD25 205 F5
Tibbs Hill Rd ABLGY WD5 187 F8 2
Tiberius Rd LTNN/LIM LU3 68 E3
Tichborne RKW/CH/CXG WD3 227 G4
Tickenhall Dr HLWE CM17 181 G1
Tilbury Md HLWS CM18 7 F5
Tilecroft WGCW AL8 122 D8
Tilegate Rd HLWS CM18 7 E6
Tilehouse Cl BORE WD6 223 J3 3
Tilehouse La RKW/CH/CXG WD3 227 H7
Tilehouse St HTCH/STOT SG5 56 C2
Tile Kiln Cl HHS/BOV HP3 9 E6 1
Tile Kiln Crs HHS/BOV HP3 9 E6
Tile Kiln La HHS/BOV HP3 9 D6
Tilgate LTNE LU2 70 E6
Tillers Link STVGE SG2 3 E6
Tillotson Rd KTN/HRWW/W HA3 231 J6
Tillwicks Rd HLWS CM18 7 E5
Tilsworth Wk STALE/WH AL4 169 F1 6
Timbercroft WGCE AL7 123 F8
Timber Orch HERT/WAS SG14 125 J7
Timber Rdg RKW/CH/CXG WD3 218 B4
Timbers Ct HARP AL5 118 B7 2
Times Cl HTCH/STOT SG5 40 B7
Timplings Rw HHW HP1 164 A4 3
Timworth Cl LTNE LU2 70 E8
Tingeys Cl STALW/RED AL3 142 B4
Tinkers La TRING HP23 160 B3
Tinsley Cl LTN LU1 89 G4
Tintagel Cl HHNE HP2 164 C1 1
LTNN/LIM LU3 69 G5
Tintern Cl HARP AL5 117 J5
KNEB SG3 96 B2
Tinwell Ms BORE WD6 224 C5 4
Tippendell La LCOL/BKTW AL2 188 C3
Tippet Ct STVG SG1 2 B5
Titan Ct LTNW/LEA LU4 68 E8
Titan Rd HHNE HP2 8 C2
Titchfield Rd PEND EN3 214 D7
Tithe Barn Cl STAL AL1 188 E1
Tithe Cl WLYN AL6 94 E8
Tithelands HLWW/ROY CM19 179 G4
Titian Av BUSH WD23 222 B7
Titmus Cl STVG SG1 2 C2
Tiverton Ct HARP AL5 144 B3 2
Tiverton Rd POTB/CUF EN6 210 E1
Toddbrook HLWW/ROY CM19 6 A5
Toddington Rd LTNW/LEA LU4 68 C4
Toland Cl LTNW/LEA LU4 68 B8
Tolcarne Dr PIN HA5 230 B8
Tollgate Cl RKW/CH/CXG WD3 217 J4
Tollgate Rd BRKMPK AL9 192 A3
CHES/WCR EN8 214 C5
STALE/WH AL4 191 J2
Tollpit End HHW HP1 163 K3
Tollsworth Wy STDN SG11 81 H6
Tolmers Av POTB/CUF EN6 195 G6
Tolmers Gdns POTB/CUF EN6 195 G7
Tolmers Rd POTB/CUF EN6 195 G5
Tolpits Cl WATW WD18 12 A4
Tolpits La WATW WD18 12 A5
Tomkins Cl BORE WD6 223 H1
Toms Cft HHNE HP2 8 B6
Toms Fld HAT AL10 170 D5
Tom's Hl KGLGY WD4 202 D6
Toms Hill Cl TRING HP23 136 E4
Toms Hill Rd TRING HP23 136 E4
Tom's La KGLGY WD4 186 C6
Tooke Cl PIN HA5 231 F7
Tooveys Mill Cl KGLGY WD4 186 A7
Topland Rd CFSP/GDCR SL9 226 A6
Topstreet Wy HARP AL5 143 K
Torquay Crs STVG SG1 75 G
Torquay Dr LTNW/LEA LU4 68 C5
Torrington Dr POTB/CUF EN6 210 E
Torrington Rd BERK HP4 161 J5
Tortoiseshell Wy BERK HP4 161 G
Torwood Cl BERK HP4 161 G5
Torworth Rd BORE WD6 223 J
Tot La BSF CM23 86 C6
Totteridge Rd PEND EN3 214 C
Totton Ms STALW/RED AL3 142 C
Totts La STVGE SG2 60 E8
Toulmin Dr STALW/RED AL3 167 K
Tovey Av HOD EN11 177 F
Tovey Cl LCOL/BKTW AL2 190 B
WAB EN9 198 E
Tower Cl BERK HP4 161 H
HTCHE/RSTV SG4 57 K
Tower Hl KGLGY WD4 184 C
MHAD SG10 103 G
Tower Hill La STALE/WH AL4 145 J
Tower Rd HTCHE/RSTV SG4 94 D
LTNE LU2 5 E
WARE SG12 127 J
Towers Rd HHNE HP2 8 B
PIN HA5 231 F
Tower St HERT/WAS SG14 151 F
Tower Vw HTCHE/RSTV SG4 93 G
Tower Wy LTNE LU2 5 E
Towne Rd ROY SG8 21 H
Town Farm LBUZ LU7 110 A2
Town Farm Crs STDN SG11 82 A
Townfield RKW/CH/CXG WD3 218 B
Town Flds HAT AL10 171 F3
Town La STVGE SG2 78 B
Townley LWTH SG6 42 C
Town Mead Rd WAB EN9 215 H
Townsend HHNE HP2 8 A
Townsend Av STAL AL1 11 D
Townsend Cl HARP AL5 118 B
ROY SG8 32 C
Townsend Dr STALW/RED AL3 10 C
Townsend La HARP AL5 117 K
Townsend Rd HARP AL5 118 C
Townsend Wy NTHWD HA6 230 A
Townshend St HERT/WAS SG14 151 H
Townsley Cl LTN LU1 4 C
Tracyes Rd HLWS CM18 180 E
Trafalgar Av BROX EN10 176 E
Trafford Cl RAD WD7 207 H2
STVG SG1 58 E
Traherne Cl HTCHE/RSTV SG4 56 D4
Trajan Ga STVG SG1 59 K
Trap Rd ROY SG8 15 H
Trapstyle Rd WARE SG12 126 E
Travellers Cl BRKMPK AL9 192 C
Travellers La BRKMPK AL9 171 C
HAT AL10 171 F
Treacle La BUNT SG9 45 H
Treacy Cl BUSH WD23 231 K
Trebellan Dr HHNE HP2 8 C
Tree Cl HHS/BOV HP3 165 C
Treehanger Cl TRING HP23 135 G5
Treetops Cl NTHWD HA6 229
Trefusis Wk WAT WD17 219 K
Tregelles Rd HOD EN11 177 F
Tremaine Gv HHNE HP2 8 B
Trent Cl RAD WD7 207 H
STVG SG1 58 E
Trent Rd LTNN/LIM LU3 69 C
Tresco Rd BERK HP4 161 C
Trescott Cl LTNE LU2 71 F7
Trevalga Wy HHNE HP2 164 C
Trevellance Wy GSTN WD25 204 E3
Trevelyan Wy BERK HP4 161
Trevor Rd HTCHE/RSTV SG4 56 E
Trevose Wy OXHEY WD19 230 D
Trewenna Dr POTB/CUF EN6 210 E
Trident Rd GSTN WD25 204 A
Triggs Wy LTNE LU2 71
Trimley Cl LTNW/LEA LU4 68 A
Trinder Rd BAR EN5 225 H
Tring Ford Rd TRING HP23 135
Tring Hl TRING HP23 134 E
Tring Rd BERK HP4 160 D
DUN/WHIP LU6 112 A
TRING HP23 109 C
Trinity Cl BSF CM23 105
NTHWD HA6 229
Trinity Gv HERT/WAS SG14 151
Trinity Hall Cl WATN WD24 13 D2

Trinity La CHES/WCR EN8 214 D2
Trinity Ms HHS/BOV HP3 165 J7 2
Trinity Rd HERT/BAY SG13 152 B6
HTCH/STOT SG5 25 J2
LTNN/LIM LU3 69 F5
STVG SG1 2 A2
WARE SG12 127 J7
Trinity St BSF CM23 105 J3 5
Trinity Wk HERT/BAY SG13 152 B6
Trinity Wy BSF CM23 105 J3
Tripton Rd HLWS CM18 7 D5
Tristram Rd HTCHE/RSTV SG4 40 E7
Triton Wy HHNE HP2 8 C3 3
Troon Gdns LTNE LU2 69 K3
Trooper Rd TRING HP23 136 D4
Trotters Bottom BAR EN5 209 F7
Trotter's Gap WARE SG12 153 K5
Trotters Rd HLWS CM18 180 D4
Trout Ri RKW/CH/CXG WD3 218 A3
Troutstream Wy
RKW/CH/CXG WD3 218 A4
Trouvere Pk HHW HP1 164 A4
Trowbridge Gdns LTNE LU2 69 K6
Trowley Bottom STALW/RED AL3 141 G1
Trowley Hill Rd STALW/RED AL3 116 B7
Trowley Ri ABLGY WD5 203 K1
Truemans Rd HTCH/STOT SG5 40 B7
Trumper Rd STVG SG1 76 A1
Trumpington Dr STAL AL1 189 F1
Trundlers Wy BUSH WD23 222 B8 1
Truro Gdns LTNN/LIM LU3 69 G4
Trust Rd CHES/WCR EN8 214 D4 4
Tucker's Rw BSF CM23 105 J3
Tucker St WATW WD18 13 D4 6
Tudor Av CHESW EN7 214 A1
WATN WD24 204 E7
Tudor Cl AMP/FLIT/B MK45 36 C5 1
CHESW EN7 214 A1
HAT AL10 170 D7
STVG SG1 58 C8
WARE SG12 154 E1
Tudor Ct BORE WD6 223 H2 1
HTCH/STOT SG5 56 B3 1
Tudor Dr WATN WD24 204 E8
Tudor Manor Gdns GSTN WD25 204 E2
Tudor Ri BROX EN10 176 D7
Tudor Rd LTNN/LIM LU3 69 G7
PIN HA5 230 D8
STALE/WH AL4 145 H1
STALW/RED AL3 168 B2
WLYN AL6 122 B6
Tudor Wk WATN WD24 204 E7
Tudor Wy HERT/WAS SG14 150 D3
RKW/CH/CXG WD3 217 K8
WAB EN9 215 J3
Tuffnells Wy HARP AL5 117 K5
Tumbler Rd HLWS CM18 7 F5
Tunfield Rd HOD EN11 153 G8
Tunnel Wood Cl WAT WD17 204 A7
Tunnel Wood Rd WAT WD17 204 A7
WATN WD24 204 A7
Tunnmeade HLW CM20 7 F3
Turf La HTCHE/RSTV SG4 58 B5
Turkey St EN EN1 213 K6
Turmore Dl WGCW AL8 147 H4
Turnberry Ct OXHEY WD19 230 D2 5
Turnberry Dr LCOL/BKTW AL2 188 A8
Turn Braemar HHNE HP2 141 G8
Turner Cl STVG SG1 58 C7
Turner Rd BUSH WD23 221 K4
Turners Cl HARP AL5 118 E5
HERT/WAS SG14 124 E5
Turners Crs BSF CM23 105 F5
Turner's Hl CHES/WCR EN8 197 H8
HHNE HP2 8 B6
Turners Rd North LTNE LU2 5 E1
Turners Rd South LTNE LU2 5 E1
Turners Wood Dr CSTG HP8 226 A2
Turneys Orch RKW/CH/CXG WD3 217 G5
Turnors HLWW/ROY CM19 6 B4
Turnpike Dr LTNN/LIM LU3 52 C8
Turnpike Gn HHNE HP2 8 C1
Turnpike La HTCH/STOT SG5 40 B6
The Turnstones GSTN WD25 205 F6
Turpins Cha WLYN AL6 123 F2
Turpins Cl HERT/WAS SG14 150 C3
Turpin's Ride ROY SG8 21 H4
WLYN AL6 122 E2
Turpin's Ri STVGE SG2 75 K8
Turpin's Wy BLDK SG7 43 F2
Tuxford Cl BORE WD6 207 H8 4
Tweed Cl BERK HP4 161 J4
Twelve Acres WGCE AL7 147 K5
Twin Foxes KNEB SG3 96 B8
Twinwoods STVG SG1 3 D4
The Twist TRING HP23 135 J7
The Twitchell BLDK SG7 43 F1 3
Two Acres WGCE AL7 148 A6
Two Dells La CSHM HP5 182 B2
Two Oaks Dr WLYN AL6 123 J3
Two Waters Rd HHS/BOV HP3 185 G1
Twyford Bury La BSF CM23 105 K5
Twyford Cl BSF CM23 105 K4
Twyford Dr LTNE LU2 70 E8
Twyford Gdns BSF CM23 105 J5
Twyford Rd BSF CM23 105 K4
STALE/WH AL4 169 F2
Tye End STVGE SG2 96 C1
Tye Green Rd RBSF CM22 87 H2
Tye Green Village HLWS CM18 180 C4 2
Tyfield Cl CHES/WCR EN8 197 G8 3
Tylers HARP AL5 119 F8
Tylers Cswy HERT/BAY SG13 173 K8
Tylers Cl BUNT SG9 63 H2 1
KGLGY WD4 185 K7
Tylersfield ABLGY WD5 204 A1
Tylers Hill Rd CSHM HP5 182 B8
Tylers Md LTNE LU2 69 K4
Tylers Rd HLWW/ROY CM19 178 E6
Tylers Wd WLYN AL6 123 J4
Tylney Cft HLWW/ROY CM19 6 A6
Tynedale LCOL/BKTW AL2 190 D5 4
Tynemouth Dr EN EN1 213 K8
Typleden Cl HHNE HP2 8 A3 7
Tysea Cl HLWS CM18 180 C4
Tysea Rd HLWS CM18 180 C4
Tysoe Av PEND EN3 214 E6
Tythe Rd LTNW/LEA LU4 68 B3
Tyttenhanger Gn STALE/WH AL4 190 B1

U

Uckfield Rd PEND EN3 214 C7
Ufford Cl KTN/HRWW/W HA3 231 J6
Ufford Rd KTN/HRWW/W HA3 231 J6
Ullswater Cl STVG SG1 59 J7
Ullswater Rd HHS/BOV HP3 165 H8
Underacres Cl HHNE HP2 9 D4
Underwood Rd STVG SG1 58 C7
Union Gn HHNE HP2 8 A4 8
Union St BAR EN5 225 K4
LTN LU1 4 C5 7
Union Ter BUNT SG9 63 J2
Unity Rd PEND EN3 214 B7
Unwin Cl LWTH SG6 41 J5
Unwin Rd STVGE SG2 76 D6
Updale Cl POTB/CUF EN6 209 K3
Upland Dr BRKMPK AL9 193 H3
Uplands LTNN/LIM LU3 68 C1
RKW/CH/CXG WD3 218 E6
STDN SG11 82 A3
STVGE SG2 76 E1
WARE SG12 127 K7
WGCW AL8 122 C7
Uplands Av HTCHE/RSTV SG4 57 F3
The Uplands HARP AL5 143 H5
LCOL/BKTW AL2 188 A8
Upper Ashlyns Rd BERK HP4 161 J6
Upper Barn HHS/BOV HP3 185 K1
Upper Bourne End La HHW HP1 183 K1
Upper Clabdens WARE SG12 127 K8
Upper Culver Rd STAL AL1 11 D2
Upper Dagnall St
STALW/RED AL3 10 C4 7
Upperfield Rd WGCE AL7 148 A4
Upper George St LTN LU1 4 B4
Upper Gn WLYN AL6 123 K5
Upper Green Rd WLYN AL6 124 A6
Upper Hall Pk BERK HP4 162 B7
Upper Heath Rd STAL AL1 11 E2
Upper Hwy ABLGY WD5 203 H2
Upper Hill Ri RKW/CH/CXG WD3 218 A6
Upper Hitch OXHEY WD19 221 F8
Upper Hook HLWS CM18 7 E6
Upper Icknield Wy TRING HP23 135 J1
Upper King St ROY SG8 21 H3
Upper Lattimore Rd STAL AL1 11 D4
Upper Lea Valley Wk LTNE LU2 69 J6
Upper Marlborough Rd
STAL AL1 11 D4 3
Upper Marsh La HOD EN11 177 F4
Upper Maylins LWTH SG6 42 C5
Upper Mealines HLWS CM18 180 D4
Upper Paddock Rd OXHEY WD19 13 F5
Upper Pk HLW CM20 6 A3
Upper Sales HHW HP1 163 J7
Upper Sean STVGE SG2 3 E5
Upper Shot WGCE AL7 148 B2
Upper Shott CHESW EN7 196 D4
Upper Station Rd RAD WD7 206 D5 3
Upperstone Cl HTCH/STOT SG5 25 K3 1
Upper Stonyfield HLWW/ROY CM19 6 A4
Upper Tail OXHEY WD19 231 F2
Upper Tilehouse St
HTCH/STOT SG5 56 B3
Upton Av STALW/RED AL3 10 C3
Upton Cl LCOL/BKTW AL2 189 F3
LTNE LU2 69 J3
Upton Lodge Cl BUSH WD23 221 K7 5
Upton Rd WATW WD18 12 C3
Upway CFSP/GDCR SL9 226 C7
Upwell Rd LTNE LU2 5 F1
Uranus Rd HHNE HP2 8 B3
Urban Rd BSF CM23 106 A2
Uxbridge Rd RKW/CH/CXG WD3 218 A8
Uxbridge Road (Harrow Weald)
KTN/HRWW/W HA3 231 J6
Uxbridge Road (Hatch End)
PIN HA5 231 G6 5
Uxbridge Road (Pinner) PIN HA5 230 E8

V

Vadis Cl LTNN/LIM LU3 68 D2 4
Valance Rd SAFWS CB11 51 J2
Vale Av BORE WD6 224 A5
Vale Cl CFSP/GDCR SL9 226 A7 3
HARP AL5 117 K5
Vale Ct STALE/WH AL4 145 G2
Valence Dr CHESW EN7 196 E6
Valency Cl NTHWD HA6 230 A3
Valerian Wy STVGE SG2 76 E1
Valerie Cl STAL AL1 168 E6
Vale Rd BUSH WD23 13 F4
Valeside HERT/WAS SG14 150 D4
The Vale CFSP/GDCR SL9 226 A7
Vallans Cl WARE SG12 127 H6
Vallansgate STVGE SG2 76 C8
Valley Cl DUN/WHIP LU6 113 K5
DUN/WHIP LU6 113 G2
HERT/BAY SG13 151 G4
PIN HA5 230 C8
WAB EN9 215 H2
WARE SG12 127 F7 1
Valley Gn HHNE HP2 141 G8
The Valley Gn WGCW AL8 147 H2
Valley La STALW/RED AL3 115 J8
Valley Ri GSTN WD25 204 C3
ROY SG8 21 J4
STALE/WH AL4 119 H7
Valley Rd BERK HP4 161 G3
DUN/WHIP LU6 113 K5
LWTH SG6 41 H2
RKW/CH/CXG WD3 217 K5
STALW/RED AL3 168 B2
WGCW AL8 147 G3
WLYN AL6 94 E8
Valley Rd South WLYN AL6 121 K1 3
Valleyside HHW HP1 163 J6
The Valley HTCHE/RSTV SG4 93 H2
Valley Vw BAR EN5 225 K6
CHESW EN7 196 A6
Valley Wk RKW/CH/CXG WD3 219 H5
Valley Wy STVGE SG2 3 D6
Vanda Crs STAL AL1 11 E5
Vantorts Cl SBW CM21 132 C7
Vantorts Rd SBW CM21 132 C8
Vardon Rd STVG SG1 76 A1
Varna Cl LTNN/LIM LU3 69 F6
Varney Cl CHESW EN7 196 E5
HHW HP1 163 J6
Varney Rd HHW HP1 163 J6
Vaughan Md STALW/RED AL3 142 B5 1
Vaughan Rd HARP AL5 118 D8
HTCH/STOT SG5 25 J3
Vauxhall Rd HHNE HP2 9 D5
LTNE LU2 5 F6
Vega Crs NTHWD HA6 230 A4
Vega Rd BUSH WD23 221 K7
Velizy Av HLW CM20 6 C3
Venetia Rd LTNE LU2 70 B5
Ventnor Gdns LTNN/LIM LU3 68 E2
Ventura Pk LCOL/BKTW AL2 189 H7
Venus Hl HHS/BOV HP3 200 D1
Vera Ct OXHEY WD19 13 E6
Ver-colne Valley Wk BUSH WD23 13 E2
HHS/BOV HP3 183 F6
STAL AL1 11 D5
STALW/RED AL3 142 C5
Verdure Cl GSTN WD25 205 F2
Veritys HAT AL10 171 F4
Verity Wy STVG SG1 59 G8
Verlum Cl WGCE AL7 148 A3 3
Verney Cl BERK HP4 161 G4
TRING HP23 135 H4
Vernon Av PEND EN3 214 D6
Vernon Dr DEN/HRF UB9 228 B7
Vernon Rd BUSH WD23 13 F4
LTN LU1 4 A3
Vernon's Cl STAL AL1 11 D5 8
Ver Rd STALW/RED AL3 10 B4
Verulam Gdns LTNN/LIM LU3 68 E3
Verulam Rd HTCH/STOT SG5 56 D1
STALW/RED AL3 10 A3
Verwood Rd RYLN/HDSTN HA2 231 K8
Vesta Av STAL AL1 188 E1
Veysey Cl HHW HP1 164 A8 2
Viaduct Rd WARE SG12 152 D1
Viaduct Wy WGCE AL7 123 F8
Vian Av PEND EN3 214 D5
Vicarage Cswy HERT/BAY SG13 152 A5
Vicarage Cl ARL/CHE SG15 24 E1
HHW HP1 164 B7 1
HHW HP1 164 B8 2
HTCH/STOT SG5 38 B1
POTB/CUF EN6 194 B8
STAL AL1 188 E1
STDN SG11 81 K7
Vicarage Gdns BERK HP4 162 E2

STALW/RED AL3 116 B8
TRING HP23 110 A7 1
Vicarage La BSF CM23 67 K1
HERT/WAS SG14 125 J6
HHS/BOV HP3 183 K4
KGLGY WD4 185 K7
LBUZ LU7 111 F4
Vicarage Rd BERK HP4 162 D2
BUNT SG9 63 J1
LBUZ LU7 110 D6
TRING HP23 109 K7
TRING HP23 135 J8
WARE SG12 127 J8
WATW WD18 12 B6
WATW WD18 12 C3
Vicarage St LTN LU1 5 D4
Vicarage Wd HLW CM20 7 E3
Vicerons Pl BSF CM23 105 G5
Victoria Cl RKW/CH/CXG WD3 218 C7
STVG SG1 2 B1
Victoria Crs ROY SG8 21 H2
Victoria Ga HLWE CM17 180 E1
Victoria Rd BERK HP4 161 K6
BUSH WD23 221 J8
HARP AL5 118 D8 2
WAB EN9 215 H4
WATN WD24 204 C8
Victoria St LTN LU1 4 C5 8
STAL AL1 11 D4
Victoria Wy HTCH/STOT SG5 56 B1
Victory Rd BERK HP4 161 H4 3
View Rd POTB/CUF EN6 210 D2
Vigors Cft HAT AL10 170 E5
Village St HTCHE/RSTV SG4 74 E8
Village Wy AMSS HP7 216 A2
Villa Rd LTNE LU2 4 B3
Villiers Crs STALE/WH AL4 169 G3
Villiers Rd OXHEY WD19 13 F5
Villiers St HERT/WAS SG14 151 H3
Villiers-sur-marne Av BSF CM23 105 G4
Vincent LWTH SG6 42 C5
Vincent Cl CHES/WCR EN8 197 J6
Vincent Rd LTNW/LEA LU4 68 C4
Vincenzo Cl BRKMPK AL9 192 C1
Vine Cl WGCW AL8 147 K1
Vine Gv HLW CM20 156 A4
Vineyards Rd POTB/CUF EN6 194 D7
The Vineyard WARE SG12 127 K7
WGCW AL8 147 J1 4
Vinters Av STVG SG1 3 D3
Violet Av ENC/FH EN2 213 G8 1
Violets La BUNT SG9 66 D5
Violet Wy RKW/CH/CXG WD3 218 B4
Virgil Dr BROX EN10 197 K1 3
Virginia Cl LTNE LU2 70 A6
Viscount Cl LTNN/LIM LU3 69 F4
Vivian Cl OXHEY WD19 230 B1
Vivian Gdns OXHEY WD19 220 B8
Vixen Dr HERT/BAY SG13 151 K3
Vyse Cl BAR EN5 225 H4

W

Wacketts CHESW EN7 196 E5 3
Waddesdon Cl LTNE LU2 70 E7 4
Waddington Rd STAL AL1 10 C4 8
Wadesmill Rd HERT/WAS SG14 126 B8
WARE SG12 127 G6
The Wades HAT AL10 171 F7
The Wade WGCE AL7 148 A6
Wadham Rd ABLGY WD5 204 A1
Wadhurst Av LTNN/LIM LU3 69 H5
Wadley Cl HHNE HP2 8 C6 2
Wadnall Wy KNEB SG3 96 A5
Wagon Rd BAR EN5 210 B5
EBAR EN4 210 C7
Wagon Wy RKW/CH/CXG WD3 218 B3
Wain Cl POTB/CUF EN6 193 H7
Walcot Av LTNE LU2 5 E1
Waldeck Rd LTN LU1 4 A3
Waldegrave Pk HARP AL5 119 F8
Walden End STVG SG1 2 C4
Walden Pl WGCW AL8 147 J1
Walden Rd WGCW AL8 147 J1
Waleys Cl LTNN/LIM LU3 68 D1
Walfords Cl HLWE CM17 157 F6
Walkern Rd HERT/WAS SG14 97 K3
STVG SG1 75 J1
STVGE SG2 77 H5
Walkers Cl HARP AL5 143 K2 5
Walkers Rd HARP AL5 143 J2
The Walk POTB/CUF EN6 210 B2
Wallace Wy HTCHE/RSTV SG4 40 E6
Waller Av LTNW/LEA LU4 68 E6
Waller Dr NTHWD HA6 230 B8 3
Wallers Wy HOD EN11 153 G8
Wallingford Wk STAL AL1 189 F1
Wallington Rd BLDK SG7 43 G1
Walnut Av BLDK SG7 43 G2
Walnut Cl HTCH/STOT SG5 25 K3 2
HTCHE/RSTV SG4 56 E3
LCOL/BKTW AL2 188 D5
LTNE LU2 70 C6
MHAD SG10 103 G7
Walnut Ct WGCE AL7 147 K6 5
Walnut Dr BSF CM23 105 G6
Walnut Gn BUSH WD23 221 G2 1
Walnut Gv HHNE HP2 8 A5
WGCE AL7 147 K6
Walnut Tree Av SBW CM21 132 C5
Walnut Tree Cl CHES/WCR EN8 214 C1
HOD EN11 177 F3 4
STVGE SG2 76 E5
Walnut Tree Crs SBW CM21 132 C6 3
Walnut Tree Rd HTCH/STOT SG5 39 F6
Walnut Tree Wk WARE SG12 152 C3
Walnut Wy HTCH/STOT SG5 40 C5
Walpole Cl PIN HA5 231 H6
Walsham Cl STVGE SG2 96 D2
Walsh Cl HTCH/STOT SG5 56 B2
Walshford Wy BORE WD6 207 K8
Walsingham Cl HAT AL10 170 E3
LTNE LU2 69 J2 4
Walsingham Wy LCOL/BKTW AL2 190 A5
Walsworth Rd HTCHE/RSTV SG4 56 E2
Waltham Gdns PEND EN3 214 B7 1
Waltham Ga CHES/WCR EN8 197 J4
Waltham Rd HTCHE/RSTV SG4 56 D3
WAB EN9 198 E4
Walton Gdns WAB EN9 215 G3
Walton Rd BUSH WD23 13 E3
HOD EN11 177 G1
WARE SG12 152 C1
Walton St STAL AL1 11 E3
Walverns Cl OXHEY WD19 13 D5 3
Wandon Cl LTNE LU2 70 D5
Wannions Cl CSHM HP5 182 C8
Wansbeck Cl HTCHE/RSTV SG4 59 G6
Wansford Pk BORE WD6 224 C4
Ward Cl CHESW EN7 196 E5 4
WARE SG12 127 G7
Ward Crs BSF CM23 105 H3
Warden Hill Cl LTNE LU2 69 H1 2
Warden Hill Gdns LTNE LU2 69 H1
Warden Hill Rd LTNE LU2 69 H1
Ward Hatch HLW CM20 156 E6 1
Wardown Crs LTNE LU2 4 C1
Warenford Wy BORE WD6 223 K1
Ware Park Rd HERT/WAS SG14 151 G1
Ware Rd HERT/BAY SG13 151 H3
HERT/WAS SG14 98 B7
HOD EN11 177 F1
WARE SG12 126 C2
WARE SG12 129 J5
WARE SG12 153 F6
Wareside HHNE HP2 141 F8 2
Wareside Cl WGCE AL7 148 C4 7
Warmark Rd HHW HP1 163 H4 1
Warminster Cl LTNE LU2 71 G8
Warneford Pl OXHEY WD19 13 F5 6
Warner Rd WARE SG12 152 C1
Warners Av HOD EN11 176 E5
Warners Cl STVGE SG2 3 F5
Warners End Rd HHW HP1 163 K6
Warren Cl HAT AL10 171 G1
LWTH SG6 41 H2
Warren Dl WGCW AL8 122 D8
Warrender Rd CSHM HP5 182 A7
The Warren Dr LTN LU1 90 C8
Warrenfield Cl CHESW EN7 213 K1 1
Warrengate La POTB/CUF EN6 209 H1
Warrengate Rd BRKMPK AL9 192 C6
Warren Gn HAT AL10 171 G1
Warren Gv BORE WD6 224 C4
Warren La BLDK SG7 43 H2
BUNT SG9 61 K3
Warren Park Rd HERT/WAS SG14 151 F2
Warren Rd BUSH WD23 221 K8
LCOL/BKTW AL2 188 E2
LTN LU1 88 E1
Warrensgreen La HTCHE/RSTV SG4 59 K4
Warren Ter HERT/WAS SG14 151 G1
The Warren CFSP/GDCR SL9 226 C6
HARP AL5 143 H4
KGLGY WD4 185 K7
RAD WD7 206 D3
ROY SG8 21 H4
Warren Wy WLYN AL6 122 E6
Warton Gn LTNE LU2 71 F7
Warwick Av POTB/CUF EN6 195 F5
Warwick Cl BUSH WD23 222 B7
HERT/BAY SG13 151 F5
POTB/CUF EN6 195 F5
Warwick Ct RKW/CH/CXG WD3 217 J3
Warwick Dr CHES/WCR EN8 197 H6
Warwick Rd BORE WD6 224 C3
BSF CM23 106 A3
PEND EN3 214 E7
STAL AL1 11 E2
STVGE SG2 76 D3
Warwick Rd East LTNW/LEA LU4 89 G1 1
Warwick Rd West LTNW/LEA LU4 69 G8
Warwick Wy RKW/CH/CXG WD3 219 H4
Washbrook Cl AMP/FLIT/B MK45 36 C8
Washington Av HHNE HP2 164 D1
Wash La BAR EN5 209 H5
POTB/CUF EN6 209 H3
The Wash BUNT SG9 67 F4
HERT/WAS SG14 151 G3 16
Watchlytes WGCE AL7 148 D3
Watchmead WGCE AL7 148 B3 1
Waterbeach WGCE AL7 148 E3 9
Watercress Cl STVGE SG2 76 E4
Waterdale HERT/BAY SG13 151 F5 3
Waterdell La HTCHE/RSTV SG4 56 D7
Waterend La STALE/WH AL4 146 B1
STALW/RED AL3 142 C4
Water End Rd BERK HP4 162 E3 1
Waterfield WGCE AL7 148 C2 7
Waterfields Wy WAT WD17 13 E3
Waterford Common
HERT/WAS SG14 125 K7
Waterford Gn WGCE AL7 148 C3
The Watergate OXHEY WD19 230 E1 1
Waterhoose Moor HLWS CM18 7 D5
Waterhouse St HHW HP1 164 B6
Water La BERK HP4 161 K5
BSF CM23 105 J1
HHS/BOV HP3 183 K7
HLWW/ROY CM19 179 F5
HTCH/STOT SG5 56 D1 6
KGLGY WD4 186 B7
STSD CM24 86 D3
WAT WD17 13 D3 12
Waterloo La HTCH/STOT SG5 39 J3
Waterman Cl OXHEY WD19 12 C5
Watermark Wy HERT/BAY SG13 151 J3 7
Watermead Rd LTNN/LIM LU3 68 E3
Watermill La HERT/WAS SG14 126 B8
Waters Dr RKW/CH/CXG WD3 218 D8 1
Waters End HTCH/STOT SG5 25 J3
Waterside KGLGY WD4 186 A7
LCOL/BKTW AL2 190 C5
RAD WD7 206 E4 1
STSD CM24 86 D3 4
WGCE AL7 148 B1
Waterside Ct KGLGY WD4 186 B7 1
Waterslade Gn LTNN/LIM LU3 69 G3 3
Watersmeet HLWW/ROY CM19 179 J5
Waterwick Hl SAFWS CB11 34 D8
Watery La HAT AL10 170 D5
STALW/RED AL3 116 E6
TRING HP23 109 K8
Watford Field Rd WAT WD17 13 D3 13
WATW WD18 13 D4
Watford Heath OXHEY WD19 13 E6
Watford Rd BORE WD6 223 F6
KGLGY WD4 186 A8
LCOL/BKTW AL2 188 C3
NTHWD HA6 230 A6
RAD WD7 206 B6
RKW/CH/CXG WD3 219 F6
STAL AL1 188 D1
Watling Cl HHNE HP2 8 B2
Watling Knoll RAD WD7 206 C3
Watling St LCOL/BKTW AL2 189 F3
STAL AL1 188 E1
Watlington Rd HLWE CM17 157 G5
Watling Vw STAL AL1 188 E1
Watson Av STALW/RED AL3 11 E1
Watson's Wk STAL AL1 11 D5
Watton Rd KNEB SG3 96 B4
WARE SG12 127 G7
Watts Cl STDN SG11 83 J7
Wauluds Bank Dr LTNN/LIM LU3 68 D2
Wavell Cl CHES/WCR EN8 197 J5
Waveney HHNE HP2 164 E
Waveney Rd HARP AL5 118 E6
Waverley Cl STVGE SG2 96 B1
Waverley Gdns NTHWD HA6 230 B7
Waverley Rd STALW/RED AL3 10 B2
Waxwell La PIN HA5 230 E8
Wayre St HLWE CM17 157 F5
Waysbrook LWTH SG6 42 B5
Wayside KGLGY WD4 185 F8
POTB/CUF EN6 210 E3
RAD WD7 207 G3
Wayside Av BUSH WD23 222 A6
The Wayside HHS/BOV HP3 9 F6
Waysmeet LWTH SG6 42 A5
Waytemore Rd BSF CM23 105 H3
Wealdwood Gdns PIN HA5 231 J5
Weall Gn GSTN WD25 204 C2
Weatherby Rd LTNW/LEA LU4 68 C7
Weavers Rd TRING HP23 134 D5
Weaver St BSF CM23 105 F5
Weavers Wy BLDK SG7 43 G1
Webb Cl LWTH SG6 42 C4
Webber Cl BORE WD6 223 G6
Webb Ri STVG SG1 3 D
Wedgewood Cl HTCHE/RSTV SG4 57 G
NTHWD HA6 229 H5
Wedgewood Dr HLWE CM17 181 G
Wedgewood Pk STVG SG1 59 J
Wedgewood Rd HTCHE/RSTV SG4 57 F
Wedgwood Ct STVG SG1 59 J
Wedgwood Ga STVG SG1 59 H
Wedgwood Wy STVG SG1 59 H
Wedhey HLWW/ROY CM19 6 B
Wedmore Rd HTCHE/RSTV SG4 56 E
Wedon Wy BLDK SG7 27 J
Weedon Cl HNLW SG16 24 A

Welbeck Cl BORE WD6 223 K3 4
Welbeck Ri HARP AL5 144 A3
Welbeck Rd LTNE LU2 4 C3 4
Welbury Av LTNN/LIM LU3 69 H2
Welch Pl PIN HA5 230 D7 1
Welclose St STALW/RED AL3 10 B4
Weldon Cl LTNE LU2 71 F8
Welham Cl BRKMPK AL9 192 C2
Welham Mnr BRKMPK AL9 192 C2
Welkin Gn HHNE HP2 9 F4 3
Wellands HAT AL10 171 F2 3
Well Ap BAR EN5 225 H5 2
Well Cft HHW HP1 164 A5
Wellcroft LBUZ LU7 111 F4
Wellcroft Cl WGCE AL7 148 B5
Wellcroft Rd WGCE AL7 148 B4
Well End Rd BORE WD6 208 B7
Wellen Ri HHS/BOV HP3 185 J1
Wellers Gv CHESW EN7 196 E6 3
Wellesley EPP CM16 179 H6
Wellesley Av NTHWD HA6 230 A4
Wellesley Crs POTB/CUF EN6 209 K3
Wellfield Av LTNN/LIM LU3 68 B1
Wellfield Cl HAT AL10 171 F3
Wellfield Rd HAT AL10 171 G3 5
Well Garth WGCE AL7 147 K4
Wellgate Rd LTNW/LEA LU4 68 C7
Well Gn HERT/WAS SG14 124 E5
Wellhouse Cl LTN LU1 89 F2
Wellhouse La BAR EN5 225 H4
Wellingham Av HTCH/STOT SG5 40 B8
Wellington Av PIN HA5 231 G7 2
Wellington Cl OXHEY WD19 231 F2
Wellington Dr WGCE AL7 148 D3
Wellington Rd LCOL/BKTW AL2 190 B4
PIN HA5 231 G7
STAL AL1 168 E7
STVGE SG2 76 D4
WAT WD17 12 C1 6
Wellington St HERT/WAS SG14 150 E2
LTN LU1 4 B4
Well La HLW CM20 179 H1
HLWW/ROY CM19 155 H8
Well Rd BAR EN5 225 H5
POTB/CUF EN6 194 A7
Well-row HERT/BAY SG13 174 C3
Wells Cl CHESW EN7 196 A3
HARP AL5 118 A5
STALW/RED AL3 10 B3
Wellside Cl BAR EN5 225 H4
Wellstones WAT WD17 12 C3 4
Wellswood Cl HHNE HP2 9 E4 2
Welsummer Wy CHES/WCR EN8 197 H5
Weltmore Rd LTNN/LIM LU3 68 E3
Welwyn by Pass Rd WLYN AL6 122 C5
Welwyn Ct HHNE HP2 8 C1 5
Welwyn Hall WLYN AL6 122 C4 7
Welwyn Rd HERT/WAS SG14 150 B2
Wendover Cl HARP AL5 119 F8 4
STALE/WH AL4 169 F1
Wendover Ct WLYN AL6 122 C4 8
Wendover Dr WLYN AL6 122 C4
Wendover Wy BUSH WD23 221 K6
LTNE LU2 70 A6
Wengeo La WARE SG12 127 F7
Wenlock St LTNE LU2 4 C3
Wensley Cl HARP AL5 144 A3
Wensleydale HHNE HP2 8 B2
Wensley Dl LTNE LU2 4 C2
Wensum Wy RKW/CH/CXG WD3 218 C8
Wentbridge Pth BORE WD6 207 K8 6
Wentworth Av BORE WD6 223 J5
LTNW/LEA LU4 68 B4
Wentworth Cl POTB/CUF EN6 210 B1 2
WAT WD17 204 A8
Wentworth Dr BSF CM23 105 G3
Wentworth Rd BAR EN5 225 J2
HERT/BAY SG13 151 F6
Wesley Cl ARL/CHE SG15 24 E5
CHESW EN7 196 A6
Wesley Rd STALW/RED AL3 115 J4
Wessex Dr PIN HA5 231 F6
Westall Cl HERT/WAS SG14 151 F4
West Aly HTCH/STOT SG5 56 C2 1
West Av BLDK SG7 42 E1
LCOL/BKTW AL2 188 D3
Westbourne Rd LTNW/LEA LU4 69 G8
Westbrook Cl ROY SG8 18 C1
West Burrowfield WGCE AL7 147 J5 1
Westbury CHES/WCR EN8 197 H8 2
Westbury Cl HTCH/STOT SG5 56 A1
Westbury Gdns LTNE LU2 69 J6
Westbury Pl LWTH SG6 41 J4
Westbury Ri HLWE CM17 181 G2
Westbury Rd NTHWD HA6 229 K3
WATW WD18 12 C4 4
Westbush Cl HOD EN11 152 E8
West Chantry RYLN/HDSTN HA2 231 J7 1
West Cl BAR EN5 225 G5
HOD EN11 177 F1
HTCHE/RSTV SG4 41 F7
STVG SG1 3 D3
West Common HARP AL5 143 J2
West Common Cl HARP AL5 143 J4 1
West Common Gv HARP AL5 143 J3
West Common Wy HARP AL5 143 H4
Westcott WGCE AL7 148 E2
Westcroft Cl PEND EN3 214 B8 2
Westcroft Ct BROX EN10 177 F5 3
West Dene DUN/WHIP LU6 139 J1
West Dr ARL/CHE SG15 24 E5
GSTN WD25 204 C6
HTCH/STOT SG5 25 F6
Westell Cl BLDK SG7 43 G1
West End BLDK SG7 17 J6
West End La BAR EN5 225 J4
BRKMPK AL9 172 D4
West End Rd BROX EN10 196 D1
LBUZ LU7 109 K2
Westerdale HHNE HP2 8 B2
LTNW/LEA LU4 68 A4
Western Cl LWTH SG6 25 J8
Western Rd LTN LU1 4 B5 5
TRING HP23 134 E6
WAB EN9 177 K8
Western Wy LWTH SG6 25 J8
Westfield BRKMPK AL9 193 G1
HLWS CM18 7 D5
WGCE AL7 148 B2
Westfield Av HARP AL5 118 C6
WATN WD24 204 E8
Westfield Cl BSF CM23 105 H1
CHES/WCR EN8 214 E1
HTCH/STOT SG5 56 B2
Westfield Ct STALE/WH AL4 169 G3 4
Westfield Dr HARP AL5 118 D5
Westfield La HTCH/STOT SG5 56 B2
Westfield Pk PIN HA5 231 G6
Westfield Pl HARP AL5 118 D5
Westfield Rd BERK HP4 161 F3
BSF CM23 105 H1
HARP AL5 118 D5
HERT/WAS SG14 151 F1
HOD EN11 176 E2
Westfields STALW/RED AL3 167 H8
West Ga HLW CM20 6 B4
West Hl HTCH/STOT SG5 56 B2
West Hill Rd HOD EN11 176 E1
LTN LU1 4 C6
Westholme LWTH SG6 41 K1
West Hyde La CFSP/GDCR SL9 226 C6
Westland Dr BRKMPK AL9 192 E5
Westland Rd KNEB SG3 96 B4
WAT WD17 12 C1 7
West La HTCH/STOT SG5 39 F4
HTCH/STOT SG5 54 E7
Westlea Av GSTN WD25 205 F7
Westlea Cl BROX EN10 197 K2 3
Westlea Rd BROX EN10 197 K1
Westlecote Gdns LTNE LU2 69 J5
West Lieth TRING HP23 134 D8
Westly Wd WGCE AL7 148 B2
West Md WGCE AL7 148 C6
Westmeade Cl CHESW EN7 197 F7
Westmill La HTCH/STOT SG5 40 A7
Westmill Lawns HTCH/STOT SG5 40 B8 1
Westmill Rd HTCH/STOT SG5 40 A7
WARE SG12 126 D4
Westminster Ct STALW/RED AL3 10 B6 1
Westmorland Av LTNN/LIM LU3 68 E4
Weston Av ROY SG8 21 G2
Weston Cl POTB/CUF EN6 210 A2 2
Weston Rd STVG SG1 58 E8
Weston Wy BLDK SG7 42 E1
Westray HHS/BOV HP3 165 H8 5
West Reach STVGE SG2 3 D6
Westridge Cl HHW HP1 163 J6 4
West Riding LCOL/BKTW AL2 188 B8
WLYN AL6 123 K4
West Rd BERK HP4 161 H4
BSF CM23 105 H3
HLW CM20 156 D5
SBW CM21 131 K6
STSD CM24 86 D4
Westron Gdns TRING HP23 135 G5
West Side BROX EN10 197 J3
West St HERT/BAY SG13 151 F4
LTNE LU2 53 K8
WARE SG12 127 H8
WAT WD17 12 C1 8
West Valley Rd HHS/BOV HP3 185 G2
West Vw HAT AL10 171 F2
LWTH SG6 41 H5
Westview Ct BORE WD6 223 G6 8
West View Gdns BORE WD6 223 G6
Westview Ri HHNE HP2 8 A4
West View Rd STALW/RED AL3 10 C3
West Wy HARP AL5 118 E7
Westway LTNE LU2 70 D5
West Wy RKW/CH/CXG WD3 218 A8
WAB EN9 215 G7
Westwick Cl HHNE HP2 165 J7
Westwick Pl GSTN WD25 204 D4
Westwick Rw HHNE HP2 165 J7
Westwood Av HTCHE/RSTV SG4 56 E3
Westwood Cl AMS HP6 216 A1
POTB/CUF EN6 193 G8
Westwood Dr AMS HP6 216 A1
Wetherby Cl STVG SG1 76 D1
Wetherby Rd BORE WD6 223 H1
Wetherfield STSD CM24 86 C2
Wetherly Cl HLWE CM17 157 F6
Wetherne Link LTNW/LEA LU4 68 B4
Wexham Cl LTNN/LIM LU3 68 D1
Weybourne Cl HARP AL5 119 F7
Weybourne Dr LTNE LU2 69 H2
Weymouth St HHS/BOV HP3 185 H2
Whaley Rd POTB/CUF EN6 210 D3
Wharfdale LTNW/LEA LU4 68 B4 6
Wharfedale HHNE HP2 8 B2
Wharf La BERK HP4 136 D8
RKW/CH/CXG WD3 218 D7
Wharf Rd BROX EN10 197 K2
BSF CM23 105 J3
HHW HP1 164 A8
Wharley Hook HLWS CM18 180 C4
Wheatbarn WGCE AL7 148 C2 8
Wheat Cl STALE/WH AL4 168 D2
Wheatcotes KNEB SG3 96 D8
Wheat Cft BSF CM23 105 H5 2
Wheatfield HAT AL10 171 G3 6
HHNE HP2 8 A3
Wheatfield Av HARP AL5 143 H4 1
Wheatfield Crs ROY SG8 21 J3 4
Wheatfield Rd HARP AL5 143 G4
Wheatfields HLWE CM17 157 G3 1
Wheathampstead Rd HARP AL5 144 A1
Wheat Hl LWTH SG6 41 J2
Wheatlands STVGE SG2 76 D2
Wheatley Cl SBW CM21 132 A8
WGCE AL7 148 B5
Wheatley Rd WGCE AL7 148 A4
Wheatleys STALE/WH AL4 169 F4 1
Wheatley Wy CFSP/GDCR SL9 226 B5
Wheatlock Md STALW/RED AL3 142 B4
Wheatsheaf Dr WARE SG12 127 F6
Wheatsheaf Rd WARE SG12 129 K7
Wheelers Cl WAB EN9 177 K8
Wheelers La HHS/BOV HP3 164 D8
Wheelers Orch CFSP/GDCR SL9 226 B5
Wheelright Cl BUSH WD23 221 J6 8
Wheelwrights Cl BSF CM23 105 F5 6
Whempstead La WARE SG12 98 E3
Whempstead Rd STVGE SG2 78 C6
Whetstone Cl WLYN AL6 122 E1 5
Whinbush Gv HTCH/STOT SG5 56 D1 7
Whinbush Rd HTCH/STOT SG5 56 D2
Whippendell Hl KGLGY WD4 185 G8
Whippendell Rd WATW WD18 12 B4
Whipperley Ring LTN LU1 89 F3
Whipperley Wy LTN LU1 89 G3
Whisper Wd RKW/CH/CXG WD3 218 A3
Whitby Rd LTNN/LIM LU3 4 A2
Whitebarns La BUNT SG9 66 C2
Whitebeam Cl CHESW EN7 196 C4 5
Whitebeams HAT AL10 171 F7 4
LCOL/BKTW AL2 188 D6
White Bear STSD CM24 86 D1 7
Whitebroom Rd HHW HP1 163 H4 2
Whitechurch Cl LTNE LU2 70 E7 5
Whitechurch Gdns LWTH SG6 42 C6
White Craig Cl PIN HA5 231 H4
Whitecroft STAL AL1 189 K1
Whitecroft Rd LTNE LU2 5 E3
White Crofts HTCH/STOT SG5 25 J2
Whitefield Av LTNN/LIM LU3 68 B2
Whitefields Rd CHES/WCR EN8 197 G6
Whitegale Cl HTCHE/RSTV SG4 56 E3 7
Whitegates Cl RKW/CH/CXG WD3 219 F4
Whitehall Cl WAB EN9 177 K8 2
Whitehall La BSF CM23 85 J8
Whitehall Rd BSF CM23 85 H8
Whitehands Cl HOD EN11 176 E3 1
White Hart Cl BUNT SG9 63 H1
White Hart Dr HHNE HP2 8 C6
White Hart Rd HHNE HP2 9 D6
White Hedge Dr STALW/RED AL3 10 B2
Whitehicks LWTH SG6 26 A8
Whitehill BERK HP4 162 A4
White Hl BERK HP4 182 E2
HHW HP1 163 J7
NTHWD HA6 229 F5
STALW/RED AL3 141 G1
STVGE SG2 60 E6
WLYN AL6 122 A7
Whitehill Av LTN LU1 4 B6
Whitehill Ct BERK HP4 162 A4
White Hill Rd AMP/FLIT/B MK45 36 C6
Whitehill Rd HTCHE/RSTV SG4 56 E3
White Horse La KNEB SG3 96 C8
LCOL/BKTW AL2 190 B4
Whitehorse St BLDK SG7 43 F1
Whitehouse Av BORE WD6 224 A4
White House Cl CFSP/GDCR SL9 226 B6
Whitehouse La ABLGY WD5 187 H4
Whitehurst Av HTCH/STOT SG5 40 D8
Whitelands Av RKW/CH/CXG WD3 216 E3
White La HTCHE/RSTV SG4 74 B3
Whiteleaf Rd HHS/BOV HP3 185 G1
Whiteley Cl WARE SG12 99 H2 1
Whiteley La BUNT SG9 47 G2
White Lion St HHS/BOV HP3 185 H2 7
White Post Fld SBW CM21 132 B7
White Shack La
RKW/CH/CXG WD3 202 E7

Whitesmead Rd *STVG* SG1 .... 2 C1
Whitestone Wk *HHW* HP1 .... 163 K3 3
White Stubbs La *BROX* EN10 .... 175 J7
Whitethorn *WGCE* AL7 .... 148 B4
Whitethorn La *LWTH* SG6 .... 42 A6
Whitethorn Wy *LTN* LU1 .... 89 F3
Whitewaits *HLW* CM20 .... 7 D3
Whitewaybottom La *LTNE* LU2 .... 92 C3
The White Wy *STVGE* SG2 .... 76 D2
Whitewebbs La *ENC/FH* EN2 .... 213 J5
Whitewebbs Rd *ENC/FH* EN2 .... 212 E5
Whitewood Rd *BERK* HP4 .... 161 H5 1
Whitfield Wy *RKW/CH/CXG* WD3 .... 217 J8
Whit Hern Ct *CHES/WCR* EN8 .... 197 G8
Whitings Cl *HARP* AL5 .... 119 F5
Whitings Rd *BAR* EN5 .... 225 H5
Whitlars Dr *KGLGY* WD4 .... 186 A6 1
Whitley Cl *ABLGY* WD5 .... 204 B2
Whitley Rd *HOD* EN11 .... 177 G1
Whitmores Wd *HHNE* HP2 .... 9 E4
Whitney Dr *STVG* SG1 .... 58 C8
Whittingham Cl *LTNE* LU2 .... 71 G8 1
Whittingstall Rd *HOD* EN11 .... 177 G1
Whittington La *STVG* SG1 .... 2 C4
Whittington Wy *BSF* CM23 .... 105 H6
Whittlesea Rd *KTN/HRWW/W* HA3 .... 231 K6
Whitwell Cl *LTNN/LIM* LU3 .... 69 G1
Whitwell Rd *GSTN* WD25 .... 204 E5
Whitworth Jones Av *HNLW* SG16 .... 24 A4
Whitworth Rd *STVG* SG1 .... 59 H6
Whomerley Rd *STVG* SG1 .... 2 C4
Whydale Rd *ROY* SG8 .... 21 J4 5
Whytingham Rd *TRING* HP23 .... 135 H5
Wick Av *STALE/WH* AL4 .... 145 G1
Wicken Flds *WARE* SG12 .... 127 G6
The Wickets *LTNE* LU2 .... 4 B2
Wickfield Cl *KNEB* SG3 .... 96 B7 4
Wickham Cl *DEN/HRF* UB9 .... 228 C7
Wickhams Whf *WARE* SG12 .... 127 J8 2
Wickham Wy *STDN* SG11 .... 81 K6 2
Wick Hl *DUN/WHIP* LU6 .... 114 D1
Wicklands Rd *WARE* SG12 .... 154 E1
Wickmere Cl *LTNE* LU2 .... 69 H2 2
Wick Rd *TRING* HP23 .... 159 H1
Wickstead Av *LTNW/LEA* LU4 .... 68 D6
The Wick *HERT/WAS* SG14 .... 125 K8
Widbury Gdns *WARE* SG12 .... 127 K8 4
Widbury Hl *WARE* SG12 .... 128 A8
Widford Rd *MHAD* SG10 .... 130 A2
WARE SG12 .... 129 K7
WGCE AL7 .... 148 C3
Widford Ter *HHNE* HP2 .... 141 F8 3
Widgeon Wy *GSTN* WD25 .... 205 F6 2
Widmore Dr *HHNE* HP2 .... 9 D3
Wieland Rd *NTHWD* HA6 .... 230 B6
Wiggenhall Rd *WATW* WD18 .... 12 C4
Wiggington Bottom *TRING* HP23 .... 159 J1
Wigmore La *LTNE* LU2 .... 70 E7
Wigmore Pl *LTNE* LU2 .... 71 F8
Wigmores North *WGCW* AL8 .... 147 J2 2
Wigram Wy *STVGE* SG2 .... 3 F4
Wilbury Cl *LWTH* SG6 .... 41 G2
Wilbury Hills Rd *LWTH* SG6 .... 41 G3
Wilbury Rd *LWTH* SG6 .... 41 H2
Wilbury Wy *HTCHE/RSTV* SG4 .... 40 E6
Wilcot Av *OXHEY* WD19 .... 13 F6
Wilcot Cl *OXHEY* WD19 .... 13 F6
Wilcox Cl *BORE* WD6 .... 224 B1
Wild Cherry Dr *LTN* LU1 .... 4 B6 3
The Wilderness *BERK* HP4 .... 161 K5 6
Wildhill Rd *BRKMPK* AL9 .... 172 A7
Wild Oaks Cl *NTHWD* HA6 .... 230 A5
Wildwood *NTHWD* HA6 .... 229 J5
Wildwood Av *LCOL/BKTW* AL2 .... 188 B8
Wildwood La *STVG* SG1 .... 2 C5
Wilford Cl *NTHWD* HA6 .... 229 J6
Wilga Rd *WLYN* AL6 .... 122 B4
Wilkin's Green La *HAT* AL10 .... 170 B5
STALE/WH AL4 .... 170 B6
Wilkins Gv *WGCW* AL8 .... 147 J4
Wilkinson Wy *HHS/BOV* HP3 .... 185 K2
Willenhall Cl *LTNN/LIM* LU3 .... 69 F2
William Ct *HHS/BOV* HP3 .... 185 H2 8
William Covell Cl *ENC/FH* EN2 .... 212 C8 3
William Pl *STVGE* SG2 .... 3 E5
Williamson Wy *RKW/CH/CXG* WD3 .... 217 K8
William St *BERK* HP4 .... 162 A5
BUSH WD23 .... 13 E2
LTNE LU2 .... 4 C2
STALW/RED AL3 .... 115 J4 3
Williams Wy *RAD* WD7 .... 207 F5
Willian Church Rd *LWTH* SG6 .... 42 A7
Willian Rd *HTCHE/RSTV* SG4 .... 41 F8
Willian Wy *BLDK* SG7 .... 42 E3 1
LWTH SG6 .... 42 A5
Willinghall Cl *WAB* EN9 .... 215 J2 1
Williton Rd *LTNE* LU2 .... 5 F1
Willoughby Cl *BROX* EN10 .... 176 D7 2
Willoughby Rd *HARP* AL5 .... 118 D5
Willoughby Wy *HTCHE/RSTV* SG4 .... 56 E3
Willowby Ct *LCOL/BKTW* AL2 .... 190 B4
Willow Cl *BSF* CM23 .... 105 H1
BUNT SG9 .... 65 G1
CHESW EN7 .... 196 C4
ROY SG8 .... 31 H4
Willow Crs *STAL* AL1 .... 169 F6
Willow Dean *PIN* HA5 .... 230 E8 2
Willow Dene *BUSH* WD23 .... 222 B7
Willowdene *CHES/WCR* EN8 .... 197 J5
Willow Dene *PIN* HA5 .... 230 E8
Willow Dr *BAR* EN5 .... 225 K4
Willow Edge *KGLGY* WD4 .... 186 A7 6
Willow End *NTHWD* HA6 .... 230 B5
Willowfield *HLWS* CM18 .... 6 C5
Willow Gv *WGCW* AL8 .... 122 D6
Willow La *HTCH/STOT* SG5 .... 56 B3
WATW WD18 .... 12 B4
Willowmead *HERT/WAS* SG14 .... 150 D4
Willow Md *SBW* CM21 .... 132 C8
Willow Pl *HLWE* CM17 .... 181 J5
Willows Cl *PIN* HA5 .... 230 D8
Willowside *LCOL/BKTW* AL2 .... 190 C5
Willowside Wy *ROY* SG8 .... 21 G1 5
Willows Link *STVGE* SG2 .... 76 B8
Willow Springs *BSF* CM23 .... 105 G1
The Willows *HTCHE/RSTV* SG4 .... 56 E4
OXHEY WD19 .... 12 C6 3
RKW/CH/CXG WD3 .... 227 K1
STAL AL1 .... 189 K2
STVGE SG2 .... 96 B1
Willow Tree Wy *HTCH/STOT* SG5 .... 40 C7
Willow Wk *WLYN* AL6 .... 122 C1
Willow Wy *HARP* AL5 .... 118 E5 3
HAT AL10 .... 170 E7
HHW HP1 .... 164 A4 4
LCOL/BKTW AL2 .... 188 C5
LTNN/LIM LU3 .... 68 D4
POTB/CUF EN6 .... 210 C3
RAD WD7 .... 206 B6
Wilsden Av *LTN* LU1 .... 4 A5
Wilshere Av *STAL* AL1 .... 188 E1
Wilshere Crs *HTCHE/RSTV* SG4 .... 57 G1
Wilshere Rd *WLYN* AL6 .... 122 A4
Wilson Cl *BSF* CM23 .... 105 J4
STVG SG1 .... 58 D8
Wilsons La *BLDK* SG7 .... 17 J5
Wilstone Br *TRING* HP23 .... 109 H8
Wilstone Dr *STALE/WH* AL4 .... 169 F1
Wilton Cl *BSF* CM23 .... 106 A2
Wilton Crs *HERT/BAY* SG13 .... 151 F6
Wilton Rd *HTCH/STOT* SG5 .... 40 C8
Wilton Wy *HERT/BAY* SG13 .... 151 F5 4
Wiltshire Rd *STVGE* SG2 .... 3 E4
Wimborne Cl *SBW* CM21 .... 132 B7 2
Wimborne Gv *WAT* WD17 .... 203 K7
Wimborne Rd *LTN* LU1 .... 89 G1
Winch Cl *WLYN* AL6 .... 121 K1 4
Winchdells *HHS/BOV* HP3 .... 186 A1
Winchester Cl *BSF* CM23 .... 105 G5
STVG SG1 .... 59 G7
Winchester Wy
RKW/CH/CXG WD3 .... 219 G5
Winchfield Wy *RKW/CH/CXG* WD3 .... 218 B7
Winch St *LTNE* LU2 .... 5 D2
Windermere Av *STAL* AL1 .... 168 E8
Windermere Cl *HHS/BOV* HP3 .... 9 F6
RKW/CH/CXG WD3 .... 217 G5
Windermere Crs *LTNN/LIM* LU3 .... 68 E4
Windhill *BSF* CM23 .... 105 H2
WGCE AL7 .... 148 B2
Windhill Old Rd *BSF* CM23 .... 105 H2
Winding Hl *MHAD* SG10 .... 103 H5
Winding Shot *HHW* HP1 .... 163 K5
Winding Shott *HERT/WAS* SG14 .... 124 E5
Windmill Av *STALE/WH* AL4 .... 169 F2
Windmill Cl *LBUZ* LU7 .... 111 F4
ROY SG8 .... 32 C4
WAB EN9 .... 215 K4
Windmill Dr *RKW/CH/CXG* WD3 .... 218 E6
Windmill Fld *WARE* SG12 .... 152 C1
Windmill Flds *HLWE* CM17 .... 157 J5
Windmill Hl *BUNT* SG9 .... 63 K3
HTCHE/RSTV SG4 .... 56 D2
KGLGY WD4 .... 201 J2
Windmill La *BAR* EN5 .... 224 E6
BUSH WD23 .... 222 B8
CHES/WCR EN8 .... 197 J8
Windmill Rd *CFSP/GDCR* SL9 .... 226 A6 3
HHNE HP2 .... 8 B5
HTCHE/RSTV SG4 .... 72 A7
LTN LU1 .... 5 E5
Windmills *WARE* SG12 .... 99 H1
Windmill St *BUSH* WD23 .... 222 B8
Windmill Wy *MHAD* SG10 .... 103 F8
TRING HP23 .... 134 E5
Windmore Av *POTB/CUF* EN6 .... 209 H1
Windridge Cl *STALW/RED* AL3 .... 167 H8
Winds End Cl *HHNE* HP2 .... 9 D3 2
Windsor Cl *CHESW* EN7 .... 196 E8
HHS/BOV HP3 .... 164 D8
HHS/BOV HP3 .... 183 J6 2
NTHWD HA6 .... 230 B8
STVGE SG2 .... 96 C2
WLYN AL6 .... 122 B6
Windsor Dr *HERT/WAS* SG14 .... 150 C2
Windsor Gdns *BSF* CM23 .... 105 F2
Windsor Rd *AMP/FLIT/B* MK45 .... 36 C5
BAR EN5 .... 225 J6
KTN/HRWW/W HA3 .... 231 K7
PEND EN3 .... 214 C6
ROY SG8 .... 21 K3
WATN WD24 .... 204 D8
WLYN AL6 .... 122 B6
Windsor St *LTN* LU1 .... 4 C5 9
Windsor Wk *LTN* LU1 .... 4 B5 6
Windsor Wy *RKW/CH/CXG* WD3 .... 217 K8
Windsor Wd *WAB* EN9 .... 215 K3 2
Windward Cl *PEND* EN3 .... 214 C5
Windy Ri *WARE* SG12 .... 99 J2 1
Winford Dr *BROX* EN10 .... 176 E8
Wingate Gdns *WLYN* AL6 .... 122 B4 1
Wingate Rd *LTNW/LEA* LU4 .... 68 E7
Wingate Wy *STAL* AL1 .... 11 F5
Wingrave Rd *TRING* HP23 .... 109 H7
Winifred Rd *HHS/BOV* HP3 .... 185 H2
Winkers Cl *CFSP/GDCR* SL9 .... 226 C7 1
Winkers La *CFSP/GDCR* SL9 .... 226 C7
Winkfield Cl *LTNW/LEA* LU4 .... 68 A8 1
Winnington Rd *PEND* EN3 .... 214 B8
Winsdon Rd *LTN* LU1 .... 4 B5
Winslow Cl *LTNN/LIM* LU3 .... 69 H5
Winston Churchill Wy
CHES/WCR EN8 .... 214 B3
Winston Cl *HTCH/STOT* SG5 .... 56 B2
Winston Ct *PIN* HA5 .... 231 J6
Winston Gdns *BERK* HP4 .... 161 G5
Winston Wy *POTB/CUF* EN6 .... 210 B3 1
Winstre Rd *BORE* WD6 .... 223 K1
Winterscroft Rd *HOD* EN11 .... 176 E2 1
Winters La *STVGE* SG2 .... 60 D8
Winton Ap *RKW/CH/CXG* WD3 .... 219 H5
Winton Cl *LTNE* LU2 .... 69 J3
LWTH SG6 .... 42 C1
Winton Crs *RKW/CH/CXG* WD3 .... 219 G5
Winton Dr *CHES/WCR* EN8 .... 197 J7
RKW/CH/CXG WD3 .... 219 H5
Winton Rd *WARE* SG12 .... 127 K8
Wisden Rd *STVG* SG1 .... 76 A1
Wiseman Cl *LTNE* LU2 .... 69 K2 1
Wisemans Gdns *SBW* CM21 .... 132 A8
Wistlea Crs *STALE/WH* AL4 .... 170 A8
Wistow Rd *LTNN/LIM* LU3 .... 69 F3
Witchford *WGCE* AL7 .... 148 E3
Withy Cl *LTNW/LEA* LU4 .... 68 A4
Withy Pl *LCOL/BKTW* AL2 .... 188 E6
Witney Cl *PIN* HA5 .... 231 G5
Witter Av *HTCH/STOT* SG5 .... 40 C5
Wiveton Cl *LTNE* LU2 .... 69 J2
Woburn Av *BSF* CM23 .... 105 F2
Woburn Cl *BUSH* WD23 .... 221 K6
STVGE SG2 .... 96 D2
Wodecroft Rd *LTNN/LIM* LU3 .... 69 G3
Wolsey Av *CHESW* EN7 .... 196 D7
Wolsey Rd *HHNE* HP2 .... 8 A6
RKW/CH/CXG WD3 .... 229 H1
Wolston Cl *LTN* LU1 .... 4 A5
Wolvescroft *KNEB* SG3 .... 96 B7
Wolves Mere *KNEB* SG3 .... 96 B7
Woodacre Dr *WLYN* AL6 .... 123 G1
Woodbank Dr *CSTG* HP8 .... 226 A2
Woodbine Cl *HLWW/ROY* CM19 .... 6 B6
Woodbine Gv *ENC/FH* EN2 .... 213 G8
Woodbridge Cl *LTNW/LEA* LU4 .... 68 D5
Woodbrook Gdns *WAB* EN9 .... 215 K3
Woodbury Hl *LTNE* LU2 .... 4 C1
Wood Cl *HAT* AL10 .... 171 G4
Woodcock Hl *RKW/CH/CXG* WD3 .... 228 D4
Woodcockhill *STALE/WH* AL4 .... 145 G8
Woodcock Rd *LTN* LU1 .... 89 F2
STVGE SG2 .... 76 E7
Wood Common *HAT* AL10 .... 171 G1
Woodcote Cl *CHES/WCR* EN8 .... 197 G8
Wood Crs *HHS/BOV* HP3 .... 8 A6
Woodcroft *HLWS* CM18 .... 6 B6
Woodcroft Av *WARE* SG12 .... 153 J5
Wood Dr *STVGE* SG2 .... 3 F6
Wood End *LCOL/BKTW* AL2 .... 188 E6
Wood End Cl *HHNE* HP2 .... 9 F4
Wood End Hl *HARP* AL5 .... 117 K6
Wood End La *STALW/RED* AL3 .... 140 E1
Wood End Rd *HARP* AL5 .... 117 K6
Wood Farm Rd *HHNE* HP2 .... 8 B5
Woodfield Av *NTHWD* HA6 .... 229 K3
Woodfield Cl *STSD* CM24 .... 86 D3
Woodfield Dr *HHS/BOV* HP3 .... 165 J8
Woodfield Gdns *HHS/BOV* HP3 .... 165 J8
Woodfield La *BRKMPK* AL9 .... 194 A1
Woodfield Ri *BUSH* WD23 .... 222 A7
Woodfield Rd *RAD* WD7 .... 206 D6
STVG SG1 .... 58 C8
WGCE AL7 .... 148 A3
Woodfields *STSD* CM24 .... 86 D3
Woodfield Ter *STSD* CM24 .... 86 D3
Woodfield Wy *STALE/WH* AL4 .... 169 F3
Woodford Crs *PIN* HA5 .... 230 C8
Woodforde Cl *BLDK* SG7 .... 18 A5
Woodford Rd *WAT* WD17 .... 12 C1
Woodgate *GSTN* WD25 .... 204 C3
Woodgate Av *POTB/CUF* EN6 .... 211 J3
Woodgate Crs *NTHWD* HA6 .... 230 B5
Wood Green Cl *LTNE* LU2 .... 70 C4
Wood Green Rd *LTNE* LU2 .... 70 C4
Woodhall Av *PIN* HA5 .... 231 F
Woodhall Cl *HERT/WAS* SG14 .... 151 F1
Woodhall Ct *WGCE* AL7 .... 147 K

Woodhall Dr *PIN* HA5 230 E7
Woodhall Ga *PIN* HA5 230 E6
Woodhall Gv *BSF* CM23 105 G3
Woodhall La *HHNE* HP2 8 B4
OXHEY WD19 230 E2
RAD WD7 207 K4 1
WGCE AL7 147 K5
Woodham Wy *WARE* SG12 153 H5 2
Woodhill *HLWS* CM18 180 B4
Woodhouse Eaves *NTHWD* HA6 230 B4 1
Wood House La *BROX* EN10 175 J7
Woodhurst *LWTH* SG6 41 K1
Woodhurst Av *GSTN* WD25 204 E5
Wooding Gv *HLWW/ROY* CM19 6 A4
Woodland Av *HHW* HP1 164 A7
LTNN/LIM LU3 69 G7
Woodland Cl *HHW* HP1 164 A7 4
TRING HP23 134 E7
Woodland Dr *STALE/WH* AL4 169 F5
WAT WD17 220 A1
Woodland La *RKW/CH/CXG* WD3 217 G3
Woodland Mt *HERT/BAY* SG13 151 J3
Woodland Pl *HHW* HP1 164 A7 5
Woodland Ri *DUN/WHIP* LU6 113 K2
WGCW AL8 147 H1
Woodland Rd *HERT/BAY* SG13 152 B6
RKW/CH/CXG WD3 227 G4
Woodlands *BRKMPK* AL9 193 H5
BSF CM23 106 B1
HARP AL5 118 A6
LCOL/BKTW AL2 188 E5
LTN LU1 88 D7
RAD WD7 206 D4 2
ROY SG8 21 J3 5
Woodlands Av *BERK* HP4 162 A6
Woodlands Cl *BORE* WD6 224 A4
HOD EN11 177 F4 4
TRING HP23 134 E7
Woodlands Dr *HOD* EN11 177 F5
Woodlands Meade
HTCHE/RSTV SG4 59 H1
Woodlands Rd *BUSH* WD23 13 F3
ENC/FH EN2 213 G8
HERT/BAY SG13 151 J3
KGLGY WD4 186 A5
WARE SG12 127 H3
Woodland Wy *BLDK* SG7 43 F3
CHESW EN7 195 K6
STVGE SG2 76 B8
WLYN AL6 123 F2
Wood La *BSF* CM23 86 D7
BUNT SG9 50 C3
HHNE HP2 8 A6
Wood Lane End *HHNE* HP2 9 E4
Woodlea *LCOL/BKTW* AL2 188 C3
Woodlea Gv *NTHWD* HA6 229 H5
Woodley Rd *WARE* SG12 127 K7
Woodman Rd *HHS/BOV* HP3 164 D8
Woodmans Yd *WAT* WD17 13 D3 14
Woodmere *LTNN/LIM* LU3 52 A8
Woodmere Av *WATN* WD24 204 E8
Woodpecker Cl *BSF* CM23 105 F3 2
BUSH WD23 221 K8
HAT AL10 170 E7 3
Woodredon Cl
HLWW/ROY CM19 178 C2 1
Woodridge Wy *NTHWD* HA6 229 K5
Woodridings Av *PIN* HA5 231 G7
Woodridings Cl *PIN* HA5 231 G6
Woods Av *HAT* AL10 171 F5
Woodshots Meadow *WATW* WD18 219 J5
Woodside *BORE* WD6 223 J4 2
BSF CM23 106 C1
CHESW EN7 213 K1
HERT/BAY SG13 152 B6
WATN WD24 204 B7
Woodside Cl *CFSP/GDCR* SL9 226 B8 2
Woodside Hl *CFSP/GDCR* SL9 226 B8
Woodside La *BRKMPK* AL9 172 B8
Woodside Rd *GSTN* WD25 204 C1
LCOL/BKTW AL2 188 B8
LTN LU1 89 F8
NTHWD HA6 230 A6
WLYN AL6 123 F6
Woods Pl *TRING* HP23 135 F6 5
The Woods *NTHWD* HA6 230 B4
RAD WD7 206 E4
Woodstock *KNEB* SG3 96 A6
Woodstock Cl *HERT/BAY* SG13 152 A5 1
Woodstock Rd *BROX* EN10 176 D5
BUSH WD23 222 B7
Woodstock Rd North *STAL* AL1 168 E4
Woodstock Rd South *STAL* AL1 168 E6
Wood St *BAR* EN5 225 H4
LTN LU1 5 D5 6
Wood V *HAT* AL10 171 G4
Wood Vw *HHW* HP1 164 A4
POTB/CUF EN6 195 G5
Woodville Court Ms *WAT* WD17 12 B1 3
Woodwards *HLWW/ROY* CM19 6 B6
Woodwaye *OXHEY* WD19 13 D6
Woodwicks *RKW/CH/CXG* WD3 227 G4 2
Woolgrove Rd *HTCHE/RSTV* SG4 40 E8
Woollam Crs *STALW/RED* AL3 167 K2
Woollard St *WAB* EN9 215 H4
Woolmans Cl *BROX* EN10 176 E8
Woolmer Cl *BORE* WD6 207 K8
Woolmerdine Ct *BUSH* WD23 13 E2
Woolmer Dr *HHNE* HP2 9 F5
Woolmers La *HERT/WAS* SG14 149 J7
Woolners Wy *STVG* SG1 2 A2
Woolston Av *LWTH* SG6 42 A5
Wootton Cl *LTNN/LIM* LU3 69 G2
Wootton Dr *HHNE* HP2 164 E1
Worboys Ct *ROY* SG8 15 G4
Worcester Rd *HAT* AL10 170 E3
Worcesters Av *EN* EN1 213 K8
Wordsworth Rd *HARP* AL5 118 C6
Works Rd *LWTH* SG6 42 B2
Worley Rd *STALW/RED* AL3 10 C3
Wormley Lodge Cl *BROX* EN10 197 K1 4
Worsdell Wy *HTCHE/RSTV* SG4 57 F2 5
Worsted La *BUNT* SG9 64 E2
Wortham Rd *ROY* SG8 21 J5
Wortham Wy *STVGE* SG2 3 F5
The Wraglins *BSF* CM23 106 A4
Wratten Cl *HTCH/STOT* SG5 56 C3 1
Wratten Rd East *HTCH/STOT* SG5 56 C3
Wratten Rd West *HTCH/STOT* SG5 56 B3
Wrayfields *HTCH/STOT* SG5 26 B2
Wraysbury Cl *LTNW/LEA* LU4 68 C6
Wrenbrook Rd *BSF* CM23 105 J4
Wren Cl *HTCHE/RSTV* SG4 92 E8
LTNE LU2 70 D3
STVGE SG2 3 F2
Wren Crs *BUSH* WD23 221 K8
Wrensfield *HHW* HP1 163 K6
The Wrens *HLWW/ROY* CM19 6 A4 1
Wren Wd *WGCE* AL7 148 C2
Wright Cl *STALE/WH* AL4 145 G2
Wright's Green La *RBSF* CM22 133 G2
Wrights Meadow *STVGE* SG2 77 J1
Wrights Orch *STVGE* SG2 77 F7
Wrotham Rd *BAR* EN5 225 K2
Wroxham Av *HHS/BOV* HP3 164 C8
Wroxham Gdns *ENC/FH* EN2 212 D5
POTB/CUF EN6 209 J1
Wroxham Wy *HARP* AL5 118 E6
Wulfrath Wy *WARE* SG12 127 G6
Wulwards Cl *LTN* LU1 89 G3
Wyatt Cl *BUSH* WD23 222 B7
HTCH/STOT SG5 40 B5
Wyatt's Cl *RKW/CH/CXG* WD3 217 K3
Wyatt's Rd *RKW/CH/CXG* WD3 217 J4
Wychdell *STVGE* SG2 96 D1
Wych Elm *HLW* CM20 6 B3
Wych Elm La *KNEB* SG3 95 K6
Wych Elms *LCOL/BKTW* AL2 188 D6
Wychford Dr *SBW* CM21 132 A8
Wychwood Av *LTNE* LU2 69 K5
Wychwood Wy *NTHWD* HA6 230 A6 4
Wycklond Cl *HTCH/STOT* SG5 25 J3 3
Wycliffe Cl *LTNN/LIM* LU3 69 H3 3
Wycombe Wy *LTNN/LIM* LU3 69 H1
STALE/WH AL4 168 E3
Wyddial Gn *WGCE* AL7 148 C3 3
Wyddial Rd *BUNT* SG9 63 J1
Wyedale *LCOL/BKTW* AL2 190 D5
Wykeham Ri *TRDG/WHET* N20 225 K8
Wyken Cl *LTNN/LIM* LU3 69 F2
Wyldwood Cl *HLWE* CM17 157 F3
Wyllyotts Pl *POTB/CUF* EN6 210 A2 3
Wylo Dr *BAR* EN5 225 F6
Wymondley Cl *HTCHE/RSTV* SG4 56 E3
Wymondley Rd *HTCHE/RSTV* SG4 56 E3
Wynches Farm Dr
STALE/WH AL4 169 G6 1
Wynchlands Crs *STALE/WH* AL4 169 G6
Wyndham Rd *LTNW/LEA* LU4 68 B7 1
Wyndhams End *BRKMPK* AL9 148 A7 1
Wynlie Gdns *PIN* HA5 230 C8
Wynn Cl *BLDK* SG7 27 G8
Wyrley Dell *LWTH* SG6 42 A6
Wyton *WGCE* AL7 148 E3
Wyvern Cl *LTNW/LEA* LU4 68 D6 1

Y

Yardley *LWTH* SG6 42 B5
Yardley Av *LBUZ* LU7 110 C5
Yarmouth Rd *STVG* SG1 75 F2
WATN WD24 204 C8
Yately Cl *LTNE* LU2 69 J2
Yearling Cl *WARE* SG12 152 E2
Yeomanry Dr *BLDK* SG7 27 G8
Yeomans Av *HARP* AL5 117 K6 1
Yeomans Cl *BSF* CM23 105 G4
Yeomans Dr *STVGE* SG2 77 F7
Yeomans Ride *HHNE* HP2 141 F8
Yeovil Rd *LTNE* LU2 5 F1
Yew Cl *CHESW* EN7 196 C5 2
Yew Gv *WGCE* AL7 148 D4
Yewlands *HOD* EN11 177 F4
SBW CM21 132 C8 3
Yewlands Dr *HOD* EN11 177 F4
Yews Av *EN* EN1 214 A6
Yew Tree Cl *CSHM* HP5 182 C8
LBUZ LU7 110 E5
Yew Tree Ct *BORE* WD6 223 G6 9
Yew Tree Dr *HHS/BOV* HP3 183 K6
Yewtree End *LCOL/BKTW* AL2 188 D5
Yew Tree Pl *BSF* CM23 105 J1
Yew Wk *HOD* EN11 177 F4
York Cl *AMP/FLIT/B* MK45 36 C5
KGLGY WD4 186 A7
York Crs *BORE* WD6 224 C2
Yorke Ga *WAT* WD17 12 B1 4
Yorke Rd *RKW/CH/CXG* WD3 219 F6
Yorkes *HLWS* CM18 7 E6
York Rd *CHES/WCR* EN8 214 D4
HTCH/STOT SG5 56 C1
NTHWD HA6 230 B8
STAL AL1 11 E3
STVG SG1 59 F8
WATW WD18 13 D4
York St *LTNE* LU2 5 D3
York Ter *ENC/FH* EN2 213 F8 2
York Wy *GSTN* WD25 204 E6
HHS/BOV HP3 8 B6
ROY SG8 21 F1
WLYN AL6 122 B6
Youngfield Rd *HHW* HP1 163 J5
Youngsbury La *WARE* SG12 127 H1
Youngs Ri *WGCW* AL8 147 G3
Yule Cl *LCOL/BKTW* AL2 188 B8

Z

Zambesi Rd *BSF* CM23 105 J4 2

Index - featured places

Abbey C of E JMI School
STALW/RED AL3 10 B5
Abbeygate Business Centre
LTNE LU2 5 D3
Abbey Mead Industrial Park
WAB EN9 215 G4
Abbey Road Surgery
CHES/WCR EN8 214 D4
Abbot's Hill School
HHS/BOV HP3 186 B3
Abbots Langley Parish Council
ABLGY WD5 204 A1
Abbots School
ABLGY WD5 187 F8
Abbotsweld Primary School
HLWS CM18 6 C6
Abbotswood Medical Centre
ABLGY WD5 204 B2
Aboyne Lodge School
STALW/RED AL3 10 C3
Adeyfield School
HHNE HP2 9 D5
Akeman Business Park
TRING HP23 135 F6
Alban Wood Infant School
GSTN WD25 204 C2
Albanwood School
GSTN WD25 204 C3
Albany School Grant Maintained
PEND EN3 214 C8
Albury School
STDN SG11 83 H3
Aldbury Junior School
TRING HP23 136 D3
Aldenham Parish Council
RAD WD7 206 D6

Aldenham School
BORE WD6 .... **222** C2
Aldwickbury Park Golf Club
HARP AL5 .... **119** G8
Algrey Trading Estate
HTCHE/RSTV SG4 .... **40** E8
Allied Business Centre
HARP AL5 .... **118** E6
All Nations Christian College
WARE SG12 .... **153** G1
All Saints C of E Junior
Middle & Infant School
BSF CM23 .... **106** A1
Almonds Hill Junior Mixed School
STVG SG1 .... **75** J1
Alpha Business Park
BRKMPK AL9 .... **192** C1
A M F Bowling
HHNE HP2 .... **9** E3
Amwell View School
WARE SG12 .... **153** G5
Andrews Lane Junior
& Infant School
CHESW EN7 .... **196** E6
Anglian Business Park
ROY SG8 .... **21** F2
Anstey School
BUNT SG9 .... **49** G3
Applecroft Junior Middle
& Infant School
WGCW AL8 .... **147** G4
Apsley Mills Retail Park
HHS/BOV HP3 .... **185** J2
Archway Surgery
HHS/BOV HP3 .... **183** J5
Ardeley School
STVGE SG2 .... **61** H6
Arndale Shopping Centre
LTN LU1 .... **4** C4
Arnetthill School
RKW/CH/CXG WD3 .... **217** K6
Arnold Middle School
AMP/FLIT/B MK45 .... **36** D7
Arseley Football Club
ARL/CHE SG15 .... **24** E6
The Arthur Findlay College
STSD CM24 .... **87** F4
The Arts Educational School
TRING HP23 .... **135** G6
Ascot Business Centre
LTN LU1 .... **4** B4
Ascot Industrial Estate
LWTH SG6 .... **42** B2
Ashcroft High School
LTNE LU2 .... **70** D7
Ashfield Junior School
BUSH WD23 .... **221** J7
Ash Industrial Estate
HLWW/ROY CM19 .... **179** G2
Ashley Business Centre
HTCH/STOT SG5 .... **56** D1
Ashlyns School
BERK HP4 .... **161** K7
Ashridge Golf Club
BERK HP4 .... **137** J2
Ashville Trading Estate
BLDK SG7 .... **27** F8
Asquith Court School
HARP AL5 .... **118** B6
Astley Cooper School
HHNE HP2 .... **165** F1
Aycliffe Drive Primary School
HHNE HP2 .... **8** B1
Aylands School
PEND EN3 .... **214** B6
Baldock Health Centre
BLDK SG7 .... **43** F2
Baldock Industrial Estate
BLDK SG7 .... **43** F2
Bancroft Business Centre
HTCH/STOT SG5 .... **56** D1
Barbara Castle Health Centre
HLWW/ROY CM19 .... **179** H5
The Barclay School
STVG SG1 .... **75** J1
The Barking Dog Theatre Co
BSF CM23 .... **105** J4
Barkway Park Golf Club
ROY SG8 .... **32** E7
Barkway Va First School
ROY SG8 .... **32** C5
Barley Vp School
ROY SG8 .... **23** G8
Barncroft JMI School
HHNE HP2 .... **164** C1

Barnet General Hospital
BAR EN5 .... **225** J4
Barnet Hospital Chest Clinic
BAR EN5 .... **225** J4
Barnfield College
LTN LU1 .... **89** G4
Barnfield College
LTNE LU2 .... **69** J4
Barnfield College
LTNN/LIM LU3 .... **69** G1
The Barn School
MHAD SG10 .... **103** G7
Barn Theatre
WGCW AL8 .... **147** H3
Barnwell School
STVGE SG2 .... **3** F6
Barracuda Swimming Club
POTB/CUF EN6 .... **210** E3
Barratt Industrial Park
LTNE LU2 .... **90** D3
Barton Industrial Estate
AMP/FLIT/B MK45 .... **36** A5
Barton Rovers Football Club
AMP/FLIT/B MK45 .... **36** C7
Batchwood Golf Club
STALW/RED AL3 .... **10** A1
Batchwood School
STALW/RED AL3 .... **10** C1
Batford JMI School
HARP AL5 .... **119** F5
Bayfordbury College
of Hertfordshire
HERT/BAY SG13 .... **150** E8
Bayford Junior Middle
& Infant School
HERT/BAY SG13 .... **174** C4
Beaumont School
STALE/WH AL4 .... **169** G5
Bedmond JMI School
ABLGY WD5 .... **187** F6
Bedwell Junior & Infant School
STVG SG1 .... **3** E2
Bedwell Medical Centre
STVG SG1 .... **3** E3
Beechfield Junior Middle
& Infant School
WATN WD24 .... **204** B7
Beech Hill Community School
LTNW/LEA LU4 .... **69** G8
Beech Hyde Junior Middle
& Infant School
STALE/WH AL4 .... **145** G2
Beechwood Infant School
LTNW/LEA LU4 .... **68** D6
Beechwood Infants
& Junior School
LTNW/LEA LU4 .... **68** D5
Beechwood Park
Preparatory School
STALW/RED AL3 .... **114** E8
Belcon Industrial Estate
HOD EN11 .... **177** H3
Bellgate JMI School
HHNE HP2 .... **8** B3
Bells House Gallery
LWTH SG6 .... **41** K3
Belswains Infant School
HHS/BOV HP3 .... **185** K2
Bengeo Junior & Infant School
HERT/WAS SG14 .... **126** A8
Benington Primary School
STVGE SG2 .... **78** A8
Bennetts End Surgery
HHS/BOV HP3 .... **186** A1
Bentfield County Primary School
STSD CM24 .... **86** C1
Berkeley Clinic
RKW/CH/CXG WD3 .... **218** B8
Berkhamsted Football Club
BERK HP4 .... **161** J4
Berkhamsted Golf Club
BERK HP4 .... **162** B2
Berkhamsted Health Centre
BERK HP4 .... **161** H4
Berkhamsted School
BERK HP4 .... **161** K5
Berkhamsted School for Girls
BERK HP4 .... **161** J5
Berkhamsted School House
BERK HP4 .... **161** K5
Berkhamsted Tennis Club
BERK HP4 .... **161** K4
Berkley Gallery
BERK HP4 .... **161** J5

Bernards Heath Infant School
STAL AL1 .... **11** E2
Beta Health Clinic
HHW HP1 .... **8** A5
Birchwood High School
BSF CM23 .... **106** B1
Birchwood Leisure Centre
HAT AL10 .... **171** G1
Bishops Hatfield Girls School
HAT AL10 .... **171** F4
Bishop's Park Health Centre
BSF CM23 .... **105** J1
Bishops Stortford College
BSF CM23 .... **105** H2
The Bishops Stortford
High School
BSF CM23 .... **105** J5
Bishops Stortford Town Council
BSF CM23 .... **105** J2
Bishops Wood Hospital
RKW/CH/CXG WD3 .... **229** F4
Bishop Wood Junior School
TRING HP23 .... **135** F6
Blackthorn Junior School
WGCE AL7 .... **148** B4
Blessed Cuthbert Mayne
RC School
HHW HP1 .... **164** A5
Blue Gold Trading Estate
ARL/CHE SG15 .... **24** E4
Bondor Business Centre
BLDK SG7 .... **42** E2
Bonneygrove Junior
& Infant School
CHESW EN7 .... **196** E8
Borehamwood Football Club
BORE WD6 .... **224** A2
Borehamwood Industrial Park
BORE WD6 .... **224** C2
The Borough Industrial Estate
LTNN/LIM LU3 .... **69** F6
Borough of Broxbourne
CHES/WCR EN8 .... **197** F8
Botany Bay Cricket Club
ENC/FH EN2 .... **212** A6
Bournehall Junior
& Infant School
BUSH WD23 .... **221** H5
Bovingdon Junior Mixed School
HHS/BOV HP3 .... **183** K5
Bovingdon Parish Council
HHS/BOV HP3 .... **183** J5
Bovingdon Primary School
HHS/BOV HP3 .... **183** K5
Bowmans Trading Estate
STVG SG1 .... **75** G4
Boxmoor Golf Club
HHW HP1 .... **184** C2
Boxmoor House School
HHS/BOV HP3 .... **184** D1
Boxwell Road Surgery
BERK HP4 .... **161** J5
Bramingham Business Park
LTNN/LIM LU3 .... **69** G1
Bramingham Medical Centre
LTNN/LIM LU3 .... **69** G1
Bramingham Park Medical Centre
LTNN/LIM LU3 .... **69** F1
Bramingham Primary School
LTNN/LIM LU3 .... **69** G1
Brandles Close School
BLDK SG7 .... **42** E2
Brays Grove
Comprehensive School
HLWS CM18 .... **180** E3
Breakspeare School
ABLGY WD5 .... **203** K1
Brickendon Grange Golf
& Country Club
HERT/BAY SG13 .... **174** E5
Brickfields Industrial Estate
HHNE HP2 .... **9** E1
Bridge Cottage Surgery
WLYN AL6 .... **122** B4
Bridger Packaging Football Club
LWTH SG6 .... **41** K6
Bridgewater School
BERK HP4 .... **161** H3
Britannia Business Centre
CHES/WCR EN8 .... **214** E4
British Museum
Zoological Museum
TRING HP23 .... **135** G6
Brittania Business Park
CHES/WCR EN8 .... **214** E4

Broadfield Infant School
HHNE HP2 .... 8 C5
Broadfield Junior School
HHNE HP2 .... 8 C5
Broadfield School
HLW CM20 .... 7 D3
Broadmead School
LTN LU1 .... 4 C6
Brockswood JMI School
HHNE HP2 .... 141 G8
Bromet School
OXHEY WD19 .... 13 E6
Brookland Junior
& Infant School
CHES/WCR EN8 .... 197 J6
Brookmans Park GM
Primary School
BRKMPK AL9 .... 192 E4
Brookmead School
LBUZ LU7 .... 110 E4
Brookside Business Centre
RBSF CM22 .... 105 J8
Broom Barns Infant School
STVG SG1 .... 2 C3
Broxbourne Borough Council
CHES/WCR EN8 .... 197 H4
Broxbourne Business Centre
CHES/WCR EN8 .... 197 H4
Broxbourne C of E JMI School
BROX EN10 .... 176 E7
Broxbourne Sailing Club
HOD EN11 .... 177 J6
The Broxbourne School
BROX EN10 .... 176 D8
Broxbourne Sports Club
BROX EN10 .... 176 E7
Brushwood Middle School
CSHM HP5 .... 182 A7
Buckinghamshire Chilterns
University College
CSTG HP8 .... 226 D1
Burleigh Primary School
CHES/WCR EN8 .... 197 H8
Burnt Mill Comprehensive School
HLW CM20 .... 7 D2
Burntmill Industrial Estate
HLW CM20 .... 6 B1
Burvill House Surgery
HAT AL10 .... 171 F4
Burydale Junior Mixed School
STVGE SG2 .... 76 C8
Bus Garage
LTN LU1 .... 4 C5
Bushey & District Synagogue
BUSH WD23 .... 221 K7
Bushey Hall School
BUSH WD23 .... 221 G6
Bushey Hall Swimming Pool
BUSH WD23 .... 221 G5
Bushey Health Centre
BUSH WD23 .... 221 G6
Bushey Heath Primary School
BUSH WD23 .... 222 A8
Bushey Manor School
BUSH WD23 .... 13 F4
Bushey Meads School
BUSH WD23 .... 221 K5
Bushey Museum & Art Gallery
BUSH WD23 .... 221 H6
Bushmead Infant School
LTNE LU2 .... 69 J4
Business Centre
RAD WD7 .... 206 E4
The Business Centre
LTNE LU1 .... 5 E2
Byfleet Industrial Estate
WATW WD18 .... 219 H8
Caddington Sports Club
LTN LU1 .... 88 E6
Caddington Surgery
LTN LU1 .... 88 D5
Calcot Medical Centre
CFSP/GDCR SL9 .... 226 A7
Camp Junior Middle
& Infant School
STAL AL1 .... 168 E7
Canary Club Football Club
HTCH/STOT SG5 .... 56 C1
Canons Brook Golf Club
HLW CM20 .... 155 H8
Canterbury Way Surgery
STVG SG1 .... 59 G7
Capel Manor Primary School
EN EN1 .... 213 K5

Capital Business Centre
WATN WD24 .... 204 E6
Cardiff Road Industrial Estate
WATW WD18 .... 12 C5
Cardinal Newman RC School
LTNE LU2 .... 52 C8
Castle (Remains)
BERK HP4 .... 162 A4
Cassio Surgery
WATW WD18 .... 12 C3
The Castlegate Surgery
HERT/BAY SG13 .... 151 F4
Castle Montessore School
BERK HP4 .... 162 A5
Castle Walk Clinic
STSD CM24 .... 86 E3
The Causeway Business Centre
BSF CM23 .... 105 J2
The Cavendish School
HHW HP1 .... 164 A5
Cedars First School
KTN/HRWW/W HA3 .... 231 K7
Cedars Middle School
KTN/HRWW/W HA3 .... 231 K7
Central Primary School
WAT WD17 .... 13 D3
Central Surgery
SBW CM21 .... 132 C7
Chalfont St Peter C of E
Middle School
CFSP/GDCR SL9 .... 226 A7
Chalfont St Peter Football Club
CFSP/GDCR SL9 .... 226 A6
Chalfonts & Gerrards Cross
Health Centre
CFSP/GDCR SL9 .... 226 A7
Challney High School for Boys
LTNW/LEA LU4 .... 68 B6
Chambersbury JMI School
HHS/BOV HP3 .... 186 B1
Chancellors School
BRKMPK AL9 .... 193 H3
Chase Farm Hospitals NHS Trust
ENC/FH EN2 .... 212 D8
Chater Infant School
WATW WD18 .... 12 B3
Chater Junior School
WATW WD18 .... 12 B3
Chaulden Junior & Infant School
HHW HP1 .... 163 J7
The Chauncy School
WARE SG12 .... 127 F7
Cheddington Lower School
LBUZ LU7 .... 110 A2
Chenies Cricket Club
RKW/CH/CXG WD3 .... 217 F1
Chenies School
RKW/CH/CXG WD3 .... 200 D8
Cherry Tree JMI School
WATN WD24 .... 204 B6
Chesham Preparatory School
CSHM HP5 .... 182 C5
Cheshunt Community Hospital
CHES/WCR EN8 .... 214 B4
Cheshunt Football Club
CHES/WCR EN8 .... 214 B2
Cheshunt School
CHES/WCR EN8 .... 197 G8
Cheshunt & Waltham
Cross Council
CHES/WCR EN8 .... 214 D4
Chesterfield Junior
& Infant School
PEND EN3 .... 214 D7
Chiltern Open Air Museum
CSTG HP8 .... 226 C1
Chinese Medical Centre
BAR EN5 .... 225 K3
Chinese Medical Centre Watford
WAT WD17 .... 13 D3
Chipperfield Junior
& Infant School
KGLGY WD4 .... 201 K1
Chorleywood Golf Club
RKW/CH/CXG WD3 .... 217 G4
Chorleywood Health Centre
RKW/CH/CXG WD3 .... 217 F4
Chorleywood Parish Council
RKW/CH/CXG WD3 .... 217 H3
Chorleywood Primary
RKW/CH/CXG WD3 .... 217 F6
Christ Church C of E
Primary School
BAR EN5 .... 225 J2

Christ Church Junior Middle
& Infant School
WARE SG12 .... 127 J8
Christ Church School
RKW/CH/CXG WD3 .... 217 J4
Churchgate C of E
Primary School
HLWE CM17 .... 157 J6
Church Langley Primary School
HLWE CM17 .... 181 F1
Church Street Surgery
WARE SG12 .... 127 H7
Cinema
LTN LU1 .... 4 C4
Civic Centre & Dacorum
Borough Council
HHW HP1 .... 164 B6
Clarklands Industrial Estate
SBW CM21 .... 132 C4
Club House
LBUZ LU7 .... 110 B4
The Club House
HERT/WAS SG14 .... 98 B6
Coach House Surgery
WATW WD18 .... 12 B3
Coates Way School
GSTN WD25 .... 205 F3
Cobden Hill Infant School
RAD WD7 .... 206 E6
Codicote Junior & Infant School
WLYN AL6 .... 94 D8
Coleman Business Centre
HTCHE/RSTV SG4 .... 93 F7
Collenswood School
STVGE SG2 .... 76 D5
The Collett School
HHW HP1 .... 164 A5
Colnbrook School
OXHEY WD19 .... 230 D1
Colne Bridge Retail Park
WAT WD17 .... 13 E4
Colney Heath JMI School
STALE/WH AL4 .... 170 B8
Colonial Business Park
WATN WD24 .... 220 D1
Commonside School
HLWS CM18 .... 180 C5
Commonswood JMI School
WGCE AL7 .... 148 C6
Community Clinic
HLWS CM18 .... 180 C4
Community Mental
Health Centre
GSTN WD25 .... 204 D4
Community Mental
Health Centre
HHNE HP2 .... 8 A4
Corn Exchange
HERT/WAS SG14 .... 151 G3
Cotswold Business Park
LTN LU1 .... 88 C7
Council Offices
OXHEY WD19 .... 230 E2
Countess Anne C of E
Primary School
HAT AL10 .... 171 H3
County Hall
HERT/BAY SG13 .... 151 F5
Cowley Hill First School
BORE WD6 .... 224 A1
CP House Business Centre
GSTN WD25 .... 221 G1
Crabtree Junior Mixed School
HARP AL5 .... 119 F8
Crabtree Lane Infant School
HARP AL5 .... 118 E8
Cranborne Industrial Estate
POTB/CUF EN6 .... 192 E8
Cranborne Primary School
POTB/CUF EN6 .... 209 K1
Cranbourne School
HOD EN11 .... 153 G8
Crawley Green Primary School
LTNE LU2 .... 5 F3
Creswick Primary School
WGCE AL7 .... 147 J6
Crews Hill Golf Club
ENC/FH EN2 .... 212 C4
Cricket Squash Tennis
& Hockey Club
BSF CM23 .... 105 F1
Crown Court
STAL AL1 .... 11 D4
Crown Prosecution Service
LTN LU1 .... 4 C4

Crown Prosecution Service
STAL AL1 .... **10** C4
Cuffley School
POTB/CUF EN6 .... **195** H8
Cunningham Hill Junior
Middle & Infant School
STAL AL1 .... **11** F6
Dacorum Athletics Track
HHS/BOV HP3 .... **164** E8
Dacorum District Sports Centre
HHW HP1 .... **164** B8
Dacre Industrial Estate
CHES/WCR EN8 .... **197** J7
Dagnall CP School
BERK HP4 .... **112** E4
Dallow Junior School
LTN LU1 .... **4** A3
Dalroad Industrial Estate
LTN LU1 .... **89** G1
Dame Alice Owens School
POTB/CUF EN6 .... **209** K3
Danesbury Park Golf Club
WLYN AL6 .... **122** C2
Datchworth School
KNEB SG3 .... **96** E6
Deer Leap Swimming Pool
BERK HP4 .... **112** D8
Delrow School
GSTN WD25 .... **221** K1
Denbigh High School
LTNN/LIM LU3 .... **4** A1
Denbigh Infant School
LTNN/LIM LU3 .... **69** G7
The Dentist Surgery
OXHEY WD19 .... **230** C4
Denture Clinic
HARP AL5 .... **117** J5
Dewhurst St Mary Junior Middle
& Infant School
CHESW EN7 .... **197** F7
Diamond Industrial Centre
LWTH SG6 .... **42** C2
Discover Bible School
GSTN WD25 .... **204** D5
Divine Saviour RC JMI School
ABLGY WD5 .... **203** J2
The Downs CP School
HLW CM20 .... **6** C4
Downside Junior & Infant School
LTNW/LEA LU4 .... **68** D8
Dr P J Walkers Surgery
HTCHE/RSTV SG4 .... **93** H2
Duncombe School
HERT/WAS SG14 .... **151** F2
Dundale Infants School
TRING HP23 .... **135** F4
Dundale J M School
TRING HP23 .... **135** F4
Dunstable Road Infant School
LTN LU1 .... **4** A3
The Earl Gallery
POTB/CUF EN6 .... **210** A2
Eastbrook Junior School
HHNE HP2 .... **164** E1
Eastbury Infant School
NTHWD HA6 .... **230** A3
Eastfield Primary
& Infant School
PEND EN3 .... **214** C8
East Herts District Council
BSF CM23 .... **105** J1
East Herts District Council
HERT/BAY SG13 .... **151** F4
East Herts District Council
HERT/WAS SG14 .... **150** C2
East Herts District Council
SBW CM21 .... **132** C7
East Herts Golf Club
BUNT SG9 .... **81** G4
East Herts Golf Clubhouse
WARE SG12 .... **152** B1
Edwinstree Middle School
BUNT SG9 .... **63** H1
Egerton Rothesay School
BERK HP4 .... **161** G5
Eleanor Estate
CHES/WCR EN8 .... **214** E4
Elliswick Lawn Tennis Club
HARP AL5 .... **118** D7
The Elms Health Centre
POTB/CUF EN6 .... **210** D1
The Elms Medical Practice
HARP AL5 .... **118** D7
The Elms Medical Practice
STALW/RED AL3 .... **142** B4

Elstree & Borehamwood
Town Council
BORE WD6 .... **224** A3
Elstree Studios
BORE WD6 .... **223** K3
Elstree Way Clinic
BORE WD6 .... **224** A2
Emmanuel C of E School
NTHWD HA6 .... **230** A6
Enfield Chace Lower School
ENC/FH EN2 .... **213** H8
Epping House School
HERT/BAY SG13 .... **173** K7
Essendon Primary School
BRKMPK AL9 .... **173** G3
Essex County Council
WAB EN9 .... **215** H3
Everest House Surgery
HHNE HP2 .... **9** D5
Everest Sports Club
CHES/WCR EN8 .... **197** F7
Eversley College
SBW CM21 .... **132** B7
Factory
STVG SG1 .... **2** A5
Fairbrook Medical Centre
BORE WD6 .... **224** A2
Fairfield Primary School
RAD WD7 .... **206** B6
Fairfields Junior Middle
& Infant School
CHESW EN7 .... **196** E5
Fairlands Junior Middle
& Infant School
STVG SG1 .... **2** B2
The Fairways
CHES/WCR EN8 .... **197** H4
Falconer School
BUSH WD23 .... **221** G5
Farley Hill Primary School
LTN LU1 .... **4** A6
Farnham School
BSF CM23 .... **85** G3
Fawbert & Barnards
Primary School
HLWE CM17 .... **157** F6
Fearnhill School
LWTH SG6 .... **41** G4
Fearnhill Sports Centre
LWTH SG6 .... **41** G4
Featherstone Wood
Primary School
STVGE SG2 .... **76** D6
Fernville Surgery
HHNE HP2 .... **8** A5
Ferrars Infant School
LTNW/LEA LU4 .... **68** A6
Fiddlebridge Industrial Centre
HAT AL10 .... **171** F3
Field Junior School
WATW WD18 .... **13** D4
Firbank Industrial Estate
LTN LU1 .... **89** F1
The Firs Junior School
BSF CM23 .... **105** H3
Fisher Industrial Estate
WATW WD18 .... **13** D4
Five Oaks School
LTN LU1 .... **88** E6
Five Springs School
LTNN/LIM LU3 .... **68** E2
Flamstead End Junior School
CHESW EN7 .... **196** E5
Flamstead Junior Middle
& Infant School
STALW/RED AL3 .... **116** B8
Fleetville Infant School
STAL AL1 .... **11** F4
Fleetville Jm School
STAL AL1 .... **11** F4
Florance Nightingale
Health Centre
HLWE CM17 .... **181** F1
Flowers Industrial Estate
LTN LU1 .... **4** C5
Football Club
TRING HP23 .... **135** J5
Football & Social Club
WGCE AL7 .... **148** C1
Forres School
HOD EN11 .... **153** G8
Forty Hill C of E School
EN EN1 .... **213** K7
Foulds Primary School
BAR EN5 .... **225** J3

The Four Swanns JMI School
CHES/WCR EN8 .... **214** D3
Foxdell Infant School
LTN LU1 .... **89** F1
Foxdell Junior School
LTN LU1 .... **88** D1
Foye Gallery
LTN LU1 .... **4** B5
Francis Bacon School
STAL AL1 .... **189** K1
Francis Combe
Secondary School
GSTN WD25 .... **204** D2
Frithwood Primary School
NTHWD HA6 .... **230** A5
Frogmore Road
Industrial Estate
HHS/BOV HP3 .... **185** H1
Furneux Pelham C of E School
BUNT SG9 .... **66** C5
Furzehill School
BORE WD6 .... **223** K4
Gaddesden Row CP School
HHNE HP2 .... **140** B2
Gade Valley JMI School
HHW HP1 .... **164** A5
The Garden City Practice
WCCW AL8 .... **147** J2
Garden City Surgery
LWTH SG6 .... **41** K3
Garden Court Business Centre
WGCE AL7 .... **148** A3
Garden Fields Junior Middle
& Infant School
STALW/RED AL3 .... **10** C1
Garston Clinic
WATN WD24 .... **204** C6
Garston JMI School
GSTN WD25 .... **204** E5
Garston Manor School
GSTN WD25 .... **204** D2
Garston Medical Centre
GSTN WD25 .... **204** D6
Gascoyne Cecil Primary School
HAT AL10 .... **171** G2
Gazelda Industrial Estate
WAT WD17 .... **13** D4
The Giles Infant & Junior School
STVG SG1 .... **59** F8
Gillmark Gallery
HERT/BAY SG13 .... **151** F4
Goffs Oak JMI School
CHESW EN7 .... **195** K6
Goffs School
CHESW EN7 .... **196** E7
Goldfield Infant School
TRING HP23 .... **134** E6
Golf Club Flat
NTHWD HA6 .... **229** J6
Gooseberry Hill Health Centre
LTNN/LIM LU3 .... **69** G7
Gorhambury
STALW/RED AL3 .... **166** C5
Gothic Mede Lower School
ARL/CHE SG15 .... **24** E4
The Gowan Gallery
SBW CM21 .... **132** C7
Grange Junior Mixed School
LWTH SG6 .... **25** K7
Grange Paddock Swimming Pool
BSF CM23 .... **85** J8
Grange Street Doctors Surgery
STALW/RED AL3 .... **10** C3
Graveley Junior Mixed School
HTCHE/RSTV SG4 .... **58** B5
Great Gaddesden JMI School
HHW HP1 .... **139** G6
Great Hormead C of E School
BUNT SG9 .... **65** F1
Green End Business Centre
RKW/CH/CXG WD3 .... **201** K7
Greenfield Primary School
OXHEY WD19 .... **230** D4
The Greenhouse Health Centre
LTN LU1 .... **4** B3
Green Lane Industrial Estate
LWTH SG6 .... **42** B2
Green Lanes School
HAT AL10 .... **146** E8
Green Side School
STVGE SG2 .... **3** E6
Greenway County First School
BERK HP4 .... **161** H5
Greenwood Park Leisure Centre
LCOL/BKTW AL2 .... **188** D3

The Greneway School
 ROY SG8 .... 21 J2
Griffin Galleries
 PIN HA5 .... 230 D8
Griffin Golf Club
 LTN LU1 .... 88 C3
Grimsdyke First & Middle School
 PIN HA5 .... 231 G5
Grimsdyke Golf Club
 PIN HA5 .... 231 H4
Grosvenor Gallery
 NTHWD HA6 .... 229 K5
Grovehill Medical Centre
 HHNE HP2 .... 8 C1
The Grove Infant School
 HARP AL5 .... 144 A1
The Grove JMI School
 HARP AL5 .... 144 A1
Grovelands Business Centre
 HHNE HP2 .... 9 F3
Grove Road Primary School
 TRING HP23 .... 135 G4
Grundy Park Leisure Centre
 CHES/WCR EN8 .... 197 J8
Guardian Industrial Centre
 LTN LU1 .... 4 A3
Guilden Morden School
 ROY SG8 .... 15 G4
Haberdashers Askes School
 for Girls
 BORE WD6 .... 222 E3
Haberdashers Rugby Club
 BORE WD6 .... 223 J2
Hadley Wood School
 EBAR EN4 .... 210 D8
Haileybury College
 HERT/BAY SG13 .... 152 C7
Hailey Hall School
 HOD EN11 .... 152 E7
The Hammond Junior
 Mixed Infant School
 HHNE HP2 .... 8 C1
Happy Valley Industrial Estate
 KGLGY WD4 .... 186 B6
Harefield Cricket Club
 DEN/HRF UB9 .... 228 C8
Harefield Health Centre
 DEN/HRF UB9 .... 228 B7
Harefield Hospital
 DEN/HRF UB9 .... 228 B7
Harefield Infant School
 DEN/HRF UB9 .... 228 A7
Harefield Junior School
 DEN/HRF UB9 .... 228 B7
Haresfoot Prep School
 BERK HP4 .... 161 J8
Haresfoot Senior School
 BERK HP4 .... 162 D3
Hare Street County Junior
 & Infant School
 HLWW/ROY CM19 .... 6 B4
Harkness Industrial Estate
 BORE WD6 .... 223 K4
Harlequin Shopping Centre
 WAT WD17 .... 13 D3
Harlowbury School
 HLWE CM17 .... 157 G5
Harlow Business Park
 HLWW/ROY CM19 .... 179 F1
Harlow College
 HLW CM20 .... 6 B4
Harlow College
 HLW CM20 .... 7 D3
Harlow Museum
 HLWS CM18 .... 6 B5
Harlow Rugby Football Club
 HLW CM20 .... 6 A2
Harlow Sports Centre
 HLW CM20 .... 6 B2
Harlow Sports Centre
 HLW CM20 .... 6 C2
Harlow Urban District
 Swimming Pool
 HLW CM20 .... 7 D2
Harpenden Common Golf Club
 HARP AL5 .... 143 J3
Harpenden Golf Club
 HARP AL5 .... 143 G4
Harpenden Health Centre
 HARP AL5 .... 118 C7
Harpenden Hospital
 HARP AL5 .... 118 C5
Harpenden Memorial Hospital
 HARP AL5 .... 118 D7

Harpenden Preparatory School
 HARP AL5 .... 118 B7
Harpenden Rugby Football Club
 HARP AL5 .... 143 F3
Harpenden Sports Centre
 HARP AL5 .... 143 H1
Harpenden Swimming Pool
 HARP AL5 .... 118 C8
Harperbury Hospital
 RAD WD7 .... 207 F1
Hart Hill Junior School
 LTNE LU2 .... 5 D3
Hartsfield Junior Middle
 & Infant School
 BLDK SG7 .... 43 F1
Hartspring Industrial Park
 GSTN WD25 .... 221 H2
Hartspring Sports Centre
 BUSH WD23 .... 221 H2
Harvey Centre
 HLW CM20 .... 6 B4
Haselmere Industrial Estate
 BSF CM23 .... 105 K5
Haslemere Industrial Estate
 HLWW/ROY CM19 .... 179 H2
Haslewood Junior School
 HOD EN11 .... 177 F2
Hatch End High School
 KTN/HRWW/W HA3 .... 231 J6
Hatfield House
 BRKMPK AL9 .... 171 J4
Hatfield London County Club
 BRKMPK AL9 .... 173 G5
Haverfield Surgery
 KGLGY WD4 .... 186 A7
Havers Infant School
 BSF CM23 .... 105 H4
Hawridge & Cholesbury
 C of E Primary School
 CSHM HP5 .... 159 J7
Hazel Grove JMI School
 HAT AL10 .... 170 E7
Heathcote School
 STVGE SG2 .... 3 E6
Heathfield Lower School
 LTN LU1 .... 88 D5
Heathlands School
 for Deaf Children
 STALW/RED AL3 .... 11 D1
Heath Mount School
 HERT/WAS SG14 .... 98 E7
Heath Sports Club
 ROY SG8 .... 21 G3
Hemel Hempstead Rugby Club
 HHW HP1 .... 163 J8
Hemel Hempstead
 General Hospital
 HHNE HP2 .... 8 A6
Hemel Hempstead
 Rugby League Club
 HHNE HP2 .... 8 C2
Hemel Hempstead School
 HHW HP1 .... 164 B7
Hemel Hempstead
 Town Cricket Club
 HHS/BOV HP3 .... 164 B8
Hemel Hempstead
 United Football Club
 HHNE HP2 .... 9 E5
Hengrove School
 TRING HP23 .... 158 B5
Heron Trading Estate
 LTNN/LIM LU3 .... 68 B2
Hertford County Hospital
 HERT/WAS SG14 .... 150 E3
Hertford Police Station
 HERT/BAY SG13 .... 151 J2
Hertford Regional College
 WARE SG12 .... 152 C1
Hertfordshire Business Centre
 LCOL/BKTW AL2 .... 190 B4
Hertfordshire Country Club
 WGCE AL7 .... 147 H6
Hertfordshire County
 Constabulary
 HHW HP1 .... 164 B6
Hertfordshire County Council
 BUSH WD23 .... 222 A7
Hertfordshire County Council
 GSTN WD25 .... 204 D6
Hertfordshire County Council
 HERT/BAY SG13 .... 151 G4
Hertfordshire County Council
 OXHEY WD19 .... 230 C2

Hertfordshire County Council
 POTB/CUF EN6 .... 210 D2
Hertfordshire County Council
 RKW/CH/CXG WD3 .... 228 A1
Hertfordshire County Council
 WAT WD17 .... 12 B1
Hertfordshire & Essex
 General Hospital
 BSF CM23 .... 106 B3
Hertfordshire
 & Essex High School
 BSF CM23 .... 106 A2
Hertfordshire Family
 Health Authority Services
 WGCW AL8 .... 147 J2
Hertford Town Football Club
 HERT/WAS SG14 .... 150 E4
Hertsmere Borough Council
 BORE WD6 .... 224 B2
Hertsmere Council
 BORE WD6 .... 223 K2
Hertsmere Jewish
 Primary School
 RAD WD7 .... 207 F8
Hertsmere Progressive
 Synagogue
 BORE WD6 .... 223 G6
Hexton Junior Middle
 & Infant School
 HTCH/STOT SG5 .... 37 G8
High Beeches JMI School
 HARP AL5 .... 144 A1
Highbury Infant School
 HTCHE/RSTV SG4 .... 56 D3
High Cross Puller Memorial
 Junior & Infant School
 STDN SG11 .... 100 D7
Highfield School
 LWTH SG6 .... 41 H6
Highfield Surgery
 HHNE HP2 .... 8 C3
Highover JMI School
 HTCHE/RSTV SG4 .... 41 G8
Hightown Recreation Centre
 LTNE LU2 .... 4 C3
Highview Surgery
 POTB/CUF EN6 .... 210 D3
Highwood Primary School
 BUSH WD23 .... 221 F1
Hillborough Junior School
 LTN LU1 .... 4 A5
Hille Business Centre
 WATN WD24 .... 220 C1
Hill Farm Industrial Estate
 GSTN WD25 .... 204 A3
Hillgrove Business Park
 WAB EN9 .... 177 H8
Hillingdon Health Authority
 NTHWD HA6 .... 230 B7
Hillmead JMI School
 BSF CM23 .... 86 B8
Hillshott Infant School
 LWTH SG6 .... 42 A3
Hillside Junior & Infant School
 NTHWD HA6 .... 230 B6
Hillside School
 BORE WD6 .... 224 B4
Hitchin Boys School
 HTCH/STOT SG5 .... 56 C1
Hitchin Cricket Club
 HTCH/STOT SG5 .... 56 A2
Hitchin Girls School
 HTCHE/RSTV SG4 .... 56 D2
Hitchin Swimming Pool
 HTCH/STOT SG5 .... 56 C1
HM Prison
 CSHM HP5 .... 183 H4
Hobbs Hill Wood Primary School
 HHS/BOV HP3 .... 165 G8
Hobletts Manor Junior School
 HHNE HP2 .... 9 D4
Hockerill Anglo European
 GM School
 BSF CM23 .... 106 A2
Hockerill Sports Club
 BSF CM23 .... 106 A4
Hockwell Surgery
 LTNW/LEA LU4 .... 68 B4
Hoddesdon Health Centre
 HOD EN11 .... 177 F4
Hoddesdon Industrial Estate
 HOD EN11 .... 177 H2
Hoddesdon Lawn Tennis Club
 HOD EN11 .... 176 E3

Hoddesdon St Pauls Infant School
HOD EN11 .... **177** G3

Holdbrook Junior Middle & Infant School
CHES/WCR EN8.................. **214** E4

Holland & Holland Shooting School
DEN/HRF UB9 .... **229** F8

Hollybush School
HERT/WAS SG14 .... **150** D3

Holly Industrial Park
WATN WD24........................ **220** D1

Holly Street Trading Estate
LTN LU1 .... **4** C5

Hollywood Bowl
STVG SG1 .... **2** A3

Holmshill School
BORE WD6......................... **224** B2

Holtsmere End Junior & Infant School
HHNE HP2 .... **165** G1

Holwell Junior & Infant School
WGCE AL7 .... **148** A4

Holy Cross Boarding & Day School
CFSP/GDCR SL9................. **226** A7

Holy Cross RC Primary School
HLWS CM18.......................... **7** F6

Holyrood Infant School
WAT WD17.......................... **203** J6

Holy Rood Junior School
WAT WD17.......................... **203** J6

Holy Trinity C of E Primary School
CHES/WCR EN8.................. **214** C2

Holy Trinity School
NTHWD HA6 .... **229** H5

Holywell School
WATW WD18 .... **12** A5

Home Farm Industrial Estate
WARE SG12 .... **154** A4

Home Park Industrial Estate
KGLGY WD4........................ **186** B8

Homerswood Junior & Infant School
WGCW AL8......................... **122** D7

Homewood School
LCOL/BKTW AL2 .... **188** D6

Honilands Junior & Infant School
EN EN1 .... **214** A6

Horseshoe Business Park
LCOL/BKTW AL2 .... **188** D8

Hospital
LTN LU1 .... **4** A4

Hospital Annexe
DEN/HRF UB9 .... **228** B6

Hot Shots Ten Pin Bowling
HHS/BOV HP3 .... **8** C6

Howard Business Park
WAB EN9 .... **215** J4

Howe Dell School
HAT AL10 .... **171** G4

Howe Green House School
RBSF CM22 .... **106** C7

How Wood Junior & Infant School
LCOL/BKTW AL2 .... **188** E5

Hurst Drive JMI School
CHES/WCR EN8.................. **214** C4

Hyatt Trading Estate
STVG SG1 .... **75** F4

Icknield High School
LTNN/LIM LU3 .... **69** H4

Icknield Infant School
LWTH SG6 .... **41** H3

Icknield Walk First School
ROY SG8 .... **21** J2

Icknield Way Industrial Estate
TRING HP23........................ **134** D5

Immanuel College
BUSH WD23........................ **222** B7

Indoor Market
WAT WD17............................ **13** D2

Industrial Estate
DEN/HRF UB9 .... **227** K5

Industrial Park
CHES/WCR EN8.................. **215** F4

International University
BUSH WD23........................ **221** G4

Ivinghoe Golf Club
LBUZ LU7 .... **111** F3

The Jamie Mosque
STAL AL1 .... **11** F4

Jerounds Junior & Infant School
HLWW/ROY CM19............... **179** J4

John F Kennedy School
HHW HP1............................ **163** H5

John Henry Newman RC School
STVG SG1 .... **58** B8

John Penrose School
DEN/HRF UB9 .... **228** C7

The John Warner School
HOD EN11 .... **153** G8

Jubilee Trading Estate
LWTH SG6 .... **42** C2

Junior & Infant School
STVG SG1 .... **2** B1

Jupiter Drive JMI School
HHNE HP2 .... **8** C3

Katherines Primary School
HLWW/ROY CM19............... **179** G3

Kenilworth Primary School
BORE WD6......................... **224** C3

Kensworth Lower School
DUN/WHIP LU6 .... **114** D1

Kevin Hinds Practice
WARE SG12 .... **127** H8

Killigrew Junior Middle & Infant School
LCOL/BKTW AL2 .... **188** D3

Kimpton Junior Middle & Infant School
HTCHE/RSTV SG4 .... **93** F8

King George Surgery
STVG SG1 .... **2** B1

King Harold Comprehensive School
WAB EN9 .... **215** K3

Kingsbury Watermill Museum & Waffle House
STALW/RED AL3 .... **10** A4

Kingshott School
HTCHE/RSTV SG4 .... **57** F4

Kings Langley Parish Council
KGLGY WD4........................ **186** A7

Kings Langley Primary School
KGLGY WD4........................ **185** K6

Kingsmoor Junior & Infant School
HLWW/ROY CM19............... **179** K5

Kingsmoor Recreation Centre
HLWW/ROY CM19............... **179** J5

The Kings Oak Private Hospital
ENC/FH EN2 .... **212** D8

Kings Park Industrial Estate
KGLGY WD4........................ **186** B7

Kingsway Industrial Estate
LTN LU1 .... **89** F1

Kingsway Junior School
GSTN WD25........................ **204** B4

Knebworth Golf Club
KNEB SG3............................ **96** A3

Knebworth Ho
KNEB SG3............................ **95** H3

Knebworth Physiotherapy Clinic
STVGE SG2 .... **96** D2

Knights Templar School
BLDK SG7 .... **42** E1

Knowl Piece
HTCHE/RSTV SG4 .... **40** E6

Knutsford Junior & Infant School
WATN WD24........................ **204** E8

Ladbroke School
POTB/CUF EN6 .... **210** C2

Lady Zia Wernher School
LTNE LU2 .... **70** C6

Laharna Trading Estate
WATN WD24........................ **204** D8

Laings Sports Ground
BAR EN5 .... **224** D4

Lakeside School
WGCW AL8......................... **147** G5

Lakeside Surgery
HTCH/STOT SG5 .... **25** J3

Langley Terrace Industrial Park
LTN LU1 .... **4** C5

Lannock JMI School
LWTH SG6 .... **42** C5

Larwood School
STVG SG1 .... **3** D1

Laser Clinic
CHESW EN7 .... **197** F8

Latton Bush Business Centre
HLWS CM18........................ **180** C4

Latton Bush Recreation Centre
HLWS CM18........................ **180** B4

Laurence Haines School
WATW WD18 .... **12** B5

Lavender Junior & Infant School
ENC/FH EN2 .... **213** H8

Layston First School
BUNT SG9 .... **63** K1

Lea Farm Junior School
GSTN WD25........................ **204** E6

Leagrave Health Centre
LTNW/LEA LU4 .... **68** B5

Leagrave Junior & Infant School
LTNW/LEA LU4 .... **68** B5

Lea Industrial Estate
HARP AL5........................... **118** E5

Lealands High School
LTNN/LIM LU3 .... **68** B1

Lea Manor High School & Community College
LTNN/LIM LU3 .... **68** E1

The Leas Junior & Infant School
HARP AL5........................... **118** C5

Lea Valley High School
PEND EN3 .... **214** B5

Leavesden Green Junior Middle & Infant School
GSTN WD25........................ **204** B4

Leavesden Hospital
ABLGY WD5........................ **204** B1

Letchworth Business Centre
LWTH SG6 .... **42** C3

Letchworth Garden City Football Club
LWTH SG6 .... **42** C4

Letchworth Golf Club
LWTH SG6 .... **41** K7

Letchworth Museum
LWTH SG6 .... **41** K4

Letchworth Swimming Pool
LWTH SG6 .... **42** A2

The Leventhorpe School
SBW CM21 .... **132** C5

Leverstock Green JMI School
HHNE HP2 .... **165** J7

Leverstock Green Lawn Tennis Club
HHS/BOV HP3 .... **165** G8

Ley Hill CP School
CSHM HP5 .... **182** D8

Ley Park CP School
BROX EN10 .... **176** E8

Leys Primary School
STVG SG1 .... **59** G7

Lime Walk JMI School
HHS/BOV HP3 .... **164** E8

Lincoln Health Surgery
HHNE HP2 .... **8** A6

Links Business Centre
BSF CM23 .... **106** B2

Lismarrine Industrial Park
BORE WD6......................... **222** E6

Lister Hospital
STVG SG1 .... **58** B7

Lister House Surgery
HAT AL10 .... **171** F3

Lister House Surgery
LTNW/LEA LU4 .... **68** E7

Lister Medical Centre
HLWS CM18........................ **179** K4

Little Chalfont CP School
AMS HP6 .... **216** B1

Little Furze School
OXHEY WD19...................... **230** C2

Little Gaddesden JMI School
BERK HP4 .... **137** K2

Little Green CP School
RKW/CH/CXG WD3 .... **219** G3

Little Hallingbury C of E Primary School
RBSF CM22 .... **133** G1

Little Heath Junior Mixed School
POTB/CUF EN6 .... **193** J8

Little Munden JMI School
WARE SG12 .... **99** H1

Little Reddings Primary School
BUSH WD23........................ **221** J5

Little St. Helens School
NTHWD HA6 .... **230** A6

Liverpool Road Health Centre
LTN LU1 .... **4** B3

Llewelyn Surgery
WAB EN9 .... **215** H3

Lochinver House School
POTB/CUF EN6 .... **193** H8

Lockers Park School
HHW HP1............................ **164** A6

Lodge Clinic
LTN LU1 .... **4** C4

Lodge Farm Infant School
STVGE SG2 .... 76 D2
Lodge Farm Junior School
STVGE SG2 .... 76 D2
Lodge Sun Sports Club
WAT WD17 .... 219 K1
Lodge Surgery
STALW/RED AL3 .... 10 C2
London Bible College
NTHWD HA6 .... 229 J5
London Colney JMI School
LCOL/BKTW AL2 .... 190 B3
London Luton Airport
LTNE LU2 .... 90 E1
London Luton Airport
LTNE LU2 .... 90 D2
London Luton Airport
LTNE LU2 .... 90 E2
Longdean School
HHS/BOV HP3 .... 186 B1
**Longlands Junior Middle
& Infant School**
BROX EN10 .... 197 J3
Long Marston JMI School
TRING HP23 .... 109 F5
**Long Meadow Infant
& Junior School**
STVGE SG2 .... 76 C8
Longrove Surgery
BAR EN5 .... 225 K3
Loreto College
STAL AL1 .... 11 D4
Lowewood Museum
HOD EN11 .... 177 F4
Lowfield Sports Ground
HOD EN11 .... 176 E3
Luton Co-operative Sports Club
LTNE LU2 .... 5 D1
Luton County Court
LTN LU1 .... 4 B4
Luton Crown Court
LTN LU1 .... 4 C4
**Luton & Dunstable Hospital
NHS Trust**
LTNW/LEA LU4 .... 68 B7
Luton Hoo
LTN LU1 .... 90 B7
Luton Leisure Park
LTN LU1 .... 4 B3
Luton Police Station
LTN LU1 .... 4 B4
Luton Sixth Form College
LTNE LU2 .... 69 K5
Luton Town Football Club
LTN LU1 .... 89 G1
Lyndhurst Middle School
BORE WD6 .... 223 J1
Madison Bowl
NTHWD HA6 .... 229 K6
Maidenhall Junior School
LTNW/LEA LU4 .... 69 F7
Maltings Arts Theatre
STAL AL1 .... 10 C4
The Maltings Industrial Estate
SBW CM21 .... 132 D7
The Maltings Surgery
STAL AL1 .... 10 C4
Malvern Way School
RKW/CH/CXG WD3 .... 219 H5
The Management Practice
STVG SG1 .... 75 G5
Mandeville Health Centre
STAL AL1 .... 189 F1
Mandeville Primary School
STAL AL1 .... 189 F1
Manland Primary School
HARP AL5 .... 118 D6
Manor Fields JMI School
BSF CM23 .... 105 G4
Manor Lodge School
RAD WD7 .... 191 G8
The Manor of Groves
SBW CM21 .... 131 H7
Manor Street Surgery
BERK HP4 .... 161 K5
Maple Cross Industrial Estate
RKW/CH/CXG WD3 .... 227 H3
**Maple Cross Junior Middle
& Infant School**
RKW/CH/CXG WD3 .... 227 G4
Maple Junior & Infant School
STAL AL1 .... 11 D3
Maple River Industrial Estate
HLW CM20 .... 156 E3

**Margaret Wix Junior
& Infant School**
STALW/RED AL3 .... 167 K2
Mark Hall Comprehensive School
HLWE CM17 .... 157 F6
Mark Hall Cycle Museum
HLW CM20 .... 156 E6
Markyate Primary School
STALW/RED AL3 .... 115 H3
Marlborough School
STAL AL1 .... 188 E1
Marlowes Health Centre
HHW HP1 .... 164 B6
Marquis Business Centre
BLDK SG7 .... 27 G8
Marriotts School
STVGE SG2 .... 3 E2
Marsworth C of E Primary School
TRING HP23 .... 110 A7
Martindale JMI School
HHW HP1 .... 163 J5
Martinfield Business Centre
WGCE AL7 .... 148 A2
Martins Wood JMI School
STVG SG1 .... 59 H8
Mary Exton JMI School
HTCHE/RSTV SG4 .... 57 G2
Maunds Wood CP School
HLWS CM18 .... 180 A5
Mayfield County Infant School
CHES/WCR EN8 .... 197 J5
The Mead Business Centre
HERT/BAY SG13 .... 151 H2
Mead Industrial Park
HLW CM20 .... 156 C5
Meadow Wood School
BUSH WD23 .... 221 K5
The Mead School
HLWS CM18 .... 7 D6
The Meads Primary School
LTNW/LIM LU3 .... 68 E3
Megabowl
STVG SG1 .... 2 B5
Mercers College
WARE SG12 .... 127 H8
Merchant Taylors School
NTHWD HA6 .... 229 K1
Meriden Primary School
GSTN WD25 .... 204 E6
Meridian School
ROY SG8 .... 21 K1
Meryfield School
BORE WD6 .... 223 J1
Micklem JMI School
HHW HP1 .... 163 J5
Middleton School
WARE SG12 .... 152 C2
Mid Herts Golf Club
STALE/WH AL4 .... 120 B5
**Millbrook Junior Middle
& Infant School**
CHES/WCR EN8 .... 197 J7
Millfield First School
BUNT SG9 .... 63 J2
Millmead Junior & Infant School
HERT/WAS SG14 .... 151 F3
Mill Studio Business Centre
WARE SG12 .... 127 J8
Millwards CP School
HLWW/ROY CM19 .... 179 J5
Milton House Surgery
BERK HP4 .... 161 J5
The Misbourne Practice
CFSP/GDCR SL9 .... 226 A7
Monksmead School
BORE WD6 .... 224 B3
Monks Walk School
WGCW AL8 .... 122 C6
Monkswood Retail Park
STVG SG1 .... 2 B5
Monro Industrial Estate
CHES/WCR EN8 .... 214 D4
Montessore School
BERK HP4 .... 161 J5
Moorlands School
LTNW/LEA LU4 .... 68 B6
Moor Park Industrial Estate
WATW WD18 .... 219 H7
Moreton Park Industrial Estate
LTNE LU2 .... 5 E1
Morgans Junior School
HERT/BAY SG13 .... 151 G5
**Morgans Walk Junior
Mixed School**
HERT/BAY SG13 .... 151 G5

**Morgans Walk Junior
Mixed School**
HERT/WAS SG14 .... 150 D5
Mosquito Aircraft
LCOL/BKTW AL2 .... 191 F7
Mosquito Aircraft Museum
LCOL/BKTW AL2 .... 190 B4
The Mountfitchet School
STSD CM24 .... 86 E5
Mount Grace GM School
POTB/CUF EN6 .... 193 H8
Mount Pleasant School
LCOL/BKTW AL2 .... 188 A8
Mount Vernon Hospital
RKW/CH/CXG WD3 .... 229 G4
Mowat Industrial Estate
WATN WD24 .... 204 D8
M S F Whitehall College
BSF CM23 .... 85 H8
Museum
WAB EN9 .... 215 H4
Musley Infant School
WARE SG12 .... 127 J7
Napsbury Hospital
LCOL/BKTW AL2 .... 189 K5
**Nascot Wood Junior
& Infant School**
WAT WD17 .... 204 B8
Nash Mills C of E Primary School
HHS/BOV HP3 .... 185 K3
**Natural Art Gallery
& Science Pictures**
HTCH/STOT SG5 .... 56 C3
Nazeing CP School
WAB EN9 .... 198 E1
Nazeing Golf Club
WAB EN9 .... 199 J2
Nazeing Parish Council
WAB EN9 .... 199 H3
Nazeing Park
WAB EN9 .... 178 D8
Neville Road Surgery
LTNN/LIM LU3 .... 69 F4
New Briars School
HAT AL10 .... 171 F4
New Court Business Park
HLWW/ROY CM19 .... 179 K5
New England Industrial Estate
HOD EN11 .... 177 H2
The New Surgery
KGLGY WD4 .... 186 A7
The New Surgery
TRING HP23 .... 135 F6
New Town Trading Estate
LTN LU1 .... 4 C6
Nicholas Breakspear RC School
STALE/WH AL4 .... 169 H7
Nicholas Hawksmoor School
BORE WD6 .... 224 A1
Nobel Secondary School
STVGE SG2 .... 76 D2
Northaw C of E School
POTB/CUF EN6 .... 194 C7
Northchurch Cricket Club
BERK HP4 .... 160 E2
**Northchurch St. Marys C of E
First School**
BERK HP4 .... 161 F3
Northfields Infant School
LWTH SG6 .... 25 K8
Northgate JMI School
BSF CM23 .... 105 H1
North Hertfordshire College
HTCHE/RSTV SG4 .... 57 F1
North Hertfordshire College
LWTH SG6 .... 41 K3
North Hertfordshire College
STVG SG1 .... 2 B4
**North Hertfordshire
Leisure Centre**
LWTH SG6 .... 42 C3
**North Hertfordshire
Secondary Centre**
LWTH SG6 .... 41 H6
North Lodge Queens School
BUSH WD23 .... 221 G3
North Luton Industrial Estate
LTNW/LEA LU4 .... 68 A2
North Mymms Cricket Club
BRKMPK AL9 .... 192 A4
North Orbital Trading Estate
STAL AL1 .... 189 J2
North Watford Health Clinic
GSTN WD25 .... 204 D4

North & West Essex Adult
  Community College
  HLW CM20 .... **6** B2
Northwood College Educational
  Foundation
  NTHWD HA6 .... **229** J6
Northwood Football Club
  NTHWD HA6 .... **230** A8
Northwood & Pinner Community
  Hospital
  NTHWD HA6 .... **230** B7
Northwood Pinner
  Liberal Synagogue
  NTHWD HA6 .... **229** K5
Northwood Preparatory School
  RKW/CH/CXG WD3 .... **229** H1
Northwood School
  NTHWD HA6 .... **230** C7
Northwood Sports Centre
  PIN HA5 .... **230** C7
Northwood United Synagogue
  NTHWD HA6 .... **229** K6
Norton Road Primary School
  LTNN/LIM LU3 .... **68** E5
Norton School
  LWTH SG6 .... **42** A1
Nucleus Gallery
  CFSP/GDCR SL9 .... **226** A7
Nup End Industrial Estate
  WLYN AL6 .... **95** G5
Oaklands College
  BORE WD6 .... **224** B2
Oaklands College
  HARP AL5 .... **118** D8
Oaklands College
  STAL AL1 .... **11** D4
Oaklands College
  STALE/WH AL4 .... **169** H5
Oaklands College
  WGCW AL8 .... **147** J2
Oaklands JMI School
  WLYN AL6 .... **122** E1
The Oakley Surgery
  LTNW/LEA LU4 .... **68** C5
Oakmere School
  POTB/CUF EN6 .... **210** E2
The Oaks Industrial Estate
  HLW CM20 .... **7** E1
Oakwood Estate
  HLW CM20 .... **7** F1
Oakwood JMI School
  STALE/WH AL4 .... **169** F5
Odeon Cinema
  HHS/BOV HP3 .... **8** C6
Odeon Cinema
  HLW CM20 .... **6** B3
Odhams Industrial Estate
  WATN WD24 .... **204** D7
Odhams Trading Estate
  WATN WD24 .... **204** B6
Old Airfield Industrial Estate
  LBUZ LU7 .... **109** K4
Old Boys School
  STDN SG11 .... **82** A2
Old Fold Manor Golf Club
  BAR EN5 .... **225** K1
Old Harlow Health Centre
  HLWE CM17 .... **157** F5
Old Merchant Taylors Sports Club
  RKW/CH/CXG WD3 .... **219** G4
Old Millhillians Sports Ground
  PIN HA5 .... **231** H7
Old Oak Close Industrial Estate
  ARL/CHE SG15 .... **24** E1
Old Verulamians
  Rugby Football Club
  LCOL/BKTW AL2 .... **190** A3
Orchard County Primary School
  WATN WD24 .... **204** A6
Oughtonhead Junior
  & Infant School
  HTCH/STOT SG5 .... **40** A8
Our Ladys Catholic
  Primary School
  WGCE AL7 .... **147** K5
Oxen Industrial Estate
  LTNE LU2 .... **5** D2
Oxhey Infant School
  BUSH WD23 .... **13** F4
Oxheywood Junior
  & Infant School
  OXHEY WD19 .... **230** D3
Palace Theatre
  WAT WD17 .... **12** C2

Panshanger Golf Club
  WGCE AL7 .... **148** D1
Panshanger JMI School
  WGCE AL7 .... **148** B2
Paramount Industrial Estate
  WATN WD24 .... **204** D8
Park Avenue Clinic
  WAT WD17 .... **12** B1
Park Avenue Industrial Estate
  LTNN/LIM LU3 .... **68** A2
Parkbury House Surgery
  STAL AL1 .... **11** D3
Park Farm Industrial Estate
  BUNT SG9 .... **47** H8
Park Farm Industrial Estate
  BUNT SG9 .... **63** H1
Parkfield Medical Centre
  POTB/CUF EN6 .... **210** C2
Parkgate Infant School
  WATN WD24 .... **204** D7
Parkgate Junior School
  WATN WD24 .... **204** D7
Park Industrial Estate
  LCOL/BKTW AL2 .... **189** G5
Park Lane Surgery
  BROX EN10 .... **176** E6
Parkside First School
  BORE WD6 .... **207** J8
Park Street C of E
  Primary School
  LCOL/BKTW AL2 .... **189** F5
Parmiters School
  GSTN WD25 .... **204** D1
Parndoni Mill Gallery
  HLW CM20 .... **6** A1
The Parochial Church
  Council of Goffs Oak St James
  CHESW EN7 .... **196** B6
Parsonage Farm
  Industrial Estate
  STSD CM24 .... **86** E6
Passmores
  Comprehensive School
  HLWS CM18 .... **6** C6
Peerglow Industrial Estate
  WATW WD18 .... **219** G7
Peterswood Junior
  & Infant School
  HLWS CM18 .... **180** A5
The Picture House
  HLW CM20 .... **6** B3
Pinehill Hospital
  HTCHE/RSTV SG4 .... **57** F2
Pine Wood School
  WARE SG12 .... **152** C2
Pin Green JMI School
  STVG SG1 .... **3** D2
Pinner Wood School
  PIN HA5 .... **230** D7
Pirton Hill Infant School
  LTNW/LEA LU4 .... **68** A3
Pirton JMI School
  HTCH/STOT SG5 .... **38** E5
Pitstone Surgery
  LBUZ LU7 .... **110** D2
Pixies Hill JMI School
  HHW HP1 .... **163** J7
Pixmore Junior School
  LWTH SG6 .... **42** A4
Ponsbourne St. Marys JMI School
  HERT/BAY SG13 .... **195** G2
Pope Paul RC Primary School
  POTB/CUF EN6 .... **210** A3
Portland Industrial Estate
  ARL/CHE SG15 .... **24** D7
Potten End School
  BERK HP4 .... **162** E3
Potterells Medical Centre
  BRKMPK AL9 .... **192** D3
Potters Bar Cricket Club
  POTB/CUF EN6 .... **210** C2
Potters Bar Golf Club
  POTB/CUF EN6 .... **210** B1
Potter Street Primary School
  HLWE CM17 .... **180** E3
Prae Wood JMI School
  STALW/RED AL3 .... **167** H7
Presdales School
  WARE SG12 .... **152** C1
Prince Hotel
  STALW/RED AL3 .... **167** H4
Prince of Wales Junior
  & Infant School
  PEND EN3 .... **214** E8

Princess Alexandra Hospital
  HLW CM20 .... **6** A3
The Princess Helena College
  HTCHE/RSTV SG4 .... **73** H3
The Print Room/Museum Books
  & Prints
  BAR EN5 .... **225** K5
Priors Wood JMI School
  WARE SG12 .... **128** A6
Priory School
  HTCH/STOT SG5 .... **40** C7
Public Swimming Pool
  OXHEY WD19 .... **231** F4
Pump House Theatre
  WAT WD17 .... **13** D4
The Purcell School
  BUSH WD23 .... **221** G2
Purford Green School
  HLWS CM18 .... **7** F6
Purwell JMI School
  HTCHE/RSTV SG4 .... **57** G1
Putteridge High School
  & Community College
  LTNE LU2 .... **70** D4
Putteridge Junior
  & Infant School
  LTNE LU2 .... **70** D4
Queen Elizabeth II Hospital
  BRKMPK AL9 .... **148** B7
Queen Elizabeths School
  BAR EN5 .... **225** J3
Queen Mother Theatre
  HTCH/STOT SG5 .... **56** D2
Queensway Health Centre
  HAT AL10 .... **171** G3
Queenswood School
  BRKMPK AL9 .... **193** K6
Queen Victoria
  Memorial Hospital
  WLYN AL6 .... **122** A5
Radburn JMI School
  LWTH SG6 .... **42** C4
Radlett & Bushey
  Reform Synagogue
  RAD WD7 .... **206** D5
Radlett Cricket Club
  RAD WD7 .... **206** E7
Radlett Lodge School
  RAD WD7 .... **206** E2
Radlett Parochial Church Council
  RAD WD7 .... **206** D6
Radlett Preparatory School
  RAD WD7 .... **207** F8
R A F Edlesborough
  DUN/WHIP LU6 .... **112** B2
Ramridge Infant School
  LTNE LU2 .... **5** F1
Ramridge Junior School
  LTNE LU2 .... **5** E1
Ramsey Manor Lower School
  AMP/FLIT/B MK45 .... **36** D7
Raynham Road Industrial Estate
  BSF CM23 .... **106** A1
Real Tennis Club
  BRKMPK AL9 .... **171** J4
Recreation Centre
  LTNE LU2 .... **70** D4
Recreation Ground
  LTN LU1 .... **5** D5
Redbourn Golf Club
  STALW/RED AL3 .... **117** H8
Redbourn Industrial Centre
  STALW/RED AL3 .... **142** C4
Redbourn Junior & Infant School
  STALW/RED AL3 .... **142** B3
Redbourn Recreation Centre
  STALW/RED AL3 .... **142** B2
Reddings JMI School
  HHS/BOV HP3 .... **164** E8
Red House Surgery
  RAD WD7 .... **206** D5
Reed First School
  ROY SG8 .... **31** J4
Regal Chambers Surgery
  HTCH/STOT SG5 .... **56** C1
Rhodes Museum
  & Commonwealth Centre
  BSF CM23 .... **105** K4
Richard Whittington JMI School
  BSF CM23 .... **105** H5
Richmond Hill School
  LTNE LU2 .... **4** C1
Rickmansworth
  Public Golf Course
  RKW/CH/CXG WD3 .... **228** E1

Rickmansworth School
RKW/CH/CXG WD3 .... 218 E6
Rickmansworth Sports Club
RKW/CH/CXG WD3 .... 218 D6
Riverside Business Park
STSD CM24 .... 86 C3
Riverside Estate
HARP AL5 .... 118 E5
Riverside Industrial Estate
LCOL/BKTW AL2 .... 190 C5
R N I B Sunshine House School
NTHWD HA6 .... 229 J5
Roaring Meg Retail Park
STVG SG1 .... 2 C5
Roaring Meg Retail Park
STVGE SG2 .... 2 C6
Robertswood County
Combined School
CFSP/GDCR SL9 .... 226 C6
Roebuck JMI School
STVGE SG2 .... 3 D6
Roecroft School
HTCH/STOT SG5 .... 26 A3
Roger Bannister Sports Ground
KTN/HRWW/W HA3 .... 231 K5
Roger De Clare School
STDN SG11 .... 81 K6
Roman Theatre
STALW/RED AL3 .... 167 H6
Rosary Priory High School
BUSH WD23 .... 222 B6
Rosedale Clinic
CHESW EN7 .... 196 E5
Roseland Junior Middle
& Infant School
HOD EN11 .... 152 E8
Rossgate JMI School
HHW HP1 .... 163 K4
Round Diamond School
STVG SG1 .... 76 C1
Roundwood Park School
HARP AL5 .... 118 A7
Rowans Junior Mixed
Infant School
WGCE AL7 .... 123 G8
The Royal Masonic School
RKW/CH/CXG WD3 .... 218 C6
Royal Veterinary College
BRKMPK AL9 .... 192 D6
Roydonbury Industrial Estate
HLWW/ROY CM19 .... 179 G1
Roydon CP School
HLWW/ROY CM19 .... 178 C1
Roydon Leisure Park
HLWW/ROY CM19 .... 154 B8
Roysia Middle School
ROY SG8 .... 21 G1
Roysia Surgery
ROY SG8 .... 21 H1
Royston & District Hospital
ROY SG8 .... 21 H5
Royston Golf Club
ROY SG8 .... 21 G3
Royston Health Centre
ROY SG8 .... 21 H3
Royston Museum
ROY SG8 .... 21 G3
Royston Swimming Pool
ROY SG8 .... 21 H3
Royston Town Football Club
ROY SG8 .... 21 H2
Rudolf Steiner School
KGLGY WD4 .... 185 J7
Rugby Club
BSF CM23 .... 85 G8
Russell Clinic
STALW/RED AL3 .... 10 C4
Russell County Primary School
RKW/CH/CXG WD3 .... 216 E4
Ryde College
WATW WD18 .... 219 K6
Ryde Junior Mixed Infant School
BRKMPK AL9 .... 171 H1
Rye House Stadium
HOD EN11 .... 177 J1
Ryelands JMI School
HOD EN11 .... 177 G2
Sacred Heart Junior Middle
& Infant School
OXHEY WD19 .... 221 G6
Sacred Heart RC Junior
& Infant School
LTNE LU2 .... 70 B6
Sacred Heart RC School
WARE SG12 .... 127 H8

Saffron Green First School
BORE WD6 .... 224 C4
St Adrians RC JMI School
STAL AL1 .... 188 E1
St Albans City Football Club
STAL AL1 .... 11 E4
St Albans City Hospital
STALW/RED AL3 .... 10 B2
St Albans Girls School
STALW/RED AL3 .... 168 B2
St Albans High School for Girls
STAL AL1 .... 11 D3
St Albans Lawn Tennis Club
STALE/WH AL4 .... 169 F4
St Albans Museum
STAL AL1 .... 10 C3
St Albans Musical Museum
LCOL/BKTW AL2 .... 188 D6
St Albans Music School
STALW/RED AL3 .... 10 C1
St Albans Organ Museum
STAL AL1 .... 168 E7
St Albans Principal Health Centre
STAL AL1 .... 10 C4
St Albans RC Primary School
HLW CM20 .... 7 E2
St Albans Retail Park
STAL AL1 .... 10 C6
St Albans School
STALW/RED AL3 .... 10 B4
St Albans & Stephen RC JMI School
STAL AL1 .... 11 F4
St Albans Synagogue
STAL AL1 .... 11 D5
St Alban & Stephen Junior
& Middle School
STAL AL1 .... 11 E5
St Albert the Great RC
Primary School
HHS/BOV HP3 .... 165 F8
St Andrews C of E Primary School
HERT/WAS SG14 .... 150 C2
St Andrews JMI School
HTCHE/RSTV SG4 .... 56 E2
St Andrews School
WARE SG12 .... 153 J5
St Anthonys RC Junior School
WATW WD18 .... 219 K5
St Bernadette JMI School
LCOL/BKTW AL2 .... 190 A5
St Catherine of Siena RC School
GSTN WD25 .... 204 E2
St Christopher School
LTWH SG6 .... 41 K6
St Clement Danes School
RKW/CH/CXG WD3 .... 217 G2
St Clements Mixed Junior School
CHES/WCR EN8 .... 197 J5
St Columbas College
Preparatory School
STALW/RED AL3 .... 10 B6
St Cross RC Primary School
HOD EN11 .... 177 F5
St Dominic RC School
HARP AL5 .... 143 J1
St Edmunds College
STDN SG11 .... 81 F8
St Elizabeths School & Home
MHAD SG10 .... 130 D3
St Francis College
LTWH SG6 .... 41 J5
St Giles C of E Primary School
POTB/CUF EN6 .... 209 F2
St Giles C of E Primary School
POTB/CUF EN6 .... 209 G3
St Helens School
NTHWD HA6 .... 229 K5
St Helens School
STALE/WH AL4 .... 145 G1
St Hildas School
HARP AL5 .... 118 B7
St Ignatius College
EN EN1 .... 213 K7
St Ippolyts School
HTCHE/RSTV SG4 .... 57 F6
St James Church School
HLWS CM18 .... 180 A5
St Joan of Arc RC School
RKW/CH/CXG WD3 .... 218 D7
St John Baptist School
WARE SG12 .... 153 F4
St John Fisher RC JMI School
STALE/WH AL4 .... 169 F3

St Johns C of E Junior
& Infant School
ENC/FH EN2 .... 212 E6
St Johns C of E Primary School
WGCW AL8 .... 146 E4
St Johns C of E Primary School
WLYN AL6 .... 123 F7
St Johns Infant School
RAD WD7 .... 206 C5
St Johns RC JMI School
BLDK SG7 .... 43 F2
St Johns RC Junior Middle
& Infant School
RKW/CH/CXG WD3 .... 218 A8
St Johns School
NTHWD HA6 .... 230 C5
St Josephs Junior & Infant School
LTNN/LIM LU3 .... 69 F5
St Josephs RC JMI School
CHES/WCR EN8 .... 214 D3
St Josephs RC Junior Middle
& Infant School
BSF CM23 .... 105 G3
St Josephs RC School
OXHEY WD19 .... 230 C2
St Lukes RC Primary School
HLWW/ROY CM19 .... 6 B6
St Luke's School
STALW/RED AL3 .... 142 B3
St Margaret Clitherow JMI School
STVGE SG2 .... 3 D6
St Margarets of Scotland
Junior School
LTN LU1 .... 89 F4
St Margarets of Scotland RC
Va Infant School
LTN LU1 .... 89 F4
St Margarets School
BUSH WD23 .... 221 H7
St Marks RC
Comprehensive School
HLWS CM18 .... 7 D5
St Martins School
NTHWD HA6 .... 229 J4
St Marys Catholic School
BSF CM23 .... 105 H2
St Marys C of E Primary School
STSD CM24 .... 86 D2
St Marys High School
CHESW EN7 .... 197 F8
St Marys Infant School
WLYN AL6 .... 122 B5
St Marys Junior & Infant School
BLDK SG7 .... 42 E3
St Marys Junior Mixed School
WARE SG12 .... 127 H6
St Marys RC JMI School
ROY SG8 .... 21 H2
St Marys School
STVGE SG2 .... 77 F6
St Marys Voluntary Lower School
HTCH/STOT SG5 .... 26 A3
St Matthews Infant School
LTNE LU2 .... 5 D2
St Meryl Junior Middle
& Infant School
OXHEY WD19 .... 231 F2
St Michaels C of E JMI School
STALW/RED AL3 .... 10 A4
St Michaels Primary School
BSF CM23 .... 105 H2
St Michaels RC School
GSTN WD25 .... 204 E2
St Nichaols Recreation Centre
STVG SG1 .... 59 H6
St Nicholas C of E
Primary School
STVG SG1 .... 3 D4
St Nicholas Health Centre
STVG SG1 .... 59 F7
St Nicholas House School
HHS/BOV HP3 .... 186 B3
St Nicholas Junior
Infant School
LTWH SG6 .... 26 C8
St Nicholas School
HLWE CM17 .... 157 J6
St Nicholas Voluntary
Primary School
HARP AL5 .... 118 C8
St Pauls Primary School
KGLGY WD4 .... 203 H4
St Pauls Roman Catholic
JMI School
CHESW EN7 .... 197 F5

St Pauls Walden Junior School
HTCHE/RSTV SG4 .... 93 G2
St Peters JMI School
STAL AL1 .... 11 D5
St Peters Junior Middle
& Infant School
RKW/CH/CXG WD3 .... 218 A8
The St Philip Howard
Catholic Primary School
HAT AL10 .... 171 G4
St Roses Infants School
HHW HP1 .... 163 K8
St Teresas RC School
KTN/HRWW/W HA3 .... 231 K7
St Thomas Moore RC JMI School
BERK HP4 .... 161 H5
St Thomas More RC Junior
& Infant School
LWTH SG6 .... 41 H5
St Thomas of Canterbury
Catholic School
STDN SG11 .... 81 H6
Salisbury Hall
LCOL/BKTW AL2 .... 191 F7
Salisbury Infant School
HAT AL10 .... 171 G2
Salisbury Lawn Tennis Club
STAL AL1 .... 168 E5
Sandon & Infant School
BUNT SG9 .... 29 K8
Sandridge Gate Business Centre
STALW/RED AL3 .... 168 C2
Sandridge JMI School
STALE/WH AL4 .... 145 G7
Sandridge Youth Club
& Sports Centre
STALW/RED AL3 .... 144 E8
Sandringham School
STALE/WH AL4 .... 168 E2
Sarbir Industrial Park
HLW CM20 .... 157 F4
Sarratt Junior Middle
& Infant School
RKW/CH/CXG WD3 .... 201 K6
Sawbridge Health Clinic
SBW CM23 .... 132 C7
Schidegger Mis College
LTN LU1 .... 4 B3
Schopwick Surgery
BORE WD6 .... 223 G6
Sebright School
STALW/RED AL3 .... 115 H5
The Sele School
HERT/WAS SG14 .... 150 C3
Service Practice
BERK HP4 .... 161 K5
Shaftesbury Industrial Centre
LWTH SG6 .... 42 B2
Shaftesbury School
KTN/HRWW/W HA3 .... 231 J7
Shakespeare Industrial Estate
WATN WD24 .... 204 B8
Sheepcot Medical Centre
GSTN WD25 .... 204 D4
Sheering C of E Primary School
RBSF CM22 .... 133 H8
Shenley JMI School
RAD WD7 .... 207 J4
Shen Nong Chinese
Medical Centre
STAL AL1 .... 10 C4
Shenval Industrial Estate
HLW CM20 .... 156 D5
Shephall Infant School
STVGE SG2 .... 3 F6
Shephall Way Surgery
STVGE SG2 .... 3 F6
Sheredes School
HOD EN11 .... 176 E4
Sherrardswood School
WLYN AL6 .... 122 D4
Shirley's Temple
LTN LU1 .... 4 B3
Silk Mill House Museum
STALW/RED AL3 .... 142 B5
Simon Balle School
HERT/BAY SG13 .... 151 H4
Sir Frederic Osborn School
WCCE AL7 .... 148 C2
Sir John Lawes School
HARP AL5 .... 118 C3
Sir John Newsom School
WCCE AL7 .... 147 K6
Ski Centre
HHS/BOV HP3 .... 164 D8

Skidmore Clinic
RKW/CH/CXG WD3 .... 218 D8
Skyswood JMI School
STALE/WH AL4 .... 169 F3
Slip End Lower School
LTN LU1 .... 89 G8
Smug Oak Green
Business Centre
LCOL/BKTW AL2 .... 188 D7
Snap Theatre
BSF CM23 .... 105 K2
Someries Castle
LTNE LU2 .... 91 F4
Someries Infant School
LTNE LU2 .... 70 D7
Someries Junior School
LTNE LU2 .... 70 D6
Sopwell House Hotel
& Country Club
STAL AL1 .... 189 H2
South Bedfordshire Golf Club
LTNE LU2 .... 52 D7
South Bedfordshire
Magistrates Court
LTN LU1 .... 4 A4
Southdown Industrial Estate
HARP AL5 .... 143 K1
Southgate Health Centre
STVG SG1 .... 2 B4
South Hill JMI School
HHW HP1 .... 164 B7
South Lodge Queens School
BUSH WD23 .... 221 H3
South Street Surgery
BSF CM23 .... 105 J3
Spellbrook JMI School
BSF CM23 .... 132 D2
Spencer Primary Jm School
STALW/RED AL3 .... 11 D1
Sphere Industrial Estate
STAL AL1 .... 11 F5
The Spinney Junior School
HLW CM20 .... 7 F3
The Spires Shopping Centre
BAR EN5 .... 225 K3
Sports Centre
BORE WD6 .... 224 B1
Sports Centre
HHS/BOV HP3 .... 8 C6
Sports Centre
LCOL/BKTW AL2 .... 205 K1
Sports Ground
BAR EN5 .... 224 D6
Springmead JMI School
WGCE AL7 .... 148 D2
Stadium Industrial Estate
LTNW/LEA LU4 .... 68 A7
Stags School
STALW/RED AL3 .... 168 B2
Stanborough School
GSTN WD25 .... 204 C5
Stanborough School
WGCW AL8 .... 147 G5
Standon Health Centre
STDN SG11 .... 81 K7
Stanmore Road Health Centre
STVG SG1 .... 2 A1
Stansted Clinic
STSD CM24 .... 86 D2
Staple Tye Shopping Centre
HLWS CM18 .... 180 A4
Steeple Morden School
ROY SG8 .... 15 H7
Stevenage Borough Football Club
STVG SG1 .... 2 B3
Stevenage Borough Football Club
STVGE SG2 .... 2 C6
Stevenage Business Park
STVG SG1 .... 59 J7
Stevenage Cricket Club
STVG SG1 .... 2 B2
Stevenage Mosque
STVG SG1 .... 2 B1
Stevenage Museum
STVG SG1 .... 2 C3
Stewards Comprehensive School
HLWS CM18 .... 179 K5
Stirling Industrial Centre
BORE WD6 .... 224 C5
Stocks Hotel Golf
& Country Club
TRING HP23 .... 136 D2
Stockwell Lodge Medical Centre
CHESW EN7 .... 196 E6

Stockwood Park Museum
LTN LU1 .... 89 J5
Stockwood Park Rugby Club
LTN LU1 .... 89 J5
Stonehill JMI School
LWTH SG6 .... 25 J8
Stopsley High School
& Community College
LTNE LU2 .... 70 A5
Stopsley Infant School
LTNE LU2 .... 70 B5
Stormont School
POTB/CUF EN6 .... 210 D1
Stortford Hall Industrial Park
BSF CM23 .... 106 A2
Stort Valley Industrial Estate
BSF CM23 .... 86 A7
Stotfold Health Centre
HTCH/STOT SG5 .... 25 J3
Strathmore Infant School
HTCH/STOT SG5 .... 40 C7
Stream Woods School
HAT AL10 .... 171 G5
Stroud Wood Business Centre
LCOL/BKTW AL2 .... 189 G5
Studham VC Lower School
DUN/WHIP LU6 .... 113 K5
Studlands Rise First School
ROY SG8 .... 21 J4
Summercroft Junior
& Infant School
BSF CM23 .... 106 B1
Summerswood Primary School
BORE WD6 .... 224 A4
Sumners Community
Recreation Centre
HLWW/ROY CM19 .... 179 H5
Sunderland Estate
KGLGY WD4 .... 186 B7
Sundon Business Park
LTNN/LIM LU3 .... 68 A1
Sundon Industrial Estate
LTNN/LIM LU3 .... 68 A1
Sundon Medical Centre
LTNN/LIM LU3 .... 68 B2
Sundon Park Junior School
LTNN/LIM LU3 .... 68 B1
Sunshine Riding School
LTNE LU2 .... 69 J1
Superstore
WAT WD17 .... 13 E4
Surrey Street School
LTN LU1 .... 5 D5
Swimming Pool
HERT/WAS SG14 .... 151 G1
Swimming Pool
STVG SG1 .... 2 B3
The Symonds Green
Health Centre
STVG SG1 .... 75 F2
Tabard Rugby Club
RAD WD7 .... 206 E7
Tanners Wood Junior
& Infant School
ABLGY WD5 .... 203 K2
Tannery Drift School
ROY SG8 .... 21 G3
Tanys Dell Junior School
HLW CM20 .... 7 F1
Telephone Exchange
WATW WD18 .... 12 C3
Telmere Industrial Estate
LTN LU1 .... 4 C5
Templewood School
WGCW AL8 .... 147 H1
Tennyson Road Primary School
LTN LU1 .... 4 C6
Tewin Road Business Centre
WGCE AL7 .... 147 K2
Tewin School
WLYN AL6 .... 124 A7
Tewin Water School
WLYN AL6 .... 123 H7
Therfield First School
ROY SG8 .... 30 D2
Thomas Alleyne School
STVG SG1 .... 75 H1
The Thomas Coram
Middle School
BERK HP4 .... 162 A7
Thomas Rivers Medical Centre
HLW CM20 .... 157 F2
The Thomas Rivers
Medical Centre
SBW CM21 .... 132 A8

Thorley Hill JMI School
BSF CM23 .... **105** J5

Thorn Grove Primary School
BSF CM23 .... **106** A3

Three Rivers District Council
OXHEY WD19 .... **230** D2

Three Rivers District Council
RKW/CH/CXG WD3 .... **218** D7

Thumbswood Infant School
WGCE AL7 .... **148** B4

Thundridge JMI School
WARE SG12 .... **127** H2

Tonwell School
WARE SG12 .... **126** C2

Town Council
HAT AL10 .... **171** F3

Town Hall & Council Offices
LTN LU1 .... **4** B4

Townsend C of E School
STALW/RED AL3 .... **167** K1

Trestle Theatre Co
STALE/WH AL4 .... **169** F7

Tricor Business Park
CHES/WCR EN8 .... **214** D4

Tricor Trading Estate
CHES/WCR EN8 .... **214** D4

Trident Industrial Estate
HOD EN11 .... **177** H3

Tring Health Centre
TRING HP23 .... **135** C5

Tring & New Mill Pre-school
TRING HP23 .... **135** C2

Tring School
TRING HP23 .... **135** C5

Tring Sports Centre
TRING HP23 .... **135** C5

Tring Town Council
TRING HP23 .... **135** F6

Trotts Hill JMI School
STVC SG1 .... **59** F8

Tudor School
HHS/BOV HP3 .... **164** D8

Turnford School
CHES/WCR EN8 .... **197** J6

Two Waters JMI School
HHS/BOV HP3 .... **185** H3

Twyford Business Centre
BSF CM23 .... **105** K4

Underhill Junior & Infant School
BAR EN5 .... **225** K5

University of Hertfordshire
GSTN WD25 .... **205** J6

University of Hertfordshire
HAT AL10 .... **170** C1

University of Hertfordshire
HAT AL10 .... **170** E5

University of Hertfordshire
HERT/BAY SG13 .... **151** J5

University of Hertfordshire
STAL AL1 .... **11** D5

University of London
ENC/FH EN2 .... **213** K6

University of Luton
LTN LU1 .... **4** C4

University of Luton
LTN LU1 .... **4** C5

University of Luton
LTNE LU2 .... **70** E3

Vale Industrial Estate
WATW WD18 .... **219** H8

Verulam Golf Club
STAL AL1 .... **11** E6

Verulam Industrial Estate
STAL AL1 .... **11** E6

Verulamium Museum
STALW/RED AL3 .... **10** A4

Verulam School
STAL AL1 .... **11** F3

Victoria C of E Primary School
BERK HP4 .... **161** K5

The Village Surgery
PIN HA5 .... **231** F8

Virgin Cinemas
HLW CM20 .... **156** C5

Waltham Abbey Swimming Pool
WAB EN9 .... **215** J5

Waltham Holy Cross Council
WAB EN9 .... **215** G3

Waltham Holy Cross
Junior School
WAB EN9 .... **215** J3

Warden Hill Infant School
LTNN/LIM LU3 .... **69** H2

Warden Hill Junior School
LTNN/LIM LU3 .... **69** H2

Warden Lodge Surgery
CHES/WCR EN8 .... **214** C1

Ward Freman School
BUNT SG9 .... **63** H1

Wardown Park Museum
LTNE LU2 .... **69** H1

Wardown Swimming
& Leisure Centre
LTNN/LIM LU3 .... **4** B1

Warrendell School
OXHEY WD19 .... **230** D2

Watchlytes JMI School
WGCE AL7 .... **148** C3

Waterside Industrial Estate
HOD EN11 .... **177** J4

Waterside (School)
BSF CM23 .... **85** H2

Waterways Heritage Museum
RKW/CH/CXG WD3 .... **218** D8

Watford Arches Retail Park
WATW WD18 .... **13** D4

Watford Borough Council
WAT WD17 .... **12** B2

Watford Business Centre
WATW WD18 .... **12** C2

Watford Central Swimming Bath
WAT WD17 .... **12** B1

Watford County Court
WAT WD17 .... **12** C1

Watford Eye Clinic
WATN WD24 .... **204** C8

Watford Football Club
WATW WD18 .... **12** C4

Watford General Hospital
WATW WD18 .... **12** C4

Watford Grammar School
for Boys
WATW WD18 .... **12** A3

Watford Grammar School
for Girls
WATW WD18 .... **13** D4

Watford Museum
WAT WD17 .... **13** D4

Watford Sports & Leisure Centre
CSTN WD25 .... **204** D3

Watford Springs Pool
WATW WD18 .... **13** D4

Watford United Synagogue
WAT WD17 .... **220** C1

Watling View School
STAL AL1 .... **189** F2

Wauluds Bank Junior
& Infant School
LTNN/LIM LU3 .... **68** D2

Wedgewood Gate
Industrial Estate
STVG SG1 .... **59** H7

Welwyn Garden City Cricket Club
WGCW AL8 .... **122** C7

Welwyn Garden City Golf Club
WGCW AL8 .... **147** G2

Welwyn Garden Hebrew
Congregation Synagogue
WGCW AL8 .... **147** G3

Welwyn Hatfield District Council
HAT AL10 .... **171** G3

Welwyn Hatfield
Museum Service
BRKMPK AL9 .... **171** K1

Welwyn Rugby Football Club
WGCW AL8 .... **147** G4

Welwyn Tennis Club
WLYN AL6 .... **122** B5

Wenlock C of E School
LTNE LU2 .... **5** F3

The Wenta Business Centre
WATN WD24 .... **204** E7

Westbrook Hay
Preparatory School
HHW HP1 .... **184** B1

Western House Hospital
WARE SG12 .... **127** H7

Westfield JMI School
HOD EN11 .... **176** E2

Westfield School
WATW WD18 .... **12** A5

West Hertfordshire College
WAT WD17 .... **204** B8

West Herts College
BUSH WD23 .... **13** E2

West Herts College
HHW HP1 .... **164** B5

Westminster Lodge
Sports Centre
STALW/RED AL3 .... **10** B6

Wheatcroft JMI School
HERT/BAY SG13 .... **151** K2

Wheatfields Junior
& Infant School
STALE/WH AL4 .... **168** E2

Whipperley Infant School
LTN LU1 .... **89** F3

Whipsnade Park Golf Club
BERK HP4 .... **113** G4

Whitefield Infant School
LTNN/LIM LU3 .... **68** D1

Whitehall Estate
HLWW/ROY CM19 .... **179** F2

Whitehill Junior School
HTCHE/RSTV SG4 .... **56** E4

The Whitewebbs Museum
of Transport & Industry
ENC/FH EN2 .... **212** E5

Whittings Hill School
BAR EN5 .... **225** H5

Whittlesea School
KTN/HRWW/W HA3 .... **231** K6

Whyllotts Council Offices
POTB/CUF EN6 .... **210** A2

Widford Junior & Infant School
WARE SG12 .... **129** K5

Wigginton JMI School
TRING HP23 .... **135** J8

Wigmore Primary School
LTNE LU2 .... **71** F7

Wilbury Junior Mixed School
LWTH SG6 .... **41** J3

William Austin Infant School
LTNN/LIM LU3 .... **69** H5

William Austin Junior School
LTNN/LIM LU3 .... **69** H5

William Penn Leisure Centre
RKW/CH/CXG WD3 .... **217** J8

William Ransom JMI School
HTCHE/RSTV SG4 .... **57** F2

Willow Field School
LTN LU1 .... **88** E5

Windermere JMI Primary School
STAL AL1 .... **168** E8

Windmill Trading Estate
LTN LU1 .... **5** D4

Wisteria House Clinic
WLYN AL6 .... **122** B3

Wodson Park Leisure Centre
WARE SG12 .... **127** G5

Wolsey Business Park
WATW WD18 .... **219** J7

Wood End JMI School
HARP AL5 .... **117** K6

Woodfield School
HHS/BOV HP3 .... **165** H8

Woodhall Farm Surgery
HHNE HP2 .... **141** G8

Woodlands Infant School
BORE WD6 .... **223** K1

Woodside Industrial Park
LWTH SG6 .... **42** B3

Woodside JMI School
CHESW EN7 .... **196** A7

Woolenwick Junior
& Infant School
STVG SG1 .... **75** G3

Woolgrove School
LWTH SG6 .... **42** D4

Worcesters Infant
& Primary School
EN EN1 .... **213** J8

Wormley JMI School
BROX EN10 .... **197** J1

Wroxham JMI School
POTB/CUF EN6 .... **209** J1

Wymondley Junior
& Infant School
HTCHE/RSTV SG4 .... **57** H5

York House School
RKW/CH/CXG WD3 .... **218** E2

Page 4

C5
1 Essex Cl
2 James Ct
3 Langley St
4 May St
5 New Town Rd
6 Oxford Rd
7 Union St
8 Victoria St
9 Windsor St

Page 8

A3
1 Andrews Cl
2 The Bounce
3 Boxhill
4 Broadcroft
5 Mead Temple
6 Sharpcroft
7 Typleden Cl

C5
1 The Queen's Sq
2 Sawyers Wy
3 Sheepcote Rd

Page 9

F6
1 Church Rd
2 Coniston Cl
3 Cumberlow Pl
4 Gravely Ct
5 Hartsbourne Wy
6 Rycroft Cl

Page 13

D1
1 Anglian Cl
2 Aston Cl
3 Keele Cl
4 Octavia Ct
5 Orphanage Rd
6 St Pauls Wy

D3
1 Cambridge Rd
2 Chapmans Yd
3 Church St
4 The Crescent
5 Derby Rd
6 Granville Rd
7 Kings Cl
8 Lower Derby Rd
9 Market Pl
10 New St
11 Smith St
12 Water La
13 Watford Field Rd
14 Woodmans Yd

E5
1 St Matthews Cl

Page 56

B3
1 Kardwell Cl
2 Kingfisher Ct
3 Lovell Cl
4 Orlando Cl
5 Riddy Hill Cl
6 South Hill Cl
7 Whitegale Cl

Page 69

F2
1 Croxton Cl
2 Cubbington Cl
3 Green Milverton
4 Quickswood

G4
1 Belvedere Rd
2 Fenwick Cl

H7
1 Chaucer Rd
2 Sheridan Rd

K8
1 Arncliffe Crs
2 Kinghamway

Page 70

E8
1 Alderton Cl
2 Barnston Cl
3 Chelsworth Cl
4 Friston Gn
5 Hickling Cl
6 Melford Cl
7 Mutford Cft
8 Pinford Dell

Page 89

J2
1 Alma Link
2 Buxton Rd
3 Gordon St
4 Hastings St
5 King St
6 Mersey Rd
7 Napier Rd
8 Regent St
9 Rothesay Rd

K2
1 Barbers La
2 Bute St
3 Castle St
4 Chapel St
5 Cheapside
6 Cheapside Sq
7 Flowers Wy
8 George St West
9 Library Rd
10 Park St
11 Stuart St

K3
1 Essex Cl
2 James Ct
3 Langley St
4 May St
5 New Town Rd
6 Oxford Rd
7 Union St
8 Victoria St
9 Windsor St

Page 105

K2
1 Fuller Ct
2 The Old Maltings

K3
1 Great Eastern Cl
2 Station Rd

Page 122

C4
1 Church Pl
2 Holly Hall Ct
3 Mimram Rd
4 Orchard Rd
5 Prospect Pl
6 St Marys Cl
7 Welwyn Hall
8 Wendover Ct

Page 147

H3
1 Barleycroft Gn
2 Handside Cl
3 Lanefield Wk
4 Palmerston Cl

H4
1 Fordwich Rd
2 Hobbs Wy
3 Honeycroft
4 Stanborough Cl

K4
1 Athelstan Wk North
2 Edgars Ct
3 Moatwood Gn
4 Oaktree Garth
5 Peartree Ct
6 Regent Cl

K7
1 Drycroft
2 Katescroft

Page 148

A3
1 Home Meadow
2 Swallowfields
3 Verlum Cl

C2
1 Buddcroft
2 Claycroft
3 Kingscroft
4 Nettlecroft
5 Smallcroft
6 Strawfields
7 Waterfield
8 Wheatbarn

C4
1 Amwell Common
2 Batford Cl
3 Bushey Cl
4 Bushey Gn
5 Graveley Dell
6 Thundridge Cl
7 Wareside Cl

D3
1 Andrewsfield
2 Bericot Wy
3 Beverley Gdns
4 Douglas Wy
5 Elizabeth Cl
6 Jackdaws
7 Lindbergh
8 Mitchell Cl

D4
1 Aspen Wy
2 Birchall Wd
3 Copperfields
4 Forresters Dr
5 Glenwood
6 High Wickfield
7 Holwell Hyde
8 Pelham Ct
9 Ploughmans End
10 Poppyfields

E3
1 Hunsdon
2 Northwood
3 Oakington
4 Roseacre Gdns
5 Somersham
6 Stapleford
7 Sylvan Wy
8 Tempsford
9 Waterbeach

Page 151

F3
1 Brewhouse La
2 Bridges Ct
3 Castle St
4 Hertingfordbury Rd
5 Mill Br
6 Old Cross
7 Old Cross B158
8 Port Hl

G3
1 Bell La
2 Bircherley Ct
3 Bluecoats Av
4 Church St
5 The Gulphs
6 Maidenhead St
7 Maidenhead Yd
8 Market Pl
9 Market St
10 Millers Yd
11 Nicholas La
12 Oldhall St
13 Parliament Sq
14 St John's St
15 Salisbury Sq
16 The Wash

J3
1 Beechwood Cl
2 Braziers Cft
3 Caxton Hl
4 Copperwood
5 Extension Rd
6 Mountsorrel
7 Watermark Wy

Page 161

H3
1 Beckets Sq
2 Dellfield
3 Dukes Wy
4 Montgomerie Cl
5 Pages Cft

J6
1 Ashlyns Ct
2 Gresham St

K5
1 Cavalier Ct
2 Clarence Rd
3 Greene Field Rd
4 Manor Cl
5 Prince Edward St
6 The Wilderness

K6
1 Old Orchard Ms
2 Pheasant Cl
3 Plover Cl

Page 164

A4
1 Cooks Vennel
2 Pierian Spring
3 Timplings Rw
4 Willow Wy

A5
1 Bards Cnr
2 Lockers Park La
3 Minstrel Cl
4 Saffron La

C5
1 The Brackens
2 Chapel Cottages
3 Fensomes Alley
4 Fensom's Cl
5 Garland Cl
6 Normandy Ct
7 Pine Tree Cl
8 Union Gn

D1
1 Helston Gv

D6
1 Chalkdell Hl
2 Quendell Wk

D8
1 Satinwood Ct

E1
1 Clyde Sq
2 Great Palmers
3 Mersey Pl
4 Robin Hood Meadow

E2
1 Cwmbran Ct
2 Kilbride Ct
3 Peterlee Ct
4 Sherwood Pl
5 Welwyn Ct

E3
1 Callisto Ct
2 Ganymede Pl
3 Pentland

E5
1 Coral Gdns
2 Hammer La
3 Rice Cl

E7
1 St Albans Rd
2 Wadley Cl

E8
1 Bennetts End Cl

Page 165

F5
1 Saracens Head
2 Southernwood Cl

H7
1 Church Rd
2 Coniston Cl
3 Cumberlow Pl
4 Gravely Ct
5 Hartsbourne Wy
6 Rycroft Cl

H8
1 Crossett Gn
2 Manan Cl
3 Stroma Cl
4 Stronsay
5 Westray

Page 168

B7
1 Approach Rd
2 Black Cut
3 Devon Ct
4 Henrys Grant
5 Hopkins Yd
6 Lime Tree Pl
7 Lower Paxton Rd
8 Vernon's Cl

D2
1 The Berries
2 Bolingbrook
3 Lay Brook

E8
1 Cell Barnes Cl

Page 171

G7
1 Downsfield
2 Richmond Ct

H1
1 Highlands
2 Lowlands

H2
1 Edward Ct
2 Frogmore Rd
3 Henry St
4 Kents Av
5 Millbank
6 St Andrew's Rd
7 White Lion St
8 William Ct

Page 185

D5
1 Bay Tree Cl
2 Glover Cl
3 Grenadine Cl
4 Lavender Cl
5 Musgrave Cl
6 Northwood Cl
7 Rennison Cl
8 Sycamore Cl

Page 196

H6
1 Campine Cl
2 The Colonnade
3 Drakes Cl
4 Faverolle Gn
5 Hamburgh Ct
6 Southbrook Dr
7 The Spur
8 Symonds Ct

J6
1 Bromleigh Cl
2 Cordell Cl
3 Fraser Rd
4 Goodwin Ct
5 Lensbury Cl

J8
1 Foster Cl
2 Guinevere Gdns
3 Roberts Cl
4 Roswell Cl

K1
1 Fern Cl
2 The Square
3 Virgil Dr
4 Wormley Lodge Cl

K3
1 Farmhouse Cl
2 Felton Cl
3 Juniper Cl

K5
1 Priory Ga

Page 204

B1
1 Lapwing Wy
2 Nightingale Cl
3 Oriole Cl
4 Redwing Gv

B3
1 Ganders Ash
2 Nottingham Cl

C2
1 Bramley Ct

C8
1 Callowland Pl
2 Halsey Pl
3 Lea Rd
4 St George's Rd

D5
1 Biddenham Turn
2 The Conifers
3 Rochester Dr

D7
1 Buckingham Cl
2 Southwold Rd

Page 214

C4
1 Dumbarton Av

C7
1 Hartmoor Ms

D4
1 Abbey Rd
2 Lodge Crs
3 Station Ap
4 Trust Rd

D7
1 Coldham Gv
2 Cornhill Dr
3 The Generals Wk
4 Johnby Cl
5 Newport Cl

Page 220

C2
1 Albert Rd North
2 Canterbury Rd
3 Franklin Rd
4 Keston Ms
5 Shady La
6 Wellington St
7 Westland Rd
8 West St

C7
1 Brookmill Cl
2 Silk Mill Rd
3 The Willows

D2
1 Anglian Cl
2 Aston Cl
3 Keele Cl
4 Octavia Ct
5 Orphanage Rd
6 St Pauls Wy

D3
1 The Broadway
2 Earl St
3 Lord St
4 Ottoman Ter
5 Queen's Pl
6 Queen's Rd
7 Shaftesbury Rd
8 Stanley Rd
9 Trinity Hall Cl

D4
1 Cambridge Rd
2 Chapmans Yd
3 Church St
4 The Crescent
5 Derby Rd
6 Granville Rd
7 Kings Cl
8 Lower Derby Rd
9 Market Pl
10 New St
11 Smith St
12 Water La
13 Watford Field Rd
14 Woodmans Yd

E2
1 Beasant House
2 Bevan House
3 Gandhi Ct
4 Mandela Pl
5 Orwell Ct

Page 221

J6
1 Baird Ct
2 The Close
3 Fidler Pl
4 Herkomer Cl
5 Meadowcroft
6 Mortimer Cl
7 Ryder Cl
8 Wheelright Cl

Page 230

A6
1 Cervantes Ct
2 Church Cl
3 Kemps Dr
4 Wychwood Wy

A7
1 Manor Cottages

D4
1 Bognor Gdns
2 Bromborough Gn
3 Darwin Gdns
4 Doncaster Cl
5 Harborne Cl
6 Huntercrombe Gdns
7 Kenilworth Gdns
8 Morriston Cl
9 Muirfield Cl

E3
1 Crowborough Pth
2 Glencorse Gn
3 Lundin Wk
4 Markeston Gn
5 Mullion Wk
6 Newport Mead
7 Piltdown Wk

E4
1 Ashford Gn
2 Falkirk Gdns
3 Gleneagles Cl
4 Letchworth Cl
5 Leven Cl

E8
1 Chesswood Wy
2 Willow Dean

Notes

Notes